THE FEDERAL ANTI-KICKBACK STATUTE AND SAFE HARBORS

ERIC FADER • GEOFFREY R. KAISER • CHRISTOPHER J. KUTNER • ADA KOZICZ • BENJAMIN P. MALERBA

THE FEDERAL ANTI-KICKBACK STATUTE AND SAFE HARBORS

AMERICAN BAR ASSOCIATION
Health Law Section

Printed in the United States of America.

24 23 22 21 20 5 4 3 2 1

Library of Congress Cataloging-in-Publication Data

Names: Kaiser, Geoffrey R., author. | Kutner, Christopher J., author. | Kozicz, Ada, author. | Malerba, Benjamin P., author. | Fader, Eric D., author. | American Bar Association. Health Law Section sponsoring body
Title: The federal anti-kickback statute and safe harbors / Geoffrey R. Kaiser, Christopher J. Kutner, Ada Kozicz, Benjamin P. Malerba, Eric D. Fader.
Description: Chicago : American Bar Association, 2020. | Includes index. | Summary: "Introduces reader to the Anti-Kickback Statute, provides specific statutory exceptions and Safe Harbors and reviews interplay between the Anti-Kickback Statute and other laws"– Provided by publisher.
Identifiers: LCCN 2020008702 (print) | LCCN 2020008703 (ebook) | ISBN 9781641056618 (hardcover) | ISBN 9781641056625 (ebook)
Subjects: LCSH: Medical care–Finance–Law and legislation–United States–Criminal provisions. | Medical referral–Law and legislation–United States–Criminal provisions. | Medicare fraud–Law and legislation. | Medicaid fraud–Law and legislation.
Classification: LCC KF9368 .K35 2020 (print) | LCC KF9368 (ebook) | DDC 345.73/0268–dc23
LC record available at https://lccn.loc.gov/2020008702
LC ebook record available at https://lccn.loc.gov/2020008703

Discounts are available for books ordered in bulk. Special consideration is given to state bars, CLE programs, and other bar-related organizations. Inquire at Book Publishing, ABA Publishing, American Bar Association, 321 N. Clark Street, Chicago, Illinois 60654-7598.

www.shopABA.org

Contents

About the Authors

Eric D. Fader

Partner

Eric Fader has represented health care providers and other corporate clients in connection with business planning and contractual issues, transactional matters, and federal and state regulatory compliance for more than 30 years. His clients include providers of intraoperative neurophysiologic monitoring (IONM) services, telehealth and telepharmacy companies, urgent care facilities, imaging centers, and private practices of all types. Eric has also represented insurers and third-party administrators, provider networks, medical device suppliers, equipment vendors, and providers of electronic medical records and other online health care services in contractual and regulatory matters.

Eric advises on billing and reimbursement questions, federal and state anti-kickback and self-referral issues, HIPAA compliance (including privacy and data breaches), payor audits, hospital privilege and medical staff issues, and state licensure and certificate of need matters. His work also includes organizational matters, corporate governance and structuring/restructuring advice, operating agreements, shareholder and partnership agreements and disputes, labor and employment law issues, private securities offerings, joint ventures, mergers, and acquisitions.

A frequent writer and commentator on health care issues, Eric has written for and has been quoted in *Bloomberg BNA, Law360* and *Thomson Reuters Westlaw*, among many others. Eric is the Editor of *Rivkin Rounds*, an electronic news bulletin for businesses, professionals, investors, and stakeholders in the health care industry.

Eric is a member of the American Society of Neurophysiological Monitoring (ASNM) and has been a webinar and symposium speaker for the

ASNM. He served on the Board of Directors of Stayhealthy, Inc., a privately owned health solutions company committed to changing the way the world measures health and fitness.

Eric began his legal career as a securities lawyer and moonlighted for several years as a professional microcap stock trader. This activity afforded him unusual insights into the OTC markets which he has used in representing small public companies and those that invest in them.

Geoffrey R. Kaiser

Senior Counsel

Geoffrey (Jeff) R. Kaiser, who has extensive experience in enforcement matters affecting the health care industry, concentrates his legal practice on health care fraud and regulatory compliance issues, white collar criminal defense, False Claims Act litigation, integrity monitoring, and internal investigations. As head of the Compliance, Investigations and White Collar Practice Group, and senior counsel in the Health Services Practice Group, Jeff is frequently called upon to handle matters implicating a range of health care fraud and abuse laws, including the False Claims Act and the Anti-Kickback Statute. The Health Services Practice Group at Rivkin Radler has been listed in the prestigious Legal 500. The practice is also recognized as "notable" by Chambers USA.

Before joining Rivkin Radler, Jeff served for nearly 10 years in the Criminal Divisions of the U.S. Attorney's Office for the Eastern District of New York and the U.S. Attorney's Office for the Southern District of New York. While at the Justice Department, he directed many white collar investigations and prosecutions, including with respect to health care fraud, securities fraud, mortgage fraud, mail and wire fraud, and bank fraud.

As Chief of Health Care Fraud Prosecutions and Deputy Chief of Public Integrity in the Eastern District U.S. Attorney's Office, Jeff directed investigations against individuals and corporations facing health care fraud allegations under a variety of criminal and civil statutes. In many instances, those investigations were rooted in allegations brought by whistleblowers under the False Claims Act. Jeff also exercised oversight responsibilities within the Public Integrity Section for all health care fraud cases within the Eastern District of New York. He received many recognitions and honors for his efforts as a federal prosecutor.

After leaving the Justice Department, Jeff served as a managing director with Navigant Consulting, Inc., a global expert services firm, in two of its practice groups: Disputes and Investigations and Healthcare Disputes, Compliance and Investigations. While at Navigant, Jeff led teams performing internal investigations and integrity monitorships of individuals and organizations in the health care, construction, and transportation industries, and supervised a major forensic review of mortgage servicing practices by a national mortgage servicer. He also oversaw the implementation of anti-counterfeiting/brand protection strategies on behalf of global brand owners.

Jeff worked as a civil litigator for more than a decade, handling commercial litigation matters involving an assortment of business disputes. He developed particular experience in the investigation and prosecution of complex civil frauds under multiple common law and statutory grounds, including the federal Racketeer Influenced and Corrupt Organizations Act (RICO). In addition, Jeff has acted as advisor to a global conglomerate in the area of anti-counterfeiting and brand protection.

Jeff received his B.A. with Honors from the University of Virginia, where he also graduated Phi Beta Kappa. He earned a J.D. from New York University School of Law, where he served on the Moot Court Board. After graduating from law school, Jeff served for two years as law clerk to the Hon. Fritz W. Alexander II, an associate judge on New York State's highest court, the New York Court of Appeals.

A frequent writer and speaker on a range of legal topics, particularly in the areas of health care fraud and compliance, Jeff was named a Super Lawyer in the Metro New York area, 2012–2019. Jeff is an adjunct professor of law at St. John's University School of Law, where he teaches Health Care Fraud.

The Health Services practice has been included in the Chambers USA directory in the Healthcare category.

Christopher J. Kutner

Partner

Christopher J. Kutner represents managed care organizations, physician groups, hospitals, and ancillary service providers, including laboratories, health care benefit administrators, and suppliers of medical equipment.

As partner in the Health Services Practice Group, Chris represents national and regional health plans in the acquisition of similar plans. He recently coordinated the acquisition and integration of a Connecticut managed care plan by a larger, New York City-based health maintenance organization (HMO). He is representing a multi-facility alcohol and substance abuse service provider in a stock sale transaction. He also represented a regional, boutique laboratory in an asset sale. Moreover, a regional laboratory-management company hired Chris to advise on acquisitions, state and federal regulatory compliance, and managed care contracting. He advises health care providers with managed care contracting and dispute resolution and with respect to compliant practice structures and permissible arrangements concerning, among other issues, referrals.

He has represented a national managed care company in connection with its acquisition of managed long term care plans (MLTCPs) and a county government in the sale of its Medicaid managed care plan including eight outpatient treatment facilities. His managed care experience makes him well-suited for advising health care consumers with benefit and medical necessity opinions as well as assisting with external appeals with state regulators.

A partner in Rivkin Radler's Compliance, Investigations & White Collar Practice Group, Chris represents health care providers who are being audited or investigated by, among others, the New York State Department of Health's Office of Professional Medical Conduct (OPMC), the New York State Medicaid Inspector General (OMIG), the U.S. Department of Health and Human Services' Office of Inspector General (OIG), the New York Attorney General, and the U.S. Attorney's Offices for all districts in New York and New Jersey.

Chris' practice includes advising providers in Western and Northern New York and he is admitted, and practices law, in Connecticut.

Beginning his career as a commercial litigator, Chris represented local, national, and global companies in complex civil litigation in state and federal courts. In 1998, he accepted an in-house counsel position with Vytra Health Plans, a managed care organization and client he represented in private practice. For eight years, Chris worked inside managed care. Among his accomplishments: He implemented Vytra's first corporate compliance program and served as compliance and privacy officer. He ultimately served as special assistant and counsel to the president and chief executive officer, focusing on health care strategic planning, product development, and regulatory compliance. He served as corporate counsel and regulatory compliance counsel for Vytra's parent organization, HIP, while assuming the role of general counsel at Vytra, where he was instrumental in working with state and federal law enforcement on investigations of individuals and entities based on health care fraud, among other claims.

Chris enlisted in the U.S. military at age 19 and served active duty in the U.S. Air Force while attending college. He earned the Air Force Commendation Medal and was honorably discharged after four years of active military service to pursue a bachelor's of mechanical engineering degree from SUNY Stony Brook, which he earned in 1987.

Chris has been named to Best Lawyers in America in Healthcare by U.S. News & World Report from 2017–2020. The Health Services Practice Group has been listed in the prestigious Legal 500. The practice also has been included in the Chambers USA directory in the Healthcare category. Chris was named a Super Lawyer in the Metro New York Area in Health Care for 2014, 2015, 2018, and 2019.

Ada Kozicz

Associate

Ada Kozicz concentrates her practice on regulatory and transactional matters within the health care industry.

An associate in Rivkin Radler's Health Services Practice Group, Ada represents health care providers, medical groups, hospitals, outpatient facilities, and other business entities that serve the health care industry. She advises clients on a wide variety of legal matters, including formation of business entities, joint ventures, employment negotiations, and compliance programs involving Medicaid and Medicare, Stark and Anti-Kickback Law, and the False Claims Act.

Ada also practices in Rivkin Radler's Privacy, Data & Cyber Law Practice Group, where she advises clients both in and outside of the health care industry on complying with HIPAA and the HITECH Act, and responding to any threats or breaches to an organization's privacy and cybersecurity.

She was honored by the Long Island Business News as a 2018 "30 Under 30" award recipient, and by the Huntington Township Chamber of Commerce as one of 30 "Celebrate Long Island's Young Professionals" honorees in 2017.

Ada is a frequent contributor to the firm's electronic health law news bulletin, *Rivkin Rounds*, available at https://www.rivkinradler.com/rivkin-rounds/.

Ada previously served as a Senior Fellow for the Gitenstein Institute for Health Law and Policy, where she worked on several community outreach projects that strived to improve access to quality care and pave the way for positive change in the health care delivery system.

During law school, Ada earned a certificate in health law and served on the Editorial Board of *Hofstra Law Review*. She also received an award for outstanding achievement in the Health Law and Policy Clinic at Hofstra, where she worked as a student-attorney and represented a nonprofit health services organization in implementing internal scope of practice and risk management policies for community health workers.

The Health Services Practice Group has been listed in the prestigious Legal 500. The practice also has been included in the Chambers USA directory in the Healthcare category.

Benjamin P. Malerba

Partner

Benjamin P. Malerba is a partner in the Health Services and Privacy, Data & Cyber Law Practice Groups. Ben counsels a cross-section of health care providers and facilities, including IPAs, ACOs, provider networks, ambulatory surgery centers, diagnostic and treatment centers, dialysis facilities, and hospitals and federally qualified health centers, on general healthcare business transactions, state licensing issues, corporate practice of medicine and fee-splitting prohibitions, regulatory compliance, disputes with managed care companies, federal and state anti-kickback statutes, self-referral statutes, and federal and state privacy laws. His practice also covers data breach and response, cybersecurity and data security, with a particular focus on security breaches related to the Health Insurance Portability and Accountability Act of 1996 (HIPAA).

Ben has particular experience representing ambulatory surgery centers (ASCs) and ambulatory surgery management companies, counseling them on a wide variety of corporate and commercial transactions, including mergers and acquisitions of existing ASCs, the establishment of de novo centers, and syndications. He regularly represents ASCs and other facilities before the New York State Department of Health and the New York State Public Health and Health Planning Council. He also has represented clients before federal and state government agencies, including the Department of Health and Human Services' Office for Civil Rights in its investigations into

HIPAA-related security breaches. Ben also counsels clients on the development and implementation of compliance programs for health care providers and business associates under HIPAA and on preparing for and responding to HIPAA breaches and investigations.

A frequent lecturer, Ben delivers presentations on health care issues before provider networks, hospitals, ASCs, medical groups, and state professional associations. He has also written articles and delivered presentations on the topic of medical marijuana. Ben has participated in the Volunteer Lawyers' Project, representing tenants in landlord/tenant proceedings. He serves on the board of directors of The Guidance Center of Westchester, whose mission is to improve the well-being of people of all ages through innovative and effective programs that enable everyone to learn, work, and thrive. Ben has also served on the board of directors of The Early Years Institute, a not-for-profit organization that promotes the impact of the early years of life on later success.

Ben has been named to Best Lawyers in America in Healthcare by *U.S. News & World Report* for 2018 through 2020. He was named a Top Healthcare Transaction Lawyer in 2015 and 2017 by the Ambulatory M&A Advisor. In 2011, Long Island Business News named him one of its "40 Rising Stars Under 40."

The Health Services Practice Group has been listed in the prestigious Legal 500. The practice also has been included in the Chambers USA directory in the Healthcare category.

1

An Introduction to the Anti-Kickback Statute

1.1. The Text and Import of the Anti-Kickback Statute

The Anti-Kickback Statute (AKS) is a criminal law that states:

(1) Whoever knowingly and willfully solicits or receives any remuneration (including any kickback, bribe, or rebate) directly or indirectly, overtly or covertly, in cash or in kind—

(A) in return for referring an individual to a person for the furnishing or arranging for the furnishing of any item or service for which payment may be made in whole or in part under a Federal health care program, or

(B) in return for purchasing, leasing, ordering, or arranging for or recommending purchasing, leasing, or ordering any good, facility, service, or item for which payment may be made in whole or in part under a Federal health care program, shall be guilty of a felony and upon conviction thereof, shall be fined not more than $25,000 or imprisoned for not more than five years, or both.

(2) Whoever knowingly and willfully offers or pays any remuneration (including any kickback, bribe, or rebate) directly or indirectly, overtly or covertly, in cash or in kind to any person to induce such person—

(A) to refer an individual to a person for the furnishing or arranging for the furnishing of any item or service for which

payment may be made in whole or in part under a Federal health care program, or

(B) to purchase, lease, order, or arrange for or recommend purchasing, leasing, or ordering any good, facility, service, or item for which payment may be made in whole or in part under a Federal health care program, shall be guilty of a felony and upon conviction thereof, shall be fined not more than $25,000 or imprisoned for not more than five years, or both.[1]

The AKS accordingly defines as felony conduct the solicitation, receipt, payment, or offer of payment of any "remuneration" to induce or in return for the referral of any individual to a person for furnishing or arranging for the furnishing of an item or service reimbursable under a federal health care program. The statute also bars a person from doing any of those things to induce or in return for purchasing, leasing, ordering, or arranging for or recommending purchasing, leasing, or ordering any item or service reimbursable under a federal health care program. An AKS violation is punishable by up to five years of imprisonment and a fine of up to $25,000. There are no exceptions to what may constitute "remuneration" under the AKS,[2] which is broadly construed to mean "anything of value."[3] The meaning of "federal health care program" is likewise broad, and includes, in addition to obvious federal health insurance programs like Medicare and Medicaid, virtually

1. 42 U.S.C. § 1320a-7b(b).

2. In this respect, the AKS is very different from, for example, the Civil Monetary Penalties Law (CMP; 42 U.S.C. § 1320a-7a). The CMP authorizes the imposition of civil penalties and sanctions for various types of health care fraud and abuse, including but not limited to violations of the AKS. Unlike the AKS, however, the CMP contains various exceptions to the definition of remuneration, and the U.S. Department of Health and Human Services, Office of Inspector General has taken the position that an exchange of remuneration having only "nominal value" will not trigger administrative sanctions under the CMP. *See* 42 U.S.C. § 1320a-7a(i)(6); OIG Special Advisory Bulletin, "Offering Gifts and Other Inducements to Beneficiaries" (Aug. 2002). Such exceptions, however, have no application to the AKS. *See* Narco Freedom, 2015 WL 1499265 at *8-9 (distinguishing the CMP from the AKS and noting that exceptions to the definition of remuneration as used in the CMP do not apply to the AKS).

3. *See, e.g.*, United States v. Narco Freedom, Inc., 2015 WL 1499265 at *8 (S.D.N.Y. 2015) (remuneration under AKS is anything of value and not limited to traditional bribes; remuneration may include an "in kind benefit [i.e., subsidized housing] provided at below market value to Medicaid beneficiaries"); Ameritox, Ltd. v. Millennium Labs., Inc., 20 F.Supp.3d 1348, 1356 (M.D. Fla. 2014) ("[T]he AKS does not contain exceptions to the broad definition of remuneration."); United States ex rel. McDonough v. Symphony Diagnostic Servs., 36 F.Supp.3d 773 (S.D. Ohio 2014) (remuneration can be "anything of value"); Klaczak v. Consol. Med. Transp., 458 F.Supp.2d 622, 678 (N.D. Ill. 2006) ("Remuneration, for purposes of the AKS, is defined broadly, meaning 'anything of value.'").

any plan or program providing health benefits which receives some degree of federal funding.[4]

To violate the AKS, a person's conduct, whether direct or indirect, covert or overt, must be knowing and willful (i.e., performed purposefully with the intention of inducing or rewarding referrals of items or services payable by a federal health care program).[5] Provided the conduct is knowing and willful, there is no requirement that the defendant have actual knowledge of or a specific intention to violate 42 U.S.C. § 1320a-7b(b) in order to trigger liability.[6]

In addition to the criminal penalties accompanying an AKS violation, violating the AKS implicates other laws as well. Conviction under the AKS brings mandatory exclusion from federal health care programs.[7] Additionally, when a person violates the AKS, the US Department of Health and Human Services, Office of Inspector General (HHS-OIG) may initiate administrative proceedings under the Civil Monetary Penalties Law (CMPL) to impose civil monetary penalties.[8] Furthermore, violating the AKS can result in liability under the Federal False Claims Act[9] for any claims submitted to federal health care programs that include any items or services resulting from a violation of the AKS. Indeed, the Patient Protection and Affordable Care Act[10] amended the AKS to state that any claim submitted in violation of the AKS "constitutes a false or fraudulent claim" for purposes of the False Claims Act.[11]

4. The AKS defines a federal health care program as: "(1) any plan or program that provides health benefits, whether directly, through insurance, or otherwise, which is funded directly, in whole or in part, by the United States Government (other than the health insurance program under chapter 89 of title 5); or (2) any State health care program, as defined in section 1320a–7(h) of this title."

5. Six Circuit Courts of Appeal that have considered the issue have held that only one purpose of the exchange of remuneration need be the inducement or reward of referrals in order to trigger the statute's provisions. This has become known as the "one purpose test." *See, e.g.*, United States v. Nagelvoort, 856 F.3d 1117, 1129-30 (7th Cir. 2017); United States v. Krikheli, 461 Fed. Appx. 7 at **3 (2d Cir. 2012); United States v. McClatchey, 217 F.3d 823, 834-35 (10th Cir. 2000); United States v. Davis, 132 F.3d 1092, 1094 (5th Cir. 1998); United States v. Kats, 871 F.2d 105, 108 (9th Cir. 1989); United States v. Greber, 760 F.2d 68, 69 (3d Cir. 1985), *cert. denied*, 474 U.S. 988 (1985); *Compare* United States v. Bay State Ambulance & Hops. Rental Serv. Inc., 874 F.2d 20, 29 (1st Cir. 1989) (affirming conviction on jury instruction requiring that jury find that "primary purpose" was to induce referrals, but leaving open the question whether the "one purpose test" is, in fact, the proper test).

6. 42 U.S.C. § 1320a-7b(h).

7. 42 U.S.C. § 1320a-7(a); 42 CFR Part 1001.

8. 42 U.S.C. § 1320a-7a(a)(7); 42 CFR §§ 1003.300 *et seq.*

9. 31 U.S.C. §§ 3729 *et seq.*

10. 42 U.S.C. §§ 18001 *et seq.*

11. 42 U.S.C. § 1320a-7b(g).

The AKS contains certain statutory and regulatory exceptions or "safe harbors" that protect selected business arrangements from prosecution under the statute.[12] Full compliance with a safe harbor is required to receive its benefits. A failure to comply with any required term of the approved business arrangement negates safe harbor protection.[13] Failing to satisfy a safe harbor, however, does not automatically result in AKS liability, which must be independently analyzed under the AKS statutory provisions.[14]

1.2. Legislative History and Public Policies Underlying the Anti-Kickback Statute and Safe Harbors

The AKS was first enacted through the Social Security Amendments of 1972 in order to combat fraud and abuse in the Medicare and Medicaid Programs.[15] The legislative history makes clear that these provisions were

---

12. *See, e.g.*, United States *ex rel.* Bartlett v. Ashcroft, 39 F. Supp. 3d 656, 676 (W.D. Pa. 2014) ("safe harbors protect certain business arrangements that might otherwise violate the Anti-Kickback Statute"); United States *ex rel.* Armfield v. Gills, 2012 WL 5340131 at *3 (M.D. Fla. 2012) (government has "promulgated regulations establishing a safe harbor for certain arrangements between healthcare providers which remove them from the scope of the Anti-Kickback Act"); United States v. Rogan, 459 F. Supp. 2d 692, 715 (N.D. Ill. 2006) (safe harbors "[list] various circumstances under which a financial relationship between a provider and a referral source would not give rise to liability under the Anti-Kickback Statute").

13. *See, e.g.*, Ashcroft, 39 F. Supp. 3d at 677 (W.D. Pa. 2014) (defendant "must prove strict compliance with a safe harbor to avoid liability for an arrangement that might otherwise violate the statute"); *Gills*, 2012 WL 5340131 at *5 ("The burden is on the party seeking protection under a safe harbor provision to demonstrate strict compliance with each and every element of the safe harbor."); United States *ex rel.* Westmoreland v. Amgen, Inc., 812 F.Supp.2d 39, 80 (D. Mass. 2011) ("To receive protection, a business arrangement must fit squarely within a safe harbor; substantial compliance is not enough . . . .").

14. *See, e.g.*, Gills, 2012 WL 5340131 at *8 n.6 (failure to satisfy a safe harbor does not mean the AKS is violated); *Westmoreland*, 812 F. Supp. 2d at 47 (safe harbor compliance "is voluntary and failure to comply is not a per se violation of the statute"); Feldstein v. Nash Cmty. Health Servs., 51 F. Supp. 2d 673, 687 (E.D.N.C. 1999) ("The failure to fall within a safe harbor . . . 'does not necessarily mean that the conduct/relationship is prohibited by the . . . anti-kickback statute.'") (citation omitted); HHS-OIG Federal Anti-Kickback Law and Regulatory Safe Harbors Fact Sheet, Nov. 1999, accessible at https://oig.hhs.gov/fraud/docs/safeharborregulations/safefs.htm ("Failure to comply with a safe harbor provision does not mean that an arrangement is *per se* illegal. Compliance with safe harbors is voluntary, and arrangements that do not comply with a safe harbor must be analyzed on a case-by-case basis for compliance with the anti-kickback statute."); Medicare and State Health Care Programs: Fraud and Abuse; Clarification of the OIG Safe Harbor Anti-Kickback Provisions, 59 Fed. Reg. 37202, 37203 (July 21, 1994) ("Whether a particular payment practice violates the statute is a question that can only be resolved by an analysis of the elements of the statute as applied to that set of facts."); Medicare and State Health Care Programs: Fraud and Abuse; OIG Anti-Kickback Provision, 56 Fed. Reg. 35952, 35955 (July 29, 1991) ("[T]he gravamen of a violation of the statute is 'inducement' and not necessarily the structure of the arrangement," and thus "case by case inquiries must necessarily focus on the intent of the parties.").

15. *See* Pub. L. No. 92-603, §242(b), 86 Stat. 1329, 1419 (1972).

intended to strengthen the legal framework for combatting practices that had "long been regarded by professional organizations as unethical, which are unlawful in some jurisdictions, and which contribute significantly to the cost of the [Medicare and Medicaid] programs."[16]

The AKS was amended in 1977 to make violations a felony, bolstering the penalties against "illegal practices by some individuals who provide services under Medicare and Medicaid" and which "contribute significantly to the cost of the programs."[17] The amendments expanded the AKS's reach to cover "*any remuneration* (including any kickback, bribe or rebate), directly or indirectly, overtly or covertly, in cash or kind,"[18] and were motivated by a rise in various health care fraud and abuse activities, including financial incentives to induce referrals of program business, medically unnecessary services, and the "*steering*" of patients to "*particular*" providers, thus violating the "*policy of freedom of choice*."[19] In 1997, additional amendments made the AKS applicable, not just to Medicare and Medicaid, but to *all* health care programs receiving federal funding.[20]

Generally, the purpose of the AKS is to remove the corrupting effects of kickbacks in health care by outlawing behavior designed to game the system through the use of financial incentives intended to direct patient referrals to particular health care providers and away from other providers rendering the same type of care. The HHS-OIG, which together with the US Department of Justice (DOJ), has primary responsibility for enforcing the AKS, has explained that violating the AKS increases risks associated with "overutilization, increased program costs, corruption of medical decision-making, patient steering and unfair competition."[21]

The AKS codifies several exceptions to the statutory prohibition, providing at 42 U.S.C. § 1320a-7b(b)(3) that the AKS "shall not apply to" the following:

> *(A) a discount or other reduction in price obtained by a provider of services or other entity under a Federal health care program if the reduction in price is properly disclosed and appropriately reflected*

---

16. H.R. Rept. No. 92-231 at p. 107 (1971).
17. H.R. 95-393 at p. 48 (1977); Pub. L. 95-142, 91 Stat. 1175 (1977).
18. *Id.* (emphasis added).
19. *Id.* at pp. 44-48 (emphasis added).
20. 42 U.S.C. §1320a-7b(f), as amended by Pub. L. No. 104-191, §204, 110 Stat. 1999-2000 (1996).
21. *See* the discussion of the AKS on the OIG website (http://oig.hhs.gov/compliance/physician-education/01laws.asp).

in the costs claimed or charges made by the provider or entity under a Federal health care program;

(B) any amount paid by an employer to an employee (who has a bona fide employment relationship with such employer) for employment in the provision of covered items or services;

(C) any amount paid by a vendor of goods or services to a person authorized to act as a purchasing agent for a group of individuals or entities who are furnishing services reimbursed under a Federal health care program if—

(i) the person has a written contract, with each such individual or entity, which specifies the amount to be paid the person, which amount may be a fixed amount or a fixed percentage of the value of the purchases made by each such individual or entity under the contract, and

(ii) in the case of an entity that is a provider of services (as defined in section 1395x (u) of this title), the person discloses (in such form and manner as the Secretary requires) to the entity and, upon request, to the Secretary the amount received from each such vendor with respect to purchases made by or on behalf of the entity;

(D) a waiver of any coinsurance under part B of subchapter XVIII of this chapter by a Federally qualified health care center with respect to an individual who qualifies for subsidized services under a provision of the Public Health Service Act [42 U.S.C. 201 et seq.];

(E) any payment practice specified by the Secretary in regulations promulgated pursuant to section 14(a) of the Medicare and Medicaid Patient and Program Protection Act of 1987 or in regulations under section 1395w–104 (e)(6) [1] *of this title;*

(F) any remuneration between an organization and an individual or entity providing items or services, or a combination thereof, pursuant to a written agreement between the organization and the individual or entity if the organization is an eligible organization under section 1395mm of this title or if the written agreement, through a risk-sharing arrangement, places the individual or entity at substantial financial risk for the cost or utilization of the items

or services, or a combination thereof, which the individual or entity is obligated to provide;

(G) *the waiver or reduction by pharmacies (including pharmacies of the Indian Health Service, Indian tribes, tribal organizations, and urban Indian organizations) of any cost-sharing imposed under part D of subchapter XVIII of this chapter, if the conditions described in clauses (i) through (iii) of section 1320a–7a (i)(6)(A) of this title are met with respect to the waiver or reduction (except that, in the case of such a waiver or reduction on behalf of a subsidy eligible individual (as defined in section 1395w–114 (a)(3) of this title), section 1320a–7a (i)(6)(A) of this title shall be applied without regard to clauses (ii) and (iii) of that section);*

(H) *any remuneration between a federally qualified health center (or an entity controlled by such a health center) and an MA organization pursuant to a written agreement described in section 1395w–23 (a)(4) of this title;*

(I) *any remuneration between a health center entity described under clause (i) or (ii) of section 1396d (l)(2)(B) of this title and any individual or entity providing goods, items, services, donations, loans, or a combination thereof, to such health center entity pursuant to a contract, lease, grant, loan, or other agreement, if such agreement contributes to the ability of the health center entity to maintain or increase the availability, or enhance the quality, of services provided to a medically underserved population served by the health center entity; and*

(J) *a discount in the price of an applicable drug (as defined in paragraph (2) of section 1395w–114a (g) of this title) of a manufacturer that is furnished to an applicable beneficiary (as defined in paragraph (1) of such section) under the Medicare coverage gap discount program under section 1395w–114a of this title.*

HHS was mandated, through legislation passed in 1987, to promulgate regulations establishing additional "safe harbors" for business arrangements and payment practices that would not be subject to prosecution under the

AKS.[22] By statute, in "modifying and establishing safe harbors," HHS may consider any of the following factors:[23]

> *(A) An increase or decrease in access to health care services.*
> *(B) An increase or decrease in the quality of health care services.*
> *(C) An increase or decrease in patient freedom of choice among health care providers.*
> *(D) An increase or decrease in competition among health care providers.*
> *(E) An increase or decrease in the ability of health care facilities to provide services in medically underserved areas or to medically underserved populations.*
> *(F) An increase or decrease in the cost to Federal health care programs (as defined in section 1320a–7b(f) of this title).*
> *(G) An increase or decrease in the potential overutilization of health care services.*
> *(H) The existence or nonexistence of any potential financial benefit to a health care professional or provider which may vary based on their decisions of—*
> *(i) whether to order a health care item or service; or*
> *(ii) whether to arrange for a referral of health care items or services to a particular practitioner or provider.*
> *(I) Any other factors the Secretary deems appropriate in the interest of preventing fraud and abuse in Federal health care programs (as so defined).*

In 1991, HHS promulgated the initial group of ten regulatory safe harbors, several of which constituted regulatory versions of statutory exceptions enacted at the time of the original AKS legislation.[24] The first group included safe harbors for investment interests, space rental, equipment rental, personal services and management contracts, sale of practice, referral services, warranties, discounts, employees, and group purchasing organizations. As HHS noted in promulgating the original regulatory safe harbors, "[t]he clear congressional intent behind the development of these safe harbor pro-

22. *See* 42 U.S.C. §1320a-7d(a); AKS regulatory safe harbors are codified at 42 CFR § 1001.952.

23. *Id.*

24. Final Rule: OIG Anti-Kickback Provisions (56 Fed. Reg. 35952; July 29, 1991): Final rulemaking promulgating the ten original safe harbor provisions.

visions is to define *innocuous arrangements* that should not be prosecuted, including the statutory exceptions."[25] The DOJ has argued the same position, maintaining that "[t]he Anti-Kickback Statute is designed to prohibit the intentional sale of patient referrals" and that "[t]he safe harbors aren't intended to undermine that principle, but, rather, to assure that legitimate economic relationships between parties who also have a referral relationship are not questioned."[26]

Over the next quarter century, additional safe harbors were created for waiver of copayment, coinsurance, and deductible amounts;[27] increased coverage, reduced cost-sharing amounts, or reduced premium amounts offered by health plans;[28] price reductions offered to health plans;[29] investment interests in rural areas;[30] practitioner recruitment;[31] obstetrical malpractice insurance subsidies;[32] investments in group practices;[33] cooperative hospital service organizations;[34] ambulatory surgical centers;[35] referral arrangements for specialty services;[36] price reductions offered to eligible managed care

25. 56 Fed. Reg. at 35957 (emphasis added); *see also* 64 Fed. Reg. 63519 (Nov. 19, 1999) (safe harbors designed to protect certain "payment and business practices" that might be seen as "technically covered" by "broad" statutory language if they are "*potentially capable* of inducing referrals of business"; explaining that "safe harbors provide a means of assuring that payment practices are not illegal . . . Payment practices that do not fully comply with a safe harbor *may still be lawful if no purpose of the payment practice is to induce referrals of Federal health care program business.*") (emphasis added); 72 Fed. Reg. 56632, 56640 (Oct. 4, 2007) (safe harbors are "meant to protect arrangements that do not pose undue risk for Federal health care programs or beneficiaries; they are not meant to protect arrangements that pose high risks to Federal health care programs.").

26. United States v. Kuchipudi, Case No. 13 CR 312 (N.D. Ill. 2016), "Government's Response to Defendant's Consolidated Post-Trial Motions," at pp. 5, 6-7, 9 (May 18, 2016).

27. Interim Final Rule: Safe Harbors for Protecting Health Plans (57 Fed. Reg. 52723; Nov. 5, 1992); Final Rule: Safe Harbors for Protecting Health Plans (61 Fed. Reg. 2122; Jan. 25, 1996): Revised final rule addressing the three managed care safe harbors originally promulgated in the Nov. 5, 1992 interim final rule; Final Rule: Medicare and State Health Care Programs: Fraud and Abuse; Revisions to the Safe Harbors Under the Anti-Kickback Statute and Civil Monetary Penalty Rules Regarding Beneficiary Inducements (81 Fed. Reg. 88368; Dec. 7, 2016).

28. *Id.*

29. *Id.*

30. Final Rule: Clarification of the Initial OIG Safe Harbor Provisions and Establishment of Additional Safe Harbor Provisions under the Anti-Kickback Statute (64 Fed. Reg. 63518; Nov. 19, 1999).

31. *Id.*

32. *Id.*

33. *Id.*

34. *Id.*

35. *Id.*

36. *Id.*

organizations;[37] price reductions offered by contractors with substantial financial risk to managed care organizations;[38] ambulance replenishing;[39] health centers;[40] electronic prescribing items and services;[41] electronic health records items and services;[42] federally qualified health centers and Medicare Advantage organizations;[43] Medicare coverage gap discount program;[44] and local transportation.[45]

Each AKS safe harbor will be examined individually in Chapter 2.[46]

1.3. Key Sources of Interpretive Guidance

A. The Advisory Opinion Process

HHS is explicitly mandated by statute[47] to issue Advisory Opinions interpreting the requirements of the AKS and safe harbors, including the following:

> *(A) What constitutes prohibited remuneration within the meaning of section 1320a–7b(b) of this title [AKS] or section 1320a–7a(i)(6) of this title [CMPL].*
>
> *(B) Whether an arrangement or proposed arrangement satisfies the criteria set forth in section 1320a–7b(b)(3) of this title [Statutory Exceptions to the AKS] for activities which do not result in prohibited remuneration.*

---

37. Interim Final Rule: Federal Health Care Programs, Fraud and Abuse, Statutory Exception to the Anti-Kickback Statute for Shared Risk Arrangements (64 Fed. Reg. 63504; Nov. 19, 1999).

38. *Id.*

39. Final Rule: Ambulance Replenishing Safe Harbor Under the Anti-Kickback Statute (66 Fed. Reg. 62979; Dec. 4, 2001).

40. Final Rule: Safe Harbor for Federally Qualified Health Centers Arrangements Under the Anti-Kickback Statute (72 Fed. Reg. 56632; Oct. 4, 2007).

41. Final Rule: Safe Harbors for Certain Electronic Prescribing and Electronic Health Records Under the Anti-Kickback Statute (71 Fed. Reg. 45110; Aug. 8, 2006); Final Rule: Medicare and State Health Care Programs: Fraud and Abuse; Electronic Health Records Safe Harbor Under the Anti-Kickback Statute (78 Fed. Reg. 79202; Dec. 27, 2013).

42. *Id.*

43. Final Rule: Medicare and State Health Care Programs: Fraud and Abuse; Revisions to the Safe Harbors Under the Anti-Kickback Statute and Civil Monetary Penalty Rules Regarding Beneficiary Inducements (81 Fed. Reg. 88368; Dec. 7, 2016).

44. *Id.*

45. *Id.*

46. OIG issued proposed rules in 2019 that would revise several AKS safe harbors and add some new ones as well. The proposed changes may be found at 84 Fed. Reg. 55694 and 84 Fed. Reg. 2340. Once these rules are finalized, the authors will update this guidance.

47. 42 U.S.C. § 1320a-7d(b)(2); 42 C.F.R. pt. 1008.

(C) *Whether an arrangement or proposed arrangement satisfies the criteria which the Secretary has established, or shall establish by regulation for activities which do not result in prohibited remuneration [Safe Harbors].*

(D) *What constitutes an inducement to reduce or limit services to individuals entitled to benefits under subchapter XVIII or subchapter XIX within the meaning of section 1320a–7a(b) of this title.*

(E) *Whether any activity or proposed activity constitutes grounds for the imposition of a sanction under section 1320a–7 [Exclusions], 1320a–7a [CMPL], or 1320a–7b [AKS] of this title.*

HHS is prohibited from opining on the fair market value of goods, services, or property, or on whether any individual is a *bona fide* employee within the requirements of the Internal Revenue Code, 26 U.S.C. § 3121(d)(2).[48] An Advisory Opinion concerning a proposed business arrangement is binding only on HHS and the party requesting the Advisory Opinion, and a party's failure to request an Advisory Opinion may not be used as evidence that the party intended to violate the AKS or the provisions of 42 U.S.C. § 1320a-7a (CMPL) or 42 U.S.C. § 1320a-7 (Exclusions).[49] Advisory Opinions are nonetheless a major source of interpretive guidance concerning the scope and limits of the AKS and the safe harbors, and they are routinely consulted for this purpose by health law practitioners.

B. Notice and Comment Rulemaking

Another key source of interpretive guidance for the AKS may be found in the preambles and responses of HHS to comments from the public that are made as part of the Notice and Comment procedure required for the adoption and modification of AKS safe harbors. Given that these agency interpretive comments are made in the exercise of safe harbor rulemaking authority delegated by Congress, and against the backdrop of broad statutory authority from Congress tasking HHS with opining on what constitutes prohibited remuneration under the AKS and on whether business arrangements will be found to satisfy safe harbor requirements, these comments are likely entitled to a significant degree of deference.[50]

48. 42 U.S.C. § 1320a-7d(b)(3).
49. 42 U.S.C. § 1320a-7d(b)(4).
50. *See, e.g.*, Chevron v. Natural Res. Def. Council, Inc., 467 U.S. 837 (1984).

C. *Special Fraud Alerts and Special Advisory Bulletins*

The OIG is charged by statute with the responsibility of issuing Special Fraud Alerts in response to a request "for a notice which informs the public of practices which [the OIG] considers to be suspect or of particular concern" under Medicare, Medicaid, or any other qualifying state health care program.[51] Upon receiving such a request, the OIG is required to investigate and determine whether a special fraud alert should be issued, and if so, the alert is published in the *Federal Register*.[52] In issuing a Special Fraud Alert, the OIG is permitted to consider "whether and to what extent" as well as the "volume and frequency" of the practices to be addressed in the alert might result in any of the consequences that are identified in the law as appropriate considerations for HHS in deciding whether to modify or adopt new AKS safe harbors.[53] Special Advisory Bulletins are another form of periodic notice utilized by the OIG to warn the health care industry against suspect practices under the AKS. These OIG advisories contain useful analysis and guidance concerning business practices that the OIG believes may violate the AKS and/or not fall within the protections of any AKS safe harbor.

D. *Case Law*

In addition to the administrative sources already described, courts are a vital source of interpretive guidance concerning the AKS and safe harbors. As previously noted, the prevailing "one purpose test," holding that just one purpose of an arrangement involving the payment or receipt of remuneration need be inducing referrals to trigger the AKS, is a product of case law development. The meaning of key statutory terms such as "remuneration," the need for strict compliance with safe harbor requirements, and whether those requirements are satisfied in particular cases likewise are issues that have been clarified in judicial opinions.

51. 42 U.S.C. § 1320a-7d(c)(1)(A).
52. 42 U.S.C. § 1320a-7d(c)(1)(B).
53. 42 U.S.C. § 1320a-7d(c)(2)(A) and (B).

2

Statutory Exceptions and Safe Harbors

2.1. Investment Interests

The Anti-Kickback Statute (AKS) includes a safe harbor for certain investment interests under special conditions.

An "investment interest" is defined to include both debt and equity and extends to any "security issued by an entity," including "shares in a corporation, interests or units in a partnership or limited liability company, bonds, debentures, notes, or other debt instruments."[54]

Who qualifies as an "investor" under the investment interest safe harbor is broadly defined by the US Department of Health and Human Services (HHS), and includes "both individuals and entities who either directly or indirectly hold an investment interest in an entity."[55] Thus, "a family member of a referring physician may hold the investment interest in the joint venture entity, or a referring physician may have a legal or beneficial interest in an entity, such as his or her group practice, a trust or a holding company, where that entity directly holds the investment interest in the joint venture entity."[56] In such cases, HHS will deem the physician "as having the ownership interest in the joint venture entity."[57]

---

54. 42 C.F.R. § 1001.952(a)(4).

55. Final Rule: HHS Anti-Kickback Provisions (56 Fed. Reg. 35952, 35963; July 29, 1991): Final rulemaking promulgating the ten original safe harbor provisions.

56. *Id.* at 35964.

57. *Id.*

The safe harbor distinguishes between active and passive investors. An active investor is defined as either one "who is responsible for the day-to-day management of the entity and is a bona fide general partner in a partnership . . . or who agrees in writing to undertake liability for the actions of the entity's agents acting within the scope of their agency."[58] A passive investor is defined as one "who is not an active investor, such as a limited partner in a partnership . . . a shareholder in a corporation, or a holder of a debt security."[59]

HHS will frequently distinguish between investors doing business with the investment entity and those who are only seeking a return on their investment. HHS deems an investor doing business "in any manner" with the investment entity to be "an investor who is in a position to make or influence referrals to, furnish items or services to, or otherwise generate business for the entity."[60] This classification is not limited to those who actually make referrals to the entity, but rather focuses "on the status of the investor and the ability to make or influence the referral stream or level of business activity for the entity."[61] These investors may include physicians, hospitals, or any other entities able to influence referrals.[62]

An investor "doing business with the entity" includes "those investors who furnish items and services to the entity" and also "those investors who otherwise generate business for the entity."[63] However, investors such as "retired physicians [who] no longer make or influence referrals," or "a physician who resides and practices in a separate service area from the entity" and likewise cannot make or influence referrals, or an investor who has agreed as a matter of contract not to make or influence referrals, may not qualify as an "investor doing business with the entity" for purposes of the safe harbor.[64] It is a fact-dependent inquiry.

Generally, HHS "will accept a written stipulation that for the life of the investment the investor will not make referrals to, furnish items or services for, or otherwise generate business for the entity."[65] Due to the potential for abuse in using such a stipulation, however, HHS has stated that "the

58. 42 C.F.R. § 1001.952(a)(4).
59. *Id.*
60. *Id.*
61. *Id.*
62. *Id.*
63. *Id.*
64. *Id.*
65. *Id.*

investor must be bound to [the] agreement for the life of the investment as long as he or she remains an investor."[66] Generally, the investment interest safe harbors "protect against possible illegal remuneration by ensuring that Interested Investors are not in a position to dominate the joint venture's business, thereby increasing the likelihood that the joint venture has an independent and legitimate business purpose, and that any return on investment derives predominately from such business."[67] "Interested investors" are investors "who make referrals or who are in a position to make referrals or furnish items or services to the entity."[68]

A. *Large Publicly Traded Entities*

The safe harbor for investment interests is codified at 42 C.F.R. § 1001.952(a). The first category of investment interest is set forth at subparagraph (1) and applies to large, publicly traded entities:

> (a) *Investment interests.* As used in section 1128B of the Act, "remuneration" does not include any payment that is a return on an investment interest, such as a dividend or interest income, made to an investor as long as all of the applicable standards are met within one of the following three categories of entities:
>
> (1) If, within the previous fiscal year or previous 12 month period, the entity possesses more than $50,000,000 in undepreciated net tangible assets (based on the net acquisition cost of purchasing such assets from an unrelated entity) related to the furnishing of health care items and services, all of the following five standards must be met -
>
> (i) With respect to an investment interest that is an equity security, the equity security must be registered with the Securities and Exchange Commission under 15 U.S.C. 78l(b) or (g).
>
> (ii) The investment interest of an investor in a position to make or influence referrals to, furnish items or services to, or otherwise generate business for the entity must be obtained on terms (including any direct or

66. *Id.*

67. Advisory Opinion No. 98-12, 1998 WL 35287767 at *4 (Sept. 16, 1998).

68. Final Rule: Clarification of the Initial OIG Safe Harbor Provisions and Establishment of Additional Safe Harbor Provisions under the Anti-Kickback Statute (64 Fed. Reg. 63518, 63533; Nov. 19, 1999).

indirect transferability restrictions) and at a price equally available to the public when trading on a registered securities exchange, such as the New York Stock Exchange or the American Stock Exchange, or in accordance with the National Association of Securities Dealers Automated Quotation System.

(iii) The entity or any investor must not market or furnish the entity's items or services (or those of another entity as part of a cross referral agreement) to passive investors differently than to non-investors.

(iv) The entity or any investor (or other individual or entity acting on behalf of the entity or any investor in the entity) must not loan funds to or guarantee a loan for an investor who is in a position to make or influence referrals to, furnish items or services to, or otherwise generate business for the entity if the investor uses any part of such loan to obtain the investment interest.

(v) The amount of payment to an investor in return for the investment interest must be directly proportional to the amount of the capital investment of that investor.

This category of investment interest was "proposed for investment interests in large public corporations where such investments are available to the general public" and requires a "minimum number of shareholders and a minimum number of assets the company must have in order to qualify."[69] HHS's intent was "to protect profit distributions made to referring investors in large publicly traded corporations where the investment interest was obtained at fair market value through trading on a publicly regulated exchange," reasoning that "[t]he remuneration received by these investors is so tangentially related to their referrals that the potential for abuse is minimal."[70] To comply with the safe harbor, the assets of the entity must be measured within the previous fiscal year or twelve-month period, which means that "growing entities will be protected as soon as they reach

69. Final Rule: HHS Anti-Kickback Provisions (56 Fed. Reg. 35952, 35953; July 29, 1991): Final rulemaking promulgating the ten original safe harbor provisions.

70. *Id.* at 35964; *see also* Advisory Opinion No. 98-12, 1998 WL 35287767 at *4 ("The requirements of the safe harbor for investments in large publicly traded entities ensure that referring investors will own such a small share of the total stock issuance that the return on investment is, at most, tangentially related to any referrals.").

compliance with all the preconditions and standards" in the safe harbor.[71] In addition, the safe harbor permits an entity "to retain safe harbor protection for a limited time period even though it is no longer in compliance with the $50 million threshold" and will be afforded "the opportunity to bring itself back into compliance."[72]

The entity further must possess that $50 million in assets in the form of undepreciated net tangible assets, which "removes many assets which [HHS] never intended to include within the scope of protection," including "all intangible assets such as the company's valuation of its name recognition and stock and other forms of goodwill."[73] HHS explained the exclusion of such assets, stating that "their valuation is too subject to 'creative' accounting or appraisal techniques."[74] Assets must also be reduced by any liabilities, such as outstanding loan obligations, but not by depreciation, as HHS decided it was "inappropriate for an entity to lose safe harbor protection as a result of the aging of its assets," and it also did not want to create incentives to replace equipment needlessly just to regain safe harbor protection.[75] The reporting of net tangible assets "must be based on net acquisition costs of purchasing such assets from an unrelated entity," a generally accepted accounting principle, and may not be based upon "a company's use of current market valuations of assets."[76] Assets that are "unrelated to a company's health care line of business cannot be used in the calculation of assets."[77] Health care–related means health care items, devices, supplies, and services as well as items or services reasonably related to the furnishing of such things, including, among other things, "non-emergency transportation, patient education, attendant services, social services . . . utilization review, quality assurance, and practice management services."[78] Marketing services are not included.[79] HHS further noted that although diversified assets could, in some cases, minimize incentives from investor referral sources, HHS "continue[d] to believe that arrangements involving ventures between

71. *Id.*
72. *Id.* at 35965.
73. *Id.*
74. *Id.*
75. *Id.*
76. *Id.*
77. *Id.*
78. Final Rule: Clarification of the Initial OIG Safe Harbor Provisions and Establishment of Additional Safe Harbor Provisions under the Anti-Kickback Statute (64 Fed. Reg. 63518, 63522; Nov. 19, 1999).
79. *Id.*

health care businesses and non-health care businesses pose an increased risk of program abuse." As an example, HHS stated that it "would be an obvious sham, inconsistent with our original intent, if a joint venture could merge with a non-health care business and have those non-health care assets, and the revenues derived from that non-health care line of business counted for the purposes of qualifying for safe harbor protection."[80] Tangible assets that are used to furnish items and services may be counted even if they are not allowable costs under Medicare.[81]

Addressing the specific elements of the safe harbor, HHS stated that element (a)(1)(i) "applies only to an investment interest in an equity security, and requires such a security to be registered with the SEC," noting that requiring actual registration "provides a clear bright-line rule, and is an indication of good-faith entry into the public securities markets, which is a significant factor underlying the rationale for this safe harbor."[82] Actual registration is also required so that certain exempt securities, which may be actively traded without being registered or subject to SEC oversight, will not receive protection under the safe harbor.[83] The registration requirement, however, does not apply to debt securities because "[p]ublicly traded debt instruments, although protected under this safe harbor, are not the type of investment interests that are the focal point of the rule," and while "the potential for abuse is present," HHS was not aware of actual abuse relating to debt securities and determined "that their usefulness as instruments for inducing investors' referrals is more limited than equity investment interests."[84]

HHS next addressed element (a)(1)(ii), commenting that the standard requiring that an investor in a position to make or influence referrals obtain his or her investment interest on terms equally available to the public through a national securities exchange was intended "to preclude safe harbor protection for securities traded through the so-called 'pink sheets' or those 'non-NASDAQ' securities that are traded through the OTC Bulletin Board Service."[85] HHS noted that this requirement

80. *Id.*

81. Final Rule: HHS Anti-Kickback Provisions (56 Fed. Reg. 35952, 35965; July 29, 1991): Final rulemaking promulgating the ten original safe harbor provisions.

82. *Id.*

83. *Id.*

84. *Id.*

85. *Id.*

> follow[ed] [its] original intent to assure that the investment interests of physicians or others in a position to influence referrals must be obtained through the kind of arms-length trading that is normally associated with actively traded public securities at . . . fair market value through a publicly regulated exchange. Such public trading assures that the entity does not obtain capital by self-selecting investors based on their status as sources of referrals.[86]

Regarding the meaning of "on terms equally available," HHS has stated that "an investment interest is obtained on equally available terms if it is obtained at the same price as is available to the general public trading on a registered exchange through a broker and is not subject to restrictions on transferability."[87] On this subject, HHS identified "two significant concerns" in relation to investments in health care–related businesses:

> First, we are concerned that limited transferability or other restrictions on the sale or disposition of stock may serve to "lock" interested investors into specific investments, thereby increasing the incentives for those investors to refer Federal health care program business to the investment entity. Second, we are concerned that interested investors who are potential referral sources for the investment entity not be permitted to obtain their investment interests at insider prices or at prices more favorable than those available to the general public when purchasing stock from a registered national securities exchange through a broker. Such favorable treatment could potentially be disguised remuneration for referrals. For example, we are aware of certain public offerings of health care companies that involve simultaneous acquisitions of physician practices in exchange for stock in the newly-public company, with the stock valued in a manner that results in the selling physician obtaining the stock at a lower price or on more advantageous terms than offered to the public. The economic benefit conferred on the physician in such an arrangement potentially violates the anti-kickback statute if one purpose of the benefit is to reward or

86. *Id.*

87. Final Rule: Clarification of the Initial OIG Safe Harbor Provisions and Establishment of Additional Safe Harbor Provisions under the Anti-Kickback Statute (64 Fed. Reg. 63518, 63522; Nov. 19, 1999).

induce referrals. The investment would not fall within the large entity investment safe harbor.[88]

HHS announced its intention to "closely scrutinize attempts to circumvent this standard," commenting that "any investment interest obtained before an entity becomes publicly traded is not protected under this provisions" and that "an investor is not protected by exchanging a limited partnership interest for shares in a newly formed entity that is publicly traded."[89] HHS further noted that the safe harbor will not protect investment interests "where physicians are afforded the opportunity to buy the available shares of an entity before other members of the public have the opportunity to invest in that entity," noting that such an entity "would have only physicians as investors" and that HHS did not wish to protect payments from that type of entity.[90] The public must have a legitimate opportunity to invest and "[w]here referring sources (or their immediate families) hold a large proportion of the shares, [HHS] will presume that this standard has not been met."[91]

Regarding element (a)(1)(iii), HHS explained that "although an entity may seek referrals or other business from passive investors, it must promote and furnish its items or services to investors and non-investors in the same manner," and "[a]n entity may not use a separate marketing approach or provide a different level of service to passive investors as opposed to non-investors" by, for example, referring to one's position as an investor or offering "special arrangements" to investors that are not offered to noninvestors.[92] Also, HHS commented that "[a]ny distribution to passive investors of individual or aggregate referral patterns" would not be protected and that "the entity or any investor must not promote the items or services of other entities as part of a cross referral agreement."[93]

Explaining the requirement in (a)(1)(iv), HHS stated that "[w]e do not believe protection should be afforded where an investor is loaned money from the entity, or from a parent or subsidiary corporation (or is guaranteed a loan by the entity or a related organization), and the investor makes an investment

88. *Id.*

89. Final Rule: HHS Anti-Kickback Provisions (56 Fed. Reg. 35952, 35965; July 29, 1991): Final rulemaking promulgating the ten original safe harbor provisions.

90. *Id.*

91. *Id.*

92. Final Rule: HHS Anti-Kickback Provisions (56 Fed. Reg. 35952, 35966; July 29, 1991): Final rulemaking promulgating the ten original safe harbor provisions.

93. *Id.*

based on that loan. . . . In such a situation, the investor is adding no real capital to the entity."[94] This prohibition "includes any such loan from another investor or a person acting on behalf of the entity or any investor."[95] HHS conceded, however, that "safe harbor protection is available where the investor borrows from other sources, such as from his or her broker or a bank."[96] Finally, addressing (a)(1)(v), HHS stated that "the amount of payment in return for the investment interest must be directly proportional to the amount of the capital investment" because "such payments are consistent with the type of corporate dividend payment that [HHS] is trying to protect."[97]

B. *Small Entities Owned by Active or Passive Investors*

The safe harbor for investment interests in small entities owned by active or passive investors is codified at 42 C.F.R. § 1001.952(a)(2):

> (2) If the entity possesses investment interests that are held by either active or passive investors, all of the following eight applicable standards must be met -
>
> (i) No more than 40 percent of the value of the investment interests of each class of investment interests may be held in the previous fiscal year or previous 12 month period by investors who are in a position to make or influence referrals to, furnish items or services to, or otherwise generate business for the entity. (For purposes of paragraph (a)(2)(i) of this section, equivalent classes of equity investments may be combined, and equivalent classes of debt instruments may be combined.)
>
> (ii) The terms on which an investment interest is offered to a passive investor, if any, who is in a position to make or influence referrals to, furnish items or services to, or otherwise generate business for the entity must be no different from the terms offered to other passive investors.
>
> (iii) The terms on which an investment interest is offered to an investor who is in a position to make or influence referrals to,

94. *Id.*

95. Final Rule: Clarification of the Initial OIG Safe Harbor Provisions and Establishment of Additional Safe Harbor Provisions under the Anti-Kickback Statute (64 Fed. Reg. 63518, 63521; Nov. 19, 1999).

96. Final Rule: HHS Anti-Kickback Provisions (56 Fed. Reg. 35952, 35966; July 29, 1991): Final rulemaking promulgating the ten original safe harbor provisions.

97. *Id.*

furnish items or services to, or otherwise generate business for the entity must not be related to the previous or expected volume of referrals, items or services furnished, or the amount of business otherwise generated from that investor to the entity.

(iv) There is no requirement that a passive investor, if any, make referrals to, be in a position to make or influence referrals to, furnish items or services to, or otherwise generate business for the entity as a condition for remaining as an investor.

(v) The entity or any investor must not market or furnish the entity's items or services (or those of another entity as part of a cross referral agreement) to passive investors differently than to non-investors.

(vi) No more than 40 percent of the entity's gross revenue related to the furnishing of health care items and services in the previous fiscal year or previous 12-month period may come from referrals or business otherwise generated from investors.

(vii) The entity or any investor (or other individual or entity acting on behalf of the entity or any investor in the entity) must not loan funds to or guarantee a loan for an investor who is in a position to make or influence referrals to, furnish items or services to, or otherwise generate business for the entity if the investor uses any part of such loan to obtain the investment interest.

(viii) The amount of payment to an investor in return for the investment interest must be directly proportional to the amount of the capital investment (including the fair market value of any pre-operational services rendered) of that investor.

This safe harbor is intended to "protect payments from investment in small entities, particularly limited and general partnership interests."[98] HHS noted that due to "the significant business investment activities in these small entities—typically joint ventures—and the advantages of permitting them in

98. *Id.* HHS further noted that the small entity investment interest safe harbor was developed, in part, based on the agency's experience enforcing the AKS, including "investigations of abusive joint venture arrangements, our Fraud Alert describing suspect features of these arrangements [*see* discussion, *infra*], and our Report to Congress entitled 'Financial Arrangements Between Physicians and Health Care Businesses' (OIG, Office of Analysis and Inspections, May 1989). [The report] disclosed in detail both the extensive ownership of joint ventures by physicians, and the additional services received by patients of these physicians as compared to all Medicare patients in general." *Id.* at 35967.

certain situations, we believe that safe harbor protection is warranted."[99] HHS, however, also sounded its alarm over "widespread abuses in many of these joint ventures," commenting that "we believe that a large number of these newly formed entities are designed to have physicians as investors specifically to induce them to use the entity in which they have invested" and that, accordingly, "any safe harbor protection must include significant safeguards to minimize any corrupting influence the investment interest may have on the physician-investor's decision where to refer a patient."[100]

HHS classified investors as either "active" or "passive":

> The definition of an "active" investor includes two categories of persons. The first category is modeled after a bona fide general partner in a partnership under the Uniform Partnership Act who is responsible for the day-to-day management of the entity.
>
> We are including a second way to qualify as an "active" investor: the individual or entity must agree in writing to undertake the liability for the partnership, including the acts of its agents acting within the scope of their agency. We believe that such an affirmative act will assure that the individual or entity performs many of the same functions that general partners do who actively manage the day-to-day operations of the joint venture entity. For example, these active investors undertake the business risk that a typical general partner does, and will be interested in assuring that the day-to-day managers of the entity engage in sound business practices and not run afoul of the statute as well as other Federal and State laws and regulations.
>
> "Passive" investors are those investors who are not active investors, such as limited partners in a partnership or shareholders in a corporation.[101]

HHS stressed that "the standards for this safe harbor must be met by all the investors in the entity" and that "to the extent that one class of investors, such as active investors, qualifies, but the passive investors do not meet one of the standards, safe harbor protection is not given to payments to any investors in the entity."[102] As an example, HHS explained that if a group of individuals were passive investors in an entity that was itself an

99. *Id.* at 35966.
100. *Id.*
101. *Id.* at 35967.
102. *Id.*

active investor in another entity, then the first entity would have to meet all requirements for active investors and the group of individuals would have to meet all requirements for passive investors.[103]

Describing its development of the small entity safe harbor standards, HHS commented:

> The standards for this provision are structured into three categories that we have identified as being of concern to us in joint venture arrangements: (1) The manner in which investors are selected and retained, (2) the nature of their business structure, and (3) the financing and profit distributions. To the extent possible, we have adopted bright line rules. We believe that this approach will facilitate compliance because investors will be able to determine easily whether they meet the conditions of safe harbor protection.[104]

The five standards contained in subparagraphs (a)(2)(i)–(v) of the safe harbor are intended to address the first category of concern. HHS explained that the first standard, limiting those "in a position to make or influence referrals to, furnish items or services to, or otherwise generate business for the entity" to 40 percent of the value of the investment interests in the entity, "requires not only that a bona fide opportunity to invest has been afforded to people not in a position to make referrals, but that these individuals hold at least 60 percent of the value of the investment interests in each class of investments."[105] HHS described this as an "outcome measure" that would "provide a bright line test which will assist all the parties to the joint venture and [HHS] in determining whether compliance with this first standard has been achieved."[106] HHS commented that "classifying investors who provide items and services together with investors who make or influence referrals to the entity" was necessary to prevent an outside vendor (e.g., durable medical equipment [DME] supplier) from forming a joint venture with referring physicians under circumstances in which all of the joint venture owners "would be doing business with the joint venture by either furnishing items or making referrals."[107] Classifying both categories of investor together means that "at least 60 percent of the value

---

103. *Id.*
104. *Id.*
105. *Id.* at 35968.
106. *Id.*
107. *Id.*

of the investment interests must be held by investors who will neither make referrals nor engage in business activity with the entity."[108]

In ensuring conformity with this requirement, "the joint venture is free to use any internal accounting principles it chooses to adopt so long as it uses such principles consistently over time so that it is not manipulating data to obscure its noncompliance."[109] The standard permits two different measurement periods. The joint venture may use either its prior fiscal year or the previous twelve-month period. If a calendar year is the venture's fiscal year, then it may look at "the number and status of investors" either in the prior year, or in the twelve-month period immediately preceding the current date.[110] HHS stressed, however, that it would be "highly unlikely" to pursue an investigation of a joint venture where it is out of compliance with the 60 and 40 percent standard based on its prior fiscal year "but is making a good-faith effort to reach compliance with this standard based on data showing compliance on a monthly basis for the most recent months of operation."[111]

The next two standards contained in (a)(2)(ii) and (a)(2)(iii) "address the problems of discriminatory marketing strategies that result in the offer of better deals, for example, more shares or a better price, to individuals who will refer a high volume of patients."[112] Standard (a)(2)(ii) "focuses on the *status* of investor and bars safe harbor protection where the terms of investment opportunities depend on whether a passive investor is in a position to influence referrals, furnish items or services, or otherwise generate business for the entity."[113] Investments may only be offered to such investors "on the same terms as those offered to other passive investors not in a position to influence the flow of business to the entity."[114] The standard does not apply to active investors in view of the fact that "it is precisely because of a physician's familiarity with the health care field that he or she may be chosen as a general partner and offered different investment terms from those offered to passive investors."[115]

Standard (a)(2)(iii) "assumes that an investment interest is being offered to a person in a position to make referrals, but bars the offering of favorable

108. *Id.*
109. *Id.*
110. *Id.*
111. *Id.*
112. *Id.*
113. *Id.*
114. *Id.*
115. *Id.*

terms based on his or her past or expected referrals or amount of business otherwise generated for the entity."[116] This standard applies to both active and passive investors based on the view of HHS that "it is inappropriate to protect all investment interests where any investor, even general partners, can obtain more shares because they can be expected to generate more business for the entity."[117]

Standards (a)(2)(iv) and (v) relate to how investors are retained:

> The fourth standard bars the entity from requiring passive investors to make referrals or remain in a position to make referrals as a condition for retaining their investment. The fifth standard parallels the new standard for publicly traded entities and requires the entity and investors not to market or furnish items or services to passive investors in any manner differently than to non-investors. . . .
>
> [The] fifth standard also requires the entity and any investor not to promote the services of other entities as part of a cross referral agreement.[118]

These two standards apply only to passive investors in recognition of the fact that "active investors are often sought out because they will help generate business for the joint venture."[119]

Standard (a)(2)(vi) relates to the second category of HHS concern, i.e., the nature of the business structure. The requirement that no more than 40 percent of the joint venture's revenue come from investor referrals stems from HHS's concern over situations in which "the referrals from investing physicians dominate the joint venture's business so that it does not have to compete for outside business and that it cannot survive without such referrals from its investing physicians," with the result that "the business purpose of the joint venture becomes suspect."[120] This sixth standard, combined with the first standard imposing a 60 and 40 percent ownership requirement, "provide clear rules which assure that no protection is afforded to joint ventures that operate primarily on the referrals of physician investors."[121] As explained by HHS:

---

116. *Id.*
117. *Id.*
118. *Id.* at 35969.
119. *Id.*
120. *Id.*
121. *Id.*

> By requiring that no more than 40 percent of the joint venture's revenue come from investors' referrals, we help assure that revenues of these joint ventures come from a wider group than referrals from physician investors. And by limiting the number of investors who make referrals, we help assure that the profits from these entities are distributed to a wider group than referring physician investors. Thus, these two standards will help assure that joint ventures are not dependent on the capital and referrals of physician-investors.[122]

This standard, like the first 40 percent standard, allows "a joint venture to use any internal accounting principle it chooses to adopt so long as it uses such principles consistently" and is "not manipulating the data to obscure its non-compliance."[123] Also, as with the first standard, the joint venture entity can measure its compliance by reference to its prior fiscal year or the previous twelve-month period.[124] And, again, HHS noted that it would be highly unlikely to initiate an investigation where the joint venture is in compliance with the other standards but is not in compliance with this standard based on prior fiscal year data, provided that it is making a "good-faith effort" to comply "based on data showing compliance on a monthly basis for the most recent months of operation."[125] HHS reiterated that in applying both 40 percent standards in situations in which the joint venture entity is owned by other entities, HHS

> will examine the ownership structure of these other entities to determine whether they are owned by physicians who are referring to the joint venture entity. In such a situation, these physicians are considered to be investors of the joint venture entity, and their ownership interest must be offset by non-referring owners and the revenue they generate for the joint venture must be offset by referrals from non-investors.

Standards (a)(2)(vii) and (viii) relate to the third category of HHS concern, i.e., financing and profit distributions. Standard (a)(2)(vii) is intended "to assure that the investments are bona fide, i.e., that investors' funds are genuinely at risk."[126] Accordingly, although the joint venture entity "may

122. *Id.*
123. *Id.*
124. *Id.*
125. *Id.*
126. *Id.* at 35970.

borrow from the investor, and investors may borrow from other sources to obtain funds to use for the capital investment," the entity "cannot lend the funds or guarantee loans used to make the investment."[127] This is because if the investment is made with capital provided by the entity, the investor is "adding no real capital to it," and the purpose of the standard is to "help assure that physicians and other investors in fact provide new needed capital and that the joint venture is not in reality a sham to facilitate the distribution of payments for referrals."[128] Moreover, HHS noted that "it is useful to analyze joint ventures on a case-by-case basis to determine what the real capital needs of the project are, and whether the capital that has been invested is merely a sham to pay investors for referrals."[129]

Standard (a)(2)(viii) provides that, in order to receive protection, "dividend payments can only be tied to the number of shares owned by an investor, and not to his or her referrals," and where investors "contribute capital in the form of pre-operational services or sweat equity, their dividend payments may reflect the fair market value of those services rendered."[130] This standard does not protect "payments to active investors for operational services they provide to the joint venture" but only "payments that represent a return on investment."[131] Protection for payments made in return for personal services is governed by the personal services and management contracts safe harbor, not the investment interests safe harbor.

The HHS, Office of Inspector General (OIG) has issued Special Fraud Alerts to discuss joint venture arrangements that it considers to be suspect and potentially violative of the AKS and outside the protection of this safe harbor. The first such Special Fraud Alert was issued in 1989 and announced that the OIG had "become aware of a proliferation of arrangements between those in a position to refer business, such as physicians, and those providing items or services for which Medicare or Medicaid pays," including "clinical diagnostic laboratory services, durable medical equipment (DME), and other diagnostic services."[132] The OIG went on to describe the nature of joint ventures and how they may be found to violate the AKS:

127. *Id.*
128. *Id.*
129. *Id.*
130. *Id.*
131. *Id.*
132. Special Fraud Alert: Joint Venture Arrangements (Issued Aug. 1989).

> A joint venture may take a variety of forms: it may be a contractual arrangement between two or more parties to cooperate in providing services, or it may involve the partnership or closely held corporation, to provide such services. Of course, there may be legitimate reasons to form a joint venture, such as raising necessary investment capital. However, [OIG] believes that some of these joint ventures may violate the [AKS].
>
> Under these suspect joint ventures, physicians may become investors in a newly formed joint venture entity. The investors refer their patients to this new entity, and are paid by the entity in the form of "profit distributions." These [suspect] joint ventures may be intended not so much to raise investment capital legitimately to start a business, but to lock up a stream of referrals from the physician investors and to compensate them indirectly for these referrals. Because physician investors can benefit financially from their referrals, unnecessary procedures and tests may be ordered or performed, resulting in unnecessary program expenditures.

The OIG identified a nonexclusive set of factors that, viewed separately or collectively, could indicate the existence of a joint venture that violates the AKS:

1. ***Investor***

- Investors are chosen because they are in a position to make referrals.
- Physicians who are expected to make a large number of referrals may be offered a greater investment opportunity in the joint venture than those anticipated to make fewer referrals.
- Physician investors may be actively encouraged to make referrals to the joint venture, and may be encouraged to divest their ownership interest if they fail to sustain an "acceptable" level of referrals.
- The joint venture tracks its sources of referrals, and distributes this information to the investors.
- Investors may be required to divest their ownership interest if they cease to practice in the service area, for example, if they move, become disabled, or retire.
- Investment interests may be nontransferable.

2. ***Business Structure***

- The structure of some joint ventures may be suspect. For example, one of the parties may be an ongoing entity already engaged in a particular line of business. That party may act as the reference laboratory or DME supplier for the joint venture. In some of these cases, the joint venture can be best characterized as a "shell."

- In the case of a shell laboratory joint venture, for example:
  - It conducts very little testing on the premises, even though it is Medicare certified.
  - The reference laboratory may do the vast bulk of the testing at its central processing laboratory, even though it also serves as the "manager" of the shell laboratory.
  - Despite the location of the actual testing, the local "shell"' laboratory bills Medicare directly for these tests.

- In the case of a shell DME joint venture, for example:
  - It owns very little of the DME or other capital equipment; rather the ongoing entity owns them.
  - The ongoing entity is responsible for all day-to-day operations of the joint venture, such as delivery of the DME and billing.

3. *Financing and Profit Distribution*

- The amount of capital invested by the physician may be disproportionately small and the returns on investment may be disproportionately large when compared to a typical investment in a new business enterprise.
- The amount of capital invested by the physician may be disproportionately small and the returns on investment may be disproportionately large when compared to a typical investment in a new business enterprise.
- Physician investors may invest only a nominal amount, such as $500 to $1500.
- Physician investors may be permitted to "borrow" the amount of the "investment" from the entity, and pay it back through deductions from profit distributions, thus eliminating even the need to contribute cash to the partnership.
- Investors may be paid extraordinary returns on the investment in comparison with the risk involved, often well over 50 to 100 percent per year.[133]

133. *Id.*

The OIG returned to the subject of suspect joint ventures in April 2003, when it issued a Special Advisory Bulletin on "Contractual Joint Ventures."[134] Referencing its 1989 bulletin, the OIG stated that it had observed the continued proliferation of joint ventures despite its prior warning. Defining a "joint venture" to be "any common enterprise with mutual economic benefit," the 2003 Special Advisory Bulletin focused on "questionable contractual arrangements where a health care provider in one line of business . . . expands into a related health care business by contracting with an existing provider of a related item or service . . . to provide the new item or service to the [first provider's] existing patient population."[135] In such arrangements, the second provider frequently "not only manages the new line of business, but may also supply it with inventory, employees, space, billing, and other services."[136] In this way, the first provider (typically an owner of the related line of business) effectively "contracts out substantially the entire operation of the related line of business" to the second provider, who might otherwise have been a competitor, and in return receives the profits of the business, including revenues earned as a result of federal health care program referrals.[137]

The OIG offered several examples of these kinds of contractual joint ventures, including (1) a hospital that establishes a DME subsidiary and contracts out the entire operation to an existing DME company; (2) a DME company that forms its own mail order pharmacy to supply nebulizer drugs and contracts with an existing mail order pharmacy to run the entire operation and sell nebulizer drugs to the DME company pharmacy for inventory; and (3) a nephrology group that establishes a wholly owned company to provide dialysis supplies to dialysis patients, and the company contracts out the entire operation to an existing home dialysis supplier.[138]

The OIG identified certain "common elements" to such suspect joint ventures:

1. the owner is expanding into a related line of business (either organized separately or as part of an existing entity) that is dependent on owner-generated referrals or other business and which serves the owner's existing patient base;

134. Special Advisory Bulletin: Contractual Joint Ventures (Issued April 2003).
135. *Id.*
136. *Id.*
137. *Id.*
138. *Id.*

2. the owner does not operate or commit significant financial or other resources to the new business, but contracts out substantially all the operations to another party that supplies management services and everything else needed to run the business, including inventory, personnel, space, and billing, which is done in the name of the owner. Contracts may include non-competition provisions that result in an exclusive dealing arrangement, and the owner does not assume meaningful business risk as a result of its ability to influence referrals to the new business.
3. the manager of the new line of business is an established provider of the same services and would, absent the joint venture, be a competitor of the new line of business, providing and billing for those services in its own name.
4. the owner and manager share in the economic benefits of the new line of business, with the manager earning revenues through its various contracts with the owner, and the owner receiving residual profits from the new line of business.
5. payments to the manager, particularly for goods and services, typically vary with the value or volume of referrals or other business generated by the owner, as will the owner's profits.[139]

The OIG warned that these suspect joint ventures may not be protected under any safe harbor, despite efforts "to carve otherwise problematic contracting arrangements into several different contracts for discrete items or services . . . and then qualify each separate contract for protection under a 'safe harbor'."[140] The OIG commented that, to the extent a manager is selling items or services to an owner as a discount, it is not protected by the discount safe harbor, which "does not protect—and has never protected—prices offered by a seller to a buyer in connection with a common enterprise."[141] Such a price reduction must be based on an arms-length transaction, and "the provision of items or services to a joint venture by a participant in the venture is not an 'arms length' transaction."[142]

The OIG also pointed out that any safe harbors that do apply would only protect the compensation flowing from the owner to the manager for actual services rendered but would not protect remuneration that "is often the

139. *Id.*
140. *Id.*
141. *Id.*
142. *Id.*

difference between the money paid by the Owner to the Manager/Supplier and the reimbursement received from the federal health care programs" since the manager, in "agreeing effectively to provide services it could otherwise provide in its own right for less than the available reimbursement . . . is providing the Owner with the opportunity to generate a fee and a profit."[143] That business opportunity "is itself remuneration that may implicate the anti-kickback statute."

The OIG summarized a nonexclusive list of characteristics that, viewed together and/or separately, potentially indicate a prohibited arrangement: (1) the new business is an expansion into a new line of health care business that can be provided to an owner's existing patients; (2) the new business is designed to exclusively or predominantly service an existing, captive patient base of the owner; (3) the owner's primary contributions are the referrals, with the entire operation delegated to the manager, and the owner taking on no real business risk and making little or no financial investment; (4) the manager/supplier would normally compete for the owner's referrals and has the ability to provide the same services and bill in its own name; (5) the manager/supplier provides all or most key services to the new business; (6) the practical effect of the arrangement is to permit the owner to bill insurers and patients for business otherwise provided by the manager/supplier; and (7) a noncompete clause exists that prohibits the owner from providing items or services to outside patients and/or prohibits the manager/supplier from providing services in its own right to the owner's patients.[144]

A significant number of Advisory Opinions have opined on the safe harbor for small entity investment interests in the context of proposed business arrangements or joint ventures.[145] One example of a venture that the OIG determined presented an unacceptable risk of violating the AKS is discussed in Advisory Opinion No. 11-15.[146] There, the OIG addressed a proposed arrangement in which a physician-owned and physician-managed company (Company A) would contract with another company that either currently operated or would form a Medicare-certified clinical anatomic pathology

143. *Id.*

144. *Id.*

145. There is also case law discussing the requirements of this safe harbor in the context of a False Claims Act lawsuit in which joint venture partners in a pharmacy business who also owned nursing homes were alleged to have arranged the investment opportunity for the purpose of securing pharmacy referrals. *See* United States *ex rel.* Nehls v. Omnicare, Inc., 2013 WL 3819671 at **14-15 (July 23, 2013, N.D. Ill.).

146. Advisory Opinion 11-15 (Issued Oct. 3, 2011).

laboratory (Company B). The physician certified that he would not refer the physician's own patients or otherwise generate business in connection with the arrangement. Company B would enter into a management services contract with Company A for at least a three-year term. Under the contract, Company A would provide Company B with all required services, including utilities, furniture, fixtures, use of lab space and equipment, marketing, billing and nonphysician support staff. Company B would pay Company A a usage fee based on a percentage of Company B's income, fixed in advance for one year, generally corresponding to the volume of Company B's use of Company's services. Company A certified that the usage fee would represent fair market value for the use of its services. The physician would offer the opportunity to invest in Company A to other physicians, most of whom would have little or no experience in clinical laboratory services, but he would hire others with the appropriate experience as employees or contractors. Physician investors in a position to refer lab specimens to Company A would account for more than 40 percent of the value of all investment interests in Company A, and more than 40 percent of Company A's gross revenue would be sourced to the referrals of such physician investors, although there would be no requirement that physician investors refer to Company A. Membership interests would be purchased based on the book value of Company A multiplied by the pro rata share purchased, and profit distributions would correspond to an investor's percentage membership interest in Company A.[147]

As the fact pattern involves "ownership of a non-public entity by interested investors," the OIG noted that the small entity investment safe harbor was "potentially applicable."[148] The OIG quickly concluded, however, that the safe harbor could not apply on these facts since both 40 percent requirements were not satisfied, commenting that "[a]s the result of noncompliance with these elements, the small entity safe harbor would be inapplicable and would not protect [Company A's] profit distributions to the new physician investors and the [physician owner/manager]."[149] The OIG

147. *Id.*

148. *Id.*

149. *Id.* The OIG further noted that the contract arrangements for all of the services provided to Company B would not satisfy other safe harbors for space rental, equipment rental, or personal services and management contracts because the compensation would not be set in advance but would instead "be calculated based on a percentage of [Company B's income]," which would impermissibly "take into account the volume or value of business generated for [Company B] by the physician investors in the form of lab referrals." *Id.*

went on to explain, concerning the risk involved, that "[t]he absence of limits on such involvement by interested investors or other safeguards to restrain the Proposed Arrangement's reliance on investor-generated business further underscores the already-noted risks of overutilization, distorted medical decision-making, and increased program costs."[150] Furthermore, the OIG noted that given the lack of any relevant experience in clinical lab services by the physician owners of the entity providing such services, but who nonetheless have the ability to refer patients for those services, the proposed arrangement "appears to have no business purpose other than to permit the physician investors to profit from the business they generate" for Company B in the form of lab specimen referrals. Further, "[t]he fact that the profits would be obtained indirectly, because [Company B], rather than [Company A], would bill for the clinical laboratory services, is immaterial."[151]

Other Advisory Opinions declined to impose administrative sanctions on proposed arrangements even though they did not comply with the small entity investment safe harbor, and despite some concerning elements that might have violated the AKS if an intent to reward or induce referrals were present. A review of these opinions reveals a variety of mitigating factors that led the OIG to conclude in a given case that the particular arrangement under review posed an acceptably low level of risk, notwithstanding its failure to comply fully with the safe harbor and despite a fact pattern that could potentially reward or induce referrals. The OIG's restraint in these cases was based on some combination of the following elements:

- Absence of individual physician investors or physician investors who were not direct referral sources[152]
- Limited number of referrals coming from joint venture partners[153]
- Affirmative measures taken by joint venture partners to limit the ability to direct or influence referrals, including not requiring or encouraging physicians to refer patients; not tracking referrals; or not compensating potential referral sources based on the volume or value of referrals[154]

---

150. *Id.*

151. *Id.*

152. *See* Advisory Opinion No. 10-15 (Issued Aug. 31, 2010); Advisory Opinion 03-12 (Issued May 22, 2003).

153. *See* Advisory Opinion No. 05-12 (Issued Oct. 31, 2005); Advisory Opinion No. 97-5 (Issued Oct. 6, 1997).

154. *See* Advisory Opinion No. 10-15 (Issued Aug. 31, 2010); Advisory Opinion No. 05-12 (Issued Oct. 31, 2005); Advisory Opinion No. 03-12 (Issued May 22, 2003); Advisory Opinion No. 98-19 (Issued Dec. 14, 1998); Advisory Opinion No. 97-5 (Issued Oct. 6, 1997).

- Return on investment that was proportional to capital investment and not based on previous or expected volume of referrals, services furnished, or amount of business that might otherwise be generated[155]
- Any ancillary service agreements were based on fair market value and did not add appreciable risk to the arrangement[156]
- Joint venture partners that were all part of one academic medical center, where the structure of the proposed arrangement would facilitate efficient integration of their respective clinical, research, and teaching missions[157]
- Inability or a limited ability to control or influence referral frequency or volume[158]
- Business opportunity that was obtained through a competitive bidding process[159]
- Arrangement promoted a public service in a location where such a service had historically been deficient or failed financially[160]
- Investor referrals well below 40 percent so that there was a low risk the arrangement relied primarily on owner referrals[161]
- Investors assumed genuine business risk by committing financial resources and agreeing to guarantee a bank line of credit[162]
- Certification that a physician, whose family members owned 70 percent of an independent diagnostic testing facility (IDTF), would not make referrals or generate business for entity, and neither physician nor IDTF would supply DME that might create incentive for physician to slant test interpretations to support medical necessity and thus risk overutilization[163]
- Fewer than 5 percent of entity patients were beneficiaries of federal health care programs and the vast majority of such group were referred

155. *See* Advisory Opinion No. 10-15 (Issued Aug. 31, 2010); Advisory Opinion No. 05-12 (Issued Oct. 31, 2005); Advisory Opinion No. 03-13 (Issued June 16, 2003); Advisory Opinion No. 03-12 (Issued May 22, 2003); Advisory Opinion No. 98-19 (Issued Dec. 14, 1998); Advisory Opinion No. 97-5 (Issued Oct. 6, 1997).

156. *See* Advisory Opinion No. 03-12 (Issued May 22, 2003).

157. *See* Advisory Opinion No. 10-15 (Issued Aug. 31, 2010).

158. *See* Advisory Opinion No. 09-17 (Issued Sept. 30, 2009); Advisory Opinion No. 03-12 (Issued May 22, 2003); Advisory Opinion No. 98-19 (Issued Dec. 14, 1998); Advisory Opinion No. 97-5 (Issued Oct. 6, 1997).

159. *See* Advisory Opinion No. 09-17 (Issued Sept. 30, 2009).

160. *See id.*

161. Advisory Opinion No. 03-13 (Issued June 16, 2003).

162. *See* Advisory Opinion No. 09-17 (Issued Sept. 30, 2009).

163. *See* Advisory Opinion No. 12-08 (Issued June 22, 2012).

by noninvestors, with any investor referrals required to undergo an independent evaluation by one whose compensation did not depend on evaluation results[164]

- Low risk of cross-referrals among physician investors, where each had independent practice providing similar services, and competed with each other[165]
- Low risk of overutilization of items or services, where federal health care program beneficiaries all belonged to capitated Medicaid health maintenance organization (HMO) plans, and no more than 2 percent of federally sourced revenues resulted from investor referrals.[166]

C. *Entities Located in Underserved Areas*

The safe harbor for entities located in underserved areas is codified at 42 C.F.R. § 1001.952(a)(3):

> (3) (i) If the entity possesses investment interests that are held by either active or passive investors and is located in an underserved area, all of the following eight standards must be met -
>
> (A) No more than 50 percent of the value of the investment interests of each class of investments may be held in the previous fiscal year or previous 12-month period by investors who are in a position to make or influence referrals to, furnish items or services to, or otherwise generate business for, the entity. (For purposes of paragraph (a)(3)(i)(A) of this section, equivalent classes of equity investments may be combined, and equivalent classes of debt instruments may be combined.)
>
> (B) The terms on which an investment interest is offered to a passive investor, if any, who is in a position to make or influence referrals to, furnish items or services to, or otherwise generate business for the entity must be no different from the terms offered to other passive investors.
>
> (C) The terms on which an investment interest is offered to an investor who is in a position to make or influence referrals to, furnish items or services to, or otherwise generate business for the entity must not be related to the previous or expected

164. Advisory Opinion No. 05-12 (Issued Oct. 31, 2005).
165. *See id.*
166. *See id.*

volume of referrals, items or services furnished, or the amount of business otherwise generated from that investor to the entity.

(D) There is no requirement that a passive investor, if any, make referrals to, be in a position to make or influence referrals to, furnish items or services to, or otherwise generate business for the entity as a condition for remaining as an investor.

(E) The entity or any investor must not market or furnish the entity's items or services (or those of another entity as part of a cross-referral agreement) to passive investors differently than to non-investors.

(F) At least 75 percent of the dollar volume of the entity's business in the previous fiscal year or previous 12-month period must be derived from the service of persons who reside in an underserved area or are members of medically underserved populations.

(G) The entity or any investor (or other individual or entity acting on behalf of the entity or any investor in the entity) must not loan funds to or guarantee a loan for an investor who is in a position to make or influence referrals to, furnish items or services to, or otherwise generate business for the entity if the investor uses any part of such loan to obtain the investment interest.

(H) The amount of payment to an investor in return for the investment interest must be directly proportional to the amount of the capital investment (including the fair market value of any pre-operational services rendered) of that investor.

(ii) If an entity that otherwise meets all of the above standards is located in an area that was an underserved area at the time of the initial investment, but subsequently ceases to be an underserved area, the entity will be deemed to comply with paragraph (a)(3)(i) of this section for a period equal to the lesser of:

(A) The current term of the investment remaining after the date upon which the area ceased to be an underserved area or

(B) Three years from the date the area ceased to be an underserved area.

The OIG initially proposed this safe harbor after learning that entities in many rural areas found it difficult with the two 60-40 tests in the small entity investment interest safe harbor.[167] The OIG commented that "[e]ntities located in rural areas may have an especially difficult time complying with these two standards, because in many cases physicians may be the primary sources of capital in the area, and those physicians may have no alternative facility to which they can refer."[168] The primary concern of the OIG was to ensure "that beneficiaries have adequate access to quality health care" given the reality that "certain communities experience shortages of health care services."[169] The safe harbor was "designed to balance the interests of those communities in facilitating the development of health care services with the anti-fraud interests that are the basis of the anti-kickback statute."[170]

The OIG observed that joint ventures in underserved areas raise the same AKS concerns as other joint ventures, namely, whether the joint venture is a *bona fide* business enterprise, whether distributions from the joint venture are merely payments for referrals from investors, and whether distributions are merely payments for referrals from one investor to another.[171] Accordingly, the OIG was mindful that "any safe harbor contain adequate safeguards and conditions against fraud and abuse," while also providing "additional flexibility for investments in underserved areas that may experience a shortage of available capital from non-referral source investors."[172] The safe harbor as adopted defines "an underserved area as any defined geographic area that is designated as a MUA [Medically Underserved Area]" by regulation, including both rural and urban areas.[173]

Other key features of the safe harbor are as follows: (1) a rule that 75 percent of the volume of the entity's business must be derived from residents of underserved areas; (2) a three-year grace period for entities that comply with the safe harbor initially but subsequently fall out of compliance; and (3) a rule requiring that at least 50 percent of the investment interests be held by nonreferral source investors.[174] The need for a grace period arises from the possibility that an entity meeting all other safe harbor requirements might be located in an area that loses its MUA designation after initially

167. Final Rule: Clarification of the Initial OIG Safe Harbor Provisions and Establishment of Additional Safe Harbor Provisions under the Anti-Kickback Statute (64 Fed. Reg. 63518, 63530; Nov. 19, 1999).

168. *Id.* at 63532.

169. *Id.*

170. *Id.*

171. *Id.*

172. *Id.*

173. *Id.*

174. *Id.*

being classified as a MUA. The grace period is designed to "afford entities that wish to maintain safe harbor protection an opportunity to restructure so as to qualify for the small entity investment interest safe harbor."[175]

Regarding the 75 percent rule found at (a)(3)(i)(F), the OIG conveyed its belief the 75 percent requirement "would adequately protect against abuses and further the purpose of this safe harbor . . . [by] requiring that at least 75 percent of the dollar volume of the entity's business in the previous fiscal year or previous 12-month period be derived from services provided to persons residing in an underserved area or persons who are member of a MUP."[176] The OIG further explained its decision to eliminate entirely the 60-40 revenue rule of the small entity investment interest safe harbor for entities operating in underserved areas, while retaining a modified interested investor rule:

> [W]e are persuaded that eliminating both 60-40 rules, and in particular the 60-40 investor rule, may lead to inappropriate financial incentives and unfair competition in some areas by allowing referral source investors, primarily physicians, to "lock up" the market for particular services in those areas. Ensuring fair competition in the health care marketplace is one of the goals of the anti-kickback statute. We are also concerned that an excessive proliferation of particular services in rural or urban underserved areas could lead to overutilization by entities competing for scarce revenue and could prompt protected entities to develop revenue streams from patients not residing in underserved areas, in contravention of the intent and spirit of the safe harbor . . .
>
> . . .
>
> In this final rule, we are adopting our original proposal to eliminate the 60-40 revenue rule, but we are retaining a modified limitation on the number of interested investors. Specifically, we are requiring, as a condition for protection, that investors who make referrals or who are in a position to make referrals or furnish items or services to the entity not own more than 50 percent of the value of investment interest within each class of investment in the entity. As with the 60-40 investor rule in the small entity investment safe harbor, we are permitting equivalent classes of stock to be aggregated for purposes of determining safe harbor compliance.

175. *Id.* at 63533.
176. *Id.* at 63534.

> We believe that eliminating the 60-40 revenue rule, thereby permitting entities to draw 100 percent of their revenue from referrals by investor-owners should make investment in such entities sufficiently attractive to non-referral source investors so as to permit the entities to meet the new 50-50 investor test.[177]

The OIG rejected a request that it allow compliance with this safe harbor in situations where an entity has certified its inability to satisfy the 60-40 standards of the small entity investment interest safe harbor despite "best efforts," commenting that "[a] mere 'best efforts' exception to the small entity investment interests safe harbor based on a certification from the investment entity would be insufficient to protect against abusive arrangements and would be impractical in application."[178] The OIG went on to say that if an entity cannot comply with the 50-50 investor rule of this safe harbor, it would still "have recourse to the advisory opinion process for guidance about their specific arrangements."[179]

There have been Advisory Opinions addressing the safe harbor for investments in underserved area entities. Advisory Opinion No. 03-13[180] analyzed a joint venture involving ownership of a magnetic resonance imaging (MRI) center that served residents of a three-county rural area that was not also designated a MUA. More than 85 percent of the MRI center's patients were residents of this region, which had not had MRI services available prior to the establishment of the center. In order to raise capital for the MRI center, limited partnership interests were offered to members of the medical community and former board members of the three area hospitals. One hospital and its supporting foundation purchased 30 percent of the partnership units. Others in a position to influence or generate referrals or provide items or services to the MRI center owned another 30 percent of the center. The remaining 40 percent of the center was owned by those who are not in a position to influence or generate referrals. The percentage of non-referring investors had increased over time. All investors were offered the opportunity to invest on the same terms, without reference to their ability to refer to or generate business for the MRI center, and return on investment was directly proportional to investor capital contributions. More than

177. *Id.* at 63533.
178. *Id.*
179. *Id.*
180. Advisory Opinion No. 03-13 (Issued June 16, 2003).

60 percent of the revenues of the MRI center was generated from referrals made by disinterested parties. Ancillary management service and space lease agreements were certified to be compliant with safe harbor requirements.

Against this factual backdrop, the OIG concluded that since 60 percent of the venture was owned by interested investors, no investment interest safe harbor was available to protect the arrangement. The small entity safe harbor requires that no more than 40 percent of the venture be owned by such investors, and while the MRI center was located in a rural area, the facility was not located in a MUA and had more than 50 percent interested investors. The OIG nonetheless determined that it would not impose administrative sanctions, as the below-enumerated factors led it to conclude that the risk of fraud and abuse was sufficiently low:

- The arrangement had indicia of a legitimate, *bona fide*, business because all investors were offered the opportunity to invest on the same terms and conditions, returns on investment interests were proportional to capital contributions and, most important, less than 40 percent of the revenue of the MRI center was derived from interested investors.
- The structure of the arrangement did not contain any suspect characteristics identified in the OIG's 1989 Special Fraud Alert on joint ventures and would have complied with the safe harbor for rural entities proposed in 1993 (although not with the final rule adopted in 1999).
- The arrangement was developed as a community-oriented effort to provide access to MRI services in the three-county region and has provided a substantial community benefit.
- The ancillary agreements have been certified as safe harbor compliant.

Advisory Opinion No. 07-20[181] involved an arrangement proposed by a physician in a Louisiana parish who had operated a medical clinic that was destroyed by Hurricane Katrina. The physician then opened a new medical practice in the parish to serve the residents there. The sole hospital in the parish had also been destroyed in the hurricane and had not reopened. The number of physicians practicing in the parish also declined precipitously after the hurricane. The physician certified that no medical imaging services were available in the parish and that patients who needed such services were required to travel outside the parish, although the health care infrastructure outside the parish was also significantly reduced after the storm. The physician proposed

181. Advisory Opinion No. 07-20 (Issued Dec. 27, 2007).

establishing an imaging center (the Center) in the same building as his medical practice. The physician and his brother would each contribute 50 percent of the capital needed to fund the Center, and they would each own 50 percent. The brother would function as the business manager and would be a *bona fide* employee receiving a salary at fair market value and unrelated to the volume or value of business generated for the Center. The physician further certified that (1) he and his brother would be active investors on terms unrelated to referral or business generation; (2) the Center would be located in a MUA and at least 75 percent of the Center's revenues would be derived from individuals residing in a MUA or who are members of a MUA population; (3) neither the Center nor any investor (or anyone acting on behalf of the Center or any investor) would loan funds to or guarantee a loan for an interested investor; and (4) returns on investment would be directly proportionate to the amount of the capital investment of the investors. The physician estimated that 35 percent of patients receiving services from the Center would be referred by him, and 65 percent would come from outside referrals, with that percentage increasing as more physicians return to the parish. The physician also certified that a proposed ancillary space lease agreement would be safe harbor compliant.

The OIG first noted that the proposed arrangement would not comply with the underserved area entity safe harbor because 100 percent of the investment interests would be held by interested investors (i.e., the physician and his brother) in a position to make or influence referrals to, furnish items or services, or generate business for the Center. The OIG concluded, however, that the risk of fraud and abuse was not materially increased by the brother's investment interest, "particularly when viewed in light of the Proposed Arrangement's substantial potential community benefits."[182] Specifically, the OIG noted:

- The brother, who was not then in the health care business, would not be compensated in any manner that depends on his generating business for the Center and would receive a fair market value salary for actual and necessary services, which would reduce the usual risk that the investor would charge the venture below-market rates to boost returns to interested investors.
- The brother would put up real capital and receive proportional returns, and the terms of investment would be unrelated to referrals, items or services furnished, or business generation.

182. *See id.*

- Because the physician already had reasons to refer patients to the Center, the sibling relationship was not viewed as likely to increase such referrals.
- Any residual risk was offset by the special conditions in which the proposed arrangement would be implemented, as an effort to improve access to care in the aftermath of Hurricane Katrina and the devastation inflicted on the local health care infrastructure.

2.2. Space Rental

The regulatory safe harbor for space rental arrangements is codified at 42 C.F.R. § 1001.952(b), which states:

> (b) *Space Rental.* As used in [the AKS], "remuneration" does not include any payment made by a lessee to a lessor for the use of premises, as long as all of the following six standards are met—
>
> (1) The lease agreement is set out in writing and signed by the parties.
>
> (2) The lease covers all of the premises leased between the parties for the term of the lease and specifies the premises covered by the lease.
>
> (3) If the lease is intended to provide the lessee with access to the premises for periodic intervals of time, rather than on a full-time basis for the term of the lease, the lease specifies exactly the schedule of such intervals, their precise length, and the exact rent for such intervals.
>
> (4) The term of the lease is for not less than one year.
>
> (5) The aggregate rental charge is set in advance, is consistent with fair market value in arms-length transactions and is not determined in a manner that takes into account the volume or value of any referrals or business otherwise generated between the parties for which payment may be made in whole or in part under Medicare, Medicaid or other Federal health care programs.
>
> (6) The aggregate space rented does not exceed that which is reasonably necessary to accomplish the commercially reasonable business purpose of the rental.
>
> Note that for purposes of paragraph (b) of this section, the term fair market value means the value of the rental property for general commercial purposes, but shall not be adjusted to reflect the

> additional value that one party (either the prospective lessee or lessor) would attribute to the property as a result of its proximity or convenience to sources of referrals or business otherwise generated for which payment may be made in whole or in part under Medicare, Medicaid and all other Federal health care programs.

This safe harbor was part of the original safe harbors enacted by HHS in 1991.[183] It was intended to protect against sham rental arrangements that purport to lease space that does not exist, is not actually used for the intended purpose, or is not large enough or otherwise suitable for its intended purpose.[184] Thus, compliance with the safe harbor predominantly turns on whether a referral relationship exists between the lessor and lessee and whether the rental fee is consistent with fair market value and does not take into account the value or volume of patients referred between the parties.

In order to determine whether a referral relationship exists, it is important to understand the direction in which referrals and remuneration flow.[185] For example, in one Advisory Opinion,[186] HHS explained that an arrangement is not suspect under the AKS when remuneration and referrals "run the same way." The proposed arrangement analyzed in the Advisory Opinion involved suppliers of DME using consignment closets in hospitals free of charge.[187] The hospitals referred patients to the suppliers, but they did not receive anything of value from the suppliers. Although the suppliers received remuneration from the hospitals in the form of free closet space, they were not in a position to refer patients to the hospital. Thus, HHS concluded that the arrangement did not implicate the AKS because there was no reason to believe that the free closet space was in fact a kickback in disguise.[188] As shown in Figure 2.1 (*see* Illustration 1), the remuneration (i.e., the free closet space) and the referrals of patients ran in the same direction (i.e., from the hospital to the supplier).

---

183. Final Rule: OIG Anti-Kickback Provisions (56 Fed. Reg. 35952, 35953; July 29, 1991) (Final rulemaking promulgating the ten original safe harbor provisions).

184. *Id.* at 35972 (providing a common example of a sham lease arrangement pursuant to which a physician rented a small, unsuitable space, such as a closet, and claimed to use the space for laboratory services, yet the space contained no laboratory equipment or personnel at any time).

185. *Id.* ("[W]here the lessor is a real estate developer or other entity *not involved in the delivery of health care services*, any arrangements that encourage referrals between the lessee and other third parties would *not be scrutinized by the OIG*." [emphasis added]).

186. OIG Advisory Opinion No. 08-20 (Nov. 19, 2008).

187. *Id.*

188. *Id.*

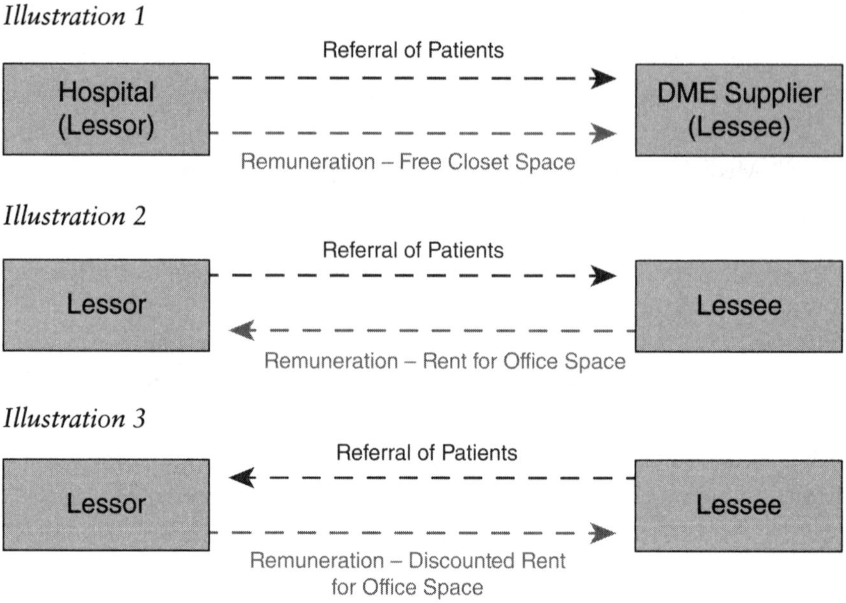

Figure 2.1

When a referral relationship does exist and the party receiving the remuneration is in a position to refer patients to the other party (see, e.g., Illustration 2 in Figure 2.1), then the AKS may be implicated because the remuneration, or a portion thereof, may be viewed as remuneration for referred patients. This analysis would apply to common rental arrangements where the lessor is in a position to refer patients to the lessee, and the lessee is giving remuneration (i.e., the rental fee) to the lessor (see Illustration 2 in Figure 2.1). However, it may also apply when the lessee is in a position to refer patients to the lessor, and the lessor is giving remuneration to the lessee by accepting a discounted rental fee from the lessee, in which case such discounted amount may be viewed as a kickback for patient referrals (see Illustration 3 in Figure 2.1).[189] In order to avoid AKS implications, such arrangements should satisfy all elements of the space rental safe harbor.

---

189. *See* United States *ex rel.* Bingham v. HCA, Inc., 2016 U.S. Dist. LEXIS 10178 at *22 (S.D. Fla. 2016) (citing United States *ex rel.* Osheroff v. Tenet Healthcare Corp., 2013 U.S. Dist. LEXIS 44235 at *9 (S.D. Fla. 2013) and explaining that a reasonable inference can be made that a landlord would not enter into a below-market rate lease if some other consideration was not involved, such as the referral of patients to the landlord).

The first element requires that the rental arrangement be set out in a written agreement that is signed by both parties.[190] In order to satisfy the second element, the written agreement must also cover all of the space leased between the parties, which would include office space leased for exclusive use and common areas to which the lessee may have access. All such leased areas must be specifically identified in the written agreement.[191]

The third element of the safe harbor states that when space is leased for periodic intervals of time, rather than a full-time basis, such intervals and the rental fee per interval must be specified in the written agreement. This requirement prohibits rental arrangements on an "as needed" basis, thereby reducing the risk that parties will modify their arrangement based on their referral patterns.[192] It is generally recommended for part-time lease agreements to include a detailed schedule, including specific days and times, when the leased space will be made available to the lessee. However, HHS has recognized that in certain circumstances it may be difficult for parties to establish a predetermined schedule for reasons other than the parties' referral patterns. Although such cases would fall outside the safe harbor protections, they would be analyzed by HHS on a case-by-case basis as to whether they are vulnerable to abuse and violation of the AKS.[193]

The fourth element of the safe harbor requires the lease agreement to be for a term of at least one year. This requirement is intended to reduce the risk that parties will periodically renegotiate short-term leases to account for changes in referral patterns.[194] Accordingly, HHS has clarified that compliance with the safe harbor does not require the services (i.e., the leased space) to be provided for at least one year, but that the terms of the lease cannot

190. *See e.g.*, United States *ex rel.* Singh v. Bradford Reg'l Med. Ctr., 752 F. Supp. 2d 602, 635-39 (W.D. Pa. 2010) (concluding that a contract proposal and preliminary invoice initialed by the parties did not constitute a formal, signed writing for purposes of compliance with the AKS safe harbor).

191. *See e.g.*, United States *ex rel.* Armfield v. Gills, 2012 U.S. Dist. LEXIS 154749 at *17-18 (M.D. Fla. 2012) (concluding that the lease at issue sufficiently specified the premises covered by the lease by identifying the total amount of square feet of the rented space, and explaining that the rented space included such office space that was sufficient and necessary for operation of physician's practice and specifically included examination rooms, waiting areas, and kitchen and bathroom facilities).

192. Final Rule: OIG Anti-Kickback Provisions, 56 Fed. Reg. 35952, 35974 (July 29, 1991) (Final rulemaking promulgating the ten original safe harbor provisions).

193. *Id.*

194. *Id.* at 35973.

be modified for such time.[195] Similarly, the lease may be terminated with or without cause by the parties prior to the expiration of the first year.[196] In the event of such early termination, the parties should refrain from entering into the same type of arrangement on substantially the same terms until the one-year period expires to ensure that the second lease is not viewed as a modification of the first, prior to expiration of the initial one-year period, which would fall outside the safe harbor protection.

The fifth element of the safe harbor relates to the rental fee. It states that the fee must be set in advance, consistent with fair market value in an arms-length transaction, and cannot be determined in a manner that takes into account the volume or value of any referrals or other business generated between the parties.[197]

With respect to the fair market value requirement, the rental fee should fall within a reasonable commercial range that does not take into account any additional value that the space may have due to its proximity or convenience to referral sources and/or patients.[198] HHS has explained that a fair inference can be drawn that payments for referrals are impermissibly disguised as rental payments when the rent is substantially higher than the cost of renting the same-sized space at a nearby location.[199] However, HHS has also acknowledged that the rental fee for space used for health care–related purposes can be justifiably higher than the fee for similar commercial property that is used for non-health care purposes.[200] For example, leasehold improvements may be required to make the space suitable for medical use, such as installation of extra plumbing and greater electrical costs due to medical equipment used at the location.[201] Such items can be considered when calculating fair market value.

In a Special Fraud Alert issued in 2000, HHS further explained that common rental arrangements involving rental of space in a physician's

195. *Id.* (recognizing that certain short-term arrangements, such as an academic physician visiting a medical university for only one semester and renting office space from the university for such time, are unlikely to implicate the AKS).

196. *Id.*

197. *See generally,* United States *ex rel.* Goodstein v. McLaren Reg'l Med. Ctr., 202 F. Supp. 2d 671 (E.D. Mich. 2002) (analyzing expert testimony regarding fair market value of a rental fee and concluding that the parties negotiated the fee at arms length).

198. Final Rule: OIG Anti-Kickback Provisions, 56 Fed. Reg. 35952, 35971-72 (July 29, 1991) (Final rulemaking promulgating the ten original safe harbor provisions).

199. *Id.*

200. *Id.*

201. *Id.*

office to referral sources, such as other practitioners or suppliers of medical equipment, are suspect under the AKS. When analyzing such arrangements, HHS considers the following factors: (i) the appropriateness of the rental agreement, (ii) the rental amount, and (iii) time and space considerations.[202]

With respect to the first factor, a threshold question for analyzing any rental arrangement is whether payment of rent is appropriate or it is in fact a disguised kickback.[203] A common example would be payment of rent for space that is traditionally provided for free or nominal charge, such as a consignment closet used for storage of medical equipment and supplies.[204] Even when payment of a fee is appropriate, the second factor also required that fee to be consistent with fair market value.[205] As a general matter, the fee should not exceed the rent paid by the physician-lessor under the underlying lease for the premises.[206] The third factor considers the amount of space that is rented and the duration of the rental arrangement. Consistent with the sixth element of the space rental safe harbor, HHS explains that the time and space should be reasonable and necessary to achieve a commercially reasonable business purpose.[207] Moreover, the rental fee should be a ratio of the length of time during which the space is rented and the amount of space that is actually used by the lessee.[208] In addition, when the lessee has exclusive use of the space then such lessee should be responsible for one hundred percent of the fair market value fee, but when use of the space is not exclusive (for example, when the lessee shares space with others, including common areas like lobbies and patient waiting rooms) the

---

202. *Special Fraud Alert: Rental of Space in Physician Offices by Persons or Entities to which Physicians Refer*, Off. Inspector Gen., Feb. 2000. https://oig.hhs.gov/fraud/docs/alertsandbulletins/office%20space.htm.

203. *Id.*

204. *Id.*; *see also* OIG Advisory Opinion No. 06-02 (Mar. 21, 2006) (stating that there is a long-standing concern that rental payments for a consignment closet may exceed fair market value and may be a disguised kickback).

205. *Special Fraud Alert: Rental of Space in Physician Offices by Persons or Entities to which Physicians Refer*, Off. Inspector Gen., Feb. 2000, https://oig.hhs.gov/fraud/docs/alertsandbulletins/office%20space.htm.

206. *Id.*

207. *Id.* Examples of unreasonable and unnecessary rental arrangements that would not qualify for the safe harbor protection include (i) when lessee only requires use of one patient examination room to meet patient demand, yet the rental payment is calculated based on use of the entire office; (ii) the rental payment includes payment for times when the space is not actually used by the lessee; and (iii) the rental payment is calculated based on the fair market value of the entire space but lessee's occupancy is not exclusive. In such shared space arrangements, fair market value should be adjusted proportionally based on the lessee's actual use of the space. *Id.*

208. *Id.*

lessee should only be responsible for his proportionate share of such shared space.[209]

By way of example, HHS has provided the following formula for calculating annual rent for *exclusive* space:

$$\frac{\text{Annual rent of underlying lease}}{\text{Number of work days per year}} \times \frac{\text{Sq. ft. used exclusively by lessee}}{\text{Total sq. ft.}} \times \frac{\text{Number of hours per day that Lessee uses the space}}{\text{Total work hours per day}} \times \text{Number of days per year that Lessee uses the space} = \text{TOTAL ANNUAL RENT FOR EXCLUSIVE SPACE}$$

Rent for *nonexclusive* space should be apportioned among all lessees who share the space.

It is also important to note that, to meet the requirements of the space rental safe harbor, the aggregate rental fee must be set in advance. Fees that are subject to fluctuation, such as percentage or "per use" fees, would not satisfy this requirement because the aggregate fee paid through the term of the lease would not be fixed (i.e., "set in advance").[210]

HHS has clarified that such percentage or "per use" rental fees are not *per se* violations of the AKS but would have to be analyzed on a case-by-case basis.[211] By way of example, the U.S. District Court in Illinois has interpreted this guidance to mean that "time-based or unit-of-service-based payments [are intended to] be protected [under the AKS], so long

209. *Id.*

210. *See* OIG Advisory Opinion No. 11-15 (Oct. 3, 2011) (analyzing a management services relationship that included the rental of office space for a fee that was based on a percentage of the lessee's income which not only did not meet the requirements of the safe harbor but also presented a substantial risk for fraud and abuse under the AKS because the fee took into account the volume and/or value of business generated between the parties).

211. Final Rule: OIG Anti-Kickback Provisions, 56 Fed. Reg. 35952, 35973 (July 29, 1991) (Final rulemaking promulgating the ten original safe harbor provisions). "[HHS] recognize[s] that legitimate considerations, such as the depreciation of equipment [or rental space], could result in some part of the payment to be based on a percentage or 'per use' payment arrangement without these payments influencing or being influenced by Medicare or Medicaid referrals. However, the more the payments appear to reflect the volume of referrals from the financially-interested party, the more suspect the arrangement becomes and the more likely [HHS] will need to examine it carefully." *Id.*

as the payment per unit is at fair market value at inception and does not subsequently change during the lease term in any manner that takes into account DHS referrals."[212] In other words, a fixed "per use" rental fee (e.g., $100 for each hour the lessee actually uses the leased space) is unlikely to violate the AKS if it is consistent with fair market value, is not increased or decreased during the term of the lease to account for changes in patient referrals, and otherwise meets the other elements of the safe harbor.

Finally, to satisfy the sixth and final element of the space harbor, the aggregate of the rented space cannot exceed what would be considered reasonable and necessary to accomplish the commercially reasonable business purpose for the rental arrangement.

Arrangements that implicate the space rental safe harbor may often implicate other safe harbors as well. For example, it is common for a lessor not only to provide office space to a lessee but to also lease medical equipment located at the premises and/or provide administrative or maintenance services necessary to operate the premises. HHS has noted that each part of such arrangement must meet the requirements of the applicable safe harbor.[213] HHS has also noted that hospitals may sometimes offer rent concessions to staff physicians which may not fall within the space rental safe harbor.[214] Such remuneration, however, may be protected under the physician recruitment safe harbor when it is offered as part of a hospital's recruitment effort.

---

212. United States *ex rel.* Perales v. St. Margaret's Hosp., 243 F. Supp. 2d 843 (C.D. Ill. 2003) (*citing* Final Rule: Medicare and Medicaid Programs; Physicians' Referrals to Health Care Entities With Which They Have Financial Relationships, 66 Fed. Reg. 856, 876 (Jan. 4, 2001)).

213. Final Rule: OIG Anti-Kickback Provisions, 56 Fed. Reg. 35952, 35972 (July 29, 1991) (Final rulemaking promulgating the ten original safe harbor provisions). To the extent rental payments include payment for office space and other equipment or services provided by the lessor, then such rental payment must reflect the fair market value of all such space, equipment, and/or services in order to qualify for each applicable safe harbor. In order to ensure that this requirement is met, parties to such arrangements may prefer to enter into multiple written agreements—a separate agreement for the space, equipment, and/or services provided—and analyze each agreement individually under its applicable safe harbor. Alternatively, if one master agreement is executed, then the fees payable under the agreement should be clearly defined and distinct based on each space/equipment/service provided. The portion of the fee attributable to the applicable space/equipment/service should reflect fair market value (FMV) of such space/equipment/services. *See also* United States *ex rel.* Armfield v. Gills, 2012 U.S. Dist. LEXIS 154749 at *14 (M.D. Fla. 2012) ("Where [ ] a single payment is made for multiple purposes (i.e., payment for rent and compensation for services), each separate aspect of the payment must comply with the respective safe harbor provisions.").

214. *Id.*

2.3. Equipment Rental

The regulatory safe harbor for equipment rental arrangements is codified at 42 C.F.R. § 1001.952(c), which states:

> (c) *Equipment Rental.* As used in [the AKS], "remuneration" does not include any payment made by a lessee of equipment to the lessor of the equipment for the use of the equipment, as long as all of the following six standards are met—
>
> (1) The lease agreement is set out in writing and signed by the parties.
>
> (2) The lease covers all of the equipment leased between the parties for the term of the lease and specifies the equipment covered by the lease.
>
> (3) If the lease is intended to provide the lessee with use of the equipment for periodic intervals of time, rather than on a full-time basis for the term of the lease, the lease specifies exactly the schedule of such intervals, their precise length, and the exact rent for such interval.
>
> (4) The term of the lease is for not less than one year.
>
> (5) The aggregate rental charge is set in advance, is consistent with fair market value in arms-length transactions and is not determined in a manner that takes into account the volume or value of any referrals or business otherwise generated between the parties for which payment may be made in whole or in part under Medicare, Medicaid or all other Federal health care programs.
>
> (6) The aggregate equipment rental does not exceed that which is reasonably necessary to accomplish the commercially reasonable business purpose of the rental.
>
> Note that for purposes of paragraph (c) of this section, the term fair market value means that the value of the equipment when obtained from a manufacturer or professional distributor, but shall not be adjusted to reflect the additional value one party (either the prospective lessee or lessor) would attribute to the equipment as a result of its proximity or convenience to sources of referrals or business otherwise generated for which payment may be made in whole or in part under Medicare, Medicaid or other Federal health care programs.

Much like the space rental safe harbor, this safe harbor was included in the original safe harbors enacted by HHS in 1991 as an effort to prevent sham rental arrangements for use of diagnostic and other medical equipment that are merely "a vehicle to provide reimbursement for referrals."[215]

The elements of this safe harbor mirror the elements of the space rental safe harbor.[216] If a referral relationship exists between a lessor and lessee who are parties to a rental arrangement for equipment, in order for such arrangement to be protected under the safe harbor, it must be set forth in a written agreement that (i) covers and specifically identifies all of the equipment leased between the parties, (ii) is for a term of at least one year, and (iii) provides for payment of a rental fee that is (A) set in advance, (B) consistent with fair market value of the leased equipment, and (C) not determined in a manner that takes into account the volume or value of referrals or other business generated between the parties.[217] In addition, the aggregate equipment rented by the lessee cannot exceed what is reasonably necessary to achieve the commercially reasonable business purpose of the rental arrangement.

If the equipment is leased for periodic intervals of time, rather than a full-time basis, the written agreement must also specify the exact intervals and the rental fee for each interval.[218] HHS has clarified that "per use" (or "per click") arrangements, in which the aggregate rental fee is not fixed and set in advance, but instead fluctuates based on the actual use of the equipment,

215. Final Rule: OIG Anti-Kickback Provisions, 56 Fed. Reg. 35952, 35953 (July 29, 1991) (Final rulemaking promulgating the ten original safe harbor provisions).

216. For a more detailed discussion of each element, see discussion on the space rental safe harbor *supra* at Chapter 2.2. *See also* OIG Advisory Opinion No. 98-18 (Nov. 25, 1998) (concluding that a rental arrangement for certain telemedicine equipment satisfied all of the elements of the equipment rental safe harbor).

217. *See generally*, United States *ex rel.* Armfield v. Gills, 2012 U.S. Dist. LEXIS 154749 at *20-22 (M.D. Fla. 2012); United States *ex rel.* Perales v. St. Margaret's Hosp., 243 F. Supp. 2d 843, 860-64 (C.D. Ill. 2003); *see also* OIG Advisory Opinion 11-17 (Nov. 16, 2011) (concluding that an arrangement that included the rental of equipment, among other things, for a fee based on percentage of collections of the lessee was not protected under the safe harbor and created a substantial risk of violating AKS).

218. *See, e.g.*, OIG Advisory Opinion No. 10-14 (Aug. 30, 2010) (explaining that a fixed "per-test" fee did not violate AKS because it was consistent with fair market value and, when taken individually and not in the aggregate, it did not take into account the value or volume of referrals or other business generated between the parties); OIG Advisory Opinion No. 04-08 (June 23, 2004) (explaining that an arrangement that involved the rental of space and equipment on an "as needed" basis failed to satisfy the elements of the applicable safe harbors and presented a substantial risk of fraud and abuse). "[P]eriodic, sporadic, or part-time leases must specify precisely the timing and duration of the rental periods and the compensation charged for each rental period." OIG Advisory Opinion No. 04-08 (June 23, 2004).

are not protected under the safe harbor and must be analyzed on a case-by-case basis.[219]

Take, for example, an arrangement where medical equipment is leased by a lessor that is in a position to refer patients to the lessee, and the aggregate rental fee increases based on the amount of procedures that are performed by the lessee that utilize the equipment. Even if the "per use" rental fee is a fixed amount consistent with fair market value, since the exact intervals of when the equipment is made available to the lessee are not predetermined at the outset of the arrangement (but instead provided on an as-needed basis), the aggregate rental fee is not "set in advance" and, therefore, does not satisfy the elements of the safe harbor. Moreover, such arrangements are considered suspect under AKS for potential fraud and abuse because they create a clear incentive for overutilization—the lessor would be incentivized to increase the amount of patient referrals that are sent to the lessee which, in turn, would increase the lessee's utilization of the equipment and the amount paid to the lessor.[220]

Similarly, some equipment rental arrangements may include "wear and tear" clauses, pursuant to which the rental fee is increased based on utilization of the equipment to account for ordinary wear and tear and depreciating value of the equipment each time it is used. However, consistent with its position on "per use" arrangements, HHS has explained that, while it "recognize[s] that equipment becomes less valuable the more it is used, and that its owner deserves compensation for such wear and tear[,] . . . it is also a relatively easy matter to disguise such a wear and tear payment as a payment for referrals."[221]

Accordingly, equipment rental fees that are based on utilization of the equipment are generally considered suspect under AKS because they present a substantial risk of fraud and abuse.

---

219. Final Rule: OIG Anti-Kickback Provisions, 56 Fed. Reg. 35952, 35973 (July 29, 1991) (Final rulemaking promulgating the ten original safe harbor provisions).

220. *See id.*; *see also* OIG Advisory Opinion No. 10-23 (Oct. 28, 2010) (analyzing an arrangement under which a hospital would provide sleep testing equipment and related services to a sleep testing provider for a "per test" fixed rental fee). In this Opinion, OIG concluded that the arrangement presented a high risk of fraud and abuse under AKS because the aggregate rental fee was not set in advance, which fell outside of the safe harbor protections, and the hospital was also providing marketing services to the sleep testing provider, which put the hospital in a position to generate patient referrals and directly linked the success of the sleep testing business to the amount of rental fees that were paid to the hospital. *Id.* at 4-6.

221. *See id.* at 35955.

2.4. Personal Services and Management Contracts

The regulatory safe harbor for personal services and management contracts is codified at 42 C.F.R. § 1001.952(d), which states:

> (d) *Personal Services and Management Contracts.* As used in [the AKS], "remuneration" does not include any payment made by a principal to an agent as compensation for the services of the agent, as long as all of the following seven standards are met—
>
> (1) The agency agreement is set out in writing and signed by the parties.
>
> (2) The agency agreement covers all of the services the agent provides to the principal for the term of the agreement and specifies the services to be provided by the agent.
>
> (3) If the agency agreement is intended to provide for the services of the agent on a periodic, sporadic or part-time basis, rather than on a full-time basis for the term of the agreement, the agreement specifies exactly the schedule of such intervals, their precise length, and the exact charge for such intervals.
>
> (4) The term of the agreement is for not less than one year.
>
> (5) The aggregate compensation paid to the agent over the term of the agreement is set in advance, is consistent with fair market value in arms-length transactions and is not determined in a manner that takes into account the volume or value of any referrals or business otherwise generated between the parties for which payment may be made in whole or in part under Medicare, Medicaid or other Federal health care programs.
>
> (6) The services performed under the agreement do not involve the counselling or promotion of a business arrangement or other activity that violates any State or Federal law.
>
> (7) The aggregate services contracted for do not exceed those which are reasonably necessary to accomplish the commercially reasonable business purpose of the services.
>
> For purposes of paragraph (d) of this section, an agent of a principal is any person, other than a bona fide employee of the principal, who has an agreement to perform services for, or on behalf of, the principal.

HHS has acknowledged that health care providers may often enter into arrangements to perform services for one another to advance a legitimate business need.[222] To protect such arrangements, HHS enacted the personal services and management contracts safe harbor in 1991 as part of its original safe harbors. Business arrangements for the provision of services and management that do not create an impermissible incentive to induce patient referrals can find protection under the safe harbor as long as they satisfy all of its elements.[223]

The first element requires a written agreement signed by the parties.[224] The agreement must cover all of the services to be provided and must describe the services in sufficient detail.[225] When the services are intended to be provided on a periodic, sporadic, or part-time basis, the agreement must also set forth the exact schedule of intervals when services will be provided, and the exact length and fee for each interval.[226]

The term of the agreement must also be for a period of at least one year. HHS has explained that in order to meet this one-year requirement, the terms of the arrangement cannot be changed during such one-year period.[227] In other words, the requirement does not necessarily preclude arrangements which by their nature can be performed in less than one

222. Final Rule: OIG Anti-Kickback Provisions, 56 Fed. Reg. 35952, 35953 (July 29, 1991) (Final rulemaking promulgating the ten original safe harbor provisions).

223. *See generally* United States *ex rel.* Perales v. St. Margaret's Hosp., 243 F. Supp. 2d 843, 859-60 (applying all of the elements of the personal services safe harbor and concluding that payment to a physician under a services arrangement did not constitute impermissible remuneration that violated the AKS).

224. *See, e.g.*, United States *ex rel.* Singh v. Bradford Reg'l Med. Ctr., 752 F. Supp. 2d 602, 635-39 (W.D. Pa. 2010) (concluding that a contract proposal and preliminary invoice initialed by the parties did not constitute a formal, signed writing for purposes of compliance with the AKS safe harbor).

225. *See, e.g.*, United States *v.* McCardell, 2018 U.S. App. LEXIS 27723 at *14-15 (5th Cir. 2018) (explaining that a service agreement did not meet the requirements of the safe harbor because it was not signed by the agent who would be responsible for providing the purported services and it failed to describe the services to be provided); United States *ex rel.* Armfield v. Gills, 2012 U.S. Dist. LEXIS 154749 at *21-23 (M.D. Fla. 2012) (concluding that a services agreement that provided the services of certain "Non-Medical Personnel" sufficiently described the services to be provided because it defined the "Non-Medical Personnel" to include support staff, such as receptionists, medical records staff, and clerical support, which in turn illustrated that the staff would provide such support services to the principal that are customary for their respective job titles).

226. *See, e.g.*, OIG Advisory Opinion 11-17 (Nov. 16, 2011) (concluding that an arrangement that included the provision of management services to operate an allergy testing laboratory on behalf of a physician practice created a substantial risk of violating AKS, and it was not protected under the applicable safe harbors because the services would be provided on an as-needed basis and the agreement failed to specify the exact schedule of intervals, length of each interval, and fee to be paid for each interval).

227. Final Rule: OIG Anti-Kickback Provisions, 56 Fed. Reg. 35952, 35973 (July 29, 1991) (Final rulemaking promulgating the ten original safe harbor provisions).

year, such as short-term medical consultation or peer review projects. As long as the terms of the arrangement are not modified within a one-year period, the services can be performed in less than one year and still fall under the safe harbor's protection. In addition, parties are free to terminate service arrangements for a legitimate business purpose during the one-year period, as long as they do not enter into a new arrangement on substantially the same terms prior to the expiration of such one-year period. As HHS explained, such limitations achieve the goal that is intended by the one-year requirement in the safe harbor, which is to prevent potential abuse when parties attempt to renegotiate terms on a frequent basis to account for changing patient referral patterns.[228]

The next element of the safe harbor requires the aggregate fee for the services to be set in advance, consistent with fair market value[229] and not determined in a manner that takes into account the volume or value of referrals or other business generated between the parties.[230] One common example of fee arrangements that would not satisfy this requirement because they are not set in advance are percentage of collection arrangements, pursuant to which the agent's service fee varies with the amount of collections

228. Final Rule: OIG Anti-Kickback Provisions, 56 Fed. Reg. 35952, 35973-74 (July 29, 1991) (Final rulemaking promulgating the ten original safe harbor provisions).

229. Parties to a proposed arrangement may also find it helpful to obtain an independent third-party valuation to determine whether the fee they are contemplating is consistent with fair market value and would satisfy this requirement under the safe harbor.

230. *See generally* United States v. Moshiri, 858 F. 3d 1077, 1082 (7th Cir. 2016) (analyzing evidence that supported the assertion that a service fee "took into account the volume or value of any referrals" and therefore did not qualify for protection under the personal services safe harbor); United States *ex rel.* Lutz v. Berkeley Heartlab, Inc., 2017 U.S. Dist. LEXIS 135678 at *8-18 (defining the "fair market value" requirement under the safe harbor and how fair market value of services should be calculated and assessed); OIG Advisory Opinion No. 16-12 (Nov. 28, 2016) (explaining that a dialysis facility's receipt of free labeling services from a laboratory had some "tangible benefit" to the facility and, therefore, failed to fall within the personal services safe harbor because the services were provided at no cost, which was unquestionably below fair market value); *see also* OIG Advisory Opinion No. 10-23 (Oct. 28, 2010) (analyzing an arrangement under which a hospital would provide sleep testing equipment and related administrative services to a sleep testing provider for a "per test" fixed rental fee). In this Opinion, OIG concluded that the arrangement presented a high risk of fraud and abuse under AKS because the aggregate fee was not set in advance, which fell outside of the safe harbor protections, and the hospital was also providing marketing services to the sleep testing provider which put the hospital in a position to generate patient referrals and directly linked the success of the sleep testing business to the amount of fees that were paid to the hospital. *Id.* at 4-6. In another Opinion, OIG found that a per-patient/per-procedure service fee similarly created a high risk of fraud and abuse because the aggregate fee was not set in advance, and it created an incentive for referrals and overutilization of reimbursable items and services under federally funded health care programs. OIG Advisory Opinion No. 03-08 (Apr. 10, 2003).

the health care provider receives from patient services. HHS has noted that such percentage of collections arrangements provide "improper incentive to refer" and are "rife with abuse."[231] Instead, to meet the safe harbor requirements, the service fee should be a fixed amount that is consistent with fair market value and not based on any referral patterns among the parties.

HHS has recently reinforced this fee requirement of the personal services safe harbor by entering into settlements with twelve individual physicians who were parties to "questionable medical directorship and office staff arrangements."[232] The physicians received payment for their services that did not reflect the fair market value of the services performed and took into account the volume or value of the physicians' referrals, which constituted improper remuneration under the AKS. Some of the physicians also entered into arrangements with affiliated health care entities pursuant to which the affiliated entities paid the salaries of the physicians' office staff. HHS explained that payment of the salaries relieved the physicians from a financial burden that they would have otherwise incurred, which also constituted improper remuneration to the physicians. HHS issued a special fraud alert as a result of the settlements to warn providers that service fees must at all times reflect fair market value and that even legitimate business arrangements may violate the AKS and result in sanctions "if even *one purpose* of the arrangement is to compensate a physician for his or her past or future referrals" (emphasis added).

Courts have also highly scrutinized physician arrangements with pharmaceutical companies that create "sham" financial arrangements that do not meet the safe harbor elements. For example, in *United States ex rel. Brown v. Pfizer, Inc.*,[233] a pharmaceutical company provided a number of improper incentives to encourage physicians and pharmacists to use and promote a drug for off-label use. The incentives included giving sales representatives large budgets to compensate physicians for promoting the drug, providing gifts to pharmacists in exchange for information on what medications

231. Final Rule: OIG Anti-Kickback Provisions, 56 Fed. Reg. 35952, 35973 (July 29, 1991) (Final rulemaking promulgating the ten original safe harbor provisions); *see also* OIG Advisory Opinion 11-17 (Nov. 16, 2011) (explaining that a fee based on percentage of collections was "inherently problematic" under the AKS and was not protected under the safe harbor).

232. *Fraud Alert: Physician Compensation Arrangements May Result in Significant Liability*, OFF. INSPECTOR GEN., June 9, 2015, https://oig.hhs.gov/compliance/alerts/guidance/Fraud_Alert_Physician_Compensation_06092015.pdf.

233. United States *ex rel.* Brown v. Pfizer, Inc., 2017 U.S. Dist. LEXIS 55656 at *23-26 (E.D. Pa. 2017).

physicians were commonly using and prescribing, paying physicians for extravagant travel, first-rate lodging, meals, and entertainment, and creating "sham" speaker programs to pay physician speakers to promote the drug to colleagues. The court found that the financial arrangements did not satisfy the fair market value requirement of the personal services safe harbor and constituted impermissible remuneration under the AKS.

Similarly, in *United States ex rel. Arnstein v. Teva Pharms. USA, Inc.*,[234] the court found that a pharmaceutical company's engagement of physicians to speak at certain programs did not fall within the safe harbor because the facts supported an inference that the compensation was not consistent with fair market value and that the parties did in fact intend to take into account the volume or value of the physicians' referrals because the physicians would only qualify to become speakers, and therefore become eligible to receive payment, if they generated a sufficient amount of prescriptions for the pharmaceutical company.

The personal services safe harbor also prohibits the services to be performed to involve the counseling or promotion of a business arrangement or other activity that violates federal or state law. HHS has noted that many marketing and advertising arrangements can find protection under the personal services safe harbor so long as they satisfy this element (in addition to the other elements) and do not involve marketing or advertising activities that encourage providers to violate laws, such as developing impermissible joint ventures or routinely waiving coinsurance and deductible amounts as an effort to generate more business.[235]

HHS also recognizes that many marketing and advertising arrangements deserve protection under the safe harbor because they do not involve direct contact with beneficiaries of federal health care programs, and/or the party providing the services is not involved in the delivery of health care and is therefore not in the same high-level position of public trust as would be a health care provider when they recommend services or products to patients.[236] Thus, such lawful promotional activities that present low risk of fraud and abuse can find protection under the personal services safe harbor.

234. United States *ex rel.* Arnstein v. Teva Pharms. USA, Inc., 2016 U.S. Dist. LEXIS 22554 at *52-53 (S.D.N.Y. 2016).

235. Final Rule: OIG Anti-Kickback Provisions, 56 Fed. Reg. 35952, 35974 (July 29, 1991) (Final rulemaking promulgating the ten original safe harbor provisions).

236. Final Rule: OIG Anti-Kickback Provisions, 56 Fed. Reg. 35952, 35974 (July 29, 1991) (Final rulemaking promulgating the ten original safe harbor provisions).

"White coat marketing," on the other hand, which relies on health care professionals to market a product or service to patients, is closely scrutinized under the AKS because "health care professionals are in an exceptional position of public trust and thus may exert undue influence when recommending health care–related items or services."[237] In such circumstances there is a high risk that patients will have difficulty distinguishing between professional medical advice and a commercial sales pitch.[238] Similarly, marketing activities that involve direct contact with patients, such as in-person sales pitches, are also considered "extremely coercive" and "highly suspect to fraud and abuse."[239] The risk of fraud and abuse is especially heightened when promoters target vulnerable patient populations, such as senior citizens or low-income Medicaid beneficiaries.[240]

Finally, in order to satisfy the last element of the personal services safe harbor, the aggregate services provided under a legitimate business arrangement cannot exceed what is reasonably necessary to accomplish the commercially reasonable business purpose of the arrangement.[241]

The HHS-OIG has opined on the personal services safe harbor in several advisory opinions. In many of these opinions, the OIG concluded that an arrangement did not satisfy all of the elements of the safe harbor but nonetheless presented a low risk of fraud and abuse under the AKS.[242] For example,

---

237. OIG Advisory Opinion No. 11-08 (June 14, 2011) (concluding that a marketing arrangement did not meet all of the requirements of the personal services safe harbor and presented a high risk of fraud and abuse which would violate the AKS); *see also* Health Choice Grp., LLC v. Bayer Corp., 2018 U.S. at *67-69 (concluding that a pharmaceutical company's use of nurse educators to market a drug constituted improper counseling and promotion of a business that violated the "white coat marketing" rules often referenced by HHS).

238. OIG Advisory Opinion No. 11-08 (June 14, 2011).

239. *Id.*

240. *Id.*

241. *See, e.g.*, OIG Advisory Opinion No. 06-02 (Mar. 21, 2006) (analyzing an arrangement under which a DME supplier leased the services of a technician to a physician's practice for a monthly fee, and finding no apparent business need for the technician to be on-site at the physician's practice and scrutinizing the arrangement for having potential "purposes not revealed on the face of the contract" which created a high risk of fraud and abuse under the AKS).

242. *See generally* OIG Advisory Opinion No. 15-10 (July 20, 2015); OIG Advisory Opinion No. 14-05 (July 21, 2014); OIG Advisory Opinion No. 03-07 (Mar. 26, 2003); *see also*, OIG Advisory Opinion No. 03-15 (Dec. 11, 2003) (explaining that a personal services arrangement was unlikely to generate impermissible remuneration under the AKS because it was not likely to generate new business between the parties as the arrangement would service largely the same group of people who were existing patients of the parties); OIG Advisory Opinion No. 01-17 (Oct. 17, 2001) (finding that a medical director agreement failed to specify the precise length and schedule of when services would be provided, but it presented a low risk of fraud and abuse because it was based on a specified hourly rate and the medical director would

in OIG Advisory Opinion No. 12-15,[243] the OIG recognized that a legitimate business need exists for physician-hospital arrangements for on-call services which by their nature must be provided on an as-needed basis and cannot satisfy all of the elements of the personal services safe harbor. The OIG explained that physician compensation models for on-call services can be structured in a way that poses minimal risk under the AKS. Based on the facts of this particular advisory opinion, the aggregate compensation was not set in advance, but the OIG concluded that it was nonetheless acceptable because, among other things, (i) the parties certified that the per diem fee was consistent with fair market value, (ii) the payments and scheduling of on-call obligations were uniformly administered among all participating physicians within the same specialty without taking into account the physician's referral patterns; and (iii) the physicians were paid only for services that were necessary and actually performed.[244]

The OIG came to a similar conclusion in Advisory Opinion No. 11-12,[245] where it analyzed an arrangement for telemedicine consultations for stroke and neurological conditions that were to be provided on an as-needed basis. The OIG explained that the arrangement failed to meet the elements of the personal services safe harbor because it did not specify an exact schedule for when services would be provided or the exact service fee for each interval. That said, the OIG determined that the arrangement presented a low risk of fraud and abuse for the following reasons: (i) it was unlikely to increase referrals between the parties and, instead, could reduce the number of transferred patients to the hospital providing such consultations; (ii) the arrangement was not conditioned on the volume or value of actual or anticipated referrals between the parties; (iii) the arrangement would improve the quality and efficiency of care provided to stroke patients, by ensuring timely consultations without the need to transfer the patient to a larger hospital; (iv) the arrangement did not require the parties to engage in any marketing that would promote their affiliation; and (v) the arrangement was unlikely to increase costs to federally funded health care programs because the parties certified that very few of their patients benefiting from the arrangement would be Medicare beneficiaries.[246]

---

only be paid upon providing written documentation specifying the hours he worked and the services he provided).

243. OIG Advisory Opinion No. 12-15 (Oct. 23, 2012).

244. *Id.*

245. OIG Advisory Opinion No. 11-12 (Aug. 29, 2011).

246. *Id.*

As illustrated by these advisory opinions, whether a proposed services arrangement satisfies all of the elements of the personal services safe harbor does not end the inquiry under the AKS. Even if an arrangement falls outside of the safe harbor protection, it may nonetheless present a low risk of violating the AKS if the underlying facts demonstrate that it presents a low risk of fraud and abuse.

It is also common for parties to enter into multiple arrangements in a single transaction that can implicate multiple safe harbors. This is especially common for arrangements that involve personal services because such arrangements often include the provision of other items or services, such as rental of office space and/or equipment. The HSS has stated that, in such cases, each part of the arrangement must meet the requirements of the applicable safe harbors.[247] By way of example, the portion of the arrangement that involves the provision of personal services must fall within the personal services safe harbor, the rental of office space must fall within the space rental safe harbor, and the rental of equipment must fall within the equipment rental safe harbor.

2.5. Sale of Practice

The safe harbor for sale of practice, codified at 42 C.F.R. § 1001.952(e), states:

(e) *Sale of practice.*

(1) As used in [the AKS], "remuneration" does not include any payment made to a practitioner by another practitioner where the former practitioner is selling his or her practice to the latter practitioner, as long as both of the following two standards are met -

(i) The period from the date of the first agreement pertaining to the sale to the completion of the sale is not more than one year.

(ii) The practitioner who is selling his or her practice will not be in a professional position to make referrals to, or otherwise generate business for, the purchasing practitioner for which payment may be made in whole or in part under Medicare, Medicaid or other Federal health care programs after 1 year from the date of the first agreement pertaining to the sale.

(2) As used in [the AKS], "remuneration" does not include any payment made to a practitioner by a hospital or other entity where

247. *See supra* note 209.

the practitioner is selling his or her practice to the hospital or other entity, so long as the following four standards are met:

(iii) The period from the date of the first agreement pertaining to the sale to the completion date of the sale is not more than three years.

(iv) The practitioner who is selling his or her practice will not be in a professional position after completion of the sale to make or influence referrals to, or otherwise generate business for, the purchasing hospital or entity for which payment may be made under Medicare, Medicaid or other Federal health care programs.

(v) The practice being acquired must be located in a Health Professional Shortage Area (HPSA), as defined in Departmental regulations, for the practitioner's specialty area.

(vi) Commencing at the time of the first agreement pertaining to the sale, the purchasing hospital or entity must diligently and in good faith engage in commercially reasonable recruitment activities that:

  (A) May reasonably be expected to result in the recruitment of a new practitioner to take over the acquired practice within a one year period and

  (B) Will satisfy the conditions of the practitioner recruitment safe harbor in accordance with paragraph (n) of this section.

In proposing this safe harbor, HHS noted that it would "exist for the sale of physician practices when occurring as the result of retirement or some other event that removes the physician from the practice of medicine or from the service area in which he or she was practicing, but not when the sale is for the purpose of obtaining an ongoing source of patient referrals."[248] As an example of a transaction not protected by the safe harbor, HHS described the purchase of a physician practice by a hospital to assure itself a steady stream of referrals for both physician and hospital services.[249] In such a transaction, HHS noted that the patients

248. Proposed Rule: OIG Anti-Kickback Provisions, 54 Fed. Reg. 3088, 3091 (Jan. 23, 1989) (Proposed original ten safe harbor provisions).

249. Another example offered by HHS of a problematic transaction was the purchase by an ophthalmologist of an optometry practice, where "the optometrist keeps practicing, only now

may be unaware of the sale, and that it may "often involve much higher rates of compensation [than] would be the case if a retiring physician sold a comparable practice to another physician," with the extra compensation "reflect[ing] the value of the referrals."[250] HHS specifically rejected the idea that these kinds of transactions deserve protection, stating that "such practices lead to increased program costs and potential conflicts between the patient's best interests and the physician's business relationship to the hospital."[251]At the same time, HHS acknowledged that "in ordinary circumstances, a hospital is not in violation of the statute if it purchases the practice of a retiring physician who no longer makes referrals to that hospital."[252] The scope of this particular safe harbor, however, is not intended to cover purchases by hospitals or other entities, except in the limited context of a rural hospital and physician recruitment, as discussed below.[253]

HHS declined to extend the period for completing the sale beyond one year given the risk of abuse, and noted that "[o]ften, sales and option agreements are designed solely to ensure referrals, and payments for the sale or option agreement are actually payments for referrals."[254] The one-year limit was designed to "protect sales where the sale occurs because the physician is no longer going to be practicing and not because the purchaser seeks an ongoing stream of referrals."[255] Payments from the sale, however, need not be completed within one year, so long as the other requirements of the safe harbor are satisfied.[256] Referrals are permitted within the one-year period.[257]

---

substantially salaried by the ophthalmologist" and where "[t]he only purpose of [the] sale [is] to lock up referrals." *Id.*

250. *Id.*

251. Final Rule: OIG Anti-Kickback Provisions (56 Fed. Reg. 35952, 35975; July 29, 1991): Final rulemaking promulgating the ten original safe harbor provisions.

252. *Id.*

253. In a letter from D. McCarty Thornton of OIG to the Internal Revenue Service (IRS) commenting on hospital acquisitions of physician practice groups, Mr. Thornton states that "[i]n the final safe harbor regulations, we expressly declined to expand the scope of the safe harbor to cover purchases of physician practices by hospitals or other types of entities or to situations where the seller remains in a continuing position to make referrals or influence referrals to the buyer because of our concerns that many of such purchases were in fact merely attempts to provide remuneration in return for a fuure stream of referrals." Letter from D. McCarty Thornton to T. J. Sullivan (Dec. 22, 1992).

254. Final Rule: OIG Anti-Kickback Provisions (56 Fed. Reg. 35952, 35975; July 29, 1991): Final rulemaking promulgating the ten original safe harbor provisions.

255. *Id.*

256. *Id.*

257. *Id.*

HHS declined to extend safe harbor protection to the sale of an individual practice to a group practice or the sale of part of a practice to a group practice or another physician when the provider is changing the scope of his or her practice, reasoning that although "some buy-out arrangements are not abusive," the agency "was also aware of abusive purchase arrangements," whereby "the sale becomes another mechanism for the buyer to profit from the stream of referrals made to the seller who previously practiced independently without dividing profits with the new 'partner.'"[258]

HHS also clarified the relationship between the sale of practice safe harbor and the employee safe harbor, explaining that "[w]here a practitioner purchases another practitioner's practice, makes payments to that other practitioner which continue for some period of time, and retains that other practitioner on his or her staff as an employee, we believe that such payments are not protected under this provision or the employee exception."[259] The payments in question are not protected by the sale of practice safe harbor because the seller "remains in a position to make referrals" and they are not protected by the employee safe harbor because "that provision only protects payments 'for employment in the provision of covered items or services' . . . [but here] these payments relate to the purchase of a practice and not to services provided pursuant to employment for the provision of items or services."[260] HHS noted, however, that if a *bona fide* employment relationship existed and the employer was making other payments for employment services, such payments could be protected.[261] If a party were attempting to comply with two separate safe harbors, then HHS stated that it "would expect separate justifications for compliance with each provision."[262]

In 1999, HHS modified the sale of practice safe harbor to protect payments made to a practitioner by a hospital or other entity to purchase the practitioner's practice in certain circumstances "to accommodate transactions involving the rural hospital purchase of a physician practice as part of a practitioner recruitment program. . . ."[263] HHS was "persuaded that a need exists to protect certain practice acquisitions by hospitals and other entities

258. *Id.*
259. *Id.*
260. *Id.*
261. *Id.*
262. *Id.*
263. Final Rule: Clarification of the Initial OIG Safe Harbor Provisions and Establishment of Additional Safe Harbor Provisions under the Anti-Kickback Statute (64 Fed. Reg. 63518, 63550; Nov. 19, 1999).

located in rural and urban underserved areas that are engaged in practitioner recruitment programs" in circumstances in which the practitioner sellers are "retiring or relocating a distance that would preclude them from being in a position to make referrals to the purchasing entity, if the acquisitions occur as part of a practitioner recruitment program that qualifies for protection under the safe harbor for practitioner recruitment."[264] HHS noted that the provider must "be retired from the practice of medicine or otherwise no longer in a position to generate referrals for the hospital" because otherwise the transaction "might result in abusive payments to induce referrals of business from the physician's new practice."[265] HHS further commented that "[r]elocation a significant distance from the practice being sold is an indicator that a physician is no longer in a position to refer patients."[266] HHS rejected calls to protect practice sales related to acquisitions by "integrated health care delivery systems," concluding that "many such arrangements may provide incentives for overutilization, increased billings to the Federal programs, and inappropriate steering of patients in circumstances where the Federal health care programs pay on a fee-for-service basis."[267] HHS also rejected a request to permit valuation of all tangible and *intangible* assets that could be used to determine a practice's fair market value, reasoning that "we remain of the opinion that payments for 'intangibles' can easily be used to disguise payments for referrals of Federal health care program business, and therefore we are unwilling to provide safe harbor protection for any particular valuation methodology."[268]

2.6. Referral Services and Referral Arrangements for Specialty Services

A. *Referral Services*

There are two safe harbors for referral services. The first, codified at 42 C.F.R. § 1001.952(f), states:

> (f) *Referral services.* As used in [the AKS], "remuneration" does not include any payment or exchange of anything of value between an individual or entity ("participant") and another entity serving as a

264. *Id.*
265. *Id.*
266. *Id.*
267. *Id.*
268. *Id.*

referral service ("referral service"), as long as all of the following four standards are met -

(1) The referral service does not exclude as a participant in the referral service any individual or entity who meets the qualifications for participation.

(2) Any payment the participant makes to the referral service is assessed equally against and collected equally from all participants and is based only on the cost of operating the referral service, and not on the volume or value of any referrals to or business otherwise generated by either party for the other party for which payment may be made in whole or in part under Medicare, Medicaid, or other Federal health care programs.

(3) The referral service imposes no requirements on the manner in which the participant provides services to a referred person, except that the referral service may require that the participant charge the person referred at the same rate as it charges other persons not referred by the referral service, or that these services be furnished free of charge or at reduced charge.

(4) The referral service makes the following five disclosures to each person seeking a referral, with each such disclosure maintained by the referral service in a written record certifying such disclosure and signed by either such person seeking a referral or by the individual making the disclosure on behalf of the referral service -

  (i) The manner in which it selects the group of participants in the referral service to which it could make a referral;
  (ii) Whether the participant has paid a fee to the referral service;
  (iii) The manner in which it selects a particular participant from this group for that person;
  (iv) The nature of the relationship between the referral service and the group of participants to whom it could make the referral; and
  (v) The nature of any restrictions that would exclude such an individual or entity from continuing as a participant.

The safe harbor for "Referral Services," was enacted in 1991 as part of the original set of safe harbors to protect service fees paid to "professional societies" and "consumer-oriented" groups that operate referral services, but instituted certain protections "to safeguard against abuse," including "by persons who would attempt to operate exclusive or selective referral services for which they would impose high participation fees."[269] The rule protects remuneration between an entity serving as a referral service and an entity or individual such as a physician participating in such a service, provided, *inter alia*, that any payment made to the referral service "is assessed equally against and collected equally from all participants, and is only based on the cost of operating the referral service, and not on the volume or value of any referrals to or business otherwise generated by either party for the other party" for which payment may be made under a federal health care program.[270]

The safe harbor also required certain disclosures to patients seeking a referral, including "[w]hether the participant has paid a fee to the referral service" and "[t]he manner in which it selects a particular participant from this group for that person."[271] HHS regarded such disclosures as essential, given that "[r]eferral services help beneficiaries make their initial contact with the health care system before a relationship of trust is established with a particular health care provider" and that without such disclosures "a consumer has very little information upon which to base his or her trust" in the provider, making the disclosures "an ethical duty" bearing upon "a patient's freedom of choice and quality of care" and which "may be necessary to enable a patient to give informed consent."[272]

HHS further noted that the safe harbor's requirements apply both to direct and indirect forms of remuneration, including in an employment setting:

> The [AKS] is implicated not only where direct payments are made in return for referrals, but also where indirect forms of remuneration are

269. Final Rule: OIG Anti-Kickback Provisions, 56 Fed. Reg. 35952, 35954 (July 29, 1991) (Final rulemaking promulgating the ten original safe harbor provisions); Proposed Rule: OIG Anti-Kickback Provisions, 54 Fed. Reg. 3088, 3091 (Jan. 23, 1989) (Proposed original ten safe harbor provisions).

270. 42 C.F.R. § 1001.952(f)(2).

271. 42 C.F.R. § 1001.952(f)(4)(ii), (iii).

272. Final Rule: OIG Anti-Kickback Provisions, 56 Fed. Reg. 35952, 35960 (July 29, 1991) (Final rulemaking promulgating the ten original safe harbor provisions).

> given for referrals. For example, hospitals often operate free referral services for members of their medical staffs as one of the benefits that comes with being on that hospital's staff. In return for the benefits of staff privileges (including the free referral service), physicians have a variety of obligations, such as sitting on various hospital committees. Depending on the circumstances, the services physicians furnish a hospital to assist in its operations may constitute a form of remuneration to the hospital for providing the referral service, and would be covered by the statute . . . "Giving a person an opportunity to earn money may well be an inducement to that person to channel potential Medicare payments towards a particular recipient." . . . Therefore, staff physicians and hospitals seeking safe harbor protection must comply with this provision when they are engaged in a referral service that does not charge a specific fee.[273]

The safe harbor for referral services applies not only to physicians but also to payments by other providers, including but not limited to chiropractors, dentists, podiatrists, psychologists, and nursing homes, to entities providing referral services.[274] Regarding the requirement that the referral service may not exclude any participant who is "qualified" for participation, HHS stated that the "determination as to whether a particular health care provider is 'qualified' to participate in the service may be made by the referral service according to its own criteria" but that it "must apply the eligibility criteria equally to all participants in the referral service."[275] Additionally, "the referral service must disclose to all persons seeking a referral the criteria it uses to determine who is qualified as a participant . . . [including] the manner in which it selects the pool of participants."[276] This includes whether the provider to whom the person is being referred "has paid a fee to participate."[277] The referral service must also disclose how the particular provider was selected for the referral (e.g., Is there a rotation system?), and what relationship exists between the provider and the referral service (e.g., Is the provider employed by the organization that operates the referral

273. *Id.* at 35976 (quoting United States v. Bay State Ambulance & Hosp. Rental Serv., Inc., 874 F.2d 20, 29 (1st Cir. 1989).
274. *Id.* at 35975.
275. *Id.* at 35975-76.
276. *Id.* at 35976.
277. *Id.*

service?).[278] Further, the referral service must disclose the criteria used to exclude a provider from participation in the service (e.g., Are there quality of care concerns?).[279] Addressing the form of the disclosure, HHS has stated that there is no one particular form that is mandated, but that it must be "effective disclosure," which "requires that the relevant information is communicated in time for the information to be used by the beneficiary before an important decision is made."[280] Accordingly, HHS has indicated that "it is unlikely that disclosure after the referral has been made would constitute effective disclosure if the beneficiary had already seen the health care provider, or in some cases, if the appointment had already been made."[281]

A written record certifying that these disclosures were made to each person seeking a referral must be maintained. The record "must be signed by either the person seeking the referral or by the individual making the disclosure on behalf of the referral service," and it will be insufficient to maintain only "a blank copy of the disclosure form or instructions to staff on how to make the disclosure."[282] The safe harbor also permits a referral service to prohibit discriminatory pricing practices by a provider participant or require that services be provided at no charge or at a reduced charge.[283] Regarding the fees that may be charged by the referral service, HHS has clarified that the safe harbor protects payments "that are related only to the cost of operating the referral service" and does not protect "fees that in any manner are based on the volume or value of Medicare or Medicaid referrals or business otherwise generated by the participant for the referral service."[284] Fees, however, need not be paid in full before referrals are made.[285] Further, the requirements of the AKS, and hence the safe harbor, apply irrespective of whether providers are charged for referral services, and the safe harbor applies to both direct and indirect forms of remuneration in exchange for referrals.[286]

This safe harbor has been addressed several times in Advisory Opinions. In Advisory Opinion No. 11-06,[287] the OIG addressed a business arrangement

278. *Id.*
279. *Id.*
280. *Id.*
281. *Id.*
282. *Id.*
283. *Id.*
284. *Id.*
285. *Id.*
286. *Id.*
287. OIG Advisory Opinion No. 11-06 (May 13, 2011).

in which a for-profit company operated an online referrals service that provided hospitals with access to a nationwide listing of post-acute care providers. Hospitals would use the service to identify and select providers for hospital patients about to be discharged and to send referral requests to selected providers. The hospitals paid a fee for the service that was equal to fair market value and not based on the volume or value of referrals or other business generated between the parties. Under the proposed arrangement, providers, who had previously not been charged for the service, would be charged a one-time implementation fee as well as a monthly fee to electronically receive or respond to hospital referral requests. Those fees would not vary based on the volume or value of referrals or other business generated between the parties, but they would be beyond the ability of some providers to pay. Although providers who elected not to pay the fees would continue to be listed by the service, they would not be able to electronically receive or respond to hospital referral requests and would be notified of such requests via facsimile, while having to respond to the requests via telephone or facsimile, thereby disadvantaging those providers and preventing them from timely communicating with hospitals.

The OIG found that the proposed arrangement did not satisfy safe harbor requirements, including the requirement that referral fees be assessed uniformly against all participants and be based only on the cost of operating the service. The OIG further determined that the arrangement posed more than a minimal risk of fraud and abuse under the AKS because the arrangement: (1) created a significant competitive advantage of paying providers over nonpaying providers in receiving patient referrals; (2) referral requests would be faxed to nonpaying providers, even though it was more expensive to do so, in order to provide paying providers a competitive advantage; and (3) pressure to recoup the costs associated with participation in the referral service could create incentives for paying providers to provide medically unnecessary services or inflate medical costs, thereby increasing costs to federal health care programs.[288]

Other Advisory Opinions examining arrangements under this safe harbor, however, have concluded that, despite failing to meet all of the requirements

288. The safe harbor has also been referenced in several court decisions. *See, e.g.*, United States *ex rel.* Young v. Suburban Homes Physicians, 2017 WL 6625940 at *2 (Dec. 28, 2017 N.D. Ill.); United States *ex rel.* DeCesare v. Americare In Home Nursing, 2011 WL 607390 at *2 (Feb. 10, 2011 E.D. Va.); Mittal v. United States, 2005 WL 2036023 at *14 n.1 (Aug. 24, 2005 S.D.N.Y.).

of the safe harbor, the arrangement at issue posed no more than a minimal risk of fraud and abuse. For example, Advisory Opinion No. 09-16[289] addressed a fact pattern in which a chiropractic association entered into an arrangement with a for-profit referral service. Under the arrangement, the cost of participation in the referral network was set at $60 per month for association members, which represented a $40 discount off the usual rate, and the network would pay the association $10 per month for each of the association's members who participated in the network, which fee would be in exchange for the association promoting the network with members and nonmembers.

While the OIG concluded that the arrangement did not fall within the safe harbor because the referral fees did "not meet the requirement that referral fees be assessed uniformly against all participants," it determined that it would not impose administrative sanctions because the arrangement posed only a minimal risk of fraud or abuse.[290] In reaching that conclusion, the OIG first noted that the arrangement was not a "typical, non-profit referral service operating for the convenience and support of patients," for which the safe harbor was designed.[291] The OIG then commented that, although not all participants would pay the same fee, the variance was not based on referrals of federal health care program business, and the providers receiving the referrals would be selected on a rotating basis by geographic area and would not be influenced by such variance. The OIG further observed that the $10 monthly fee for participating association members, while varying with the amount of business generated for the network, would not vary with referrals and that, in fact, the network did not provide reimbursable items or services, and therefore the payment did not implicate the AKS.[292] Finally, the OIG noted that the referral service would be open to participation by any state-licensed chiropractor, participating providers would receive referrals on an equal basis, there would be no requirements on the manner in which providers could furnish services, and all disclosures required by the referral services safe harbor would be made.[293]

Consistent with the OIG's reasoning in Advisory Opinion No. 09-16, those Advisory Opinions that have determined not to impose administrative sanctions on arrangements, notwithstanding the failure to meet all of

289. OIG Advisory Opinion No. 09-16 (Sept. 17, 2009).
290. *Id.* at 2.
291. *Id.* at 4.
292. *Id.* at 5.
293. *Id.*

the requirements of the safe harbor, have relied on some combination of the following factors:

- Fees paid by providers did not vary based on the volume or value of referrals and were unrelated to inducement of referrals.[294]
- Notices to prospective patients indicated that the provider was not being endorsed and advised of patients' freedom of choice.[295]
- There was a low risk of a cross-referral arrangement between parties to the arrangement.[296]
- No extra charge was to be included in a provider network.[297]
- Although fees charged in connection with referrals were on a "per click" basis, such transaction-based pricing was charged each time an ordering provider made a referral, regardless of whether the patient followed through and actually received items or services from the receiving provider—not a "success" fee.[298]
- Fees charged to ordering providers in a referral service were low and also capped, making it unlikely to influence the ordering provider's referral decisions.[299]
- There were no artificial limitations on which providers may participate in referral network, which was intended to be as complete as possible, and therefore there was no negative impact on patient or provider freedom of choice.[300]
- The fee structure of the referral service did not provide those participating in the service with enhanced access to a patient referral stream.[301]

B. *Referral Arrangements for Specialty Services*

The second referral services safe harbor, codified at 42 C.F.R. § 1001.952(s), states:

> (s) *Referral arrangements for specialty services.* As used in [the AKS], "remuneration" does not include any exchange of value among

---

294. OIG Advisory Opinion No. 11-18 (Nov. 30, 2011); OIG Advisory Opinion No. 09-16 (Sept. 17, 2009).
295. OIG Advisory Opinion No. 99-8 (July 6, 1999).
296. *Id.*
297. OIG Advisory Opinion No. 11-18 (Nov. 30, 2011).
298. *Id.*
299. *Id.*
300. *Id.*
301. *Id.*

individuals and entities where one party agrees to refer a patient to the other party for the provision of a specialty service payable in whole or in part under Medicare, Medicaid or any other Federal health care programs in return for an agreement on the part of the other party to refer that patient back at a mutually agreed upon time or circumstance as long as the following four standards are met -

(1) The mutually agreed upon time or circumstance for referring the patient back to the originating individual or entity is clinically appropriate.

(2) The service for which the referral is made is not within the medical expertise of the referring individual or entity, but is within the special expertise of the other party receiving the referral.

(3) The parties receive no payment from each other for the referral and do not share or split a global fee from any Federal health care program in connection with the referred patient.

(4) Unless both parties belong to the same group practice as defined in paragraph (p) of this section, the only exchange of value between the parties is the remuneration the parties receive directly from third-party payors or the patient compensating the parties for the services they each have furnished to the patient.

The safe harbor for specialty services was adopted in 1999 to allow for the referral of patients to those with specialized medical knowledge. In discussing the need for the safe harbor, HHS noted that patient freedom of choice could be compromised if patients are not given access to specialty care and that physicians might decline to make such referrals for fear of permanently losing patients to specialists.[302] For that reason, the safe harbor protects an agreement between general and specialized providers by which the general provider refers a patient to the specialist for needed treatment, provided that the specialist refers the patient back to the general provider when the specialty treatment is completed.[303] HHS made clear, however, that "protection

302. Final Rule: Clarification of the Initial OIG Safe Harbor Provisions and Establishment of Additional Safe Harbor Provisions under the Anti-Kickback Statute, 64 Fed. Reg. 63518, 63548 (Nov. 19, 1999).

303. *Id.*

under this safe harbor is limited to referral arrangements for patients of the physician making referrals to the specialist" and that the "safe harbor does not protect generalized cross-referral arrangements of the 'you send me your patients and I'll send you mine' variety."[304] Instead, the safe harbor "protects an agreement to refer patients to a specialist in return for an agreement or understanding that the specialist will refer those *same* patients back at the agreed upon time or circumstance (*e.g.*, completion of the specialist services for which the patient was referred)."[305]

The safe harbor applies to solo practitioners as well as members of group practices, with the difference being that members of group practices who refer among themselves "may share revenues from specialty services performed as a result of the intra-group referrals," whereas solo practitioners "may not give anything of value to a specialist in exchange for the referral back of his or her original patient, except for the opportunity to receive compensation for services directly from third parties or patients."[306]

When the rule was first proposed in 1993, HHS commented on the criteria developed for satisfying the safe harbor, emphasizing the importance of permitting payments only for the services rendered, and not for the referrals themselves, commenting that "[t]he . . . standard[s] . . . proposed prohibit[] any actual *payment* to be made between the parties for the referral [and] requires that the only exchange of value between the parties . . . is the opportunity to obtain monetary remuneration directly from third-party payors or the patient, as compensation for his or her respective professional services."[307] In the final rule, HHS commented on the importance of prohibiting referral payments to ensure "preservation of patient freedom of choice" and stated that referral arrangements protected by the safe harbor posed only a minimal risk of abuse, provided that "no payment is made between the referring and receiving parties."[308] HHS expressed particular concern with "the potential for abuse when the referring physician and the specialty physician receiving the referral split a global payment from a Federal health

304. *Id.*

305. *Id.*

306. *Id.* at 63549.

307. Proposed Rule: Additional Safe Harbor Provisions Under the Anti-Kickback Statute, 58 Fed. Reg. 49008, 49012 (Sept. 21, 1993) (Proposed rule designed to incorporate seven additional safe harbor provisions) (emphasis in original).

308. Final Rule: Clarification of the Initial OIG Safe Harbor Provisions and Establishment of Additional Safe Harbor Provisions under the Anti-Kickback Statute, 64 Fed. Reg. 63518, 63548 (Nov. 19, 1999).

care program," citing complaints from ophthalmology providers about certain abusive arrangements with optometrists who use their ability to control referrals to insist on the right to receive the postoperative portion of the Medicare global fee for eye surgery.[309] The final version of the safe harbor excluded such remuneration from protection.[310] In making that exclusion, HHS noted that it was not suggesting that all referral arrangement involving the splitting of a global fee violate the AKS, which would depend, *inter alia*, on "whether the specialty services are medically necessary, whether the timing of the referrals is clinically appropriate, and whether the services performed are commensurate with the portion of the global fee received."[311]

In adopting the final rule, HHS noted, in response to concerns that the safe harbor could encourage arrangements that required patients to be referred back to the primary physician regardless of clinical appropriateness, that "clinical appropriateness should be the touchstone of all referrals, specialty or otherwise," and inserted a requirement that referrals back to the primary provider must be clinically appropriate.[312] HHS declined, however, to define "clinically appropriate," concluding that "whether a referral is clinically appropriate will depend on the particular facts and circumstances."[313]

2.7. Warranties

The safe harbor for warranties is codified at 42 C.F.R. § 1001.952(g):

(g) *Warranties.* As used in section 1128B of the Act, "remuneration" does not include any payment or exchange of anything of value under a warranty provided by a manufacturer or supplier of an item to the buyer (such as a health care provider or beneficiary) of the item, as long as the buyer complies with all of the following standards in paragraphs (g)(1) and (g)(2) of this section and the manufacturer or supplier complies with all of the following standards in paragraphs (g)(3) and (g)(4) of this section -

(1) The buyer must fully and accurately report any price reduction of the item (including a free item), which was obtained as part of the warranty, in the applicable cost reporting

309. *Id.*
310. *Id.*
311. *Id.* at 63548-49.
312. *Id.* at 63548.
313. *Id.*

mechanism or claim for payment filed with the Department or a State agency.

(2) The buyer must provide, upon request by the Secretary or a State agency, information provided by the manufacturer or supplier as specified in paragraph (g)(3) of this section.

(3) The manufacturer or supplier must comply with either of the following two standards -

(i) The manufacturer or supplier must fully and accurately report the price reduction of the item (including a free item), which was obtained as part of the warranty, on the invoice or statement submitted to the buyer, and inform the buyer of its obligations under paragraphs (a) (1) and (a)(2) of this section.

(ii) Where the amount of the price reduction is not known at the time of sale, the manufacturer or supplier must fully and accurately report the existence of a warranty on the invoice or statement, inform the buyer of its obligations under paragraphs (g)(1) and (g)(2) of this section, and, when the price reduction becomes known, provide the buyer with documentation of the calculation of the price reduction resulting from the warranty.

(4) The manufacturer or supplier must not pay any remuneration to any individual (other than a beneficiary) or entity for any medical, surgical, or hospital expense incurred by a beneficiary other than for the cost of the item itself.

For purposes of paragraph (g) of this section, the term *warranty* means either an agreement made in accordance with the provisions of 15 U.S.C. 2301(6),[314] or a manufacturer's or supplier's agreement to replace another manufacturer's or supplier's defective item (which is covered by an agreement

314. 15 U.S.C. § 2301(6) states: "The term 'written warranty' means—(A) any written affirmation of fact or written promise made in connection with the sale of a consumer product by a supplier to a buyer which relates to the nature of the material or workmanship and affirms or promises that such material or workmanship is defect free or will meet a specified level of performance over a specified period of time, or (B) any undertaking in writing in connection with the sale by a supplier of a consumer product to refund, repair, replace, or take other remedial action with respect to such product in the event that such product fails to meet the specifications set forth in the undertaking, which written affirmation, promise, or undertaking becomes part of the basis of the bargain between a supplier and a buyer for purposes other than resale of such product."

> made in accordance with this statutory provision), on terms equal to the agreement that it replaces.

In adopting the safe harbor for warranties, the OIG declared that "[i]t is in the public interest to have companies offer warranties as an inducement to the consumer to purchase a product."[315] Responding to a device manufacturer's suggestion that its warranty complied with the discount safe harbor and thus did not need to comply with the warranty provision as well, the OIG replied that it did "not believe that warranty arrangements fit within the 'discount' safe harbor provision," although the OIG agreed that "some of the policies underlying the discount exception should apply to warranties" and therefore "with respect to any reduction of equipment prices offered as part of a warranty agreement, we are requiring the same disclosure requirements as contained in the discount provision."[316] Rejecting the request of commenters urging the OIG to protect "competitive replacement agreements" under which a company might, for example, offer inducements to a hospital or physician to replace a defective medical device with the company's product, the OIG stated:

> [W]e remain concerned that many of these programs either provide additional incentives beyond the original warranty or impose additional costs on the Medicare and Medicaid programs. For example, while some competitive replacement programs replace the item, such as a pacemaker, only on the same terms as those in the warranty of the original manufacturer, others replace the item under other conditions as well; while some provide the replacement item free of charge, others provide a discount on the replacement item capped at a specified dollar amount; and while some make no payments for medical expenses, others assist patients (either directly or by paying the health care provider) with their unreimbursed medical expenses up to a specified dollar amount. Depending on the original manufacturer's warranty, some of these programs do much more than merely put the beneficiary in the same position he or she would be in if he or she bought a replacement item from the original manufacturer under the terms of that warranty.

---

315. Final Rule: HHS Anti-Kickback Provisions (56 Fed. Reg. 35952, 35953; July 29, 1991): Final rulemaking promulgating the ten original safe harbor provisions.

316. *Id.* at 35976.

> We believe that safe harbor protection is proper where a replacement program honors the original manufacturer's warranty, which qualifies by itself under this provision, and the agreement provides remuneration on the same terms as the original manufacturer's warranty without providing additional incentives or shifting additional costs to the Medicare and Medicaid programs.
>
> Under such programs, any incentive to replace a product under warranty stems from the original warranty, and not from the competitive replacement agreement. We remain concerned about potential abuse in one additional area. Some competitive replacement agreements pay the health care provider or practitioner directly for the beneficiary's medical expenses. We believe that such direct payments are potentially abusive because the health care provider or practitioner knows that the warranty insures against beneficiaries' bad debts. Thus, we are adding paragraph (g)(4) so that safe harbor protection is not provided when payments are made to any health care provider (such as a hospital or ASC) for expenses such as medical, surgical or hospital expenses incurred by the beneficiary. Payments made to the health care provider or practitioner for the item itself, or price reductions on that item, are protected.[317]

Rejecting a request that the safe harbor not be interpreted to protect middlemen suppliers/wholesalers who expand the protection afforded by the manufacturer's warranty, the OIG reiterated that "warranties generally benefit consumers as well as the Medicare and Medicaid program[s] even though they may constitute a technical violation of the statute," and that the agency did not "see the harm when it provides greater benefits than those provided by the manufacturer," as is frequently the case in other industries, and that such expanded protection "should be encouraged."[318]

Several Advisory Opinions have addressed the safe harbor for warranties, and the scope of the arrangements to which the safe harbor has been viewed as potentially applicable has broadened over time. In 2001, the OIG issued Advisory Opinion No. 01-08,[319] which addressed the application of this safe harbor to a proposed arrangement involving a manufacturer of therapeutic mattresses and other support surfaces for the treatment and prevention of pressure ulcers. As part of a multifaceted program involving its

317. *Id.* at 35977.
318. *Id.*
319. Advisory Opinion No. 01-08 (Issued July 3, 2001).

products and services that it offered to nursing facilities, the manufacturer offered a program warranty, pursuant to which the manufacturer agreed to reimburse a facility for insurance deductibles paid by the facility as a result of judgments for skin care or wound care deficiencies, provided that the facility complied with all of the requirements of the program. The OIG noted that the safe harbor for warranties was potentially applicable to the program warranty, as the safe harbor applies to "payments made by a manufacturer or supplier to settle claims or satisfy judgments arising out of product liability claims . . . to the extent they comply with all of the other conditions of" the safe harbor, and the OIG found the other conditions were satisfied.[320] The OIG noted, however, that "[s]ince the warranty safe harbor only protects warranties on 'items', a warranty on a combination of items and services [like the program warranty] does not technically qualify for protection."[321] The OIG nonetheless concluded that "the linchpin" to the program was items like mattresses and other support surfaces, rather than services, and thus the program warranty "[did] not significantly increase the risk of fraud and abuse."[322]

Advisory Opinion No. 02-6[323] addressed a proposed refund program by a device company for hospital customers who purchased a blood-filtering device for the treatment of rheumatoid arthritis. Notwithstanding a National Coverage Determination (NCD) from the Centers for Medicare and Medicaid Services (CMS) permitting reimbursement of the device in specified circumstances, some hospitals resisted purchasing the device because of its high cost for a course of treatment and the uncertainty of reimbursement. The device company, therefore, wished to offer a full refund of the purchase price of any device to a hospital if an insurer denied payment for treatments with the device under certain conditions. The device company would report the existence of the refund program on invoices to each hospital and the refund offer would expire on the earlier of 120 days after initial delivery of the device or the hospital's first receipt of notice from a payer that payment had been denied for a patient who qualified for treatment under the NCD.

The OIG initially noted that the refund program represented a financial inducement under the AKS, and that the program would not be protected under the warranty safe harbor because "[f]or purposes of the safe harbor,

320. *See id.*
321. *See id.*
322. *See id.*
323. Advisory Opinion No. 02-6 (Issued May 14, 2002).

the warranty must be related to product failure" and the refund program "does not relate to product failure, but to the purchaser's resale of the product," meaning that the refund program did "not meet the definition of warranty and cannot fit in the safe harbor."[324] Notwithstanding this fact, the OIG concluded that the program contained certain safeguards that sufficiently reduced the risk of fraud and abuse: (1) the refund offer was limited in time in reference to the initial delivery of the device or the initial payment denial; (2) the refund offer was limited in scope to treatments that met the conditions of the NCD and to Medicare claims denied through the first level of appeal; (3) the refund offer was limited in amount to the purchase price of the columns; and (4) the device company certified that it would report the refund program on invoices to each hospital and would condition each hospital's participation in the program on the hospital's compliance with all relevant regulatory obligations.

Advisory Opinion No. 17-03[325] addressed the warranty safe harbor in the context of a proposed arrangement involving a group of affiliated companies (the Company) that manufactured and sold biologics and other products, some of which required reconstitution in a controlled environment due to product changes that could be caused by temperature, sunlight, or movement. The product labels listed specific storage and handling requirements and, if reconstitution were required, time limits between when the product was reconstituted and when it was administered to the patient in order to avoid spoilage. Under the proposed arrangement, the company would replace at no cost products purchased by providers if the products spoiled or became unusable after purchase. To qualify for replacement, the product could not have been administered to a patient after having been rendered unusable as a result of any of several enumerated reasons (Spoiled Product). The company certified that it would develop a written policy setting for all the conditions that needed to be satisfied to qualify for a replacement and that customers would be notified before they purchased a product. Only replacement of Spoiled Products would be permitted. Customers would not

324. *See id.*. This conclusion by the OIG appeared to limit the scope of warranty safe harbor protection to product defects and correspondingly limit any understanding of "undertaking" relative to product "specifications" contained in the second paragraph of the warranty definition contained in 15 U.S.C. § 2301(6)(B) to a promise related to a product defect. As discussed earlier, however, in Advisory Opinion No. 17-03, the OIG appeared to broaden the scope of "undertaking" such that a product could fail to meet "specifications" for many reasons other than a defect in material or workmanship.

325. Advisory Opinion No. 17-02 (Issued Aug. 18, 2017).

receive credit for Spoiled Products or replacements for free samples, nor would a replacement be available if the customer administered a Spoiled Product or billed an insurer or patient for a Spoiled Product. The arrangement only applied to single Spoiled Product claims, and not to multiunit losses, except in cases of refrigeration failure, when the customer would be limited to a maximum loss of five Spoiled Products. The customer would be required to submit documentation detailing how spoilage occurred and return the Spoiled Product, except if the product was not returnable, in which case the customer was required to attest as to how the product became unusable and include a photograph, if available. The customer would also be required to sign an acknowledgement that neither the patient nor a payor was billed for the Spoiled Product.

The OIG proceeded to analyze the proposed arrangement under the warranty safe harbor, noting that while "[t]he safe harbor for warranties protects remedial actions by suppliers to address products that fail to meet bargained-for requirements," the Spoiled Products to be replaced under the proposed arrangement "would not be defective or substandard" nor would they fail "to meet the specifications set forth in the undertaking" as required under the definition of warranty in 15 U.S.C. § 2301(6). Rather, the proposed arrangement applied to products that were unusable after delivery due to customer error or the customer's unforeseen inability to administer the product after it was prepared for the patient. Accordingly, the spoilage would occur as a result of the customer's failure to implement the product specifications, and not as a result of the product's failure to meet those specifications. The OIG hastened to add, however, that in other circumstances a product could fail to meet specifications in a manner that would be protected by the safe harbor, noting that a product might "'fail to meet the specifications in the undertaking' for many reasons, including failure to meet quality standards or failing to achieve patient clinical results specified as targets at the time of sale."[326]

Despite concluding that the arrangement at issue did not satisfy the warranty safe harbor, however, the OIG determined that the proposed arrangement posed a low risk of fraud and abuse and would not warrant the imposition of administrative sanctions because:

- Replacement of Spoiled Products would be restricted to unintentional, unplanned circumstances that could increase patient safety and quality

326. *See id.*

of care, and in cases of accidental spoilage, could decrease the risk that customer administers a Spoiled Product to avoid financial loss.

- Since the arrangement applies only to products that customers already selected and intended to use but did not administer or bill, there was a low risk that it could lead to increased costs or overutilization.
- Since the arrangement would cover only individual claims of Spoiled Products and not large losses, and the only remedy would be product replacement, there was a low risk that a customer would be prompted to select the company's product over that of a competitor.
- The arrangement would function similarly to an insurance policy, the cost of which the company certified would be bundled into the price of its products, and it was no more likely to cause a customer to rely on the warranty by cutting corners on spoilage prevention than it would be for a driver or homeowner to act recklessly in reliance on insurance.
- The OIG also noted that the requirement that customers complete an administrative process, provide proof of spoilage, and return the product, or explain why the product could not be returned, further reduced the risk that the arrangement might unduly influence a customer's purchase of the product.

2.8. Discounts

The safe harbor for discounts is codified both by statute and regulation. 42 U.S.C. § 1320a-7b(b)(3)(A) states that the AKS "shall not apply to":

> (A) a discount or other reduction in price obtained by a provider of services or other entity under a Federal health care program if the reduction in price is properly disclosed and appropriately reflected in the costs claimed or charges made by the provider or entity under a Federal health care program

The analogous, though far more detailed, regulatory safe harbor for discounts may be found at 42 C.F.R. § 1001.952(h), which states:

> **(h)** *Discounts.* As used in section 1128B of the Act, "remuneration" does not include a discount, as defined in paragraph (h)(5) of this section, on an item or service for which payment may be made in whole or in part under Medicare, Medicaid or other Federal health care programs for a buyer as long as the buyer complies with the applicable standards of paragraph (h)(1) of this section;

a seller as long as the seller complies with the applicable standards of paragraph (h)(2) of this section; and an offeror of a discount who is not a seller under paragraph (h)(2) of this section so long as such offeror complies with the applicable standards of paragraph (h)(3) of this section.

(1) With respect to the following three categories of buyers, the buyer must comply with all of the applicable standards within one of the three following categories -

(i) If the buyer is an entity which is a health maintenance organization (HMO) or a competitive medical plan (CMP) acting in accordance with a risk contract under section 1876(g) or 1903(m) of the Act, or under another State health care program, it need not report the discount except as otherwise may be required under the risk contract.

(ii) If the buyer is an entity which reports its costs on a cost report required by the Department or a State health care program, it must comply with all of the following four standards -

(A) The discount must be earned based on purchases of that same good or service bought within a single fiscal year of the buyer;

(B) The buyer must claim the benefit of the discount in the fiscal year in which the discount is earned or the following year;

(C) The buyer must fully and accurately report the discount in the applicable cost report; and

(D) the buyer must provide, upon request by the Secretary or a State agency, information provided by the seller as specified in paragraph (h)(2)(ii) of this section, or information provided by the offeror as specified in paragraph (h)(3)(ii) of this section.

(iii) If the buyer is an individual or entity in whose name a claim or request for payment is submitted for the discounted item or service and payment may be made, in whole or in part, under Medicare, Medicaid or other Federal health care programs (not including individuals or entities defined as buyers in paragraph (h)(1)(i) or

(h) (1)(ii) of this section), the buyer must comply with both of the following standards -

(A) The discount must be made at the time of the sale of the good or service or the terms of the rebate must be fixed and disclosed in writing to the buyer at the time of the initial sale of the good or service; and

(B) the buyer (if submitting the claim) must provide, upon request by the Secretary or a State agency, information provided by the seller as specified in paragraph (h)(2)(iii)(B) of this section, or information provided by the offeror as specified in paragraph (h)(3)(iii)(A) of this section.

(2) The seller is an individual or entity that supplies an item or service for which payment may be made, in whole or in part, under Medicare, Medicaid or other Federal health care programs to the buyer and who permits a discount to be taken off the buyer's purchase price. The seller must comply with all of the applicable standards within one of the following three categories-

(i) If the buyer is an entity which is an HMO a CMP acting in accordance with a risk contract under section 1876(g) or 1903(m) of the Act, or under another State health care program, the seller need not report the discount to the buyer for purposes of this provision.

(ii) If the buyer is an entity that reports its costs on a cost report required by the Department or a State agency, the seller must comply with either of the following two standards -

(A) Where a discount is required to be reported to Medicare or a State health care program under paragraph (h)(1) of this section, the seller must fully and accurately report such discount on the invoice, coupon or statement submitted to the buyer; inform the buyer in a manner that is reasonably calculated to give notice to the buyer of its obligations to report such discount and to provide information upon request under paragraph (h)(1) of this section; and refrain from doing anything that would impede the buyer from meeting its obligations under this paragraph; or

(**B**) Where the value of the discount is not known at the time of sale, the seller must fully and accurately report the existence of a discount program on the invoice, coupon or statement submitted to the buyer; inform the buyer in a manner reasonably calculated to give notice to the buyer of its obligations to report such discount and to provide information upon request under paragraph (h)(1) of this section; when the value of the discount becomes known, provide the buyer with documentation of the calculation of the discount identifying the specific goods or services purchased to which the discount will be applied; and refrain from doing anything which would impede the buyer from meeting its obligations under this paragraph.

(**iii**) If the buyer is an individual or entity not included in paragraph (h)(2)(i) or (h)(2)(ii) of this section, the seller must comply with either of the following two standards -

(**A**) Where the seller submits a claim or request for payment on behalf of the buyer and the item or service is separately claimed, the seller must provide, upon request by the Secretary or a State agency, information provided by the offeror as specified in paragraph (h)(3)(iii)(A) of this section; or

(**B**) Where the buyer submits a claim, the seller must fully and accurately report such discount on the invoice, coupon or statement submitted to the buyer; inform the buyer in a manner reasonably calculated to give notice to the buyer of its obligations to report such discount and to provide information upon request under paragraph (h)(1) of this section; and refrain from doing anything that would impede the buyer from meeting its obligations under this paragraph.

(**3**) The offeror of a discount is an individual or entity who is not a seller under paragraph (h)(2) of this section, but promotes the purchase of an item or service by a buyer under paragraph (h)(1) of this section at a reduced price for which payment may be made, in whole or in part, under Medicare,

Medicaid or other Federal health care programs. The offeror must comply with all of the applicable standards within the following three categories -

(i) If the buyer is an entity which is an HMO or a CMP acting in accordance with a risk contract under section 1876(g) or 1903(m) of the Act, or under another State health care program, the offeror need not report the discount to the buyer for purposes of this provision.

(ii) If the buyer is an entity that reports its costs on a cost report required by the Department or a State agency, the offeror must comply with the following two standards -

(A) The offeror must inform the buyer in a manner reasonably calculated to give notice to the buyer of its obligations to report such a discount and to provide information upon request under paragraph (h)(1) of this section; and

(B) The offeror of the discount must refrain from doing anything that would impede the buyer's ability to meet its obligations under this paragraph.

(iii) If the buyer is an individual or entity in whose name a request for payment is submitted for the discounted item or service and payment may be made, in whole or in part, under Medicare, Medicaid or other Federal health care programs (not including individuals or entities defined as buyers in paragraph (h)(1)(i) or (h)(1)(ii) of this section), the offeror must comply with the following two standards -

(A) The offeror must inform the individual or entity submitting the claim or request for payment in a manner reasonably calculated to give notice to the individual or entity of its obligations to report such a discount and to provide information upon request under paragraphs (h)(1) and (h)(2) of this section; and

(B) The offeror of the discount must refrain from doing anything that would impede the buyer's or seller's ability to meet its obligations under this paragraph.

(4) For purposes of this paragraph, a *rebate* is any discount the terms of which are fixed and disclosed in writing to the

buyer at the time of the initial purchase to which the discount applies, but which is not given at the time of sale.

(5) For purposes of this paragraph, the term *discount* means a reduction in the amount a buyer (who buys either directly or through a wholesaler or a group purchasing organization) is charged for an item or service based on an arms-length transaction. The term *discount* does not include -

(i) Cash payment or cash equivalents (except that rebates as defined in paragraph (h)(4) of this section may be in the form of a check);

(ii) Supplying one good or service without charge or at a reduced charge to induce the purchase of a different good or service, unless the goods and services are reimbursed by the same Federal health care program using the same methodology and the reduced charge is fully disclosed to the Federal health care program and accurately reflected where appropriate, and as appropriate, to the reimbursement methodology;

(iii) A reduction in price applicable to one payer but not to Medicare, Medicaid or other Federal health care programs;

(iv) A routine reduction or waiver of any coinsurance or deductible amount owed by a program beneficiary;

(v) Warranties;

(vi) Services provided in accordance with a personal or management services contract; or

(vii) Other remuneration, in cash or in kind, not explicitly described in paragraph (h)(5) of this section.[327]

It is the OIG's position that "the regulatory safe harbor protects *all* discounts or reductions in price protected by Congress in the statutory exception," but that it also "expands upon the statutory safe harbor by defining additional discounting practices not included in the statutory exception that are not abusive," and thus "both incorporates and enlarges upon

327. On February 6, 2019, the OIG published a proposed rule that amended the discount safe harbor to explicitly exclude from the definition of a discount certain reductions in price or other remuneration from a manufacturer of prescription pharmaceutical products to plan sponsors under Medicare Part D, Medicaid managed care organizations, and pharmacy benefit managers under contract with them.

the statutory exception."[328] The OIG has noted that "[a]s a general rule, discounts for health care items and services are encouraged under the Federal health care programs so long as the Federal health care programs share in the discount where appropriate, and as appropriate, to the reimbursement methodology."[329] Arrangements in which federal programs "get less than their proportional share of cost-savings on items or services payable by the programs are seriously abusive," result in "the programs being overcharged, and are not protected by either the statutory exception or regulatory safe harbor for discounts."[330] According to the OIG, "the discount exception was intended to encourage price competition that benefits the Medicare and Medicaid programs" and "was limited in application to reductions in the amount a seller charges for a good or service to the buyer."[331] The discount "could take the form of a specified price break, or the inclusion of an extra quantity of the item purchased 'at no extra charge'" but was not intended "to protect many kinds of marketing incentive programs such as cash rebates, free goods or services, redeemable coupons, or credits."[332] Regarding credits and coupons, the OIG later clarified that "[i]f a coupon or credit fits within the definition of a discount, it is included within the safe harbor (assuming all safe harbor conditions are satisfied)" but that the OIG "did not intend to protect credits or coupons that are merely surrogate cash payments, such as credits or coupons that can be used like cash to purchase unspecified goods or services from the seller or offeror."[333] Accordingly "a coupon good for a reduced price on a designated item could be included in the definition, so long as it meets all of the other requirements of the regulation; however, a coupon good for a certain dollar amount off any goods sold by the seller is not included in the definition."[334] The OIG further noted that the safe harbor for discounts demonstrated that Congress intended to prohibit transactions even "where there is no direct payment at all from the party receiving the

328. Final Rule: Clarification of the Initial OIG Safe Harbor Provisions and Establishment of Additional Safe Harbor Provisions under the Anti-Kickback Statute (64 Fed. Reg. 63518, 63528; Nov. 19, 1999).

329. *Id.* at 63526.

330. *Id.*

331. Final Rule: HHS Anti-Kickback Provisions (56 Fed. Reg. 35952, 35953; July 29, 1991): Final rulemaking promulgating the ten original safe harbor provisions.

332. *Id.*

333. Final Rule: Clarification of the Initial OIG Safe Harbor Provisions and Establishment of Additional Safe Harbor Provisions under the Anti-Kickback Statute (64 Fed. Reg. 63518, 63529; Nov. 19, 1999).

334. *Id.*

referrals" since "the remuneration in a discount is merely a lowered price that a purchaser would otherwise obtain from a seller, which is made as an inducement to purchase larger quantities."[335]

Responding to industry concerns over ambiguity in the safe harbor concerning the requirements needed to be satisfied for protection, in 1999 the OIG clarified the safe harbor "by dividing the parties to a discount arrangement into three groups—buyers, sellers, and offerors of discounts—with descriptions of each party's obligations in separate paragraphs."[336] "An 'offeror' may be any individual or entity that provides a discount on an item or service to a buyer, but that is not the seller of the item or service."[337] In clarifying the safe harbor, however, the OIG reiterated its view that "[t]he most important aspect of the discount safe harbor is that the Federal health care programs share in the discount in proportion to the percentage the programs pay of the total cost," that "Congress intended *only* to protect discounts that could fairly benefit the Federal health care programs," and that the intention of the discount safe harbor regulation is "to ensure that the only discounts protected are those where the Federal programs receive such benefit."[338]

The OIG stated that the statutory exception for discounts was "intended to cover discounts and other price reductions offered by a seller through an arms-length transaction to induce a buyer to purchase goods (including items) or services for which the discount applies or other goods or services payable under Medicare or Medicaid."[339] As explained by the OIG, "[a] discount typically is the difference in the price at which a good or service is normally sold compared to the price at which it is actually sold when the inducement is given."[340] The safe harbor, moreover, "applies only to discounts obtained by health care providers who submit claims to the Medicare and Medicaid programs. We believe that this exception was not intended to cover the offering of discounts by health care providers who submit claims, for example, to beneficiaries as part of a routine waiver

335. Final Rule: HHS Anti-Kickback Provisions (56 Fed. Reg. 35952, 35958; July 29, 1991): Final rulemaking promulgating the ten original safe harbor provisions.

336. Final Rule: Clarification of the Initial OIG Safe Harbor Provisions and Establishment of Additional Safe Harbor Provisions under the Anti-Kickback Statute (64 Fed. Reg. 63518, 63526; Nov. 19, 1999).

337. *Id.* at 63528.

338. *Id.* at 63529.

339. Final Rule: HHS Anti-Kickback Provisions (56 Fed. Reg. 35952, 35977; July 29, 1991): Final rulemaking promulgating the ten original safe harbor provisions.

340. *Id.*

program for coinsurance and deductible amounts."[341] Discounts, according to the OIG, "are distinct from across-the-board price reductions offered to all buyers where the inducement that is made is so diffuse that it does not appear intended to encourage a particular buyer to purchase or order a particular good or service payable under Medicare or Medicaid."[342] Nor was the safe harbor intended "to apply to price reductions offered to one payor but not to Medicare or Medicaid," offering as an example a situation where a laboratory offers a discount to a physician who bills the patient but does not offer the same discount to the government.[343] Since such a discount "does not benefit Medicare," protecting it would be "inconsistent with the statutory intent for discounts to be reported to the programs with costs and charges reduced appropriately to reflect the discounts."[344]

Although the safe harbor applies to rebates, in 1999 the OIG clarified the definition of "rebate" to make clear that a rebate is "any discount not given at the time of sale" and that, accordingly, "a rebate transaction would not be covered by the safe harbor if it involves a buyer under §1001.952(h)(1)(iii) that is neither a cost-reporter nor a [Health Maintenance Organization] or [Competitive Medical Plan], because for such buyers, all discounts must be given at the time of sale."[345] By modifying the definition of rebate "to include any discount the terms of which are fixed at the time of the sale of the good or service and disclosed to the buyer, but which is not received at the time of the sale of the good or service," the OIG explained that it could "extend safe harbor protection to certain charge-based buyers and buyers reimbursed on the basis of fee schedules who obtain rebates."[346] The OIG acknowledged that in the case of some rebates, "the exact dollar amount of the rebate may not be known until the rebate is paid" and that "[i]n some circumstances, a rebate may be paid only after some number of successive purchases of particular goods or services," in which case "the terms of the rebate must be fixed and disclosed to the buyer at the time of the first sale of a good or service to which the rebate applies."[347]

341. *Id.*
342. *Id.*
343. *Id.*
344. *Id.*
345. Final Rule: Clarification of the Initial OIG Safe Harbor Provisions and Establishment of Additional Safe Harbor Provisions under the Anti-Kickback Statute (64 Fed. Reg. 63518, 63526; Nov. 19, 1999).
346. *Id.*
347. *Id.*

The OIG further clarified that the discount safe harbor may only be used to protect "transactions made on an arms-length basis" and may not be used to protect "discounts" provided to a joint venture by an entity that is both a provider/supplier and a joint venture partner as a way of sharing profits with referring physician partners, since such an arrangement is not an arms-length transaction "where the joint venture entity shops around for the best price on a good or service."[348] Providing services or supplies "at a discount" does not, therefore, automatically make the arrangement subject to the safe harbor, and the OIG noted that many such arrangements should more appropriately be analyzed under the safe harbor for personal services or management contracts.[349] The OIG specifically declined "to broaden the scope of [the safe harbor] to include discounts on bundled goods" in recognition of the "enormous potential for abuse" in "the practice of a seller giving away, or reducing the price of, one good in connection with the purchase of a different good."[350] However, the OIG has recognized that "in certain circumstances, discounts offered on one good or service to induce the purchase of a different good or service where the net value can be properly reported do not pose risk of program abuse and may benefit the programs through lower costs or charges achieved through volume purchasing and other economies of scale . . . where the goods and services are reimbursed by the same Federal health care program in the same manner."[351]

While the discount safe harbor is applicable to rebate checks, redeemable coupons, and credits, the OIG noted that the reporting of credits "presents an unusual situation because the monetary value of the credit only applies to future purchases of goods or services" and that, therefore, "the buyer must report the credits on the applicable cost report or claim form covering the goods or services for which the credit is being used."[352] The OIG noted that the safe harbor generally "does not permit end-of-year discounts" after the good is purchased or the service is provided due to practical difficulties in "retrospectively" determining the price impact of such discounts,

348. Final Rule: HHS Anti-Kickback Provisions (56 Fed. Reg. 35952, 35977-78; July 29, 1991): Final rulemaking promulgating the ten original safe harbor provisions.

349. *Id.* at 35978.

350. *Id.*

351. Final Rule: Clarification of the Initial OIG Safe Harbor Provisions and Establishment of Additional Safe Harbor Provisions under the Anti-Kickback Statute (64 Fed. Reg. 63518, 63530; Nov. 19, 1999).

352. Final Rule: HHS Anti-Kickback Provisions (56 Fed. Reg. 35952, 35979; July 29, 1991): Final rulemaking promulgating the ten original safe harbor provisions.

but that when a provider is required to maintain cost reports, "end of year calculations of discounts on purchases of the same good or service can be fully and accurately reported, as well as those discounts obtained at the time of the purchase," and the safe harbor thus protects end-of-year discounts for cost report providers.[353] The OIG explained that this protection "complies with the most important statutory requirement of the discount exception—full reporting—and accommodates many of these end-of-year discounting programs," and that it is also "consistent with [CMS's] prudent buyer rules, which are not applicable to charge-based health care providers."[354]

Regarding "prompt pay" discounts, the OIG declined to include them in the safe harbor because "by definition, they are designed to induce prompt payment, and thus do not appear to violate the statute" but noted that the OIG "will continue to scrutinize closely 'prompt pay' discounts to make sure that they are not payments made for an illegal purpose cloaked under a legitimate label."[355] Commenting on the "special attention" due to HMOs and CMPs having risk contracts with the CMS or a state health care program, the OIG noted that under the safe harbor such entities "need not report discounts they receive except as may otherwise be required under their risk contract."[356]

Commenting on discount reporting requirements, the OIG noted that such requirement "is limited to items or services that are separately claimed as a line item for payment with [HHS] or a State agency" and that "we will not require health care providers to report discounts they receive on goods purchased for which a line item charge is not separately made, but rather is included in the professional charge."[357] Explaining why the safe harbor does not require that providers submitting cost reports reduce their costs by the amount of any discount, the OIG stated that the reason is that "the cost reporting requirements accomplish the statutory purpose of having the amount of the discount 'appropriately reflected in the costs claimed'" and that "[w]hether a provider submits cost reports . . . or submits a seller's invoice to demonstrate its acquisition costs . . . the amount of the discount is passed along to the Medicare and Medicaid programs."[358] Therefore, the

353. *Id.*
354. *Id.*
355. *Id.*
356. *Id.*
357. *Id.* at 35980.
358. *Id.*

safe harbor "treats items and services reimbursed on the basis of charges differently from those reimbursed on the basis of costs, because costs will be reduced by the amounts of discounts whereas charges will not be affected."[359] The OIG also explained that sellers, other than in situations involving HMOs or CMPs, "must . . . fully and accurately report the discount on the invoice or statement" and "must inform the buyer of its obligations under" (h)(1) of the safe harbor, although sellers will not be held "liable for the reporting omissions of health care providers."[360] Indeed, in the 1999 rule clarifying the original safe harbor, the OIG clarified the scope of protection "for sellers in situations where buyers have not fully complied with their obligations," commenting that "[i]f a seller has done everything that it reasonably could under the circumstances to ensure that the buyer understands its obligation to report the discount accurately, the seller is protected irrespective of the buyer's omissions."[361] A condition of receiving such protection is that "the seller must report the discount to the buyer and inform the buyer of its obligation to report the discount."[362] However, "if the seller, in good faith, meets its obligations under the safe harbor and the buyer does not meet its obligations due to no fault of the seller, the seller would receive safe harbor protection."[363] "An offeror of a discount would similarly receive safe harbor protection if it meets all of its safe harbor obligations, but its buyer or seller does not meet its obligations due to no fault of the offeror."[364]

According to the OIG, "[t]he fundamental test for complying with the reporting requirement is whether the actual purchase price net of any discount is fully and accurately reported by the seller on the invoice or statement (or, where applicable for end-of-year discounts, on a reconciliation statement) and by the purchaser on the claim or request for payment submitted to Medicare and Medicaid."[365] It is not necessary that "all the information in the calculation of the discount . . . be noted specifically on the invoice, statement, claim or request for payment; rather, a notation may be made that the actual purchase price is 'net discount,'" which will satisfy

359. *Id.*

360. *Id.*

361. Final Rule: Clarification of the Initial OIG Safe Harbor Provisions and Establishment of Additional Safe Harbor Provisions under the Anti-Kickback Statute (64 Fed. Reg. 63518, 63526-27; Nov. 19, 1999).

362. *Id.*

363. *Id.*

364. *Id.*

365. Final Rule: HHS Anti-Kickback Provisions (56 Fed. Reg. 35952, 35981; July 29, 1991): Final rulemaking promulgating the ten original safe harbor provisions.

the safe harbor.[366] Moreover, "where a practitioner obtains a discount . . . for a good that is included as part of his or her professional service charge, such discounts need not be reported" since the good itself is not separately reported, but if the practitioner "purchases an item or service at a discount and such item or service is separately claimed as a line item on the applicable claim form, the discounted price must be fully and accurately reported."[367] The OIG offered as an example a surgeon who performs cataract surgery in his or her office and implants an intraocular lens, which would require that the surgeon report any discount received on the lens. Finally, the OIG noted that just as it was unwilling "to protect the offering of a free good different from the one that is being purchased," it likewise was unwilling "to protect the offering of free computers even when named as 'office supplies' to induce the purchase of other items that are reimbursable separately."[368]

The discount safe harbor has been discussed in numerous OIG Advisory Opinions.[369] In one opinion (Advisory Opinion No. 99-13), a pathology services business had implemented a billing arrangement whereby the business billed federal health care programs directly for services provided to program patients, but for nonprogram patients would afford referring physicians two payment options. Under one option, the business would bill charges directly to the third-party payor, and under the other option (referred to as "account billing"), the business would bill the physicians at a discount and accept that payment as payment in full. The physicians would then bill the third-party payors and patients for the services. The business represented that

366. *Id.* In the 1999 clarifying rule, however, the OIG noted that "for purposes of submitting a claim or request for payment . . . what is necessary is that the value of the discount be accurately reflected in the actual purchase price" and that it is "not necessary to distinguish whether this price is the result of a discount or to state 'net discount' . . . as long as the actual purchase price accurately reflects the discount." Final Rule: Clarification of the Initial OIG Safe Harbor Provisions and Establishment of Additional Safe Harbor Provisions under the Anti-Kickback Statute (64 Fed. Reg. 63518, 63527; Nov. 19, 1999); *see also* United States v. Carroll, 320 F. Supp. 2d 748, 756 (S.D. Ill. 2004) (noting that 1999 rule "dropped the requirement of including the notation 'net discount' and now requires only that 'the value of the discount be accurately reflected in the actual purchase price'") (citation omitted).

367. Final Rule: HHS Anti-Kickback Provisions (56 Fed. Reg. 35952, 35977; July 29, 1991): Final rulemaking promulgating the ten original safe harbor provisions.

368. *Id.*

369. *See, e.g.*, Advisory Opinion No. 13-07 (Issued June 24, 2013); Advisory Opinion No. 12-02 (Issued Mar. 20, 2012); Advisory Opinion No. 12-01 (Issued Mar. 8, 2012); Advisory Opinion No. 02-10 (Issued July 30, 2002); Advisory Opinion No. 01-8 (Issued July 3, 2001); Advisory Opinion No. 99-13 (Issued Nov. 30, 1999); Advisory Opinion No. 99-3 (Issued Mar. 16, 1999); Advisory Opinion No. 99-2 (Issued Feb. 26, 1999); Advisory Opinion No. 98-5 (Issued Apr. 24, 1998); Advisory Opinion No. 98-2 (Posted Apr. 8, 1998).

the discount offered to physicians under the account billing arrangement reflected its cost savings realized through that billing method. Most physicians who participated in the account billing arrangement referred all their patients to the business, including both nonprogram patients (billed to the physicians at a discount) and program patients (billed to the federal health care programs). Under the proposed arrangement, the business wished to offer its account billing customers discounts greater than its cost savings, in order to match the prices of competitors and, in some cases, the discounts would be greater than the actual cost of providing services. The profit margin for non-federal health care program business would be less than the profit margin for program business.

The OIG analyzed the proposed arrangement under the discount safe harbor, which it noted "reflects the intent of Congress to encourage price competition that benefits the Medicare and Medicaid programs," and concluded that the safe harbor did not protect the arrangement, which offered price reductions "to one payor but not . . . to Medicare or Medicaid." The OIG commented that "[s]uch price reductions create a risk that a laboratory may be offering remuneration in the form of discounts on business for which the purchaser pays the laboratory, in exchange for the opportunity to service and bill for higher paying Federal health care program business reimbursed directly by the program to the laboratory." The OIG further noted that in such an arrangement, "neither Medicare nor Medicaid benefits from the discount; to the contrary, Medicare and Medicaid may, in effect, subsidize the other payor's discounted rates . . . [and] laboratories may have an incentive to engage in abusive billing practices to recoup losses on the discounted business."[370] Having concluded that the arrangement was not protected by the safe harbor, the OIG proceeded to find that it also might violate the AKS because the circumstances surrounding the arrangement suggested that "a nexus may exist between the discount to the physicians for non-Federal health care program business and referrals of Federal health care program business."[371]

Similar reasoning has led the OIG to deny safe harbor protection to other arrangements as well.[372] Where the OIG has approved arrangements despite the failure to satisfy the elements of the discount safe harbor, it cited various

370. Advisory Opinion No. 99-13 at pp. 2-4.

371. *Id.* at 4.

372. *See, e.g.*, Advisory Opinion No. 99-2 (proposed arrangement under which ambulance company would offer substantial discounts to nursing home for Part A capitated business

factors that mitigated the risk of fraud and abuse, including (1) uniform pricing that did not discriminate on the basis of the payor; (2) any bundling of items and services did not prejudice federal health care programs; and (3) there was no risk of "swapping" discounted prices for an opportunity to provide and bill for unrelated items or services.[373]

The discount safe harbor also has been analyzed in a number of court decisions.[374] A particularly lengthy discussion of the origins and requirements of the safe harbor can be found in *United States v. Shaw*, 106 F. Supp. 2d 103, 113-123 (D. Mass. 2000). The *Shaw* decision provides the following insightful discussion of the discount safe harbor's purpose:

> As stated in the House Report on the Medicare–Medicaid Anti–Fraud and Abuse amendments, the reason for excluding certain "practice[s] of discounting the normal course of business transactions" from criminal liability under the statute was to "encourage providers to seek discounts as a good business practice which results in savings to medicare and medicaid program costs."[375] The exception, then, reflects a predictive understanding that competitive pricing schemes

---

reflected possible intention of inducing nursing home referrals of more lucrative Part B business billed by ambulance company to Medicare in illicit "swapping" arrangement).

373. *See, e.g.*, Advisory Opinion No. 01-08 (involving arrangement between manufacturer of therapeutic mattresses and nursing facilities); Advisory Opinion No. 99-3 (involving arrangement between therapeutic mattress distributor and nursing facilities).

374. *See, e.g.*, United States *ex rel.* Banigan v. Organon USA Inc., 883 F. Supp. 2d 277, 296 (D. Mass. 2012) (analyzing discount safe harbor in the context of the purchase of pharmaceuticals and noting that discount "does not embrace collateral kickbacks or reductions in price which are not passed on to Medicaid"); United States v. Shaw, 106 F. Supp. 2d 103, 113-123 (D. Mass. 2000) (extensive analysis of the discount safe harbor); United States v. Carroll, 320 F. Supp. 2d 748, 756-57 (S.D. Ill. 2004) (in criminal fraud case involving sale of medical supplies, court noted that defendant could not satisfy safe harbor since the transaction involved a "rental," which does not qualify as a discount, and the transaction also was not accurately disclosed); United States *ex rel.* Klaczak v. Consol. Med. Transp., 458 F. Supp. 2d 622, 679-680 (N.D. Ill. 2006) (in case alleging that ambulance companies paid kickbacks in the form of reduced rates to hospitals for referrals, court noted that "the statutory exception for discounts does not require that Medicare receive the same discount, just that any discount is properly accounted for and disclosed on the cost reports" and that the safe harbor "does not require that Medicare receive the same rate—it states that a reduction in price does not qualify as a discount if it is not offered to 'Medicare or Medicaid.'") (citation omitted); United States *ex rel.* Schmidt, M.D. v. Zimmer, Inc., 386 F.3d 235, 241 (3d Cir. 2004) (provision of cash or cash equivalents does not qualify as discount under the safe harbor); United States *ex rel.* Gale v. Omnicare, Inc., 2013 WL 3822152 at **5-6 (N.D. Ohio July 23, 2013) (in order to show that its arrangement was protected, Ominicare could show "either that its pricing was that of an arms-length transaction *or* that the discount . . . was not intended to induce a referral").

375. H.R. Rep. No. 95–393, pt. 2, at 54 (1977), *reprinted in* 1977 U.S.C.C.A.N. 3039, 3056.

within the health care field will lower the cost of health care services and goods.

For these competitively low prices (in the form of discounts or "other reductions") to be exempt from criminal liability, however, they must enure to the benefit of Medicare and Medicaid and of their beneficiaries. Thus, one essential component of this exception is that the federal or state health program share in and benefit from the reduced cost of the services or goods that are being provided at a discount or other reduced price.[376] The only way to pass on those benefits, however, is if Medicare and Medicaid are made aware of the competitively low costs so that the federal or state system reimburses the provider the percentage of only the reduced price. This is the purpose of the phrase in the exception "properly disclose and appropriately reflected.". . . .

In the context of the entire statute, the discount exception makes good sense. The statute was passed to curtail fraud and abuse in Medicare and Medicaid reporting, in particular. It was passed to prevent health care service and good suppliers and providers from depriving the federal and state health care subsidy system of the benefits that a free market for health care services and goods can provide. By allowing for suppliers and providers of health care service and goods to compete with one another in limited forms, the statute strikes a balance: on the one hand, it provides for some of the benefits of a market economy by encouraging limited forms of price competition; on the other hand, it deters and penalizes other types of conduct that would lower the cost of some health care services and goods for some suppliers and providers but would not pass on that lowered cost to the federal and state health systems or to its patients.[377]

2.9. Employees

Although Congress intended that "remuneration" under the AKS be construed "broadly,"[378] the 1977 legislation also included several exceptions,

376. *See* 64 Fed. Reg. 63,518, 63,529 (1999) ("Congress intended only to protect discounts that could fairly benefit the Federal health care programs.").

377. *Id.* at 115.

378. H.R. 95-393 at p. 49 (1977).

commonly known as "safe harbors," from AKS prosecution. One such exception, codified at 42 U.S.C. §1320a-7b(b)(3)(B), states as follows:

> *(3) [The AKS] shall not apply to-*
>
> . . .
>
> *(B) any amount paid by an employer to an employee (who has a bona fide employment relationship with such employer) for employment in the provision of covered items or services. . . .*

The initial set of safe harbors published in the 1991 final rule included a regulatory version of this exception, which may be found at 42 C.F.R. § 1001.952(i). The regulatory safe harbor generally tracks the statutory language:

> *As used in [the AKS], "remuneration" does not include any amount paid by an employer to an employee, who has a bona fide employment relationship with the employer, for employment in the furnishing of any item or service for which payment may be made in whole or in part under Medicare, Medicaid or other Federal health care programs. For purposes . . . of this section, the term employee has the same meaning as it does for purposes of [the Internal Revenue Code].*

Thus, the safe harbor has two independently mandated elements: (1) there must be a *bona fide* employment relationship; and (2) the remuneration paid must be for employment in the furnishing or provision of items or services reimbursable under a federal health care program.

Regarding the first requirement, the regulatory safe harbor states that "the term employee has the same meaning as it does for purposes" of the Internal Revenue Code.[379] HHS, however, is barred by statute from opining, during the Advisory Opinion process, on whether an individual is a *bona fide* employee within the meaning of the IRS Code provision.[380]

Regarding the second requirement, there has been disagreement in the case law over its precise meaning and scope, with some courts ruling that a *bona fide* employee may be paid in any manner chosen by an employer,

379. 42 C.F.R. § 1001.952(i) ("the term *employee* has the same meaning as it does for purposes of 26 U.S.C. § 3121(d)(2)"); 26 U.S.C. § 3121(d)(2) ("[T]he terms "employee" means . . . an individual who, under the usual common law rules applicable in determining the employer-employee relationship, has the status of an employee").

380. 42 U.S.C. § 1320a-7d(b)(3)(B).

which may even include payments for referrals,[381] while other courts have ruled that the safe harbor only protects payments to employees that are tied to the employees' furnishing or provision of items and services reimbursable under a federal health care program, and not simply payments made in exchange for referrals.[382]

Some have taken the view that the latter position is more consistent with the legislative purpose and design of the AKS and the other safe harbors, with HHS interpretations of the employee safe harbor and with the text of the employee safe harbor itself. On this view, permitting an employer's purchase of patient referrals from an employee who otherwise qualified as *bona fide* within the meaning of the safe harbor could allow the employee safe harbor to undermine the remedial purposes of the AKS by effectively permitting employers to hire their co-conspirators and swallowing the general statutory prohibition against making payments to induce or reward referrals. Furthermore, such an interpretation arguably does not make sense by reference to the text of the safe harbor itself. Under this reasoning, if the intent of the safe harbor were to allow referral payments, there would have been no need to limit the reach of the safe harbor by requiring that payment be for "employment in the furnishing [or provision]" of covered items or services, a clause presumably meant to tie the specific remuneration paid to an employee's "furnishing" or "providing" particular reimbursable items or services, which do not include referrals. Instead, the safe harbor could simply have required evidence of a *bona fide* employment relationship, with no additional showing needed. The inclusion of that additional language, this reasoning continues, was not an inadvertence, but a requirement that compensation, even that paid to *bona fide* employees, must be for the furnishing or providing of covered items and services in order to receive safe harbor protection. Additionally, if the employee safe harbor were intended to shield referral payments, one might expect to see exceptions included in other safe harbors permitting such payments to *bona fide* employees. Yet,

---

381. *See, e.g.*, Wall v. Vista Hospice Care Inc., 2016 WL 3449833 (N.D. Tex. June 20, 2016) (upholding legality of referral payments under employee safe harbor); United States v. Crinel, 2015 WL 3755896 (E.D. La. June 16, 2015) (upholding legality of referral payments under employee safe harbor, provided services rendered are otherwise reimbursable under federal health care program).

382. *See, e.g.*, Obert-Hong v. Advocate Health Care, 211 F.Supp.2d 1045, 1050-51 (N.D. Ill. 2002) (employee safe harbor protects "typical hospital-physician employment relationships," provided that compensation arrangements are "based on personally performed services" and are not "directly related to referrals").

one will search in vain for any such exceptions. For example, a safe harbor for free or discounted local transportation services that became effective on January 6, 2017, contains an explicit prohibition against paying drivers transporting patients on a "per head" basis, and that safe harbor contains no exception for *bona fide* employee drivers of health care organizations offering such transportation services.[383]

These are some of the reasons that a persuasive argument can be made in support of the view that the employee safe harbor is an exception intended to protect, not the purchase of patient referrals at the expense of patient choice and other competing providers in the health care marketplace, but rather traditional compensation arrangements such as those between physicians and employers like hospitals and group practices which, even while compensating the employee for personally performed services, might still be "potentially capable of inducing referrals of business under Medicare."[384]

To protect these kinds of arrangements, Congress and HHS required not only that there be a *bona fide* employment relationship but also that the money paid by the employer be for employment in the furnishing or provision of covered items and services. On this view, satisfying the former requirement without satisfying the latter requirement will not trigger the safe harbor's protections. Nor would it be sufficient to invoke the safe harbor for a *bona fide* employee to receive a fee in connection with a patient referral unless that fee has some relation to covered items or services that are being personally furnished by that employee. Where the fee is disconnected from the furnishing by the employee of any covered item or service outside the referral itself, such that the fee can only be reasonably viewed as a referral payment (i.e., a payment made solely for the purpose of inducing or rewarding a decision to steer a patient to a particular provider), the protections of the safe harbor would not be available.

The view that the safe harbor does not protect payments made only for referrals and for no other purpose finds support in multiple judicial decisions as well as by opinions issued by the agency charged by statute with the safe harbor's interpretation and enforcement.

---

383. 42 C.F.R. § 1001.952(b)(b).

384. Proposed Rule: OIG Anti-Kickback Provisions, 54 Fed. Reg. 3088 (Jan. 23, 1989); *See* Obert-Hong v. Advocate Health Care, 211 F. Supp. 2d 1045, 1050-51 (N.D. Ill. 2002) (employee safe harbor protects "typical hospital-physician employment relationships," provided that compensation arrangements are "based on personally performed services" and are not "directly related to referrals").

Among judicial decisions, one particularly lucid discussion may be found in a district court decision from the Southern District of Florida, *United States v. Luis*.[385] In *Luis*, the government moved for a preliminary injunction in a case seeking to restrain the assets of a defendant under criminal prosecution for health care fraud and violating the AKS by paying employee nurses to recruit Medicare patients. Opposing the motion, the defendant argued that the payments were protected by the employee safe harbor. The court, relying both on the text of the safe harbor and the Eleventh Circuit's 1998 decision in *United States v. Starks*,[386] rejected this argument:

> For either safe-harbor provision to apply, the remuneration must have been made to the employee for furnishing or providing covered items or services or for items or services payable under Medicare. This is evident from the text of the safe-harbor provisions, as well as the Eleventh Circuit's decision in [*Starks*]. The text of the safe-harbor provision upon which Luis relies states that "remuneration" does not include "any amount paid by an employer to an employee . . . *in the furnishing* of any item or service for which payment may be made in whole or in part under Medicare." 42 C.F.R. §1001.952 (emphasis added). Similarly, the safe harbor contained in §1320a–7b states that it will apply to "any amount paid by an employer to an employee . . . *for employment in the provision* of covered items or services." §1320a–7b(b)(3)(B) (emphasis added). The emphasized language in both of these provisions makes clear that the safe-harbor provisions will only apply when payments made to an employee compensate the employee for furnishing or providing covered items or services or items or services payable by Medicare, not simply for referring patients.
>
> This was also the Eleventh Circuit's view in [*Starks*] where the court considered a vagueness challenge to the employee safe-harbor provisions. In that case, two individuals (Angela Starks and Barbara Henry) were paid for referring patients to Future Steps, Inc. [a drug addiction services business owned by Andrew Siegel] . . . Although Starks and Henry referred patients, they did not personally provide any medical services . . . Starks and Siegel appealed their [Anti-Kickback Statute] convictions, arguing that the [employee safe harbor] . . . is

385. United States v. Luis, 966 F. Supp. 2d 1321 (S.D. Fla. 2013) (Huck, J.), *aff'd*, 564 Fed. Appx. 493 (11th Cir. 2014), *vacated and remanded on other grounds*, 136 S.Ct. 1083 (2016).

386. United States v. Starks, 157 F.3d 833 (11th Cir. 1998).

> unconstitutionally vague. Rejecting this argument the court found that, even if Starks and Siegel believed they were bona fide employees, the safe-harbor was not vague, as applied, because Starks and Henry were not compensated for providing "covered items or services." . . .
>
> . . .
>
> Here, Special Agent Warren's declaration states that [the nurse employees] were paid for recruiting patients. Even if these patients ultimately received legitimate medical care, payments to these nurse/recruiters for referring patients . . . violate the Anti-kickback statute . . . Therefore, it is irrelevant whether the nurses were bona fide employees paid for "covered items or services" because the payments to them were, at least in part, for their illegal patient referrals.[387]

Advisory Opinions issued by HHS likewise have consistently interpreted the safe harbor as requiring that compensation qualifying for its protections must be paid for the employee's furnishing or provision of covered items or services.[388] That is significant because, as previously discussed, HHS is statutorily mandated, as part of the Advisory Opinion process, to opine

387. *Luis*, 966 F. Supp. 2d at 1330-31 (emphasis added); *see also* United States v. Jackson, 220 Fed. Appx. 317 (5th Cir. 2007) (affirming conviction under the AKS based on payments for patient referrals that were paid to employee in checks separate from employee's regular payroll checks written for patient-related services).

388. *See, e.g.*, Advisory Opinion No. 12-08, 2012 WL 4753655 (issued June 22, 2012) (analyzing proposed compensation arrangement between a physician and an independent diagnostic testing facility providing home sleep testing services in which facility would pay physician to read and perform sleep studies and perform administrative duties and, after assuming physician would be *bona fide* employee, concluding arrangement was protected under safe harbor because the physician "*would be compensated for furnishing a service for which payment may be made in whole or in part under Medicare, Medicaid or other Federal health care program*") (emphasis added); Advisory Opinion No. 04-09, 2004 WL 5701854 (issued July 15, 2004) (proposed arrangement between geriatric practice group and referring primary care physicians under which the latter would provide consulting services at an hourly rate was protected under employee safe harbor because, assuming *bona fide* status of employees, physicians would be paid "*for the furnishing of covered items and services*"; noting that AKS "*disfavors payment structures that tie compensation, even for services, to patients referred by the compensated party*" but creates exception where services are furnished by *bona fide* employees) (emphasis added); Advisory Opinion No. 98-9, 1998 WL 35287764 (issued July 13, 1998) (proposed arrangement under collective bargaining agreement, whereby nurse employees would receive additional compensation based on the number of union members and dependents admitted to hospital as inpatients over set periods, was protected under employee safe harbor because, assuming nurses were *bona fide* employees, the compensation was based on the performance of covered "*nursing and other health care related services,*" the extra compensation was "*tied to aggregate admissions and not to specific admissions or services,*" and to be eligible to receive the money, a nurse could not be "*in a position to refer patients to the Hospital*") (emphasis added).

on "[w]hat constitutes prohibited remuneration within the meaning of section 1320a-7b(b) [i.e., the AKS]."[389] Thus, interpretive guidance from the agency concerning what kinds of remuneration are and are not protected by the safe harbor is likely entitled to substantial deference.[390]

However, the need to link employee compensation to the furnishing or provision of covered items or services in order to trigger the employee safe harbor does not mean that employee compensation formulas may not contain incentive elements that could potentially induce patient referrals. On the contrary, this is where the real impact of the safe harbor is felt by providing broad discretion to employers in how they choose to compensate their employees for furnishing or providing those covered items or services.

The reason underpinning this grant (both statutory and regulatory) of employer autonomy is alluded to in HHS commentary within the final rule promulgating the original regulatory safe harbors. HHS declared its confidence "that the employer-employee relationship is unlikely to be abusive, in part because the employer is generally fully liable for the actions of its employees and is therefore more motivated to supervise and control them."[391]

In other commentary, HHS has stated that the safe harbor "permits an employer to pay an employee in whatever manner he or she chooses for having that employee assist in the solicitation of . . . health care program business" and "if individuals and entities desire to pay a salesperson on the basis of the amount of business they generate, then to be exempt from civil or criminal prosecution, they should make these salespersons employees where they can and should exert appropriate supervision for the individual's acts."[392]

In some quarters, this commentary has been construed as supporting virtually unlimited discretion by employers in devising compensation formulas, to include payments to employees in exchange for patient referrals. As discussed earlier, however, such a view might be a "bridge too far" in interpreting the scope and reach of the employee safe harbor. The commentary may

---

389. *See* 42 U.S.C. § 1320a-7d(b)(2)(A) (emphasis added).

390. *See, e.g.*, Chevron v. Natural Res. Def. Council, Inc., 467 U.S. 837 (1984).

391. Final Rule: OIG Anti-Kickback Provisions (56 Fed. Reg. 35952; July 29, 1991): Final rulemaking promulgating the ten original safe harbor provisions.

392. Proposed Rule: OIG Anti-Kickback Provisions (54 Fed. Reg. 3088; Jan. 23, 1989): Proposed original ten safe harbor provisions. Medicare and Medicaid Programs, Fraud and Abuse OIG Anti-Kickback Provisions, 54 Fed. Reg. 3088, 3093 (Jan. 23, 1989).

also be understood as speaking to an employer's flexibility in structuring employee compensation for furnishing covered items or services, rather than an employer's authority to pay for referrals alone. Notably, the cited commentary does not purport to address the safe harbor's requirement that the remuneration be tied to the furnishing or provision of covered items or services but instead focuses on the employer's freedom in structuring the compensation even where the compensation formula is related to "the solicitation of . . . health care program business." That would be consistent, for example, with paying physician employees based on a percentage of revenue collections generated from their personally performed services,[393] or with permitting such employees to participate in a bonus pool composed of revenues related to their personally performed services.[394] It is also consistent with an employer paying commissions to an employed sales force responsible for selling various reimbursable "items" (e.g., DME, pharmaceuticals, etc.) directly to medical providers.

Whereas one can at least understand a rationale for not protecting under the employee safe harbor a payment that is solely and exclusively for referrals, and not related to any covered item or service, what of a payment that is made for both reasons? For example, it is certainly conceivable that a hospital employer could choose to structure an employed physician's compensation, both to compensate the physician for personally performed services and also to encourage the physician to refer more patients to his or her hospital employer. Both motivations could underlie a hospital employer's decision to allow a physician to participate in a bonus pool composed of collections by the hospital on the physician's personally performed services. Does the motivation to encourage the physician to refer more patients to the hospital taint the entire compensation formula under the AKS? A strict application of the "one purpose test" might suggest so, and there is some case law and Advisory Opinion language that could support such an outcome, focusing on whether *any* purpose of the remuneration is to induce referrals.[395] Such

---

393. Obert-Hong v. Advocate Health Care, 211 F. Supp. 2d 1045, 1051 (N.D. Ill. 2002) (approving compensation formula based on percentage of collections).

394. Baklid-Kunz v. Halifax Hosp., 2013 WL 6196562 at *2 (M.D. Fla. Nov. 26, 2013) (approving compensation formula involving payments to medical oncologists consisting of revenues from "outpatient medical oncology services" including "physician services" of the oncologists and paid out of an "Incentive Compensation pool [that] was divided . . . based on each individual oncologist's personally performed services.").

395. *See* United States v. Borrasi, 639 F.3d 774, 782 (7th Cir. 2011) (payments intended to induce referrals violated AKS "even if the payments were also intended to compensate for professional services").

an interpretation might, however, intrude upon the legislative and regulatory scope of the employee safe harbor by allowing prosecution under the AKS for payments made to *bona fide* employees, even if those payments are intended to compensate for an employee's furnishing of covered items or services, so long as the payments are also intended to induce referrals. Yet, since the employee safe harbor contains no specific language requiring that the remuneration paid, in order to receive protection, be paid *exclusively* for the purpose of providing covered items or services, it is fair to ask whether a more commonsense interpretation would require only that at least one purpose of the compensation be for the furnishing of a covered item or service. On this view, if the facts indicated that the sole purpose of the compensation was to reward or induce referrals, the employee safe harbor would not apply, but if the remuneration had a dual purpose to compensate for personally performed services and also to induce referrals to the employer, the payment could still receive protection under the safe harbor.

Another situation involves compensation that is paid only for a single purpose (i.e., personally performed services) but that may fall within more than one safe harbor (e.g., employee safe harbor and personal services safe harbor). In such a situation, HHS has stated that if the payment practice does not qualify for protection under the employee safe harbor, "it still may receive safe harbor protection under the personal services and management contract safe harbor," and "if the payment practice fits into either one of the safe harbors, it is exempt from criminal prosecution and program exclusion."[396]

Concerning the relationship between the employee safe harbor and the safe harbor for sale of practice, in cases where a practitioner purchases another's practice and retains the other practitioner on staff as an employee, HHS has stated that payments to the other practitioner for the practice

---

396. Final Rule: OIG Anti-Kickback Provisions (56 Fed. Reg. 35952, 35957; July 29, 1991): Final rulemaking promulgating the ten original safe harbor provisions. It is important to distinguish whether an AKS analysis involves *one* arrangement that may fall within multiple safe harbors or *multiple* arrangements between the same parties, whereby each separate arrangement would fall under a different safe harbor. In the example discussed here, a compensation arrangement (i.e., a single arrangement) can fall under multiple safe harbors, including the safe harbor for employee compensation and personal services arrangements. In such an example, only one applicable safe harbor must be satisfied for the arrangement to be protected under AKS. By comparison, when parties have multiple arrangements in place, for example, a landlord may provide office space and certain administrative services to a tenant, then each part of the arrangement must fall within an applicable safe harbor. In this example, the provision of office space would need to fall under the space rental safe harbor, and the administrative services would need to fall under the personal services safe harbor. *See supra* note 209.

itself do not qualify under either safe harbor because those payments are made to one who is still in a position to make referrals (see Chapter 2.5 on Sale of Practice), and they are not payments made "for employment in the provision of covered items or services" since the payments "relate to the purchase of a practice and not to services provided pursuant to employment for the provision of items or services."[397] However, any salary payments to the practitioner for services, assuming the existence of a *bona fide* employment relationship, would be protected under the employee safe harbor.[398]

In explaining the decision to defer to the IRS definition of "employee," HHS stated that the IRS definition "is a longstanding one that has been developed by both agency and court rulings" and that the definition "is sufficiently narrow that it excludes certain types of relationships that we believe tend to be associated with violations of the statute."[399] HHS clarified that the meaning of "employee" will be defined not only by the IRS Code (26 U.S.C. § 3121(d)(2)), "but also by the IRS's interpretation of that provision as codified in its regulations and other interpretive sources."[400] Part-time as well as full-time employment can qualify for protection.[401] Independent contractor relationships are not protected by the safe harbor, although they may receive protection under the safe harbor for personal services (see Chapter 2.4 on Personal Services and Management Contracts).[402]

2.10. Group Purchasing Organizations

The safe harbor for group purchasing organizations is codified both in statute and regulation. 42 U.S.C. § 1320a-7b(b)(3)(C) states:

> (C) any amount paid by a vendor of goods or services to a person authorized to act as a purchasing agent for a group of individuals or entities who are furnishing services reimbursed under a Federal health care program if—
>
> (i) the person has a written contract, with each such individual or entity, which specifies the amount to be paid the person, which amount may be a fixed amount or a fixed percentage

397. *Id.* at 35975.
398. *Id.*
399. *Id.* at 35981.
400. *Id.*
401. *Id.*
402. *Id.* at 35981-82.

of the value of the purchases made by each such individual or entity under the contract, and

(ii) in the case of an entity that is a provider of services (as defined in section 1395x (u) of this title), the person discloses (in such form and manner as the Secretary requires) to the entity and, upon request, to the Secretary the amount received from each such vendor with respect to purchases made by or on behalf of the entity. . . .

The regulatory equivalent of this safe harbor is codified at 42 C.F.R. § 1001.952(j):

(j) *Group purchasing organizations.* As used in [the AKS], "remuneration" does not include any payment by a vendor of goods or services to a group purchasing organization (GPO), as part of an agreement to furnish such goods or services to an individual or entity as long as both of the following two standards are met -

(1) The GPO must have a written agreement with each individual or entity, for which items or services are furnished, that provides for either of the following -

(i) The agreement states that participating vendors from which the individual or entity will purchase goods or services will pay a fee to the GPO of 3 percent or less of the purchase price of the goods or services provided by that vendor.

(ii) In the event the fee paid to the GPO is not fixed at 3 percent or less of the purchase price of the goods or services, the agreement specifies the amount (or if not known, the maximum amount) the GPO will be paid by each vendor (where such amount may be a fixed sum or a fixed percentage of the value of purchases made from the vendor by the members of the group under the contract between the vendor and the GPO).

(2) Where the entity which receives the goods or service from the vendor is a health care provider of services, the GPO must disclose in writing to the entity at least annually, and to the Secretary upon request, the amount received from each vendor with respect to purchases made by or on behalf of the entity. Note that for purposes of paragraph (j) of this section,

> the term *group purchasing organization* (GPO) means an entity authorized to act as a purchasing agent for a group of individuals or entities who are furnishing services for which payment may be made in whole or in part under Medicare, Medicaid or other Federal health care programs, and who are neither wholly-owned by the GPO nor subsidiaries of a parent corporation that wholly owns the GPO (either directly or through another wholly-owned entity).

As explained by Congress in adopting the statutory safe harbor[403]:

> Group Purchasing organizations (GPOs) purchase goods and services for participating hospitals and other institutions at costs below those which the members would be able to obtain individually. To cover costs, GPOs either charge administrative fees to member institutions, or they require vendors from whom they purchase services or supplies to pay them a fixed percentage of the value of the business that they refer to the vendors. The Inspector General of the Department of Health and Services has determined that this latter arrangement—the vendor-paid fee—represents a "technical" violation of the anti-kickback provisions. In the IG's view, both the vendor who agrees to such a condition and a GPO who solicits such an agreement are violating the law. The IG does not consider these payments exempt from criminal liability as "discounts" under sections 1877(b) and 1909(b) of the Act because they are not reductions in price, the value of which are passed on to the purchaser. Under group purchasing agreements, the amount paid by the vendor to the agent may not be passed along to the hospitals.
>
> Pending Congressional clarification on this point, the IG requested that the Justice Department announce it would refrain from prosecuting such arrangements, but the Department, by letter dated October 30, 1985, declined, arguing that "this would be tantamount to saying that conduct which Congress in its wisdom has made a crime is not a crime." It is clear that Congressional action is warranted.
>
> The Committee believes that GPOs can help reduce health care costs for the government and the private sector alike by enabling a group

403. H.R. Rep. 99-727, Omnibus Budget Reconciliation Act of 1986 (July 31, 1986) (1986 WL 31979 at **3662-63).

> of purchasers to obtain substantial volume discounts on the prices they are charged. The Committee understands that the amount of the price reductions exceeds the fees the vendors must pay the GPOs. The Committee can see no justification for prohibiting such cost-saving arrangements, and believes that the uncertainty resulting from the Justice Department's position on this issue should be eliminated.
>
> The Committee bill therefore creates an exception to the antikickback provisions for amounts paid by vendors of goods and services to authorized purchasing agents for groups of hospitals, nursing homes, or other entities receiving Medicare and Medicaid reimbursement, if the following conditions are met. First, the purchasing agent must have a written contract with each vendor and with each Medicare or Medicaid provider or practitioner in the group specifying the amount paid to the agent. The amount may be either a fixed sum or a fixed percentage (not to exceed 3 percent) of the value of the purchase made by each practitioner or provider under the contract. Second, the purchasing agent must disclose to each practitioner or provider in the group the amount received from each vendor with respect to that individual's or entities purchases. These limitations are intended to assure that only reasonable and above-board vendor-paid GPO fee arrangements receive the protection of this exclusion.
>
> The purpose of this provision is to assure GPOs and the vendors who contract with them, that they do not risk prosecution as a result of the fees the GPO's collection from the vendors. The provision is therefore effective with respect to payments made before, on, or after enactment.

In adopting the regulatory version of the GPO safe harbor, HHS commented that the safe harbor "was designed to apply to payments from vendors to entities authorized to act as a GPO for individuals or entities who are furnishing Medicare or Medicaid services. The exception required a written agreement between the GPO and the individual or entity that specifies the amounts vendors will pay the GPO."[404] In response to a comment, HHS clarified that the exception was not designed to protect a nursing home chain that requested payments from laboratories as GPO fees in return for laboratory referrals from member nursing homes:

404. Final Rule: OIG Anti-Kickback Provisions (56 Fed. Reg. 35952, 35953; July 29, 1991): Final rulemaking promulgating the ten original safe harbor provisions.

> [W]e do not believe it appropriate for a nursing home chain to qualify as a GPO and request "GPO fees" for referrals. If a nursing home directly requested such a fee it would appear to represent an illegal inducement. We see no reason how such a solicitation sanitizes the illegality when it is made indirectly by a wholly-owned subsidiary of the nursing home, instead of directly by the nursing home itself.
>
> In addition, we believe that Congress did not intend this exception to apply where it is the vendor and not the health care provider who is furnishing services and directly billing the Medicare or Medicaid program. For example, in addition to services furnished by the nursing home, other health care providers furnish many part B services to nursing home patients, such as laboratory services and durable medical equipment (DME). We believe that a GPO, acting on behalf of a group of nursing homes, is not serving as a GPO when it receives a "GPO fee" from a laboratory or DME supplier that is supplying goods or services to nursing home patients and billing Medicare or Medicaid directly.[405]

Responding to comments requesting that GPOs be permitted to specify a fee range rather than the actual fee amount, HHS agreed that "it is not necessary in all circumstances, to specify the exact fees the GPO will receive from its vendors as a result of a particular member's purchases."[406] To guard against excessive GPO fees, however, which HHS noted was a specific concern of Congress, HHS explained that a GPO "needs to specify the administrative fee it is paid from vendors only if any fee will be above 3 percent" and that "[i]n the event that the fee cannot be ascertained at the time of the contract or the fee is not fixed at 3 percent or less, the contract must state the maximum amount that could be paid to the GPO by the vendor."[407] HHS noted that "this mechanism will permit some flexibility in payments made to the GPO, yet retain the focus on excessive fees about which Congress was concerned."[408]

Addressing the relationship between the GPO safe harbor and the discount safe harbor, HHS noted that "[t]his is an example of an arrangement where two safe harbor provisions could apply, i.e., one applicable

405. *Id.* at 35982.
406. *Id.*
407. *Id.*
408. *Id.*

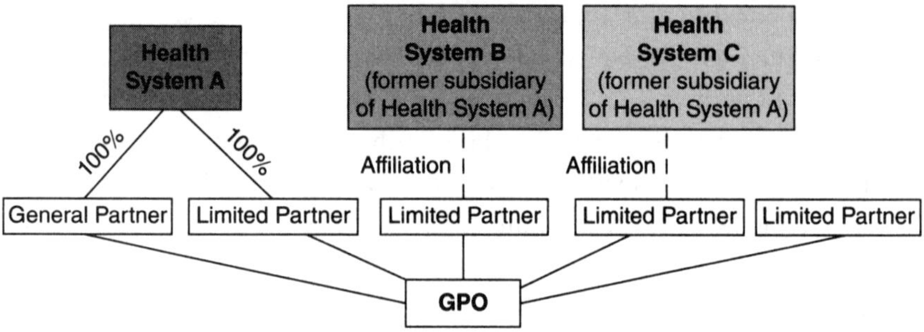

Figure 2.2

to discounts, and one applicable to GPOs" but that "the GPO provision applies only to payments made by a vendor of goods or services to a person authorized to act as a GPO [whereas] [p]ayments, such as discounts, made by vendors of goods or services to health care providers must qualify under the discount exception."[409]

Several Advisory Opinions have been issued on the subject of the GPO safe harbor. In Advisory Opinion No. 01-6, the OIG addressed a business arrangement (see Figure 2.2) involving a GPO organized as a limited partnership owned by entities affiliated with four health care systems that purchased items and services through the GPO, which negotiated discounted prices with vendors. The general partner and one of the limited partners were wholly owned by a health system (Health System) that owned a health care provider that purchased items and services through, and provided advisory and consulting services, space, and personnel to, the GPO. Two of the limited partners were affiliated with health care systems that were formerly subsidiaries of Health System, and the fourth limited partner was an entity having no affiliations with Health System or any other limited partner. In addition to the health care systems affiliated with the GPO, other nonaffiliated health care providers also contracted with the GPO to purchase health care products and services from vendors. Each purchaser entered into an agreement permitting the GPO to act as purchasing agent and disclosing that the GPO would receive quarterly fees from the vendors in connection with purchases made through the GPO. The party requesting the opinion certified that (a) the GPO agreement identified the vendors paying a fee of

409. *Id.*

3 percent or less to the GPO and, for those paying more than 3 percent, specified the exact percentage; (b) the GPO made an annual written disclosure to purchasers of the amounts received from each vendor relating to purchases attributable to each purchaser; (c) none of the purchasers was wholly owned by the GPO or was a subsidiary of a parent corporation that wholly owned the GPO; and (d) the GPO would promptly advise the Affiliated Purchasers that the regulations governing costs to related organizations (42 C.F.R. § 413.17) might apply to them. Finding that all of the requirements of the GPO safe harbor would be satisfied under the facts certified, the OIG concluded that the GPO fees paid by the vendors would not constitute prohibited remuneration under the AKS.

In Advisory Opinion No. 12-01, the OIG addressed a somewhat different GPO fact pattern (see Figure 2.3) that did not elicit the same unqualified approval from the OIG but still avoided the prospect of administrative sanctions in the absence of any intention to induce or reward referrals. The fact pattern involved a corporate parent (Parent Organization) of a national health system consisting of multiple nonprofit corporations operating local health care facilities (Nonprofits). Each of the Nonprofits was a separate legal entity and indirect subsidiary of the Parent Organization. A direct subsidiary of the Parent Organization (Subsidiary) exercised oversight over the Nonprofits and wholly owned another entity (LLC) that was responsible for supply chain, resource, and materials management functions on behalf

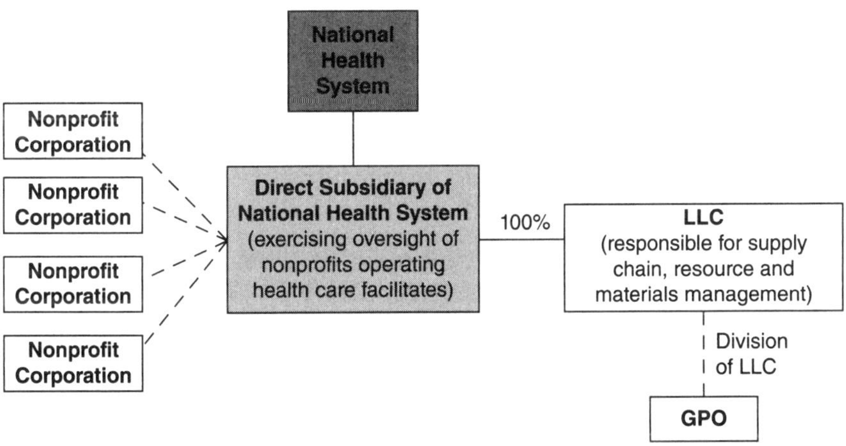

Figure 2.3

of the Parent Organization, Subsidiary, and the Nonprofits. The LLC sought to form and operate a GPO, as a division of the LLC, to benefit the Nonprofits and other affiliated organizations in the health care industry, while continuing through a separate division to be responsible for resource and supply management functions. The initial participants of the GPO would likely be the Nonprofits and other affiliates of the Parent Organization or Subsidiary, but the GPO would also be open to participation by unrelated health systems and organizations (affiliated and nonaffiliated entities, collectively "Participants"). The LLC would not charge GPO participation fees to the Participants. To accomplish its goals, the GPO represented, among other things, that it would enter into written agreements with Participants and suppliers, pursuant to which the GPO would arrange for discounts. The GPO might also provide rebates to Participants by distributing administrative fees to Participants that it collects in excess of its costs, and it would inform vendors directly of this practice.

The OIG concluded that the administrative fees paid to the GPO would *not* be protected by the GPO safe harbor "because the Proposed GPO and most of the Affiliated Participants would be wholly owned by the Parent Organization or the Subsidiary," which is not permitted under the safe harbor and which creates "an increased risk that administrative fees collected by the GPO could be illegal inducements to induce referrals or recommendations." Notwithstanding this fact, however, the OIG determined that the proposed arrangement "present[ed] an acceptably low level or risk to Federal health care programs" because (a) the Nonprofits are separate legal entities, the GPO would function as a purchasing agent for those entities and charge vendors fees for those services, and the GPO would not retain all of the administrative fees but would distribute fees exceeding its costs to Participants, which, in turn, would be required to report their fees as rebates under the discount safe harbor, thereby removing any incentive for the GPO to negotiate higher fees in lieu of discounts; (b) there was a certification that all Medicare cost reporting rules would be satisfied by affiliated participants and thus there was no risk that those participants would not fully account for their distributions from the GPO, and nonaffiliated participants would be provided with the information necessary to accurately report their costs; (c) vendors would be informed that administrative fees in excess of the GPO's costs may be passed through to participants, and thus vendors would be on notice to obtain specific information regarding passed-through fees in order to comply with their own price

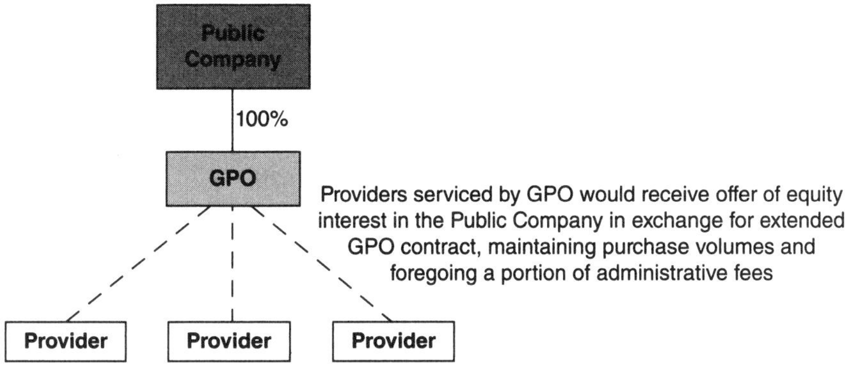

Figure 2.4

reporting requirements; (d) there was a certification that the GPO would not be restricted to affiliated participants, and its expanded roster of participants would serve as additional motivation for the GPO to be competitive in the marketplace and seek out the best prices and services; and (e) there was a certification that the Parent Organization would continue to direct its purchasing volume through independent GPOs whenever those independent GPOs could obtain better value from suppliers, and the LLC would continue to contract directly on behalf of the Nonprofits whenever necessary to meet their needs, thereby ensuring that multiple resources would be used to obtain the best value for Participants, whether or not that was through the proposed GPO, which made it more likely that Participants would receive the benefits intended by Congress.

Advisory Opinion No. 13-09 involved a publicly traded company (the "Company") that provided financial and performance improvement products and services to hospitals and health systems (see Figure 2.4). A wholly owned subsidiary of the Company operated a GPO. The GPO served various providers, the largest among them being hospital and integrated delivery systems. The GPO accounted for about 60 percent of the Company's revenues. The GPO's fees paid by vendors range from 0.25 to 3 percent. The GPO has different contract models a fee-for-service model under which members pay the GPO a negotiated fee but have no minimum purchase requirements, and the GPO passes 100 percent of the administrative fees paid by vendors through to members; and a "shareback" model, under which the GPO passes through to members a negotiated percentage (usually 50 percent) of the administrative fees collected from vendors, and although members often do have minimum purchase requirements, they do not pay any fees to the GPO. If the member does not meet its minimum purchase requirements, then the percentage pass-through of administrative fees is reduced. The GPO pass-through fees are treated as discounts under both models. Under the new proposed arrangement, the Company wanted to offer current and prospective GPO members an equity interest in the Company in exchange for the member extending the existing (or, in the case of a new member, entering into a new) GPO agreement for five to seven years and committing not to decrease the volume of its purchases through the GPO. Those members accepting the equity interest would forgo a portion of the administrative fees that they otherwise would have received. The new arrangement would be presented as an option, with the member also being allowed to keep its current arrangement with no change, accept 66 percent of the current "shareback" amount and receive equity approximating the market value of the forfeited shareback, or accept 33 percent of the current shareback and receive equity approximating the market value of the forfeited shareback. Fee-for-service members would be permitted to enter into shareback arrangements under these terms.

The OIG concluded that the offer of an equity interest in the Company was a form of remuneration to induce members to order federally reimbursable products under the GPO's contracts and to extend those contracts under new terms. The OIG determined that this particular form of remuneration did not meet any safe harbor and could not be said to present a minimal risk of fraud and abuse. The OIG noted that while administrative fees passed through to GPO members could be treated as discounts and members could meet reporting requirements under the discount safe harbor, the same was not true of the equity interest. The OIG cited Government Accountability Office (GAO) reports raising concerns that the "financial flows between hospitals, GPOs, and vendors might result in divergent interests between GPOs and hospitals" and that GPOs might "have an incentive not to seek the lowest price, because the GPO could earn higher administrative fees on higher-priced products."[410]

OIG observed that when administrative fees are passed through to members, savings to federal health care programs may still be realized even when the GPO is not obtaining the lowest cost on products and services, because those distributions must be treated as either discounts or rebates, but if the

410. Advisory Opinion 13-09 at pp. 5-6.

distributions take the form of equity in the Company, that equity would have no potential to benefit payers. Additionally, OIG noted that under the proposed arrangement, equity received was tied to past purchases and members would be required to extend their contracts by five to seven years and could not reduce their volume of purchases, regardless of whether the GPO was obtaining the best price. Further, even though return on investment in the Company would not be directly tied to future purchases, since the GPO's revenues were a substantial percentage of the Company's revenues, and the GPO would be retaining more administrative fees, that might increase Company revenue and result in higher returns for investors referring to the GPO. OIG, therefore, ultimately concluded that the proposed arrangement was non-compliant since it would use Company equity to reward past referrals and induce members to continue purchasing items through the GPO for an extended period of time.

Advisory Opinion No. 16-06 involved a national GPO with more than 84,000 members, including hospitals, nursing facilities, clinics, physician practices, laboratories, and home care or equipment organizations (*see* Figure 2.5). Through a series of corporate transactions, the GPO was 95 percent owned by a health system (Health System) and 5 percent by another holding company (Holdings). Under the proposed arrangement, the Health System would purchase the remaining ten shares of the GPO currently held by Holdings. It was certified that the GPO would continue to serve the same market in the same way, "including negotiating with vendors regarding products and pricing to be offered to the GPO . . . members, and receiving administrative fee from vendors based on a small percentage of the value of

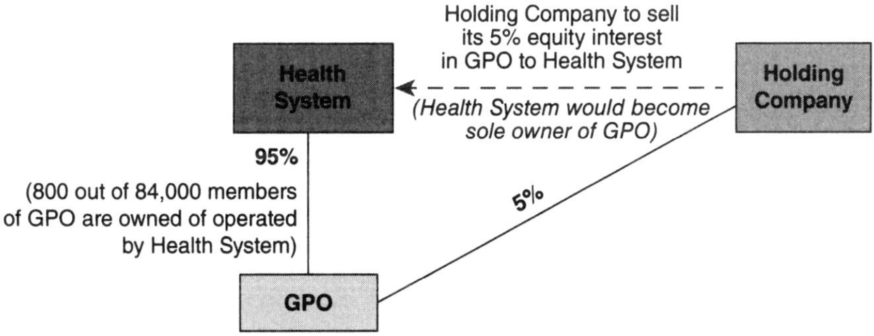

Figure 2.5

sales to members."[411] It was further certified that members of the GPO "that are owned or operated by the Health System . . . are, and would continue to be, subject to GPO contract terms and conditions negotiated on the same basis as members unaffiliated with the Health System," and that various other requirements of the GPO and discount safe harbors would be satisfied, except "that the GPO . . . would be wholly owned by the same entity that also wholly owns approximately one percent of the pool of the [GPO's] members."[412]

The OIG first commented that, even if discounts offered and given to members and administrative fees passed through to members qualified for protection under the discount safe harbor, that safe harbor would not protect the administrative fees received by the GPO from vendors, because those fees must be analyzed under the GPO safe harbor. The OIG then acknowledged that under the proposed arrangement, the GPO would no longer meet the regulatory requirement that the GPO members not be either "wholly-owned by the GPO nor [be] subsidiaries of a parent corporation that wholly owns the GPO" since Health System owned the GPO as well as some of the GPO members (about 800 out of 84,000 members). The OIG, however, determined that this circumstance did not create a heightened risk. The OIG noted that even though the GPO would be wholly owned by the same entity that owns some of the GPO's members, those wholly owned members only comprised 1 percent of the GPO's total membership, and all the members would continue to be subject to GPO "contract terms and conditions negotiated on the same basis as members unaffiliated with the Health System."[413] Accordingly, the GPO "would continue to operate as a purchasing agent for a group of individuals and entities, the vast majority of which are unrelated to the GPO."[414]

2.11. Waiver of Beneficiary Copayment, Coinsurance and Deductible Amounts

The regulatory safe harbor for space rental arrangements is codified at 42 C.F.R. § 1001.952(k), which states:

> (k) *Waiver of beneficiary copayment, coinsurance and deductible amounts.* As used in [the AKS], "remuneration" does not

411. Advisory Opinion No. 16-06, at p. 3.
412. *Id.*
413. *Id.* at pp. 6-7.
414. *Id.*

include any reduction or waiver of a Federal health care program beneficiary's obligation to pay copayment, coinsurance or deductible (for purposes of this subparagraph (k) "cost-sharing") amounts as long as all the standards are met within one of the following categories of health care providers or suppliers.

(1) If the cost-sharing amounts are owed to a hospital for inpatient hospital services for which a Federal health care program pays under the prospective payment system, the hospital must comply with all of the following three standards:

  (i) The hospital must not later claim the amount reduced or waived as a bad debt for payment purposes under a Federal health care program or otherwise shift the burden of the reduction or waiver onto a Federal health care program, other payers, or individuals;

  (ii) The hospital must offer to reduce or waive the cost-sharing amounts without regard to the reason for admission, the length of stay of the beneficiary, or the diagnostic related group for which the claim for reimbursement is filed; and

  (iii) The hospital's offer to reduce or waive the cost-sharing amounts must not be made as part of a price reduction agreement between a hospital and a third-party payer (including a health plan as defined in paragraph (l)(2) of this section), unless the agreement is part of a contract for the furnishing of items or services to a beneficiary of a Medicare supplemental policy issued under the terms of section 1882(t)(1) of the [Social Security Act].

(2) If the cost-sharing amounts are owed by an individual who qualifies for subsidized services under a provision of the Public Health Services Act or under Titles V or XIX of the [Social Security Act] to a federally qualified health care center or other health care facility under any Public Health Services Act grant program or under Title V of the [Social Security Act], the health care center or facility may reduce or waive the cost-sharing amounts for items or services for which payment may be made in whole or in part by a Federal health care program.

(3) If the cost-sharing amounts are owed to a pharmacy (including, but not limited to, pharmacies of the Indian Health Service, Indian tribes, tribal organizations, and urban Indian organizations) for cost-sharing imposed under a Federal health care program, the pharmacy may reduce or waive the cost-sharing amounts if:
   (i) The waiver or reduction is not offered as part of an advertisement or solicitation; and
   (ii) Except for waivers or reductions offered to subsidy-eligible individuals (as defined in section 1860D-14(a)(3)) to which only requirement in paragraph (k)(3)(i) of this section applies:
      (A) The pharmacy does not routinely waive or reduce cost-sharing amounts; and
      (B) The pharmacy waives the cost-sharing amounts only after determining in good faith that the individual is in financial need or after failing to collect the cost-sharing amounts after making reasonable collection efforts.

(4) If the cost-sharing amounts are owed to an ambulance provider or supplier for emergency ambulance services for which a Federal health care program pays under a fee-for-service payment system and all the following conditions are met:
   (i) The ambulance provider or supplier is owned and operated by a State, a political subdivision of a State, or a tribal health care program, as that term is defined in section 4 of the Indian Health Care Improvement Act;
   (ii) The ambulance provider or supplier engaged in an emergency response, as defined in 42 CFR 414.605;
   (iii) The ambulance provider or supplier offers the reduction or waiver on a uniform basis to all of its residents or (if applicable) tribal members, or to all individuals transported; and
   (iv) The ambulance provider or supplier must not later claim the amount reduced or waived as a bad debt for payment purposes under a Federal health care program or otherwise shift the burden of the reduction or waiver

onto a Federal health care program, other payers, or individuals.

The cost-sharing waiver safe harbor was included as part of the original safe harbors that were enacted by HHS in 1991.[415] HHS has made numerous amendments to the safe harbor since its enactment. As it currently stands, the safe harbor protects waivers and reductions[416] of cost-sharing amounts that are offered by the following four types of providers and suppliers, as long as all of the requirements of the safe harbor are met: (1) hospitals for inpatient services, (2) federally qualified health centers (FQHCs) or other health care facilities under a Public Health Services Act grant program or under Title V of the Social Security Act ("Qualifying Facilities"), (3) pharmacies, and (4) ambulance provider or supplier of emergency ambulance services.[417]

A. *Cost-Sharing Waivers Offered by a Hospital*

The first category of providers and suppliers that are protected by the cost-sharing waiver safe harbor are hospitals. This category is further limited to waivers offered by hospitals for inpatient services only.

When enacting the safe harbor, HHS explained that it is aware that hospitals routinely waive deductibles and coinsurance charges in order to attract patients and that such practice is considered an inducement to utilize the hospital's services.[418] However, HHS also noted that such inducement can present a low risk of fraud and abuse if certain risk-mitigating factors are present. For example, HHS stated that there is a relatively fixed level of patient demand for hospital inpatient services. As such, permitting hospitals to waive a patient's deductible or coinsurance amount is not likely to significantly increase the utilization of hospital inpatient services. For this reason, HHS limited the applicability of the safe harbor to waivers for inpatient hospital services only.[419] Other risk-mitigating factors

415. Final Rule: OIG Anti-Kickback Provisions, 56 Fed. Reg. 35952.

416. Although the safe harbor is often referred to as the cost-sharing "waiver" safe harbor, it applies equally to both waivers and reductions of deductibles, copayments, and coinsurance amounts. *See* 81 Fed. Reg. 88368, 88374.

417. Originally, the safe harbor only applied to waivers of cost-sharing amounts offered by a hospital for inpatient services and by FQHCs and other Qualifying Facilities. *Id.* In 2016, it was expanded to also include protections for waivers offered by pharmacies and ambulance service providers. 81 Fed. Reg. 88368, at 88376.

418. 56 Fed. Reg. 35952.

419. *Id.* For this same reason, HHS declined to expand the safe harbor protections to other types of providers at the time the safe harbor was originally enacted in 1991. HHS believed that other types of providers did not have a fixed level of patient demand for their services

noted by HHS are addressed in the other three requirements of the safe harbor summarized below.[420]

The first requirement prohibits the hospital from claiming the waived amount as bad debt for payment purposes under a federal health care program or otherwise shifting the burden of the waived amount onto a federal health care program or other payor. By prohibiting hospitals from claiming the waived amount as bad debt, it ensures that the waiver "cause[s] no direct financial harm to the Medicare program [or other federal health care program or payor]."[421]

The second requirement of the safe harbor prohibits the hospital from taking into account the following factors when making decisions whether to waive cost-sharing amounts for a particular patient: (i) the patient's reason for admission, (ii) length of hospital stay, and (iii) the type of disease or diagnostic group for which the patient is seeking treatment and for which reimbursement will be sought.[422] HHS has long reiterated its position that hospital waiver policies should be applied uniformly to all patients and should not take into account the foregoing factors.[423]

The last requirement states that the waiver of cost-sharing amounts cannot be made as part of a price reduction agreement between a hospital and a third-party payor, including a health plan,[424] unless the agreement is part of a contract for the furnishing of items or services to a beneficiary of a Medicare supplemental policy issued under Section 1882(t)(1) of the Social

---

as hospitals did for inpatient services such that a waiver of cost-sharing amounts would not present a risk of overutilization. However, HHS also noted that it has no purpose in interfering with other providers or hospitals that offer waivers of cost-sharing amounts to indigent patient populations in order to promote access to care for such patient populations. Such practices "would not likely violate the statute so long as the partial forgiveness of the copayment obligation was strictly a pragmatic financial decision and not an inducement to patients to purchase medical services." *Id.*

420. HHS also declined to extend the safe harbor protections to other forms of remuneration that might be offered by hospitals to patients, such as free meals, presurgical overnight stays, sample products, or other free items or services because such inducements "could easily become excessive." *Id.* Unlike a waiver of coinsurance or deducible, which is limited to the fixed amount of the coinsurance or deductible, free items or services have "no distinct financial or other cut-off point below which [HHS] can be sure that [such] gifts remain non-abusive." *Id.*

421. 56 Fed. Reg. 35952.

422. *Id.*

423. *Id.*; *see also* 81 Fed. Reg. 88368, at 88373 (explaining that all decisions regarding waivers of cost-sharing amounts for "financial need" must be made "on a good faith, individualized, case-by-case basis in accordance with a reasonable set of income guidelines uniformly applied in all cases").

424. HHS enacted a separate safe harbor that protects reductions in cost-sharing amounts offered by health plans. *See* 42 C.F.R. § 1001.952(l) (summarized herein in Chapter 2.12).

Security Act. Generally speaking, the cost-sharing waiver safe harbor was only intended to protect waivers offered directly to patients and not third-party payors.[425] However, in 1992, HHS revised the safe harbor to provide one exception that permits cost-sharing waiver arrangements with a Medicare supplemental policy that is issued by Medicare SELECT insurers, provided that the first two requirements of the safe harbor are also satisfied.[426] HHS also clarified that the waiver arrangement with the Medicare SELECT insurer must only be applicable to beneficiaries covered by the insurer's Medicare SELECT policy.[427]

In addition, the OIG has often concluded that waivers offered to third-party payors, which do not satisfy the third requirement for safe harbor protection, can nonetheless present a low risk of fraud and abuse if the following factors are present:

1. The waiver will not affect payments made by a federal health care program (e.g., by increasing the amount owed by a federal health care program for the inpatient hospital service or otherwise shifting the burden of the waived amount);
2. The arrangement is unlikely to increase overutilization of a service;[428]
3. The arrangement will not unfairly affect competition among hospitals;
4. The arrangement is unlikely to affect professional medical judgement of providers; and
5. The arrangement would operate transparently, meaning that patients would be clearly informed about their freedom to choose any hospital to receive inpatient services.

Based on the OIG's position in numerous advisory opinions, if the foregoing factors are present in a proposed cost-sharing waiver arrangement

425. *See, e.g.*, OIG Advisory Opinion 18-04 (June 7, 2018) ("[The] safe harbor specifically excludes [coinsurance and deductible] waivers when they are part of an agreement with insurers.").

426. 57 Fed. Reg. 52723. Medicare SELECT policies are intended to reduce costs for beneficiaries by encouraging providers to become preferred providers of the plan in order to be able to treat Medicare SELECT patients in exchange for accepting a reduced payment for such treatment. *Id.* The safe harbor protection for waivers of coinsurance and deductions between hospitals and the plans is consistent with the plan's intent to reduce overall health care costs. *See id.; see also* 61 Fed. Reg. 2122 at 2127.

427. *Id.*

428. With respect to inpatient hospital services, the OIG notes that it has long held that due to the relatively fixed demand for inpatient services, waivers of cost-sharing amounts are unlikely to increase demand or utilization of such services. *See supra* note 5.

between a hospital and a third-party payor, such arrangement is unlikely to violate the AKS or result in sanctions imposed by the OIG.[429]

B. *Cost-Sharing Waivers Offered by a Federally Qualified Health Center or Other Qualifying Facility*

The second category under the safe harbor permits FQHCs and other Qualifying Facilities (as defined earlier) to waive cost-sharing amounts owed by patients for subsidized services for which payment may be made in whole or in part by a federal health care program.[430]

C. *Cost-Sharing Waivers Offered by a Pharmacy*

The third category under the cost-sharing waiver safe harbor applies to pharmacies. Pharmacies are permitted to reduce or waive cost-sharing amounts imposed under a federal health care program if the waiver or reduction is not offered as part of an advertisement or solicitation.

HHS explained that the terms "advertisement" and "solicitation" as used in the safe harbor should be interpreted in accordance with "their common usage in the health care industry," and "whether a particular means of communication constitutes an advertisement or solicitation will depend on the [particular] facts and circumstances."[431] By way of example, information posted on websites regarding cost-sharing waivers would likely be considered an advertisement.[432] In comparison, responding to a specific patient inquiry about cost-sharing waivers and/or discussing the patient's

---

429. *See, e.g.*, OIG Advisory Opinion 18-04 (June 7, 2018); OIG Advisory Opinion 18-12 (Oct. 22, 2018); OIG Advisory Opinion 18-09 (Aug. 14, 2018); OIG Advisory Opinion 18-06 (July 11, 2018); OIG Advisory Opinion 17-06 (Nov. 9, 2017); OIG Advisory Opinion 17-04 (Aug. 24, 2017); OIG Advisory Opinion 16-11 (Oct. 27, 2016); OIG Advisory Opinion 16-05 (Apr. 26, 2016); OIG Advisory Opinion 16-04 (Apr. 12, 2016); OIG Advisory Opinion 16-03 (Mar. 11, 2016); OIG Advisory Opinion 16-01 (Jan. 7, 2016); OIG Advisory Opinion 15-09 (July 16, 2015); OIG Advisory Opinion 15-08 (June 12, 2015); OIG Advisory Opinion 15-05 (Apr. 22, 2015); OIG Advisory Opinion 15-03 (Feb. 23, 2015); OIG Advisory Opinion 14-10 (Oct. 14, 2014); OIG Advisory Opinion 14-08 (Sept. 17, 2014); OIG Advisory Opinion 14-07 (Aug. 18, 2014); OIG Advisory Opinion 14-04 (Apr. 9, 2014); OIG Advisory Opinion 14-02 (Feb. 12, 2014); OIG Advisory Opinion 13-06 (June 20, 2013); OIG Advisory Opinion 13-01 (May 8, 2013); OIG Advisory Opinion 11-09 (July 14, 2011); OIG Advisory Opinion 10-21 (Sept. 21, 2010); OIG Advisory Opinion 10-01 (Feb. 12, 2010); OIG Advisory Opinion 09-10 (July 24, 2009); OIG Advisory Opinion 08-13 (Sept. 23, 2008); OIG Advisory Opinion 07-15 (Dec. 3, 2007); OIG Advisory Opinion 03-10 (May 8, 2003).

430. *See* 42 C.F.R. § 1001.952(k)(2); 57 Fed. Reg. 52723.

431. 81 Fed. Reg. 88368, at 88372.

432. *Id.*

financial needs would generally not be considered an advertisement or solicitation.[433]

In addition, in order to qualify for the safe harbor protection, the pharmacy offering the waiver must satisfy the following two requirements: (i) it cannot routinely waive or reduce cost-sharing amounts; and (ii) it can only waive or reduce cost-sharing amounts after (A) determining in good faith that the patient receiving the waiver or reduction is in financial need or (B) failing to collect the cost-sharing amounts from the patient after making reasonable collection efforts. However, the foregoing requirements in sub-clause (i) and (ii) are not applicable if the pharmacy offers the cost-sharing waiver to subsidy-eligible patients, as defined under Section 1860D-14(a)(3) of the Social Security Act. When cost-sharing waivers are offered to such subsidy-eligible patients, the pharmacy is permitted to make the waiver as long as the first element of the safe harbor is met, i.e., the waiver was not part of an advertisement or solicitation.[434]

With respect to the prohibition on "routine waivers," HHS has declined to explicitly define what constitutes a "routine" waiver.[435] However, it has stated that waivers should not become commonplace and should only be offered "occasionally" when patients meet certain objective criteria, such as financial need.[436] Yet, HHS has also declined to define a particular method for determining "financial need."[437] What constitutes a "routine waiver" or "financial need" will be determined by HHS on a case-by-case basis after considering the underlying facts and circumstances.

HHS has noted that, under the safe harbor, pharmacies must make a "good faith" determination of financial need. Such determinations should be made on a "case-by-case basis in accordance with a reasonable set of income guidelines [that are] uniformly applied."[438] Further, pharmacies should not only accept a patient's statement that they are in financial need but should perform an independent assessment of the patient's financial need.[439] Such assessment may include verifying the patient's financial resources and/or

433. *Id.*

434. *Id.* at 88371.

435. *Id.* at 88372.

436. *Id.*; *see also* OIG Special Fraud Alert (Dec. 19, 1994), https://oig.hhs.gov/fraud/docs/alertsandbulletins/121994.html.

437. *Id.* at 88373.

438. *Id.* The guidelines should be objective and appropriate for the applicable locality so as to ensure that inflated income guidelines are not used. *Id.*

439. *Id.* Although HHS acknowledges that performing a financial assessment may be costly, it also believes that it is an "important safeguard" in mitigating potential fraud and abuse.

collecting financial documents from the patient such as pay stubs, tax forms, or evidence of other expenses.[440]

As an alternative to performing a financial need assessment, the second element of the cost-sharing waiver safe harbor permits pharmacies to waive or reduce cost-sharing amounts after making reasonable collection efforts (and assuming that all other requirements of the safe harbor are satisfied). HHS defines "reasonable collection efforts" as "those efforts that a reasonable provider would undertake to collect amounts owed for items and services provided to patients."[441] HHS also relies on the collection guidelines established by the CMS *Provider Reimbursement Manual*, which requires providers to issue bills to patients and take other reasonable actions to collect payment for such bills, including issuance of subsequent bills, collection letters, telephone calls, and other contact with the patient.[442] In other words, to qualify for safe harbor protection, the pharmacies must make a "genuine" collection effort before waiving or reducing cost-sharing amounts.[443]

D. *Cost-Sharing Waivers Offered by an Emergency Ambulance Service Provider*

The fourth and final category of the cost-sharing waiver safe harbor applies to providers or suppliers of emergency ambulance services for which payment is made under a federal health care program. The safe harbor applies only to waivers or reductions of cost-sharing amounts offered by an ambulance provider or supplier that is owned and operated by a state, a political subdivision of a state, or a tribal health care program (as the term is defined under the Indian Health Care Improvement Act). The safe harbor does not apply to privately owned ambulance companies.[444]

In addition, the safe harbor protects only cost-sharing waivers for emergency ambulance services. "Emergency ambulance services" are defined

440. "By way of example only, one pharmacy might choose to apply a multiple of the poverty guidelines, which take into account family size, for determining financial need, while another pharmacy might prefer to take into account a combination of the poverty guidelines, adjusted for the cost of living in the pharmacy's locality, plus family medical expenses. We emphasize, however, whatever guideline is applied by the pharmacy must be reasonable and applied uniformly." *Id.* at 88374.

441. *Id.* (citing *Provider Reimbursement Manual* (CMS Pub. 15-1) § 310).

442. *Id.*

443. *Id.* HHS also noted that "[t]he amount of the copayment or historical inability to collect cost-sharing amounts for a particular beneficiary might be factors that are considered in determining what reasonable collection efforts are, but they do not justify forgoing all collection efforts." *Id.*

444. *Id.*

as ambulance transports initiated by a 911 call or other emergency access number.[445] Further, the ambulance provider or supplier must be engaged in an "emergency response" that is defined as a response to a 911 call or equivalent call system that requires BLS (basic life support) or ALS1 (advanced life support) level of service.[446]

Further, to qualify for the safe harbor protection, the cost-sharing waiver must be applied on a uniform basis to all patients. HHS has also clarified that the applicability of the waiver should not be based on patient-specific factors.[447] An ambulance provider cannot decide to waive cost-sharing amounts due to a patient's health condition, age, or insurance or financial status.[448] Notably, the latter prohibition is distinguishable from other categories of the cost-sharing waiver safe harbor. The category for pharmacies (discussed earlier), for example, states that, under certain circumstances, pharmacies are permitted to waive cost-sharing amounts only after determining the patient's financial need. Yet, under the same safe harbor, ambulance providers are prohibited from taking into account the financial need or insurance status of a patient.[449]

HHS has also stated that ambulance providers are not prohibited from considering the residency of a patient in a particular municipality or government unit when making cost-sharing waiver decisions.[450]

The final requirement of the safe harbor, as applicable to ambulance providers, is the same as the requirement applicable to hospitals (as discussed earlier)—the ambulance provider cannot claim the waived cost-sharing amount as bad debt for payment under a federal health care program, or otherwise shift the burden onto a federal health care program or other payor or individual.[451]

When analyzing proposed arrangements that did not meet all of the elements of the cost-sharing waiver safe harbor for ambulance services, the OIG

445. *Id.* at 88376; *see also* 42 C.F.R. § 1001.952(u)(i)(E)(4)(iv).

446. 42 C.F.R. § 1001.952(k); 42 C.F.R. § 414.605.

447. 81 Fed. Reg. 88368, at 88376.

448. *Id.*

449. *Id.*

450. *Id.* ("[A]n ambulance provider or supplier could waive cost-sharing amounts for all residents, but charge cost-sharing amounts to nonresidents. However, the ambulance provider or supplier cannot discriminate on the basis of any factor other than residency or, if applicable, tribal membership. For example, an ambulance provider or supplier cannot waive cost-sharing amounts for patients transported for an emergency that required only outpatient treatment, but charge cost-sharing amounts for patients transported for a condition that requires hospitalization (or vice versa)."); *see also* OIG Advisory Opinion 13-11 (Aug. 14, 2014).

451. 81 Fed. Reg. 88368, at 88376.

has considered whether the arrangement presented a risk of overutilization of services and increased costs to federal health care programs. Where the risk of overutilization is low, the OIG has concluded that there was a low risk of fraud and abuse under the AKS.[452] Generally speaking, routine waivers are likely to be considered suspect under the AKS, while "unscheduled and sporadic waivers" are less likely to present a risk of fraud and abuse.[453]

Similarly, the OIG has previously found that arrangements that do not influence demand for ambulance services would not be considered suspect under the AKS.[454] By way of example, one arrangement analyzed by the OIG involved an ambulance provider offering backup services to adjoining fire departments and waiving patient cost-sharing amounts.[455] The backup services were provided as needed by the fire departments and were not based on the value or volume of referrals between the parties.[456] Moreover, the ambulance provider would use the same billing practices as the fire departments for all backup services it provided.[457] The OIG concluded that the arrangement presented a low risk of fraud and abuse because it did not influence demand for ambulance services, since the services would have to be provided regardless if they were provided by the fire departments or as backup services, and in either event, they would be billed using the same billing practices, without potential for increasing costs to federal health care programs.[458]

2.12. Increased Coverage, Reduced Cost-Sharing Amounts, or Reduced Premium Amounts Offered by Health Plans

The safe harbor for price reductions offered to health plans is codified at 42 C.F.R. § 1001.952(l):

(l) *Increased coverage, reduced cost-sharing amounts, or reduced premium amounts offered by health plans.*

452. *See, e.g.*, OIG Advisory Opinion 13-11 (Aug. 14, 2014) (explaining that when waivers were offered on an "unscheduled and sporadic basis" they were unlikely to result in overutilization).

453. *Id.*

454. *See* OIG Advisory Opinion 18-08 (Aug. 7, 2018).

455. *Id.*

456. *Id.*

457. *Id.*

458. *Id.*

(1) As used in [the AKS], "remuneration" does not include the additional coverage of any item or service offered by a health plan to an enrollee or the reduction of some or all of the enrollee's obligation to pay the health plan or a contract health care provider for cost-sharing amounts (such as coinsurance, deductible, or copayment amounts) or for premium amounts attributable to items or services covered by the health plan, the Medicare program, or a State health care program, as long as the health plan complies with all of the standards within one of the following two categories of health plans:

(i) If the health plan is a risk-based health maintenance organization, competitive medical plan, prepaid health plan, or other health plan under contract with CMS or a State health care program and operating in accordance with section 1876(g) or 1903(m) of the Act, under a Federal statutory demonstration authority, or under other Federal statutory or regulatory authority, it must offer the same increased coverage or reduced cost-sharing or premium amounts to all Medicare or State health care program enrollees covered by the contract unless otherwise approved by CMS or by a State health care program.

(ii) If the health plan is a health maintenance organization, competitive medical plan, health care prepayment plan, prepaid health plan or other health plan that has executed a contract or agreement with CMS or with a State health care program to receive payment for enrollees on a reasonable cost or similar basis, it must comply with both of the following two standards -

(A) The health plan must offer the same increased coverage or reduced cost-sharing or premium amounts to all Medicare or State health care program enrollees covered by the contract or agreement unless otherwise approved by CMS or by a State health care program; and

(B) The health plan must not claim the costs of the increased coverage or the reduced cost-sharing or premium amounts as a bad debt for payment purposes under Medicare or a State health care program or otherwise shift the burden of the increased coverage or reduced cost-sharing or premium amounts to the extent that increased payments are claimed from Medicare or a State health care program.

(2) For purposes of paragraph (1) of this section, the terms -

Contract health care provider means an individual or entity under contract with a health plan to furnish items or services to enrollees who are covered by the health plan, Medicare, or a State health care program.

Enrollee means an individual who has entered into a contractual relationship with a health plan (or on whose behalf an employer, or other private or governmental entity has entered into such a relationship) under which the individual is entitled to receive specified health care items and services, or insurance coverage for such items and services, in return for payment of a premium or a fee.

Health plan means an entity that furnishes or arranges under agreement with contract health care providers for the furnishing of items or services to enrollees, or furnishes insurance coverage for the provision of such items and services, in exchange for a premium or a fee, where such entity:

(i) Operates in accordance with a contract, agreement or statutory demonstration authority approved by CMS or a State health care program;

(ii) Charges a premium and its premium structure is regulated under a State insurance statute or a State enabling statute governing health maintenance organizations or preferred provider organizations;

(iii) Is an employer, if the enrollees of the plan are current or retired employees, or is a union welfare fund, if the enrollees of the plan are union members; or

(iv) Is licensed in the State, is under contract with an employer, union welfare fund, or a company furnishing health insurance coverage as described in conditions (ii) and (iii) of this definition, and is paid a fee for the administration of the plan which reflects the fair market value of those services.

In 1992, the OIG published an interim final rule establishing a safe harbor for "Increased Coverage, Reduced Cost-sharing Amounts, or Reduced Premium Amounts Offered by Health Plans."[459] This was one of three safe harbor provisions protecting health plans and dealt "with the relationship of health plans to enrollees."[460] The OIG noted that while the AKS "is generally not implicated when a health plan offers a premium to a Medicare or State health care program beneficiary to provide an insurance package, the statute is implicated when discounts on premiums or other incentives are offered."[461] This safe harbor "was created to protect certain incentives to enrollees (including increased benefits and waiver of deductible and coinsurance amounts) offered by health plans . . . [and] contained two parts designed to protect incentives offered by health care plans under contract with the Health Care Financing Administration (HCFA) [now CMS] or a State health care program."[462]

According to the OIG, the "first part of this safe harbor protected risk-based health plans, like HMOs, competitive medical plans (CMPs) and prepaid health plans (PHPs)" and "the only standard for such health plans was that the health care plan could not discriminate in the offering of these incentives, but [had to] offer the same incentives to all enrollees unless otherwise specifically approved by HCFA or a State health care program."[463] The second part of the safe harbor "protected incentives offered to enrollees by HMOs, CMPs, PHPs and health care prepaid plans (HCPPs) . . . that are paid on a reasonable cost or similar basis" provided that "the same incentives [are] offered to all enrollees for all covered services" and that "the health plan [does] not claim the cost of these incentives as bad debts or otherwise shift the burden of these incentives onto Medicare, the State health care programs, other payers or individuals."[464]

459. Interim Final Rule: Safe Harbors for Protecting Health Plans (57 Fed. Reg. 52723, 52725; Nov. 5, 1992) (sets forth three new safe harbors addressing managed care plans through interim final rulemaking).

460. *Id.*

461. *Id.*

462. Final Rule: Safe Harbors for Protecting Health Plans (61 Fed. Reg. 2122, 2123; Jan. 25, 1996) (revised final rule addressing the three managed care safe harbors originally promulgated in the Nov. 5, 1992, interim final rule).

463. *Id.*

464. *Id.*

Regarding the safe harbor's requirement that incentives be provided to all enrollees, the OIG explained that its purpose was "to restrict the ability of health plans to target particular Medicare or Medicaid beneficiaries or groups of such beneficiaries and induce them to enroll in the plan by providing incentives."[465] The OIG did not want plans to "target health beneficiaries by offering them increased services or reductions in cost sharing and attempt to avoid older or sicker beneficiaries or those with expensive or chronic health conditions requiring a high utilization of services by offering only the same services available through a fee-for-service plan."[466] Nor did the OIG limit the safe harbor to any specific type of insurance product because it believed that "the same type of abuses could occur where health plans offered several different products."[467] In addition, the OIG required that any incentives offered by health plans "be offered to all Medicare or State health care program enrollees of the plan" in order to "safeguard against the possibility that health plans may improperly favor certain healthy beneficiaries or use incentives to improperly encourage utilization when the item or service is furnished."[468]

The OIG emphasized that the safe harbor did nothing to "change[] reimbursement rules" and that "[i]f a provider chooses to . . . comply with [the safe harbor], such action may very well have reimbursement implications." The OIG further commented:

> Many program beneficiaries are now served by a wide variety of managed care plans, such as various models of HMOs, CMPs, and health care prepayment plans (HCPPs) . . . and prepaid health plans (PHPs) . . . as well as PPOs, and we agree that additional safe harbor protection is warranted . . . We are promulgating . . . safe harbor provisions to protect the essential activities of prepaid health plans ("health plans") . . . [This safe harbor] protects the contractual relationships between health plans and "contract health care providers" for the furnishing of covered items and services at reduced prices.[469]

465. *Id.* at 2130.
466. *Id.*
467. *Id.*
468. *Id.*
469. *Id.* Definitions of key terms used in the safe harbor are as follows:
Contract health care provider means an individual or entity under contract with a health plan to furnish items or services to enrollees who are covered by the health plan, Medicare, or a State health care program.
Enrollee means an individual who has entered into a contractual relationship with a health plan (or on whose behalf an employer, or other private or governmental entity

The OIG noted that "health care providers will contract with health plans and agree to furnish items and services to enrollees of the health plan at a discount from the provider's usual fee in return for obtaining a large volume of patients."[470] As with the safe harbor codified at 42 CFR § 1001.952(l), "protecting incentives to enrollees," this safe harbor "is divided into two separate parts for risk-based and cost-reimbursed health plans that operate in accordance with a contract or agreement with [CMS] or a State health care program."[471] A third part of the safe harbor protects "other health plans that do not have [such] contracts or agreement . . . where additional standards are met."[472]

The remuneration protected by the safe harbor is a provider's reduction of its usual charges and "only applies to reductions in the total amount charged by" the provider, rather than "reductions which are applicable only to a specific part of portion of the health care provider's charge, such as coinsurance and deductibles."[473] The OIG continued:

> Furthermore, we are only protecting the remuneration which represents the price reduction offered by the contract health care provider to make clear that any other forms of remuneration offered or paid by a contract health care provider to a health plan are not protected under this safe harbor provision. Indeed, we will closely review any forms of other such remuneration to ensure that improper payments

---

has entered into such a relationship) under which the individual is entitled to receive specified health care items and services, or insurance coverage for such items and services, in return for payment of a premium or a fee.

Health plan means an entity that furnishes or arranges under agreement with contract health care providers for the furnishing of items or services to enrollees, or furnishes insurance coverage for the provision of such items and services, in exchange for a premium or a fee, where such entity:

(i) Operates in accordance with a contract, agreement or statutory demonstration authority approved by CMS or a State health care program;

(ii) Charges a premium and its premium structure is regulated under a State insurance statute or a State enabling statute governing health maintenance organizations or preferred provider organizations;

(iii) Is an employer, if the enrollees of the plan are current or retired employees, or is a union welfare fund, if the enrollees of the plan are union members; or

(iv) Is licensed in the State, is under contract with an employer, union welfare fund, or a company furnishing health insurance coverage as described in conditions (ii) and (iii) of this definition, and is paid a fee for the administration of the plan which reflects the fair market value of those services.

42 CFR § 1001.952(l).

470. *Id.* at 52726.

471. *Id.*

472. *Id.*

473. *Id.*

are not employed to induce the health plan to issue a contract or otherwise steer patients to the person paying the remuneration.[474]

The safe harbor's second requirement that the agreement with the parties be in writing "is intended to assist [HHS] in understanding the intent of the parties" and, if needed, the OIG "will look behind the contract to determine if the real intent of the parties is not fully disclosed in the written agreement."[475] A third requirement that the agreement must be for the sole purpose of having the provider furnish to enrollees items or services covered by the health plan, Medicare, or Medicaid is to ensure that the safe harbor does not protect contracts for services other than "covered benefits."[476]

Noncovered services such as "peer review," "marketing services," and "pre-enrollment screening" would need to satisfy another safe harbor, such as the safe harbor for personal services and management contracts, and "where protection is sought from more than one safe harbor, separate justifications must be clearly set forth for each provision for which protection is sought."[477] The OIG explained the need for this requirement as stemming from its "experience with some HMOs that have abused their contractual relationships with medical groups where individuals in the groups have engaged in abusive or illegal activities on behalf of the HMO . . . by conducting pre-enrollment screening."[478] The OIG indicated its intention to "use [its] authorities aggressively to monitor closely and penalize where appropriate any abusive relationships between health plans and contract health care providers to assure the medically necessary services of a high quality are available and accessible to all enrollees."[479]

The first part of the safe harbor was designed to protect risk-based HMOs, CMPs, and PHPs under contract with [CMS] or a State health care program and operating in accordance with specified provisions of the Social Security Act or under a federal demonstration authority or under other federal statutory or regulatory authority.[480] In addition to risk-based contract health plans having to satisfy the requirements described earlier, the interim final rule required that contract providers "not separately bill Medicare, Medicaid

474. *Id.*
475. *Id.*
476. *Id.*
477. *Id.*
478. *Id.*
479. *Id.*
480. *Id.*

or another State health care program for items or services furnished under the agreement with the health plan . . . [or] otherwise shift the burden of the agreement onto Medicare, Medicaid, other payors, or individuals."[481] Moreover, "[a]ny claim for reimbursement made directly to Medicare, Medicaid or other State health care program for items or services for which payment was made by the health plan would constitute an unlawful false claim."[482]

The second part of the safe harbor protected health plans that had executed a contract or agreement with the CMS or a state health care program to have payment made on a reasonable cost or similar basis, provided that any price reduction agreement satisfied four enumerated standards.

The third part of the safe harbor protected price reductions offered by contract health care providers to all other health plans, provided that six enumerated standards were satisfied.

In 1996, the OIG revised and clarified the rule in response to public comments.[483] In its general comments, the OIG clarified, in response to concerns that this and other safe harbors affecting health plans could "chill" the activities of such plans if they find themselves unable to fit within the safe harbor, that the safe harbors "did not expand the zone of illegal conduct" under the AKS and that "[l]egally and logically, the safe harbors can only make the zone of illegal conduct smaller."[484] The OIG further explained that "compliance with the safe harbors is completely voluntary" and "[i]f a practice or arrangement does not fall within a safe harbor, it has precisely the same legal risk that it had before the safe harbor was promulgated."[485] The safe harbors "are designed to provide a means through which plans and providers can be assured that their arrangements are immune from potential criminal and administrative sanctions under the anti-kickback statute."[486] The OIG further assured the public that the fact that certain activities of health plans are not referenced in the safe harbors does not mean the OIG regards such activities as unlawful or that they would be subjected to heightened scrutiny.[487] The OIG made clear that, being voluntary, the safe harbors "do not

481. *Id.* at 52727.

482. *Id.*

483. Final Rule: Safe Harbors for Protecting Health Plans (61 Fed. Reg. 2122; Jan. 25, 1996) (revised final rule addressing the three managed care safe harbors originally promulgated in the Nov. 5, 1992, interim final rule).

484. *Id.* at 2124.

485. *Id.*

486. *Id.*

487. *Id.*

create affirmative obligations on individuals or entities" and that "failure to comply with a safe harbor means only that the practice or arrangement does not have the absolute assurance of protection from [AKS] liability."

Addressing the overall need for the safe harbor, the OIG commented that

> Enrollment in a health plan falls within the scope of the anti-kickback statute where such enrollment involves Medicare or Medicaid beneficiaries and results from various incentives offered to these individuals by the managed care plan.
>
> The incentives offered to beneficiaries constitute remuneration with the meaning of the statute. Once enrolled, the plan is entitled to receive Medicare or Medicaid reimbursement for the services directly provided to program beneficiaries. Alternatively, the plan steers enrollees to certain providers who furnish reimbursable services. The incentives offered to program beneficiaries can be in return for obtaining reimbursable program business and, therefore, are covered by the statute.[488]

Responding to comments protesting the safe harbor's requirement that health plans not shift the burden of increased coverage, reduced cost-sharing, or price reductions to other payers, the OIG reaffirmed its view "that enrollee incentives and provider price reductions should be economically sensible, i.e., they should not be driven by a motive to shift costs to the government or other payers."[489] The OIG continued:

> A health plan should not be offering incentives or provider discounts unless they believe the cost of those incentives or discounts can be recovered through lower operating costs resulting from increased volume, economies of scale or other efficiencies. We also believe that practices should be protected only if they do not cause harm to the Medicare and Medicaid programs. Accordingly, we are only willing to protect incentives and price reductions that do not result in increased costs to the programs. In order to ensure that result, we believe it is necessary to include a requirement which prohibits cost shifting to the Medicare and Medicaid programs.[490]

The OIG did agree, however, that the bar against burden shifting did not need to be broader than necessary to protect Medicare and Medicaid and

488. *Id.*
489. *Id.* at 2126.
490. *Id.* at 2126-27.

thus narrowed the scope of the prohibition in the revised final rule to make clear that cost shifting occurs "when an arrangement or agreement results in increased payments being claimed from the Medicare or State health care programs."[491] The OIG declined to establish standards for determining when cost shifting has occurred but noted that "in any case where a plan or provider raises its costs or fees to others or reduces the services it provides to others as a result of an incentive or a discount, prohibited cost shifting has occurred" and that "[c]laiming certain costs, such as waivers of coinsurance or deductibles, as bad debt would also constitute impermissible cost shifting."[492]

2.13. Price Reductions Offered to Health Plans

The safe harbor for price reductions offered to health plans is codified at 42 C.F.R. § 1001.952(m):

> (m) *Price reductions offered to health plans.*
>
> (1) As used in section 1128B of the Act, "remuneration" does not include a reduction in price a contract health care provider offers to a health plan in accordance with the terms of a written agreement between the contract health care provider and the health plan for the sole purpose of furnishing to enrollees items or services that are covered by the health plan, Medicare, or a State health care program, as long as both the health plan and contract health care provider comply with all of the applicable standards within one of the following four categories of health plans:
>
> (i) If the health plan is a risk-based health maintenance organization, competitive medical plan, or prepaid health plan under contract with CMS or a State agency and operating in accordance with section 1876(g) or 1903(m) of the Act, under a Federal statutory demonstration authority, or under other Federal statutory or regulatory authority, the contract health care provider must not claim payment in any form from the Department or the State agency for items or services furnished in accordance with the agreement except as approved

491. *Id.* at 2127.
492. *Id.*

by CMS or the State health care program, or otherwise shift the burden of such an agreement to the extent that increased payments are claimed from Medicare or a State health care program.

(ii) If the health plan is a health maintenance organization, competitive medical plan, health care prepayment plan, prepaid health plan, or other health plan that has executed a contract or agreement with CMS or a State health care program to receive payment for enrollees on a reasonable cost or similar basis, the health plan and contract health care provider must comply with all of the following four standards -

(A) The term of the agreement between the health plan and the contract health care provider must be for not less than one year;

(B) The agreement between the health plan and the contract health care provider must specify in advance the covered items and services to be furnished to enrollees, and the methodology for computing the payment to the contract health care provider;

(C) The health plan must fully and accurately report, on the applicable cost report or other claim form filed with the Department or the State health care program, the amount it has paid the contract health care provider under the agreement for the covered items and services furnished to enrollees; and

(D) The contract health care provider must not claim payment in any form from the Department or the State health care program for items or services furnished in accordance with the agreement except as approved by CMS or the State health care program, or otherwise shift the burden of such an agreement to the extent that increased payments are claimed from Medicare or a State health care program.

(iii) If the health plan is not described in paragraphs (m)(1)(i) or (m)(1)(ii) of this section and the contract health care provider is not paid on an at-risk, capitated basis, both the health plan and contract health care provider must comply with all of the following six standards -

(A) The term of the agreement between the health plan and the contract health care provider must be for not less than one year;

(B) The agreement between the health plan and the contract health care provider must specify in advance the covered items and services to be furnished to enrollees, which party is to file claims or requests for payment with Medicare or the State health care program for such items and services, and the schedule of fees the contract health care provider will charge for furnishing such items and services to enrollees;

(C) The fee schedule contained in the agreement between the health plan and the contract health care provider must remain in effect throughout the term of the agreement, unless a fee increase results directly from a payment update authorized by Medicare or the State health care program;

(D) The party submitting claims or requests for payment from Medicare or the State health care program for items and services furnished in accordance with the agreement must not claim or request payment for amounts in excess of the fee schedule;

(E) The contract health care provider and the health plan must fully and accurately report on any cost report filed with Medicare or a State health care program the fee schedule amounts charged in accordance with the agreement and, upon request, will report to the Medicare or a State health care program the terms of the agreement and the amounts paid in accordance with the agreement; and

(F) The party to the agreement, which does not have the responsibility under the agreement for filing claims or requests for payment, must not claim or request payment in any form from the Department or the State health care program for items or services furnished in accordance with the agreement, or otherwise shift the burden of such an agreement to the extent that increased payments are claimed from Medicare or a State health care program.

(iv) If the health plan is not described in paragraphs (m)(1)(i) or (m)(1)(ii) of this section, and the contract health care provider is paid on an at-risk, capitated basis, both the health plan and contract health care provider must comply with all of the following five standards -

(A) The term of the agreement between the health plan and the contract health provider must be for not less than one year;

(B) The agreement between the health plan and the contract health provider must specify in advance the covered items and services to be furnished to enrollees and the total amount per enrollee (which may be expressed in a per month or other time period basis) the contract health care provider will be paid by the health plan for furnishing such items and services to enrollees and must set forth any copayments, if any, to be paid by enrollees to the contract health care provider for covered services;

(C) The payment amount contained in the agreement between the health care plan and the contract health care provider must remain in effect throughout the term of the agreement;

(D) The contract health care provider and the health plan must fully and accurately report to the Medicare and State health care program upon request, the terms of the agreement and the amounts paid in accordance with the agreement; and

(E) The contract health care provider must not claim or request payment in any form from the Department, a State health care program or an enrollee (other than copayment amounts described in paragraph (m)(2)(iv)(B) of this section) and the health plan must not pay the contract care provider in excess of the amounts described in paragraph (m)(2)(iv)(B) of this section for items and services covered by the agreement.

(2) For purposes of this paragraph, the terms *contract health care provider, enrollee,* and *health plan* have the same meaning as in paragraph (l)(2) of this section.

In 1992, the OIG published an interim final rule establishing a safe harbor for price reductions offered to health plans. The OIG emphasized that the safe harbor did nothing to "change[] reimbursement rules" and that "[i]f a provider chooses to . . . comply with [the safe harbor], such action may very well have reimbursement implications."[493] The OIG further commented:

> Many program beneficiaries are now served by a wide variety of managed care plans, such as various models of HMOs, CMPs, and health care prepayment plans (HCPPs) . . . and prepaid health plans (PHPs) . . . as well as PPOs, and we agree that additional safe harbor protection is warranted . . . We are promulgating . . . safe harbor provisions to protect the essential activities of prepaid health plans ("health plans") . . . [This safe harbor] protects the contractual relationships between health plans and "contract health care providers" for the furnishing of covered items and services at reduced prices.[494]

---

493. Interim Final Rule: Safe Harbors for Protecting Health Plans (57 Fed. Reg. 52723, 52724-25; Nov. 5, 1992) (sets forth three new safe harbors addressing managed care plans through interim final rulemaking).

494. *Id.* Definitions of key terms used in the safe harbor are as follows:

Contract health care provider means an individual or entity under contract with a health plan to furnish items or services to enrollees who are covered by the health plan, Medicare, or a State health care program.

Enrollee means an individual who has entered into a contractual relationship with a health plan (or on whose behalf an employer, or other private or governmental entity has entered into such a relationship) under which the individual is entitled to receive specified health care items and services, or insurance coverage for such items and services, in return for payment of a premium or a fee.

Health plan means an entity that furnishes or arranges under agreement with contract health care providers for the furnishing of items or services to enrollees, or furnishes insurance coverage for the provision of such items and services, in exchange for a premium or a fee, where such entity:

(i) Operates in accordance with a contract, agreement or statutory demonstration authority approved by CMS or a State health care program;

(ii) Charges a premium and its premium structure is regulated under a State insurance statute or a State enabling statute governing health maintenance organizations or preferred provider organizations;

(iii) Is an employer, if the enrollees of the plan are current or retired employees, or is a union welfare fund, if the enrollees of the plan are union members; or

(iv) Is licensed in the State, is under contract with an employer, union welfare fund, or a company furnishing health insurance coverage as described in conditions (ii) and (iii) of this definition, and is paid a fee for the administration of the plan which reflects the fair market value of those services.

42 CFR § 1001.952(l).

The OIG noted that "health care providers will contract with health plans and agree to furnish items and services to enrollees of the health plan at a discount from the provider's usual fee in return for obtaining a large volume of patients."[495] As with the safe harbor codified at 42 CFR § 1001.952(l), "protecting incentives to enrollees," this safe harbor "is divided into two separate parts for risk-based and cost-reimbursed health plans that operate in accordance with a contract or agreement with [CMS] or a State health care program."[496] A third part of the safe harbor protects "other health plans that do not have [such] contracts or agreement . . . where additional standards are met."[497]

The remuneration protected by the safe harbor is a provider's reduction of its usual charges and "only applies to reductions in the total amount charged by" the provider, rather than "reductions which are applicable only to a specific part of portion of the health care provider's charge, such as coinsurance and deductibles."[498] The OIG continued:

> Furthermore, we are only protecting the remuneration which represents the price reduction offered by the contract health care provider to make clear that any other forms of remuneration offered or paid by a contract health care provider to a health plan are not protected under this safe harbor provision. Indeed, we will closely review any forms of other such remuneration to ensure that improper payments are not employed to induce the health plan to issue a contract or otherwise steer patients to the person paying the remuneration.[499]

The safe harbor's second requirement that the agreement with the parties be in writing "is intended to assist [HHS] in understanding the intent of the parties" and, if needed, the OIG "will look behind the contract to determine if the real intent of the parties is not fully disclosed in the written agreement."[500] A third requirement that the agreement must be for the sole purpose of having the provider furnish to enrollees items or services covered by the health plan, Medicare or Medicaid is to ensure that the safe harbor does not protect contracts for services other than "covered benefits."[501]

---

495. *Id.* at 52726.
496. *Id.*
497. *Id.*
498. *Id.*
499. *Id.*
500. *Id.*
501. *Id.*

Noncovered services such as "peer review," "marketing services," and "pre-enrollment screening" would need to satisfy another safe harbor, such as the safe harbor for personal services and management contracts, and "where protection is sought from more than one safe harbor, separate justifications must be clearly set forth for each provision for which protection is sought."[502] The OIG explained the need for this requirement as stemming from its "experience with some HMOs that have abused their contractual relationships with medical groups where individuals in the groups have engaged in abusive or illegal activities on behalf of the HMO . . . by conducting pre-enrollment screening."[503] The OIG indicated its intention to "use [its] authorities aggressively to monitor closely and penalize where appropriate any abusive relationships between health plans and contract health care providers to assure the medically necessary services of a high quality are available and accessible to all enrollees."[504]

The first part of the safe harbor was designed to protect risk-based HMOs, CMPs, and PHPs under contract with [CMS] or a state health care program and operating in accordance with specified provisions of the Social Security Act or under a federal demonstration authority or under other federal statutory or regulatory authority.[505] In addition to risk-based contract health plans having to satisfy the requirements described earlier, the interim final rule required that contract providers "not separately bill Medicare, Medicaid or another State health care program for items or services furnished under the agreement with the health plan . . . [or] otherwise shift the burden of the agreement onto Medicare, Medicaid, other payors, or individuals."[506] Moreover, "[a]ny claim for reimbursement made directly to Medicare, Medicaid or other State health care program for items or services for which payment was made by the health plan would constitute an unlawful false claim."[507]

The second part of the safe harbor protected health plans that had executed a contract or agreement with the CMS or a state health care program to have payment made on a reasonable cost or similar basis, provided that any price reduction agreement satisfied four enumerated standards.

502. *Id.*
503. *Id.*
504. *Id.*
505. *Id.*
506. *Id.* at 52727.
507. *Id.*

The third part of the safe harbor protected price reductions offered by contract health care providers to all other health plans, provided that six enumerated standards were satisfied.

In 1996, the OIG revised and clarified the rule in response to public comments.[508] In its general comments, the OIG clarified, in response to concerns that this and other safe harbors affecting health plans could "chill" the activities of such plans if they find themselves unable to fit within the safe harbor, that the safe harbors "did not expand the zone of illegal conduct" under the AKS and that "[l]egally and logically, the safe harbors can only make the zone of illegal conduct smaller."[509] The OIG further explained that "compliance with the safe harbors is completely voluntary" and "[i]f a practice or arrangement does not fall within a safe harbor, it has precisely the same legal risk that it had before the safe harbor was promulgated."[510] The safe harbors "are designed to provide a means through which plans and providers can be assured that their arrangements are immune from potential criminal and administrative sanctions under the anti-kickback statute."[511] The OIG further assured the public that the fact that certain activities of health plans are not referenced in the safe harbors does not mean the OIG regards such activities as unlawful or that they would be subjected to heightened scrutiny.[512] The OIG made clear that, being voluntary, the safe harbors "do not create affirmative obligations on individuals or entities" and "failure to comply with a safe harbor means only that the practice or arrangement does not have the absolute assurance of protection from [AKS] liability."

Addressing the overall need for the safe harbor, the OIG commented that

> Enrollment in a health plan falls within the scope of the anti-kickback statute where such enrollment involves Medicare or Medicaid beneficiaries and results from various incentives offered to these individuals by the managed care plan.
>
> The incentives offered to beneficiaries constitute remuneration with the meaning of the statute. Once enrolled, the plan is entitled to receive Medicare or Medicaid reimbursement for the services directly provided

508. Final Rule: Safe Harbors for Protecting Health Plans (61 Fed. Reg. 2122; Jan. 25, 1996) (revised final rule addressing the three managed care safe harbors originally promulgated in the Nov. 5, 1992, interim final rule).

509. *Id.* at 2124.

510. *Id.*

511. *Id.*

512. *Id.*

to program beneficiaries. Alternatively, the plan steers enrollees to certain providers who furnish reimbursable services. The incentives offered to program beneficiaries can be in return for obtaining reimbursable program business and, therefore, are covered by the statute.[513]

Responding to comments protesting the safe harbor's requirement that health plans not shift the burden of increased coverage, reduced cost-sharing, or price reductions to other payers, the OIG reaffirmed its view "that enrollee incentives and provider price reductions should be economically sensible, i.e., they should not be driven by a motive to shift costs to the government or other payers."[514] The OIG continued:

> A health plan should not be offering incentives or provider discounts unless they believe the cost of those incentives or discounts can be recovered through lower operating costs resulting from increased volume, economies of scale or other efficiencies. We also believe that practices should be protected only if they do not cause harm to the Medicare and Medicaid programs. Accordingly, we are only willing to protect incentives and price reductions that do not result in increased costs to the programs. In order to ensure that result, we believe it is necessary to include a requirement which prohibits cost shifting to the Medicare and Medicaid programs.[515]

The OIG did agree, however, that the bar against burden shifting did not need to be broader than necessary to protect Medicare and Medicaid and thus narrowed the scope of the prohibition in the revised final rule to make clear that cost shifting occurs "when an arrangement or agreement results in increased payments being claimed from the Medicare or State health care programs."[516] The OIG declined to establish standards for determining when cost shifting has occurred, but noted that "in any case where a plan or provider raises its costs or fees to others or reduces the services it provides to others as a result of an incentive or a discount, prohibited cost shifting has occurred" and that "[c]laiming certain costs, such as waivers of coinsurance or deductibles, as bad debt would also constitute impermissible cost shifting."[517]

---

513. *Id.*
514. *Id.* at 2126.
515. *Id.* at 2126-27.
516. *Id.* at 2127.
517. *Id.*

2.14. Practitioner Recruitment

The safe harbor for practitioner recruitment, codified at 42 C.F.R. § 1001.952(n),[518] states:

(n) *Practitioner recruitment.* As used in [the Anti-Kickback Statute], "remuneration" does not include any payment or exchange of anything of value by an entity in order to induce a practitioner who has been practicing within his or her current specialty for less than one year to locate, or to induce any other practitioner to relocate, his or her primary place of practice into a Health Professional Shortage Area (HPSA) for his or her specialty area, as defined in Departmental regulations, that is served by the entity, as long as all of the following nine standards are met -

(1) The arrangement is set forth in a written agreement signed by the parties that specifies the benefits provided by the entity, the terms under which the benefits are to be provided, and the obligations of each party.

(2) If a practitioner is leaving an established practice, at least 75 percent of the revenues of the new practice must be generated from new patients not previously seen by the practitioner at his or her former practice.

(3) The benefits are provided by the entity for a period not in excess of 3 years, and the terms of the agreement are not renegotiated during this 3-year period in any substantial aspect; provided, however, that if the HPSA to which the practitioner was recruited ceases to be a HPSA during the term of the written agreement, the payments made under the written agreement will continue to satisfy this paragraph for the duration of the written agreement (not to exceed 3 years).

(4) There is no requirement that the practitioner make referrals to, be in a position to make or influence referrals to, or otherwise generate business for the entity as a condition for receiving the benefits; provided, however, that for purposes of this paragraph, the entity may require as a condition for receiving benefits that the practitioner maintain staff privileges at the entity.

518. 42 C.F.R. § 1001.952(n).

(5) The practitioner is not restricted from establishing staff privileges at, referring any service to, or otherwise generating any business for any other entity of his or her choosing.

(6) The amount or value of the benefits provided by the entity may not vary (or be adjusted or renegotiated) in any manner based on the volume or value of any expected referrals to or business otherwise generated for the entity by the practitioner for which payment may be made in whole or in part under Medicare, Medicaid or any other Federal health care programs.

(7) The practitioner agrees to treat patients receiving medical benefits or assistance under any Federal health care program in a nondiscriminatory manner.

(8) At least 75 percent of the revenues of the new practice must be generated from patients residing in a HPSA or a Medically Underserved Area (MUA) or who are part of a Medically Underserved Population (MUP), all as defined in paragraph (a) of this section.

(9) The payment or exchange of anything of value may not directly or indirectly benefit any person (other than the practitioner being recruited) or entity in a position to make or influence referrals to the entity providing the recruitment payments or benefits of items or services payable by a Federal health care program.

The safe harbor for practitioner recruitment was enacted in 1999 with the intent to "promote beneficiary access to quality health care by permitting communities that have difficulty attracting needed medical professionals to offer inducements to those professionals without running afoul of the anti-kickback statute."[519] This intention was an expansion of the original proposed rule of 1993, which sought only to protect recruitment in communities defined as "rural" by the Office of Management and Budget.[520] The final rule is intended to allow areas that have shown a need for the practitioners,

519. Final Rule: Clarification of the Initial OIG Safe Harbor Provisions and Establishment of Additional Safe Harbor Provisions under the Anti-Kickback Statute, 64 Fed. Reg. 63518, 63541 (Nov. 19, 1999).

520. Proposed Rule: Additional Safe Harbor Provisions under the Anti-Kickback Statute, 58 Fed. Reg. 49008 49010 (Sept. 21, 1993) (proposed rule designed to incorporate seven additional safe harbor provisions).

and for practitioners who "actually serve" the affected community.[521] HHS updated and clarified that the designation of demonstrated need is limited to HPSAs and MUAs, as defined by the Health Resources and Services Administration (HRSA), as opposed to simply a disproportionate share hospital (DSH) or the original "rural" designation. This is due to the fact that while DSH payments indicate the number of low-income patients, they do not necessarily indicate a shortage of practitioners.[522] In order to fit within the safe harbor, a physician's relocation must be to a HPSA; a service area consisting exclusively of areas designated as MUAs is not sufficient to satisfy the relocation standard.

HHS affirmatively stated that failure to meet the standards of this safe harbor does not determine whether or not an arrangement violates the AKS. Arrangements for remuneration to physicians for recruitment need to be evaluated on a case-by-case basis if they do not meet the standards of the safe harbor.[523]

In response to concerns over the meaning of the clause "the terms of the agreement are not renegotiated during this 3-year period in any substantial aspect," HHS clarified that "substantial aspect" means any manner that would materially affect the payments and benefits to be made to the practitioners that were recruited, per the written agreement.[524] The terms "payment" and "benefit" are used in §§ 1001.952(n)(1), (3), and (6). HHS clarified that these terms could not be given a definitive specification due to the necessity of evaluating the recruitment process and the degree of variation associated with it in each case. The three-year limit does not allow for incentives to be offered after that period for the purpose of retention.[525] "[P]ayments for retention purposes require closer scrutiny than initial recruitment payments."[526]

When the rule was proposed in 1993, it required a relocating practitioner to move at least 100 miles from the previous place of practice, and derive 85 percent of the new practice's revenue from new patients "not previously

521. Final Rule: Clarification of the Initial OIG Safe Harbor Provisions and Establishment of Additional Safe Harbor Provisions under the Anti-Kickback Statute, 64 Fed. Reg. 63518, 63541 (Nov. 19, 1999).

522. *Id.* at 63542.

523. *Id.* at 63545.

524. *Id.* at 63543.

525. *Id.* at 63544.

526. *Id.* at 63543.

seen by the practitioner at his or her former practice."[527] The final version of the rule, when changing its methodology in determining which areas were to be covered, removed the 100-mile requirement as it could have led to arbitrary results in rural areas and made it difficult to serve urban areas in need. The enacted rule allows for even a short move, providing it is into a HPSA. HHS cautioned that the area of practitioner recruitment is particularly vulnerable to abuse, and "experienced practitioners" could relocate a short distance to a HPSA with the purpose of qualifying for the safe harbor rather than to serve the affected community.[528] This potential abuse would not have been mitigated with the proposed 85 percent new patient revenue. The final version rectifies this issue by requiring that "75 percent of the revenues of the new practice must be generated from patients residing in a HPSA or a MUA or who are members of a MUP." HHS further clarified where the patients of the new practice may come from: "The patients do not necessarily have to reside in the specific HPSA in which the practitioner's new practice is located, but may reside instead in a nearby MUA or HPSA. In sum, to qualify for the safe harbor, a new or relocating physician must substantially treat patients who are new to the physician's practice and who reside in underserved areas, or are members of medically-underserved populations designated by HRSA."[529]

For times when the recruitment process does not strictly meet the requirements of this safe harbor, the OIG has offered advisory opinions on how to move forward and whether or not a hospital would be subject to administrative sanctions. OIG Advisory Opinion No. 01-4[530] emphasized four points as being of particular importance:

> Whether there is documented evidence of an objective need for the practitioner's services . . . , Whether the practitioner has an existing stream of referrals within the recruiting entity's service area . . . , Whether the benefit is narrowly tailored so that it does not exceed that which is reasonably necessary to recruit a practitioner . . . , [and] Whether the remuneration directly or indirectly benefits other referral sources.[531]

---

527. Proposed Rule: Additional Safe Harbor Provisions under the Anti-Kickback Statute, 58 Fed. Reg. 49008 49010 (Sept. 21, 1993) (proposed rule designed to incorporate seven additional safe harbor provisions).

528. *Id.* at 63543.

529. *Id.*

530. OIG Advisory Opinion No. 01-4 (May 10, 2001).

531. *Id.* at 8.

These factors are meant to weigh the level of risk of abuse presented by a given arrangement but are not determinative in and of themselves, as each case is subject to the OIG's discretion.[532]

2.15. Obstetrical Malpractice Insurance Subsidies

The safe harbor for obstetrical malpractice insurance subsidies is codified at 42 C.F.R. § 1001.952(o):

(o) *Obstetrical malpractice insurance subsidies.* As used in [the AKS] "remuneration" does not include any payment made by a hospital or other entity to another entity that is providing malpractice insurance (including a self-funded entity), where such payment is used to pay for some or all of the costs of malpractice insurance premiums for a practitioner (including a certified nurse-midwife as defined in section 1861(gg) of the Act) who engages in obstetrical practice as a routine part of his or her medical practice in a primary care HPSA, as long as all of the following seven standards are met -

(1) The payment is made in accordance with a written agreement between the entity paying the premiums and the practitioner, which sets out the payments to be made by the entity, and the terms under which the payments are to be provided.

(2)

(i) The practitioner must certify that for the initial coverage period (not to exceed one year) the practitioner has a reasonable basis for believing that at least 75 percent of the practitioner's obstetrical patients treated under the coverage of the malpractice insurance will either -

(A) Reside in a HPSA or MUA, as defined in paragraph (a) of this section; or

(B) Be part of a MUP, as defined in paragraph (a) of this section.

(ii) Thereafter, for each additional coverage period (not to exceed one year), at least 75 percent of the practitioner's obstetrical patients treated under the prior coverage period (not to exceed one year) must have -

532. The safe harbor has also been referenced in several court decisions. *See, e.g.*, McDonnell v. Cardiothoracic & Vascular Surgical Assoc., Inc., 2004 WL 3733402 at *7 (July 28, 2004 S.D. Ohio); United States v. AIDS Healthcare Found., Inc., 262 F. Supp. 3d 1353 (June 9, 2017 S.D. Fla.); United States *ex rel.* Jacobs v. CDS, P.A., 2015 WL 5698395 at *4 (Sept. 28, 2015 D. Idaho).

(A) Resided in a HPSA or MUA, as defined in paragraph (a) of this section; or

(B) Been part of a MUP, as defined in paragraph (a) of this section.

(3) There is no requirement that the practitioner make referrals to, or otherwise generate business for, the entity as a condition for receiving the benefits.

(4) The practitioner is not restricted from establishing staff privileges at, referring any service to, or otherwise generating any business for any other entity of his or her choosing.

(5) The amount of payment may not vary based on the volume or value of any previous or expected referrals to or business otherwise generated for the entity by the practitioner for which payment may be made in whole or in part under Medicare, Medicaid or any other Federal health care programs.

(6) The practitioner must treat obstetrical patients who receive medical benefits or assistance under any Federal health care program in a nondiscriminatory manner.

(7) The insurance is a bona fide malpractice insurance policy or program, and the premium, if any, is calculated based on a bona fide assessment of the liability risk covered under the insurance. For purposes of paragraph (o) of this section, *costs of malpractice insurance premiums* means:

(i) For practitioners who engage in obstetrical practice full-time, any costs attributable to malpractice insurance; or

(ii) For practitioners who engage in obstetrical practice on a part-time or sporadic basis, the costs:

(A) Attributable exclusively to the obstetrical portion of the practitioner's malpractice insurance and

(B) Related exclusively to obstetrical services provided in a primary care HPSA.

As explained by the OIG, "[t]his safe harbor is intended to facilitate access to obstetrical services for Federal health care program beneficiaries in primary care health professional shortage areas by protecting from the reach of the antikickback statute subsidized malpractice insurance for practitioners who are primarily engaged in obstetrical practices in those areas."[533]

The OIG noted that, by limiting such protection to obstetrical malpractice insurance subsidies, the safe harbor "does not call into question the legality of all other types of practitioner malpractice insurance subsidies" and that those subsidies "may qualify for protection under other safe harbors, such as practitioner recruitment, personal services contracts or employee compensation."[534] At the same time, however, the OIG noted "that malpractice insurance subsidies paid to or on behalf of potential referral sources may be suspect under the anti-kickback statute."[535] In proposing the rule, the OIG explained that "nothing in the safe harbor would authorize payment by the Federal health care programs to hospitals or other institutional providers for costs they may incur in providing malpractice insurance" and that "[a]ny allowable costs for such insurance are governed strictly by Federal health care program rules."[536]

The OIG noted that safe harbor protection is "appropriate for family practitioners and other physicians and certified nurse midwives who deliver babies as routine part of their medical practices."[537] The OIG defined "routine" as requiring "that the practitioner must provide substantial and regular obstetrical services; we do not intend to protect obstetrical insurance subsidies for practitioners who practice obstetrical medicine on only an occasional basis."[538] For certified nurse midwives and practitioners who do not practice obstetrical medicine full time, the safe harbor "will protect payments for *obstetrical* malpractice insurance only" and not "subsidies for other types of medical malpractice liability" so that "the protected subsidy will be the difference between the cost of malpractice insurance that includes obstetrical coverage and the cost of malpractice insurance that includes obstetrical coverage and the cost of malpractice insurance that does not include such coverage."[539] The safe harbor also protects insurance subsidies paid for practitioners who are engaged only in part-time obstet-

533. Final Rule: Clarification of the Initial OIG Safe Harbor Provisions and Establishment of Additional Safe Harbor Provisions under the Anti-Kickback Statute (64 Fed. Reg. 63518, 63545; Nov. 19, 1999).

534. *Id.* at 63546.

535. *Id.*

536. *Id.* at 63545.

537. *Id.*

538. *Id.*

539. *Id.*

rical practice within a health professional shortage area (HPSA), protecting subsidies for insurance coverage that is "related exclusively to services provided in the HPSA."[540] Further, "[i]f the practitioner is covered by a single insurance policy or program, the safe harbor covers subsidies for that portion of the insurance premium that is reasonably allocable to obstetrical services provided in a HPSA."[541] The OIG limited the safe harbor "to primary care HPSAs so as to ensure as much as possible that the benefits protected by this safe harbor are extended to practitioners in areas where there is a well-founded, documented shortage of obstetrical practitioners."[542] The OIG further commented that "nothing in this safe harbor prevents protection of malpractice insurance subsidies for practitioners engaged in practice outside primary care HPSAs as part of an arms-length, fair market value compensation package that meets the requirements of the personal services safe harbor or the employee compensation exception to the anti-kickback statute."[543]

Regarding the safe harbor's protection of "*bona fide*" insurance products, such as "*bona fide* self-funded obstetrical malpractice insurance programs, including risk-retention groups that qualify under the Liability Risk Retention Act, 15 U.S.C. 3901, and . . . *bona fide* offshore insurance products," the OIG stated that although it was "not defining the full scope of *bona fide* insurance products, [it] believe[s] that certification by a qualified actuary that the program is adequate relative to the risk insured would be an indicator of a *bona fide* insurance program."[544] Finally, responding to a comment raising concern that the safe harbor did not sufficiently protect group practices, the OIG commented that "[a] group practice that provides obstetrical malpractice insurance subsidies may qualify as an 'entity' for purposes of this safe harbor" but that the safe harbor "is not intended to protect group practices for any payment practice that does not satisfy all of the safe harbor criteria."[545]

This safe harbor also has been addressed in an Advisory Opinion. In Advisory Opinion No. 04-11,[546] the OIG elected not to impose administrative sanctions on an arrangement under which a medical center would subsidize malpractice insurance expenses for four community-based obstetricians. The

540. *Id.*
541. *Id.*
542. *Id.* at 63546.
543. *Id.*
544. *Id.* at 63547.
545. *Id.*
546. Advisory Opinion No. 04-11 (Issued Sept. 2, 2004).

medical center wished to provide the benefit because it was concerned that rising malpractice costs might cause the obstetricians to stop providing care, which would cause a sharp decrease in access to obstetrical care. The OIG acknowledged that the arrangement did not satisfy the requirements of the safe harbor because the obstetricians did not practice in a "primary care" HPSA, and instead practiced in a community having different HPSA designations for low-income populations, migrant agricultural workers, and homeless individuals. Nevertheless, the OIG concluded that this one discrepancy did not increase the risk of fraud and abuse and was consistent "with the intent of the safe harbor to ensure access to needed obstetrical care . . . in places and for populations that do not have sufficient access to care."[547] The OIG also determined that there were other factors that mitigated any residual risk, including that (1) the insurance subsidies were a response to sharply escalating premium costs and would only be provided on a temporary basis for a fixed period; (2) the subsidies would only cover a portion of the obstetricians' increased premium expense and would not result in a "windfall"; and (3) the subsidies would be provided irrespective of whether the obstetricians performed services at a facility affiliated with the medical center.

2.16. Investments in Group Practices

The safe harbor for investments in group practices is codified at 42 C.F.R. § 1001.952(p) and states:

> (p) *Investments in group practices.* As used in [the AKS], "remuneration" does not include any payment that is a return on an investment interest, such as a dividend or interest income, made to a solo or group practitioner investing in his or her own practice or group practice if the following four standards are met -
>
> (1) The equity interests in the practice or group must be held by licensed health care professionals who practice in the practice or group.
>
> (2) The equity interests must be in the practice or group itself, and not some subdivision of the practice or group.
>
> (3) In the case of group practices, the practice must:
>
> (i) Meet the definition of "group practice" in section 1877(h)(4) of the Social Security Act and implementing regulations; and

547. *Id.*

(ii) Be a unified business with centralized decision-making, pooling of expenses and revenues, and a compensation/ profit distribution system that is not based on satellite offices operating substantially as if they were separate enterprises or profit centers.

(4) Revenues from ancillary services, if any, must be derived from "in-office ancillary services" that meet the definition of such term in section 1877(b)(2) of the Act and implementing regulations.

The safe harbor for investments in group practices was added in 1999 and "protects returns on investments in the group practice itself (i.e., not in separately owned health care services), if the group practice meets the Stark Law definition of a group practice . . . and if the group practice investors are all licensed professionals who practice in the group."[548] The safe harbor "also protects investments in solo practices where the practice is conducted through the solo practitioner's professional corporation or other separate legal entity."[549] While not viewing investments in group or solo practices as "suspect per se," the OIG recognized that the "plain language of the anti-kickback statute is sufficiently broad so as potentially to include payments from a group [or solo] practice to an investor in the practice."[550] Profits derived from in-office ancillary services, as defined under the Stark Law, are also protected.[551] Equity interests "may be held by an individual professional corporation if the corporation is exclusively owned by a single individual."[552] The safe harbor, however, "does not protect investments made jointly by group members in separate entities."[553] The OIG specifically chose not to use this safe harbor to protect group practice investments in outside entities providing ancillary services due to concerns over "anti-competitive effects and . . . abusive arrangements and incentives to overutilize" such services, but acknowledged that such investments could still receive protection under the small entity investment interest safe harbor.[554] The OIG further

548. Final Rule: OIG Anti-Kickback Provisions, 64 Fed. Reg. 63518, 63540 (Nov. 19, 1999) (Final Rule: Clarification of the Initial OIG Safe Harbor Provisions and Establishment of Additional Safe Harbor Provisions under the Anti-Kickback Statute).

549. *Id.*

550. *Id.*

551. *Id.*

552. *Id.*

553. *Id.*

554. *Id.*

noted that, while the group practice safe harbor imposed no restrictions on whether the investment interest could be related to previous or expected referrals, since such a restriction was deemed unnecessary in the context of a physician group practice, the safe harbor still requires that any return on investment comply with the Stark Law, "which limits compensation to physician investors that is based on the volume or value of referrals by the physician."[555]

The OIG addressed the group practice investment safe harbor in Advisory Opinion No. 08-24.[556] There, the OIG was asked to opine upon a shared medical practice (the Practice) involving twenty-three physicians and podiatrists that offered medical care, consultation, diagnosis, and treatment services through shared office space, facilities, equipment, and personnel. Among other things, the Practice provided urgent care consultation on a walk-in basis, clinical laboratory services, and diagnostic radiology services. All the physician investors in the Practice, except for one, treated patients at the practice, but none of them worked there full time, instead spending time at different office locations that were not affiliated with the practice. Each investor owned a fixed percentage stake in the Practice and shared in profits or losses in direct proportion to that stake. The Practice had a central governing board that made key decisions, maintained control over assets and liabilities, handled finance-related matters, and developed clinical and nonclinical policies and procedures. The Practice also had a centralized accounting system and pooled all expenses and revenues. The Practice certified that it would shortly meet the definition of "group practice" under the Stark Law and that any revenues from ancillary services would meet the Stark Law definition of "in-office ancillary services."

The OIG noted that, since one of the physician investors (holding one percent equity) did not treat patients and performed only an administrative function, the Practice could not satisfy the group practice investment safe harbor. The OIG also noted that "it may be necessary, in order to meet the minimum percentage of physician-patient encounters conducted by practice members under [the group practice definition], for the Practice" to hire additional physicians.[557] The OIG, however, determined that the Practice would

555. *Id.* at 63541.
556. Advisory Opinion No. 08-24 (Issued Dec. 29, 2008).
557. *See id.*, at n.3.

comply with the safe harbor "in nearly all respects" and that several factors sufficiently reduced the risk of fraud and abuse:

- All equity interests, save for one, were held by health care professionals who work at the Practice.
- All equity interests are held in the Practice and not a subdivision, and each investor held a fixed percentage stake in the entire Practice, rather than in a specialty group or other subdivision.
- It was certified that the arrangement would comply fully in all respects with the requirements of the group practice definition under the Stark Law.
- It was certified that the ancillary service revenues were derived from "in-office ancillary services" that meet the Stark Law definition.

Given these facts, the OIG concluded that the lone physician investor who performed only administrative services at the Practice "[did] not pose appreciable additional risks," commenting that his returns were directly proportional to his investment interest that the provided "substantial services integral to the Practice's operation and administration, thus minimizing the risk that his small equity interest reflects referrals."[558] While the OIG did not specifically cite this factor as a justification, it nonetheless bears mentioning that the OIG's decision not to impose administrative sanctions in this case could have been influenced by the fact that the Practice at issue was located in a rural HPSA.[559]

2.17. Cooperative Hospital Service Organizations

The safe harbor for cooperative hospital service organizations is codified at 42 C.F.R. § 1001.952(q):

> (q) *Cooperative hospital service organizations.* As used in [the AKS], "remuneration" does not include any payment made between a cooperative hospital service organization (CHSO) and its patron-hospital, both of which are described in section 501(e) of the Internal Revenue Code of 1986 and are tax-exempt under section 501(c)(3) of the Internal Revenue Code, where the CHSO is wholly owned by two or more patron-hospitals, as long as the following standards are met -

558. *See id.*
559. *See id.*

(1) If the patron-hospital makes a payment to the CHSO, the payment must be for the purpose of paying for the bona fide operating expenses of the CHSO, or

(2) If the CHSO makes a payment to the patron-hospital, the payment must be for the purpose of paying a distribution of net earnings required to be made under section 501(e)(2) of the Internal Revenue Code of 1986.

The OIG proposed this safe harbor in 1993 "for most cooperative hospital service organizations (CHSOs) that qualify under section 501(c)(3) of the Internal Revenue Code."[560] Pursuant to that Code provision and related regulations (26 CFR 1.501(e)-1), "these organizations are formed by two or more tax exempt hospitals (known as "patron-hospitals") to provide specifically enumerated services, such as purchasing, billing, and clinical services solely for the benefit of its patron-hospitals."[561] The organizations also are "required to distribute 'all net earnings to patrons on the basis of services performed.'"[562]

The proposed provision was intended to "protect payments from a patron-hospital to a CHSO to support the CHSO's operational costs and those payments from a CHSO to a patron-hospital that are required under IRS rules."[563] In order for protection to attach, "the CHSO must be wholly owned by its patron-hospitals" since such a condition "protects against potentially abusive joint venture arrangements that are formed under the guise of CHSOs."[564]

The OIG explained that "[w]ith respect to the payments the CHSO makes to its patron-hospitals . . . the level of discretion given to these providers as to what payment formula to use warrants safe harbor protection."[565]

---

560. Proposed Rule: Additional Safe Harbor Provisions Under the Anti-Kickback Statute (58 Fed. Reg. 49008, 49012; Sept. 21, 1993) (proposed rule designed to incorporate seven additional safe harbor provisions); *see also* Final Rule: Clarification of the Initial OIG Safe Harbor Provisions and Establishment of Additional Safe Harbor Provisions under the Anti-Kickback Statute (64 Fed. Reg. 63518, 63549; Nov. 19, 1999) (adopting proposed rule without modification).

561. *Id.*

562. *Id.*

563. *Id.*

564. *Id.*

565. *Id.* On the issue of discretion, the OIG commented: "Where a health care provider engages in an activity which is specifically required by another statutory provision and the provider is afforded no discretion in the manner of compliance, such a requirement is a valid defense to an alleged violation of the anti-kickback statute. However, where the health care provider is engaging in the activity to fulfill a general statutory obligation, but is afforded

The OIG also pointed out that "[t]o the extent a CHSO acts as a group purchasing organization or a patron-hospital obtains discounts as a result of the CHSO's activities, CHSOs and patron-hospitals must comply with the respective safe harbor provisions applicable to group purchasing organizations and discounts to be fully protected."[566]

The OIG declined to extend safe harbor protection to other cooperative organizations that do not qualify under section 501(e) of the Internal Revenue Code because there would be "no limits on the types of services that may be shared, nor are there restrictions on the identity of shareholders."[567] The OIG concluded that "the limitations imposed under section 501(e) are necessary to protect against potentially abusive joint ventures or referral arrangements."[568]

2.18. Ambulatory Surgical Centers

The regulatory safe harbor for ambulatory surgical centers (ASCs)[569] is codified at 42 C.F.R. § 1001.952(r), which states:

> (r) *Ambulatory surgical centers.* As used in section 1128B of the Act, "remuneration" does not include any payment that is a return on an investment interest, such as a dividend or interest income, made to an investor, as long as the investment entity is a certified ambulatory surgical center (ASC) under part 416 of this title, whose operating and recovery room space is dedicated exclusively to the ASC, patients referred to the investment entity by an investor are fully informed of the investor's investment interest, and all of the applicable standards are met within one of the following four categories –
>
> (1) Surgeon-owned ASCs – If all of the investors are general surgeons or surgeons engaged in the same surgical specialty, who

discretion in the manner of compliance, such a defense is not available because the provider's choice in the method of compliance may be motivated by an intent to generate program-related business." *Id.*

566. *Id.*

567. Final Rule: Clarification of the Initial OIG Safe Harbor Provisions and Establishment of Additional Safe Harbor Provisions under the Anti-Kickback Statute (64 Fed. Reg. 63518, 63549; Nov. 19, 1999).

568. *Id.*

569. An ASC is defined as any distinct entity that operates exclusively for the purpose of providing surgical services to patients not requiring hospitalization and in which the expected duration of services would not exceed 24 hours following an admission. *See* 42 C.F.R. § 416.2.

are in a position to refer patients directly to the entity and perform surgery on such referred patients; surgical group practices (as defined in this paragraph) composed exclusively of such surgeons; or investors who are not employed by the entity or by any investor, are not in a position to provide items or services to the entity or any of its investors, and are not in a position to make or influence referrals directly or indirectly to the entity or any of its investors, all of the following six standards must be met –

(i) The terms on which an investment interest is offered to an investor must not be related to the previous or expected volume of referrals, services furnished, or the amount of business otherwise generated from that investor to the entity.

(ii) At least one-third of each surgeon investor's medical practice income from all sources for the previous fiscal year or previous 12-month period must be derived from the surgeon's performance of procedures (as defined in this paragraph).

(iii) The entity or any investor (or other individual or entity acting on behalf of the entity or any investor) must not loan funds to or guarantee a loan for an investor if the investor uses any part of such loan to obtain the investment interest.

(iv) The amount of payment to an investor in return for the investment must be directly proportional to the amount of the capital investment (including the fair market value of any pre-operational services rendered) of that investor.

(v) All ancillary services for Federal health care program beneficiaries performed at the entity must be directly and integrally related to primary procedures performed at the entity, and none may be separately billed to Medicare or other Federal health care programs.

(vi) The entity and any surgeon investors must treat patients receiving medical benefits or assistance under any Federal health care program in a nondiscriminatory manner.

(2) Single-Specialty ASCs – If all of the investors are physicians engaged in the same medical practice specialty who are in a position to refer patients directly to the entity and perform procedures on such referred patients; group practices (as defined in this paragraph) composed exclusively of such physicians; or investors who are not employed by the entity or by any investor, are not in a position to provide items or services to the entity or any of its investors, and are not in a position to make or influence referrals directly or indirectly to the entity or any of its investors, all of the following six standards must be met –

(i) The terms on which an investment interest is offered to an investor must not be related to the previous or expected volume of referrals, services furnished, or the amount of business otherwise generated from that investor to the entity.

(ii) At least one-third of each physician investor's medical practice income from all sources for the previous fiscal year or previous 12-month period must be derived from the surgeon's performance of procedures (as defined in this paragraph).

(iii) The entity or any investor (or other individual or entity acting on behalf of the entity or any investor) must not loan funds to or guarantee a loan for an investor if the investor uses any part of such loan to obtain the investment interest.

(iv) The amount of payment to an investor in return for the investment must be directly proportional to the amount of the capital investment (including the fair market value of any pre-operational services rendered) of that investor.

(v) All ancillary services for Federal health care program beneficiaries performed at the entity must be directly and integrally related to primary procedures performed at the entity, and none may be separately billed to Medicare or other Federal health care programs.

(vi) The entity and any physician investors must treat patients receiving medical benefits or assistance under any Federal health care program in a nondiscriminatory manner.

(3) Multi-Specialty ASCs – If all of the investors are physicians who are in a position to refer patients directly to the entity and perform procedures on such referred patients; group practices, as defined in this paragraph, composed exclusively of such physicians; or investors who are not employed by the entity or by any investor, are not in a position to provide items or services to the entity or any of its investors, and are not in a position to make or influence referrals directly or indirectly to the entity or any of its investors, all of the following seven standards must be met –

(i) The terms on which an investment interest is offered to an investor must not be related to the previous or expected volume of referrals, services furnished, or the amount of business otherwise generated from that investor to the entity.

(ii) At least one-third of each physician investor's medical practice income from all sources for the previous fiscal year or previous 12-month period must be derived from the physician's performance of procedures (as defined in this paragraph).

(iii) At least one-third of the procedures (as defined in this paragraph) performed by each physician investor for the previous fiscal year or previous 12-month period must be performed at the investment entity.

(iv) The entity or any investor (or other individual or entity acting on behalf of the entity or any investor) must not loan funds to or guarantee a loan for an investor if the investor uses any part of such loan to obtain the investment interest.

(v) The amount of payment to an investor in return for the investment must be directly proportional to the amount of the capital investment (including the fair market value of any pre-operational services rendered) of that investor.

(vi) All ancillary services for Federal health care program beneficiaries performed at the entity must be directly and integrally related to primary procedures performed at the entity, and none may be separately billed to Medicare or other Federal health care programs.

(vii) The entity and any physician investors must treat patients receiving medical benefits or assistance under any Federal health care program in a nondiscriminatory manner.

(4) Hospital/Physician ASCs – If at least one investor is a hospital, and all of the remaining investors are physicians who meet the requirements of paragraphs (r)(1), (r)(2) or (r)(3) of this section; group practices (as defined in this paragraph) composed of such physicians; surgical group practices (as defined in this paragraph); or investors who are not employed by the entity or by any investor, are not in a position to provide items or services to the entity or any of its investors, and are not in a position to refer patients directly or indirectly to the entity or any of its investors, all of the following eight standards must be met –

(i) The terms on which an investment interest is offered to an investor must not be related to the previous or expected volume of referrals, services furnished, or the amount of business otherwise generated from that investor to the entity.

(ii) The entity or any investor (or other individual or entity acting on behalf of the entity or any investor) must not loan funds to or guarantee a loan for an investor if the investor uses any part of such loan to obtain the investment interest.

(iii) The amount of payment to an investor in return for the investment must be directly proportional to the amount of the capital investment (including the fair market value of any pre-operational services rendered) of that investor.

(iv) The entity and any hospital or physician investor must treat patients receiving medical benefits or assistance under any Federal health care program in a nondiscriminatory manner.

(v) The entity may not use space, including, but not limited to, operating and recovery room space, located in or owned by any hospital investor, unless such space is leased from the hospital in accordance with a lease that complies with all the standards of the space rental safe harbor set forth in paragraph (b) of this section; nor may it use equipment owned by or services provided by the hospital unless such equipment is leased in accordance with a lease that complies with the equipment rental safe harbor set forth in paragraph (c) of this section, and such services are provided in accordance with a contract that complies with the personal services and management contracts safe harbor set forth in paragraph (d) of this section.

(vi) All ancillary services for Federal health care program beneficiaries performed at the entity must be directly and integrally related to primary procedures performed at the entity, and none may be separately billed to Medicare or other Federal health care programs.

(vii) The hospital may not include on its cost report or any claim for payment from a Federal health care program any costs associated with the ASC (unless such costs are required to be included by a Federal health care program).

(viii) The hospital may not be in a position to make or influence referrals directly or indirectly to any investor or the entity.

(5) For purposes of paragraph (r) of this section, procedures means any procedure or procedures on the list of Medicare-covered procedures for ambulatory surgical centers in accordance with regulations issued by the Department and group practice means a group practice that meets all of the standards of paragraph (p) of this section. Surgical group practice means a group practice that meets all of the standards of paragraph (p) of this section and is composed exclusively of surgeons who meet the requirements of paragraph (r)(1) of this section.

The ASC safe harbor has four categories: Surgeon-Owned ASCs, Single-Specialty ASCs, Multi-Specialty ASCs, and Hospital/Physician ASCs. In order to establish safe harbor protection, all requirements of a given category must be met. The following requirements are shared by all four categories:

(i) the ASC must be certified under 42 C.F.R. part 416;
(ii) loans from the ASC or other investors for the purpose of investing are prohibited;

(iii) investment interests must be offered on terms not related to the volume or value of referrals;
(iv) all ancillary services must be directly and integrally related to primary procedures performed at the ASC and none may be separately billed to Medicare or other Federal health care programs; and
(v) neither the ASC nor physicians practicing at the ASC are permitted to discriminate against Federal health care program beneficiaries.

Further, the ASC's operating and recovery room space must be exclusive to use by the ASC,[570] and physician investors must inform all patients referred to an ASC of the physician investor's ownership interest in such ASC with written notice prior to the date of a procedure at the ASC, absent exigent circumstances.

A. *Surgeon-Owned Ambulatory Surgical Centers*

The first category of the safe harbor is the Surgeon-Owned ASC. Generally, this category protects investments in ASCs where all physician investors are general surgeons or surgeons engaged in the same surgical specialty who are in a position to refer patients directly to the ASC to perform procedures on these patients, group practices that are composed of such physicians and who meet all requirements of the group practice safe harbor,[571] or investors who:

(i) do not provide services to the ASC or its investors;
(ii) are not employed by the ASC or any investor; and
(iii) are not in a position to refer patients directly or indirectly to, or generate business for, the ASC or any of its investors.[572]

Importantly, in order for surgeon investors to qualify for safe harbor protection, they must perform at least one-third of their medical practice income from all sources for the previous fiscal year or twelve-month period through the physician's performance of surgical procedures at an ASC or other hospital setting ("1/3 Income Test").[573]

570. *See* 42 C.F.R. § 1001.952(r).
571. *See* Group Practice Safe Harbor 42 C.F.R. § 1001.952(p).
572. *See* 64 Fed. Reg. 63518, at 63518-63519.
573. *See id.*

B. *Single-Specialty Ambulatory Surgical Centers*

The second category is the Single-Specialty ASC. This category protects investment entities in the same way the Surgeon-Owned ASC category does, without requiring the physician investor to be a general surgeon.[574] Generally, it is designed to protect ASC investments by physician investors engaged in the same medical practice specialty who perform ASC procedures as a significant part of their practice (e.g., gastroenterologists).[575] Specifically, it protects investments in ASCs by physicians who are in a position to refer patients directly to the ASC to perform procedures on these patients, group practices that are composed of such physicians and meet all requirements of the group practice safe harbor,[576] or investors who:

(i) do not provide services to the ASC or its investors;
(ii) are not employed by the ASC or any investor; and
(iii) are not in a position to refer patients directly or indirectly to, or generate business for, the ASC or any of its investors.[577]

As with the Surgeon-Owned ASC category, each physician investor must meet the 1/3 Income Test.[578]

C. *Multispecialty Ambulatory Surgical Centers*

The third category of the safe harbor is the Multispecialty ASC. Its requirements are similar to the Surgeon-Owned ASC and Single-Specialty ASC categories but allows for a variation in the types of physicians and their specialties that are eligible for protection.[579] Specifically, it extends protection to (a) both surgeons or nonsurgeons who are in a position to refer patients directly to the ASC and who perform procedures on these patients, (b) group practices that are composed of such physicians and meet all requirements of the group practice safe harbor,[580] or (c) investors who:

(i) do not provide services to the ASC or its investors;
(ii) are not employed by the ASC or any investor; and

574. Compare Surgeon-Owned ASC safe harbor with Single-Specialty ASC safe harbor.
575. *See* 64 Fed. Reg. 63518, 63518-19.
576. *See* Group Practice Safe Harbor, 42 C.F.R. § 1001.952(p).
577. *See* 64 Fed. Reg. 63518, 63518-19.
578. *See id.*
579. *See id.*
580. *See* Group Practice Safe Harbor, 42 C.F.R. §1001.952(p).

(iii) are not in a position to refer patients directly or indirectly to, or generate business for, the ASC or any of its investors.[581]

As with the previous two categories, each physician investor must meet the 1/3 Income Test[582] and, due to the increased risk of remuneration for referrals among physicians with different specialties, physicians in this category are also required to perform at least one-third (1/3) of their procedures that require an ASC or hospital surgical setting to be performed at the ASC in which the physician is investing ("1/3 Procedure Test"). The 1/3 Procedure Test helps to ensure that the ASC serves as an extension of the physician's office so as to mitigate concerns that the physician investors may be incentivized to refer surgical procedures to other investors in order to receive an additional return on their investment in the ASC from the referral.[583]

D. Hospital/Physician Ambulatory Surgical Centers

The fourth category is the Hospital/Physician ASC. It protects certain joint venture ASC investments by hospitals, physicians, and/or other investors. In order to qualify for protection, at least one investor must be a hospital and the other investors must be:

(i) physicians who meet the requirements of Surgeon-Owned ASCs, Single-Specialty ASCs, or Multi-Specialty ASCs, as applicable: or
(ii) non-referral source investors.[584]

Moreover, the hospital must not be in a position to refer patients directly or indirectly to any physician investor or to the ASC to be eligible. The ASC space must be for the exclusive use of the ASC,[585] and the space must not be used by the hospital for the hospital's inpatient or outpatient treatments.[586] Finally, the ASC may lease space and/or equipment owned by or located in a hospital investor's premises as long as the lease of space and the equipment meets all requirements of those respective safe harbors.[587]

---

581. *See* 64 Fed. Reg. 63518, 63518-19.
582. *See id.*
583. *See id.*
584. *See id.*
585. *See id.*
586. *See id.*
587. *See* Space Rental Safe Harbor at 42 C.F.R. §1001.952(b), and Equipment Rental Safe Harbor at 42 C.F.R. §1001.952(c).

E. Regulatory Guidance, Policy, and Advisory Opinions

The ASC safe harbor was included as an additional safe harbor proposed as an amendment by HHS in 1993.[588] As explained in the preamble to the final rule providing safe harbor protection for returns on investment interests in ASCs, the decision to extend this protection derives in large measure from HHS's long-standing policy of promoting greater utilization of ASCs, where appropriate, because of the substantial cost savings that the federal health care programs may achieve when procedures are performed in ASCs rather than in more costly hospital inpatient or outpatient facilities.[589] When promulgating the ASC safe harbor, the OIG stated that its chief concern was that "a return on investment in an ASC might be a disguised payment for referrals."[590] However, recognizing that some physician-owned ASCs may be beneficial to the federal health care programs and their beneficiaries, the OIG stated:

> The gravamen of an anti-kickback offense is payment of remuneration to induce the referral of Federal health care program business. In the context of an ASC, our chief concern is that a return on an investment in an ASC might be disguised as payment for referrals . . . [P]hysicians in specialties that typically refer to one another could jointly invest in an ASC so that they are positioned to earn a profit from such referrals or so that one physician specialty provides the ASC services and the other provides the referrals. In such cases, medical decision-making may be corrupted by financial incentives offered to potential referral sources who stand to profit from services provided by another physician.[591]

For example, indirect kickbacks might flow to investor physicians, by means of receiving a return through the ASC's profit distribution, who refer patients to other investors in an ASC that perform surgical procedures at that ASC.[592]

---

588. 64 Fed. Reg. 63518; *see also Fact Sheet: Federal Anti-Kickback Law and Regulatory Safe Harbors*, U.S. Off. Inspector Gen., Nov. 1999, https://oig.hhs.gov/fraud/docs/safeharborregulations/safefs.htm.

589. *See* 64 Fed. Reg. 63518, 63537; *see also* OIG Advisory Opinion No. 12-06 at 7 (June 1, 2012).

590. 64 Fed. Reg. 63518, 63536 (providing two illustrative examples of potentially problematic arrangements).

591. *Id.*

592. *See id.*

However, so long as an arrangement does not violate these core principles, coupled with the strong policy support for the promotion of ASCs, the OIG has ruled favorably in several advisory opinions notwithstanding the failure of the arrangement to meet each and every requirement of the applicable ASC safe harbor. In doing so, the OIG has recognized that the absence of safe harbor protection is not fatal provided that the arrangement would pose more than a minimal risk of fraud and abuse under the AKS. This is particularly the case "[w]here the ASC is functionally an extension of a physician's office, so that the physician personally performs services at the ASC on his or her own patients as a substantial part of his or her medical practice."[593] It is also important to note that while many ASC arrangements will fit within the advised safe harbor requirements, some legitimate ASC arrangements that do not meet the safe harbor requirements may still be protected under the small entity investments safe harbor or the safe harbor for investments in underserved areas.[594]

In Advisory Opinion 08-08, the OIG determined not to impose administrative sanctions on a proposed physician/hospital joint venture ASC that did not qualify for safe harbor protection.[595] Specifically, of the eighteen surgeon investors involved in the proposed ASC, only fourteen met the 1/3 Income Test and would regularly practice at the ASC. The four surgeons who would not be utilizing the ASC primarily performed surgeries at a hospital on an inpatient basis. In finding that the proposed arrangement posed little risk of fraud and abuse, the OIG reasoned that notwithstanding the failure of the four inpatient surgeons to meet the 1/3 Income Test, the ASC was unlikely to be a vehicle for them to profit from referrals.[596] This was because as practitioners in subspecialties of orthopedic surgery that require a hospital operating room setting, the inpatient surgeons rarely have occasion to refer patients for ASC-qualified procedures,

593. OIG Advisory Opinion No. 12-06 at 7 (June 1, 2012).

594. 64 Fed. Reg. 63518, 63536 (discussing the small entity investments safe harbor (42 C.F.R. § 1001.952(a)(2)-(3)).

595. *See* OIG Advisory Opinion No. 08-08 (July 25, 2008).

596. *See id.* at 5 (finding that the arrangement did not qualify for the protection of the hospital-/physician-owned ASC safe harbor because the surgeon investors did not hold their investment interests in the ASC either directly or through a group practice). However, the OIG opined that since the surgeon investor's ownership interest in the pass through entity "[was] proportioned to his or her capital investment, the surgeon's ownership interest in the ASC was, in turn, proportional to its capital investment." *Id.* As a result, the individual surgeon investors received a return in their ASC investments that was the same as if they had invested directly.

with the exception of pain management procedures.[597] Moreover, like the other surgeon investors, the inpatient surgeons were regularly engaged in a genuine surgical practice, deriving at least one-third of their medical practice income from procedures requiring a hospital operating room setting. The inpatient surgeons were qualified to perform surgeries at the ASC and had a choice to do so (and earn the professional fees) in medically appropriate cases. Also, the inpatient surgeons comprised a small proportion of the surgeon investors, and a majority of them would use the ASC on a regular basis as part of their medical practice. The OIG found that this arrangement was distinguishable from potentially riskier arrangements in which few investing physicians actually used the ASC on a regular basis or in which investing physicians were significant potential referral sources for other investors or the ASC, as when primary care physicians invest in a surgical ASC or cardiologists invest in a cardiac surgery ASC.

Similarly, in finding that a joint venture ASC between a hospital and physicians was unlikely to be a vehicle for the investors to profit from referrals where the proposed ASC did not satisfy all of the elements of the Hospital/Physician ASC safe harbor because the hospital was in a position to refer patients to either the ASC or its investors, the OIG ruled in Advisory Opinion 01-17 that four safeguards proposed by the hospital mitigated any concerns about the hospital's ability to direct or influence referrals to the ASC.[598] These safeguards included:

(i) the hospital's restraint from requiring or encouraging hospital-affiliated physicians from referring patients to the ASC, the investing ophthalmologists, or their group practices;
(ii) the hospital's commitment not to track referrals made by hospital-affiliated physicians to the ASC, investing ophthalmologists, or their group practices;
(iii) compensation paid to hospital-affiliated physicians was determined at arm's length and at a fair market value and not related to the volume or value of referrals or other business generated by these physicians

597. *See id.* at 6 (determining that the potential for abusive referrals was sufficiently mitigated by a stipulation from the requestors certifying that no surgeon investor would refer patients for pain management procedures to be performed at the ASC, unless the procedure would be performed personally by the referring surgeon investor).

598. *See* OIG Advisory Opinion No. 01-17 (Oct. 10, 2001).

to or for the ASC, the investing ophthalmologists, or their group practices; and

(iv) hospital-affiliated physicians were informed of these measures.[599]

With the implementation of these safeguards, the OIG found that the ASC was unlikely to be a vehicle for the investors to profit from referrals by the hospital. However, by way of comparison, in OIG Advisory Opinion No. 03-5, the OIG found that the proposed arrangement would pose more than a minimal risk of fraud and abuse under the AKS.[600] This was because the proposed ASC was to be owned by a multispecialty group comprised of surgeons and fourteen family practitioners, eleven internists, six pediatricians, five obstetricians/gynecologists, two general surgeons, three orthopedic surgeons, and two ophthalmologists. The OIG opined that since the group was a multispecialty group, there was a substantial likelihood of cross-specialty referrals for services performed in the ASC, principally because few of the physician owners would actually use the ASC on a regular basis as part of their medical practice. The proposed arrangement would allow those physician owners for whom the ASC was not an extension of their office practices to profit from their referrals to the ASC or to their partners who perform procedures there. In this respect, the OIG reasoned that the proposed arrangement posed the same risks as an ASC owned directly by surgeons and primary care physicians in the same community.[601]

2.19. Price Reductions Offered to Eligible Managed Care Organizations

The safe harbor for price reductions offered to eligible managed care organizations (MCOs) is codified in statute and regulation. The AKS, at 42 U.S.C. § 1320a-7b(b)(3)(F), states that the AKS will not apply to "any remuneration between an organization and an individual or entity providing items or services, or a combination thereof, pursuant to a written agreement between the organization and the individual or entity if the organization is an eligible

599. *See id.*; *see also* OIG Advisory Opinion No. 03-2 (Jan. 13, 2003) (determining that the OIG would not impose administrative sanctions on a proposed ASC arrangement that included safeguards that limited the risk of fraud and abuse).

600. OIG Advisory Opinion No. 03-5 (Feb. 6, 2003).

601. *See generally* OIG Adv. Op. No. 07-13 (concluding that the proposed arrangement composed of optometrists and ophthalmologists had "no discernible safeguards to minimize significant risk" that investment in the ASC was for the purpose of inducing or rewarding referrals).

organization under section 1395mm of this title [authorizing payments to health maintenance organizations and competitive medical plans]. . . ." Consistent with this statutory protection, 42 C.F.R. § 1001.952(t) provides as follows:

(t) *Price reductions offered to eligible managed care organizations.*
(1) As used in section 1128(B) of the Act, "remuneration" does not include any payment between:
(i) An eligible managed care organization and any first tier contractor for providing or arranging for items or services, as long as the following three standards are met -
(A) The eligible managed care organization and the first tier contractor have an agreement that:
(1) Is set out in writing and signed by both parties;
(2) Specifies the items and services covered by the agreement;
(3) Is for a period of at least one year; and
(4) Specifies that the first tier contractor cannot claim payment in any form directly or indirectly from a Federal health care program for items or services covered under the agreement, except for:
(i) HMOs and competitive medical plans with cost-based contracts under section 1876 of the Act where the agreement with the eligible managed care organization sets out the arrangements in accordance with which the first tier contractor is billing the Federal health care program;
(ii) Federally qualified HMOs without a contract under sections 1854 or 1876 of the Act, where the agreement with the eligible managed care organization sets out the arrangements in accordance with which the first tier contractor is billing the Federal health care program; or
(iii) First tier contractors that are Federally qualified health centers that claim supplemental payments from a Federal health care program.
(B) In establishing the terms of the agreement, neither party gives or receives remuneration in return for

or to induce the provision or acceptance of business (other than business covered by the agreement) for which payment may be made in whole or in part by a Federal health care program on a fee-for-service or cost basis.

(C) Neither party to the agreement shifts the financial burden of the agreement to the extent that increased payments are claimed from a Federal health care program.

(ii) A first tier contractor and a downstream contractor or between two downstream contractors to provide or arrange for items or services, as long as the following four standards are met -

(A) The parties have an agreement that:

(1) Is set out in writing and signed by both parties;

(2) Specifies the items and services covered by the agreement;

(3) Is for a period of at least one year; and

(4) Specifies that the party providing the items or services cannot claim payment in any form from a Federal health care program for items or services covered under the agreement.

(B) In establishing the terms of the agreement, neither party gives or receives remuneration in return for or to induce the provision or acceptance of business (other than business covered by the agreement) for which payment may be made in whole or in part by a Federal health care program on a fee-for-service or cost basis.

(C) Neither party shifts the financial burden of the agreement to the extent that increased payments are claimed from a Federal health care program.

(D) The agreement between the eligible managed care organization and first tier contractor covering the items or services that are covered by the agreement between the parties does not involve:

(1) A Federally qualified health center receiving supplemental payments;

(2) A HMO or CMP with a cost-based contract under section 1876 of the Act; or

(3) A Federally qualified HMO, unless the items or services are covered by a risk based contract under sections 1854 or 1876 of the Act.

(2) For purposes of this paragraph, the following terms are defined as follows:

(i) *Downstream contractor* means an individual or entity that has a subcontract directly or indirectly with a first tier contractor for the provision or arrangement of items or services that are covered by an agreement between an eligible managed care organization and the first tier contractor.

(ii) *Eligible managed care organization*[602] means -

(A) A HMO or CMP with a risk or cost based contract in accordance with section 1876 of the Act;

(B) Any Medicare Part C health plan that receives a capitated payment from Medicare and which must have its total Medicare beneficiary cost sharing approved by CMS under section 1854 of the Act;

(C) Medicaid managed care organizations as defined in section 1903(m)(1)(A) that provide or arrange for items or services for Medicaid enrollees under a contract in accordance with section 1903(m) of the Act (except for fee-for-service plans or medical savings accounts);

(D) Any other health plans that provide or arrange for items and services for Medicaid enrollees in accordance with a risk-based contract with a State agency subject to the upper payment limits in § 447.361 of this title or an equivalent payment cap approved by the Secretary;

(E) Programs For All Inclusive Care For The Elderly (PACE) under sections 1894 and 1934 of the Act, except for for-profit demonstrations under sections 4801(h) and 4802(h) of Pub. L. 105-33; or

(F) A Federally qualified HMO.

602. The eligible managed care organizations in paragraphs (u)(2)(ii)(A)-(F) of this section are only eligible with respect to items or services covered by the contracts specified in those paragraphs.

(iii) *First tier contractor* means an individual or entity that has a contract directly with an eligible managed care organization to provide or arrange for items or services.

(iv) *Items and services* means health care items, devices, supplies or services or those services reasonably related to the provision of health care items, devices, supplies or services including, but not limited to, non-emergency transportation, patient education, attendant services, social services (e.g., case management), utilization review and quality assurance. Marketing and other pre-enrollment activities are not "items or services" for purposes of this section.

In 1999, OIG published an interim final rule establishing the above-quoted safe harbor, which corresponds to one of two statutory safe harbors relating to managed care arrangements found in 42 U.S.C. § 1320a-7b(b)(3)(F).[603] The first of these safe harbors, set forth in § 1001.952(t), "protects various financial arrangements between managed care entities that receive a fixed or capitated amount from the Federal health care programs and individuals and entities with whom the managed care entity contracts for the provision of health care items or services."[604] The OIG commented that both safe harbors were designed to "protect remuneration between parties where the remuneration is a price reduction for the provision of health care items or services" and that the safe harbors do not protect "[o]ther remuneration, such as profit distributions from investment interests in an entity with a risk sharing arrangement."[605] The OIG further clarified that any arrangement that protects remuneration that is covered by the safe harbors, and also remuneration that is not covered, would still receive protection for the former type of remuneration," and that "an arrangement that potentially falls within more than one safe harbor need only meet the requirements of one safe harbor."[606] The OIG also made a point of stating that the safe harbors "do not apply to other laws, such as State licensure laws, antitrust laws or other Federal and State health care fraud laws."[607]

For purposes of the safe harbor, an "eligible organization" includes federally qualified HMOs and competitive medical plans "that have entered into

603. Interim Final Rule: Federal Health Care Program, Fraud and Abuse, Statutory Exception to the anti-Kickback Statute for Shared Risk Arrangements (64 Fed. Reg. 63504, Nov. 19, 1999).

604. *Id.* at 63505.

605. *Id.* at 63506.

606. *Id.*

607. *Id.*

either risk or cost-based managed care contracts" with the CMS since the OIG recognized that eligible organizations with risk-based contracts "presented little or no risk of overutilization or increased costs to the Federal Health care programs, given applicable payment arrangements and regulatory oversight."[608] The OIG noted that "[w]hen plans are paid a capitated amount for all of the services they provide regardless of the dates, frequency or type of services, there is no incentive to overutilize" and that "even if overutilization occurs, the Federal health care programs are not at risk for these increased costs."[609] The safe harbor "extends protection from the anti-kickback statute beyond the managed care arrangements" specifically protected under the statutory exception by including "other programs where the Federal health care programs pay on a capitated or fixed aggregate basis, such as certain Medicare Part C plans."[610] The safe harbor also extends protection downstream to "subcontracts with other providers and entities to provide items and services in accordance with a protected managed care arrangement" and "regardless of the payment methodology" underlying the subcontracting arrangement, provided that the "aggregate financial exposure [to the Federal health care program] is fixed in accordance with its contract with the managed care organization."[611]

The safe harbor, however, also contains certain limitations. The protections for subcontractors "is limited to risk-based managed care plans that do not claim any payment from a Federal health care program" other than the capitated amount set forth in the agreement between MCO and the federal program.[612] Protections are not afforded to subcontractor arrangements that are "cost-based or where the prime contract is protected solely because the contracting entity is a Federally-qualified HMO" because in the former situation, reimbursement is "based on costs," and in the latter situation reimbursement is made "on a fee-for-service basis," both of which involve scenarios in which "reimbursement will increase with utilization, thus providing the same incentive to overutilize as any fee-for-service payment methodology."[613] Additionally, the safe harbor "only applies to remuneration for health care items and services and those items or services reasonably related to the

608. *Id.*
609. *Id.*
610. *Id.* at 63507.
611. *Id.*
612. *Id.*
613. *Id.*

provision" of such services and "does not cover marketing services or any services provided prior to a beneficiary's enrollment in a health plan."[614] Furthermore, "there is no protection if the financial arrangements under the managed care agreement are implicitly or explicitly part of a broader agreement to steer fee-for-service Federal health care program business to the entity giving the discount to induce the referral of managed care business."[615] The concern underlying these comments involves "swapping," whereby in "managed care arrangements low capitation rates could be traded for access to additional fee-for-service lines of business."[616] The OIG expressed concern for arrangements in which "discounts are in exchange for access to fee-for-service lines of business, where there is an incentive to overutilize services provided to Federal health care program beneficiaries."

2.20. Price Reductions Offered by Contractors with Substantial Financial Risk to Managed Care Organizations

The safe harbor for price reductions offered by contractors with substantial financial risk to managed care organizations is codified in statute and regulation. The AKS, at 42 U.S.C. § 1320a-7b(b)(3)(F), states that the AKS will not apply to "any remuneration between an organization and an individual or entity providing items or services, or a combination thereof, pursuant to a written agreement between the organization and the individual or entity . . . if the written agreement, through a risk-sharing arrangement, places the individual or entity at substantial financial risk for the cost or utilization of the items or services, or a combination thereof, which the individual or entity is obligated to provide." Consistent with this statutory protection, 42 C.F.R. § 1001.952(u) provides as follows:

> (u) *Price reductions offered by contractors with substantial financial risk to managed care organizations.*
>
> (1) As used in section 1128(B) of the Act, "remuneration" does not include any payment between:
>
> (i) A qualified managed care plan and a first tier contractor for providing or arranging for items or services, where the following five standards are met -

614. *Id.* This limitation also applies to § 1001.952(u).
615. *Id.*
616. *Id.*

(A) The agreement between the qualified managed care plan and first tier contractor must:
  (1) Be in writing and signed by the parties;
  (2) Specify the items and services covered by the agreement;
  (3) Be for a period of a least one year;
  (4) Require participation in a quality assurance program that promotes the coordination of care, protects against underutilization and specifies patient goals, including measurable outcomes where appropriate; and
  (5) Specify a methodology for determining payment that is commercially reasonable and consistent with fair market value established in an arms-length transaction and includes the intervals at which payments will be made and the formula for calculating incentives and penalties, if any.

(B) If a first tier contractor has an investment interest in a qualified managed care plan, the investment interest must meet the criteria of paragraph (a)(1) of this section.

(C) The first tier contractor must have substantial financial risk for the cost or utilization of services it is obligated to provide through one of the following four payment methodologies:
  (1) A periodic fixed payment per patient that does not take into account the dates services are provided, the frequency of services, or the extent or kind of services provided;
  (2) Percentage of premium;
  (3) Inpatient Federal health care program diagnosis-related groups (DRGs) (other than those for psychiatric services);
  (4) Bonus and withhold arrangements, provided -
    (i) The target payment for first tier contractors that are individuals or non-institutional providers is at least 20 percent greater than the minimum payment, and for first tier

contractors that are institutional providers, i.e., hospitals and nursing homes, is at least 10 percent greater than the minimum payment;

(ii) The amount at risk, *i.e.,* the bonus or withhold, is earned by a first tier contractor in direct proportion to the ratio of the contractor's actual utilization to its target utilization;

(iii) In calculating the percentage in accordance with paragraph (u)(1)(i)(C)(*4*)(*i*) of this section, both the target payment amount and the minimum payment amount include any performance bonus, e.g., payments for timely submission of paperwork, continuing medical education, meeting attendance, etc., at a level achieved by 75 percent of the first tier contractors who are eligible for such payments;

(iv) Payment amounts, including any bonus or withhold amounts, are reasonable given the historical utilization patterns and costs for the same or comparable populations in similar managed care arrangements; and

(v) Alternatively, for a first tier contractor that is a physician, the qualified managed care plan has placed the physician at risk for referral services in an amount that exceeds the substantial financial risk threshold set forth in 42 CFR 417.479(f) and the arrangement is in compliance with the stop-loss and beneficiary survey requirements of 42 CFR 417.479(g).

(D) Payments for items and services reimbursable by Federal health care program must comply with the following two standards -

(1) The qualified managed care plan (or in the case of a self-funded employer plan that contracts with a qualified managed care plan to provide administrative services, the self-funded employer plan) must submit the claims directly to the Federal health care program, in accordance with a valid reassignment agreement, for items or services reimbursed by the Federal health care program. (Notwithstanding the foregoing, inpatient hospital services, other than psychiatric services, will be deemed to comply if the hospital is reimbursed by a Federal health care program under a DRG methodology.)

(2) Payments to first tier contractors and any downstream contractors for providing or arranging for items or services reimbursed by a Federal health care program must be identical to payment arrangements to or between such parties for the same items or services provided to other beneficiaries with similar health status, provided that such payments may be adjusted where the adjustments are related to utilization patterns or costs of providing items or services to the relevant population.

(E) In establishing the terms of an arrangement -

(1) Neither party gives or receives remuneration in return for or to induce the provision or acceptance of business (other than business covered by the arrangement) for which payment may be made in whole or in part by a Federal health care program on a fee-for-service or cost basis; and

(2) Neither party to the arrangement shifts the financial burden of such arrangement to the extent that increased payments are claimed from a Federal health care program.

(ii) A first tier contractor and a downstream contractor, or between downstream contractors, to provide or arrange for items or services, as long as the following three standards are met -

(A) Both parties are being paid for the provision or arrangement of items or services in accordance with one of the payment methodologies set out in paragraph (u)(1)(i)(C) of this section;

(B) Payment arrangements for items and services reimbursable by a Federal health care program comply with paragraph (u)(1)(i)(D) of this section; and

(C) In establishing the terms of an arrangement -

(1) Neither party gives or receives remuneration in return for or to induce the provision or acceptance of business (other than business covered by the arrangement) for which payment may be made in whole or in part by a Federal health care program on a fee-for-service or cost basis; and

(2) Neither party to the arrangement shifts the financial burden of the arrangement to the extent that increased payments are claimed from a Federal health care program.

(2) For purposes of this paragraph, the following terms are defined as follows:

(i) *Downstream contractor* means an individual or entity that has a subcontract directly or indirectly with a first tier contractor for the provision or arrangement of items or services that are covered by an agreement between a qualified managed care plan and the first tier contractor.

(ii) *First tier contractor* means an individual or entity that has a contract directly with a qualified managed care plan to provide or arrange for items or services.

(iii) *Is obligated to provide* for a contractor refers to items or services:

(A) Provided directly by an individual or entity and its employees;

(B) For which an individual or entity is financially responsible, but which are provided by downstream contractors;

(C) For which an individual or entity makes referrals or arrangements; or

(D) For which an individual or entity receives financial incentives based on its own, its provider group's, or its qualified managed care plan's performance (or combination thereof).

(iv) *Items and services* means health care items, devices, supplies or services or those services reasonably related to the provision of health care items, devices, supplies or services including, but not limited to, non-emergency transportation, patient education, attendant services, social services (e.g., case management), utilization review and quality assurance. Marketing or other pre-enrollment activities are not "items or services" for purposes of this definition in this paragraph.

(v) *Minimum payment* is the guaranteed amount that a provider is entitled to receive under an agreement with a first tier or downstream contractor or a qualified managed care plan.

(vi) *Qualified managed care plan* means a health plan as defined in paragraph (l)(2) of this section that:

(A) Provides a comprehensive range of health services;

(B) Provides or arranges for -

(1) Reasonable utilization goals to avoid inappropriate utilization;

(2) An operational utilization review program;

(3) A quality assurance program that promotes the coordination of care, protects against underutilization, and specifies patient goals, including measurable outcomes where appropriate;

(4) Grievance and hearing procedures;

(5) Protection of enrollees from incurring financial liability other than copayments and deductibles; and

(6) Treatment for Federal health care program beneficiaries that is not different than treatment for other enrollees because of their status as Federal health care program beneficiaries; and

(C) Covers a beneficiary population of which either -

(1) No more than 10 percent are Medicare beneficiaries, not including persons for whom a Federal health care program is the secondary payer; or

(2) No more than 50 percent are Medicare beneficiaries (not including persons for whom a Federal health care program is the secondary payer), provided that payment of premiums is on a periodic basis that does not take into account the dates services are rendered, the frequency of services, or the extent or kind of services rendered, and provided further that such periodic payments for the non-Federal health care program beneficiaries do not take into account the number of Federal health care program fee-for-service beneficiaries covered by the agreement or the amount of services generated by such beneficiaries.

(vii) *Target payment* means the fair market value payment established through arms length negotiations that will be earned by an individual or entity that:

(A) Is dependent on the individual or entity's meeting a utilization target or range of utilization targets that are set consistent with historical utilization rates for the same or comparable populations in similar managed care arrangements, whether based on its own, its provider group's or the qualified managed care plan's utilization (or a combination thereof); and

(B) Does not include any bonus or fees that the individual or entity may earn from exceeding the utilization target.

In 1999, the OIG published an interim final rule establishing the above-quoted safe harbor, which corresponds to one of two statutory safe harbors relating to managed care arrangements found in 42 U.S.C. § 1320a-7b(b)(3)(F).[617] The second of these safe harbors, set forth in § 1001.952(u), "protects contractual relationships between managed care entities and their

617. Interim Final Rule: Federal Health Care Program, Fraud and Abuse, Statutory Exception to the Anti-Kickback Statute for (64 Fed. Reg. 63504, Nov. 19, 1999).

contractors and subcontractors where the contractors and subcontractors are at *substantial financial risk* for the cost or utilization of items or services they provide or order for Federal health care program beneficiaries."[618] The OIG recognized that "there are few existing managed care arrangements that would qualify under [this safe harbor] that are not otherwise covered by the safe harbor in [§ 1001.952(t)]" because most such arrangements "do *not* place their contractors and subcontractors at substantial financial risk for the cost or utilization of items or services to Federal health care program beneficiaries" and usually such contractors and subcontractors "are reimbursed directly by the Federal payor on a fee-for-service basis."[619]

Notwithstanding this fact, the OIG decided to adopt this safe harbor in order to protect "a category of arrangements that *could* qualify for protection."[620] The OIG commented that both safe harbors were designed to "protect remuneration between parties where the remuneration is a price reduction for the provision of health care items or services" and that the safe harbors do not protect "[o]ther remuneration, such as profit distributions from investment interests in an entity with a risk sharing arrangement."[621] The OIG further clarified that any arrangement that protects remuneration that is covered by the safe harbors, and also remuneration that is not covered, would still receive protection for the former type of remuneration, and that "an arrangement that potentially falls within more than one safe harbor need only meet the requirements of one safe harbor."[622] The OIG also made a point of stating that the safe harbors "do not apply to other laws, such as State licensure laws, antitrust laws or other Federal and State health care fraud laws."[623]

2.21. Ambulance Replenishing

The safe harbor for ambulance replenishment services, codified at 42 C.F.R. § 1001.952(v), states:

(v) Ambulance replenishing

(1) As used in section 1128B of the Act, "remuneration" does not include any gift or transfer of drugs or medical supplies

618. *Id.* at 63505.
619. *Id.* at 63505-06.
620. *Id.*
621. *Id.* at 63506.
622. *Id.*
623. *Id.*

(including linens) by a hospital or other receiving facility to an ambulance provider for the purpose of replenishing comparable drugs or medical supplies (including linens) used by the ambulance provider (or a first responder) in connection with the transport of a patient by ambulance to the hospital or other receiving facility if all of the standards in paragraph (v)(2) of this section are satisfied and all of the applicable standards in either paragraph (v)(3)(i), (v)(3)(ii) or (v)(3)(iii) of this section are satisfied. However, to qualify under paragraph (v), the ambulance that is replenished must be used to provide emergency ambulance services an average of three times per week, as measured over a reasonable period of time. Drugs and medical supplies (including linens) initially used by a first responder and replenished at the scene of the illness or injury by the ambulance provider that transports the patient to the hospital or other receiving facility will be deemed to have been used by the ambulance provider.

(2) To qualify under paragraph (v) of this section, the ambulance replenishing arrangement must satisfy all of the following four conditions -

(i) (A) Under no circumstances may the ambulance provider (or first responder) and the receiving facility both bill for the same replenished drug or supply. Replenished drugs or supplies may only be billed (including claiming bad debt) to a Federal health care program by either the ambulance provider (or first responder) or the receiving facility.

(B) All billing or claims submission by the receiving facility, ambulance provider or first responder for replenished drugs and medical supplies used in connection with the transport of a Federal health care program beneficiary must comply with all applicable Federal health care program payment and coverage rules and regulations.

(C) Compliance with paragraph (v)(2)(i)(B) of this section will be determined separately for the receiving facility and the ambulance provider (and first responder, if any), so long as the receiving facility, ambulance provider (or first responder) refrains from doing anything that would impede the other party or parties from meeting their obligations under paragraph (v)(2)(i)(B).

(ii) (A) The receiving facility or ambulance provider, or both, must

(1) Maintain records of the replenished drugs and medical supplies and the patient transport to which the replenished drugs and medical supplies related;

(2) Provide a copy of such records to the other party within a reasonable time (unless the other party is separately maintaining records of the replenished drugs and medical supplies); and

(3) Make those records available to the Secretary promptly upon request.

(B) A pre-hospital care report (including, but not limited to, a trip sheet, patient care report or patient encounter report) prepared by the ambulance provider and filed with the receiving facility will meet the requirements of paragraph (v)(2)(ii)(A) of this section, provided that it documents the specific type and amount of medical supplies and drugs used on the patient and subsequently replenished.

(C) For purposes of paragraph (v)(2)(ii) of this section, documentation may be maintained and, if required, filed with the other party in hard copy or electronically. If a replenishing arrangement includes linens, documentation need not be maintained for their exchange. If documentation is not maintained for the exchange of linens, the receiving facility will be presumed to have provided an exchange of comparable clean linens for soiled linens for each ambulance transport of a patient to the receiving facility. Records required under paragraph (v)(2)(ii)(A) of this section must be maintained for 5 years.

(iii) The replenishing arrangement must not take into account the volume or value of any referrals or business otherwise generated between the parties for which payment may be made in whole or in part under any Federal health care program (other than the referral of the particular patient to whom the replenished drugs and medical supplies were furnished).

(iv) The receiving facility and the ambulance provider otherwise comply with all Federal, State, and local laws regulating ambulance services, including, but not limited to, emergency services, and the provision of drugs and medical supplies, including, but not limited to, laws relating to the handling of controlled substances.

(3) To qualify under paragraph (v) of this section, the arrangement must satisfy all of the standards in one of the following three categories:

(i) General replenishing

(A) The receiving facility must replenish medical supplies or drugs on an equal basis for all ambulance providers that bring patients to the receiving facility in any one of the categories described in paragraph (v)(3)(i)(A)(1), (2), or (3) of this section. A receiving facility may offer replenishing to one or more of the categories and may offer different replenishing arrangements to different categories, so long as the replenishing is conducted uniformly within each category. For example, a receiving facility may offer to replenish a broader array of drugs or supplies for ambulance providers that do no not charge for their services than for ambulance providers that charge for their services. Within each category, the receiving facility may limit its replenishing arrangements to the replenishing of emergency ambulance transports only. A receiving facility may offer replenishing to one or more of the categories -

(1) All ambulance providers that do not bill any patient or insurer (including Federal health care programs) for ambulance services, regardless of the payor or the patient's ability to pay (i.e., ambulance providers, such as volunteer

companies, that provide ambulance services without charge to any person or entity);

(2) All not-for-profit and State or local government ambulance service providers (including, but not limited to, municipal and volunteer ambulance services providers); or

(3) All ambulance service providers.

(B) (1) The replenishing arrangement must be conducted in an open and public manner. A replenishing arrangement will be considered to be conducted in an open and public manner if one of the following two conditions are satisfied:

(i) A written disclosure of the replenishing program is posted conspicuously in the receiving facility's emergency room or other location where the ambulance providers deliver patients and copies are made available upon request to ambulance providers, Government representatives, and members of the public (subject to reasonable photocopying charges). The written disclosure can take any reasonable form and should include the category of ambulance service providers that qualifies for replenishment; the drugs or medical supplies included in the replenishment program; and the procedures for documenting the replenishment. A sample disclosure form is included in appendix A to subpart C of this part for illustrative purposes only. No written contracts between the parties are required for purposes of paragraph (v)(3)(i)(B)(1)(i) of this section; or

(ii) The replenishment arrangement operates in accordance with a plan or protocol of general application promulgated by an Emergency Medical Services (EMS) Council or comparable entity, agency or organization,

provided a copy of the plan or protocol is available upon request to ambulance providers, Government representatives and members of the public (subject to reasonable photocopying charges). While parties are encouraged to participate in collaborative, comprehensive, community-wide EMS systems to improve the delivery of EMS in their local communities, nothing in this paragraph shall be construed as requiring the involvement of such organizations or the development or implementation of ambulance replenishment plans or protocols by such organizations.

(2) Nothing in this paragraph (v)(3)(i) shall be construed as requiring disclosure of confidential proprietary or financial information related to the replenishing arrangement (including, but not limited to, information about cost, pricing or the volume of replenished drugs or supplies) to ambulance providers or members of the general public.

(ii) Fair market value replenishing

(A) Except as otherwise provided in paragraph (v)(3)(ii)(B) of this section, the ambulance provider must pay the receiving facility fair market value, based on an arms-length transaction, for replenished medical supplies; and

(B) If payment is not made at the same time as the replenishing of the medical supplies, the receiving facility and the ambulance provider must make commercially reasonable payment arrangements in advance.

(iii) Government mandated replenishing. The replenishing arrangement is undertaken in accordance with a State or local statute, ordinance, regulation or binding protocol that requires hospitals or receiving facilities in the area subject to such requirement to replenish ambulances that deliver patients to the hospital with drugs or medical supplies (including linens) that are used during the transport of that patient.

(4) For purposes of paragraph (v) of this section -

(i) A receiving facility is a hospital or other facility that provides emergency medical services.

(ii) An ambulance provider is a provider or supplier of ambulance transport services that provides emergency ambulance services. The term does not include a provider of ambulance transport services that provides only non-emergency transport services.

(iii) A first responder includes, but is not limited to, a fire department, paramedic service or search and rescue squad that responds to an emergency call (through 9-1-1 or other emergency access number) and treats the patient, but does not transport the patient to the hospital or other receiving facility.

(iv) An emergency ambulance service is a transport by ambulance initiated as a result of a call through 9-1-1 or other emergency access number or a call from another acute care facility unable to provide the higher level care required by the patient and available at the receiving facility.

(v) Medical supplies includes linens, unless otherwise provided.

The safe harbor provision for Ambulance Replenishing was enacted in 2001. Ambulance restocking deals before the passage of this safe harbor were often deemed to violate the AKS by giving a material benefit to those that bring in patients to hospitals. HHS noted that there was a potential for abuse with these arrangements, even though the vast majority of ambulance restocking arrangements are believed to be lawful under the AKS.[624] HHS acknowledged the need for this safe harbor in the final version by saying, "We fully recognize the importance of ambulances being restocked and ready for emergency use at all times. Properly structured restocking arrangements contribute to this laudable goal without significant risk of fraud or

624. Final Rule: OIG Ambulance Replenishing Safe Harbor Under the Anti-Kickback Statute, 66 Fed. Reg. 233, 62979, 62980 (Dec. 4, 2001).

abuse."[625] The intention of this safe harbor was to provide protection for the "vast majority of ambulance restocking arrangements" and subsequently enhance the ability of EMS to benefit the entire community.[626] The safe harbor covers drugs, supplies, and linens used for the care of patients either on the scene or in transit in an ambulance. The final rule was written as an expansion of the scope of the safe harbor, with less ambiguity, and granted more autonomy for those who enter a replenishing agreement.[627]

The federal government's first public mention of ambulance replenishing arrangements was in a 1997 advisory opinion that indicated that a certain ambulatory restocking arrangement would be in violation of the AKS.[628] This led to fear among the medical community that ambulance replenishment would not be a protected agreement.[629] However, following this negative document, the OIG offered several positive advisory opinions on the matter. A proposal for an ambulance replenishing safe harbor was offered in a 2000 advisory opinion, before the final rule was enacted.[630]

The final rule outlines regulations for three categories of replenishing arrangements: (1) general restocking, (2) fair market value restocking, and (3) government-mandated restocking. "Parties need only satisfy the conditions applicable to any one of these categories."[631] All three categories are first governed by certain overarching regulations, codified at § 1001.952(v)(2), and then by the arrangement-specific regulations, codified at § 1001.952(v)(3).[632]

There are four conditions that apply to all replenishing arrangements:

1. Appropriate billing of federal health care programs. The ambulance provider and the hospital are not allowed to both bill for the same restocked drugs or supplies. However, improper billing by one party does not necessitate improper billing by the other party. "For example, if a hospital improperly bills for restocked supplies, the ambulance provider who received the supplies may still be protected, so long as the

625. *Id.*

626. Proposed Rule: OIG Ambulance Replenishing Safe Harbor Under the Anti-Kickback Statute, 65 Fed. Reg. 99, 32060, 32061 (May 22, 2000).

627. Final Rule: OIG Ambulance Replenishing Safe Harbor Under the Anti-Kickback Statute, 66 Fed. Reg. 233, 62979,62980 (Dec. 4, 2001).

628. OIG Advisory Opinion No. 97-6 (Oct. 8, 1997).

629. Final Rule: OIG Ambulance Replenishing Safe Harbor Under the Anti-Kickback Statute, 66 Fed. Reg. 233, 62979,62982 (Dec. 4, 2001).

630. OIG Advisory Opinion No. 00-9 (Dec. 8, 2000).

631. Final Rule: OIG Ambulance Replenishing Safe Harbor Under the Anti-Kickback Statute, 66 Fed. Reg. 233, 62979,62981 (Dec. 4, 2001).

632. 42 C.F.R. § 1001.952.

provider has not done anything to impede the hospital's compliance with the billing rules."[633]

2. Documentation requirements. "Under the final rule, either the hospital or the ambulance provider may generate the necessary documentation, so long as the other party receives and maintains a copy of it for 5 years."[634]
3. No ties or referrals. This condition is a safeguard that prohibits any restocking arrangement from being predicated on, or taking into account, the volume or value of referrals or other business between the parties.
4. Compliance with all other laws. Both the receiving facility and ambulance provider must comply with all other federal and state laws.[635]

For general restocking, an agreement in which a provider pays either nothing or some discounted amount for restocked drugs and supplies, the agreement must adhere to two conditions. First, the receiving party must restock supplies and drugs on an equal basis for ambulance providers in one or more of the following three categories: "(i) All ambulance providers; (ii) all non-profit and governmental providers; or (iii) all non-charging providers (typically volunteers and municipal providers)."[636] A receiving facility can offer restocking to any number of the three categories and may offer different programs to the different categories. However, within each category, the program must be the same for any provider.

Second, all restocking agreements must be made public. An agreement will be considered public if, "(i) The arrangement is memorialized in a conspicuously posted writing that outlines the terms of the restocking program and copies are available publicly (a sample disclosure form is included in the regulations); or (ii) The restocking program operates in accordance with a plan or protocol of general application promulgated by an EMS council or comparable organization."[637] Confidential or proprietary information does not need to be disclosed in these writings.[638]

633. Final Rule: OIG Ambulance Replenishing Safe Harbor Under the Anti-Kickback Statute, 66 Fed. Reg. 233, 62979, 62981 (Dec. 4, 2001).

634. *Id.*

635. *Id.*

636. *Id.*

637. *Id.*

638. *Id.*

Fair market value restocking, agreements that have ambulance providers paying fair market value for restocked medical supplies (though the resale of drugs is not included, as that is covered by the Prescription Drug Marketing Act), must satisfy two conditions: "(i) The restocking must be at fair market value, and (ii) payment arrangements must be commercially reasonable and made in advance."[639]

Government-mandated restocking, agreements that are ordered by local statutes, has no additional conditions to be met other than adherence to the regulation.[640]

As with all safe harbors, failure to meet the terms of the ambulance replenishment safe harbor does not necessarily mean an arrangement would be in violation of the AKS. Instead, such arrangements must be evaluated on a case-by-case basis.[641] Further, HHS clarified that participation in restocking agreements by either party is not required. "All ambulance providers in a service area are not required to participate in order for an arrangement to fit in the safe harbor. Under the proposed rule, we did not intend to require all ambulance providers and receiving facilities in a service area actually to participate in a restocking arrangement in order for the arrangement to qualify for safe harbor protection."[642]

Two Advisory Opinions have been issued regarding this safe harbor since its enactment. The first, Advisory Opinion No. 02-2, addressed concerns about free replenishing for emergency ambulances from a receiving facility. The arrangement was deemed acceptable because of the general replenishment subsection, which allows for free or discounted rates of restocking, provided that the offer is made to all ambulance providers.[643] This opinion further solidifies the comprehensive and clear language of the statute at § 1001.952(v)(3)(i).[644] The second, Advisory Opinion No. 02-3, further clarifies the general replenishment category of arrangements. A formal region-wide policy of ambulance replenishment was implemented that satisfied the criteria of the safe harbor. All of the ambulances of the same category were offered the same arrangement, and the definition of emergency transports met the standards of the safe harbor.[645]

639. *Id.* at 62981-82.
640. *Id.* at 62982.
641. *Id.*
642. *Id.* at 62984.
643. OIG Advisory Opinion No. 02-2 (Apr. 11, 2002).
644. 42 C.F.R. § 1001.952(v)(3)(i).
645. OIG Advisory Opinion No. 02-3 (Apr. 11, 2002).

2.22. Health Centers

The safe harbor for health centers is codified at 42 C.F.R. § 1001.952(w):

(w) *Health centers.* As used in [the AKS], "remuneration" does not include the transfer of any goods, items, services, donations or loans (whether the donation or loan is in cash or in-kind), or combination thereof from an individual or entity to a health center (as defined in this paragraph), as long as the following nine standards are met -

(1)

(i) The transfer is made pursuant to a contract, lease, grant, loan, or other agreement that -

(A) Is set out in writing;

(B) Is signed by the parties; and

(C) Covers, and specifies the amount of, all goods, items, services, donations, or loans to be provided by the individual or entity to the health center.

(ii) The amount of goods, items, services, donations, or loans specified in the agreement in accordance with paragraph (w)(1)(i)(C) of this section may be a fixed sum, fixed percentage, or set forth by a fixed methodology. The amount may not be conditioned on the volume or value of Federal health care program business generated between the parties. The written agreement will be deemed to cover all goods, items, services, donations, or loans provided by the individual or entity to the health center as required by paragraph (w)(1)(i)(C) of this section if all separate agreements between the individual or entity and the health center incorporate each other by reference or if they cross-reference a master list of agreements that is maintained centrally, is kept up to date, and is available for review by the Secretary upon request. The master list should be maintained in a manner that preserves the historical record of arrangements.

(2) The goods, items, services, donations, or loans are medical or clinical in nature or relate directly to services provided by the health center as part of the scope of the health center's section 330 grant (including, by way of example, billing

services, administrative support services, technology support, and enabling services, such as case management, transportation, and translation services, that are within the scope of the grant).

(3) The health center reasonably expects the arrangement to contribute meaningfully to the health center's ability to maintain or increase the availability, or enhance the quality, of services provided to a medically underserved population served by the health center, and the health center documents the basis for the reasonable expectation prior to entering the arrangement. The documentation must be made available to the Secretary upon request.

(4) At reasonable intervals, but at least annually, the health center must re-evaluate the arrangement to ensure that the arrangement is expected to continue to satisfy the standard set forth in paragraph (w)(3) of this section, and must document the re-evaluation contemporaneously. The documentation must be made available to the Secretary upon request. Arrangements must not be renewed or renegotiated unless the health center reasonably expects the standard set forth in paragraph (w)(3) of this section to be satisfied in the next agreement term. Renewed or renegotiated agreements must comply with the requirements of paragraph (w)(3) of this section.

(5) The individual or entity does not

(i) Require the health center (or its affiliated health care professionals) to refer patients to a particular individual or entity, or

(ii) restrict the health center (or its affiliated health care professionals) from referring patients to any individual or entity.

(6) Individuals and entities that offer to furnish goods, items, or services without charge or at a reduced charge to the health center must furnish such goods, items, or services to all patients from the health center who clinically qualify for the goods, items, or services, regardless of the patient's payor status or ability to pay. The individual or entity may impose reasonable limits on the aggregate volume or value of the goods, items, or services furnished under the arrangement with the

health center, provided such limits do not take into account a patient's payor status or ability to pay.

(7) The agreement must not restrict the health center's ability, if it chooses, to enter into agreements with other providers or suppliers of comparable goods, items, or services, or with other lenders or donors. Where a health center has multiple individuals or entities willing to offer comparable remuneration, the health center must employ a reasonable methodology to determine which individuals or entities to select and must document its determination. In making these determinations, health centers should look to the procurement standards for beneficiaries of Federal grants set forth in 45 CFR 75.326 through 75.340.

(8) The health center must provide effective notification to patients of their freedom to choose any willing provider or supplier. In addition, the health center must disclose the existence and nature of an agreement under paragraph (w)(1) of this section to any patient who inquires. The health center must provide such notification or disclosure in a timely fashion and in a manner reasonably calculated to be effective and understood by the patient.

(9) The health center may, at its option, elect to require that an individual or entity charge a referred health center patient the same rate it charges other similarly situated patients not referred by the health center or that the individual or entity charge a referred health center patient a reduced rate (where the discount applies to the total charge and not just to the cost-sharing portion owed by an insured patient).

Note to paragraph (w):

For purposes of this paragraph, the term "health center" means a Federally Qualified Health Center under section 1905(l)(2)(B)(i) or 1905(l)(2)(B)(ii) of the Act, and "medically underserved population" means a medically underserved population as defined in regulations at 42 CFR 51c.102(e).

The OIG proposed this safe harbor in 2005[646] in compliance with section 431 of the Medicare Prescription Drug, Improvement, and Modernization Act of 2003 (MMA). As explained by the OIG in the Final Rule:

> Section 431 of MMA amended the anti-kickback statute to create a new safe harbor for certain agreements involving health centers. Specifically, section 431(a) of MMA excludes from the reach of the anti-kickback statute any remuneration between: (i) A health center described under section 1905(l)(2)(B)(i) or 1905(l)(2)(B)(ii) of the Act; and (ii) an individual or entity providing goods, items, services, donations, loans, or a combination of these to the health center pursuant to a contract, lease, grant, loan, or other agreement, provided that such agreement contributes to the health center's ability to maintain or increase the availability, or enhance the quality, of services provided to a medically underserved population served by the health center.
>
> In other words, Congress intended to permit health centers to accept certain remuneration that would otherwise implicate the anti-kickback statute when the remuneration furthers a core purpose of the Federal health centers program: ensuring the availability and quality of safety net health care services to otherwise underserved populations.[647]

The OIG further explained the history of the federal health center initiative:

> Beginning in the 1960s, Congress enacted various health center programs to assist the large number of individuals living in medically underserved areas, as well as the growing number of special populations with limited access to preventive and primary health care services. . . .
>
> . . .
>
> Health centers receiving section 330 grant funding must provide, either directly or through contracts or cooperative arrangements, a broad range of required primary health care services, including clinical services by physicians, and, where appropriate, physician assistants, nurse practitioners, and nurse midwives; diagnostic laboratory and radiological services; preventive health services; emergency medical

646. Proposed Rule: Safe Harbor for Federally Qualified Health Centers Under the Anti-Kickback Statute (70 Fed. Reg. 38081; July 1, 2005).

647. Final Rule: Safe Harbor for Federally Qualified Health Centers Arrangements Under the Anti-Kickback Statute (72 Fed. Reg. 56632, 56634; Oct. 4, 2007).

> services; certain pharmaceutical services; referrals to other providers (including substance abuse and mental health services); patient case management; services that enable individuals to use the services of the health center (*e.g.*, outreach, transportation, and translation services); and patient and community education services. 42 U.S.C. 254b(b)(1). They may also provide certain additional health services that are appropriate to serve the health needs of the population served by the health center. 42 U.S.C. 254b(b)(2). These additional health services may include mental health and substance abuse services; recuperative care services; environmental health services; special occupation-related health services for migratory and seasonal agricultural workers; programs to control infectious disease; and injury prevention programs.
>
> Consistent with their mission and the terms of their PHS grants, section 330 grant recipients serve predominantly low-income individuals, including some beneficiaries of the Medicare and Medicaid programs. . . .
>
> . . .
>
> Frequently, health centers are provided with, or seek out, opportunities to enter into arrangements with hospitals or other providers or suppliers to further the health centers' patient care mission. For example, providers or suppliers may agree to provide health centers with capital development grants, low cost (or no cost) loans, reduced price services, or in-kind donations of supplies, equipment, or space.
>
> Some providers and suppliers expressed concern that remuneration offered to health centers might be viewed as suspect under the anti-kickback statute, because the health centers are frequently in a position to refer Federal health care program beneficiaries to the provider or supplier. Accordingly, Congress enacted section 431 of MMA to enable some health centers to conserve section 330 and other monies by accepting needed goods, items, services, donations, or loans for free or at reduced rates from willing providers and suppliers.[648]

As adopted, the safe harbor regulation "protects remuneration in the form of goods, items, services, donations or loans (whether the donation or loan is in cash or in-kind), or a combination thereof provided by a Donor to a qualifying health center."[649] The remuneration "must be medical or clinical in nature or relate directly to services provided by the health center as

648. *Id.* at 56633-34.
649. *Id.* at 56635.

part of the scope of the health center's section 330 grant," and a "protected arrangement must contribute to the ability of the health center to maintain or increase the availability of, or enhance the quality of, services provided to a medically underserved population."[650] The OIG further explains:

> Protected arrangements must be pursuant to a contract, lease, grant, loan, or other agreement that is written, signed by the parties, and covers all of the remuneration to be provided. The amount of the remuneration must be specified and not be conditioned on the volume or value of Federal health care program business generated between the parties.
>
> Health centers must reasonably expect before entering into an agreement that the arrangement is likely to contribute to the health center's ability to maintain or increase the availability, or enhance the quality, of services provided to a medically underserved population as defined at 42 U.S.C. 254b(b)(3). Health centers must document the basis for their determination that the arrangement will yield such a benefit. Health centers must periodically reevaluate agreements to ensure ongoing compliance with the benefit standard. These determinations must be contemporaneously documented.
>
> Health centers must not be required to refer patients to a particular provider or supplier under the arrangement, and must be free to refer patients to any provider or supplier. In addition, Donors that offer to furnish goods, items, or services for health center patients must furnish those goods, items, or services to all health center patients who clinically qualify for them, regardless of payor status or ability to pay.
>
> Health centers are required to provide effective notification to patients of their freedom to choose any willing provider or supplier and to disclose to patients, upon request, the existence and nature of the arrangement with the Donor.
>
> The safe harbor makes clear that a health center may, at its option, require a Donor that enters into a protected arrangement to charge a referred health center patient the same rate it charges other similarly situated persons not referred by the health center or furnish items or services to health center patients at a reduced rate (where the discount applies to the total charge and not just the cost-sharing portion owed by an insured patient).[651]

650. *Id.*
651. *Id.*

The OIG clarified that protected remuneration under the safe harbor "would generally extend to community benefit grants or similar payments, even where such grants or payments are subject to a reconciliation provision . . . [if] the reconciliation methodology is fixed in advance and does not hinge on the volume or value of referrals from the health center to the Donor."[652] Further, "[d]onations and loans need not be limited to in-kind goods or services, and indeed may be in monetary form."[653] Donations, however, must be for the purpose of benefiting the health center to receive protection. According to the OIG, "Congress did not intend the safe harbor to protect arrangements where the donation primarily creates a benefit to the Donor instead of to the health center."[654] Likewise, the OIG stated that the safe harbor "would not protect an arrangement where a Donor used the health center as a conduit to transfer remuneration to a particular recruited physician; to transfer remuneration specifically for the purpose of recruiting a physician to join the Donor's medical staff, or to practice in the Donor's service area; or to transfer remuneration to existing group practices."[655] Nor does the safe harbor "protect remuneration transferred to an individual affiliated with a health center" or "remuneration transferred from a health center to an individual or entity."[656]

The OIG also set forth guidelines for health centers to follow when evaluating arrangements with potential donors for funds to support physician recruitment, commenting that "health centers should consider whether the remuneration would be used for expenses commonly or typically borne by the health center, such that the arrangement results in measurable savings that will benefit a medically underserved population, or would be used to recruit a health care professional needed by the health center to serve a medically underserved population, or would be used to recruit a health care professional needed by the health center to serve a medically underserved population."[657] The OIG noted that if a recruited physician joined a health center's staff, that "would be some evidence that the benefit primarily runs to medically underserved populations served by the health center as opposed to the Donor."[658]

652. *Id.* at 56637.
653. *Id.*
654. *Id.*
655. *Id.*
656. *Id.*
657. *Id.*
658. *Id.*

Regarding the transfer of goods, items, services, donations, or loans that are "medical or clinical in nature," the OIG explained that this category

> broadly covers all medical or clinical services (*e.g.*, physician services, nurse practitioner and physician assistant services, diagnostic services, therapeutic services, etc.); medical or clinical goods and items (*e.g.*, pharmaceuticals, knee braces, stethoscopes, x-ray machines, etc.); donations of money or other forms of remuneration that the health center can use to furnish medical or clinical services or to acquire goods, items, or services that are medical or clinical in nature; and loans of money or other forms of remuneration that the health center can use to furnish medical or clinical services or to acquire goods, items, or services that are medical or clinical in nature.[659]

Commenting on the safe harbor's writing requirement, the OIG clarified that the safe harbor "requires the documentation of all arrangements for the transfer of goods, items, services, donations, or loans from a Donor to a health center."[660]

As to the requirement in subparagraph (3) that the center "reasonably expects the arrangement to contribute meaningfully to the health center's ability to maintain or increase the availability, or enhance the quality, of services provided to a medically underserved population served by the health center," the OIG confirmed that the rule "does not require a financial gain to the health center and does not require direct savings of [health center] funding."[661] Satisfying this requirement will depend on the "specific facts and circumstances," but the OIG believes that "health centers are well-situated in the first instance to make a reasonable determination whether an arrangement contributes meaningfully to the health center's ability to maintain or increase the availability, or enhance the quality of, services provided to a medically underserved population," and that they "should have flexibility in making these determinations."[662] The OIG listed several "exemplar" considerations that could factor into this determination, although it made clear that it is not necessary to satisfy each one:

- Does the arrangement directly benefit a medically underserved population?
- Does the arrangement involve goods, items, or services of a type that are commonly or typically purchased by the health center, such that the

659. *Id.* at 56638.
660. *Id.*
661. *Id.* at 56639.
662. *Id.*

arrangement results in measurable savings that will benefit a medically underserved population?

- If the arrangement involves a donation to the health center, would the donation result in the increased availability of an item, good, device, service, technology, or treatment needed by a medically underserved population but not previously available in sufficient quantities due to financial limitations?
- Does the health center need the donated items, goods, or services, or the loaned funds to satisfy the scope of its section 330 grant?[663]

Regarding the requirement in (w)(3) that the health center document the basis for its reasonable expectation of benefits to a medically underserved population, the OIG indicated that it "may, as a matter of prudent business practice, develop standards that are reasonable, uniform, and consistently applied as part of the methodology [it uses] in assessing the expected benefit to a medically underserved population."[664] In this regard, the OIG noted that a "health center can document its determination of a meaningful benefit to a medically underserved population . . . by maintaining written or electronic records of the data and methodology used to assess the expected maintenance of, increase in, or enhanced quality of services to a medically underserved population and the outcome of such assessment."[665] Further, if the arrangement falls out of compliance with this requirement, "the continuation of such an arrangement would fall outside of the safe harbor and its legality under the anti-kickback statute would be determined on a case-by-case basis, based on all the facts and circumstances, including intent of the parties."[666]

The OIG clarified that nothing in the safe harbor "limits a health center's ability to contract with one supplier consistent with the procurement rules."[667] Nor does the safe harbor "prohibit the health center from entering into an exclusive arrangement with a provider or supplier when the health center so chooses, and when it can do so in compliance with relevant procurement rules."[668] As an example, the OIG stated that a health center could enter into an exclusive contract with one laboratory supplier to the

663. *Id.* at 56639.
664. *Id.*
665. *Id.*
666. *Id.* at 56640.
667. *Id.*
668. *Id.*

exclusion of other suppliers in order to accept an offer of free laboratory services for uninsured patients, "provided all other safe harbor conditions are met."[669] The OIG stressed, however, that the safe harbor was "unique to Federally Qualified Health Centers" and that "[i]n general, arrangements where a provider or supplier offers free or discounted items or services to a potential referral source that would otherwise incur out-of-pocket costs for such items or services pose a substantial risk of fraud under the anti-kickback statute."[670]

Regarding the requirement in (w)(6) that donors that are offering free or reduced charge goods or services furnish them to all patients of the health center who clinically qualify without regard for payer status or ability to pay, the OIG commented that the safe harbor "does not protect arrangements through which Donors limit their financial risk by cherry picking which health center patients will receive their goods or services based on the patient's insurance status."[671] The OIG further clarified that this requirement applies only to goods, items, or services furnished by donors, and not donations or loans.[672]

Regarding the patient notification requirement in (w)(8), the OIG clarified that "health centers can satisfy the notification requirement through broad disclosures" such as "directing patients to a written disclosure notice posted in a conspicuous place in the health center . . . provided that the written notice is reasonably calculated to provide effective notice and to be understood by the parties."[673] Broad disclosures, however, "are not required."[674]

The provision set forth in (w)(9), which affords health centers the option of requiring that donors charge a referred health center patient either a reduced rate or the same rate charged other similarly situated patients, was intended to "allow health centers to protect their patients from price gouging" by "being charged prices higher than they would be charged in the absence of the health center's participation in the safe harbored arrangement."[675] The OIG indicated its concern that, without such an option, donors "might otherwise seek to recoup part of the cost of remuneration offered to a health center by charging health center patients inflated

669. *Id.*
670. *Id.* at 56640-41.
671. *Id.* at 56641.
672. *Id.*
673. *Id.* at 56642.
674. *Id.*
675. *Id.*

rates."[676] The OIG further confirmed that the safe harbor would not keep health centers "from offering health center patients waivers or reductions of cost sharing obligations, as permitted in the safe harbor for waiver of beneficiary coinsurance and deductible amounts [1001.952(k)]" or reducing patient cost sharing amounts "based on individualized good faith assessments of financial need."[677]

This safe harbor was the subject of Advisory Opinion No. 08-01.[678] That opinion addressed the program of a nonprofit corporation that arranged for pharmaceutical manufacturer patient assistance programs (PAPs) to provide donated drugs to free clinics and FQHCs for use by needy patients without outpatient prescription drug coverage. The program was not open to Medicare or Medicaid patients; therefore, donated pharmaceuticals could not be dispensed to such patients. The OIG analyzed the arrangement under § 1001.952(w), concluding that the safe harbor was "potentially applicable" to the portion of the arrangement involving FQHCs. The OIG concluded, however, that the arrangement, while sharing "many features of the safe harbor," did not "fit squarely for several reasons," including that the arrangement does not require the FQHC "to make the requisite determinations regarding benefit to underserved populations" and "the free drugs offered by [donors] are not offered to all FQHC patients regardless of payer status."[679]

Notwithstanding these failings, however, the OIG elected not to impose sanctions. Although the OIG recognized that the arrangement could be a vehicle through which a pharmaceutical donor offers or pays remuneration to "induce FQHCs to purchase or order" donor products reimbursable by a federal health care program or to "influence the prescribing patterns of the FQHC physicians with respect to" such products, the OIG concluded that certain other characteristics of the arrangement mitigated this risk. Specifically, the OIG first noted that "the FQHCs receive no compensation from any [donor] for dispensing or administrative services under the Arrangement, and the FQHCs are not permitted to bill any insurer or patient for the [donor] drugs," making any remuneration to the FQHC indirect, such as

---

676. *Id.*

677. *Id.*

678. Advisory Opinion No. 08-01 (Issued Feb. 1, 2008). The safe harbor also was referenced in United States v. IASIS Healthcare LLC, 2016 WL 6610675 at *7 (D. Ariz. Nov. 9, 2016) (under safe harbor, "FQHCs may receive payments pursuant to written contracts designated for administrative and case management services").

679. *Id.* at p. 4.

"through the offsetting of drug costs otherwise borne by the FQHC."[680] The OIG further commented that the arrangement did not warrant the imposition of sanctions for the following additional reasons:

- The structure of the arrangement mitigated the risk that the FQHCs "might obtain excess stocks of drugs" by limiting drug supplies to the provision of outpatient prescription drugs that are shipped monthly "based on amounts dispensed to eligible patients during the previous month or based on projected usage (with subsequent reconciliation)."[681]
- The arrangement was transparent and documented in a signed agreement covering all the free drugs to be provided, the drugs were shipped to each FQHC "pursuant to a fixed methodology that is unrelated to the volume or value of referrals of Federal business generated by the FQHC for the [donor]," and the FQHCs were required to segregate inventory and maintain detailed records that create an audit trail for the distribution of PAP drugs to eligible patients.[682]
- The donors do not control the selection of FQHCs which participate in the arrangement, and pharmaceutical donors that participate in the arrangement must provide drugs "uniformly to all participating affiliated FQHCs." As a result, the arrangement "prevents [donors] from cherry-picking certain FQHCs to receive donated drugs. The nonprofit certified that "the availability of drugs . . . is not conditioned on the volume or value of Federal health care program business generated by an FQHC or on the inclusion of other non-[patient assistance program] products of the [donors] on the FQHC's formulary."[683]
- The physicians prescribing drugs for FQHC patients "do not receive any compensation that takes into account in any manner the physicians' prescribing patterns for [donor] products and the FQHCs do not track any physician's prescribing patterns." Physicians are encouraged to choose PAP drugs for eligible patients to minimize financial hardship, but only when the drug would be clinically appropriate. The nonprofit certified that the affiliated FQHCs would adopt a policy ensuring that physicians "are made aware of these protections by written

680. *Id.* at p. 6.
681. *Id.*
682. *Id.*
683. *Id.*

notice provided annually" in order to protect physician independent professional judgment.[684]

- The nonprofit insulates the FQHCs from the donors by not permitting "any of its staff or the staff of any participating [donors] to be involved in the formulary decision-making process of any affiliated FQHC," the participating FQHCs adopted conflict of interest policies "[prohibiting] employees involved in the formulary decision-making process from accepting employment with, or remuneration from, any participating [donor]," and the nonprofit "does not permit sales or marketing representatives of any participating [donor] to communicate with affiliated FQHCs, or their physicians, with respect to the Arrangement."[685]
- The ultimate recipients of the drugs are limited to "financially-needy patients who lack outpatient prescription drug coverage," "the PAP drugs are targeted at precisely the type of vulnerable, financially-needy patients the FQHCs are commissioned to serve," and so the arrangement did "not involve the kind of cherry-picking of patients on the basis of payer status or ability to pay that raises concerns in other contexts."[686]
- The nonprofit certified that there were no other undeclared arrangements or understandings among the parties that might result in FQHC physicians prescribing donor products to insured patients or FQHCs agreeing to place donor products on their formularies.[687]
- The arrangement related "directly to the core clinical services provided by the FQHCs and helps ensure the availability of safety net health services for otherwise underserved populations."[688]

2.23. Electronic Prescribing Items and Services

The safe harbor provision for electronic prescribing items and services is codified at 42 C.F.R. § 1001.952(x), including a supplemental definition paragraph:

> (x) *Electronic prescribing items and services.* As used in section 1128B of the Act, "remuneration" does not include nonmonetary remuneration (consisting of items and services in the form of hardware, software, or information technology and training services)

684. *Id.* at p. 7.
685. *Id.*
686. *Id.*
687. *Id.*
688. *Id.*

necessary and used solely to receive and transmit electronic prescription information, if all of the following conditions are met:

(1) The items and services are provided by a -
   (i) Hospital to a physician who is a member of its medical staff;
   (ii) Group practice to a prescribing health care professional who is a member of the group practice; and
   (iii) A PDP sponsor or MA organization to pharmacists and pharmacies participating in the network of such sponsor or organization and to prescribing health care professionals.

(2) The items and services are provided as part of, or are used to access, an electronic prescription drug program that meets the applicable standards under Medicare Part D at the time the items and services are provided.

(3) The donor (or any person on the donor's behalf) does not take any action to limit or restrict the use or compatibility of the items or services with other electronic prescribing or electronic health records systems.

(4) For items or services that are of the type that can be used for any patient without regard to payor status, the donor does not restrict, or take any action to limit, the recipient's right or ability to use the items or services for any patient.

(5) Neither the beneficiary nor the recipient's practice (or any affiliated individual or entity) makes the receipt of items or services, or the amount or nature of the items or services, a condition of doing business with the donor.

(6) Neither the eligibility of a beneficiary for the items or services, nor the amount or nature of the items or services, is determined in a manner that takes into account the volume or value of referrals or other business generated between the parties.

(7) The arrangement is set forth in a written agreement that -
   (i) Is signed by the parties;
   (ii) Specifies the items and services being provided and the donor's cost of the items and services; and
   (iii) Covers all of the electronic prescribing items and services to be provided by the donor (or affiliated parties). This requirement will be met if all separate agreements

between the donor (and affiliated parties) and the beneficiary incorporate each other by reference or if they cross-reference a master list of agreements that is maintained and updated centrally and is available for review by the Secretary upon request. The master list should be maintained in a manner that preserves the historical record of agreements.

(8) The donor does not have actual knowledge of, and does not act in reckless disregard or deliberate ignorance of, the fact that the beneficiary possesses or has obtained items or services equivalent to those provided by the donor.

Note to paragraph (x):
For purposes of paragraph (x) of this section, *group practice* shall have the meaning set forth at 42 CFR 411.352; *member of the group practice* shall mean all persons covered by the definition of "member of the group or member of a group practice" at 42 CFR 411.351, as well as other prescribing health care professionals who are owners or employees of the group practice; *prescribing health care professional* shall mean a physician or other health care professional licensed to prescribe drugs in the State in which the drugs are dispensed; *PDP sponsor or MA organization* shall have the meanings set forth at 42 CFR 423.4 and 422.2, respectively; *prescription information* shall mean information about prescriptions for drugs or for any other item or service normally accomplished through a written prescription; and *electronic health record* shall mean a repository of consumer health status information in computer processable form used for clinical diagnosis and treatment for a broad array of clinical conditions.

This safe harbor was finalized simultaneously with the Electronic Health Records safe harbor, 42 C.F.R. § 1001.952(y), with the intention of expanding the use and modernization of technology in the health care field. These safe harbors were passed following the adoption of the MMA of 2003. Following this new drug benefit, Congress required that HHS establish standards for electronic prescriptions in an effort to improve the efficiency and effectiveness of patient care. This direction came with the assumption of donations of electronic prescription-capable technology to hospitals and other health care groups, which would create the potential for AKS violations. Therefore, a safe harbor was added to protect the growth of technology in the medical field that had to be in compliance with the new law.[689]

The rule that was initially proposed in 2005 was significantly more restrictive than the final rule. The scope of the safe harbor and the latitude afforded to the donor and donee were expanded with the passage of the final rule in 2006.[690] The limit on the value of donated goods was removed along with the required written statement ensuring that donated technology was not equivalent to technology already possessed by the recipient, or was instead a significant upgrade over said possessed technology.[691]

The proposed written certification was originally included to make the donation process as transparent as possible, in an effort to reduce the potential for abuse. However, this was omitted from the final rule because it was "unnecessarily burdensome" for the recipient.[692] It is difficult to distinguish between "significant" improvements as opposed to other beneficial improvements, and the difficult distinction made the certification overly complex.[693] The potential abuse of this system is severely mitigated by the burden shifting to the donor not to "have actual knowledge of, and . . . [not to] act in reckless disregard or deliberate ignorance of, the fact that the beneficiary possesses or has obtained items or services equivalent to those provided by the donor."[694] It is further mitigated by the use of the term "necessary," further defined later in this section.[695]

The OIG expressed concern over the lack of a hard limit for value of donated goods, stating, "in our experience, the risk of fraud and abuse generally (although not always) increases with the value of the remuneration

689. Final Rule: Medicare and State Health Care Programs: Fraud and Abuse; Safe Harbors for Certain Electronic Prescribing and Electronic Health Records Arrangements Under the Anti-Kickback Statute, 71 Fed. Reg. 45110, 45110 (Aug. 8, 2006).

690. Proposed Rule: Medicare and State Health Care Programs: Fraud and Abuse; Safe Harbor for Certain Electronic Prescribing Arrangements Under the Anti-Kickback Statute, 70 Fed. Reg. 59015, 59015 (Oct. 11, 2005).

691. Final Rule: Medicare and State Health Care Programs: Fraud and Abuse; Safe Harbors for Certain Electronic Prescribing and Electronic Health Records Arrangements Under the Anti-Kickback Statute, 71 Fed. Reg. 45110, 45115 (Aug. 8, 2006).

692. *Id.* at 45123.

693. *Id.* at 45116.

694. 42 C.F.R.§ 1001.952(x)(8).

695. Final Rule: Medicare and State Health Care Programs: Fraud and Abuse; Safe Harbors for Certain Electronic Prescribing and Electronic Health Records Arrangements Under the Anti-Kickback Statute, 71 Fed. Reg. 45110, 45123 (Aug. 8, 2006).

offered."[696] Despite this, the OIG agreed that the fair market value of certain goods would be difficult to ascertain, particularly in the rapidly developing field of technology. In an effort to stay within the spirit of the law and to not stunt the growth of technology in the health care field, the limit was removed, with the provision that "necessary and used solely" should be sufficient to prevent abuse. "Under the final safe harbor, any upgrade that is necessary and used solely to transmit and receive electronic prescribing information will be protected."[697]

The final rule allows for the donation of electronic prescribing technology including, but not limited to, hardware, software, and information technology and/or training services, that are necessary and solely used for receiving and sending electronic prescription information.[698] The OIG declined to be more specific in its terminology for this rule. "While a specific list would provide a 'bright line' rule, in this case it would also impede the ability of the safe harbor to accommodate novel or rapidly evolving technologies in the marketplace. For these reasons, we are not promulgating a specific list of protected items and services."[699] The terms "necessary" and "used solely" were more narrowly defined by the OIG. "We believe . . . that Congress intended for all donated technology to be necessary for the receipt and transmission of electronic prescription information and to be used solely for that purpose."[700] This definition removes devices that can be used for prescription purposes but also serve other uses from the acceptable list of donations. The OIG stated that this was done intentionally so as to reduce the risk of abuse by donors. Further, the electronic prescription technology must meet the applicable standards under Medicare Part D.[701]

This safe harbor covers four donor-recipient relationships: "hospital to its medical staff; . . . medical group practice to its members; . . . a [prescription drug plan] sponsor or [Medicare Advantage] organization to prescribing health care professionals, as well as to pharmacies and pharmacists in

696. *Id.* at 45118.

697. *Id.* at 45116.

698. 42 C.F.R.§ 1001.952(x).

699. Final Rule: Medicare and State Health Care Programs: Fraud and Abuse; Safe Harbors for Certain Electronic Prescribing and Electronic Health Records Arrangements Under the Anti-Kickback Statute, 71 Fed. Reg. 45110, 45116 (Aug. 8, 2006).

700. *Id.* at 45115.

701. 42 C.F.R. § 1001.952(x)(2).

the plan's network."[702] Having this relationship does not necessarily confer safe harbor protection unless all of the remaining requirements are satisfied. The goal of this safe harbor was to promote technological use and development in health care, which led to the broad scope of protected donors. The intention was to "protect any donor that is an individual or entity that provides patients with health care items or services covered by a Federal health care program and submits claims or requests for payment for those items or services (directly or pursuant to reassignment) to Medicare, Medicaid, or other Federal health care programs."[703] The OIG still held reservations about the potential for abuse, particularly with respect to "laboratories, durable medical equipment suppliers, and others."[704] It was clarified that these protected donors will be under particular scrutiny for abuse, and the OIG may revisit the issue should the need arise, though no revisions have been made since the safe harbor's enactment.[705] This is a "bright-line" rule, intended to directly clarify who the protected donors are, while simultaneously achieving the goal of the safe harbor.

The donor is not allowed to attach restrictions to the donation it provides. The donor may not donate in a manner that takes into account the volume or value of referrals generated between the two parties, nor can the donor take action to limit the use of the electronic prescribing technology. Likewise, the recipient is not allowed to condition doing business with the donor based on the receipt of electronic prescribing technology.[706] These restrictions are made clear by the OIG:

> The safe harbor would not protect arrangements that seek to induce a recipient to change loyalties from other providers or plans to the donor (e.g., a hospital using an electronic prescribing technology arrangement to induce a physician who is on the medical staff of another hospital to join the donor hospital's medical staff), because such arrangements take into account business generated for the donor.[707]

---

702. Final Rule: Medicare and State Health Care Programs: Fraud and Abuse; Safe Harbors for Certain Electronic Prescribing and Electronic Health Records Arrangements Under the Anti-Kickback Statute, 71 Fed. Reg. 45110, 45114 (Aug. 8, 2003).

703. *Id.* at 45127.

704. *Id.* at 45128.

705. *Id.*

706. 42 C.F.R. §§ 1001.952(x)(4), (5), (6).

707. Final Rule: Medicare and State Health Care Programs: Fraud and Abuse; Safe Harbors for Certain Electronic Prescribing and Electronic Health Records Arrangements Under the Anti-Kickback Statute, 71 Fed. Reg. 45110, 45118 (Aug. 8, 2003).

2.24. Electronic Health Records

The electronic health records safe harbor, codified at 42 C.F.R. § 1001.952(y), states:

> (y) Electronic health records items and services. As used in section 1128B of the Act, "remuneration" does not include nonmonetary remuneration (consisting of items and services in the form of software or information technology and training services) necessary and used predominantly to create, maintain, transmit, or receive electronic health records, if all of the following conditions are met:
>
> (1) The items and services are provided to an individual or entity engaged in the delivery of health care by -
>
> (i) An individual or entity, other than a laboratory company, that provides services covered by a Federal health care program and submits claims or requests for payment, either directly or through reassignment, to the Federal health care program; or
>
> (ii) A health plan.
>
> (2) The software is interoperable at the time it is provided to the recipient. For purposes of this subparagraph, software is deemed to be interoperable if, on the date it is provided to the recipient, it has been certified by a certifying body authorized by the National Coordinator for Health Information Technology to an edition of the electronic health record certification criteria identified in the then-applicable version of 45 CFR part 170.
>
> (3) The donor (or any person on the donor's behalf) does not take any action to limit or restrict the use, compatibility, or interoperability of the items or services with other electronic prescribing or electronic health records systems (including, but not limited to, health information technology applications, products, or services).
>
> (4) Neither the beneficiary nor the recipient's practice (or any affiliated individual or entity) makes the receipt of items or services, or the amount or nature of the items or services, a condition of doing business with the donor.
>
> (5) Neither the eligibility of a beneficiary for the items or services, nor the amount or nature of the items or services, is determined

in a manner that directly takes into account the volume or value of referrals or other business generated between the parties. For the purposes of this paragraph (y)(5), the determination is deemed not to directly take into account the volume or value of referrals or other business generated between the parties if any one of the following conditions is met:

(i) The determination is based on the total number of prescriptions written by the beneficiary (but not the volume or value of prescriptions dispensed or paid by the donor or billed to a Federal health care program);

(ii) The determination is based on the size of the recipient's medical practice (for example, total patients, total patient encounters, or total relative value units);

(iii) The determination is based on the total number of hours that the beneficiary practices medicine;

(iv) The determination is based on the recipient's overall use of automated technology in his or her medical practice (without specific reference to the use of technology in connection with referrals made to the donor);

(v) The determination is based on whether the beneficiary is a member of the donor's medical staff, if the donor has a formal medical staff;

(vi) The determination is based on the level of uncompensated care provided by the recipient; or

(vii) The determination is made in any reasonable and verifiable manner that does not directly take into account the volume or value of referrals or other business generated between the parties.

(6) The arrangement is set forth in a written agreement that -

(i) Is signed by the parties;

(ii) Specifies the items and services being provided, the donor's cost of those items and services, and the amount of the recipient's contribution; and

(iii) Covers all of the electronic health records items and services to be provided by the donor (or any affiliate). This requirement will be met if all separate agreements between the donor (and affiliated parties) and the beneficiary incorporate each other by reference or if they cross-reference a master list of agreements that is maintained and updated centrally and is available for review by the Secretary upon request. The master list should be maintained in a manner that preserves the historical record of agreements.

(7) The donor does not have actual knowledge of, and does not act in reckless disregard or deliberate ignorance of, the fact that the beneficiary possesses or has obtained items or services equivalent to those provided by the donor.

(8) For items or services that are of the type that can be used for any patient without regard to payor status, the donor does not restrict, or take any action to limit, the recipient's right or ability to use the items or services for any patient.

(9) The items and services do not include staffing of the recipient's office and are not used primarily to conduct personal business or business unrelated to the recipient's clinical practice or clinical operations.

(10)[Reserved]

(11)Before receipt of the items and services, the beneficiary pays 15 percent of the donor's cost for the items and services. The donor (or any affiliated individual or entity) does not finance the recipient's payment or loan funds to be used by the beneficiary to pay for the items and services.

(12)The donor does not shift the costs of the items or services to any Federal health care program.

(13)The transfer of the items and services occurs, and all conditions in this paragraph (y) have been satisfied, on or before December 31, 2021.

Note to paragraph (Y):

For purposes of paragraph (y) of this section, *health plan* shall have the meaning set forth at § 1001.952(l)(2); *interoperable* shall mean able to communicate and exchange data accurately, effectively, securely, and consistently with different information technology systems, software applications, and networks, in various settings, and exchange data such that the clinical or operational purpose and meaning of the data are preserved and unaltered; and

> *electronic health record* shall mean a repository of consumer health status information in computer processable form used for clinical diagnosis and treatment for a broad array of clinical conditions.

This safe harbor rule was originally proposed in 2005, following the passage of the MMA of 2003, and enacted in 2006. An amendment to the existing rule was proposed and enacted in 2013.[708] The amended rule updated the original rule by modernizing the provision under which electronic health records software is deemed interoperable. Further, the requirement related to electronic prescribing capability from the safe harbor was removed; the sunset date of the safe harbor was extended to December 31, 2021; the scope of protected donors was limited to exclude laboratory companies; and the text was changed to clarify the condition that prohibits a donor from taking any action to limit or restrict the use, compatibility, or interoperability of the donated items or services.[709]

The list of acceptable donations is fairly limited in scope, allowing only "items and services in the form of software or information technology and training services."[710] This definition excludes hardware and storage devices among others from being protected donations.[711] Additionally, these nonmonetary donations must be "necessary" and used "predominantly" to create, maintain, transmit, or receive electronic health records.[712] The OIG noted that "predominantly" was more forgiving than the "used solely" restriction in 42 C.F.R. § 1001.952(x), due to the nature and wider scope of electronic health record technologies.[713] Originally, the software needed to have e-prescribing capability, though the 2013 amendment eliminated this prerequisite.[714] The OIG defined "electronic health records" in a broad sense as "[a] repository of consumer health status information in computer

708. Final Rule: Medicare and State Health Care Programs: Fraud and Abuse; Electronic Health Records Safe Harbor Under the Anti-Kickback Statute, 78 Fed. Reg. 79202, 79202 (Dec. 27, 2013).

709. *Id.*

710. 42 C.F.R. § 1001.952(y).

711. Final Rule: Medicare and State Health Care Programs: Fraud and Abuse; Safe Harbors for Certain Electronic Prescribing and Electronic Health Records Arrangements Under the Anti-Kickback Statute, 71 Fed. Reg. 45110, 45125 (Aug. 8, 2006).

712. 42 C.F.R. § 1001.952(y).

713. Final Rule: Medicare and State Health Care Programs: Fraud and Abuse; Safe Harbors for Certain Electronic Prescribing and Electronic Health Records Arrangements Under the Anti-Kickback Statute, 71 Fed. Reg. 45110, 45125 (Aug. 8, 2006).

714. Final Rule: Medicare and State Health Care Programs: Fraud and Abuse; Electronic Health Records Safe Harbor Under the Anti-Kickback Statute, 78 Fed. Reg. 79202, 79202 (Dec. 27, 2013).

processable form used for clinical diagnosis and treatment for a broad array of clinical conditions."[715] The term "necessary" was added to restrict potential abuse by more clearly defining what is acceptable. Equivalent technologies are not sufficient to warrant necessity, and as such, donations may only be an improvement technologically.[716] What follows to further prevent abuse is "the donor must not have actual knowledge of, and not act in reckless disregard or deliberate ignorance of, the fact that the recipient possessed or had obtained items and services that were technically or functionally equivalent to those donated by the donor."[717]

The protection for donors and recipients uses intentionally broad wording in an effort to carry out the safe harbor's purpose of expanding technological usage.[718] "[T]he safe harbor should protect any donor that is an individual or entity that provides patients with health care items or services covered by a Federal health care program and submits claims or requests for payment for those items or services (directly or pursuant to reassignment) to Medicare, Medicaid, or other Federal health care programs."[719] The reasoning is that these parties have a substantial stake in electronic health records and therefore are most readily able to advance their implementation. Likewise, health plans, as defined at § 1001.952(l)(2), are protected by this safe harbor.[720] The OIG expressed concern for abuse with this group of donors: "We note that our decision to include health plans as protected donors does not reflect our endorsement of the proposition that health plans necessarily present a lower risk of fraud and abuse because they have economic incentives to limit utilization. Rather, our decision reflects the direction provided by Congress with respect to PDP sponsors and MA organizations, as well as the important and central role health plans play in the adoption and use of electronic prescribing and health records systems."[721] In the original rule, laboratories were part of the protected donors, though the potential for abuse was noted: "We remain concerned about the potential for abuse by

715. Final Rule: Medicare and State Health Care Programs: Fraud and Abuse; Safe Harbors for Certain Electronic Prescribing and Electronic Health Records Arrangements Under the Anti-Kickback Statute, 71 Fed. Reg. 45110, 45122 (Aug. 8, 2006).

716. *Id.* at 45123.

717. *Id.*

718. *Id.* at 45127.

719. *Id.*

720. 42 C.F.R. § 1001.952(l)(2).

721. Final Rule: Medicare and State Health Care Programs: Fraud and Abuse; Safe Harbors for Certain Electronic Prescribing and Electronic Health Records Arrangements Under the Anti-Kickback Statute, 71 Fed. Reg. 45110, 45128 (Aug. 8, 2006).

laboratories, durable medical equipment suppliers, and others, but believe that the safe harbor conditions in the final rule and the fact that the safe harbor is temporary should adequately address our concerns. We intend to monitor the situation. If abuses occur, we may revisit our determination."[722] The amended rule acted on these concerns and removed laboratory companies from protection, due to complaints of abuse.[723] Manufacturers were intentionally not covered as they do not provide health services and also had a history of abuse in the form of remuneration of free goods for referrals.[724] Protected recipients include individuals or entities that engage in the delivery of health care, "without regard to whether the recipient is on a medical staff, is a member of a group practice, or is in network of a PDP sponsor or MA organization."[725]

Neither the eligibility for items or services nor the amount or nature of the items or services can be determined based on the volume or value of referrals between the parties. However, the factors listed at 42 C.F.R. 1001.952(y)(5) serve as a bright-line rule that is neither too restrictive nor too soft on potential abuse. There is also a general provision that permits other "reasonable and verifiable" selection criteria, to ensure that this safe harbor encourages the growth of electronic health records rather than dissuades it.[726]

The safe harbor does not allow for the donor to take any action that would limit the use of the items or services with other electronic health records systems. In addition, the relationship between the parties cannot be conditioned, by either donor or recipient, on the amount of items or services donated.

When the safe harbor was first proposed in 2005, there was to be a cap on the protected value of the donation, but this concept was eliminated in the final rule due to the difficulty in valuing technologies.[727] To further prevent abuse, there is a cost-sharing provision in the safe harbor:

> Specifically, the final rule offers safe harbor protection only if the recipient pays 15 percent of the donor's cost of the technology.

722. *Id.*

723. Final Rule: Medicare and State Health Care Programs: Fraud and Abuse; Electronic Health Records Safe Harbor Under the Anti-Kickback Statute, 78 Fed. Reg. 79202, 79208 (Dec. 27, 2013).

724. Final Rule: Medicare and State Health Care Programs: Fraud and Abuse; Safe Harbors for Certain Electronic Prescribing and Electronic Health Records Arrangements Under the Anti-Kickback Statute, 71 Fed. Reg. 45110, 45128 (Aug. 8, 2006).

725. *Id.* at 45129.

726. *Id.* at 45130.

727. *Id.* at 45132.

> We believe the 15 percent cost sharing requirement is high enough to encourage prudent and robust electronic health records arrangements, without imposing a prohibitive financial burden on recipients. Requiring financial participation by a recipient should result in selection of technology appropriate for the recipient's practice and increase the likelihood that the recipient will actually use the technology. Moreover, this approach requires recipients to contribute toward the benefits they may experience from the adoption of interoperable electronic health records (for example, a decrease in practice expenses or access to incentive payments related to the adoption of health information technology).[728]

The OIG expressed concern that a differential in the amount of cost sharing a donor could impose upon recipients could be tied to referrals and other business between the parties, and cautioned that these situations must be carefully scrutinized.[729]

The OIG discussed this safe harbor in Advisory Opinion No. 12-19,[730] which addressed four proposed arrangements involving a pharmacy company's provision of items and services to community homes in which the customers resided. Of the four, proposed arrangements B, C, and D related to the Electronic Health Records safe harbor.[731] These three arrangements all had the requesting party providing free electronic health records items or services to the community homes. However, none of the software provided was interoperable as defined in the safe harbor, disqualifying them from this protection. Despite this issue, the OIG determined that whether or not these arrangements violated the AKS would require case-by-case analysis.[732] For arrangement B, it was determined that the software provided no benefit independent of the essential work functions it offered and therefore was not likely to result in fraud or abuse.[733] Arrangement C provided software for the same cost to all recipients, as well as built-in safeguards to ensure that prices stayed at market value, making it unlikely to result in an AKS violation.[734] Arrangement D offered expensive software at no cost, contrary

728. *Id.*
729. *Id.*
730. OIG Advisory Opinion No. 12-19 (Dec. 7, 2012).
731. *Id.* at 8.
732. *Id.*
733. *Id.* at 11-12.
734. *Id.* at 12.

to industry standards. Further, it was not interoperable with other software, effectively forcing the community homes to continue using this system. Due to these factors, this proposed arrangement could be subject to administrative sanctions.[735]

2.25. Federally Qualified Health Centers and Medicare Advantage Organizations

The regulatory safe harbor for FQHCs and Medicare Advantage Organizations is codified at 42 C.F.R. § 1001.952(z), which states:

> (z) *Federally Qualified Health Centers and Medicare Advantage Organizations.* As used in [the AKS], "remuneration" does not include any remuneration between a federally qualified health center (or an entity controlled by such a health center) and a Medicare Advantage organization pursuant to a written agreement described in section 1853(a)(4) of [the Social Security Act].

Section 1853(a)(4) of the Social Security Act[736] states that when a patient is enrolled in a Medicare Advantage plan and receives services from an FQHC that has a written agreement in place with the Medicare Advantage Organization, HHS will pay the amounts owed for such services directly to the FQHC on at least a quarterly basis.

This is a relatively new safe harbor that was enacted in December 2016 and became effective in January 2017. When enacting the safe harbor, HHS explained that the level and amount of payment made to the FQHC for patient services must be "not less than the level and amount of payment that the [Medicare Advantage Organization] would make for such services if the services had been furnished by an entity other than an FQHC."[737] HHS further clarified that this requirement sets a minimum, but not a maximum, with respect to the payments received by an FQHC.[738] Medicare Advantage Organizations and FQHCs can sign agreements that specify various payment levels and amounts, so long as they meet this minimum threshold. HHS also noted that this safe harbor

735. *Id.* at 13.

736. Codified at 42 U.S.C. § 1395w-23(a)(4).

737. Final Rule: Revisions to the Safe Harbors Under the Anti-Kickback Statute and Civil Monetary Penalty Rules, 81 Fed. Reg. 88368, 88377 (Dec. 7, 2016).

738. *Id.*

does not include a fair market value requirement, unlike many other safe harbors under the AKS.[739]

Moreover, this safe harbor applies only to payments received by an FQHC for services rendered to patients enrolled in a Medicare Advantage plan. Other types of arrangements between an FQHC and a Medicare Advantage Organization, such as leasing of office space or provision of administrative services, would have to be analyzed independently and may need to rely on other safe harbors for protection under the AKS.[740]

2.26. Medicare Coverage Gap Discount Program

The safe harbor for Medicare coverage gap discount program is codified at 42 C.F.R. § 1001.952(aa):

> (aa) *Medicare Coverage Gap Discount Program.* As used in [the AKS], "remuneration" does not include a discount in the price of a drug when the discount is furnished to a beneficiary under the Medicare Coverage Gap Discount Program established in section 1860D-14A of the Act, as long as all the following requirements are met:
>
> (1) The discounted drug meets the definition of "applicable drug" set forth in section 1860D-14A(g) of the Act;
>
> (2) The beneficiary receiving the discount meets the definition of "applicable beneficiary" set forth in section 1860D-14A(g) of the Act; and
>
> (3) The manufacturer of the drug participates in, and is in compliance with the requirements of, the Medicare Coverage Gap Discount Program.

Under the Medicare Coverage Gap Discount Program (MCGDP), "prescription drug manufacturers enter into an agreement with the Secretary to provide certain beneficiaries access to discounts on drugs at the point of sale."[741] The Patient Protection and Affordable Care Act (PPACA) amended the AKS by adding a provision "to protect the discounts provided for under the [MCGDP]" and this safe harbor was proposed to "codify this

739. *Id.*

740. *Id.* For example, if an FQHC leased office space from the Medicare Advantage Organization, such an arrangement would fall under the space rental safe harbor.

741. Proposed Rule: Medicare and State Health Care Programs: Fraud and Abuse; Revisions to Safe Harbors under the Anti-Kickback Statute, and Civil Monetary Penalty Rules Regarding Beneficiary Inducements and Gainsharing (79 Fed. Reg. 59717, 59721; Oct. 3, 2014).

self-implementing exception" in the law.[742] The safe harbor is designed "to protect a discount in the price of an 'applicable drug' of a manufacturer that is furnished to an 'applicable beneficiary' under the [MCGDP]."[743] The safe harbor incorporates by reference the definitions of "applicable beneficiary" and "applicable drug" MCGDP statute.[744]

In adopting the final rule, the OIG clarified that "minor administrative or technical non-compliance [with the requirements of the MCGDP] should not preclude safe harbor protection."[745] However, the OIG also stated that "[w]hile we do not contemplate that missing a payment deadline by one day would subject a manufacturer to sanctions under the anti-kickback statute, the safe harbor only protects discounts offered in connection with this program" and that "[a] manufacturer that knowingly and willfully provided discounts without complying with the requirements of the [MCGDP] could be subject to sanctions, unless such discounts are protected by another safe harbor."[746]

---

742. *Id.*

743. Final Rule: Medicare and State Health Care Programs: Fraud and Abuse; Revisions to the Safe Harbors Under the Anti-Kickback Statute and Civil Monetary Penalty Rules Regarding Beneficiary Inducements (81 Fed. Reg. 88368, 88378; Dec. 7, 2016).

744. (1) Applicable beneficiary.—The term "applicable beneficiary" means an individual who, on the date of dispensing an applicable druga covered part D drug—

(A) is enrolled in a prescription drug plan or an MA–PD plan;

(B) is not enrolled in a qualified retiree prescription drug plan;

(C) is not entitled to an income-related subsidy under section 1860D–14(a);

(D) who—

(i) has reached or exceeded the initial coverage limit under section 1860D–2(b)(3) during the year; and

(ii) has not incurred costs for covered part D drugs in the year equal to the annual out-of-pocket threshold specified in section 1860D–2(b)(4)(B).

(2) Applicable drug.—The term "applicable drug" means, with respect to an applicable beneficiary, a covered part D drug—

(A) approved under a new drug application under section 505(b) of the Federal Food, Drug, and Cosmetic Act or, in the case of a biologic product, licensed under section 351 of the Public Health Service Act (other than a product licensed under subsection (k) of such section 351); and

(B) (i) if the PDP sponsor of the prescription drug plan or the MA organization offering the MA–PD plan uses a formulary, which is on the formulary of the prescription drug plan or MA–PD plan that the applicable beneficiary is enrolled in;

(ii) if the PDP sponsor of the prescription drug plan or the MA organization offering the MA–PD plan does not use a formulary, for which benefits are available under the prescription drug plan or MA–PD plan that the applicable beneficiary is enrolled in; or

(iii) is provided through an exception or appeal.

745. *Id.*

746. *Id.*

2.27. Local Transportation

The safe harbor for local transportation is codified at 42 C.F.R. § 1001.952(bb):

(**bb**) *Local Transportation.* As used in [the AKS], "remuneration" does not include free or discounted local transportation made available by an eligible entity (as defined in this paragraph (bb)):

(**1**) To Federal health care program beneficiaries if all the following conditions are met:

(i) The availability of the free or discounted local transportation services—

(**A**) Is set forth in a policy, which the eligible entity applies uniformly and consistently; and

(**B**) Is not determined in a manner related to the past or anticipated volume or value of Federal health care program business;

(ii) The free or discounted local transportation services are not air, luxury, or ambulance-level transportation;

(iii) The eligible entity does not publicly market or advertise the free or discounted local transportation services, no marketing of health care items and services occurs during the course of the transportation or at any time by drivers who provide the transportation, and drivers or others arranging for the transportation are not paid on a per-beneficiary-transported basis;

(iv) The eligible entity makes the free or discounted transportation available only:

(**A**) To an individual who is:

(**1**) An established patient (as defined in this paragraph (bb)) of the eligible entity that is providing the free or discounted transportation, if the eligible entity is a provider or supplier of health care services; and

(**2**) An established patient of the provider or supplier to or from which the individual is being transported;

(**B**) Within 25 miles of the health care provider or supplier to or from which the patient would be transported, or within 50 miles if the patient resides in a rural area, as defined in this paragraph (bb); and

(C) For the purpose of obtaining medically necessary items and services.

(v) The eligible entity that makes the transportation available bears the costs of the free or discounted local transportation services and does not shift the burden of these costs onto any Federal health care program, other payers, or individuals; and

(2) In the form of a "shuttle service" (as defined in this paragraph (bb)) if all of the following conditions are met:

(i) The shuttle service is not air, luxury, or ambulance-level transportation;

(ii) The shuttle service is not marketed or advertised (other than posting necessary route and schedule details), no marketing of health care items and services occurs during the course of the transportation or at any time by drivers who provide the transportation, and drivers or others arranging for the transportation are not paid on a per-beneficiary-transported basis;

(iii) The eligible entity makes the shuttle service available only within the eligible entity's local area, meaning there are no more than 25 miles from any stop on the route to any stop at a location where health care items or services are provided, except that if a stop on the route is in a rural area, the distance may be up to 50 miles between that that stop and all providers or suppliers on the route; and

(iv) The eligible entity that makes the shuttle service available bears the costs of the free or discounted shuttle services and does not shift the burden of these costs onto any Federal health care program, other payers, or individuals.

Note to paragraph (bb):

For purposes of this paragraph (bb), an "eligible entity" is any individual or entity, except for individuals or entities (or family members or others acting on their behalf) that primarily supply health care items; "established patient" is a person who has selected and initiated contact to schedule an appointment with a provider or supplier to schedule an appointment, or who previously has attended an appointment with the provider or supplier; "shuttle service" is a vehicle that runs on a set route, on a set schedule; "rural area" is an area that is not an urban area, as defined in this rule; and "urban area" as: (a) A Metropolitan Statistical Area (MSA) or New England County Metropolitan Area (NECMA), as defined by the Executive Office of Management and Budget; or (b) the following New England counties, which are deemed to be parts of urban areas under section 601(g) of the Social Security Amendments of 1983 (Pub. L. 98-21, 42 U.S.C. 1395ww (note)): Litchfield County, Connecticut; York County, Maine; Sagadahoc County, Maine; Merrimack County, New Hampshire; and Newport County, Rhode Island.

The safe harbor for local transportation was proposed by the OIG to "protect free or discounted local transportation made available by an 'eligible entity' to established patients (and, if needed, a person to assist the patient) to obtain medically necessary items or services."[747] While acknowledging that Congress did not intend to prohibit offering local transportation having only nominal value in the context of the Civil Monetary Penalties Law (42 U.S.C. § 1320a-7a), the OIG noted that the AKS "does not have any exceptions for items or services of nominal value" and thus "a safe harbor is warranted to protect complimentary local transportation that meets certain requirements that limit the risk of fraud and abuse."[748]

A. *Eligible Entities*

The OIG explained that, provided all requirements of the safe harbor are satisfied, "the safe harbor would protect transportation both to a provider or supplier of services and back to a patient's home" and that "an eligible entity offering free or discounted local transportation need not require that transportation be planned in advance."[749] Further, "a transportation

747. Final Rule: Medicare and State Health Care Programs: Fraud and Abuse; Revisions to the Safe Harbors Under the Anti-Kickback Statute and Civil Monetary Penalty Rules Regarding Beneficiary Inducements, 81 Fed. Reg. 88378 (Dec. 7, 2016).

748. *Id.* at 88379.

749. *Id.*

program could use vouchers rather than having the transportation provided directly by the eligible entity."[750]

Regarding the meaning of "eligible entity," the OIG noted that the safe harbor excludes entities that "primarily supply health care items" such as pharmacies, which "would be excluded from the definition."[751] Other kinds of entities that "may not directly render health care services to patients," including "MA organizations, MCOs, accountable care organizations (ACOs), clinically integrated networks, and charitable organizations," would remain eligible to provide transportation pursuant to the safe harbor.[752] Generally, the OIG expressed concern that "allowing individuals and entities that primarily supply health care items to offer transportation to patients presents a heightened risk of using such transportation to generate referrals, potentially in a way that increases costs for patients and Federal health care program."[753] An eligible entity may impose limitations on the transportation services offered, so long as those limitations are consistent with the safe harbor's requirements. For example, an eligible entity can "set restrictions on the distance it is willing to transport the patient," among other restrictions.[754] The OIG noted that an eligible entity "might be willing to transport patients only within a 10-mile radius of its location, or willing to transport patients only to primary care providers, or only for visits included in a discharge plan . . . [and] [t]hese types of limitations are acceptable and do not limit patient choice or steer to particular providers or suppliers."[755]

The OIG commented that "an eligible entity that does not itself provide health care services (such as a charitable organization, health plan, ACO, or other entity) is not required to have an established relationship with a patient in order to provide transportation that is protected by this safe harbor."[756] The OIG further explained that "an eligible entity can transport patients to another provider or supplier that is a referral source; the transportation offer, however, cannot be contingent on the patient choosing a referral source."[757]

750. *Id.*
751. *Id.* at 88382.
752. *Id.*
753. *Id.*
754. *Id.* at 88385.
755. *Id.* at 88382.
756. *Id.* at 88385.
757. *Id.*

B. Established Patients

The safe harbor requires that the offer of transportation services be made to "established patients." "The purpose of limiting the local transportation offers to established patients is to offer flexibility to improve patient care while limiting the risk of the transportation being used as a recruiting tool, or to bring patients in for unnecessary services."[758] An "established patient" is one who either has previously attended an appointment with the provider or has selected and initiated contact with a provider or supplier to schedule an appointment.[759] "If a patient is unable to call a provider or supplier himself, or has otherwise given consent for a person (*e.g.*, a family member, a case manager, or a provider or supplier where the patient is attending an appointment) to schedule appointments for him, then a request for an appointment made on behalf of the patient is sufficient to meet this criterion."[760] The OIG further stressed that transportation cannot be used as a recruiting tool, and that a provider or supplier may *not* "reach[] out to the patient (or to the patient's case manager) and ask[] to have a new patient come in, coupled with an offer of transportation," and still receive safe harbor protection.

The OIG commented that it will not deem a patient established with a specific physician practice also to be established "with respect to the entire integrated health care system of which that practice is a part" such that "the system would be able to provide transportation limited to entities within the system."[761] The OIG noted, however, that shuttle transportation is not subject to the established patient requirement and thus a health care system "could offer a shuttle service to the public that made stops at its own facilities, but not at any health care facilities outside the system."[762] The OIG also observed that "an ACO or similar entity may assist its affiliates in providing transportation (*e.g.*, by having a fleet of vehicles available for the use of its affiliates in transporting their patients)" and that, in such a situation, "the transportation would be provided by the affiliates, who could limit the transportation offers to their own patients."[763] In that event, however, the affiliates, as the eligible entities, would have to bear the cost of the transportation they provide, which could be accomplished, as one example, by

758. *Id.* at 88382.
759. *Id.*
760. *Id.*
761. *Id.*
762. *Id.*
763. *Id.*

"having the affiliates pay to the ACO a fixed amount per mile or per trip for their transported patients."[764]

The OIG cautioned that "transportation for marketing purposes, offered to a patient who has not yet selected the facility, would not be protected by the safe harbor."[765] However, a patient who was either admitted to a hospital or received outpatient care there would be "established" under the safe harbor, as would a patient who was discharged from the hospital and was offered transportation for follow-up care or a patient who was being transported home after a visit to the emergency room.[766] In sum, "[a] patient who has received a service is an established patient, and transportation of such a patient could be protected by this safe harbor."[767] The OIG further commented that while the safe harbor "does not require documentation that the patients receiving transportation are established patients . . . maintaining documentation that demonstrates compliance with the safe harbor may be best practice."[768]

C. *Purpose of the Transportation*

The OIG commented that to receive the protection of the safe harbor, an eligible entity's "provision of transportation must be for medically necessary services" and comply with all other safe harbor conditions.[769] The OIG rejected a request to extend safe harbor protection to transportation for reasons other than medically necessary items or services, reasoning that "[a] transportation program offered by a provider or supplier inherently poses a risk both of inducing patients to get items or services that they might otherwise not have obtained and to get the services from that provider or supplier."[770] The OIG concluded that such a risk was acceptable "[i]n the case of transportation for medically necessary items or services" but was "too high when the transportation for an individual (as opposed to a shuttle) is for non-health-related purposes."[771]

764. *Id.* The OIG also noted that, in some cases, an ACO "in the [Medicare Shared Savings Program] and certain CMS demonstration programs may use waivers of the fraud and abuse laws to cover some transportation arrangements, provided all waiver conditions are met." *Id.* at 88382-83.

765. *Id.* at 88383.

766. *Id.*

767. *Id.*

768. *Id.*

769. *Id.* at 88382.

770. *Id.* at 88384.

771. *Id.*

Addressing the concern of one commenter that eligible entities not be permitted to discriminate on the basis of insurance type, the OIG observed:

> [A]n eligible entity could take into account an individual patient's need for transportation, even if this resulted in the transportation being disproportionately made available to elderly or low-income patients who are more likely to be Federal health care program beneficiaries. It would be necessary for the determination of transportation to be made on an individual basis, however, and not on the basis of insurance type. For example, a geriatric practice might provide transportation almost exclusively to Medicare beneficiaries where most of its practice is Medicare beneficiaries, so long as the practice does not discriminate based on insurance type. In other words, any non-Medicare patients of the practice must be eligible for transportation assistance on the same terms as the Medicare patients.[772]

The OIG further acknowledged the importance of "allowing one eligible entity to transport patients to another provider or supplier," provided all elements of the safe harbor are satisfied.[773] The OIG cautioned, however, that "if the patient is being transported to a different provider than the eligible entity that is providing the transportation, and the eligible entity providing the transportation is itself a provider or supplier of federally payable services, then there must be an established patient relationship between the eligible entity providing the transportation and the patient being transported, as well an established patient relationship between the patient and the provider to which the patient is being transported."[774] The OIG reasoned that "[i]f a provider with no established relationship with a patient provides or offers to provide transportation, there is a risk that a purpose of the transportation is to market its own services to the patient or induce referrals from the provider to whom the patient is being transported."[775]

D. *Need for the Transportation*

Although eligible entities must have a set policy concerning the availability of transportation assistance, they "are not required to maintain individualized documentation for each patient to whom transportation is provided,"

772. *Id.*
773. *Id.*
774. *Id.* at 88385.
775. *Id.*

although such would be a "best practice to demonstrate compliance with the requirements of the policy and the consistent and uniform application."[776] The OIG did not mandate parameters for a transportation policy, requiring only that it comply with the terms of the safe harbor and "be applied uniformly and consistently," reasoning that the safe harbor imposes requirements designed to protect federal health care programs and that "eligible entities should have the flexibility to develop policies to suit their patient populations' needs within those requirements."[777]

The OIG did, however, take the position that a patient's status as a Medicaid or Medicare beneficiary should not "be used as a proxy for establishing transportation need, in part because this would result in transportation being offered on the basis of volume or value of Federal health care program business."[778] According to the OIG, Medicaid or Medicare status does not establish that a patient has, or does not have, a need for the transportation.[779] Thus, although "eligible entities are free to tailor their transportation programs to the needs of their own patient populations and communities (including setting caps on available transportation), they may not do so in a way that is linked to status as a Federal health care program beneficiary."[780]

E. Payment and Marketing

Regarding payment for the transportation, the OIG commented that transportation offered through a driver or private company hired by the eligible entity may not be paid for on a "per-patient-transported basis" but that if it is public transportation such as a taxi or bus, payment could be paid for or reimbursed to patients using vouchers or bus fare or cash reimbursement "if the patient has a receipt to show that he or she incurred the cost of the transportation."[781]

Responding to a comment inquiring whether donor acknowledgment is permitted, the OIG stated that "[i]f a donor is a health care provider or supplier, or makes, markets, or sells health care items or supplies, an acknowledgment of that donor's contribution would be prohibited," but

776. *Id.*
777. *Id.*
778. *Id.* at 88386.
779. *Id.*
780. *Id.*
781. *Id.* at 88387.

that if the donor does not fall into that category, the acknowledgment would be proper.[782]

F. *Local Transportation*

The safe harbor was designed to protect "local transportation." The OIG commented as follows regarding its decision to adopt specific mileage limits to establish a "bright line" rule:

> We believe that expanding the distance to 50 miles for patients in rural areas should protect transportation that meets the vast majority of patients' needs, while still being "local" for their communities.
>
> We believe that a 25-mile distance should be sufficient for patients in urban areas to access quality health care, and can be fairly characterized as "local." We recognize that there may be areas within urban areas, as we are defining that term in this regulation, that are generally underserved, or underserved as to particular types of health care services. However, we believe using definitions of "rural area" and "urban area" in this safe harbor that are consistent with definitions of the same terms used in connection with the physician self-referral law . . . will be simplest for providers to work with and encourage the widest use of this safe harbor.
>
> Individuals and entities anticipating a need to transport over longer distances and believing that they have sufficient safeguards in place to avoid abusive outcomes, such as steering of patients and inducements to obtain unnecessary care, may seek an advisory opinion for a determination on whether the program is sufficiently low risk.
>
> We are sensitive to the fact that patients living in rural areas may have fewer health care providers and suppliers in their immediate areas, and that transportation might provide these patients with more choices and better access to quality care. We note that the requirement for a longer distance is that the patient resides in a rural area. Thus, the eligible entity (or the provider or supplier to whom the patient is transported) may or may not be in a rural area.
>
> . . .
>
> While we understand that a set mileage limit is not a one-size-fits-all solution, we believe that a bright-line rule is easier for all parties to apply . . .

782. *Id.*

> . . .
>
> The purpose of this safe harbor is to protect free or discounted local transportation. We do not consider distances greater than 25 miles to be "local" in urban areas, or 50 miles in rural areas, for purposes of this safe harbor. We understand that there may be beneficial, low-risk transportation arrangements that the mileage limit will exclude from protection under the safe harbor. Entities desiring to implement an arrangement that implicates the statute and does not meet the terms of the safe harbor may submit an advisory opinion request so that we can determine, on a case-by-case basis, whether the arrangement is sufficiently low risk to be protected.[783]

G. *Prohibition on Cost Shifting*

The safe harbor requires that eligible entities bear the costs of the free or discounted transportation and not shift those costs to federal health care programs or other payers. Responding to questions regarding whether providers may pool resources to pay for transportation or may receive transportation-related donations from third parties, the OIG agreed "that providers and suppliers should not have to bear the full cost of transportation, if they can get donations or contributions from appropriate sources."[784] The OIG continued:

> However, in the absence of an agreement among entities to share costs, entered into voluntarily and without any tie to referrals, the costs should not be shifted to any payer, individual, or other provider or supplier. This prohibition is not intended to bar entities from voluntarily joining together to offer transportation.
>
> Investing in transportation is not necessarily different than making any other investment (and donating transportation is not different than making any other donation). For example, a charity might donate a vehicle to a hospital, or a health system or an ACO might purchase vehicles that would be available for use by its providers or suppliers (at their cost pursuant to the safe harbor requirement that the eligible entity bear the costs of the transportation) to transport their patients (i.e., the ACO or health system would not be acting as the eligible

783. *Id.* at 88388.
784. *Id.* at 88389.

entity; the transporting provider or supplier would be). Any agreement parties enter into to make this investment would not be covered under this safe harbor (which protects the transportation itself), but it also would not disqualify the transportation from the protection of this safe harbor, as long as the terms of the agreement would not result in transportation that fails to meet the conditions of the safe harbor (e.g., if the agreement involved tying the availability of transportation to referrals). Parties would need to ensure that the agreement does not violate the anti-kickback statute or other fraud and abuse laws.

H. *Shuttle Transportation*

Regarding the provisions of the safe harbor addressing shuttle transportation, the OIG commented that "shuttle vans or buses should be permitted" and that it would not dictate the "particular types of stops as appropriate for a shuttle service" nor would it "mandate who runs the shuttles (whether it is the eligible or a contractor of the eligible entity operating the shuttle service)."[785] The OIG further stated that it was "not requiring that the shuttle be limited to established patients . . . [because] unlike door-to-door transportation in which a driver is sent to pick up a specific patient, a shuttle would run on a regular route," and that it would be "burdensome if [OIG] required shuttle drivers to determine whether individuals using the shuttle were established patients of one of the facilities where the shuttle would stop."[786] Additionally, the OIG observed that "a shuttle service may be used for reasons other than to obtain health care items or services, or to obtain such items or services from a particular provider, practitioner, or supplier," such as providing transportation to employees of and visitors to the eligible entity.[787] The OIG did not see any material increased potential for abuse by making a shuttle service "available to the general public."[788] However, if an eligible entity wished to voluntarily limit the shuttle service to established patients, that would be permitted under the safe harbor.[789]

785. *Id.* at 88390.
786. *Id.*
787. *Id.*
788. *Id.*
789. *Id.*

3
Interplay Between the Anti-Kickback Statute and Other Laws

3.1. The False Claims Act

The False Claims Act (FCA) (31 U.S.C. §§ 3729 *et seq.*), known as the "Lincoln Law," was passed during the Civil War in response to profiteering by companies that sold worthless supplies to the Union Army like guns that did not shoot, ammunition filled with sawdust, and uniforms that disintegrated in the rain. President Lincoln advocated passage of the law, which contained "*qui tam*" provisions that allowed private citizens to sue on the government's behalf. "*Qui tam*" is short for a Latin phrase meaning "he who brings an action for the king as well as for himself." The FCA is the federal government's primary enforcement tool to recover monies lost to health care fraud and other government fraud. In 2017, the federal government recovered more than $3.7 billion in judgments and settlements under the FCA.[790] Of that amount, $2.4 billion came from the health care industry.[791] Between 2009 and 2017, the federal government recovered about $22.1 billion in fraudulent health care claims under the FCA.[792]

790. Press Release, Department of Justice, Justice Department Recovers Over $3.7 Billion from False Claims Act Cases in Fiscal Year 2017 (Dec. 21, 2017).

791. *Id.*

792. *Id.*

The FCA creates civil liability for knowingly submitting, *or* causing others to submit, *or* agreeing with others to submit, false claims seeking reimbursement from the government.[793] "Claim" is defined extremely broadly to include any request for money or property that is presented to the government or made to a contractor or grantee if the money or property is being spent on the government's behalf or to advance a governmental interest, and the government either funds or reimburses the contractor or grantee for any portion of the money or property being requested.[794] Failing to return overpayments received from the government can also be a false claim; this is called a "reverse false claim."[795] Proving an intent to defraud is not required, provided that the action was undertaken knowingly, which means acting with actual knowledge or in deliberate ignorance or reckless disregard of the truth.[796]

The FCA authorizes recovery of three times the amount of the damages actually sustained by the government.[797] The FCA also imposes a mandatory civil penalty of not less than $5,500 (or $11,181 for claims submitted after November 2, 2015) or more than $11,000 (or $22,363 for claims submitted after November 2, 2015) for each false claim submitted.[798] Violators are also subject to possible exclusion from participating in federal health care programs.[799] If a violator promptly self-discloses its misconduct to government, and cooperates in the investigation prior to any criminal prosecution, civil action, or administrative action being commenced, and if that person had no knowledge of an investigation at the time such information was provided, damages may be reduced to twice the amount of loss.[800]

Pursuant to the statute's *qui tam* provisions, a person with knowledge of government fraud may bring an action on behalf of the government.[801] That person, referred to as a "relator," will collect a portion of the government's recovery if the action results in a settlement or verdict. The complaint is filed under seal, and a copy of the complaint and a disclosure statement of all material information possessed by the relator is served on the

793. 31 U.S.C. § 3729(a).
794. 31 U.S.C. § 3729(b)(2).
795. 31 U.S.C. § 3729(b)(3).
796. 31 U.S.C. § 3729(b)(1).
797. 31 U.S.C. § 3729(a).
798. 15 C.F.R. § 6.3(a)(3).
799. 42 U.S.C. § 1320a-7(a)(7).
800. 31 U.S.C. § 3729(a)(2).
801. 31 U.S.C. § 3730(b).

government.[802] The initial seal is for 60 days while the government considers whether to intervene in the action. Extensions of the initial seal are routinely requested and granted while the government investigates.

The government may choose to intervene in the action and assume control over the litigation, or it may choose to decline intervention. When the government declines intervention, the relator may proceed with the action independently, although the government continues to monitor the case as it proceeds and retains ultimate control over the government's claim, including the power to approve or reject any settlement reached between the parties. Even if the government declines intervention, it may reenter the case at a later date for good cause.[803] If the FCA action is successful (whether by settlement or judgment), the relator's share of the recovery is between 15 and 25 percent if the government intervenes and between 25 and 30 percent if the government declines intervention.[804] If the relator planned and initiated the activity underlying the violation, the court may reduce the relator's share of the recovery. If the relator is convicted of an offense arising from an FCA violation, the relator receives nothing under the FCA.[805]

The AKS can form the basis of an FCA claim and is frequently cited as the legal predicate for FCA lawsuits and settlements. All claims for services submitted to Medicare or Medicaid include express certifications that such claims comply with the AKS, rendering such claims false when they instead arose as a result of kickbacks paid to induce patient referrals. Furthermore, the AKS includes a provision that states that "a claim that includes items or services resulting from a violation of [the AKS] constitutes a false or fraudulent claim for purposes of [the FCA]."[806]

3.2. The Civil Monetary Penalties Law

The Civil Monetary Penalties Law (CMPL) was enacted in 1981 to provide the US Department of Health and Human Services (HHS) with an administrative remedy corresponding to the FCA to combat Medicare and Medicaid fraud.[807] The Health Insurance Portability and Accountability Act of 1996 (HIPAA) made the CMPL applicable to virtually all federal health

802. *Id.*
803. 31 U.S.C. § 3730(c).
804. 31 U.S.C. § 3730(d).
805. *Id.*
806. 42 U.S.C. § 1320a-7b(g).
807. Omnibus Budget Reconciliation Act of 1981, Pub. L. No. 97-35, §2105(a). *See* S. Rep. No. 97-139, 97th Cong., 1st Sess. 461-2 (1981), reprinted in 1981 U.S.C.C.A.N. 727-28.

care programs.[808] The CMPL covers a broad range of misconduct, including violations of the AKS.[809] Each such AKS violation, under the CMPL, carries a penalty of $50,000, plus damages of not more than three times the total amount of remuneration offered, paid, solicited, or received without regard to whether such act was done for a lawful purpose.[810]

In addition, HHS may exclude the violator from participating in federal health care programs and direct the relevant state agency to do the same for state programs.[811]

3.3. Administrative Exclusions

Another administrative remedy available to combat Medicare and Medicaid fraud is the exclusion authority granted HHS in 42 U.S.C. § 1320a-7. There are both mandatory and permissive exclusions for misconduct enumerated in the statute.[812] In the case of mandatory exclusions, the period of exclusion must be for at least five years but will be for at least ten years if the individual was previously convicted of a mandatory exclusion offense and will be permanent if the individual had two or more such prior convictions.[813] In many ways, the exclusion authority is the most powerful weapon available to the government because the ability to seek reimbursement from federal health care programs is frequently essential in order for a health care provider to maintain a viable business operation. Exclusion thus can effectively end a corporate provider's business and an individual provider's career. A conviction under the AKS would require mandatory exclusion under 42 U.S.C. § 1320a-7(a)(1) or (3).

3.4. Physician Self-Referral Law ("Stark Law")

The Stark Law is a civil statute that, together with its accompanying regulations, generally prohibits physicians[814] from making referrals for certain

808. The only exception is the Federal Employees Health Benefits Program (FEHBP). The CMPL incorporates the definition of federal health care program contained in 42 U.S.C. § 1320a-7b(f), which excludes the FEHBP.

809. 42 U.S.C. § 1320a-7a(a)(7) (CMPL covers conduct "described in paragraph (1) or (2) of section 1320a-7b(b)").

810. 42 U.S.C. § 1320a-7a(a).

811. *Id.*

812. 42 U.S.C. § 1320a-7(a) and (b).

813. 42 U.S.C. § 1320a-7(c)(3)(B) and (G).

814. Physician is defined as "a doctor of medicine or osteopathy, a doctor of dental surgery or dental medicine, a doctor of podiatric medicine, a doctor of optometry, or a chiropractor." 42 C.F.R. § 411.351.

designated health services (DHSs) payable by Medicare or Medicaid[815] to an entity with which he or she has a financial relationship, unless an exception to the law applies.[816] The Stark Law prohibits entities from presenting a claim to Medicare or Medicaid for those referred services.[817] A "financial relationship" of a physician includes (1) an ownership or investment interest in the entity or (2) a compensation arrangement between the physician and the entity.[818]

DHS includes the following services: (i) clinical laboratory services; (ii) physical therapy, occupational therapy, and outpatient speech-language pathology services; (iii) radiology and certain other imaging services; (iv) radiation therapy services and supplies; (v) durable medical equipment and supplies; (vi) parenteral and enteral nutrients, equipment, and supplies; (vii) prosthetics, orthotics, and prosthetic devices and supplies; (viii) home health services; (ix) outpatient prescription drugs; and (x) inpatient and outpatient hospital services.

The Stark Law is a strict liability statute, meaning that liability does not depend on the knowledge or intent of the individual violating the law. No payment may be made for any DHS billed in violation of the Stark Law, and any person who collects amounts billed in violation of the Stark Law is liable for and must refund such amounts. Moreover, anyone knowingly presenting a claim in violation of the Stark Law is subject to a civil monetary penalty of up to $15,000 for each service unlawfully billed. The Stark Law provides more severe penalties for engaging in a "circumvention scheme," described as "an arrangement or scheme (such as a cross-referral arrangement) which the physician or entity knows or should know has a principal purpose of assuring referral by the physician to a particular entity which, if the physician directly made referrals to such entity, would" violate the law. A physician or entity engaging in a circumvention scheme is subject to a civil monetary penalty of up to $100,000 for each such scheme.

The Stark Law and the AKS are frequently implicated in the same fact patterns, as both laws regulate financial relationships with patient referral sources. Like the AKS, the Stark Law may support liability under the FCA,

---

815. The Stark Law is extended to Medicaid claims through 42 U.S.C. § 1396b(s), which denies federal funding for claims submitted to state Medicaid programs in violation of the Stark Law.

816. 42 USC § 1395nn.

817. *Id.*

818. *Id.*

and *qui tam* cases brought against health care providers frequently include allegations under both statutes. The Stark Law, however, is considerably narrower in scope than the AKS, as it only applies to referrals made by physicians (whereas the AKS applies to anyone), and the Stark Law covers only DHS, and not all items and services reimbursable by a federal health care program as with the AKS.

3.5. State Analogs

Many jurisdictions have adopted state-law versions of the AKS, which focus on the payment of kickbacks in Medicaid and/or commercial payer cases.[819] Additionally, similar prohibitions are frequently incorporated into professional misconduct rules barring licensed professionals from paying, offering, soliciting, or receiving payment for referrals.

---

819. See e.g.,

AK ST § 09.58.010

CA GOVERNMENT CODE SECTIONS 12650-12656

CO Added by Laws 2010, Ch. 296, § 14, eff. May 26, 2010. Amended by Laws 2017, Ch. 175, § 3, eff. Aug. 9, 2017CO C. R. S. A. § 25.5-4-310, CO ST § 25.5-4-310. CT ST Title 4, CHAPTER 55e

DE ST tit. 6, subtit. II, ch. 12. D.C. Law 19-317, 60 DCR 2064. FL False Claims Act tit. 6, § 68.081-68.092. GA Taxpayer Protection False Claims Act, codified at 23-3-120 to 23-3-127 (as amended Ga. L. 2014, p. 866, SB 340). GA State False Medicaid Claims Act, codified at 49-4-168 TO 49-4-168.6 (as amended Ga. L. 2014, p. 77, HB 973). HI False Claims to the State (**661-21** *et seq.*) (as amended by Laws 2012 ch. 294.). HI False Claims to the Counties (46-171 *et seq.*) (as amended by Laws 2012 ch. 294.). IL False Claims Act 740 ILCS 175/1 from ch. 127, ¶ 4101.

IL 740 ILCS 175/2 from Ch. 127, ¶ 4102. IN False Claims and Whistleblower Protection Act, codified at 5-11-5.5 *et seq.* (as amended through P.L. 109-2014); and IN Medicaid False Claims and Whistleblower Protection Act, codified at 5-11-5.7 *et seq.* (as amended through P.L. 109-2014). IA False Claims Act Title XV, Subtitle 5, ch. 685. LA ST Title 46, Part VI-A, Subpart A, § 437.1 and 437.2. MD False Health Claims Act, Health, tit. 2, subtit. 6, § 2-601– 2-611. MA False Claims Act, Part 1, tit. II, ch. 12, § 5-50. MI the Medicaid False Claim Act, 400.601, § 1-15. MN False Claims Act § 15C.01–15C.145. MT False Claims Act ch. 388, L.2013. 17-8-401. NV False Claims Act ch. 357. NH False Claims Act § 167. NJ False Claims Act § 1-15, 17-18, 2A:32C-1 Short title. NM Medicaid False Claims Act §§ 27-14-1 to 27-14-15, as enacted by Laws 2004, ch. 49. NM Fraud Against Taxpayers Act §§ 44-9-1 to 44-9-14, as amended by Laws 2015, ch. 128. NY False Claims Act, NYS Finance Law, Chapter 56, Article XIII, § 187-194. NC False Claims Act § 1-605–1-618. OK 63 Okl. St. Ann. § 5053.1. RI False Claims Act ch. 1.1, § 9-1.1-1 through 9-1.1-9. TN False Claims Act 4-18-101 *et seq.* (through Acts 2012, ch. 1061). TN Medicaid False Claims Act 71-5-181 *et seq.* (through Acts 2013, ch. 99). TN False Claims Act as amended by Acts 2012, ch. 1061. TX Human Resources Code ch. 36, subch. A, § 36.0001. VT False Claims Act (H.120) Sec. 1. 32 V.S.A. ch. 7, subch. 8

VA Fraud Against Taxpayers Act § 8.01-216.1-18. WA Medicaid Fraud False Claims Act RCW 74.66.0005 [2012 c 241 § 214.].

APPENDICES

A. Selected Legislative History
B. Selected Advisory Opinions
C. Selected Fraud Alerts and Special Advisory Bulletins
D. Selected Judicial Opinions

APPENDIX A
Selected Legislative History

H.R. REP. 95-393(II), H.R. REP. 95-393, H.R. Rep. No. 393(II), 95TH Cong., 1ST Sess. 1977, 1977 U.S.C.C.A.N. 3039, 1977 WL 16075 (Leg.Hist.)
****3039** P.L. 95-142, MEDICARE-- MEDICAID
ANTIFRAUD AND ABUSE AMENDMENTS
House Report (Ways and Means Committee) No. 95-393(I),
June 7, 1977 (To accompany H.R. 3)
House Report (Interstate and Foreign Commerce Committee No. 95-393 (II),
July 12, 1977 (To accompany H.R. 3)
Senate Report (Finance Committee) No. 95-453,
Sept. 26, 1977 (To accompany S. 143)
House Conference Report No. 95-673,
Oct. 11, 1977 (To accompany H.R. 3)
Cong. Record Vol. 123 (1977)
DATES OF CONSIDERATION AND PASSAGE
House September 23, October 13, 1977
Senate September 30, October 13, 1977
The House bill was passed in lieu of the Senate bill. House Report
No. 95-393(II), and the House Conference Report are set out.

(CONSULT NOTE FOLLOWING TEXT FOR INFORMATION ABOUT OMITTED MATERIAL. EACH COMMITTEE REPORT IS A SEPARATE DOCUMENT ON WESTLAW.)

HOUSE REPORT NO. 95-393(II)

July 12, 1977

TABULAR OR GRAPHIC MATERIAL SET FORTH AT THIS POINT IS NOT DISPLAYABLE

****3040** ***1** The Committee on Interstate and Foreign Commerce, to whom was referred the bill (H.R. 3) to strengthen the capability of the Government to detect, prosecute, and punish fraudulent activities under the medicare and medicaid programs, and for other purposes, having considered the same, report favorably thereon with four amendments and recommend that the bill as amended do pass.

* * * *

***38** I. LEGISLATIVE BACKGROUND

Legislation to amend the Social Security Act to strengthen the capability of the Government to detect, prosecute and punish fraudulent activities under the medicare and medicaid programs was introduced on January 4, 1977, by Mr. Rogers, Chairman of the Subcommittee and the Environment, and by Mr. Rostenkowski, Chairman of the Subcommittee on Health of the Ways and Means Committee. The bill was subsequently reintroduced as H.R. 3020, H.R. 3021, H.R. 3022, H.R. 3023, H.R. 4087, and H.R. 5702, with an additional 93 members of the House joining as co-sponsors, including 7 members of the Subcommittee on Health and the Environment. Joint hearings were ****3041** held by the Health Subcommittees of the Interstate and Foreign Commerce Committee and the Ways and Means Committee on March 3 and 7. The bill was subsequently considered in open executive sessions by the Subcommittee on Health and the Environment, amended, and reported on April 28, 1977. The Subcommittee convened to reconsider the bill after the Ways and Means Committee had completed action, adopted additional amendments, and reported H.R. 3 with amendments on June 13, 1977. H.R. 3 was considered by the Interstate and Foreign Commerce Committee, and ordered reported by voice vote, on June 28, 1977.

The legislation reported by the Committee is a product of close consultation and cooperation throughout the stages of its development with the Committee on Ways and Means. In addition to holding joint hearings, the two Health Subcommittees held sequential executive sessions to consider the bill in the light of the actions taken by the other Committee members. As a result, both Committees are recommending very similar Committee amendments in reporting the bill to the House.

In order to minimize the differences in the amendments reported by each committee, the Committee on Interstate and Foreign Commerce ***39** has included in its reported amendments some provisions which relate solely to part A of the medicare program (Hospital Insurance Benefits for the Aged and Disabled), which is in the jurisdiction of the Committee on Ways and Means. (Similarly, that committee, has included in its reported amendments provisions relating solely to medicaid, which is the jurisdiction of the Interstate and Foreign Commerce Committee). It should be noted that substantive action on the amendments in these cases were carried out by the committee on jurisdiction. Adoption by the other committee was generally done pro forma. All provisions which were within both committees' jurisdiction, however, were fully considered by each.

II. SUMMARY OF THE BILL

As reported, the provisions of H.R. 3, the Medicare-Medicaid Antifraud and Abuse Amendments, are focused on six major areas: Strengthened program penalty sanctions, increased disclosure of information, needed improvements in the Professional Standards Review program, administrative reform, and other Medicaid amendments.

The summary presented below briefly outlines the principal features of the bill as reported.

PROGRAM PENALTY SANCTIONS

1. The bill modifies the penalty provisions in existing law which relate to those persons providing services under medicare and medicaid. Most fraudulent acts now classified as misdemeanors are to become felonies. Penalties are to be increased to a maximum $25,000 fine, up to five years imprisonment, or both. The types of financial arrangements and conduct to be classified as illegal have been clarified. In addition, States will now be permitted to suspend the eligibility of medicaid recipients convicted of defrauding the program. However, the misdemeanor penalty presently provided under existing law for ****3042** conviction of such individuals is retained, as is the misdemeanor penalty for the conviction of a beneficiary under the medicare program. The bill also requires the Health, Education, and Welfare Inspector General to include in his annual report an evaluation of the effort of the Department of Justice in the investigation and prosecution of fraud in the medicare and medicaid programs and his recommendations for improvement of that effort. (Section 4)

2. The bill requires the Secretary of Health, Education, and Welfare to suspend, for such period as he deems appropriate, from participation under medicare and medicaid, an individual practitioner who has been convicted of a criminal offense related to such individual's involvement in medicare or medicaid. When the Secretary suspends an individual, he must also notify the appropriate State licensing authorities, requesting that investigation be made and sanctions invoked in accordance with the State's law and public policy. (Section 7)

1.(a) The bill requires, as a condition of participation or certification in either medicare, medicaid or the maternal and child health program, the annual disclosure to the Secretary or the appropriate State agency by the participating entity of the identity of any person ***40** who has a five percent or more ownership interest in the entity. These disclosure of ownership provisions will apply to medicare and medicaid providers of services (including independent clinical laboratories and renal disease facilities), entities furnishing services for which payment may be claimed under medicaid or the maternal and child health program (but not including any individual or group of practitioners), and medicare carriers or intermediaries and medicaid fiscal agents. Providers of services would also have to disclose similar ownership information about any subcontractor, five percent or more of which is owned by the provider. (Section 3)

(b) Furthermore, the bill modifies existing medicare and medicaid provisions relating to termination of medicare provider agreements or suspension of medicaid payments to health care entities by adding a requirement that a provider must comply with a request specifically addressed to it by the Secretary or the medicaid State agency for full and complete information as to any significant business transactions between it and any subcontractors or between it and wholly-owned suppliers. Finally, in the case of subcontractors having more than $25,000 in annual business transactions with a provider, compliance would be required with similar requests related to ownership information pertaining to the subcontractor. (Section 3)

2. The bill requires all institutional providers of services, or other agencies, institutions, or organizations, as a condition of participation or certification in medicare, medicaid or the social services programs under Title XX of the Social Security Act to disclose, in the application for participation or certification, the names of owners, officers, directors, agents, or managing employees who have been convicted of fraud against the medicare, medicaid, or State social service grant programs. Where an application contains the name of any such previously convicted individual, the Secretary or the State agency can refuse to enter into an agreement or refuse to contract with the applicant. The Inspector General of the Department of Health, Education, ****3043** and Welfare must be informed of the receipt of any such applications and of any action taken on them. (Section 8)

3. The bill authorizes the Comptroller General of the United States to sign and issue subpenas in order to obtain necessary information and facilitate review of Social Security Act health programs. The Comptroller General will also be authorized, upon resistance or refusal by an individual to obey a subpena, to request a court order requiring compliance with the subpena. The bill would impose criminal sanctions for unauthorized disclosure by the GAO of individually identifiable personal medical records and would protect such records from subpena or discovery proceedings in connection with a civil suit. (Section 6)

4. The bill requires any provider of services participating in medicare to promptly notify the Secretary of its employment of an individual who, at any time during the preceding year, was employed in a managerial, accounting, auditing, or similar capacity by a medicare fiscal intermediary or carrier that services the provider. (Section 15)

5. The bill allows Federal access to the records of persons or institutions providing services under medicaid in the same manner that such access is presently provided to State agencies. (Section 9)

***41** PROFESSIONAL STANDARDS REVIEW

The bill includes several provisions designed to clarify the nature and scope of PSRO review responsibilities, to enhance the capacity of PSRO'S to perform reviews of the necessity and appropriateness of services more effectively, and to improve the administration and coordination of review activities so as to assure that program funds are properly expended. Thus, section 5 of the bill provides:

(1) for the termination of other duplicative review activities when the Secretary determines that a PSRO is competent to perform its review responsibilities; that the determinations of PSRO'S so recognized by the Secretary with respect to the necessity and appropriateness of care are conclusive for purposes of program payment; and that the role of the State in the process of establishing and evaluating PSRO review of services provided through the medicaid program will be increased and made more specific;

(2) that a PSRO may be conditionally designated for a period not to exceed 48 months (with authority for the Secretary to extend the period for an additional 24 months where warranted by unusual circumstances); and that PSRO'S must assume review responsibilities for institutional services during this period;

(3) for the Secretary to develop ambulatory care review methodologies for use by PSRO's and to make such methodologies available within 2 years; to require a PSRO, where he finds it is capable of undertaking ambulatory care review, to undertake such review no later than 2 years after it becomes fully operational; and to give priority to requests by PSRO's to review services in 'shared health facilities';

(4) that the Federal Government may assume the defense costs incurred by a PSRO in a liability suit related to the performance of its functions;

****3044** (5) for the disclosure of information with respect to evidence of fraud to designated Federal and State law enforcement agencies (with a prohibition against access to PSRO records in the case of subpena or discovery proceedings in a civil action), and for the disclosure of aggregate statistical data to Federal and State health planning agencies;

(6) for the annual submission to the Congress by the Secretary of a comprehensive report on the administration, cost, and impact of the PSRO program;

(7) for a prohibition against any PSRO disclosing to a Federal official, or a Federal official having access to, any individually identifiable medical record in the possession of a PSRO relating to medical care not provided or paid for by the Federal Government without the specific consent of the patient. The Department of HEW would also be required to submit its legislative recommendations to the Congress as to the appropriate procedure for maintaining the confidentiality of individual medical records. These recommendations would be made after taking into consideration the final report of the Privacy Protection Study Commission and must be submitted to the Congress no later than 90 days after the Privacy Commission's report is issued; and

***42** (8) for several clarifying administrative and technical changes designed to enhance a PSRO's operational capacity. (Section 5)

ADMINISTRATIVE REFORM

1. The bill authorizes the Secretary to assign and reassign providers to available intermediaries, after taking into account any preferences expressed by the providers and after applying objective performance standards to the original nominee of the provider prior to making a reassignment. Any assignment action he takes must be based on a finding that it will result in more efficient and effective administration of the program. Before making any assignment or reassignment that is not in accord with the provider's choice, the Secretary must furnish to the provider and its chosen intermediary a full explanation of his findings with respect to efficiency and effectiveness and provide an appropriate opportunity for a hearing, which is subject to judicial review.

The Secretary is also authorized to designate regional intermediaries or a national intermediary with respect to a class of providers (e.g., home health agencies) where he determines that, after applying objective performance standards to agencies or organizations that would be adversely affected, such designation will result in more efficient and effective administration of the program. In a similar manner to that mentioned above, this authority to designate with respect to a class of providers is subject to a requirement that the Secretary fully explain to the affected parties his findings with respect to efficiency and effectiveness and provide an appropriate opportunity for a hearing which is subject to judicial review. (Section 14)

2. The bill requires the Secretary to establish for each of the different types of health services institutions a uniform system for the reporting of such items as cost of operation, volume of services, rates, ****3045** capital assets and bill data. This reporting system would be mandated for use by medicare and medicaid providers and such use would be phased in by type of provider. (Section 19)

3. The bill repeals the program review team provisions of present law. The functions formerly performed by such teams with respect to the quality and utilization of services will be performed by Professional Standards Review Organizations. (Section 13)

4. The bill would encourage each State to establish an office separate from the medicaid program agency to prepare and prosecute cases of suspected fraud and abuse in the program by providing for 90 percent Federal matching funds for expenditures to establish and operate State medicaid fraud control units. (Section 17)

5. The bill also requires States to make provision in their State medicaid plan for claims payment procedures which ensure that 90 percent of the bills submitted by eligible noninstitutionally-based providers will be reimbursed within 30 days, and 99 percent within 60 days. The State would not be cited for noncompliance if the Secretary found the State was acting in good faith to achieve this goal. (Section 2)

6. The bill directs the Comptroller General to conduct a comprehensive review of the administrative structure for the processing of medicare claims. (Section 12)

***43** 7. The bill requires the Secretary of Health, Education, and Welfare to report to the Congress within 12 months after enactment of this legislation with an analysis and recommendations relating to all aspects (including the availability, administration, provision, reimbursement procedures and cost) of the delivery of home health services under medicare, medicaid and the title XX social services program. (Section 18)

TECHNICAL REVISION

1. Your committee's bill clarifies existing law to insure that a power of attorney cannot be used to circumvent the prohibition in existing law against the use of 'factoring' arrangements in connection with the payment of provider claims by the medicare and medicaid programs. (Section 2)

2. The bill modifies the provisions of existing law related to the rental or purchase of durable medical equipment to mandate that the Secretary require the purchase of such equipment where purchase will be less costly than extended rental payments. (Section 16)

3. The bill increases individual state's incentives to adopt a computerized medicaid claims processing and information retrieval system by modifying one current requirement for higher Federal matching funds for the development and operation of

this system. The bill would require such systems to provide explanation of benefits information to only a sample group of medicaid recipients rather than to each recipient as is currently required. (Section 10)

4. The bill would preclude Federal matching of State medicaid expenditures that result from State laws or contracts which exclude or limit insurance benefits because an individual is eligible for medicaid. (Section 11)

****3046** OTHER MEDICAID AMENDMENTS

The bill provides an additional six-month period to States to meet the requirements of the current law concerning review of care delivered in long-term care institutions. The section provides that is a State is in compliance for the year period ending December 31, 1977, the Secretary shall waive all (or such part as is appropriate) of the reduction which would otherwise be imposed on those States that failed to fulfill the requirements of the law during previous periods. Further the section specifies: 1) that the Secretary must provide States with a 30-day notice before reducing funds, 2) that the Secretary must complete his validation surveys of State reviews and give notice of any reduction resulting from his findings within 9 months of the close of the year in question, and 3) that good faith attempts to perform reviews of all institutions, and actual review of all large institutions and 98 percent of all other institutions, will be considered full compliance with the requirements of the law. (Section 20)

III. COST OF LEGISLATION

As reported by the Committee, H.R. 3 as amended provides authorization for an increase in the Federal matching rate for the Medicaid program as follows:

(a) It provides 90 percent Federal matching for State expenditures to support programs of educational and technical assistance to expedite ***44** the filing and payment of claims. The higher Federal matching is authorized for a 3-year period only. A maximum of $5 million in aggregate expenditures annually is placed on funds available at the higher matching rate.

(b) It provides 90 percent Federal matching for expenditures to establish and operate State Medicaid fraud control units which meet certain specified standards. The higher Federal matching is authorized for a 3-year period only. A maximum on the annual amount any State could receive at the higher matching rate is established at one-quarter of 1 percent of Medicaid expenditures in the State, or $500,000, whichever is greater.

The bill also delays reductions of Medicaid matching funds imposed on the States because of failure to meet the requirements of the law for review in long-term care institutions. The reduction is waived if a State comes into compliance with the requirements of the law by December 31, 1977.

However, because the provisions of the law are designed to increase program efficiency and ability to detect and prosecute fraud, reductions in program expenditures resulting from H.R. 3 are expected to offset any increase in expenditures resulting from the provisions of the bill. As set forth in the Congressional Budget Office estimate which appears later in this report, no increase in cost is estimated to occur.

IV. PURPOSE AND BACKGROUND OF THE BILL

In recent years, numerous hearings, studies, and investigations undertaken by this committee and other committees of the Congress, the General Accounting Office, and other Federal and State agencies ****3047** have demonstrated that there exist, to a disturbing degree, fraudulent and abusive practices associated with thc provision of health services financed by the medicare and medicaid programs. The disclosures to date have focused on a broad range of improper activities which are not restricted to one particular class of providers or treatment settings. In whatever form it is found, however, fraud in these health care financing programs adversely impacts on all Americans. It cheats taxpayers who must ultimately bear the financial burden of misuse of funds in any government-sponsored program. It diverts from those most in need, the nation's elderly and poor, scarce program dollars that were intended to provide vitally needed quality health services. The wasting of program funds through fraud also further erodes the financial stability of those state and local governments whose budgets are already overextended and who must commit an ever-increasing portion of their financial resources to fulfill the obligations of their medical assistance programs. In addition to these adverse financial consequences, the activities of those who seek to defraud these programs unfairly call into question and honesty and integrity of the vast majority of practitioners and health care institutions.

Fraud and abuse can occur in a number of different medical settings. Recent investigations have demonstrated the pervasiveness of the problem.

***45** A. SHARED HEALTH FACILITIES

Many of the more flagrant examples of fraud and abuse activities have been uncovered in so-called 'shared health facilities,' also referred to as medicaid 'mills.' Typically, these are unregulated, unlicensed, and poorly equipped storefront units located in ghetto areas of large metropolitan cities. Such mills derive their primary business from welfare patients.

Owners of these facilities are usually individuals who have joined together in a partnership or corporation arrangement. Some may own more than one facility. Some may also be providers on the facility premises or at another location. They may also own pharmacies or laboratories which are often used as the exclusive lab or pharmacy service by all practitioners in the facilities. In certain instances there is overlapping ownership between medicaid mills and factoring companies.

Many medicaid practitioners in urban areas, with little working capital and often holding foreign medical degrees, turn to medicaid mills. These are usually owned by real estate operators who have sufficient capital to purchase the land, office space, and equipment necessary to operate a medical practice. In turn, the average practitioner will pay from 30 to 40 percent of gross income as rent, will lose 12 percent of his income to the factoring agency, and in a large number of cases be asked to divide the remaining net 50-50 with the mill owner. In some mills, the practitioners' total medicaid income is turned over to the mill operator and the practitioner receives a commission based on dollar volume, (an average of 20 to 40 percent to the practitioner and 60 to 80 percent to the mill operator).

****3048** The most common violations in the mills include:

(1) 'ping-ponging'-- referring of patients from one practitioner to another within the facility even though there is no medical reason for doing so;

(2) 'ganging'-- billing for multiple services to relatives who accompany a family member who alone had sought treatment at the mill;

(3) 'upgrading' billing for a service more extensive than that actually provided;

(4) 'steering'-- directing a patient to a particular pharmacy, a violation of the medicaid program's policy of freedom of choice; and

(5) billing for services not rendered-- either adding services not performed onto an invoice carrying legitimate billings or submitting a totally fraudulent claim.

Other violations include soliciting offering, or receiving kickbacks; billing twice or more for the same service; and billing both medicare and medicaid for the same service.

Fee splitting and percentage lease arrangements are common practices and often go hand-in-hand with medicaid mills. Percentage lease arrangements are a basic economic incentive to form these facilities. Percentage lease arrangements give the landlord a percentage of the provider's gross income in return for office, space, equipment, shared waiting rooms, laboratory services, custodial and office help, and often administrative services. Studies have shown that the average percentage ***46** lease in New York City, for example, appeared to range from 30 to 40 percent of the providers' gross fees for most medical disciplines. While the American Medical Association has ruled this practice unethical, it is not considered illegal in most States and is not prohibited under Federal law or regulations.

Factoring is also a very common practice associated with medicaid mills. Although factoring was outlawed under the Social Security Amendments of 1972, factoring firms have evaded statutory intent by working under a power of attorney arrangement.

B. CLINICAL LABORATORIES

Both medicare and medicaid provide coverage for laboratory services provided by independent clinical laboratories. Over the past several years, there has been increasing concern over the potential for fraud and abuse among clinical laboratories, particularly for services funded by the medicaid program. Several State commissions and legislative investigative committees have focused attention on this issue. At the Federal level, two congressional committees and the General Accounting Office have also examined service and billing patterns in these facilities.

The House Committee on Interstate and Foreign Commerce reviewed the question of fraud and abuse in clinical laboratories within the context of overall improvements needed in such facilities. Testimony presented to the committee by the executive director of the New Jersey State Commission of Investigation indicated that physicians often determined which laboratories would do the test work for their medicaid patients by the amount of the kickbacks and rebates offered ****3049** by the laboratory. Testimony before the committee's Subcommittee on Oversight and Investigations indicated that these kickbacks are in the neighborhood of 25 percent.

Kickbacks take a number of forms including cash, long-term credit arrangements, gifts, supplies and equipment, and the furnishing of business machines. The most common practice, however, involves the 'rental' of small office space in a medical clinic for amounts which are far in excess of the reasonable value of the space. Frequently, the 'rent' is determined by paying a percentage of the business sent to the laboratory, often in amounts as high as 30 to 45 percent of the medicaid billings of the physician or clinic sent to the laboratory.

C. NURSING HOMES

Nursing home fraud and abuse has also been the subject of extensive study and investigation. Numerous reports and hearings have been published by congressional committees, Federal agencies, and State commissions which document such activities as patient abuse, substandard homes, deceptive real estate practices, false cost reporting, and kickback practices.

Fraudulent and abusive practices relating to program costs involve the intentional misrepresentation or falsification of the costs involved in providing patient care. These practices may take many forms. Examples include: deceptive real estate practices which artifically inflate property costs, false or misleading cost reports which hide nonallowable ***47** costs, inadequate accounting procedures which prohibit effective auditing, kickbacks from vendors, and failure to disclose ownership interests. Among other questionable activities engaged in by some nursing home owners and operators are:

(1) Deceptive non-arms-length transactions.-- Increased medicaid reimbursement can result from failure to disclose a 'non-arms-length transaction' for services, realty or goods provided to the nursing home. This type of transaction is defined as an arrangement in which the nursing home operator has at least a 10 percent interest in the equity of a company providing real property, goods, or services to the facility.

(2) Reporting other business expenses on the nursing home's books.-- Some nursing home owners attempt to put the expense of other business interests on the nursing home's records. These include real estate taxes, maintenance supplies, and insurance and fuel expenses.

(3) Unauditable books.-- The books of some nursing homes are practically unauditable. A case was reported where an owner kept one set of books for three of his homes with records so jumbled that according to the State auditor 'they defied all ordinary auditing procedures.'

D. INDEPENDENT PRACTITIONERS

An independent practitioner's income from medicaid and medicare is based in part on the volume and complexity of the services he provides. Thus, for the practitioner, program fraud and abuse covers a broad spectrum of practices, ranging from the rendering of services ****3050** of arguable medical necessity to such criminal offenses as filing false claims.

There is much less evidence of fraud and abuse among practitioners than by nursing homes, medicaid mills, and independent laboratories. However, there is no way to estimate the extent to which fraud and abuse by practitioners has gone undetected. Much of the evidence that has been collected in these other areas has been based on the testimony of associates, a review of business records, and other investigative techniques that are impractical or less suitable for the review of an individual practitioner's activities. Detection and proof of fraud or abuse by an individual practitioner must often depend on the patient, who may well be both old and sick, and without medical knowledge. In any case, whatever its true extent might be, it is clear that the potential for exploitation exists for those practitioners that choose to cheat medicaid and medicare.

Perhaps the most flagrant fraud involves billings for patients whom the practitioner has not treated. A related form of fraud involves claims for services to a practitioner's patients that were not actually furnished and intentionally billing more than once for the same service.

Furnishing excessive services is probably the most costly noncriminal abuse faced by health benefit programs. At the same time, it is relatively difficult to prove and correct. Since the medical needs of a particular patient can be highly judgmental, it is difficult to identify program abuse as a practical manner unless the overutilization is grossly unreasonable.

***48** H.R. 3 is designed to strengthen the ability of the Federal and State governments to find and correct abuse and to detect and prosecute fraud. Fraud involves an intentional deception or misrepresentation, with the intent of receiving some unauthorized benefit for the individual engaged in fraud. In the health area, examples of fraud may include: billing for services not rendered, misrepresentation of services rendered, kickbacks, deliberate duplicate billing, false or misleading entries on cost reports, and so forth. Program abuse is less clearly defined and includes activity wherein providers, practitioners, and suppliers of services operate in a manner inconsistent with accepted, sound medical or business practices resulting in excessive and unreasonable financial cost to either medicare or medicaid. Included in the area of abuse are the provision of unnecessary health services and the provision of necessary care in unnecessarily costly settings.

To deal with the problem of fraud, more effective prosecution efforts and stiffer criminal penalties are proposed. Additionally, since issues of medical necessity and quality of care may be present in cases of possible program abuse (as distinct from criminal fraud). PSRO's can be a valuable resource for the exercise of the professional medical judgment that may need to be made in certain of such cases. The committee believes that every effort must be made to encourage the rapid implementation of the PSRO program. To achieve this end, H.R. 3 includes several provisions making modifications in the administrative structure of the program to enhance the capacity of individual PSRO'S to effectively review matters of quality and necessity.

****3051** V. COMMITTEE PROPOSAL

EXPLANATION, JUSTIFICATION, AND COMPARISON WITH PRESENT LAW

Prohibition Against Assignment by Physicians and Others of Claims for Services; Claims Payment Procedures for Medicaid Program (Section 2)

The Committee's bill would modify existing law to preclude the use of a power of attorney as a device to circumvent the existing ban on the use of 'factoring' arrangements in connection with the payment of claims by the medicare and medicaid programs. The bill further requires State medicaid programs to provide for timely claims payment procedures and provides higher Federal matching funds for a three-year period to assist States with programs of educational and technical assistance to expedite the filing and payment of claims.

In 1972, the Congress took action to stop a practice under which some physicians and other persons providing services under medicare and medicaid reassigned their medicare and medicaid receivables to other organizations or groups. Under the conditions of these reassignments, the organizations or groups purchased the receivables for a percentage of their face value, submitted claims and received payments in their name. By 1972, it had become apparent that such reassignments were a significant source of incorrect and inflated claims for services paid by medicare and medicaid. In addition, cases of fraudulent billings by collection agencies and substantial overpayments to these so-called 'factoring' agencies were also found.

***49** Congress concluded that such arrangements were not in the best interest of the government or the beneficiaries served by the medicare and medicaid programs.

H.R. REP. 92-231, H.R. Rep. No. 231, 92ND Cong., 2ND Sess.
1972, 1972 U.S.C.C.A.N. 4989, 1971 WL 11290 (Leg.Hist.)
***4989** P.L. 92-603, SOCIAL SECURITY AMENDMENTS OF 1972
House Report (Ways and Means Committee) No. 92-231,
May 26, 1971 (To accompany H.R. 1)
Senate Report (Finance Committee) No. 92-1230,
Sept. 26, 1972 (To accompany H.R. 1)
House Conference Report No. 92-1605,
Oct. 14, 1972 (To accompany H.R. 1)
Cong. Record Vol. 117 (1971)
Cong. Record Vol. 118 (1972)
DATES OF CONSIDERATION AND PASSAGE
House June 22, 1971; October 17, 1972
Senate October 5, 6, 17, 1972
The House Report and the Conference Report are set out.

(CONSULT NOTE FOLLOWING TEXT FOR INFORMATION ABOUT OMITTED MATERIAL. EACH COMMITTEE REPORT IS A SEPARATE DOCUMENT ON WESTLAW.)

HOUSE REPORT NO. 92-231

May 26, 1971

THE Committee on Ways and Means, to whom was referred the bill (H.R. 1) to amend the Social Security Act to provide increases in benefits improve computation methods, and raise the earnings base under the OASDI program to make improvements in the medicare, medicaid, and maternal and child health programs with emphasis on improvements in their operating effectiveness, to authorize a family assistance plan providing basic benefits to low-income families with children with incentives for employment and training to improve the capacity for employment of members of such families, to achieve more uniform treatment of recipients under the Federal-State public assistance programs and otherwise improve such programs, and for other purposes, having considered the same, report favorably thereon with amendments and recommend that the bill as amended do pass.

The amendments are as follows:

The amendment to the text of the bill strikes out all after the enacting clause and inserts a substitute which appears in the reported bill in italic type.

Your committee agrees with the Secretary that appropriate criteria as prima facie evidence of competence are necessary. However, your committee is concerned that reliance solely on specific formal education or training, or membership in private professional organizations might serve to disqualify people whose work experience and training might make them equally or better qualified than those who meet the existing requirements. Your committee believes that failure to make the fullest use of competent health personnel is of particular concern because of the shortage of such personnel.

Your committee's bill, therefore, requires the Secretary to explore, develop, and apply appropriate means of determining the proficiency of health personnel disqualified or limited in responsibility under present regulations. A proficiency testing program would help to make greater use of otherwise qualified health personnel and technicians who do not now meet medicare's formal criteria for judging professional competency and qualifications. Appropriate methods and procedures are capable of being promptly developed and applied to determine qualifications and to upgrade skills to qualifying levels.

Your committee obtained agreement from the Department last year to institute such a program with respect to clinical laboratory personnel and asked for a report on the matter by July 1, 1971. Your committee is looking forward to receiving that report.

The amendment would be effective upon enactment.

(v) Penalties for fraudulent acts and false reporting under medicare and medicaid.--Under present law, a false statement or representation of a material fact in any application for payment under social security programs is defined as a misdemeanor and carries a penalty of up to one year of imprisonment, a fine of $1,000, or both.

Your committee believes that a specific provision defining acts subject to penalty under the medicare and medicaid programs should be included to provide penalties for certain practices which have long been regarded by professional organizations as unethical, as well as unlawful in some jurisdictions, and which contribute appreciably to the cost of the medicare and medicaid programs. Thus, under the committee bill, the criminal penalty provision would include such practices as the soliciting, offering, or accepting or kickbacks or bribes, including the rebating of a portion of a fee or charge for a patient referral, involving providers of health care services. In addition, the provision would include penalties for concealing or failing to disclose knowledge of any event affecting a persons' right to any benefit payment with the intent to defraud, or for knowingly and willfully converting benefits or payments to improper use. Under the bill, the penalty for such acts, as well as false statements or representations ***5094** of material facts in any application for payment under the medicare and medicaid programs, would be a fine of $10,000, 1 year of imprisonment, or both.

Continuing investigation and review of reports by the General Accounting Office have indicated that false statements may have been made by individuals and institutions with respect to health and safety conditions and operating conditions in health care facilities in order to secure approval for participation in the medicare and medicaid programs. While the numbers of different individuals and institutions involved in such fraud may not be large in relation to the number participating in the program, your committee believes that a specific penalty for such acts should be provided to deter the making or inducing of such statements. Thus, your committee's bill includes specific provisions under title XVIII (medicare) and under title XIX (medicaid) of the Social Security Act whereby anyone who knowingly and willfully makes, or induces or seeks to induce the making of, a false statement of material fact with respect to the conditions and operation of a health care facility or agency in order to secure certification or approval to participate in the medicare and medicaid programs would be subject to imprisonment for up to 6 months, a fine not to exceed $2,000 or both.

These provisions would be in addition to and not in lieu of any other penalty provisions in State or Federal law.

The amendment is effective upon enactment.

(w) Provider reimbursement review board.-- Under present law there is no specific provision for an appeal by a provider of services of a fiscal intermediary's final reasonable cost determination. Although the HEW has developed administrative procedures to assist providers and intermediaries to reach reasonable and mutually satisfactory settlements of disputed reimbursement items, your committee believes that it is desirable to prescribe in law a specific procedure for settling disputed final determinations applying to the amount of program reimbursement. This procedure would not apply to questions of coverage or disputes involving individual beneficiary claims.

Your committee's bill, therefore, provides for the establishment of a Provider Reimbursement Review Board. The Board would be composed of 5 members, knowledgeable in the field of cost reimbursement appointed by the Secretary of Health, Education, and Welfare. At least one member of the Board would have to be a certified public accountant, and two members would be representative of providers of services.

APPENDIX B
Selected Advisory Opinions

[*We redact certain identifying information and certain potentially privileged, confidential, or proprietary information associated with the individual or entity, unless otherwise approved by the requester.*]

Issued: November 30, 1999
Posted: December 7, 1999

[name and address redacted]

Re: OIG Advisory Opinion No. 99-13

Dear [name redacted]:

We are writing in response to your request for an advisory opinion regarding certain arrangements for discounted pathology services provided to physicians (the "Proposed Arrangement"). You have asked whether the Proposed Arrangement would result in prohibited remuneration under the anti-kickback statute, section 1128B(b) of the Social Security Act (the "Act") or would constitute grounds for the imposition of sanctions under the anti-kickback statute, section 1128B(b) of the Act, the exclusion authority related to kickbacks, section 1128(b)(7) of the Act, or the civil monetary penalty provision for kickbacks, section 1128A(a)(7) of the Act. In addition, you have asked whether the Proposed Arrangement would constitute grounds for a permissive exclusion for charging Medicare or Medicaid substantially in excess of the usual charges, section 1128(b)(6)(A) of the Act.

In issuing this opinion, we have relied solely on the facts and information presented to us. We have not undertaken an independent investigation of such information. This opinion is limited to the facts presented. If material facts have not been disclosed or have been misrepresented, this opinion is without force and effect.

Based on the facts certified in your request for an advisory opinion, we conclude that the Proposed Arrangement might constitute prohibited remuneration under the anti-kickback statute if the requisite intent to induce referrals of Federal health care program business were present and might be subject to sanctions arising under sections 1128B(b), 1128(b)(7), and 1128A(a)(7) of the Act, as well as grounds for a permissive exclusion under section 1128(b)(6)(A) of the Act.

This opinion may not be relied on by any person other than the addressee and is further qualified as set out in Part IV below and in 42 C.F.R. Part 1008.

I. FACTUAL BACKGROUND

A. [Company A]

Company A is a State X professional corporation with three shareholders, all of whom are specialists in pathology and are licensed to practice medicine in State X. Company A employs five pathologists and fourteen technicians. It provides pathology services (including clinical and anatomic pathology services)[(1)] to five hospitals, as well as to the patients of physicians in private practice.

B. Billing Procedures

Company A has several billing methodologies depending upon the payor. For Federal health care program patients, Company A bills its charges to the government payor and bills the patients for any applicable copayments or deductibles.

For non-Federal health care program patients, referring physicians have two payment options. One option is for Company A to bill its charges directly to the applicable third-party payor, and bill the patients for any copayments or deductibles. The alternative is for Company A to bill the physicians for the pathology services and accept that payment as payment in full. The physicians then bill the third-party payors and patients for the purchased pathology services. This option is commonly referred to as "account billing".

Under its account billing arrangements, Company A has traditionally offered physicians a discount off its usual charges which reflects the cost savings it realizes. Company A generates a single monthly statement to the referring physician who is required to pay on a prompt basis. Company A has represented that an account billing arrangement saves time and expense because: (i) claims are not submitted to a wide range of payors; (ii) Company A need not consider the claims submission criteria of the various payors; and (iii) Company A is not responsible for determining and collecting applicable copayments and deductibles owed by the patients. In addition, Company A realizes a better collection rate under account billing. Most physicians who have an account billing arrangement with Company A refer virtually all of their patients to Company A, whether the patients' specimens are covered under the account billing arrangement or are directly billed to the Federal health care programs.[(2)]

C. The Proposed Arrangement

Under the Proposed Arrangement, Company A will offer its account billing customers discounts that are greater than its cost savings, in order to match the prices of its competitors. Some of the discounted charges will be below the actual cost of providing the pathology services. In addition, Company A's profit margin for the non-Federal health care program business under the Proposed Arrangement would be less than the profit margin on the services that it bills directly to Federal health care programs. The discount will not be conditioned upon the physicians sending Company A its Federal health care program business. However, Company A has assumed that the physicians receiving discounts under the Proposed Arrangement will send virtually all of their patients to Company A. If Company A does not match the discounts of its competitors, Company A has represented that it will lose both the account billing business and the Federal health care program business of those clients.

II. LEGAL ANALYSIS

A. The Anti-Kickback Statute

The anti-kickback statute makes it a criminal offense knowingly and wilfully to offer, pay, solicit, or receive any remuneration to induce referrals of items or services reimbursable by Federal health care programs. See section 1128B(b) of the Act. Where remuneration is paid purposefully to induce referrals of items or services paid for by a Federal health care program, the anti-kickback statute is violated. By its terms, the statute ascribes liability to parties on both sides of an impermissible "kickback" transaction. For purposes of the anti-kickback statute, "remuneration" includes the transfer of anything of value, in cash or in-kind, directly or indirectly, covertly or overtly.

The statute has been interpreted to cover any arrangement where one purpose of the remuneration is to obtain money for referral of services or to induce further referrals. United States v. Kats, 871 F.2d 105 (9th Cir. 1989); United States v. Greber, 760 F.2d 68 (3d Cir.), cert. denied, 474 U.S. 988 (1985). Violation of the statute constitutes a felony punishable by a maximum fine of $25,000, imprisonment up to five years or both. Conviction will also lead to automatic exclusion from Federal health care programs, including Medicare and Medicaid. This Office may also initiate administrative proceedings to exclude persons from Federal health care programs or to impose civil monetary penalties for fraud, kickbacks, and other prohibited activities under sections 1128(b)(7) and 1128A(a)(7) of the Act.[(3)]

1. Special Fraud Alert Relating to Arrangements for the Provision of Clinical Laboratory Services

In 1994, we issued a Special Fraud Alert describing certain laboratory practices that implicated the anti-kickback statute. The Special Fraud Alert set forth our analysis that when a laboratory offers or gives to a referral source anything of value for less than fair market value, an inference may be made that the thing of value is offered to induce the referral of business. Specifically, we gave the example of laboratories waiving charges for laboratory tests to physicians for managed care patients, in order to retain the high-paying non-managed care business. In that example, the free laboratory services for managed care patients could be a kickback between the laboratory and the physician for the fee-for-service patients.

2. The Discount Exception and Safe Harbor

The anti-kickback statute contains a statutory exception for "a discount or other reduction in price obtained by a provider of services or other entity under a Federal health care program if the reduction in price is properly disclosed and appropriately reflected in the costs claimed or charges made by the provider or entity under a Federal health care program." Section 1128B(b)(3)(A) of the Act. This discount exception reflects the intent of Congress to encourage price competition that benefits the Medicare and Medicaid programs. The Department of Health and Human Services has published regulations implementing this discount "safe harbor" exception. See 42 C.F.R. § 1001.952(h).

To determine whether Company A's proposed discount practice implicates the anti-kickback statute, we must determine whether the Proposed Arrangement fits within the discount safe harbor. We conclude that the Proposed Arrangement does not fit within the safe harbor. The statutory exception for discounts, as implemented by the regulatory safe harbor, does not protect price reductions -- like those at issue here -- offered to one payor but not offered to Medicare or Medicaid. See 42 C.F.R. § 1001.952(h)(3)(iii).

Specifically, the preamble to the discount safe harbor illustrated the potential problem with laboratory price reductions:

> [W]e are aware of cases where laboratories offer a discount to physicians who then bill the patient, but do not offer the same discount to the Medicare program. In some of these cases, the discount offered to the physician is explicitly conditioned on the physician's referral of all of his or her laboratory business. Such a "discount" does not benefit Medicare, and is therefore inconsistent with the statutory intent for discounts to be reported to the programs with costs and charges reduced appropriately to reflect the discounts. 56 Fed. Reg. 35977 (July 29, 1991).

Such price reductions create a risk that a laboratory may be offering remuneration in the form of discounts on business for which the purchaser pays the laboratory, in exchange for the opportunity to service and bill for higher paying Federal health care program business reimbursed directly by the program to the laboratory. In such circumstances, neither Medicare nor Medicaid benefits from the discount; to the contrary, Medicare and Medicaid may, in effect, subsidize the other payor's discounted rates. Moreover, laboratories may have an incentive to engage in abusive billing practices to recoup losses on the discounted business. Accordingly, the Proposed Arrangement does not fit in the discount safe harbor.

Having concluded that the Proposed Arrangement does not fit in the safe harbor, we must consider whether the discount arrangement between Company A and physicians utilizing account billing under the Proposed Arrangement may involve illegal remuneration to the physicians for their referrals of Federal health care program business not covered by the account billing arrangement and not subject to the discount. We conclude that it may.

The circumstances surrounding the Proposed Arrangement suggest that a nexus may exist between the discount to the physicians for non-Federal health care program business and referrals of Federal health care program business. First, the physicians are in a position to direct a significant amount of Federal health care program business to Company A that is not covered by the account billing component of the Proposed Arrangement. Second, both parties have obvious motives for agreeing to trade business: the physicians have the opportunity to make a larger profit on the non-Federal health care program business, and Company A is able to secure profitable Federal health care program business in a highly competitive market. Third, Company A has represented that it is likely that physicians who have account billing arrangements with Company A will refer Federal health care program business to Company A as a matter of practical convenience.

In evaluating whether an improper nexus exists between a discount and referrals of Federal business in a particular arrangement, neither the size nor structure of the discount is determinative of an anti-kickback violation. Rather, the appropriate question to ask is whether the discount -- regardless of its size or structure -- is tied or linked directly or indirectly to referrals of other Federal health care program business. Evidence that the discount is not commercially reasonable in the absence of other, non-discounted business is highly probative. In this regard, discounts on account billing business that are particularly suspect include, but are not limited to:

- discounted prices that are below the laboratory's cost,(4) and
- discounted prices that are lower than the prices that the laboratory offers to a buyer that (i) generates a volume of business for the supplier that is the same or greater than the volume of account billing business generated by the physician, but (ii) does not have any potentially available Federal health care program business.

This is an illustrative, not exhaustive, list of suspect discounts; other arrangements may be equally suspect. Each of the above pricing arrangements independently gives rise to an inference that the laboratory and the physicians may be "swapping" discounts on account billing business in exchange for profitable non-discounted Federal health care program business.

Based on the facts presented here, we are unable to exclude the possibility that Company A may be offering improper discounts under the Proposed Arrangement with the intent to induce referrals of more lucrative Federal health care program business. Nor are we able to exclude the possibility that the physicians may be soliciting improper discounts on business for which they have the opportunity to earn money in exchange for referrals of business for which they have no opportunity, but for which the laboratories can receive additional revenue. Indeed, the Proposed Arrangement poses a significant risk of such improper "swapping" of business, especially in light of Company A's representation that many of its competitors are agreeing to such discounts. These competitor discount arrangements may similarly run afoul of the anti-kickback statute. The risk of improper "swapping" is compounded by the likelihood that physicians will refer Federal health care program business to their account billing laboratory as a matter of practical convenience.

B. Permissive Exclusion for Billing Medicare Substantially in Excess of Usual Charges

Price reductions offered to physicians that are not offered to Medicare or Medicaid raise additional issues under section 1128(b)(6)(A) of the Act, which provides for permissive exclusion from the Federal health care programs of individuals or entities that submit or cause to be submitted bills or requests for payment (based on charges or costs) under Medicare or Medicaid that are substantially in excess of such individual's or entity's usual charges or costs, unless the Secretary finds good cause for such bills or requests. In determining an individual's or entity's "usual" charges, we will look at the amounts charged to non-Federal payors, including physicians. If the charge to Medicare or Medicaid substantially exceeds the amount the laboratory most frequently charges or has contractually agreed to accept from non-Federal payors, the laboratory may be subject to exclusion under section 1128(b)(6)(A) of the Act.

The limited information submitted by Company A is insufficient to make a determination as to whether the Proposed Arrangement may run afoul of section 1128(b)(6)(A).(5)

III. CONCLUSION

Based on the facts certified in the request for an advisory opinion and supplemental submissions, we conclude that the Proposed Arrangement might constitute prohibited remuneration under the anti-kickback statute, if the requisite intent to induce referrals of Federal health care program business were present, and might be subject to sanctions arising under the anti-kickback statute pursuant to sections 1128(b)(7), 1128A(a)(7), or 1128B(b) of the Act, and the permissive exclusion provision under section 1128(b)(6)(A).

IV. LIMITATIONS

The limitations applicable to this opinion include the following:

- This advisory opinion is issued only to Company A, the requester of this opinion. This advisory opinion has no application to, and cannot be relied upon by, any other individual or entity.
- This advisory opinion may not be introduced into evidence in any matter involving an entity or individual that is not a requester to this opinion.
- This advisory opinion is applicable only to the statutory provisions specifically noted above. No opinion is herein expressed or implied with respect to the application of any other Federal, state, or local statute, rule, regulation, ordinance, or other law that may be applicable to the Proposed Arrangement.
- This advisory opinion will not bind or obligate any agency other than the U.S. Department of Health and Human Services.
- This advisory opinion is limited in scope to the specific arrangement described in this letter and has no applicability to other arrangements, even those that appear similar in nature or scope.
- No opinion is expressed herein regarding the liability of any party under the False Claims Act or other legal authorities for any improper billing, claims submission, cost reporting, or related conduct.

This opinion is also subject to any additional limitations set forth at 42 C.F.R. Part 1008.

The Office of Inspector General reserves the right to reconsider the questions and issues raised in this advisory opinion and, where the public interest requires, rescind, modify, or terminate this opinion.

Sincerely,
/s/
D. McCarty Thornton
Chief Counsel to the Inspector General

1. Throughout this opinion, the term pathology services is synonymous with laboratory services.

2. We express no opinion regarding the legality of their existing account billing arrangement under the anti-kickback statute, permissive exclusion, or any other legal authority.

3. Because both the criminal and administrative sanctions related to the Proposed Arrangement are based on violations of the anti-kickback statute, the analysis for purposes of this advisory opinion is the same for both.

4. In determining whether a discount is below cost, we look, for example, at the total of all costs (including labor, overhead, equipment, etc.) divided by the total number of laboratory tests.

5. We express no opinion regarding the legality of the current account billing arrangement under the permissive exclusion or any other legal authority.

[*We redact certain identifying information and certain potentially privileged, confidential, or proprietary information associated with the individual or entity, unless otherwise approved by the requestor.*]

Issued: July 3, 2001

Posted: July 10, 2001

[name and address redacted]

Re: OIG Advisory Opinion No. 01-8

Dear [name redacted]:

We are writing in response to your request for an advisory opinion regarding a comprehensive program (the "Program") that [company's name redacted] (the "Company") markets and sells to State-licensed nursing facilities ("Facilities") to manage pressure ulcers. Specifically, the Program couples the purchase of the Company's therapeutic mattresses with the purchase of skin and wound care products and a Program warranty. The question raised by your request is whether the Program constitutes grounds for the imposition of sanctions under the exclusion authority at section 1128(b)(7) of the Social Security Act (the "Act") or the civil monetary penalty provision at section 1128A(a)(7) of the Act, as those sections relate to the commission of acts described in section 1128B(b) of the Act.

You have certified that all of the information provided in your request, including all supplementary letters, is true and correct and constitutes a complete description of the relevant facts and agreements among the parties.

In issuing this opinion, we have relied solely on the facts and information presented to us. We have not undertaken an independent investigation of such information. This opinion is limited to the facts presented. If material facts have not been disclosed or have been misrepresented, this opinion is without force and effect.

Based on the facts certified in your request for an advisory opinion and supplemental submissions, we conclude that the Program could potentially generate prohibited remuneration under the anti-kickback statute, if the requisite intent to induce or reward referrals of Federal health care program business were present, but that the Office of Inspector General ("OIG") would not impose administrative sanctions on [company's name redacted] under sections 1128(b)(7) or 1128A(a)(7) of the Act (as those sections relate to the commission of acts described in section 1128B(b) of the Act) in connection with the Program. This opinion is limited to the Program and, therefore, we express no opinion about any ancillary agreements or arrangements disclosed or referenced in your request letter or supplemental submissions.

This opinion may not be relied on by any persons other than [company's name redacted], the requestor of this opinion, and is further qualified as set out in Part IV below and in 42 C.F.R. Part 1008.

I. FACTUAL BACKGROUND

The Company, a wholly-owned subsidiary of [parent company's name redacted], manufactures and sells therapeutic mattresses and other support surfaces used for the treatment and prevention of pressure ulcers. The Program is a 3-year contractual arrangement consisting of three conjoined components: (i) the discounted sale of the Company's therapeutic mattresses and other support surfaces, together with limited replacement warranties; (ii) a prospectively-fixed, per resident/per diem payment for skin and wound care products; and (iii) a limited warranty (the "Program Warranty") for certain monetary liabilities resulting from the Program's failure to meet its stated objective: managing pressure ulcers. The Company offers the Program only to Facilities, some of which are Medicare-certified skilled nursing facilities ("SNFs").

The crux of the Program is the replacement of all of a Facility's existing mattresses with the Company's therapeutic mattresses. More specifically, the first component of the Program requires the Facility to pay a negotiated, fixed, discounted price per bed in exchange for which the Facility receives: (i) a non-powered therapeutic mattress for each bed; (ii) a specified number of wheelchair cushions and therapy pads ("other support surfaces") based upon the number of residents in the Facility; (iii) a sufficient quantity of advanced powered therapeutic mattresses to address residents' wound care needs; and (iv) online access to a wound documentation system and a certified wound care specialist.[1] Under the Program, ownership of the non-powered mattresses and the other support surfaces is transferred from the Company to the participating Facility; ownership of the powered mattresses remains with the Company. The non-powered mattresses and other support surfaces are subject to a 7-year and 3-year replacement warranty, respectively. The Company has certified that the aggregate payment for the first component of the Program represents a fair market value payment.[2]

The second component of the Program requires a participating Facility to pay a fixed, daily fee per resident in exchange for an extensive skin and wound care program which includes all non-

[1]The Company permits Facilities to finance the aggregate payment for the first component of the Program and, if financed, the Company adjusts the aggregate payment to include the cost of financing.

[2]We are precluded by statute from opining on whether fair market value shall be or was paid for goods, services, or property. See 42 U.S.C. § 1320a-7d(b)(3)(A). For purposes of this advisory opinion, we rely on the Company's certification of fair market value.

Page 3 -- OIG Advisory Opinion No. 01-08

prescription skin and wound care products required to meet the needs of the Facility's residents.[3] In addition to the skin and wound care products, the Company also furnishes to participating Facilities certain support services relating to skin and wound care, including protocols[4] and in-service training and continuing education for the Facility's staff. The Company has certified that the capitation fee represents a fair market value payment for the skin and wound care products and services, based on its good faith estimation of the costs of the Program, taking into account the average quantity of goods typically consumed in the clinically sound care of residents and the projected decrease in incidence of pressure ulcers attributable to use of the Company's therapeutic mattresses.[5]

The final component of the Program is the Program Warranty. Under the Program Warranty, the Company agrees to reimburse a participating Facility for the first $[X] of liability insurance deductibles actually paid (excluding legal and research costs and liability resulting from medical, surgical, or hospital expenses incurred by a Facility resident) per incident during the contract term and resulting from judgments for skin or wound care deficiencies. In order to qualify for the Program Warranty, a participating Facility must comply with Program obligations and objectives, including following Company-approved skin and wound care protocols, providing certain in-service training to Facility staff, using the Company's online wound documentation tools and, when necessary, using the services of the Company's certified wound specialist.

The items and services provided under the Program are potentially reimbursable by Medicare and State health care programs ("Medicaid"). They are not, however, separately reimbursable under Medicare Part A. Rather, all costs resulting from a Medicare Part A covered stay, including Program costs for mattresses, other support surfaces, and skin and wound care products, are included in a per diem payment under the SNF prospective payment system ("PPS"). If a resident is not eligible for a Medicare Part A covered stay, then, except for reimbursement for certain wound care supplies in limited situations, Medicare Part B provides no reimbursement for Program items or services.[6] The Company has further certified that, typically, Program-provided wound care supplies that are potentially reimbursable under Medicare Part B (the "surgical wound

---

[3]A participating Facility must use the generic and brand name skin and wound care products provided by the Company. In addition, if a resident of a participating Facility develops pressure ulcers and if non-prescription products other than those ordinarily provided under the Program are required, the Company will supply those products at no additional charge.

[4]A participating Facility may continue to use its own pre-existing skin and wound care protocols only if the protocols are approved by the Company.

[5]See supra note 2.

[6]The Company has certified that wound care supplies are reimbursable under Medicare Part B only if they are used for treatment of surgical or debrided wounds, in which case they might be reimbursable as a surgical dressings.

supplies") should represent substantially less than 1% of the Program's price. Because Medicaid reimbursement varies from state to state, some of the items and services provided under the Program may be separately reimbursable in some states. Most states, however, use a fixed, per diem reimbursement methodology for nursing facility residential care that would not reimburse Facilities separately for the vast majority of items and services (by number or value) provided under the Program.[7]

The Company has certified that: (i) the Company will have no financial arrangements with any Facility that participates in the Program apart from the Program; (ii) the Program will not be marketed or sold by any other party, including any durable medical equipment supplier; (iii) the Company does not directly or indirectly market or provide to Facilities other items or services that are reimbursable under Medicare Part A or Part B; (iv) the Company fully and accurately reports the Program's pricing arrangement and the existence of the Program Warranty on the invoice provided to each participating Facility; (v) with respect to the Program Warranty, the invoice also contains a statement informing the purchasing Facility that the Facility must fully and accurately report any payments made under the Program Warranty in accordance with the rules governing the applicable Federal health care program, and that the Facility must provide, upon request by the Secretary of the Department of Health and Human Services or a State agency, information regarding the Program Warranty provided to the Facility by the Company; and (vi) if any payment is made in connection with the Program Warranty, the remittance statement will reflect the amount of the payment and the specific formal action for which payment is being made.

II. LEGAL ANALYSIS

A. Law

The anti-kickback statute makes it a criminal offense knowingly and willfully to offer, pay, solicit, or receive any remuneration to induce or reward referrals of items or services reimbursable by Federal health care programs. See section 1128B(b) of the Act. Where remuneration is paid purposefully to induce or reward referrals of items or services paid for by a Federal health care program, the anti-kickback statute is violated. By its terms, the statute ascribes criminal liability to parties on both sides of an impermissible "kickback" transaction. For purposes of the anti-kickback statute, "remuneration" includes the transfer of anything of value, in cash or in-kind, directly or indirectly, covertly or overtly.

The statute has been interpreted to cover any arrangement where one purpose of the remuneration was to obtain money for the referral of services or to induce further referrals. United States v. Kats, 871 F.2d 105 (9th Cir. 1989); United States v. Greber, 760 F.2d 68 (3d Cir.), cert. denied, 474 U.S. 988 (1985). Violation of the statute constitutes a felony punishable by a maximum fine

---

[7]The Company has certified that, to its knowledge, only three State Medicaid programs (i.e., New York, Ohio, and California) may, in infrequent circumstances, provide separate reimbursement for mattresses and other support surfaces provided under the Program.

of $25,000, imprisonment up to five years, or both. Conviction will also lead to automatic exclusion from Federal health care programs, including Medicare and Medicaid. Where a party commits an act described in section 1128B(b) of the Act, the OIG may initiate administrative proceedings to impose civil monetary penalties on such party under section 1128A(a)(7) of the Act. The OIG may also initiate administrative proceedings to exclude such party from the Federal health care programs under section 1128(b)(7) of the Act.

The Department of Health and Human Services has promulgated safe harbor regulations that define practices that are not subject to the anti-kickback statute because such practices would be unlikely to result in fraud or abuse. See 42 C.F.R. § 1001.952. The safe harbors set forth specific conditions that, if met, assure entities involved of not being prosecuted or sanctioned for the arrangement qualifying for the safe harbor. However, safe harbor protection is afforded only to those arrangements that precisely meet all of the conditions set forth in the safe harbor.

The safe harbor for warranties, 42 C.F.R. § 1001.952(g), is potentially applicable to the Program Warranty. Safe harbor protection is available as long as the buyer complies with the standards of 42 C.F.R. § 1001.952(g)(1)-(2) and the manufacturer or supplier complies with the following standards of 42 C.F.R. § 1001.952(g)(3)-(4):

- The manufacturer or supplier must comply with either of the following two standards -- (i) The manufacturer or supplier must fully and accurately report the price reduction of the item (including a free item), which was obtained as part of the warranty, on the invoice or statement submitted to the buyer, and inform the buyer of its obligations under paragraphs (g)(1) and (g)(2) of this section.[8] (ii) Where the amount of the price reduction is not known at the time of sale, the manufacturer or supplier must fully and accurately report the existence of a warranty on the invoice or statement, inform the buyer of its obligations under paragraphs (g)(1) and (g)(2) of this section, and, when the price reduction becomes known, provide the buyer with documentation of the calculation of the price reduction resulting from the warranty.

- The manufacturer or supplier must not pay any remuneration to any individual (other than a beneficiary) or entity for any medical, surgical, or hospital expense incurred by a beneficiary other than for the cost of the item itself.

B. Analysis

---

[8]Paragraph (g)(1) of 42 C.F.R. § 1001.952 provides that the buyer must fully and accurately report any price reduction of the item (including a free item), which was obtained as part of the warranty, in the applicable cost reporting mechanism or claim for payment filed with the Department or a State agency. Paragraph (g)(2) of 42 C.F.R. § 1001.952 provides that the buyer must provide, upon request by the Secretary or a State agency, information provided by the manufacturer or supplier in paragraph (g)(3) of that section.

Page 6 -- OIG Advisory Opinion No. 01-08

The advent of the SNF PPS has sparked a variety of innovative arrangements between ancillary suppliers and SNFs seeking to control and reduce their costs for PPS-covered items and services. The Program is one such response and addresses an obvious marketing problem facing the Company: how to convince Facility operators to buy the Company's therapeutic mattresses when the Facilities are being paid primarily on a fixed, all-inclusive, per diem rate. As a practical matter, the Program is designed to show potential customers that the Company is willing to put its money at risk if its therapeutic mattresses do not perform as intended by reducing substantially the incidence of pressure ulcers. Specifically, the Program's pricing arrangement puts the Company at risk for: (i) the costs of powered mattresses necessary to treat pressure ulcers; (ii) the costs of skin and wound care products that result from the failure of the non-powered and powered mattresses to reduce the incidence of pressure ulcers; and (iii) to a limited extent, the costs of legal liability resulting from pressure ulcers.

As a threshold matter, we will consider the Program's pricing arrangement and the Program Warranty separately. The Program's pricing arrangement cannot fit into the discount safe harbor, 42 C.F.R. § 1001.952(h), since it bundles several distinct items and services. The OIG has consistently stated that the provision of one item or service for free or at less than fair market value to induce the purchase of another item or service constitutes remuneration within the meaning of the anti-kickback statute and is not protected by the discount safe harbor. Therefore, we must carefully scrutinize the Program's pricing arrangement in its entirety to determine whether, based upon a totality of the facts and circumstances presented, it poses a risk of fraud and abuse.

The Program's pricing arrangement contains the following factors which, taken together, lead us to conclude that the Program's pricing arrangement for therapeutic mattresses, other support surfaces, and skin and wound care products poses minimal risk of fraud or abuse.

- First, the Program covers all beds and all residents of a participating Facility and pricing is uniform, regardless of the resident's payor.
- Second, participating Facilities are reimbursed pursuant to a global, all-inclusive rate, either by Medicare Part A or State Medicaid programs, for the vast majority of the items and services included in the Program. Thus, there is little apparent risk of abuse from the bundling of items and services all of which are reimbursed primarily by a single, global, all-inclusive rate, since the financial incentive for the Facility receiving a fixed payment is to reduce total costs. To the extent that a State uses a cost-based reimbursement system to determine the global rate, the total cost of the Program should be reflected on the participating Facility's cost report.[9]

---

[9]We express no opinion regarding liability of any Facility under the False Claims Act or other legal authorities in connection with any improper billing or claims submission directly or indirectly related to, or arising from, the Program.

Page 7 -- OIG Advisory Opinion No. 01-08

- Third, of all of the items and services provided in connection with the Program's bundled pricing arrangement, only surgical wound supplies are potentially separately reimbursable under Medicare Part B. In general, we are concerned with bundled payments for items and services that are separately reimbursable because it is difficult to ensure that Federal health care programs receive their appropriate share of any savings. Bundled arrangements are especially problematic in cases where the financial benefit inures primarily to the purchaser and not to the Federal fisc, or where the bundled arrangement increases utilization of a particular item or service on which profit margins from Federal reimbursement are unusually high. However, in this case, the Company has certified that (i) except for surgical wound supplies, no separate reimbursement is available for the items and services provided under the Program, so the opportunity to bill separately for any of the Program's items or services is rare, and (ii) the value of the surgical wound supplies provided under the Program represents a very small percentage of the Program's price. The foregoing makes it highly unlikely that the limited opportunity to separately bill surgical wound supplies under Medicare Part B will significantly increase the risk of fraud and abuse.[10]

- Fourth, the Program is the only financial arrangement between the Company and the participating Facilities. Accordingly, there is no risk of potential "swapping" of low Program prices for the Company's opportunity to provide other unrelated items or services to participating Facilities.

With respect to the Program Warranty, we begin with the warranty safe harbor, 42 C.F.R. § 1001.952(g). The definition of warranty in the warranty safe harbor incorporates the Federal Trade Commission's definition of warranty which includes "any undertaking in writing . . . to refund, repair, replace, or take other remedial action with respect to such product in the event that such product fails to meet the specifications set forth in the undertaking." 15 U.S.C. § 2301(6)(B). In the instant case, for each purchasing Facility, the "product" is the entire Program. The promise to indemnify a participating Facility from certain liabilities resulting from judgments for skin or wound care deficiencies, notwithstanding the Facility's strict adherence to the Program, constitutes remedial action resulting from failure of the Program to perform as promised. Specifically, in the preamble to the final warranty safe harbor, we stated that payments made by a manufacturer or supplier to settle claims or satisfy judgments arising out of product liability claims were protected by the warranty safe harbor to the extent they comply with all of

[10]For purposes of this opinion, we assume that any Medicare Part B claim submitted by a participating Facility will accurately describe the item and include the appropriate code from the HCFA Common Procedure Coding System ("HCPCS"). See 42 C.F.R. § 424.32(a)(5). We express no opinion regarding liability of the Company or any Facility under the False Claims Act or other legal authorities in connection with any improper billing or claims submission directly or indirectly related to, or arising from, the Program.

the other conditions of that safe harbor. See 56 Fed. Reg. at 35977 (July 29, 1991). In this case, all other conditions are met.[11]

The sole issue with respect to the Program Warranty is that the "product" is a combination of items (i.e., the support surfaces, skin and wound care products, and protocols) and some services (i.e., the wound specialist's advice and in-service training). Since the warranty safe harbor only protects warranties on "items", a warranty on a combination of items and services does not technically qualify for protection. In this case, however, the Program's items, especially its mattresses and other support services, are the linchpin of the Program and the Program Warranty. The vast majority of the costs of the Program are for the items and the anticipated benefit is principally attributed to the mattresses and other support surfaces. Thus, we conclude that the fact that the Program Warranty covers a small service component, as well as items, does not significantly increase the risk of fraud and abuse.

Finally, if the Program works as intended and reduces the incidence of pressure ulcers, patients and Federal health care programs will benefit. In many respects, global payments are intended to encourage Facility operators to re-engineer the delivery of care to reduce costs and increase quality. Given the absence of any identifiable opportunity for abuse, we are reluctant to chill innovative and potentially beneficial arrangements. We caution, however, that if we subsequently become aware of problems not apparent to us today, we reserve the right, as provided by regulation, to modify this opinion.

For all of the foregoing reasons, we will not subject the Company to administrative sanctions under sections 1128(b)(7) or 1128A(a)(7) of the Act (as those sections relate to the commission of acts described in section 1128B(b) of the Act) in connection with the Program.

III. CONCLUSION

Based on the facts certified in your request for an advisory opinion and supplemental submissions, we conclude that the Program could potentially generate prohibited remuneration under the anti-kickback statute, if the requisite intent to induce or reward referrals of Federal health care program business were present, but that the OIG would not impose administrative sanctions on [company's name redacted] under sections 1128(b)(7) or 1128A(a)(7) of the Act (as those sections relate to the commission of acts described in section 1128B(b) of the Act) in connection with the Program. This opinion is limited to the Program and, therefore, we express no opinion about any ancillary agreements or arrangements disclosed or referenced in your request letter or supplemental submissions.

IV. LIMITATIONS

---

[11]The Program Warranty expressly prohibits the Company from making any payments for liability resulting from medical, surgical, or hospital expenses incurred by a Facility resident.

Page 9 -- OIG Advisory Opinion No. 01-08

The limitations applicable to this opinion include the following:

- This advisory opinion is issued only to [company's name redacted], who is the requestor of this opinion. This advisory opinion has no application to, and cannot be relied upon by, any other individual or entity.

- This advisory opinion may not be introduced into evidence in any matter involving an entity or individual that is not a requestor of this opinion.

- This advisory opinion is applicable only to the statutory provisions specifically noted above. No opinion is herein expressed or implied with respect to the application of any other Federal, state, or local statute, rule, regulation, ordinance, or other law that may be applicable to the Program.

- This advisory opinion will not bind or obligate any agency other than the U.S. Department of Health and Human Services.

- This advisory opinion is limited in scope to the specific arrangement described in this letter and has no applicability to other arrangements, even those which appear similar in nature or scope.

- No opinion is expressed herein regarding the liability of any party under the False Claims Act or other legal authorities for any improper billing, claims submission, cost reporting, or related conduct.

This opinion is also subject to any additional limitations set forth at 42 C.F.R. Part 1008.

The OIG will not proceed against the Company with respect to any action that is part of the Program taken in good faith reliance upon this advisory opinion as long as all of the material facts have been fully, completely, and accurately presented, and the Program in practice comports with the information provided. The OIG reserves the right to reconsider the questions and issues raised in this advisory opinion and, where the public interest requires, rescind, modify or terminate this opinion. In the event that this advisory opinion is modified or terminated, the OIG will not proceed against the Company with respect to any action taken in good faith reliance upon this advisory opinion, where all of the relevant facts were fully, completely, and accurately presented and where such action was promptly discontinued upon notification of the modification or termination of this advisory opinion. An advisory opinion may be rescinded only if the relevant and material facts have not been fully, completely, and accurately disclosed to the OIG.

Sincerely,

/s/

D. McCarty Thornton

Chief Counsel to the Inspector General

DEPARTMENT OF HEALTH & HUMAN SERVICES

Office of Inspector General

Washington, D.C. 20201

[*We redact certain identifying information and certain potentially privileged, confidential, or proprietary information associated with the individual or entity, unless otherwise approved by the requestors*.]

Issued: October 10, 2001

Posted: October 17, 2001

[names and addresses redacted]

Re: [Surgical Center X]
OIG Advisory Opinion No. 01-17

Dear Sirs:

We are writing in response to your request for an advisory opinion regarding whether an existing ambulatory surgical center ("ASC") joint venture between a hospital-affiliated entity and an entity owned indirectly by five ophthalmologists, together with the execution of three related ancillary agreements (the "Arrangement"), constitutes grounds for the imposition of sanctions under the exclusion authority at section 1128(b)(7) of the Social Security Act (the "Act") or the civil monetary penalty provision at section 1128A(a)(7) of the Act, as those sections relate to the commission of acts described in section 1128B(b) of the Act.

You have certified that all of the information provided in your request, including all supplementary letters, is true and correct and constitutes a complete description of the relevant facts and agreements among the parties.

Page 2 — OIG Advisory Opinion No. 01-17

In issuing this opinion, we have relied solely on the facts and information presented to us. We have not undertaken an independent investigation of such information. This opinion is limited to the facts presented. If material facts have not been disclosed or have been misrepresented, this opinion is without force and effect.

Based on the facts certified in your request for an advisory opinion and supplemental submissions, we conclude that the Arrangement could potentially generate prohibited remuneration under the anti-kickback statute if the requisite intent to induce or reward referrals were present, but that the Office of Inspector General ("OIG") will not impose administrative sanctions on [Surgical Center X] or [Hospital Y] (collectively, the "Requestors") under sections 1128(b)(7) or 1128A(a)(7) of the Act (as those sections relate to the commission of acts described in section 1128B(b) of the Act) in connection with the Arrangement.

This opinion may not be relied on by any persons other than [Surgical Center X] and [Hospital Y], the requestors of this opinion, and is further qualified as set out in Part V below and in 42 C.F.R. Part 1008.

I. FACTUAL BACKGROUND

A. The Investment Interests

[Surgical Center X] (the "Surgical Center") is a freestanding eye surgery center indirectly owned by [Hospital Y] (the "Hospital")[1] and five individual ophthalmologic surgeons (the "Investing Ophthalmologists"),[2] each of whom is a member of one of two group practices. Through holding companies, the Hospital owns 25% of the Surgical Center and the Investing Ophthalmologists jointly own 75%. For the Hospital and each Investing

---

[1]The Hospital owns and operates an acute care hospital and employs twelve physicians and twenty-one residents. The Hospital is part of a group of affiliated entities owned and controlled, directly or indirectly, by [Parent Entity Z]. Affiliated entities include two physician practices and a real estate company. For purposes of this advisory opinion, we consider all of the foregoing and all other affiliated entities owned and controlled in whole or in part, directly or indirectly, by any of the foregoing to be sufficiently related to be treated as a single entity, which will be referred to individually and collectively as the "Hospital".

[2]The Investing Ophthalmologists are [3 names redacted] (affiliated with a group practice known as [group name redacted]) and [2 names redacted] (affiliated with a group practice known as [group name redacted]).

Page 3 — OIG Advisory Opinion No. 01-17

Ophthalmologist, the return on the Surgical Center investment is directly proportional to the amount of capital that the applicable investor contributed to the respective holding company compared to the total capital contributions to the Surgical Center from all investors.

The Investing Ophthalmologists own their interests in the Surgical Center indirectly. Each Investing Ophthalmologist's direct investment is in one of two limited liability companies, depending on their group practice. In turn, these two limited liability companies jointly own a third limited liability company that is the actual investor in the Surgery Center. The Requestors have certified that: (i) the terms on which the investment interests in the three limited liability companies were offered to the Investing Ophthalmologists were not related to the previous or expected volume of referrals, services furnished, or business otherwise generated to or for the Hospital or the Surgical Center; and (ii) none of the capital contributed by the Investing Ophthalmologists was obtained with funds loaned or guaranteed by the Surgical Center, any direct or indirect investor, or any individual or entity acting on behalf of the Surgical Center or any direct or indirect investor. Each Investing Ophthalmologist meets the "one-third practice income test" set forth at 42 C.F.R. § 1001.952(r)(2)(ii).[3]

The Requestors have certified that the Surgical Center meets all of the requirements of the hospital-physician ASC safe harbor, 42 C.F.R. § 1001.952(r)(4), except for the requirement that the hospital must not be in a position to make or influence referrals directly or indirectly to any investor or the ASC and the requirement that the physicians' interests must be held directly by physicians or their group practices.[4] In particular, the Hospital has a number of affiliations with referring physicians as employees, independent contractors, and medical staff members (collectively, "Hospital-Affiliated Physicians"). Consequently, the Hospital has certified that it will implement the following measures:

---

[3]Under the one-third practice income test, at least one-third of each physician investor's medical practice income from all sources for the previous fiscal year or previous 12-month period must be derived from the physician's performance of procedures. <u>See</u> 42 C.F.R. § 1001.952(r)(2)(ii). The term "procedures" is defined at 42 C.F.R. § 1001.952(r)(5).

[4]Since all of the Investing Ophthalmologists are engaged in the same medical practice specialty, they are not required to meet the additional "one-third of the procedures test" for multi-specialty ASCs, 42 C.F.R. § 1001.952(r)(3)(iii).

- Physicians employed by the Hospital will not make referrals directly to the Surgical Center, although they may refer patients to the Investing Ophthalmologists or their group practices.

- The Hospital will refrain from taking any actions to require or encourage Hospital-Affiliated Physicians to refer patients to the Surgical Center, the Investing Ophthalmologists, or their group practices.

- The Hospital will not track referrals made by Hospital-Affiliated Physicians to the Surgical Center, the Investing Ophthalmologists, or their group practices.

- Compensation paid to Hospital-Affiliated Physicians, whether pursuant to employment or personal services contracts, will not be related directly or indirectly to the volume or value of referrals or other business generated by such physicians to or for the Surgical Center, the Investing Ophthalmologists, or their group practices. Such compensation will be consistent with fair market value in arm's-length transactions.

On an annual basis, the Hospital will notify all Hospital-Affiliated Physicians of these measures.

The Requestors have certified that the Surgical Center, each Investing Ophthalmologist, and the Investing Ophthalmologists' group practices have agreed to treat Federal health care program beneficiaries in a nondiscriminatory manner and that the Investing Ophthalmologists will fully inform patients referred to the Surgical Center by them or their group practices of the Hospital's and the Investing Ophthalmologists' investment interests through a written disclosure to each such patient and through a notice posted in each Investing Ophthalmologist's office.

B. The Ancillary Agreements

In addition to the investment interests, the Surgical Center leases space from the Hospital for the Surgical Center's ASC and shares its reception area with the Hospital's outpatient endoscopy ASC. These arrangements are structured in two agreements: (i) a lease of a surgical suite and an adjacent reception area suite from the Hospital to the Surgical Center; and (ii) a partial leaseback agreement under which the Surgical Center agrees to share its reception area with the Hospital's endoscopy ASC, in exchange for a proportional payment equal to half of the reception area rent payment under the primary

Page 5 — OIG Advisory Opinion No. 01-17

lease to the Surgical Center.[5] The Requestors have certified that the lease and the partial leaseback agreement meet all of the requirements of the space rental safe harbor, 42 C.F.R. § 1001.952(b), and that payments under each agreement are consistent with fair market value in arm's-length transactions.

Finally, the Surgical Center has engaged one of the Investing Ophthalmologists to serve as medical director of the Surgical Center for approximately three to fours hours per week. Based upon the medical director's daily log of services rendered and time spent, the Surgical Center pays the medical director $[m] per hour, subject to a cap of $[n] per month. The Requestors have certified that such services are provided through a medical director agreement, which meets all of the requirements of the personal services and management contracts safe harbor, 42 C.F.R. § 1001.952(d), except for (i) the requirement that, for services provided on a periodic, sporadic, or part-time basis, the contract must specify the exact schedule, precise length, and exact charge for the intervals, and (ii) the requirement that the aggregate compensation paid over the term of the contract must be set in advance. The Requestors have also certified that compensation paid under the medical director agreement is consistent with fair market value in arm's-length transactions for the services rendered.

II. THE LAW

The anti-kickback statute makes it a criminal offense knowingly and willfully to offer, pay, solicit, or receive any remuneration to induce or reward referrals of items or services reimbursable by Federal health care programs. See section 1128B(b) of the Act. Where remuneration is paid purposefully to induce or reward referrals of items or services payable by a Federal health care program, the anti-kickback statute is violated. By its terms, the statute ascribes criminal liability to parties on both sides of an impermissible "kickback" transaction. For purposes of the anti-kickback statute, "remuneration" includes the transfer of anything of value, in cash or in-kind, directly or indirectly, covertly or overtly.

The statute has been interpreted to cover any arrangement where one purpose of the remuneration was to obtain money for the referral of services or to induce further referrals. United States v. Kats, 871 F.2d 105 (9th Cir. 1989); United States v. Greber, 760 F.2d 68 (3d Cir.), cert. denied, 474 U.S. 988 (1985). Violation of the statute constitutes a felony punishable by a maximum fine of $25,000, imprisonment up to five years, or both. Conviction will also lead to automatic exclusion from Federal health care

---

[5]The Surgical Center and the Hospital's endoscopy ASC have hired separate receptionists.

Page 6 — OIG Advisory Opinion No. 01-17

programs, including Medicare and Medicaid. Where a party commits an act described in section 1128B(b) of the Act, the OIG may initiate administrative proceedings to impose civil monetary penalties on such party under section 1128A(a)(7) of the Act. The OIG may also initiate administrative proceedings to exclude such party from the Federal health care programs under section 1128(b)(7) of the Act.

The Department of Health and Human Services has published "safe harbor" regulations that define practices that are not subject to the anti-kickback statute because such practices would be unlikely to result in fraud or abuse. See section 1128B(b)(3) of the Act; 42 C.F.R. § 1001.952. The safe harbors set forth specific conditions that, if met, assure entities involved of not being prosecuted or sanctioned for the arrangement qualifying for the safe harbor. Strict compliance with all elements is required for safe harbor protection. See 56 Fed. Reg. 35952, 35954 (July 29, 1991).

Three safe harbors are relevant to the Arrangement. First, with respect to the Arrangement's investment interests, the safe harbor for investment interests in ambulatory surgical centers jointly-owned by hospitals and physicians, 42 C.F.R. § 1001.952(r)(4), is relevant. Three of the conditions of the hospital-physician ASC safe harbor require that: (i) a hospital investor must not be in a position to refer directly or indirectly to, or otherwise generate business for, the ASC or any investor; (ii) investing physicians who are in a position to refer patients to the ASC can only invest as individuals who meet the requirements for surgeon-owned ASCs, single-specialty ASCs, or multi-specialty ASCs set forth at 42 C.F.R. § 1001.952(r)(1), (r)(2), or (r)(3) or as group practices composed of such physicians or surgical group practices; and (iii) any services, equipment, or space provided by the hospital to the ASC must comply with a safe harbor. Second, in cases, such as the instant case, where the ASC is located in space owned by the hospital, the space rental safe harbor, 42 C.F.R. § 1001.952(b), is relevant. Third, for services provided by the medical director, the safe harbor for personal services and management contracts, 42 C.F.R. § 1001.952(d), is relevant. Two of the conditions of this safe harbor are that (i) for services provided on a periodic, sporadic, or part-time basis, the contract must specify the exact schedule, precise length, and exact charge for the intervals, and (ii) the aggregate compensation paid over the term of the contract must be set in advance. See 42 C.F.R. § 1001.952(d)(3), (d)(5).

III. ANALYSIS

Although joint ventures by physicians and hospitals are often susceptible to fraud and abuse, the OIG recognizes that precluding joint ownership of ASCs may place hospitals at a competitive disadvantage by forcing them to compete with ASCs owned by physicians, who principally control referrals. Thus, the Department promulgated a safe harbor for ASCs that meet all of the applicable safe harbor conditions. However, the

Page 7 — OIG Advisory Opinion No. 01-17

Arrangement does not qualify for safe harbor protection because it fails to satisfy two such conditions (i.e., the Hospital is a potential referral source and the Investing Ophthalmologists are investing through holding companies, instead of investing directly as individuals or through their group practices). Therefore, we must carefully scrutinize the Arrangement in its entirety to determine whether, based upon a totality of the facts and circumstances presented, the potential risk of fraud and abuse is sufficiently low.

As a threshold matter, we consider the Arrangement's investment interests and ancillary agreements separately. With respect to the investment interests, a primary concern is that the Hospital may potentially direct or influence referrals to the Surgical Center or the Investing Ophthalmologists by using its control and influence over Hospital-Affiliated Physicians. However, the Hospital has certified that it will take the following steps to limit its ability to direct or influence referrals to the Surgical Center, the Investing Ophthalmologists, or their group practices:

- The Hospital will refrain from taking any actions to require or encourage Hospital-Affiliated Physicians to refer patients to the Surgical Center, the Investing Ophthalmologists, or their group practices.
- The Hospital will not track referrals made by Hospital-Affiliated Physicians to the Surgical Center, the Investing Ophthalmologists, or their group practices.
- Compensation paid to Hospital-Affiliated Physicians, whether pursuant to employment or personal services contracts, will not be related directly or indirectly to the volume or value of referrals or other business generated by such physicians to or for the Surgical Center, the Investing Ophthalmologists, or their group practices. Such compensation will be consistent with fair market value in arm's-length transactions.
- On an annual basis, the Hospital will inform Hospital-Affiliated Physicians of the foregoing measures.

In light of these safeguards, the Hospital's ability to direct or influence the referrals of its Hospital Affiliated Physicians will be significantly constrained.

With respect to the investment interests of the Investing Ophthalmologists, in this case, the use of "pass through" entities rather than direct ownership does not substantively increase the risk of fraud or abuse. Each Investing Ophthalmologist meets the "one-third practice income" test. Each Investing Ophthalmologist will receive a return on his or her Surgical Center investment that is directly proportional to the percentage that his or her contribution bears to the total investment contributions in the Surgery Center. Moreover,

Page 8 — OIG Advisory Opinion No. 01-17

the terms on which the Investing Ophthalmologists were offered their direct and indirect investment interests were not based on the volume or value of referrals to the Surgery Center or the Hospital.

With respect to the ancillary agreements, the Requestors have certified that the lease for the Surgical Center's suites and the partial leaseback agreement for the Surgical Center's reception area meet all of the requirements of the space rental safe harbor at 42 C.F.R. § 1001.952(b). The Requestors have also certified that the medical director agreement meets all of the requirements of the personal services and management contract safe harbor at 42 C.F.R. § 1001.952(d), except for the requirement that, for services provided on a periodic, sporadic, or part-time basis, the contract must specify the exact schedule, precise length, and exact charge for the intervals and the requirement that the aggregate compensation paid over the term of the contract must be set in advance. See 42 C.F.R. §§ 1001.952(d)(3), (d)(5). However, the risk is substantially reduced in the instant case because the medical director agreement involves compensation that is certified to be consistent with fair market value, based upon a specified hourly rate, subject to a monthly payment cap, and paid only if there is written documentation of the hours and the services provided. Thus, given the totality of facts and circumstances presented, the ancillary agreements do not significantly increase the risk of fraud and abuse.

For all of the foregoing reasons, we conclude that, while the Arrangement poses some risk, the safeguards put in place by the Requestors make that risk sufficiently low that we would not subject the Arrangement to administrative sanctions in connection with the anti-kickback statute.

IV. CONCLUSION

For all of the above reasons, and based on the facts certified in your request for an advisory opinion and supplemental submissions, we conclude that the Arrangement could potentially generate prohibited remuneration under the anti-kickback statute if the requisite intent to induce or reward referrals were present, but that the OIG will not impose administrative sanctions on [Surgical Center X] or [Hospital Y] under sections 1128(b)(7) or 1128A(a)(7) of the Act (as those sections relate to the commission of acts described in section 1128B(b) of the Act) in connection with the Arrangement.

V. LIMITATIONS

The limitations applicable to this opinion include the following:

Page 9 — OIG Advisory Opinion No. 01-17

- This advisory opinion is issued only to [Surgical Center X] and [Hospital Y], which are the requestors of this opinion. This advisory opinion has no application, and cannot be relied upon, by any other individual or entity.

- This advisory opinion may not be introduced into evidence in any matter involving an entity or individual that is not a requestor of this opinion.

- This advisory opinion is applicable only to the statutory provisions specifically noted above. No opinion is expressed or implied herein with respect to the application of any other Federal, state, or local statute, rule, regulation, ordinance, or other law that may be applicable to the Arrangement.

- This advisory opinion will not bind or obligate any agency other than the U.S. Department of Health and Human Services.

- This advisory opinion is limited in scope to the specific arrangement described in this letter and has no applicability to other arrangements, even those which appear similar in nature or scope.

- No opinion is expressed herein regarding the liability of any party under the False Claims Act or other legal authorities for any improper billing, claims submission, cost reporting, or related conduct.

This opinion is also subject to any additional limitations set forth at 42 C.F.R. Part 1008.

The OIG will not proceed against the Requestors with respect to any action that is part of the Arrangement taken in good faith reliance upon this advisory opinion as long as all of the material facts have been fully, completely, and accurately presented, and the Arrangement in practice comports with the information provided. The OIG reserves the right to reconsider the questions and issues raised in this advisory opinion and, where the public interest requires, to rescind, modify or terminate this opinion. In the event that this advisory opinion is modified or terminated, the OIG will not proceed against the Requestors with respect to any action taken in good faith reliance upon this advisory opinion, where all of the relevant facts were fully, completely, and accurately presented and where such action was promptly discontinued upon notification of the modification or termination of this advisory opinion. An advisory opinion may be rescinded only if the relevant and material facts have not been fully, completely and accurately disclosed to the OIG.

Sincerely,

Page 10 — OIG Advisory Opinion No. 01-17

/s/

D. McCarty Thornton
Chief Counsel to the Inspector General

DEPARTMENT OF HEALTH & HUMAN SERVICES Office of Inspector General

Washington, D.C. 20201

[We redact certain identifying information and certain potentially privileged, confidential, or proprietary information associated with the individual or entity, unless otherwise approved by the requestor.]

Issued: May 14, 2002

Posted: May 22, 2002

[name and address redacted]

Re: OIG Advisory Opinion No. 02-6

Dear [name redacted]:

We are writing in response to your request for an advisory opinion regarding your proposal to offer a refund program to hospital customers who purchase your blood-filtering device for treatment of rheumatoid arthritis (the "Refund Program"). Specifically, you have inquired whether the Refund Program would constitute grounds for the imposition of sanctions under the exclusion authority at section 1128(b)(7) of the Social Security Act (the "Act") or the civil monetary penalty provision at section 1128A(a)(7) of the Act, as those sections relate to the commission of acts described in section 1128B(b) of the Act.

You have certified that all of the information provided in your request, including all supplementary letters, is true and correct and constitutes a complete description of the relevant facts and agreements among the parties.

In issuing this opinion, we have relied solely on the facts and information presented to us. We have not undertaken an independent investigation of such information. This opinion is limited to the facts presented. If material facts have not been disclosed or have been misrepresented, this opinion is without force and effect.

Based on the facts certified in your request for an advisory opinion and supplemental submissions, we conclude that the Refund Program could potentially generate prohibited remuneration under the anti-kickback statute, if the requisite intent to induce or reward referrals of Federal health care program business were present, but that the Office of Inspector General ("OIG") would not impose administrative sanctions on [name redacted] under sections 1128(b)(7) or 1128A(a)(7) of the Act (as those sections relate to the commission of acts described in section 1128B(b) of the Act) in connection with the Refund Program.

This opinion may not be relied on by any persons other than [name redacted], the requestor of this opinion, and is further qualified as set out in Part IV below and in 42 C.F.R. Part 1008.

I. FACTUAL BACKGROUND

[Name redacted] (the "Requestor") has developed and sells to health care providers a Protein A column for the filtering of blood in the treatment of rheumatoid arthritis (the "Column"). In a process similar to kidney dialysis, a rheumatoid arthritis patient's blood is filtered through the Column, which removes anti-platelet antibodies from the patient's plasma. A course of treatment typically consists of twelve blood-filtering sessions (one Column per session), given at weekly intervals.

The Centers for Medicare and Medicaid Services ("CMS") (formerly the Health Care Financing Administration) issued a National Coverage Decision ("NCD") that extracorporeal immunoadsorption using Protein A columns is a reasonable and necessary treatment for rheumatoid arthritis that is covered if the following two criteria are met:

- the patient has severe rheumatoid arthritis; and
- the disease has failed to respond to an adequate course of a minimum of three disease-modifying drugs.

See Medicare Coverage Policy – National Coverage Decisions, CAG-00057N (HCFA April 27, 2000).

The Requestor has represented that some hospitals have been reluctant to purchase Columns because of the high cost of the Columns for a course of treatment and uncertainty regarding coverage, notwithstanding the NCD. In such circumstances, the Requestor proposes to refund the full purchase price of any Column to a purchasing hospital if a fiscal intermediary denies payment for treatments with the Column, subject to the following limitations and restrictions:

Page 3 - OIG Advisory Opinion No. 02-6

- The treatments must meet the coverage criteria of the NCD;
- The payment denial must be sustained through the first level of appeal;[1]
- Medicare must be the primary insurer of the patient for whom payment is denied;
- The patient for whom payment is denied must be a registered outpatient of the hospital;
- The hospital must have maintained and submitted all documentation to Medicare necessary to establish the Medicare conditions of coverage;
- In the event that the Requestor provides a refund under the Refund Program, the hospital must agree to: (1) report the refund to the appropriate government payor (e.g., the Medicare contractor) and any secondary insurer; (2) return any collected deductibles and copayments to the patient and/or adjust the statement submitted to the government payor or any secondary insurer to reflect the return of any collected cost-sharing amounts; (3) upon request, provide the Requestor with proof of such reports, refunds, or adjustments; and (4) upon request, provide all information related to the Refund Program to Federal and state health care officials.

The Requestor will report the existence of the Refund Program on invoices to each hospital. For each hospital, the refund offer would be for a limited time and would expire on the earlier of (i) the one-hundred and twentieth (120th) day after the first delivery to the hospital of purchased Columns, or (ii) the hospital's first receipt of notice of a denial by the fiscal intermediary for a patient qualified for the treatment under the NCD. In other words, the Refund Program would be limited to the period of the Column's initial introduction in each hospital.

Virtually all of the hospitals that are potential purchasers of the Columns participate in Medicare. Therefore, it is expected that at least some of the Columns sold to hospitals will be used to provide services reimbursed by Medicare.

---

[1]In connection with the first level of appeal at which the denial is upheld, the hospital must have submitted all relevant portions of the patient's medical records necessary to demonstrate that the patient met Medicare standards for coverage of treatments with the Column.

Page 4 - OIG Advisory Opinion No. 02-6

II. LEGAL ANALYSIS

B. Law

The anti-kickback statute makes it a criminal offense knowingly and willfully to offer, pay, solicit, or receive any remuneration to induce or reward referrals of items or services reimbursable by a Federal health care program. See section 1128B(b) of the Act. Where remuneration is paid purposefully to induce or reward referrals of items or services payable by a Federal health care program, the anti-kickback statute is violated. By its terms, the statute ascribes criminal liability to parties on both sides of an impermissible "kickback" transaction. For purposes of the anti-kickback statute, "remuneration" includes the transfer of anything of value, directly or indirectly, overtly or covertly, in cash or in kind.

The statute has been interpreted to cover any arrangement where one purpose of the remuneration was to obtain money for the referral of services or to induce further referrals. United States v. Kats, 871 F.2d 105 (9th Cir. 1989); United States v. Greber, 760 F.2d 68 (3d Cir.), cert. denied, 474 U.S. 988 (1985). Violation of the statute constitutes a felony punishable by a maximum fine of $25,000, imprisonment up to five years, or both. Conviction will also lead to automatic exclusion from Federal health care programs, including Medicare and Medicaid. Where a party commits an act described in section 1128B(b) of the Act, the OIG may initiate administrative proceedings to impose civil monetary penalties on such party under section 1128A(a)(7) of the Act. The OIG may also initiate administrative proceedings to exclude such party from the Federal health care programs under section 1128(b)(7) of the Act.

The Department of Health and Human Services has promulgated safe harbor regulations that define practices that are not subject to the anti-kickback statute because such practices would be unlikely to result in fraud or abuse. See 42 C.F.R. § 1001.952. The safe harbors set forth specific conditions that, if met, assure entities involved of not being prosecuted or sanctioned for the arrangement qualifying for the safe harbor. However, safe harbor protection is afforded only to those arrangements that precisely meet all of the conditions set forth in the safe harbor. The safe harbor for warranties, 42 C.F.R. § 1001.952(g), is potentially applicable to the Refund Program.

B. Analysis

Extracorporeal adsorption using Protein A columns is a Medicare-covered service for treatment of rheumatoid arthritis, and the hospitals that purchase the Columns are expected to use them to provide treatment to some Medicare patients. Therefore, the

Page 5 - OIG Advisory Opinion No. 02-6

Refund Program is an offer of remuneration to induce the hospitals to purchase items indirectly reimbursable by a Federal health care program. Accordingly, the Refund Program implicates the anti-kickback statute.

The Refund Program would not be protected under the warranty safe harbor to the anti-kickback statute. See 42 C.F.R. § 1001.952(g). For purposes of the safe harbor, the warranty must be related to product failure.[2] By contrast, the Refund Program does not relate to product failure, but to the purchaser's resale of the product. Thus, the Refund Program does not meet the definition of warranty and cannot fit in the safe harbor.

Nevertheless, the Refund Program contains a number of safeguards that reduce the risk of fraud and abuse. First, the reimbursement guarantee for each hospital is limited in time with reference to the initial delivery of purchased Columns or the initial payment denial. Second, the guarantee is limited in scope to treatments that meet the conditions of coverage in the NCD. Given the constraints on coverage in the NCD, this limitation should reduce the risk of improper utilization. Third, the guarantee is also limited to Medicare claims denied through the first level of appeal. Fourth, the guarantee is limited to a refund of the purchase price of the Columns. The Requestor will not reimburse the purchasers for any patient care expenses (i.e., medical, surgical, or hospital expenses) or for any other costs that the hospital may have incurred related to the therapy. Fifth, the Requestor will report the existence of the Refund Program on invoices to each hospital and, as a condition of participation in the Refund Program, will require each hospital to uphold its regulatory obligations related to the Refund Program, including (1) reporting the refund to the appropriate government payor and secondary insurer, (2) returning any collected deductibles and copayments to the patient, and/or adjusting the statement submitted to the government payor or any secondary insurer to reflect the return of any collected cost-sharing amounts, and (3) providing all information related to the Refund Program to Federal and state health care officials upon request.

---

[2]The safe harbor incorporates the definition of warranty in 15 U.S.C. § 2301(6), namely:

> any undertaking in writing in connection with the sale by a supplier of a consumer product to refund, repair, replace, or take other remedial action with respect to such product in the event that such product fails to meet the specifications set forth in the undertaking, which written affirmation, promise, or undertaking becomes part of the basis of the bargain between a supplier and a buyer for purposes other than resale of such product.

See 15 U.S.C. § 2301(6)(b).

Page 6 - OIG Advisory Opinion No. 02-6

These safeguards and the limited nature of the Refund Program serve to reduce the risk of fraud or abuse related to the anti-kickback statute. In particular, the Refund Program presents a low risk of fraud and abuse because it is not open-ended and is restricted to a time limit that is tied to the initial introduction and product launch of the Column within each hospital.

III. CONCLUSION

Based on the facts certified in your request for an advisory opinion and supplemental submissions, we conclude that the Refund Program could potentially generate prohibited remuneration under the anti-kickback statute, if the requisite intent to induce or reward referrals of Federal health care program business were present, but that the OIG would not impose administrative sanctions on [name redacted] under sections 1128(b)(7) or 1128A(a)(7) of the Act (as those sections relate to the commission of acts described in section 1128B(b) of the Act) in connection with the Refund Program.

IV. LIMITATIONS

The limitations applicable to this opinion include the following:

- This advisory opinion is issued only to [name redacted], which is the requestor of this opinion. This advisory opinion has no application to, and cannot be relied upon by, any other individual or entity.

- This advisory opinion may not be introduced into evidence in any matter involving an entity or individual that is not a requestor of this opinion.

- This advisory opinion is applicable only to the statutory provisions specifically noted above. No opinion is expressed or implied herein with respect to the application of any other Federal, state, or local statute, rule, regulation, ordinance, or other law that may be applicable to the Refund Program, including, without limitation, the physician self-referral law, section 1877 of the Act.

- This advisory opinion will not bind or obligate any agency other than the U.S. Department of Health and Human Services.

- This advisory opinion is limited in scope to the specific arrangement described in this letter and has no applicability to other arrangements, even those which appear similar in nature or scope.

Page 72 - OIG Advisory Opinion No. 02-6

- No opinion is expressed herein regarding the liability of any party under the False Claims Act or other legal authorities for any improper billing, claims submission, cost reporting, or related conduct.

This opinion is also subject to any additional limitations set forth at 42 C.F.R. Part 1008.

The OIG will not proceed against [name redacted] with respect to any action that is part of the Refund Program taken in good faith reliance upon this advisory opinion, as long as all of the material facts have been fully, completely, and accurately presented, and the Refund Program in practice comports with the information provided. The OIG reserves the right to reconsider the questions and issues raised in this advisory opinion and, where the public interest requires, to rescind, modify, or terminate this opinion. In the event that this advisory opinion is modified or terminated, the OIG will not proceed against [name redacted] with respect to any action taken in good faith reliance upon this advisory opinion, where all of the relevant facts were fully, completely, and accurately presented and where such action was promptly discontinued upon notification of the modification or termination of this advisory opinion. An advisory opinion may be rescinded only if the relevant and material facts have not been fully, completely, and accurately disclosed to the OIG.

Sincerely,

\S\

D. McCarty Thornton
Chief Counsel to the Inspector General

DEPARTMENT OF HEALTH & HUMAN SERVICES

Office of Inspector General

Washington, D.C. 20201

[*We redact certain identifying information and certain potentially privileged, confidential, or proprietary information associated with the individual or entity, unless otherwise approved by the requestor.*]

Issued: February 6, 2003

Posted: February 13, 2003

[name and address redacted]

Re: OIG Advisory Opinion No. 03-5

Dear [name redacted]:

We are writing in response to your request for an advisory opinion regarding an ambulatory surgery center (an "ASC") that would be jointly owned by a hospital and a multi-specialty group practice that has a substantial number of physician members who would not personally use the ASC (the "Proposed Arrangement"). Specifically, you have inquired whether the Proposed Arrangement would constitute grounds for the imposition of sanctions under the exclusion authority at section 1128(b)(7) of the Social Security Act (the "Act") or the civil monetary penalty provision at section 1128A(a)(7) of the Act, as those sections relate to the commission of acts described in section 1128B(b) of the Act.

You have certified that all of the information provided in your request, including all supplementary letters, is true and correct and constitutes a complete description of the relevant facts and agreements among the parties.

In issuing this opinion, we have relied solely on the facts and information presented to us. We have not undertaken an independent investigation of such information. This opinion is limited to the facts presented. If material facts have not been disclosed or have been misrepresented, this opinion is without force and effect.

Based on the facts certified in your request for an advisory opinion and supplemental submissions, we conclude that the Proposed Arrangement could potentially generate prohibited remuneration under the anti-kickback statute and that the Office of Inspector General ("OIG") could potentially impose administrative sanctions on [Company X] under sections 1128(b)(7) or 1128A(a)(7) of the Act (as those sections relate to the commission of acts described in section 1128B(b) of the Act) in connection with the Proposed Arrangement. Any definitive conclusion regarding the existence of an anti-kickback violation requires a determination of the parties' intent, which determination is beyond the scope of the advisory opinion process.

This opinion may not be relied on by any persons other than [Company X], the requestorof this opinion, and is further qualified as set out in Part IV below and in 42 C.F.R. Part 1008.

I. FACTUAL BACKGROUND

[Company X] (the "Surgical Center") is an [state redacted] ("State") limited liability company formed for the purpose of planning, developing, and operating an ASC that will be certified by Medicare under 42 C.F.R. part 416. [Company Y], an acute care hospital (the "Hospital"), owns 49% of the Surgical Center, and [Company Z], a multi-specialty clinic (the "Group") owns 51% of the Surgical Center.[1] For each investor, the return on the Surgical Center investment will be directly proportional to the amount of capital that the investor contributed. The Surgical Center will maintain an open medical staff. It will be located on land owned by the Hospital and leased to the Surgical Center pursuant to a written lease.

The Group has fifty-two shareholders (the "Group Shareholders"), each of whom is a licensed physician and an employee of the Group. Each Group Shareholder owns one share of the Group's stock, and any dividends paid by the Group are divided equally among the Group Shareholders. In addition, the Group employs other physicians who do not own Group stock (the "Group Associates") and other health care professionals, such as physical therapists, optometrists, and licensed nurse practitioners. Group Shareholders and Group Associates are collectively referred to herein as "Group Physicians." Some Group Physicians are surgeons; however, most are not. For example, there are fourteen family practitioners, eleven internists, six pediatricians, five obstetricians/gynecologists, two general surgeons, three orthopedic surgeons, and two ophthalmologists. The Surgical Center has certified that the salaries, bonuses, and any other forms of employment-related remuneration payable to Group Physicians will not take into account the physicians' referrals of patients to the Surgical Center or the volume of surgical procedures

[1]The Surgical Center has two classes of members: the voting, Class A Members, consisting solely of the Hospital and the Group, and the non-voting, Class B Members, each of whom must be either a State-licensed physician eligible for credentialing at the Surgical Center or a State legal entity with a majority of its owners being physicians who meet the foregoing requirements. No Class B memberships have been sold.

performed by the physicians at the Surgical Center or elsewhere.

The Hospital is wholly owned by a nonprofit corporation that is also the sole owner of two other hospitals. The Hospital employs forty-two physicians, including eight family practitioners, twelve internal medicine practitioners, eight obstetricians/gynecologists, and two pediatricians. Currently, the Hospital has eight operating suites for both inpatient and outpatient surgery, and physicians employed by the Group perform approximately 25% of all surgeries performed at the Hospital.

II. LEGAL ANALYSIS

A. Law

The anti-kickback statute makes it a criminal offense knowingly and willfully to offer, pay, solicit, or receive any remuneration to induce or reward referrals of items or services reimbursable by a federal health care program. See section 1128B(b) of the Act. Where remuneration is paid purposefully to induce or reward referrals of items or services payable by a federal health care program, the anti-kickback statute is violated. By its terms, the statute ascribes criminal liability to parties on both sides of an impermissible "kickback" transaction. For purposes of the anti-kickback statute, "remuneration" includes the transfer of anything of value, directly or indirectly, overtly or covertly, in cash or in kind.

The statute has been interpreted to cover any arrangement where one purpose of the remuneration was to obtain money for the referral of services or to induce further referrals. United States v. Kats, 871 F.2d 105 (9th Cir. 1989); United States v. Greber, 760 F.2d 68 (3d Cir.), cert. denied, 474 U.S. 988 (1985). Violation of the statute constitutes a felony punishable by a maximum fine of $25,000, imprisonment up to five years, or both. Conviction will also lead to automatic exclusion from federal health care programs, including Medicare and Medicaid. Where a party commits an act described in section 1128B(b) of the Act, the OIG may initiate administrative proceedings to impose civil monetary penalties on such party under section 1128A(a)(7) of the Act. The OIG may also initiate administrative proceedings to exclude such party from the federal health care programs under section 1128(b)(7) of the Act.

The Department of Health and Human Services has promulgated safe harbor regulations that define practices that are not subject to the anti-kickback statute because such practices would be unlikely to result in fraud or abuse. See 42 C.F.R. § 1001.952. The safe harbors set forth specific conditions that, if met, assure entities involved of not being prosecuted or sanctioned for the arrangement qualifying for the safe harbor. However, safe harbor protection is afforded only to those arrangements that precisely meet all of the conditions set forth in the safe harbor.

The safe harbor for investment interests in ambulatory surgical centers jointly owned by hospitals and physicians, 42 C.F.R. §1001.952(r)(4), is relevant to the Proposed Arrangement.[2] One condition of the hospital-physician ASC safe harbor is that investing physicians who are in a position to refer patients to the ASC can only invest as individuals who meet the requirements for surgeon-owned ASCs, single-specialty ASCs, or multi-specialty ASCs set forth at 42 C.F.R. § 1001.952(r)(1), (r)(2), or (r)(3), as applicable, or as group practices composed of such physicians or surgical group practices.[3] Since the Surgical Center's investing physicians are investing through a multi-specialty group practice, for safe harbor protection the group practice (i.e., the Group) must meet all the requirements of the group practice safe harbor at 42 C.F.R. § 1001.952(p) and the group practice must be composed of physicians who meet both the one-third practice income test at 42 C.F.R. § 1001.952(r)(3)(ii) and the one-third practice test at 42 C.F.R. § 1001.952(r)(3)(iii).[4]

B. Analysis

Surgical center joint ventures that include physician-investors in a position to generate surgical business are susceptible to fraud and abuse. Notwithstanding, in recognition that some physician-owned ASC ventures may be beneficial to the federal programs and their beneficiaries, the Department issued a narrow safe harbor for physician-owned ASCs that meet criteria carefully tailored to mitigate the risks of fraud and abuse. With respect to physician-investors, the safe harbor is carefully circumscribed to apply only to physicians who are unlikely to use the investment as a vehicle for profiting from their referrals to other physicians using the ASC. Accordingly, safe harbor protection is limited to physician-investors who actually use the ASC on a regular basis as part of their medical practices or who practice the same specialty as other physician-investors and are therefore unlikely to refer substantial business to "competing" physician-investors when they can earn the fees themselves.

---

[2]In cases, such as the instant case, where the ASC is located in space owned by the hospital, the space rental safe harbor, 42 C.F.R. § 1001.952(b), is also relevant.

[3]The terms "group practice" and "surgical group practice" are defined at 42 C.F.R. § 1001.952(r)(5).

[4]Under the one-third practice income test, 42 C.F.R. § 1001.952(r)(3)(ii), at least one-third of each physician investor's medical practice income from all sources for the previous fiscal year or previous 12-month period must be derived from the physician's performance of procedures. Under the one-third practice test, 42 C.F.R. § 1001.952(r)(3)(iii), at least one-third of the procedures performed by each physician investor for the previous fiscal year or previous 12-month period must be performed at the investment entity. The term "procedures" is defined at 42 C.F.R. § 1001.952(r)(5).

The majority of the Group Physicians fit neither category. Since the Group is a multi-specialty group, there is a substantial likelihood of cross-specialty referrals for services performed in the ASC. Moreover, few of the Group Physicians will actually use the Surgical Center on a regular basis as part of their medical practice. In other words, the Proposed Arrangement would allow those Group Physicians for whom the Surgical Center is not an extension of their office practices to profit from their referrals to the Surgical Center or to their partners who perform procedures there. In this respect, the Proposed Arrangement poses the same risks as an ASC owned directly by surgeons and primary care physicians in the same community. In these circumstances, the fact that the ownership of the ASC is held indirectly through a group practice whose membership includes both surgeons and other potential referring physicians does not reduce the risk that the venture may be used to reward referrals.

Accordingly, we cannot conclude that the Proposed Arrangement poses a minimal risk of fraud and abuse.

III. CONCLUSION

Based on the facts certified in your request for an advisory opinion and supplemental submissions, we conclude that the Proposed Arrangement could potentially generate prohibited remuneration under the anti-kickback statute and that the OIG could potentially impose administrative sanctions on [Company X] under sections 1128(b)(7) or 1128A(a)(7) of the Act (as those sections relate to the commission of acts described in section 1128B(b) of the Act) in connection with the Proposed Arrangement. Any definitive conclusion regarding the existence of an anti-kickback violation requires a determination of the parties' intent, which determination is beyond the scope of the advisory opinion process.

IV. LIMITATIONS

The limitations applicable to this opinion include the following:

- This advisory opinion is issued only to [Company X], the requestor of this opinion. This advisory opinion has no application to, and cannot be relied upon by, any other individual or entity.

- This advisory opinion may not be introduced into evidence in any matter involving an entity or individual that is not a requestor of this opinion.

- This advisory opinion is applicable only to the statutory provisions specifically noted above. No opinion is expressed or implied herein with respect to the application of any other federal, state, or local statute, rule, regulation, ordinance, or other law that may be applicable to the Proposed Arrangement, including, without limitation, the physician self-referral law, section 1877 of the Act.

- This advisory opinion will not bind or obligate any agency other than the U.S. Department of Health and Human Services.

- This advisory opinion is limited in scope to the specific arrangement described in this letter and has no applicability to other arrangements, even those which appear similar in nature or scope.

- No opinion is expressed herein regarding the liability of any party under the False Claims Act or other legal authorities for any improper billing, claims submission, cost reporting, or related conduct.

This opinion is also subject to any additional limitations set forth at 42 C.F.R. Part 1008. The OIG reserves the right to reconsider the questions and issues raised in this advisory opinion and, where the public interest requires, to rescind, modify, or terminate this opinion.

Sincerely,

/s/

Lewis Morris
Chief Counsel to the Inspector General

DEPARTMENT OF HEALTH & HUMAN SERVICES Office of Inspector General

Washington, D.C. 20201

[*We redact certain identifying information and certain potentially privileged, confidential, or proprietary information associated with the individual or entity, unless otherwise approved by the requestor*.]

Issued: June 16, 2003

Posted: June 23, 2003

[name and address redacted]

Re: OIG Advisory Opinion Request No. 03-13

Dear [name redacted]:

We are writing in response to your request for an advisory opinion regarding joint venture ownership of a freestanding magnetic resonance imaging center located on the campus of a rural community hospital (the "Arrangement"). You have asked whether the Arrangement would constitute grounds for the imposition of sanctions under the exclusion authority at section 1128(b)(7) of the Social Security Act (the "Act") or the civil monetary penalty provision at section 1128A(a)(7) of the Act, as those sections relate to the commission of acts described in section 1128B(b) of the Act.

You have certified that all of the information provided in your request, including all supplementary letters, is true and correct and constitutes a complete description of the relevant facts and agreements among the parties.

In issuing this opinion, we have relied solely on the facts and information presented to us. We have not undertaken an independent investigation of such information. This opinion is limited to the facts presented. If material facts have not been disclosed or have been misrepresented, this opinion is without force and effect.

Based on the facts certified in your request for an advisory opinion and supplemental submissions, we conclude that the Arrangement could potentially generate prohibited remuneration under the anti-kickback statute if the requisite intent to induce or reward referrals were present, but that the Office of Inspector General ("OIG") would not impose administrative sanctions on [name redacted] under sections 1128(b)(7) or 1128A(a)(7) of the Act (as those sections relate to the commission of acts described in section 1128B(b) of the Act) in connection with the past and present investment interests relating to the Arrangement. We express no opinion about any future changes in investment interests relating to the Arrangement or about any other agreements or arrangements disclosed or referenced in your request letter or supplemental submissions.

This opinion may not be relied on by any persons other than [name redacted], the requestor of this opinion, and is further qualified as set out in Part V below and in 42 C.F.R. Part 1008.

I. FACTUAL BACKGROUND

[Name redacted] (the "Requestor") is a limited partnership that has owned and operated a freestanding center for magnetic resonance imaging services (the "MRI Center") in a three-county rural area since 1990. The three-county area is a federally designated rural area, but is not a medically underserved area ("MUA") under the regulations at 42 C.F.R. Part 51c. More than 85% of the MRI Center's patients are residents of the three-country area. The MRI Center was established at a time when no MRI services were available in the three-county area.[1]

To raise capital for the MRI Center, all members of the medical community in the three-county area, regardless of hospital affiliation, as well as all former members of the boards of directors of the three area hospitals, were offered limited partnership interests in the Requestor. All potential investors were offered the opportunity to purchase the partnership interests for $[x] per unit on the same terms and conditions of ownership, regardless of their ability to refer patients to, or otherwise generate business for, the MRI Center. Under the terms of the partnership, returns on investments are, have been, and will continue to be directly proportional to the investors' capital contributions.

[1]Although other MRI service providers now exist in the area, the nearest MRI facility comparable to the MRI Center is twenty miles away from the town in which the MRI Center is located. The Requestor has certified that termination of the MRI Center's services would create a hardship for many of the area's poor and elderly residents, who would have to travel a significant distance to obtain comparable MRI services.

A large number of individuals and entities purchased units in the MRI Center.[2] [Name redacted] (the "Hospital"), a local nonprofit hospital, and its supporting foundation, [name redacted] (the "Foundation"), a tax-exempt organization, together own approximately 30% of the partnership units. The Foundation is the venture's managing partner. Various parties in a position to influence or generate referrals, or provide items or services, to the MRI Center also own approximately 30% of the units. The remaining units (approximately 40% of the total) are owned by various community members or physicians who are not in a position to influence or generate referrals to the MRI Center, because they either have retired or practice in the area of radiology. The percentage of interests owned by non-referring investors has increased over time.

Investors generated approximately 37% of the MRI Center's revenues in 2000 and 2001; approximately 24% of total revenues were generated by the Hospital, which contracts with the MRI Center for MRI services, while approximately 13% of total revenues were generated by investing physicians. The MRI Center's remaining revenues (over 60% of the total) were generated from referrals by disinterested parties. The Requestor does not provide information on the sources of its referrals to any of its investors (other than aggregate numbers of referrals from interested and disinterested investors).

The MRI Center is located on the campus of the Hospital pursuant to a space lease (the "Space Lease"). The Requestor has certified that the Space Lease meets all of the conditions of the space rental safe harbor at 42 C.F.R. § 1001.952(b). The MRI Center is managed pursuant to a written contract (the "Management Agreement") with [name redacted] (the "Management Company"), a radiology group practice that provides radiology services to, and clinical operation of, the MRI Center. Neither the Management Company, nor any of its physician members, is an investor in the MRI Center, and neither the Hospital, nor the Foundation, has any direct or indirect ownership interest in the Management Company. The Requestor has certified that the Management Agreement meets all of the conditions of the personal services and management contracts safe harbor at 42 C.F.R. § 1001.952(d).

II. THE LAW

The anti-kickback statute makes it a criminal offense knowingly and willfully to offer, pay, solicit, or receive any remuneration to induce or reward referrals of items or services reimbursable by federal health care programs. See section 1128B(b) of the Act. Where remuneration is paid purposefully to induce or reward referrals of items or services

---

[2]A complete list of current investors is attached to this opinion as Appendix A.

payable by a federal health care program, the anti-kickback statute is violated. By its terms, the statute ascribes criminal liability to parties on both sides of an impermissible "kickback" transaction. For purposes of the anti-kickback statute, "remuneration" includes the transfer of anything of value, in cash or in kind, directly or indirectly, covertly or overtly.

The statute has been interpreted to cover any arrangement where one purpose of the remuneration was to obtain money for the referral of services or to induce further referrals. United States v. Kats, 871 F.2d 105 (9th Cir. 1989); United States v. Greber, 760 F.2d 68 (3d Cir.), cert. denied, 474 U.S. 988 (1985). Violation of the statute constitutes a felony punishable by a maximum fine of $25,000, imprisonment up to five years, or both. Conviction will also lead to automatic exclusion from federal health care programs, including Medicare and Medicaid. Where a party commits an act described in section 1128B(b) of the Act, the OIG may initiate administrative proceedings to impose civil monetary penalties on such party under section 1128A(a)(7) of the Act. The OIG may also initiate administrative proceedings to exclude such party from the federal health care programs under section 1128(b)(7) of the Act.

The Department of Health and Human Services has promulgated safe harbor regulations that define practices that are not subject to the anti-kickback statute because such practices would be unlikely to result in fraud or abuse. See 42 C.F.R. § 1001.952. The safe harbors set forth specific conditions that, if met, assure entities involved of not being prosecuted or sanctioned for the arrangement qualifying for the safe harbor. However, safe harbor protection is afforded only to those arrangements that precisely meet all of the conditions set forth in the safe harbor. The safe harbors for investments in small entities and rural area ventures, 42 C.F.R. § 1001.952(a)(2) and (3), respectively, are potentially applicable to the Arrangement.

III. ANALYSIS

This Office has long expressed concern about health care joint ventures in which investors are sources of referrals for, or suppliers of items or services to, the joint venture or other co-investors. Distributions from the joint venture may be disguised remuneration paid in return for referrals. Like any kickback scheme, such arrangements can lead to overutilization of services, increased costs for federal health care programs, corruption of professional judgment, and unfair competition.

Notwithstanding our concerns about joint ventures, the OIG has established several "safe harbors" applicable to joint ventures, two of which are potentially relevant to the Arrangement. The first, a safe harbor for small entity investments at 42 C.F.R. §

1001.952(a)(2), protects certain investments so long as interested investors[3] own no more than 40% of the ownership interests in the entity and generate no more than 40% of the entity's revenues. In other words, the safe harbor looks to indicia that the joint venture represents something substantially more than an appendage of its referring investors. In addition, in recognition of the practical difficulties in raising capital for health care ventures in rural areas, the OIG has established a safe harbor at 42 C.F.R. § 1001.952(a)(3) that protects investments in medically underserved areas ("MUAs"), if interested investors own no more than 50% of the entity, even if all revenues are generated by interested investors.

In this opinion, we consider a rural joint venture that, while deriving less than 40% of its revenues from investors, cannot fit in the small entity safe harbor because interested investors own approximately 60% of the venture, and, while located in a clearly rural area and primarily serving rural patients, cannot fit in the rural entity safe harbor because it is not located in a MUA and has more than 50% interested investors.

Notwithstanding, based on a totality of the facts and circumstances presented, we conclude that, while the Arrangement poses some risk, the combination of factors described below sufficiently vitiates the potential for fraud and abuse under the anti-kickback statute.

First, the Arrangement possesses indicia of a legitimate, bona fide business. All potential investors, both physicians and non-physicians, were offered the opportunity to purchase investment interests on the same terms and conditions. Returns on the investment interests are, have been, and will continue to be proportional to the investors' capital contributions. Most importantly, less than 40% of revenue of the MRI Center is derived from business generated by interested investors. While not determinative, these revenue characteristics, in conjunction with the substantial participation of non-business-generating investors, provide strong evidence that the MRI Center is a legitimate, bona fide business venture.

---

[3]For purposes of the ownership test under the safe harbor, interested investors include parties in a position to make or influence referrals to, furnish items or services to, or otherwise generate business for the entity. See 42 C.F.R. § 1001.952(a)(2)(i). Under the safe harbor's tainted revenues test, revenues derived from items or services furnished by investors would not be included. See 42 C.F.R. § 1001.952(a)(2)(vi); see also 64 Fed. Reg. 63518, 63521 (Nov. 19, 1999).

Second, the structure of the Arrangement comports with then-extant guidance related to the application of the anti-kickback statute to rural joint ventures. In particular, the joint venture's structure has none of the suspect characteristics identified in the OIG's 1989 Special Fraud Alert on Joint Ventures, such as nominal capital contributions, disproportionate return on investment, or selective investment opportunities based on referral volumes. See Special Fraud Alert, "Joint Venture Arrangements" (OIG-89-4), reprinted in 59 Fed. Reg. 65372 (Dec. 19, 1994). In addition, while not determinative, the fact that the Arrangement would have complied with the 1993 proposed safe harbor for rural entities (58 Fed. Reg. 49008 (Sept. 21, 1993)) – although not with the final safe harbor issued in 1999 – bears on the issue of the Arrangement's potential risk.

Third, the Arrangement was developed as a community-oriented effort to provide access to MRI services in the rural three-county area and has provided a substantial community benefit. The MRI Center continues to serve a large majority of rural patients, many of whom are elderly or indigent patients for whom travel to a distant MRI facility would be a hardship.

Fourth, the Requestor has certified that the Management Agreement and Space Lease comply with the relevant safe harbors.

Based on the totality of the facts and circumstances presented, we conclude that, while the Arrangement poses some risk, a combination of factors exists that renders that risk sufficiently low. Therefore, we would not subject the Requestor to administrative sanctions arising under the anti-kickback law in connection with the past and present investment interests under the Arrangement.

IV. CONCLUSION

Based on the facts certified in your request for an advisory opinion and supplemental submissions, we conclude that the Arrangement could potentially generate prohibited remuneration under the anti-kickback statute if the requisite intent to induce or reward referrals were present, but that the OIG would not impose administrative sanctions on [name redacted] under sections 1128(b)(7) or 1128A(a)(7) of the Act (as those sections relate to the commission of acts described in section 1128B(b) of the Act) in connection with the past and present investment interests relating to the Arrangement. This opinion is limited to the past and present investment interests relating to the Arrangement. We express no opinion about any future changes in investment interests relating to the

Arrangement or about any other agreements or arrangements disclosed or referenced in your request letter or supplemental submissions.

V. LIMITATIONS

The limitations applicable to this opinion include the following:

- This advisory opinion is issued only to [name redacted], the requestor of this opinion. This advisory opinion has no application, and cannot be relied upon, by any other individual or entity.

- This advisory opinion may not be introduced into evidence in any matter involving an entity or individual that is not a requestor to this opinion.

- This advisory opinion is applicable only to the statutory provisions specifically noted above. No opinion is expressed or implied herein with respect to the application of any other federal, state, or local statute, rule, regulation, ordinance, or other law that may be applicable to the Arrangement, including, without limitation, the physician self-referral law, section 1877 of the Act.

- This advisory opinion will not bind or obligate any agency other than the U.S. Department of Health and Human Services.

- This advisory opinion is limited in scope to the specific arrangement described in this letter and has no applicability to other arrangements, even those which appear similar in nature or scope.

- No opinion is expressed herein regarding the liability of any party under the False Claims Act or other legal authorities for any improper billing, claims submission, cost reporting, or related conduct.

This opinion is also subject to any additional limitations set forth at 42 C.F.R. Part 1008.

Page 8 — OIG Advisory Opinion No. 03-13

The OIG will not proceed against [name redacted] with respect to any action that is part of the Arrangement taken in good faith reliance upon this advisory opinion as long as all of the material facts have been fully, completely, and accurately presented, and the Arrangement in practice comports with the information provided. The OIG reserves the right to reconsider the questions and issues raised in this advisory opinion and, where the public interest requires, rescind, modify, or terminate this opinion. In the event that this advisory opinion is modified or terminated, the OIG will not proceed against [name redacted] with respect to any action taken in good faith reliance upon this advisory opinion, where all of the relevant facts were fully, completely, and accurately presented and where such action was promptly discontinued upon notification of the modification or termination of this advisory opinion. An advisory opinion may be rescinded only if the relevant and material facts have not been fully, completely, and accurately disclosed to the OIG.

Sincerely,

/s/

Lewis Morris

Chief Counsel to the Inspector General

DEPARTMENT OF HEALTH & HUMAN SERVICES **Office of Inspector General**

Washington, D.C. 20201

[*We redact certain identifying information and certain potentially privileged, confidential, or proprietary information associated with the individual or entity, unless otherwise approved by the requestor*.]

Issued: December 27, 2007

Posted: January 3, 2008

[Name and address redacted]

Re: OIG Advisory Opinion No. 07-20

Dear [name redacted]:

We are writing in response to your request for an advisory opinion regarding a proposal to establish an imaging center in the same building as your medical practice in a hurricane-devastated area (the "Proposed Arrangement"). Specifically, you have inquired whether the Proposed Arrangement would constitute grounds for the imposition of sanctions under the exclusion authority at section 1128(b)(7) of the Social Security Act (the "Act"), or the civil monetary penalty provision at section 1128A(a)(7) of the Act, as those sections relate to the commission of acts described in section 1128B(b) of the Act, the Federal anti-kickback statute.

You have certified that all of the information provided in your request, including all supplementary letters, is true and correct and constitutes a complete description of the relevant facts and agreements among the parties.

In issuing this opinion, we have relied solely on the facts and information presented to us. We have not undertaken an independent investigation of such information. This opinion is limited to the facts presented. If material facts have not been disclosed or have been misrepresented, this opinion is without force and effect.

Based on the facts certified in your request for an advisory opinion and supplemental submissions, we conclude that while the Proposed Arrangement could potentially generate prohibited remuneration under the anti-kickback statute, if the requisite intent to induce or reward referrals of Federal health care program business were present, the Office of

Page -2- OIG Advisory Opinion No. 07-20

Inspector General ("OIG") would not impose administrative sanctions on you under sections 1128(b)(7) or 1128A(a)(7) of the Act (as those sections relate to the commission of acts described in section 1128B(b) of the Act) in connection with the Proposed Arrangement.

This opinion may not be relied on by any persons other than you, the requestor of this opinion, and is further qualified as set out in Part IV below and in 42 C.F.R. Part 1008.

I. FACTUAL BACKGROUND

You have certified that you are a physician practicing in [name redacted] Parish, Louisiana (the "Parish"). The Parish is in the area hardest hit by Hurricane Katrina in August 2005. Shortly before Hurricane Katrina struck, you had opened [type redacted] clinic in the Parish. That clinic was completely destroyed in the aftermath of the hurricane. You have since opened [name redacted] (the "Medical Practice"), also in the Parish. You are the sole physician employee of the Medical Practice, which you co-own with your wife. You have certified that most of your patients reside in the Parish.

In July 2005, the U.S. Census Bureau officially estimated the population of the Parish to exceed [number redacted]. The Census Bureau's July 2006 estimate for the Parish, however, was less than one-quarter of the 2005 number. While the Census Bureau has not issued an updated population estimate since that for 2006, a recent private study indicates that the population of the Parish remains well below 50 percent of its pre-Katrina level, and that the Parish's population recovery rate lags behind that of other nearby jurisdictions affected by hurricane damage in 2005.[1]

The sole hospital in the Parish was destroyed by Hurricane Katrina and has not reopened. You have certified that there were approximately [number redacted] physicians practicing in the Parish prior to Hurricane Katrina and that you are one of fewer than [one-sixth the previous number] physicians now practicing there.

You have certified that, at the present time, there are no medical imaging services available in the Parish. Patients who need such imaging services are required to travel outside the Parish. As a result of hurricane damage, however, the healthcare infrastructure of the entire region has been significantly reduced, making it also more difficult to obtain services in the immediate area outside the Parish.

You propose to establish a medical imaging center (the "Imaging Center") in the same building as your Medical Practice. You have certified that you and your brother will each

[1] [Citation redacted.]

contribute 50 percent of the capital necessary to fund the Imaging Center and will each own 50 percent of it.

Your brother will be employed as business manager of the Imaging Center. You have certified that he will be a bona fide employee and will be paid a salary that will be fair market value for actual and necessary services rendered and will not take into account the volume or value of business generated for the Imaging Center. Your brother has not previously been employed or invested in the health care industry.

You have certified that: (1) both you and your brother will be active investors in the Imaging Center; (2) the terms on which an investment interest is offered to you and your brother will not be related to the previous or expected volume of referrals, items or services furnished, or the amount of business otherwise generated from either of you to the Imaging Center; (3) the Imaging Center will be located in a Medically Underserved Area, as designated in accordance with regulations issued by the Department, and at least 75 percent of the dollar volume of the Imaging Center's business will be derived from the service of persons who reside in a Medically Underserved Area or are members of a Medically Underserved Population, in accordance with regulations issued by the Department; (4) neither the Imaging Center nor any investor (or other individual or entity acting on behalf of the Imaging Center or any investor in the Imaging Center) will loan funds to or guarantee a loan for an investor who is in a position to make or influence referrals to, furnish items or services to, or otherwise generate business for the Imaging Center if the investor uses any part of such loan to obtain the investment interest; and (5) the amount of payments to each investor in return for the investment interest will be directly proportional to the amount of the capital investment (including the fair market value of any pre-operational services rendered) of that investor.

You state that the Imaging Center will be available to provide services to patients other than those of the Medical Practice. You estimate that initially about 35 percent of the patients receiving services from the Imaging Center will be referred by you,[2] and 65 percent will come from outside referrals. As more physicians return to or establish new medical practices in the Parish, you expect that the percentage of patients referred by other physicians will increase.

The building in which the Medical Practice is located and the Imaging Center is proposed to be located is owned by [name redacted], which you co-own with your wife. You have

---

[2] You have certified that the Proposed Arrangement will comply with the requirements of the Physician Self-Referral Law, Section 1877 of the Act, 42 U.S.C. § 1395nn and with the billing requirements of the Center for Medicare and Medicaid Services. We express no opinion with regard to these issues.

certified that the Imaging Center will lease space from [name redacted] in compliance with each of the conditions of the space rental safe harbor to the anti-kickback statute, 42 C.F.R. § 1001.952(b).

II. LEGAL ANALYSIS

A. Law

The anti-kickback statute makes it a criminal offense knowingly and willfully to offer, pay, solicit, or receive any remuneration to induce or reward referrals of items or services reimbursable by a Federal health care program. See section 1128B(b) of the Act. Where remuneration is paid purposefully to induce or reward referrals of items or services payable by a Federal health care program, the anti-kickback statute is violated. By its terms, the statute ascribes criminal liability to parties on both sides of an impermissible "kickback" transaction. For purposes of the anti-kickback statute, "remuneration" includes the transfer of anything of value, directly or indirectly, overtly or covertly, in cash or in kind.

The statute has been interpreted to cover any arrangement where one purpose of the remuneration was to obtain money for the referral of services or to induce further referrals. United States v. Kats, 871 F.2d 105 (9th Cir. 1989); United States v. Greber, 760 F.2d 68 (3d Cir.), cert. denied, 474 U.S. 988 (1985). Violation of the statute constitutes a felony punishable by a maximum fine of $25,000, imprisonment up to five years, or both. Conviction will also lead to automatic exclusion from Federal health care programs, including Medicare and Medicaid. Where a party commits an act described in section 1128B(b) of the Act, the OIG may initiate administrative proceedings to impose civil monetary penalties on such party under section 1128A(a)(7) of the Act. The OIG may also initiate administrative proceedings to exclude such party from the Federal health care programs under section 1128(b)(7) of the Act.

The Department of Health and Human Services has promulgated safe harbor regulations that define practices that are not subject to the anti-kickback statute because such practices would be unlikely to result in fraud or abuse. See 42 C.F.R. § 1001.952. The safe harbors set forth specific conditions that, if met, assure entities involved of not being prosecuted or sanctioned for the arrangement qualifying for the safe harbor. However, safe harbor protection is afforded only to those arrangements that precisely meet all of the conditions set forth in the safe harbor.

The safe harbor for investment in small entities in underserved areas, 42 C.F.R. § 1001.952(a)(3), is potentially applicable to the Proposed Arrangement. This safe harbor applies to an investment entity located in an underserved area, if all of the following eight standards are met: (1) No more than 50 percent of the value of the investment interests of each class of investments may be held in the previous fiscal year or previous 12-month period by investors who are in a position to make or influence referrals to, furnish items or services to, or otherwise generate business for, the entity; (2) the terms on which an investment interest is offered to a passive investor, if any, who is in a position to make or influence referrals to, furnish items or services to, or otherwise generate business for the entity must be no different from the terms offered to other passive investors; (3) the terms on which an investment interest is offered to an investor who is in a position to make or influence referrals to, furnish items or services to, or otherwise generate business for the entity must not be related to the previous or expected volume of referrals, items or services furnished, or the amount of business otherwise generated from that investor to the entity; (4) there is no requirement that a passive investor, if any, make referrals to, be in a position to make or influence referrals to, furnish items or services to, or otherwise generate business for the entity as a condition for remaining as an investor; (5) the entity or any investor must not market or furnish the entity's items or services (or those of another entity as part of a cross-referrals agreement) to passive investors differently than to non-investors); (6) at least 75 percent of the dollar volume of the entity's business in the previous fiscal year or previous 12-month period must be derived from the service of persons who reside in an underserved area or are members of medically underserved populations; (7) the entity or any investor (or other individual or entity acting on behalf of the entity or any investor in the entity) must not loan funds to or guarantee a loan for a investor who is in a position to make or influence referrals to, furnish items or services to, or otherwise generate business for the entity if the investor uses any part of such loan to obtain the investment interest; and (8) the amount of payment to an investor in return for the investment interest must be directly proportional to the amount of the capital investment (including the fair market value of any pre-operational services rendered) of that investor.

B. Analysis

The Proposed Arrangement does not qualify for protection by the safe harbor for investment in small entities in underserved areas, because it does not meet the first condition of the safe harbor, that no more than 50 percent of investment interests in an entity may be held by investors who are in a position to make or influence referrals to, furnish items or services to, or otherwise generate business for, the entity. In the Proposed Arrangement, 100 percent of the investment interests are to be held by investors who are in a position to make or influence referrals to, furnish items or services to, or otherwise generate business for, the Imaging Center. You, who will own 50 percent of the Imaging Center, are a physician who is in a position to refer patients. Your brother, who will also own 50 percent, will be employed as the Imaging Center's business manager, and thus provide services to it. In addition, your brother, through his family relationship with you, may be in a position to influence patient referrals.

Page -6- OIG Advisory Opinion No. 07-20

The fact that the Proposed Arrangement does not fit in the safe harbor does not end the inquiry, and we must examine the totality of facts and circumstances to determine the extent of the risk posed by the Proposed Arrangement. In the singular circumstances presented here, the fact that 50% of the venture is owned by your brother who will be employed as the Imaging Center's business manager – rather than by a wholly disinterested investor -- does not materially increase the risk of fraud and abuse, particularly when viewed in light of the Proposed Arrangement's substantial potential community benefits.

Your brother is not currently in the health care business, will not be compensated as business manager in any manner that depends on his generating business for the Imaging Center, and will receive a fair market value salary for actual and necessary services rendered to the Imaging Center.[3] This latter fact reduces a usual risk that arises when an investor provides items or services to a venture, namely that the investor will charge the venture below market rates in order artificially to boost the profitability of the venture and the size of returns available to investors who are referral sources. In addition, your brother, like you, will put up real capital and receive returns that are proportional to his capital contributions. You have certified that the terms the investment will not be related to the previous or expected volume of referrals, items or services furnished, or amount of business otherwise generated by an investor for the Imaging Center.

We recognize that, as the relative of a physician, your brother may be in a position to influence referrals. He can do so, however, only through his relationship with you, who are also an investor in the Imaging Center. Because you already have substantial independent reasons to refer patients to the Imaging Center, on the facts presented your family relationship should not increase the capacity of the investors, as a whole, to influence referrals.[4]

Finally, any residual risk posed by the Proposed Arrangement is offset by the special conditions in which the Proposed Arrangement is to be implemented. As noted in the preamble to the safe harbor for investment in entities in underserved areas, "[p]aramount among OIG's concerns is that beneficiaries have adequate access to quality health care." 64 FR 63518, 63532 (Nov. 19, 1999).

---

[3]We are precluded by statute from opining on whether fair market value shall be or was paid for goods, services, or property. See 42 U.S.C. § 1320a-7d(b)(3)(A). For purposes of this advisory opinion, we rely on your certifications of fair market value. If the compensation is not fair market value, this opinion is without force and effect.

[4]We are mindful that unscrupulous parties sometimes use family members as fronts to funnel money to referral sources. Here, however, we are persuaded, based on the totality of facts and circumstances – including your certification that your brother will invest his own capital in the venture -- that such subterfuge is unlikely.

The devastation to health care services in the area to be served by the proposed Imaging Center is well-known. Two years after Hurricane Katrina, the one hospital that had operated in the Parish has not reopened. You have certified that fewer than [number redacted] physicians now practice in the Parish, which previously was served by approximately [number redacted] practitioners. It is possible – even likely – that the limited availability of health care services discourages the return of some former residents and the rebuilding of the community as a whole.

For all of these reasons, we conclude that the risk of fraud and abuse posed by the Proposed Agreement is relatively low and offset by potential improvements in access to care in an area still recovering from catastrophic damage to its healthcare infrastructure.

III. CONCLUSION

Based on the facts certified in your request for an advisory opinion and supplemental submissions, we conclude that while the Proposed Arrangement could potentially generate prohibited remuneration under the anti-kickback statute, if the requisite intent to induce or reward referrals of Federal health care program business were present, the OIG would not impose administrative sanctions on you under sections 1128(b)(7) or 1128A(a)(7) of the Act (as those sections relate to the commission of acts described in section 1128B(b) of the Act) in connection with the Proposed Arrangement. This opinion is limited to the Proposed Arrangement and, therefore, we express no opinion about any ancillary agreements or arrangements disclosed or referenced in your request letter or supplemental submissions.

IV. LIMITATIONS

The limitations applicable to this opinion include the following:

- This advisory opinion is issued only to you, [name redacted], the requestor of this opinion. This advisory opinion has no application to, and cannot be relied upon by, any other individual or entity.

- This advisory opinion may not be introduced into evidence in any matter involving an entity or individual that is not a requestor of this opinion.

- This advisory opinion is applicable only to the statutory provisions specifically noted above. No opinion is expressed or implied herein with respect to the application of any other Federal, state, or local statute, rule, regulation, ordinance, or other law that may be applicable to the Proposed

Arrangement, including, without limitation, the physician self-referral law, section 1877 of the Act.

- This advisory opinion will not bind or obligate any agency other than the U.S. Department of Health and Human Services.

- This advisory opinion is limited in scope to the specific arrangement described in this letter and has no applicability to other arrangements, even those which appear similar in nature or scope.

- No opinion is expressed herein regarding the liability of any party under the False Claims Act or other legal authorities for any improper billing, claims submission, cost reporting, or related conduct.

This opinion is also subject to any additional limitations set forth at 42 C.F.R. Part 1008.

The OIG will not proceed against you with respect to any action that is part of the Proposed Arrangement taken in good faith reliance upon this advisory opinion, as long as all of the material facts have been fully, completely, and accurately presented, and the Proposed Arrangement in practice comports with the information provided. The OIG reserves the right to reconsider the questions and issues raised in this advisory opinion and, where the public interest requires, to rescind, modify, or terminate this opinion. In the event that this advisory opinion is modified or terminated, the OIG will not proceed against you with respect to any action taken in good faith reliance upon this advisory opinion, where all of the relevant facts were fully, completely, and accurately presented and where such action was promptly discontinued upon notification of the modification or termination of this advisory opinion. An advisory opinion may be rescinded only if the relevant and material facts have not been fully, completely, and accurately disclosed to the OIG.

Sincerely,

/s/

Lewis Morris
Chief Counsel to the Inspector General

DEPARTMENT OF HEALTH & HUMAN SERVICES **Office of Inspector General**

Washington, D.C. 20201

[*We redact certain identifying information and certain potentially privileged, confidential, or proprietary information associated with the individual or entity, unless otherwise approved by the requestor*.]

Issued: July 18, 2008

Posted: July 25, 2008

To: ATTACHED DISTRIBUTION LIST

Re: OIG Advisory Opinion No. 08-08

Ladies and Gentlemen:

We are writing in response to your request for an advisory opinion regarding an investment in an ambulatory surgery center by a group of surgeons and a health care corporation that owns hospitals (the "Arrangement"). Specifically, you have inquired whether the Arrangement constitutes grounds for the imposition of sanctions under the exclusion authority at section 1128(b)(7) of the Social Security Act (the "Act"), or the civil monetary penalty provision at section 1128A(a)(7) of the Act, as those sections relate to the commission of acts described in section 1128B(b) of the Act, the Federal anti-kickback statute.

You have certified that all of the information provided in your request, including all supplementary letters, is true and correct and constitutes a complete description of the relevant facts and agreements among the parties.

In issuing this opinion, we have relied solely on the facts and information presented to us. We have not undertaken an independent investigation of such information. This opinion is limited to the facts presented. If material facts have not been disclosed or have been misrepresented, this opinion is without force and effect.

Based on the facts certified in your request for an advisory opinion and supplemental submissions, we conclude that while the Arrangement could potentially generate prohibited remuneration under the anti-kickback statute, if the requisite intent to induce or reward referrals of Federal health care program business were present, the Office of

Page 2 - OIG Advisory Opinion No. 08-08

Inspector General ("OIG") will not impose administrative sanctions on [names redacted] (the "Requestors") under sections 1128(b)(7) or 1128A(a)(7) of the Act (as those sections relate to the commission of acts described in section 1128B(b) of the Act) in connection with the Arrangement. This opinion is limited to the Arrangement and, therefore, we express no opinion about any ancillary agreements or arrangements disclosed or referenced in your request letter or supplemental submissions, except as explicitly stated in this opinion.

This opinion may not be relied on by any persons other than the Requestors of this opinion, and is further qualified as set out in Part IV below and in 42 C.F.R. Part 1008.

I. FACTUAL BACKGROUND

[Name redacted] (the "Hospital Corporation")[1] is [state redacted] not-for-profit corporation that owns three hospitals and other healthcare-related entities, including a large physician group practice consisting of primary-care and specialty-care physicians (the "Hospital-Owned Physician Practice").

[Name redacted] (the "Surgeon Partnership"), is [state redacted] limited liability company whose members (the "Surgeon Investors") are also members of two divisions of [name redacted], a large, multi-site physician group (the "Surgeon Group"). (The Surgeon Group is not the Hospital-Owned Physician Practice, nor do their memberships overlap.) All of the Surgeon Investors are orthopedic surgeons. Each Surgeon Investor made an initial capital contribution of $50,000 and a subsequent capital contribution of $11,000 to the Surgeon Partnership. Each of the Surgeon Investors owns an equal share of the Surgeon Partnership.

[Name redacted] (the "Company") is an entity owned 70 percent by the Surgeon Partnership and 30 percent by the Hospital Corporation. Under the Arrangement, the Company owns and operates an ambulatory surgery center (the "ASC"). The Surgeon Partnership and the Hospital Corporation made financial contributions to the Company proportional to their ownership interests, in order to finance the development and operation of this ASC.

There are eighteen Surgeon Investors, of whom fourteen meet the following test: Each received at least one-third of his or her medical practice income for the previous fiscal year or previous 12-month period from the performance of procedures payable by

---

[1] For the purpose of this opinion, "Hospital Corporation" will refer to [name redacted] and entities owned or controlled by it.

Medicare when performed in an ambulatory surgery center ("ASC-Qualified Procedures"). The four remaining Surgeon Investors (the "Inpatient Surgeons") do not meet this test. Each of the Inpatient Surgeons derives at least one-third of his or her medical practice income from procedures requiring a hospital operating room setting, but receives little or no medical practice income from the performance of ASC-Qualified Procedures. The Requestors have certified that the Inpatient Surgeons rarely have the occasion to refer patients to other physicians for ASC-Qualified Procedures, except for pain management procedures. The Requestors also have certified that none of the Surgeon Investors will refer patients for pain management procedures to be performed at the ASC, unless the pain management procedure is to be performed personally by the referring Surgeon Investor.

The Surgeon Investors inform patients of their ownership interest in the ASC by posting notices in the two offices in which the Surgeon Investors practice and through a written notice to each individual patient. The Requestors have certified that, in the future, in the absence of exigent circumstances, such written notice to individual patients will be provided prior to the date of the procedure in the ASC.

The Hospital Corporation is in a position to make or influence referrals to the ASC. The Requestors have certified that, in order to limit such ability, the Hospital Corporation has refrained and will refrain from any actions to require or encourage physicians who are employees, independent contractors, and medical staff members ("Hospital-Affiliated Physicians") to refer patients to the ASC or to its Surgeon Investors, and has not and will not track referrals, if any, by Hospital-Affiliated Physicians to the ASC or to its Surgeon Investors. The Requestors have further certified that any compensation paid by the Hospital Corporation to Hospital-Affiliated Physicians has been and will be consistent with fair market value and has not been and will not be related, directly or indirectly, to the volume or value of any referrals Hospital-Affiliated Physicians may make to the ASC, its Surgeon Investors, or the Surgeon Group. The Hospital Corporation will inform Hospital-Affiliated Physicians annually of these measures.

The Company entered a written agreement (the "Anesthesia Agreement") with the Hospital-Owned Physician Practice to be the exclusive provider of anesthesiology (except for pain management services) at the ASC through its employed anesthesiologists and certified registered nurse anesthetists. The Hospital-Owned Physician Practice obtains payment for anesthesia services from third-party payers, including Federal health care programs, and from patients for uninsured amounts. Pursuant to the Anesthesia Agreement, one of the anesthesiologists employed by the Hospital-Owned Physician Practice serves, on a part-time basis, as Director of Anesthesiology and Medical Director of the ASC, for an annual fixed stipend paid by the Company to the Department of

Anesthesiology of the Hospital-Owned Physician Practice. The duties of this individual, which are administrative and supervisory, are described in detail in the Anesthesia Agreement, and the Requestors have certified that the stipend is fair market value for these services and not determined in a manner that takes into account the volume or value of any referrals or business otherwise generated between the parties.

II. LEGAL ANALYSIS

A. Law

The anti-kickback statute makes it a criminal offense knowingly and willfully to offer, pay, solicit, or receive any remuneration to induce or reward referrals of items or services reimbursable by a Federal health care program. See section 1128B(b) of the Act. Where remuneration is paid purposefully to induce or reward referrals of items or services payable by a Federal health care program, the anti-kickback statute is violated. By its terms, the statute ascribes criminal liability to parties on both sides of an impermissible "kickback" transaction. For purposes of the anti-kickback statute, "remuneration" includes the transfer of anything of value, directly or indirectly, overtly or covertly, in cash or in kind.

The statute has been interpreted to cover any arrangement where one purpose of the remuneration was to obtain money for the referral of services or to induce further referrals. United States v. Kats, 871 F.2d 105 (9th Cir. 1989); United States v. Greber, 760 F.2d 68 (3d Cir.), cert. denied, 474 U.S. 988 (1985). Violation of the statute constitutes a felony punishable by a maximum fine of $25,000, imprisonment up to five years, or both. Conviction will also lead to automatic exclusion from Federal health care programs, including Medicare and Medicaid. Where a party commits an act described in section 1128B(b) of the Act, the OIG may initiate administrative proceedings to impose civil monetary penalties on such party under section 1128A(a)(7) of the Act. The OIG may also initiate administrative proceedings to exclude such party from the Federal health care programs under section 1128(b)(7) of the Act.

The Department of Health and Human Services has promulgated safe harbor regulations that define practices that are not subject to the anti-kickback statute because such practices would be unlikely to result in fraud or abuse. See 42 C.F.R. § 1001.952. The safe harbors set forth specific conditions that, if met, assure entities involved of not being prosecuted or sanctioned for the arrangement qualifying for the safe harbor. However, safe harbor protection is afforded only to those arrangements that precisely meet all of the conditions set forth in the safe harbor.

The safe harbor for ambulatory surgery centers jointly owned by physicians and hospitals, 42 C.F.R. § 1001.952(r)(4), and the safe harbor for personal services and management contracts, 42 C.F.R. § 1001.952(d), are potentially applicable to our analysis of the Arrangement.

B. Analysis

Although joint ventures by physicians and hospitals are susceptible to fraud and abuse, the OIG recognizes that hospitals may be at a competitive disadvantage when they compete with ASCs owned by physicians, who principally control referrals. Thus, the OIG promulgated a safe harbor for investment income from ASCs jointly-owned by physicians and hospitals that meet certain conditions, 42 C.F.R. § 1001.952(r)(4). Among the ownership arrangements potentially protected by this safe harbor are ASCs jointly owned by hospitals and general surgeons or surgeons engaged in the same surgical specialty. Because all the Surgeon Investors in the ASC are engaged in the same surgical specialty (orthopedics), the safe harbor is potentially applicable to the Arrangement. The Arrangement does not qualify for protection by this safe harbor, however, for the reasons noted below. Because no safe harbor would protect the investment income from the ASC, we must determine whether, given all the relevant facts, the Arrangement poses a minimal risk under the anti-kickback statute.

First, the Arrangement does not qualify for the protection of the hospital/physician-owned ASC safe harbor, because the Surgeon Investors do not hold their investment interests in the ASC either directly or through a group practice composed of qualifying physicians. Rather, the Surgeon Investors hold their individual ownership interests in the Surgeon Partnership. The Surgeon Partnership, in turn, holds an interest in the Company that owns and operates the ASC. We have previously expressed concern that intermediate investment entities could be used to redirect revenues to reward referrals or otherwise vitiate the safeguards provided by direct investment, including distributions of profits in proportion to capital investment. However, in this case, the use of a "pass-through" entity does not substantially increase the risk of fraud or abuse. Each Surgeon Investor's ownership in the Surgeon Partnership is proportional to his or her capital investment.[2] The Surgeon Partnership's ownership interest in the Company is, in turn, proportional to its capital investment. Thus the individual Surgeon Investors receive a return on their ASC investments that is exactly the same as if they had invested directly.

---

[2] We express no opinion with regard to any future sales of membership interests in the Surgeon Partnership that may result in individual investors having ownership interests that are not proportional to their investment.

Second, four of the eighteen Surgeon Investors (the Inpatient Surgeons) fail to meet the safe harbor requirement that at least one-third of a physician investor's income from medical practice for the previous fiscal year or previous 12-month period be derived from the performance of ASC-Qualified Procedures.[3] This "one third" test helps ensure that the safe harbor applies only to investment income to physicians who are unlikely to use the investment as a vehicle for profiting from their referrals to other physicians using the ASC. Safe harbor protection is limited to physician-investors who, because they perform a substantial number of ASC-Qualified Procedures, are likely to use the ASC on a regular basis as part of their medical practices.

In the circumstances presented, notwithstanding that four Inpatient Surgeons will not regularly practice at the ASC, we conclude that the ASC is unlikely to be a vehicle for them to profit from referrals. The Requestors have certified that, as practitioners of sub-specialties of orthopedic surgery that require a hospital operating room setting, the Inpatient Surgeons rarely have occasion to refer patients for ASC-Qualified Procedures (other than pain management procedures, which are discussed below).[4] Moreover, like the other Surgeon Investors, the Inpatient Surgeons are regularly engaged in a genuine surgical practice, deriving at least one-third of their medical practice income from procedures requiring a hospital operating room setting. The Inpatient Surgeons are qualified to perform surgeries at the ASC and may choose to do so (and earn the professional fees) in medically appropriate cases. Also, the Inpatient Surgeons comprise a small proportion of the Surgeon Investors, a majority of whom will use the ASC on a regular basis as part of their medical practice. This Arrangement is readily distinguishable from potentially riskier arrangements in which few investing physicians actually use the ASC on a regular basis or in which investing physicians are significant potential referral sources for other investors or the ASC, as when primary care physicians invest in a surgical ASC or cardiologists invest in a cardiac surgery ASC.

As noted above, the Inpatient Surgeons do have occasion to refer patients for pain management procedures that are ASC-Qualified Procedures. This raises the possibility that an Inpatient Surgeon or other Surgeon Investor might refer patients to other practitioners for pain management procedures performed at the ASC, for the purpose of generating a facility fee for the ASC. The Requestors have certified, however, that no Surgeon Investor will refer patients for pain management procedures to be performed at

---

[3] The safe harbor for hospital/physician-owned ASCs (42 C.F.R. § 1001.952(r)(4)) incorporates by reference this requirement of the safe harbor for surgeon-owned ASCs (42 C.F.R. § 1001.952(r)(1)(ii)).

[4] If this certification proves incorrect, this advisory opinion is without force and effect.

the ASC, unless the procedure is to be performed personally by the referring Surgeon Investor. This serves to mitigate the potential for abusive referrals, with regard to this type of procedure.

Third, the Arrangement does not qualify for the safe harbor for ASCs jointly owned by physicians and hospitals, because the Hospital Corporation is in a position to make or influence referrals to the ASC and to the Surgeon Investors. However, the Arrangement includes certain commitments limiting the ability of the Hospital Corporation to direct or influence such referrals. The Hospital Corporation refrains from any actions to require or encourage Hospital-Affiliated Physicians to refer patients to the ASC or to its Surgeon Investors; it does not track referrals, if any, by Hospital-Affiliated Physicians to the ASC or to its Surgeon Investors; any compensation paid to Hospital-Affiliated Physicians is at fair market value and does not take into account any referrals Hospital-Affiliated Physicians may make to the ASC or to its Surgeon Investors; and the Hospital Corporation informs Hospital-Affiliated Physicians annually of these measures. In light of these safeguards, the ability of the Hospital Corporation to direct or influence referrals to the ASC is significantly constrained.

Fourth, the Arrangement does not meet the requirement of the hospital/physician-owned ASC safe harbor that any services provided by the Hospital Corporation to the ASC must be pursuant to a contract that complies with the personal services and management contracts safe harbor set forth at 42 C.F.R. § 1001.952(d). Among the conditions of the personal services and management contracts safe harbor is that, if the agreement is intended to provide for services on a periodic, sporadic or part-time basis, rather than on a full-time basis for the term of the agreement, the agreement must specify exactly the schedule of such intervals, their precise length, and the exact charge for such intervals.

The Anesthesia Agreement does not meet this requirement. It provides for an employee of the Hospital-Owned Physician Practice to serve as Director of Anesthesiology and Medical Director of the ASC on less than a full-time basis, but does not specify a schedule for the services to be provided by this individual. However, all of the services to be provided are set out in the Anesthesia Agreement in detail, and the Requestors have certified that the services are reasonable and necessary for the ASC. They have further certified that the amount to be paid under the agreement – a fixed fee set in advance in the contract – is fair market value for the services described, as determined in an arms length transaction, and not determined in a manner that takes into account the volume or value of any referrals or business otherwise generated between the parties.[5] The parties will keep accurate and contemporaneous records, such as time cards, of the services provided by the Medical Director, and make them available to the Secretary and the OIG upon request. In these circumstances and given the nature of the contracted services, the lack of specificity of the schedule of services does not raise the risk of fraud and abuse under the Arrangement.

For all of the foregoing reasons, we conclude that, while the Arrangement poses some risk, the safeguards put in place by the Requestors make that risk sufficiently low that we would not subject the Arrangement to administrative sanctions in connection with the anti-kickback statute.

III. CONCLUSION

Based on the facts certified in your request for an advisory opinion and supplemental submissions, we conclude that while the Arrangement could potentially generate prohibited remuneration under the anti-kickback statute, if the requisite intent to induce or reward referrals of Federal health care program business were present, the OIG will not impose administrative sanctions on the Requestors under sections 1128(b)(7) or 1128A(a)(7) of the Act (as those sections relate to the commission of acts described in section 1128B(b) of the Act) in connection with the Arrangement.

IV. LIMITATIONS

The limitations applicable to this opinion include the following:

- This advisory opinion is issued only to the Requestors of this opinion. This advisory opinion has no application to, and cannot be relied upon by, any other individual or entity.

- This advisory opinion may not be introduced into evidence in any matter involving an entity or individual that is not a requestor of this opinion.

---

[5] We are precluded by statute from opining on whether fair market value shall be or was paid for goods, services, or property. See 42 U.S.C. § 1320a-7d(b)(3)(A). For purposes of this advisory opinion, we rely on the Requestors' certifications of fair market value. If the compensation is not fair market value, this opinion is without force and effect.

- This advisory opinion is applicable only to the statutory provisions specifically noted above. No opinion is expressed or implied herein with respect to the application of any other Federal, state, or local statute, rule, regulation, ordinance, or other law that may be applicable to the Arrangement, including, without limitation, the physician self-referral law, section 1877 of the Act.

- This advisory opinion will not bind or obligate any agency other than the U.S. Department of Health and Human Services.

- This advisory opinion is limited in scope to the specific arrangement described in this letter and has no applicability to other arrangements, even those which appear similar in nature or scope.

- No opinion is expressed herein regarding the liability of any party under the False Claims Act or other legal authorities for any improper billing, claims submission, cost reporting, or related conduct.

This opinion is also subject to any additional limitations set forth at 42 C.F.R. Part 1008.

The OIG will not proceed against the Requestors with respect to any action that is part of the Arrangement taken in good faith reliance upon this advisory opinion, as long as all of the material facts have been fully, completely, and accurately presented, and the Arrangement in practice comports with the information provided. The OIG reserves the right to reconsider the questions and issues raised in this advisory opinion and, where the public interest requires, to rescind, modify, or terminate this opinion. In the event that this advisory opinion is modified or terminated, the OIG will not proceed against the Requestors with respect to any action taken in good faith reliance upon this advisory opinion, where all of the relevant facts were fully, completely, and accurately presented and where such action was promptly discontinued upon notification of the modification or termination of this advisory opinion. An advisory opinion may be rescinded only if the relevant and material facts have not been fully, completely, and accurately disclosed to the OIG.

Sincerely,

/s/

Lewis Morris
Chief Counsel to the Inspector General

Page 10 - OIG Advisory Opinion No. 08-08

DISTRIBUTION LIST

OIG ADVISORY OPINION 08-8

[Names and addresses redacted]

DEPARTMENT OF HEALTH & HUMAN SERVICES Office of Inspector General

Washington, D.C. 20201

[*We redact certain identifying information and certain potentially privileged, confidential, or proprietary information associated with the individual or entity, unless otherwise approved by the requestor.*]

Issued: December 29, 2008

Posted: January 7, 2009

To: Attached Distribution List

Re: OIG Advisory Opinion No. 08-24

Ladies and Gentlemen:

We are writing in response to your request for an advisory opinion regarding investments in a shared medical practice by 23 physicians and podiatrists (the "Proposed Arrangement"). Specifically, you have inquired whether the Proposed Arrangement would constitute grounds for the imposition of sanctions under the exclusion authority at section 1128(b)(7) of the Social Security Act (the "Act"), or the civil monetary penalty provision at section 1128A(a)(7) of the Act, as those sections relate to the commission of acts described in section 1128B(b) of the Act, the Federal anti-kickback statute.

You have certified that all of the information provided in your request, including all supplementary letters, is true and correct and constitutes a complete description of the relevant facts and agreements among the parties.

In issuing this opinion, we have relied solely on the facts and information presented to us. We have not undertaken an independent investigation of such information. This opinion is limited to the facts presented. If material facts have not been disclosed or have been misrepresented, this opinion is without force and effect.

Based on the facts certified in your request for an advisory opinion and supplemental submissions, we conclude that while the Proposed Arrangement could potentially generate prohibited remuneration under the anti-kickback statute, if the requisite intent to induce or reward referrals of Federal health care program business were present, the Office of the Inspector General ("OIG") would not impose administrative sanctions on [facility name redacted] or its members [practitioner names redacted] (referred to collectively herein as the "Requestors") under sections 1128(b)(7) or 1128A(a)(7) of the Act (as those sections relate to the commission of acts described in section 1128B(b) of the Act) in connection with the Proposed Arrangement. This opinion is limited to the Proposed Arrangement and, therefore, we express no opinion about any ancillary agreements or arrangements disclosed or referenced in your request letter or supplemental submissions.

This opinion may not be relied on by any persons other than the Requestors of this opinion, and is further qualified as set out in Part IV below and in 42 C.F.R. Part 1008.

I. FACTUAL BACKGROUND

[Facility name redacted] (the "Practice") is a limited liability company that was formed under [state name redacted] law by 23 investor physicians and podiatrists. The Practice is located in [county and state names redacted] in a rural Health Professional Shortage Area. It offers various medical care, consultation, diagnosis, and treatment services by means of shared office space, facilities, equipment, and personnel. The Practice's operations include physician consultation on a walk-in urgent care basis, and various clinical laboratory and diagnostic radiology services.

With one exception,[1] all equity interests in the Practice are held by licensed physicians and podiatrists who treat patients at the Practice. None of the investors works at the Practice full-time, however. Each investor in the Practice also sees patients separately at different office locations not affiliated with the Practice. Each investor owns a fixed percentage investment stake in the entire Practice. Each shares in the Practice's profits or losses in direct proportion to his or her individual investment stake.

The Practice is organized as a limited liability company with a central governing Board of Managers (the "Board") comprised of managing Practice members. The Board meets regularly and has sole authority to make decisions for the Practice.[2] It maintains control over Practice assets and liabilities. It develops, drafts, and approves the company budget, compensation rates, and staff salaries. Significant expenses undertaken by the Practice must

---

[1] A one percent (1%) interest in the entire Practice is held by [Stakeholder name redacted], who is licensed to practice medicine in [state name redacted], but whose duties at the Practice are administrative. [Stakeholder name redacted] incurs profits and losses in direct proportion to his investment interest.

[2] Nearly all major business decisions made by the Practice require consent of the majority of the Board.

receive formal Board approval. The Board also formulates and approves Practice policies and procedures regarding both clinical matters (e.g., how walk-in patients who appear at the Practice are evaluated and treated) and business matters (e.g., how and when debts to the Practice are collected or written-off).

The Practice maintains a single consolidated accounting system for managing billing and finances. All expenses and revenues are pooled across the Practice and not separated in relation to individual Practice members.

The Requestors have certified that revenues generated by the Practice from ancillary services are derived from "in-office ancillary services" as defined in section 1877(b)(2) of the Act and implementing regulations. The Requestors have certified that the Practice has achieved or will shortly achieve compliance with the definition of "group practice" in section 1877(h)(4) of the Act and corresponding regulations.[3] As described in section II.A below, these certifications related to the physician self-referral statute at section 1877 of the Act are relevant to the inquiry under the anti-kickback statute. It is beyond the scope of this advisory opinion to assess whether the Proposed Arrangement, in fact, meets the terms of section 1877 of the Act (also known as the "physician self-referral law") and the corresponding regulations.[4]

---

[3]Specifically, it may be necessary, in order to meet the minimum percentage of physician-patient encounters conducted by practice members under 42 C.F.R. § 411.352(h), for the Practice to bring onboard as members a number of urgent care physicians who are not among the Requestors and who are currently working as independent contractors. The Requestors have certified that they will shortly do so. It is for this reason that we describe the facts on which this opinion is based as a Proposed Arrangement. No opinion is expressed on the existing arrangement. Nor is any opinion expressed with respect to any employment or independent contractor arrangements with these physicians.

[4]Questions pertaining to compliance with the physician-self referral law and regulations come within the jurisdiction of the Centers for Medicare & Medicaid Services ("CMS"). See 42 C.F.R. §§ 411.370 –.389. The Practice has been the subject of a favorable advisory opinion from CMS in connection with issues under the physician self-referral law. See CMS Advisory Opinion 2008-02 (June 2008). That opinion addressed the Practice's compliance with the rural provider exception in section 1877(d)(2) of the Act and 42 C.F.R. § 411.356(c)(1). It did not address whether the revenues generated by the Practice from ancillary services will be derived from "in-office ancillary services" as defined in section 1877(b)(2) of the Act and corresponding regulations or whether the Practice complies with the definition of "group practice" in section 1877(h)(4) of the Act and corresponding regulations. We rely on the certifications of the Requestors with respect to these issues. If the certifications are not accurate, this opinion is without force and effect.

Page 4 – OIG Advisory Opinion No. 08-24

II. LEGAL ANALYSIS

A. Law

The anti-kickback statute makes it a criminal offense knowingly and willfully to offer, pay, solicit, or receive any remuneration to induce or reward referrals of items or services reimbursable by a Federal health care program. See section 1128B(b) of the Act. Where remuneration is paid purposefully to induce or reward referrals of items or services payable by a Federal health care program, the anti-kickback statute is violated. By its terms, the statute ascribes criminal liability to parties on both sides of an impermissible "kickback" transaction. For purposes of the anti-kickback statute, "remuneration" includes the transfer of anything of value, directly or indirectly, overtly or covertly, in cash or in kind.

The statute has been interpreted to cover any arrangement where one purpose of the remuneration was to obtain money for the referral of services or to induce further referrals. United States v. Kats, 871 F.2d 105 (9th Cir. 1989); United States v. Greber, 760 F.2d 68 (3d Cir.), cert. denied, 474 U.S. 988 (1985). Violation of the statute constitutes a felony punishable by a maximum fine of $25,000, imprisonment up to five years, or both. Conviction will also lead to automatic exclusion from Federal health care programs, including Medicare and Medicaid. Where a party commits an act described in section 1128B(b) of the Act, the OIG may initiate administrative proceedings to impose civil monetary penalties on such party under section 1128A(a)(7) of the Act. The OIG may also initiate administrative proceedings to exclude such party from the Federal health care programs under section 1128(b)(7) of the Act.

The Department of Health and Human Services has promulgated safe harbor regulations that define practices that are not subject to the anti-kickback statute because such practices would be unlikely to result in fraud or abuse. See 42 C.F.R. § 1001.952. The safe harbors set forth specific conditions that, if met, assure entities involved of not being prosecuted or sanctioned for the arrangement qualifying for the safe harbor. However, safe harbor protection is afforded only to those arrangements that precisely meet all of the conditions set forth in the safe harbor.

The safe harbor for investments in group practices, 42 C.F.R. § 1001.952(p), is potentially applicable to the Proposed Arrangement. The safe harbor applies if the following four standards are met:

> (1) The equity interests in the . . . group must be held by licensed health care professionals who practice in the . . . group.
> (2) The equity interests must be in the . . . group itself, and not some subdivision of the . . . group.

Page 5 – OIG Advisory Opinion No. 08-24

(3) [A group practice] must: (i) [m]eet the definition of "group practice" in section 1877(h)(4) of the . . . Act and implementing regulations; and (ii) [b]e a unified business with centralized decision-making, pooling of expenses and revenues, and a compensation/profit distribution system that is not based on satellite offices operating substantially as if they were separate enterprises or profit centers.

(4) Revenues from ancillary services, if any, must be derived from "in-office ancillary services" that meet the definition of such term in section 1877(b)(2) of the Act and implementing regulations.

42 C.F.R. § 1001.952(p). If all of the conditions of the safe harbor are met, it protects "any payment that is a return on investment interest, such as a dividend or interest income, made to an investor" in the group practice.

B. Analysis

Our opinion is based on the facts presented, including, but not limited to, the Requestors' certifications that they have or will shortly achieve compliance with the group practice definition of the physician self-referral law.

The Proposed Arrangement cannot fit in the investments in group practices safe harbor because [Stakeholder name redacted], who holds one percent of equity, does not treat patients at the Practice. However, the absence of safe harbor protection is not fatal. Instead, the Proposed Arrangement must be evaluated based on the totality of its facts.

Under the Proposed Arrangement, the Practice will comply with the requirements of the safe harbor for investments in group practices in nearly all respects. First, all equity interests except [Stakeholder name redacted]'s one percent stake are held by health care professionals who practice in the Practice. Second, all equity interests are held in the Practice and not some subdivision thereof. Each investor (including [Stakeholder name redacted]) holds a fixed percentage stake in the entire Practice, rather than in particular specialty groups or other subdivisions. To a degree directly proportionate to their individual stake in the Practice, each investor shares in the entire enterprise's risks and returns. Third, the Requestors have certified that the Proposed Arrangement will comply fully in all respects with the requirements of the "group practice" definition under the physician self-referral law. As described in the facts, the Practice is structured and operated as a unified business. For example, central decision-making authority rests with the Board, which determines both clinical and financial policies. Expenses and revenues are pooled across the enterprise and are not separated in relation to satellite offices maintained by individual

Practice members. Fourth, the Practice has certified that revenues from ancillary services are derived from "in-office ancillary services" that meet the definition of that term under the physician self-referral law.

Given the totality of facts and circumstances described above, [Stakeholder name redacted]'s one percent stake in the Practice does not pose any appreciable additional risks to Federal programs or beneficiaries. His returns are directly proportional to his investment interest, and he provides substantial services integral to the Practice's operation and administration, thus minimizing the risk that his small equity interest reflects referrals.

For a combination of the above reasons, we conclude that the Proposed Arrangement presents a minimal risk of Federal health care program abuse, and we would not seek to seek to impose administrative sanctions in connection with the statutes discussed above. This favorable opinion is conditioned on the Practice's full compliance with relevant provisions under the physician self-referral law regulations. (See infra note 4.) This opinion only applies to returns on investment interests made to the current investors in the Practice. It does not apply to any other remuneration arising out of this venture, including compensatory income paid physicians for services.

III. CONCLUSION

Based on the facts certified in your request for an advisory opinion and supplemental submissions, we conclude that, while the Proposed Arrangement could potentially generate prohibited remuneration under the anti-kickback statute, if the requisite intent to induce or reward referrals of Federal health care program business were present, the OIG would not impose administrative sanctions on the Requestors under sections 1128(b)(7) or 1128A(a)(7) of the Act (as those sections relate to the commission of acts described in section 1128B(b) of the Act) in connection with the Proposed Arrangement.

IV. LIMITATIONS

The limitations applicable to this opinion include the following:

- This advisory opinion is issued only to the Requestors of this opinion. This advisory opinion has no application to, and cannot be relied upon by, any other individual or entity.

- This advisory opinion may not be introduced into evidence in any matter involving an entity or individual that is not a requestor of this opinion.

Page 7 – OIG Advisory Opinion No. 08-24

- This advisory opinion is applicable only to the statutory provisions specifically noted above. No opinion is expressed or implied herein with respect to the application of any other Federal, state, or local statute, rule, regulation, ordinance, or other law that may be applicable to the Proposed Arrangement, including, without limitation, the physician self-referral law, section 1877 of the Act.

- This advisory opinion will not bind or obligate any agency other than the U.S. Department of Health and Human Services.

- This advisory opinion is limited in scope to the specific arrangement described in this letter and has no applicability to other arrangements, even those which appear similar in nature or scope.

- No opinion is expressed herein regarding the liability of any party under the False Claims Act or other legal authorities for any improper billing, claims submission, cost reporting, or related conduct.

This opinion is also subject to any additional limitations set forth at 42 C.F.R. Part 1008.

The OIG will not proceed against the Requestors with respect to any action that is part of the Proposed Arrangement taken in good faith reliance upon this advisory opinion, as long as all of the material facts have been fully, completely, and accurately presented, and the Proposed Arrangement in practice comports with the information provided. The OIG reserves the right to reconsider the questions and issues raised in this advisory opinion and, where the public interest requires, to rescind, modify, or terminate this opinion. In the event that this advisory opinion is modified or terminated, the OIG will not proceed against the Requestors with respect to any action taken in good faith reliance upon this advisory opinion, where all of the relevant facts were fully, completely, and accurately presented and where such action was promptly discontinued upon notification of the modification or termination of this advisory opinion. An advisory opinion may be rescinded only if the relevant and material facts have not been fully, completely, and accurately disclosed to the OIG.

Sincerely,

/Lewis Morris/

Lewis Morris
Chief Counsel to the Inspector General

Page 8 – OIG Advisory Opinion No. 08-24

[Distribution List redacted]

DEPARTMENT OF HEALTH & HUMAN SERVICES **Office of Inspector General**

Washington, D.C. 20201

[*We redact certain identifying information and certain potentially privileged, confidential, or proprietary information associated with the individual or entity, unless otherwise approved by the requestor*.]

Issued: September 17, 2009

Posted: September 24, 2009

[Name and address redacted]

Re: OIG Advisory Opinion No. 09-16

Ladies and Gentlemen:

We are writing in response to your request for an advisory opinion regarding a proposed arrangement between your professional organization and a referral service (the "Proposed Arrangement"). Specifically, you have inquired whether the Proposed Arrangement would constitute grounds for the imposition of sanctions under the exclusion authority at section 1128(b)(7) of the Social Security Act (the "Act"), or the civil monetary penalty provision at section 1128A(a)(7) of the Act, as those sections relate to the commission of acts described in section 1128B(b) of the Act, the Federal anti-kickback statute.

You have certified that all of the information provided in your request, including all supplemental submissions, is true and correct and constitutes a complete description of the relevant facts and agreements among the parties.

In issuing this opinion, we have relied solely on the facts and information presented to us. We have not undertaken an independent investigation of such information. This opinion is limited to the facts presented. If material facts have not been disclosed or have been misrepresented, this opinion is without force and effect.

Based on the facts certified in your request for an advisory opinion and supplemental submissions, we conclude that while the Proposed Arrangement could potentially generate prohibited remuneration under the anti-kickback statute, if the requisite intent to induce or reward referrals of Federal health care program business were present, the Office of

Page 2 – OIG Advisory Opinion No. 09-16

Inspector General ("OIG") would not impose administrative sanctions on the [name redacted] under sections 1128(b)(7) or 1128A(a)(7) of the Act (as those sections relate to the commission of acts described in section 1128B(b) of the Act) in connection with the Proposed Arrangement. This opinion is limited to the Proposed Arrangement and, therefore, we express no opinion about any ancillary agreements or arrangements disclosed or referenced in your request for an advisory opinion or supplemental submissions. This opinion may not be relied on by any persons other than the [name redacted], the requestor of this opinion, and is further qualified as set out in Part IV below and in 42 C.F.R. Part 1008.

I. FACTUAL BACKGROUND

The requestor is the [name redacted] (the "Association"), a [state redacted] not-for-profit corporation formed under section 501(c)(6) of the Internal Revenue Code. Under the Association's by-laws, any chiropractor of good character, licensed to practice in [state redacted], is eligible for membership. Approximately [number redacted] chiropractors are licensed to practice in [state redacted], and approximately [number redacted] of these are members of the Association.

The [name redacted] (the "Network") is a [state redacted] for-profit corporation. It does not provide any items or services payable by Federal health care programs, and it is not affiliated with any individual or entity that provides such items or services. It is a start-up entity that intends to advertise chiropractic services in the [state redacted] metropolitan area and provide referrals for such services. The Network intends to advertise its chiropractor referral service through internet, print, radio, or television advertising. A prospective patient who contacts the Network for a chiropractor referral will be asked to provide a zip code. The Network will provide contact information for a participating chiropractor who practices in that zip code or, if no participating chiropractor practices in that zip code, in a nearby zip code. If more than one participating chiropractor is in the particular zip code, a name will be provided in sequence from a rotating list.

The Association has certified that the Network will make all the disclosures required by the safe harbor for referral services at 42 C.F.R. § 1001.952(f)(4). These disclosures will be made on the Network's website and orally when the Network receives telephone requests for referrals to chiropractors. The Association also has certified that written records for the website will be maintained and that voice recordings will be made for the call center, with written notations documenting the above-described disclosures and signed by the person making the disclosures. The Network will impose no requirements on the manner in which participating chiropractors provide services to referred persons.

Page 3 – OIG Advisory Opinion No. 09-16

The referral service will be open to participation by any chiropractor licensed to practice in [state redacted], for a standard flat fee of $200 per month. Under the Proposed Arrangement, the Association and the Network would enter an agreement by which the Association's members would have access to the Network's referral service for a reduced fee of $60 per month. Except for this discount, the Association's members would not be treated any differently than other chiropractors who participate in the referral service. Their names would be provided to prospective patients who contact the Network on exactly the same basis as the names of participating chiropractors who are not members of the Association.

Also under the Proposed Arrangement, the Association would form a for-profit subsidiary (the "Subsidiary"). The Network would pay the Subsidiary a flat fee of $10 per month for each of the Association's members who participate in the Network's referral service. In return for this compensation, the Association would advertise and promote the Network's referral service through e-mails and faxes to its members and to non-members, through its quarterly publication, and at its statewide conventions, conference calls, webinars, and other meetings.

II. LEGAL ANALYSIS

A. Law

The anti-kickback statute makes it a criminal offense knowingly and willfully to offer, pay, solicit, or receive any remuneration to induce or reward referrals of items or services reimbursable by a Federal health care program. See section 1128B(b) of the Act. Where remuneration is paid purposefully to induce or reward referrals of items or services payable by a Federal health care program, the anti-kickback statute is violated. By its terms, the statute ascribes criminal liability to parties on both sides of an impermissible "kickback" transaction. For purposes of the anti-kickback statute, "remuneration" includes the transfer of anything of value, directly or indirectly, overtly or covertly, in cash or in kind.

The statute has been interpreted to cover any arrangement where one purpose of the remuneration was to obtain money for the referral of services or to induce further referrals. United States v. Kats, 871 F.2d 105 (9th Cir. 1989); United States v. Greber, 760 F.2d 68 (3d Cir.), cert. denied, 474 U.S. 988 (1985). Violation of the statute constitutes a felony punishable by a maximum fine of $25,000, imprisonment up to five years, or both. Conviction will also lead to automatic exclusion from Federal health care programs, including Medicare and Medicaid. Where a party commits an act described in section 1128B(b) of the Act, the OIG may initiate administrative proceedings to impose civil monetary penalties on such party under section 1128A(a)(7) of the Act. The OIG may also initiate administrative proceedings to exclude such party from the Federal health care programs under section 1128(b)(7) of the Act.

The Department of Health and Human Services has promulgated safe harbor regulations that define practices that are not subject to the anti-kickback statute because such practices would be unlikely to result in fraud or abuse. See 42 C.F.R. § 1001.952. The safe harbors set forth specific conditions that, if met, assure entities involved of not being prosecuted or sanctioned for the arrangement qualifying for the safe harbor. However, safe harbor protection is afforded only to those arrangements that precisely meet all of the conditions set forth in the safe harbor.

The safe harbor for referral services, 42 C.F.R. § 1001.952(f), is potentially applicable to the Proposed Arrangement. It provides that, for purposes of the anti-kickback statute, the term "remuneration" does not include payments or exchanges of anything of value between a referral service and a participant in the service, provided certain conditions are met. Among these conditions are requirements that the referral service not exclude any person or entity that meets its qualifications for participation; that referral fees be assessed uniformly against all participants, be based only on the cost of operating the referral service, and not vary with the volume or value of referrals of Federal health care program business; and that the referral service make certain disclosures to persons seeking a referral.

B. Analysis

The Proposed Arrangement does not qualify for protection by the safe harbor for referral services. It does not meet the requirement that referral fees be assessed uniformly against all participants. See 42 C.F.R. § 1001.952(f)(2). The fact that the Proposed Arrangement does not fit in a safe harbor does not end the inquiry, however. We must examine the totality of facts and circumstances to determine the extent of the risk posed.

We note, at the outset, that the Proposed Arrangement has certain characteristics in common with the facts addressed in OIG Advisory Opinion 08-19, in which an internet advertiser forwarded e-mails and calls to chiropractors who paid a fee for each such contact. We analyzed those facts as an advertising arrangement, noting that the arrangement "is unlike a typical, non-profit referral service operating for the convenience and support of patients and is not the type of referral service for which the safe harbor at 42 C.F.R. § 1001.952(f) was designed." The Proposed Arrangement also does not involve a non-profit referral service and has some characteristics of an advertising arrangement. Whether we analyze the Proposed Arrangement as an advertising arrangement or as a referral service is not determinative of the outcome, however; the critical question is to what extent the Proposed Arrangement poses a risk of fraud or abuse.

Page 5 – OIG Advisory Opinion No. 09-16

To answer this question, we first address the fact that the Network would not charge the same fee to all participants in its referral service; members of the Association would receive a discount. The participation fee would not vary, however, on the basis of referrals of Federally payable business. Referral of potential patients to participating chiropractors would be on a rotating basis, by geographic area, and would not be influenced by the variation in fees paid by participants. Under these circumstances, we find that the variation in fees charged to participating chiropractors poses a minimal risk of fraud or abuse.

We next address the Network's proposed payment to the Association's for-profit Subsidiary of $10 per month for each Association member who participates in the Network. This compensation paid to the Association would vary with the amount of business generated for the Network, but would not vary with referrals of items or services payable by Federal health care programs. Indeed, unlike some sponsors of referral services, such as hospitals, the Network does not provide items or services payable by Federal health care programs. Under the circumstances of the Proposed Arrangement, we conclude that this payment does not implicate the anti-kickback statute.

The Network's referral service will be open to participation by any chiropractor licensed to practice in the state, and participating chiropractors will receive referrals on an equal basis. The Network will impose no requirements on the manner in which participating chiropractors provide services to referred persons, and the Network will make all the disclosures required by the safe harbor for referral services at 42 C.F.R. § 1001.952(f)(4). Given these particular facts and circumstances, we conclude that the Proposed Arrangement poses a minimal risk of fraud and abuse.

III. CONCLUSION

Based on the facts certified in your request for an advisory opinion and supplemental submissions, we conclude that while the Proposed Arrangement could potentially generate prohibited remuneration under the anti-kickback statute, if the requisite intent to induce or reward referrals of Federal health care program business were present, the OIG would not impose administrative sanctions on the [name redacted] under sections 1128(b)(7) or 1128A(a)(7) of the Act (as those sections relate to the commission of acts described in section 1128B(b) of the Act) in connection with the Proposed Arrangement. This opinion is limited to the Proposed Arrangement and, therefore, we express no opinion about any ancillary agreements or arrangements disclosed or referenced in your request for an advisory opinion or supplemental submissions.

IV. LIMITATIONS

The limitations applicable to this opinion include the following:

- This advisory opinion is issued only to the [name redacted], the requestor of this opinion. This advisory opinion has no application to, and cannot be relied upon by, any other individual or entity.
- This advisory opinion may not be introduced into evidence in any matter involving an entity or individual that is not a requestor of this opinion.
- This advisory opinion is applicable only to the statutory provisions specifically noted above. No opinion is expressed or implied herein with respect to the application of any other Federal, state, or local statute, rule, regulation, ordinance, or other law that may be applicable to the Proposed Arrangement, including, without limitation, the physician self-referral law, section 1877 of the Act.
- This advisory opinion will not bind or obligate any agency other than the U.S. Department of Health and Human Services.
- This advisory opinion is limited in scope to the specific arrangement described in this letter and has no applicability to other arrangements, even those which appear similar in nature or scope.
- No opinion is expressed herein regarding the liability of any party under the False Claims Act or other legal authorities for any improper billing, claims submission, cost reporting, or related conduct.

This opinion is also subject to any additional limitations set forth at 42 C.F.R. Part 1008.

The OIG will not proceed against the [name redacted] with respect to any action that is part of the Proposed Arrangement taken in good faith reliance upon this advisory opinion, as long as all of the material facts have been fully, completely, and accurately presented, and the Proposed Arrangement in practice comports with the information provided. The OIG reserves the right to reconsider the questions and issues raised in this advisory opinion and, where the public interest requires, to rescind, modify, or terminate this opinion. In the event that this advisory opinion is modified or terminated, the OIG will not proceed against the [name redacted] with respect to any action taken in good faith reliance upon this advisory opinion, where all of the relevant facts were fully, completely, and accurately presented and where such action was promptly discontinued upon notification of the modification or termination of this advisory opinion. An advisory opinion may be rescinded only if the relevant and material facts have not been fully, completely, and accurately disclosed to the OIG.

Sincerely,

/Lewis Morris/

Lewis Morris
Chief Counsel to the Inspector General

DEPARTMENT OF HEALTH & HUMAN SERVICES **Office of Inspector General**

Washington, D.C. 20201

[*We redact certain identifying information and certain potentially privileged, confidential, or proprietary information associated with the individual or entity, unless otherwise approved by the requestor.*]

Issued: May 13, 2011

Posted: May 20, 2011

[Name and address redacted]

Re: OIG Advisory Opinion No. 11-06

Dear [Name redacted]:

We are writing in response to your request for an advisory opinion regarding an online referral service operated by [name redacted], whereby post-acute care providers would pay a fee to electronically receive and respond to referral requests from hospitals for post-discharge care (the "Proposed Arrangement"). Specifically, you have inquired whether the Proposed Arrangement would constitute grounds for the imposition of sanctions under the exclusion authority at section 1128(b)(7) of the Social Security Act (the "Act"), or the civil monetary penalty provision at section 1128A(a)(7) of the Act, as those sections relate to the commission of acts described in section 1128B(b) of the Act, the Federal anti-kickback statute.

You have certified that all of the information provided in your request, including all supplemental submissions, is true and correct and constitutes a complete description of the relevant facts and agreements among the parties.

In issuing this opinion, we have relied solely on the facts and information presented to us. We have not undertaken an independent investigation of such information. This opinion is limited to the facts presented. If material facts have not been disclosed or have been misrepresented, this opinion is without force and effect.

Based on the facts certified in your request for an advisory opinion and supplemental submissions, we conclude that the Proposed Arrangement could potentially generate prohibited remuneration under the anti-kickback statute and that the Office of Inspector General ("OIG") could potentially impose administrative sanctions on [name redacted] under sections 1128(b)(7) or 1128A(a)(7) of the Act (as those sections relate to the commission of acts described in section 1128B(b) of the Act) in connection with the Proposed Arrangement. Any definitive conclusion regarding the existence of an anti-kickback violation requires a determination of the parties' intent, which determination is beyond the scope of the advisory opinion process.

Page 2 – OIG Advisory Opinion No. 11-06

This opinion may not be relied on by any persons other than [name redacted], the requestor of this opinion, and is further qualified as set out in Part IV below and in 42 C.F.R. Part 1008.

I. FACTUAL BACKGROUND

[Name redacted] (the "Requestor") is a for-profit corporation that provides software, online tools, and related discharge planning support services to hospitals across the nation. It operates an online referral service, [name redacted] (the "System"), that provides hospitals with access to a nationwide listing of all licensed post-acute care providers, including skilled nursing facilities, home health agencies, and assisted living facilities ("Providers"). The Requestor typically compiles this listing by reviewing state licensure databases of post-acute care providers.

Hospitals use the System to identify and select the Providers that are best-suited to meet the post-acute care needs of hospital patients who are ready to be discharged, including Federal health care program beneficiaries, and to send referral requests to the selected Providers. When initiating a referral, a hospital provides to the Requestor, via the System, the patient's name and identifying information, as well as any medical records a Provider needs to make an informed decision regarding whether to accept the patient. The Requestor then forwards this information to the Providers selected by the hospital.[1] According to the Requestor, many hospitals provide referrals to post-acute care providers on a first-come, first-served basis; consequently, the first Provider that responds to the hospital's inquiry typically will receive that patient.

Hospitals pay a fee to the Requestor to utilize the System. The Requestor has certified that the amounts paid by the hospitals are equal to fair market value and are not tied, directly or indirectly, to the volume or value of referrals or other business generated between the parties. The Requestor further certified that the revenues it collects under its arrangements with the hospitals exceed the associated costs of the System.[2]

Currently, Providers are not charged a fee to use the System to electronically receive or respond to hospital referral requests. Under the Proposed Arrangement, the Requestor would begin charging Providers that wish to use these online capabilities a one-time implementation fee of approximately [amount redacted], and a monthly fee of

---

[1] We have not been asked to opine on, and we offer no opinion regarding, whether the transmission of patient information from the hospital to the Requestor, and from the Requestor to the Providers, complies with state and Federal privacy laws.

[2] We have not been asked to opine on, and express no opinion about, the arrangement between the Requestor and the participating hospitals.

approximately [amount redacted]. The Requestor has certified that the fees would not vary based on the volume or value of referrals or other business generated between the parties.

Providers that choose not to pay the Requestor's fees would continue to be listed in the System but would not be able to electronically receive or respond to the hospitals' referral requests. Rather, the Requestor would notify non-paying Providers of hospital referral requests via facsimile. Non-paying Providers that wished to respond to hospital referral requests would then be required to either call or fax the hospital. According to the Requestor, non-paying Providers would be significantly disadvantaged vis-à-vis paying Providers under the Proposed Arrangement—and may effectively be eliminated from any chance of receiving the patient—because they would not be able to communicate with hospital discharge planners and accept referrals in a timely manner.

The Requestor set the implementation and monthly fees based on research it performed regarding the System's value to Providers. According to the Requestor, some Providers indicated that they would be willing to pay the estimated fees to electronically receive and respond to hospital referral requests, whereas other Providers indicated that their profit margins are so slim that they could not afford to pay for such online access. The Requestor has certified that, once it has recouped the System's development costs, it would be more expensive to fax referral requests to non-paying Providers than it would be to transmit them electronically.

II. LEGAL ANALYSIS

A. Law

The anti-kickback statute makes it a criminal offense knowingly and willfully to offer, pay, solicit, or receive any remuneration to induce or reward referrals of items or services reimbursable by a Federal health care program. See section 1128B(b) of the Act. Where remuneration is paid purposefully to induce or reward referrals of items or services payable by a Federal health care program, the anti-kickback statute is violated. By its terms, the statute ascribes criminal liability to parties on both sides of an impermissible "kickback" transaction. For purposes of the anti-kickback statute, "remuneration" includes the transfer of anything of value, directly or indirectly, overtly or covertly, in cash or in kind.

The statute has been interpreted to cover any arrangement where one purpose of the remuneration was to obtain money for the referral of services or to induce further referrals. United States v. Kats, 871 F.2d 105 (9th Cir. 1989); United States v. Greber, 760 F.2d 68 (3d Cir. 1985), cert. denied, 474 U.S. 988 (1985). Violation of the statute

Page 4 – OIG Advisory Opinion No. 11-06

constitutes a felony punishable by a maximum fine of $25,000, imprisonment up to five years, or both. Conviction will also lead to automatic exclusion from Federal health care programs, including Medicare and Medicaid. Where a party commits an act described in section 1128B(b) of the Act, the OIG may initiate administrative proceedings to impose civil monetary penalties on such party under section 1128A(a)(7) of the Act. The OIG may also initiate administrative proceedings to exclude such party from the Federal health care programs under section 1128(b)(7) of the Act.

The Department of Health and Human Services has promulgated safe harbor regulations that define practices that are not subject to the anti-kickback statute because such practices would be unlikely to result in fraud or abuse. See 42 C.F.R. § 1001.952. The safe harbors set forth specific conditions that, if met, assure entities involved of not being prosecuted or sanctioned for the arrangement qualifying for the safe harbor. However, safe harbor protection is afforded only to those arrangements that precisely meet all of the conditions set forth in the safe harbor.

The safe harbor for referral services, 42 C.F.R. § 1001.952(f), is potentially applicable to the Proposed Arrangement. It provides that, for purposes of the anti-kickback statute, the term "remuneration" does not include payments or exchanges of anything of value between a referral service and a participant in the service, provided certain conditions are met. Among those conditions are requirements that referral fees be assessed uniformly against all participants, be based only on the cost of operating the referral service, and not vary with the volume or value of referrals of Federal health care program business.

B. Analysis

Under the Proposed Arrangement, Providers would pay the Requestor in return for the opportunity to use the System to electronically receive and respond to hospital referral requests for post-acute care services, including post-acute care services for Federal health care program beneficiaries. The Proposed Arrangement would implicate the anti-kickback statute, because the Requestor would be soliciting and accepting, and Providers would be paying, remuneration in return for the Requestor's arranging for the furnishing of post-acute care services for which payment would be made by a Federal health care program.

The Proposed Arrangement does not qualify for protection under the safe harbor for referral services. It fails to satisfy several of the safe harbor's requirements, including the requirement that referral fees be assessed uniformly against all participants and be based only on the cost of operating the referral service. See 42 C.F.R. § 1001.952(f)(2).

Page 5 – OIG Advisory Opinion No. 11-06

Because no safe harbor would protect the Proposed Arrangement, we must determine whether, given all of the relevant facts, the Proposed Arrangement would pose no more than a minimal risk under the anti-kickback statute. For the following reasons, we conclude that it would not.

First, based on the Requestor's certification, hospitals often discharge patients to Providers on a first-come, first-served basis, which means that Providers with the ability to electronically receive and respond to referral requests through the System would have a significant competitive advantage over non-paying Providers. In fact, according to the Requestor, non-paying Providers may effectively be eliminated from any chance of receiving the patient under the Proposed Arrangement. Thus, Providers that pay the Requestor's fees would be more likely to get the patients—not because they provide superior care but because they paid for the opportunity.

Second, the costs that the Requestor would incur to fax the referral requests to non-paying Providers would exceed the costs that it would incur to transmit them electronically. The Requestor would fax referral requests to non-paying Providers not because it would be easier or cheaper to do so, but rather to provide the paying Providers with a competitive advantage in obtaining referrals or, conversely, to penalize Providers that do not pay.[3]

Finally, the Requestor reported that some Providers indicated that they cannot afford to pay for online access to the System. Under the Proposed Arrangement, these Providers would be required to pay fees they cannot afford for services they require to remain competitive, or risk substantial loss of business. These—and indeed all—Providers that choose to participate in the Proposed Arrangement could face pressure to recoup the costs associated with participation. This pressure could create incentives to, among other things, prolong patient stays, provide separately billable, unnecessary services, or upcode resident Resource Utilization Group assignments—all of which could result in increased costs to the Federal health care programs.

For the above reasons, we cannot conclude that the Proposed Arrangement poses a sufficiently low level of risk that we should protect it.

---

[3] This fact, together with the fact that the revenues the Requestor collects under its arrangements with the hospitals exceed the associated costs of the System, demonstrates that the proposed fees for Providers are not based only on the cost of operating the System. See 42 C.F.R. § 1001.952(f)(2).

Page 6 – OIG Advisory Opinion No. 11-06

III. CONCLUSION

Based on the facts certified in your request for an advisory opinion and supplemental submissions, we conclude that the Proposed Arrangement could potentially generate prohibited remuneration under the anti-kickback statute and that the OIG could potentially impose administrative sanctions on [name redacted] under sections 1128(b)(7) or 1128A(a)(7) of the Act (as those sections relate to the commission of acts described in section 1128B(b) of the Act) in connection with the Proposed Arrangement. Any definitive conclusion regarding the existence of an anti-kickback violation requires a determination of the parties' intent, which determination is beyond the scope of the advisory opinion process.

IV. LIMITATIONS

The limitations applicable to this opinion include the following:

- This advisory opinion is issued only to [name redacted], the requestor of this opinion. This advisory opinion has no application to, and cannot be relied upon by, any other individual or entity.

- This advisory opinion may not be introduced into evidence in any matter involving an entity or individual that is not a requestor of this opinion.

- This advisory opinion is applicable only to the statutory provisions specifically noted above. No opinion is expressed or implied herein with respect to the application of any other Federal, state, or local statute, rule, regulation, ordinance, or other law that may be applicable to the Proposed Arrangement, including, without limitation, the physician self-referral law, section 1877 of the Act.

- This advisory opinion will not bind or obligate any agency other than the U.S. Department of Health and Human Services.

- This advisory opinion is limited in scope to the specific arrangement described in this letter and has no applicability to other arrangements, even those which appear similar in nature or scope.

- No opinion is expressed herein regarding the liability of any party under the False Claims Act or other legal authorities for any improper billing, claims submission, cost reporting, or related conduct.

Page 7 – OIG Advisory Opinion No. 11-06

This opinion is also subject to any additional limitations set forth at 42 C.F.R. Part 1008. The OIG reserves the right to reconsider the questions and issues raised in this advisory opinion and, where the public interest requires, to rescind, modify, or terminate this opinion.

Sincerely,

/Lewis Morris/

Lewis Morris
Chief Counsel to the Inspector General

DEPARTMENT OF HEALTH & HUMAN SERVICES **Office of Inspector General**

Washington, D.C. 20201

[*We redact certain identifying information and certain potentially privileged, confidential, or proprietary information associated with the individual or entity, unless otherwise approved by the requestor.*]

Issued: August 29, 2011

Posted: September 6, 2011

[Name and address redacted]

Re: OIG Advisory Opinion No. 11-12

Dear [Name redacted]:

We are writing in response to your request for an advisory opinion regarding a health system's proposal to enter into arrangements to provide neuro emergency clinical protocols and immediate consultations with stroke neurologists via telemedicine technology to certain community hospitals (the "Proposed Arrangement"). Specifically, you have inquired whether the Proposed Arrangement would constitute grounds for the imposition of sanctions under the exclusion authority at section 1128(b)(7) of the Social Security Act (the "Act"), or the civil monetary penalty provision at section 1128A(a)(7) of the Act, as those sections relate to the commission of acts described in section 1128B(b) of the Act, the Federal anti-kickback statute.

You have certified that all of the information provided in your request, including all supplemental submissions, is true and correct and constitutes a complete description of the relevant facts and agreements among the parties.

In issuing this opinion, we have relied solely on the facts and information presented to us. We have not undertaken an independent investigation of such information. This opinion is limited to the facts presented. If material facts have not been disclosed or have been misrepresented, this opinion is without force and effect.

Based on the facts certified in your request for an advisory opinion and supplemental submissions, we conclude that, while the Proposed Arrangement could potentially generate prohibited remuneration under the anti-kickback statute if the requisite intent to induce or reward referrals of Federal health care program business were present, the Office of Inspector General ("OIG") would not impose administrative sanctions on [name redacted] under sections 1128(b)(7) or 1128A(a)(7) of the Act (as those sections relate to the commission of acts described in section 1128B(b) of the Act) in connection with the Proposed Arrangement. This opinion is limited to the Proposed Arrangement and, therefore, we express no opinion about any ancillary agreements or arrangements disclosed or referenced in your request for an advisory opinion or supplemental submissions.

This opinion may not be relied on by any persons other than [name redacted], the requestor of this opinion, and is further qualified as set out in Part IV below and in 42 C.F.R. Part 1008.

I. FACTUAL BACKGROUND

[Name redacted] (the "Requestor") is an operating division of the not-for-profit corporation [name redacted]. Through its flagship hospital, the Requestor provides nationally-ranked neuroscience care. The Requestor states that part of its mission is to spread the availability of its quality and excellence throughout the region in which it is located, including by developing programs that foster enhanced access to high-quality tertiary/quaternary neuroscience services.

Recent statistics indicate that stroke is the third leading cause of death in the nation and a leading cause of serious, long-term disability.[1] The Requestor states that, for legal reasons, community hospitals frequently transfer suspected stroke patients to comprehensive stroke centers that have the medical resources to treat acute stroke and other neuro emergencies that may present with stroke-like symptoms. The Requestor also states that, although acute stroke is a treatable illness, time is of the essence in its treatment and, therefore, treatment is most effective when commenced in the emergency department. Hospitals with the proper support of a comprehensive stroke center can safely and effectively treat simple stroke cases, rather than transfer them to a comprehensive stroke center, thus allowing treatment to begin at the time that it is most effective.

Comprehensive stroke centers frequently offer local community hospital emergency departments access to stroke neurologists 24 hours a day, seven days a week, 365 days a year ("24/7/365"); however, according to the Requestor, consultations between emergency physicians and stroke neurologists typically take place over the telephone, thus limiting the quality of information the parties can exchange. The Requestor further

---

[1] See, e.g., Centers for Disease Control and Prevention, "Stroke Facts," available at http://www.cdc.gov/stroke/facts.htm.

states that consultation arrangements between comprehensive stroke centers and local community hospitals have, historically, been informal and ad hoc.

Under the Proposed Arrangement, the Requestor would provide, at its expense, the following items and services to certain community hospitals in the Requestor's service area (each, a "Participating Hospital"): (i) neuro emergency telemedicine technology; (ii) neuro emergency clinical consultations; (iii) acceptance of neuro emergency transfers; and (iv) neuro emergency clinical protocols, training, and medical education (collectively, the "Program"). In addition, the Requestor and the Participating Hospitals would have the opportunity to use each other's trademarks and service marks for certain marketing activities in connection with the Program.

The Program initially would be offered to community hospitals in the Requestor's service area with which the Requestor has pre-existing, significant contractual relationships[2] ("Affiliated Hospitals"). The Requestor has certified that neither the continued transfer of stroke patients to the Requestor nor the value or volume of any other business generated between the parties would be a condition of participation. The Requestor further certified that, to the extent that it elects to make participation in the Program available to community hospitals with which it does not have pre-existing, significant contractual relationships ("Non-Affiliated Hospitals"), the decision as to which Non-Affiliated Hospitals to offer the Program would not be based on the volume or value of the Non-Affiliated Hospital's previous referrals, or on any arrangement or understanding regarding anticipated referrals. Rather, Program participation would be extended to Non-Affiliated Hospitals based on rational access-to-care considerations, including the Non-Affiliated Hospital's location, the location of other stroke programs, the local population density, and the Requestor's resources for the Program.

The Requestor has certified that the Program aims to reduce the mortality and morbidity rates of stroke in the Requestor's metropolitan area and lower the costs associated with transfers of stroke cases that, with the Program's support, could be managed at the Participating Hospitals. The Requestor certified that it receives a significant volume of transfers of stroke patients who could effectively be treated in their local community hospitals with the appropriate clinical support. The Requestor expects that the Program would reduce the volume of these transfers and that this reduction would, in turn, free up resources for patients who require the level of tertiary care that the Requestor's hospital can provide.

The Requestor would enter into a written agreement with each Participating Hospital that sets forth all of the services to be provided by each party under the Program. In recognition of the Requestor's investment of time and capital in the Program, the

[2] According to the Requestor, these contractual relationships typically involve some sort of clinical affiliation, such as participation in the Requestor's cancer network.

Participating Hospitals must agree not to participate in any other neuro emergency telemedicine service without the Requestor's prior approval for the length of the agreement, which the Requestor anticipates would be two years. The Requestor has certified that this exclusivity requirement would not: (i) restrict a Participating Hospital's emergency or attending physician from consulting by phone or in-person with any stroke specialist of his or her choice; (ii) require either party or any physician on its medical staff to refer patients to the other party; or (iii) restrict the freedom of a patient or the patient's physician to request a transfer to a stroke center other than the Requestor's stroke center.

We provide a brief description of each of the Program's components, below.

Neuro Emergency Telemedicine

The Requestor's contracted telemedicine service provider would, at the Requestor's expense, install neuro emergency telemedicine technology, including both hardware and software, in the Participating Hospitals' emergency departments. The telemedicine service provider would provide maintenance, upgrades, technical training, and support services pursuant to a contract between it and the Requestor. Central to the telemedicine technology is a web-enabled stroke treatment consultation and decision support system with integrated audio-visual capabilities (the "Tele-Stroke Application") that would enable the Requestor's neurologists, who have extensive training and experience in the treatment of stroke, to consult, in real time, with the Participating Hospitals' emergency physicians.

Each Participating Hospital would be required to, among other things: (i) enter into, and comply with, an end user license agreement with the telemedicine service provider; (ii) at its own expense, install and maintain the communication links and connectivity necessary for the telemedicine technology to link with the Requestor; and (iii) at its own expense, install and maintain at least one computed tomography ("CT") scanner capable of transmitting CT scan images to a remote server, thereby permitting the Requestor's neurologists to view the images remotely. The Requestor has certified that neither it nor any Participating Hospital would bill any patient or third party payor for the cost of the telemedicine technology.

Neuro Emergency Clinical Consultations

The Requestor would, at its expense, furnish the Participating Hospitals' emergency physicians with 24/7/365 access to the Requestor's stroke expertise, via both telephone and the Tele-Stroke Application. If medically necessary, one of the Requestor's neurologists would examine the patient in real-time using the Tele-Stroke Application, view the CT scans performed in the Participating Hospital's emergency department through remote access, and make recommendations based on his or her clinical assessment. The Participating Hospitals would be required to, among other things, facilitate the medical staff credentialing of the Requestor's neurologists and their appointments as consulting physicians on an expedited basis. The Requestor states that although few, if any, of the consultations would be billable to Medicare, to the extent the consultations are covered and payable by third party payors, it would bill and collect for them.[3]

Acceptance of Neuro Emergency Transfers

The Requestor would, at its expense, ensure that neurosurgeons and neuro intensivists are on call and available to accept transfers of acute stroke patients from the Participating Hospitals. Each Participating Hospital must represent and warrant to the Requestor that: (i) it would at all times respect the independence of its emergency physicians' clinical judgment and its patients' freedom of choice; (ii) no emergency physician's compensation would take into account the volume or value of the physician's referrals to the Requestor; and (iii) no emergency physician would receive additional remuneration as a result of the Program.

Neuro Emergency Clinical Protocols, Training, and Medical Education

The Requestor would, at its expense, furnish neuro emergency clinical protocols to the Participating Hospitals and offer access to neuro emergency training and medical education programs to the Participating Hospitals' emergency department staffs. The programs would include: (i) initial training sessions designed to ensure that the Participating Hospitals' staffs are well-versed in the use of the Tele-Stroke Application and stroke assessment protocols, and (ii) opportunities for the Participating Hospitals' staffs to participate in Requestor-run events intended to further the physicians' education, such as the ability to participate in grand rounds and special stroke-related events.[4] The Requestor has certified that the training and medical education programs would take place either at the Participating Hospital or at the Requestor's hospital, as appropriate.

---

[3] The Requestor has certified that: (i) this policy would not represent a change from its current billing practices, and (ii) it does not anticipate that the use of the Tele-Stroke Application would allow it to bill for consultations for which it otherwise could not have billed if performed using the telephone.

[4] The Requestor certified that the medical education programs likely would be informal and collaborative in nature and consistent with the ordinary course of the Requestor's internal education and training programs, and would not be comparable to the type of continuing medical education that is available for commercial purchase.

Marketing and Advertising

Subject to the Participating Hospital's prior approval of each specific use of its name and marks, each Participating Hospital would grant the Requestor a limited, non-exclusive, royalty-free license to use the Participating Hospital's trademarks and service marks for purposes of marketing the Program. Conversely, subject to the Requestor's prior approval of each specific use of its name and marks, the Requestor would grant the Participating Hospital a limited, non-exclusive, royalty-free license to use [trademark redacted] and associated trademarks and service marks for purposes of marketing the Participating Hospital's stroke service line. The Requestor has certified that neither party would be required to engage in marketing activities under the Proposed Arrangement and that each party would be responsible for the cost of its own marketing, including any marketing involving the use of the other party's name or marks.

II. LEGAL ANALYSIS

A. Law

The anti-kickback statute makes it a criminal offense knowingly and willfully to offer, pay, solicit, or receive any remuneration to induce or reward referrals of items or services reimbursable by a Federal health care program. See section 1128B(b) of the Act. Where remuneration is paid purposefully to induce or reward referrals of items or services payable by a Federal health care program, the anti-kickback statute is violated. By its terms, the statute ascribes criminal liability to parties on both sides of an impermissible "kickback" transaction. For purposes of the anti-kickback statute, "remuneration" includes the transfer of anything of value, directly or indirectly, overtly or covertly, in cash or in kind.

The statute has been interpreted to cover any arrangement where one purpose of the remuneration was to obtain money for the referral of services or to induce further referrals. United States v. Kats, 871 F.2d 105 (9th Cir. 1989); United States v. Greber, 760 F.2d 68 (3d Cir. 1985), cert. denied, 474 U.S. 988 (1985). Violation of the statute constitutes a felony punishable by a maximum fine of $25,000, imprisonment up to five years, or both. Conviction will also lead to automatic exclusion from Federal health care programs, including Medicare and Medicaid. Where a party commits an act described in section 1128B(b) of the Act, the OIG may initiate administrative proceedings to impose civil monetary penalties on such party under section 1128A(a)(7) of the Act. The OIG may also initiate administrative proceedings to exclude such party from the Federal health care programs under section 1128(b)(7) of the Act.

The Department of Health and Human Services has promulgated safe harbor regulations that define practices that are not subject to the anti-kickback statute because such practices would be unlikely to result in fraud or abuse. See 42 C.F.R. § 1001.952. The safe harbors set forth specific conditions that, if met, assure entities involved of not being prosecuted or sanctioned for the arrangement qualifying for the safe harbor. However, safe harbor protection is afforded only to those arrangements that precisely meet all of the conditions set forth in the safe harbor.

The safe harbor for personal services and management contracts, 42 C.F.R. § 1001.952(d), is potentially applicable to the Proposed Arrangement. Among the conditions of the personal services and management contracts safe harbor is that agreements for services to be provided on a periodic, sporadic, or part-time basis must specify exactly the schedule of such intervals, their precise length, and the exact charge for such intervals. See 42 C.F.R. § 1001.952(d)(3).

B. Analysis

The Requestor and the Participating Hospitals are potential sources of referrals of Federal health care program business to one another. As such, the exchange of anything of value between them potentially implicates the anti-kickback statute.

As a threshold matter, safe harbor protection is not available for the Proposed Arrangement. Under the safe harbor for personal services and management contracts, agreements for services to be provided on a periodic or sporadic basis must specify the schedule of such intervals, their precise length, and the exact charge for such intervals. Because the Participating Hospitals' physicians would use the Tele-Stroke Application to consult with the Requestor's neurologists—and, if medically necessary, to facilitate the Requestor's neurologists' examination of the patient—on an unscheduled, as-needed basis, the Proposed Arrangement cannot fit squarely within the terms of the safe harbor. We therefore must analyze the Proposed Arrangement for compliance with the anti-kickback statute by taking into account the totality of the facts and circumstances.

For the reasons set forth below, we conclude that the facts and circumstances of the Proposed Arrangement, in combination, adequately reduce the risk that the remuneration provided under the Proposed Arrangement could be an improper payment for referrals of Federal health care program business.

First, the Requestor would be unlikely to generate appreciable referrals through the Proposed Arrangement. Neither the Participating Hospitals nor their physicians would be required or encouraged to refer patients to the Requestor's hospital as a condition of Program participation, and no emergency physician would receive additional compensation under the Program. Further, the Requestor has stated that an express objective of the Program is to reduce the number of transfers of stroke patients to the Requestor's hospital in circumstances where those patients may be managed, with the appropriate clinical support, by a Participating Hospital. Although the Participating Hospitals must commit to a period of exclusivity under the Proposed Arrangement, the exclusivity requirement would prohibit the Participating Hospitals only from participating in another neuro emergency telemedicine service without the Requestor's prior approval; the exclusivity provision would not prohibit the Participating Hospitals' emergency physicians from consulting with other neurologists in-person or by telephone. Further, the Participating Hospitals' physicians would remain free at all times to refer their patients to a facility other than the Requestor's hospital.

Second, under the Proposed Arrangement, Program participation initially would be offered to Affiliated Hospitals—i.e., hospitals with which the Requestor typically has some sort of clinical affiliation. If resources permit, Program participation would be offered to Non-Affiliated hospitals based on rational access-to-care considerations. With respect to both Affiliated Hospitals and Non-Affiliated hospitals, neither the volume or value of a hospital's previous or anticipated referrals, nor the volume or value of any other business generated between the parties, would be a condition of Program participation.

Third, while both the Participating Hospitals and the Requestor might benefit from the Proposed Arrangement, the primary beneficiaries would be the stroke patients who, with the Program's support, could be treated at the Participating Hospitals' emergency departments, when treatment is most effective.[5] Further, because the Program likely would reduce the volume of transfers of stroke patients to the Requestor's hospital, patients who need the level of tertiary care that the Requestor's hospital can provide, but who might not otherwise have been able to receive it due to capacity issues, might also benefit.

Fourth, although the Proposed Arrangement would afford the Requestor and the Participating Hospitals the opportunity to engage in marketing activities using each other's marks, neither the Requestor nor any Participating Hospital would be required to engage in any marketing activities, and each party would be responsible for the costs associated with its own marketing activities.

---

[5] The Participating Hospitals' physicians might also benefit from the Proposed Arrangement, as they would have the opportunity to enhance their professional skills by attending medical education programs offered as part of the Program. However, the medical education programs would not be comparable to the type of continuing medical education that is available for commercial purchase, and thus would differ substantially from those that pose a greater risk of fraud or abuse, such as continuing medical education services sponsored or funded by pharmaceutical manufacturers. See, e.g., "OIG Compliance Program Guidance for Pharmaceutical Manufacturers," 68 Fed. Reg. 23,731 (May 5, 2003), available at http://oig.hhs.gov/authorities/docs/03/050503FRCPGPharmac.pdf.

Finally, the Proposed Arrangement is unlikely to result in increased costs to the Federal health care programs. The Requestor certified that few—if any—of the consultations it would provide under the Program would be billable to Medicare. Further, because the Program is designed to reduce the volume of transfers of stroke patients to the Requestor's hospital, the costs associated with these transfers, such as ambulance services, would correspondingly decrease. The timely treatment of stroke patients would also likely decrease the incidence of stroke-related disabilities, which, in turn, would likely decrease the costs associated with treating and supporting such patients. The Federal health care programs would be likely to benefit from these decreased costs.

In short, as structured, the Proposed Arrangement appears to contain sufficient safeguards to reduce the risk that it would result in improper payments for referrals of Federal health care program business for the Requestor. Moreover, the Proposed Arrangement promotes the obvious public benefit of promoting timely access to specialty care for acute stroke patients. In light of the totality of the facts and circumstances presented, we would not subject the Requestor to sanctions under the anti-kickback statute in connection with the Proposed Arrangement.

III. CONCLUSION

Based on the facts certified in your request for an advisory opinion and supplemental submissions, we conclude that, while the Proposed Arrangement could potentially generate prohibited remuneration under the anti-kickback statute if the requisite intent to induce or reward referrals of Federal health care program business were present, the OIG would not impose administrative sanctions on [name redacted] under sections 1128(b)(7) or 1128A(a)(7) of the Act (as those sections relate to the commission of acts described in section 1128B(b) of the Act) in connection with the Proposed Arrangement. This opinion is limited to the Proposed Arrangement and, therefore, we express no opinion about any ancillary agreements or arrangements disclosed or referenced in your request for an advisory opinion or supplemental submissions.

IV. LIMITATIONS

The limitations applicable to this opinion include the following:

- This advisory opinion is issued only to [name redacted], the requestor of this opinion. This advisory opinion has no application to, and cannot be relied upon by, any other individual or entity.

- This advisory opinion may not be introduced into evidence in any matter involving an entity or individual that is not a requestor of this opinion.

- This advisory opinion is applicable only to the statutory provisions specifically noted above. No opinion is expressed or implied herein with respect to the application of any other Federal, state, or local statute, rule, regulation, ordinance, or other law that may be applicable to the Proposed Arrangement, including, without limitation, the physician self-referral law, section 1877 of the Act.

- This advisory opinion will not bind or obligate any agency other than the U.S. Department of Health and Human Services.

- This advisory opinion is limited in scope to the specific arrangement described in this letter and has no applicability to other arrangements, even those which appear similar in nature or scope.

- No opinion is expressed herein regarding the liability of any party under the False Claims Act or other legal authorities for any improper billing, claims submission, cost reporting, or related conduct.

This opinion is also subject to any additional limitations set forth at 42 C.F.R. Part 1008.

The OIG will not proceed against [name redacted] with respect to any action that is part of the Proposed Arrangement taken in good faith reliance upon this advisory opinion, as long as all of the material facts have been fully, completely, and accurately presented, and the Proposed Arrangement in practice comports with the information provided. The OIG reserves the right to reconsider the questions and issues raised in this advisory opinion and, where the public interest requires, to rescind, modify, or terminate this opinion. In the event that this advisory opinion is modified or terminated, the OIG will not proceed against [name redacted] with respect to any action taken in good faith reliance upon this advisory opinion, where all of the relevant facts were fully, completely, and accurately presented and where such action was promptly discontinued upon notification of the modification or termination of this advisory opinion. An advisory opinion may be rescinded only if the relevant and material facts have not been fully, completely, and accurately disclosed to the OIG.

Sincerely,

/Lewis Morris/

Lewis Morris
Chief Counsel to the Inspector General

DEPARTMENT OF HEALTH & HUMAN SERVICES **Office of Inspector General**

Washington, D.C. 20201

[*We redact certain identifying information and certain potentially privileged, confidential, or proprietary information associated with the individual or entity, unless otherwise approved by the requestor.*]

Issued: October 3, 2011

Posted: October 11, 2011

[Name and address redacted]

Re: OIG Advisory Opinion No. 11-15

[Salutation redacted]:

We are writing in response to your request for an advisory opinion regarding a proposal under which physicians would invest in a company that would provide pathology laboratory management services to a third party (the "Proposed Arrangement"). Specifically, you have inquired whether the Proposed Arrangement would constitute grounds for the imposition of sanctions under the exclusion authority at section 1128(b)(7) of the Social Security Act (the "Act") or the civil monetary penalty provision at section 1128A(a)(7) of the Act, as those sections relate to the commission of acts described in section 1128B(b) of the Act, the Federal anti-kickback statute.

You have certified that all of the information provided in your request, including all supplemental submissions, is true and correct and constitutes a complete description of the relevant facts and agreements among the parties.

In issuing this opinion, we have relied solely on the facts and information presented to us. We have not undertaken an independent investigation of such information. This opinion is limited to the facts presented. If material facts have not been disclosed or have been misrepresented, this opinion is without force and effect.

Based on the facts certified in your request for an advisory opinion and supplemental submissions, we conclude that the Proposed Arrangement could potentially generate prohibited remuneration under the anti-kickback statute and that the Office of Inspector General ("OIG") could potentially impose administrative sanctions on [name redacted] under sections 1128(b)(7) or 1128A(a)(7) of the Act (as those sections relate to the commission of acts described in section 1128B(b) of the Act) in connection with the

Proposed Arrangement. Any definitive conclusion regarding the existence of an anti-kickback violation requires a determination of the parties' intent, which determination is beyond the scope of the advisory opinion process.

This opinion may not be relied on by any persons other than [name redacted], the requestor of this opinion, and is further qualified as set out in Part IV below and in 42 C.F.R. Part 1008.

I. FACTUAL BACKGROUND

[Name redacted] (the "Requestor") is a Delaware limited liability company owned and managed by a physician (the "Owner/Manager"). Under the Proposed Arrangement, the Requestor would contract with another company, the identity of which has not yet been determined (the "Path Lab"), that either currently operates a licensed, Medicare-certified clinical anatomic pathology laboratory, or would form one for the purpose of doing business with the Requestor. The Owner/Manager cannot refer his or her own patients or otherwise generate business in connection with the Proposed Arrangement.

The Path Lab would enter into a management services contract (the "Management Contract") with the Requestor for a term of at least three years. Under the Management Contract, the Requestor would furnish the Path Lab the complete array of clinical laboratory pathology services for a fixed maximum number of hours each year, as well as utilities, furniture, fixtures, and the exclusive use of laboratory space and equipment. The Requestor would also provide the Path Lab marketing and billing services, and essential non-physician staff. In turn, the Path Lab would pay the Requestor a usage fee that would be calculated based on a percentage of the Path Lab's income, fixed in advance for a term of 12 months, which generally would correspond to the volume of the Path Lab's use of the Requestor's services, personnel, and equipment. The Path Lab's income could include payments from Federal health care programs for laboratory services provided to program beneficiaries. The Requestor has certified that any usage fees paid to it by the Path Lab would represent fair market value for the use of the Requestor's space, equipment, and services.[1]

The Owner/Manager would offer the opportunity to invest in the Requestor to various additional, as-yet undetermined physicians, including urologists, gastroenterologists and dermatologists (each, individually, a "New Physician Investor," and collectively, the "New Physician Investors"). The Requestor stated that, while the Owner/Manager has some experience in the clinical laboratory services field, it anticipates that most of the New Physician Investors would have little or no such background. The Requestor stated that it plans to recruit individuals with the appropriate experience and expertise to

---

[1] We are not authorized to opine on whether fair market value shall be, or was, paid or received for any goods, services, or property. <u>See</u> section 1128D(b)(3) of the Act.

Page 3 – OIG Advisory Opinion No. 11-15

provide clinical laboratory services and retain them as employees or contractors. The Requestor certified that the value of the investment interests in the Requestor that would be held by physician investors in a position to generate business for the Requestor through referrals of laboratory specimens to the Path Lab would exceed 40 percent. The Requestor further anticipates that substantially more than 40 percent of the Requestor's gross revenue related to the furnishing of health care items and services would derive from business generated by its physician investors through referrals of laboratory specimens to the Path Lab.

The Requestor certified that each of the New Physician Investors would have the option of referring specimens to the Path Lab but that there would be no implicit or explicit agreement or condition that a New Physician Investor make referrals to, or use the services of, the Requestor or the Path Lab. Each New Physician Investor would purchase membership interests in the Requestor at a cost equal to the Requestor's book value times the pro rata share of the Requestor being purchased. The Requestor certified that the book value, and thus the per-share price, would not vary from investor to investor (including the Owner/Manager). All profit distributions would correspond to an investor's percentage membership interest in the Requestor.

II. LEGAL ANALYSIS

A. Law

The anti-kickback statute makes it a criminal offense knowingly and willfully to offer, pay, solicit, or receive any remuneration to induce or reward referrals of items or services reimbursable by a Federal health care program. See section 1128B(b) of the Act. Where remuneration is paid purposefully to induce or reward referrals of items or services payable by a Federal health care program, the anti-kickback statute is violated. By its terms, the statute ascribes criminal liability to parties on both sides of an impermissible "kickback" transaction. For purposes of the anti-kickback statute, "remuneration" includes the transfer of anything of value, directly or indirectly, overtly or covertly, in cash or in kind.

The statute has been interpreted to cover any arrangement where one purpose of the remuneration was to obtain money for the referral of services or to induce further referrals. United States v. Kats, 871 F.2d 105 (9th Cir. 1989); United States v. Greber, 760 F.2d 68 (3d Cir. 1985), cert. denied, 474 U.S. 988 (1985). Violation of the statute constitutes a felony punishable by a maximum fine of $25,000, imprisonment up to five years, or both. Conviction will also lead to automatic exclusion from Federal health care programs, including Medicare and Medicaid. Where a party commits an act described in section 1128B(b) of the Act, the OIG may initiate administrative proceedings to impose civil monetary penalties on such party under section 1128A(a)(7) of the Act. The OIG may also initiate administrative proceedings to exclude such party from the Federal health care programs under section 1128(b)(7) of the Act.

The Department of Health and Human Services has promulgated safe harbor regulations that define practices that are not subject to the anti-kickback statute because such practices would be unlikely to result in fraud or abuse. See 42 C.F.R. § 1001.952. The safe harbors set forth specific conditions that, if met, assure entities involved of not being prosecuted or sanctioned for the arrangement qualifying for the safe harbor. However, safe harbor protection is afforded only to those arrangements that precisely meet all of the conditions set forth in the safe harbor. Potentially applicable to the Proposed Arrangement are the safe harbors for: small entity investments, 42 C.F.R. § 1001.952(a)(2); space rental, 42 C.F.R. § 1001.952(b); equipment rental, 42 C.F.R. § 1001.952(c); and personal services and management contracts, 42 C.F.R. § 1001.952(d).

B. Analysis

We note, first, similarities between the Proposed Arrangement and questionable joint venture arrangements that have been the subject of OIG guidance. The OIG has in past publications warned the public about arrangements in which a health care provider expands into clinical diagnostic laboratory services by contracting with an existing provider of that laboratory services to operate a newly formed laboratory subsidiary on essentially a turn-key basis. See, e.g., OIG's 1989 Special Fraud Alert on Joint Venture Arrangements, reprinted in the Federal Register in 1994 (59 Fed. Reg. 65,372, 65,373 (Dec. 19, 1994); OIG's Special Advisory Bulletin on "Contractual Joint Ventures," 68 Fed. Reg. 23,148 (Apr. 30, 2003); OIG Advisory Opinion 04-17. The Proposed Arrangement is the converse of such an arrangement; rather than contracting with an existing provider to obtain turn-key laboratory services for which a physician-owned entity would bill Federal health care programs, the Requestor, a physician-owned entity, would contract to provide such services to an entity that would, in turn, bill Federal health care programs. Under both types of arrangements, however, the income of the physician-owned entity would vary with the volume or value of referrals from physician investors. We therefore evaluate the Proposed Arrangement for compliance with any applicable safe harbor, and for the potential for abuse.

Under the Proposed Arrangement, the New Physician Investors would join the Owner/Manager as investors in the Requestor. Because the Proposed Arrangement would involve ownership of a non-public entity by interested investors, the small entity investment safe harbor, 42 C.F.R. § 1001.952(a)(2), is potentially applicable. This safe harbor protects profit distributions paid on investments in small entities; if applicable to the Proposed Arrangement, this safe harbor would protect the Requestor's profit distributions to the New Physician Investors and the Owner/Manager.

Two of the small entity investment safe harbor's eight elements are of particular relevance here: first, no more than 40 percent of an entity's investment interests may be

Page 5 – OIG Advisory Opinion No. 11-15

held by investors that are in a position to make or influence referrals to, or otherwise generate business for, the entity; and second, no more than 40 percent of an entity's gross revenue may come from referrals or business otherwise generated from investors. 42 C.F.R. § 1001.952(a)(2)(i) & (vi). The Requestor certified that more than 40 percent of the Requestor would be held by physician investors in a position to generate business for the Requestor through referrals of laboratory specimens to the Path Lab, and, further, that substantially more than 40 percent of the Requestor's gross revenue related to furnishing health care items and services would come from laboratory business generated by its physician investors. As the result of noncompliance with these elements, the small entity safe harbor would be inapplicable and would not protect the Requestor's profit distributions to the New Physician Investors and the Owner/Manager.

Under the Proposed Arrangement, the Requestor would enter the Management Contract with the Path Lab to provide the Path Lab with the complete range of clinical laboratory management services, along with administrative and marketing personnel, rental space, furniture, and equipment in return for usage fees. The safe harbors for space rental, for equipment rental, and for personal services and management contracts—at 42 C.F.R. § 1001.952(b), (c), & (d), respectively—therefore are potentially applicable to the Proposed Arrangement. If applicable, these safe harbors would protect the usage fees paid by the Path Lab to the Requestor for space and equipment rental, and the payments made pursuant to the personal services and management contracts.

The safe harbors for space rental, for equipment rental, and for personal services and management contracts all share six basic elements: (i) the agreement must be set out in writing and signed by the parties; (ii) the agreement must specify the services to be performed; (iii) if the services are to be performed on a part-time basis, the schedule for performance must be specified in the contract; (iv) the agreement must be for not less than one year; (v) the aggregate amount of compensation must be fixed in advance, consistent with fair market value in an arms'-length transaction, and must not be determined in a manner that takes into account the volume or value of any referrals or business otherwise generated between the parties for which payment may be made by Medicare or a State health care program; and (vi) the services contracted for must not exceed those reasonably necessary to accomplish the commercially reasonable business purpose of the services.[2] 42 C.F.R. § 1001.952(b), (c), & (d).

The Proposed Arrangement would not satisfy the requirements of the safe harbors for space rental, equipment rental, or personal services and management contracts because, among other reasons, the aggregate usage fees paid to the Requestor would not be set in advance; instead, the usage fees would be calculated based on a percentage of the Path

---

[2] The personal services and management contracts safe harbor adds a seventh element: the services performed under the agreement must not involve the promotion of business that violates any Federal or State law. 42 C.F.R. § 1001.952(d).

Page 6 – OIG Advisory Opinion No. 11-15

Lab's income. As a result, none of the three safe harbors would protect the fees paid by the Path Lab to the Requestor. Absent any safe harbor protection for the Proposed Arrangement, we must apply careful scrutiny to determine whether it poses no more than a minimal risk of fraud and abuse under the anti-kickback statute. For the combination of the following reasons, we conclude that the Proposed Arrangement would pose more than a minimal risk of fraud and abuse.

First, the usage fees to be paid by the Path Lab to the Requestor under the Management Contract would take into account the volume or value of business generated for the Path Lab by the New Physician Investors in the form of laboratory specimen referrals directed to the Path Lab. This fee structure would effectively link the New Physician Investors' profit distributions to the laboratory business they send the Path Lab, posing considerable risks of overutilization of laboratory services, distorted medical decision-making, and increased costs to Federal health care programs.

Second, the Requestor certified that more than 40 percent of the Requestor's investment interests would be held by physician investors in a position to generate business for the Path Lab in the form of referrals of laboratory specimens. The Requestor also anticipates that substantially more than 40 percent of its gross revenue would come from business generated from its investors. The absence of limits on such involvement by interested investors or other safeguards to restrain the Proposed Arrangement's reliance on investor-generated business further underscores the already-noted risks of overutilization, distorted medical decision-making, and increased program costs.

Third, the Requestor would be an entity largely owned by persons with no experience in providing clinical pathology services but with the ability to refer patients for these services. It would furnish the Path Lab, a company which may already operate a clinical anatomic pathology lab, the entire range of key services connected with the Path Lab's laboratory operation: day-to-day management; marketing and billing services; equipment; personnel and related administrative services; space, fixtures, and furniture; and the complete array of clinical laboratory pathology services. The Proposed Arrangement appears to have no business purpose other than to permit the physician investors to profit from the business they generate for the Path Lab in the form of their laboratory specimen referrals. The fact that the profits would be obtained indirectly, because the Path Lab, rather than the Requestor, would bill for the clinical laboratory services, is immaterial.[3]

[3] We express no opinion regarding the legality of the Proposed Arrangement under the Stark Law or any payment rule. The Stark Law and the anti-kickback statute are independent legal authorities and each must be evaluated separately. See, e.g., 66 Fed. Reg. 855, 863 (Jan. 4, 2001); 69 Fed. Reg. 16,053, 16,063 (Mar. 26, 2004) (reflecting clear distinction between the statutes).

Page 7 – OIG Advisory Opinion No. 11-15

III. CONCLUSION

Based on the facts certified in your request for an advisory opinion and supplemental submissions, we conclude that the Proposed Arrangement could potentially generate prohibited remuneration under the anti-kickback statute and that the OIG could potentially impose administrative sanctions on [name redacted] under sections 1128(b)(7) or 1128A(a)(7) of the Act (as those sections relate to the commission of acts described in section 1128B(b) of the Act) in connection with the Proposed Arrangement. Any definitive conclusion regarding the existence of an anti-kickback violation requires a determination of the parties' intent, which determination is beyond the scope of the advisory opinion process.

IV. LIMITATIONS

The limitations applicable to this opinion include the following:

- This advisory opinion is issued only to [name redacted], the requestor of this opinion. This advisory opinion has no application to, and cannot be relied upon by, any other individual or entity.

- This advisory opinion may not be introduced into evidence in any matter involving an entity or individual that is not a requestor of this opinion.

- This advisory opinion is applicable only to the statutory provisions specifically noted above. No opinion is expressed or implied herein with respect to the application of any other Federal, state, or local statute, rule, regulation, ordinance, or other law that may be applicable to the Proposed Arrangement, including, without limitation, the physician self-referral law, section 1877 of the Act.

- This advisory opinion will not bind or obligate any agency other than the U.S. Department of Health and Human Services.

- This advisory opinion is limited in scope to the specific arrangement described in this letter and has no applicability to other arrangements, even those which appear similar in nature or scope.

- No opinion is expressed herein regarding the liability of any party under the False Claims Act or other legal authorities for any improper billing, claims submission, cost reporting, or related conduct.

This opinion is also subject to any additional limitations set forth at 42 C.F.R. Part 1008.

Page 8 – OIG Advisory Opinion No. 11-15

The OIG reserves the right to reconsider the questions and issues raised in this advisory opinion and, where the public interest requires, to rescind, modify, or terminate this opinion.

Sincerely,

/Lewis Morris/

Lewis Morris
Chief Counsel to the Inspector General

DEPARTMENT OF HEALTH AND HUMAN SERVICES

OFFICE OF INSPECTOR GENERAL

WASHINGTON, DC 20201

[*We redact certain identifying information and certain potentially privileged, confidential, or proprietary information associated with the individual or entity, unless otherwise approved by the requestor*.]

Issued: March 8, 2012

Posted: March 15, 2012

[Name and address redacted]

Re: OIG Advisory Opinion No. 12-01

Dear [Name redacted]:

We are writing in response to your request for an advisory opinion regarding your proposal to establish a group purchasing organization ("GPO") that would be wholly owned by an entity that also wholly owns many of the potential participants in the GPO, and to pass through to participants in the GPO a portion of the payments received by the GPO from vendors (the "Proposed Arrangement"). Specifically, you have inquired whether the Proposed Arrangement would constitute grounds for the imposition of sanctions under the exclusion authority at section 1128(b)(7) of the Social Security Act (the "Act"), or the civil monetary penalty provision at section 1128A(a)(7) of the Act, as those sections relate to the commission of acts described in section 1128B(b) of the Act, the Federal anti-kickback statute.

You have certified that all of the information provided in your request, including all supplemental submissions, is true and correct and constitutes a complete description of the relevant facts and agreements among the parties.

In issuing this opinion, we have relied solely on the facts and information presented to us. We have not undertaken an independent investigation of such information. This opinion is limited to the facts presented. If material facts have not been disclosed or have been misrepresented, this opinion is without force and effect.

Page 2—OIG Advisory Opinion No. 12-01

Based on the facts certified in your request for an advisory opinion and supplemental submissions, we conclude that, although the Proposed Arrangement could potentially generate prohibited remuneration under the anti-kickback statute if the requisite intent to induce or reward referrals of Federal health care program business were present, the Office of Inspector General ("OIG") would not impose administrative sanctions on [Name redacted], [Name redacted], or [Name redacted] under sections 1128(b)(7) or 1128A(a)(7) of the Act (as those sections relate to the commission of acts described in section 1128B(b) of the Act) in connection with the Proposed Arrangement. This opinion is limited to the Proposed Arrangement and, therefore, we express no opinion about any ancillary agreements or arrangements disclosed or referenced in your request for an advisory opinion or supplemental submissions.

This opinion may not be relied on by any persons other than [Name redacted], [Name redacted], or [Name redacted], the requestors of this opinion, and is further qualified as set out in Part IV below and in 42 C.F.R. Part 1008.

I. FACTUAL BACKGROUND

[Name redacted] (the "Parent Organization") is the parent organization of a national health system consisting primarily of nonprofit corporations (the "Nonprofit Corporations") that own and operate local health care facilities. Each Nonprofit Corporation is a separate legal entity, and each is an indirect subsidiary of the Parent Organization. [Name redacted] (the "Subsidiary") is a first tier subsidiary of the Parent Organization and holds governance and oversight responsibility for the Nonprofit Organizations. [Name redacted] (the "LLC") is a wholly owned subsidiary of the Subsidiary. Collectively, the Parent Organization, the Subsidiary, and the LLC are the "Requestors." The LLC houses the [Name redacted] (the "Resource Group"), which is responsible for the Parent Organization, the Subsidiary, and the Nonprofit Corporations' supply chain, resource, and materials management functions and operations. Currently, the LLC contracts on behalf of the Nonprofit Corporations to allow the Nonprofit Corporations to participate in the system-wide contracts. The Subsidiary also maintains a GPO arrangement with an independent GPO under which the Subsidiary opts into certain GPO contracts with various suppliers on behalf of the Nonprofit Corporations and other affiliated organizations.

The LLC seeks to form and operate a GPO (the "Proposed GPO") for the benefit of the Nonprofit Corporations and other related and affiliated organizations in the health care industry. The Proposed GPO would be a division of the LLC, and the leadership of the Proposed GPO would be the same as the leadership of the LLC. The Resource Group would continue to exist as a separate division of the LLC and would continue to be responsible for the Parent Organization, the Subsidiary, and the Nonprofit Corporations' resource and supply management functions and operations. If the Parent Organization can obtain a better cost value from suppliers through independent GPOs, the Parent

Page 3—OIG Advisory Opinion No. 12-01

Organization has certified that it would direct its purchasing volume through independent GPOs for those supplies.[1] Similarly, the LLC has certified that it would continue its current practice of contracting directly with vendors on behalf of individual Nonprofit Corporations (without going through the Proposed GPO) when such process would be necessary to meet the Nonprofit Corporations' needs. Other departments and groups within the health system would continue to work collaboratively with the LLC to share knowledge about appropriate product utilization, generate cost-savings, and seek out opportunities that would lead to improvement in the delivery of patient care. This collaboration occurs at the system level through decision teams and a clinical excellence department, and extends down to the individual hospitals, many of which are represented by "clinical sponsors" who are designated to work with the Resource Group and be available to discuss clinically sensitive initiatives.

Although the initial participants of the Proposed GPO likely would be the Nonprofit Corporations and other organizations related to, or affiliated with, the Parent Organization or the Subsidiary (the "Affiliated Participants"[2]), the Proposed GPO would also be open to participation by unrelated health systems and other health organizations (the "Non-Affiliated Participants," and collectively with the Affiliated Participants, the "Participants"). The LLC would not charge the Participants fees to participate in the Proposed GPO.

The Requestors have certified that the purposes of the Proposed GPO would be, in part, as follows: (1) to utilize the purchasing power of the Participants to obtain discounts and realize efficiencies from suppliers based upon the collective buying power of the Participants, thereby reducing spending and controlling costs; (2) to negotiate contracts and develop a contract portfolio to provide for the procurement of supplies, services, and goods necessary and desirable for the successful operation of medical and associated facilities; and (3) to allow Participants to obtain savings by standardizing and streamlining purchasing, thus reducing administrative costs currently associated with their individual supply chain operations and to have the potential for receiving distributions of administrative fees received by the Proposed GPO from suppliers.

---

[1] We have not been asked, and we express no opinion, about these independent GPO arrangements.

[2] The vast majority of the related and affiliated entities constituting "Affiliated Participants" are wholly owned by the Parent Organization or the Subsidiary and/or are nonprofit entities in which the Parent Organization or the Subsidiary is the sole corporate member. Those Affiliated Participants that are not wholly owned by the Parent Organization or the Subsidiary may be affiliated through management agreements, joint venture agreements, or similar contractual arrangements. We have not been asked about, and we express no opinion regarding, any of these agreements or relationships.

To accomplish these goals, the Proposed GPO would enter into written agreements with Participants ("Participation Agreements") and suppliers ("Supplier Agreements"). Pursuant to the Participation Agreements and Supplier Agreements, the Proposed GPO would arrange for initial discounts when Participants purchase discounted products directly from the suppliers and may also provide rebates to its Participants by distributing administrative fees to Participants that it collects in excess of its costs.

The Supplier Agreements would specify the method for calculating any administrative fees owed by the supplier to the Proposed GPO, which could be a percentage of the purchases of products by Participants or a flat fee. If the fee would not be fixed at three percent or less of the purchase price of the goods or services, the Supplier Agreement would specify the amount (or maximum amount) that the Proposed GPO would be paid by the supplier. The Proposed GPO would also require suppliers to provide the Proposed GPO with records and reports detailing each Participant's spending and purchasing volume under the contracts for purposes of calculating and allocating such fees.[3] The terms of any rebate would be fixed at the time of the first sale, and the Proposed GPO would disclose to each Participant the aggregate administrative fees that the Proposed GPO received from each supplier during that annual period with respect to purchases made by or on behalf of that Participant. The Proposed GPO would also make such disclosures available to the Secretary upon request. Further, the Proposed GPO would inform Participants in a manner reasonably calculated to give the Participants notice of their obligations to report such discounts and rebates to satisfy the discount safe harbor to the Federal anti-kickback statute, described in more detail in Part II below, and the Proposed GPO would refrain from doing anything that would impede the Participants' ability to meet their obligations under that safe harbor.

The Proposed GPO would maintain a website containing general information about its structure and operations. The website would include access points for vendors to obtain and provide information about the contracts maintained with the Proposed GPO and the purchasing activity of its Participants. The Proposed GPO would include on its website, along with the other general information, a statement indicating that it attempts to operate as efficiently as possible to minimize its costs and that the Proposed GPO may, in its discretion, distribute all or portions of administrative fees it receives from vendors to its Participants. Some vendors that contract with the Proposed GPO may have reporting requirements related to administrative fees that do not qualify as bona fide service fees,

---

[3] This tracking of the spending and purchasing volume for each Participant and the associated administrative fees will allow the Proposed GPO to determine what, if any, portion of a particular vendor's administrative fees were passed through to Participants, which will enable the Proposed GPO and the Participants to comply with any reporting obligations. The tracking will also enable Participants to comply with any disclosure requirements imposed through vendor contracts to enable vendors to comply with their own reporting obligations related to Average Manufacturer Price and Best Price.

such as the requirements imposed on pharmaceutical manufacturers with respect to price reporting. The Proposed GPO would inform such vendors directly that administrative fees in excess of the Proposed GPO's operating costs may be passed through to the Participants.

The Participation Agreements would require compliance with any contractual obligations contained in the Supplier Agreements, as well as compliance with all applicable laws, regulations, and the rules, standards and policies of the Proposed GPO, including cost reporting rules.[4] Pursuant to the Participation Agreements, Non-Affiliated Participants would be required to report the full amount of actual distributions as rebates and net such amounts against the cost of purchases. Affiliated Participants would be required to: (1) report the full amounts of their allocated administrative fees as rebates; and (2) net such amounts against the costs of purchases, whether or not the administrative fees were distributed.[5] The Requestors certified that the Parent Organization, the Subsidiary, the LLC, the Proposed GPO, and the Affiliated Participants would comply with the Medicare cost reporting rules applicable to central purchasing activities[6] (i.e., for Affiliated Participants, all discounts, allowances, refunds, and rebates received from vendors would be credited directly against the costs of the purchasing providers, even if these amounts are not distributed to the purchasing providers).

II. LEGAL ANALYSIS

A. Law

The anti-kickback statute makes it a criminal offense to knowingly and willfully offer, pay, solicit, or receive any remuneration to induce or reward referrals of items or services reimbursable by a Federal health care program. See section 1128B(b) of the Act. Where remuneration is paid purposefully to induce or reward referrals of items or services payable by a Federal health care program, the anti-kickback statute is violated. By its

---

[4] Similar provisions would be included in the Supplier Agreements, including agreements with drug manufacturers.

[5] As explained above, the tracking reports the vendors would provide regarding each Participant's spending would allow the Proposed GPO to allocate the earned fees among Participants. However, only the administrative fees the Proposed GPO collects in excess of its costs would be distributed to the Participants.

[6] The Requestors certified that the Proposed GPO would constitute a "central purchasing organization" under chapter 8, section 808 of the CMS Provider Reimbursement Manual. Under section 808 and the home office cost reporting process, the Affiliated Participants would be required to report the administrative fees as cost reductions, whether or not these amounts are actually distributed to the purchasing providers.

terms, the statute ascribes criminal liability to parties on both sides of an impermissible "kickback" transaction. For purposes of the anti-kickback statute, "remuneration" includes the transfer of anything of value, directly or indirectly, overtly or covertly, in cash or in kind.

The statute has been interpreted to cover any arrangement where one purpose of the remuneration was to obtain money for the referral of services or to induce further referrals. See, e.g., United States v. Borrasi, 639 F.3d 774 (7th Cir. 2011); United States v. McClatchey, 217 F.3d 823 (10th Cir. 2000); United States v. Davis, 132 F.3d 1092 (5th Cir. 1998); United States v. Kats, 871 F.2d 105 (9th Cir. 1989); United States v. Greber, 760 F.2d 68 (3d Cir. 1985), cert. denied, 474 U.S. 988 (1985). Violation of the statute constitutes a felony punishable by a maximum fine of $25,000, imprisonment up to five years, or both. Conviction will also lead to automatic exclusion from Federal health care programs, including Medicare and Medicaid. Where a party commits an act described in section 1128B(b) of the Act, the OIG may initiate administrative proceedings to impose civil monetary penalties on such party under section 1128A(a)(7) of the Act. The OIG may also initiate administrative proceedings to exclude such party from the Federal health care programs under section 1128(b)(7) of the Act.

The Department of Health and Human Services has promulgated safe harbor regulations that define practices that are not subject to the anti-kickback statute because such practices would be unlikely to result in fraud or abuse. See 42 C.F.R. § 1001.952. The safe harbors set forth specific conditions that, if met, assure entities involved of not being prosecuted or sanctioned for the arrangement qualifying for the safe harbor. However, safe harbor protection is afforded only to those arrangements that precisely meet all of the conditions set forth in the safe harbor.

Two safe harbors, both of which were created by statute and interpreted by regulation, potentially apply to the Proposed Arrangement. The Proposed Arrangement would involve: (1) discounts that the Proposed GPO would negotiate from vendors on behalf of its Participants; (2) the Proposed GPO's distribution to Participants of administrative fees that exceed its costs, which the Proposed GPO would also require the Participants to treat as discounts; and (3) the administrative fees that the Proposed GPO would collect from vendors and retain. The discount safe harbor, 42 C.F.R. § 1001.952(h) could apply to remuneration included in items (1) and (2), and the GPO safe harbor, 42 C.F.R. § 1001.952(j), could apply to the remuneration included in item (3).

The discount safe harbor excludes from the definition of "remuneration," for purposes of the anti-kickback statute, a discount on an item or service for which payment may be made in whole or in part under Medicare, Medicaid, or other Federal health care programs for a buyer, seller, or offeror of a discount who is not a seller, as long as the relevant entity complies with certain standards. Under the safe harbor, the term "discount" includes a "rebate," which is defined, for purposes of the discount safe harbor,

Page 7—OIG Advisory Opinion No. 12-01

as "any discount the terms of which are fixed and disclosed in writing to the buyer at the time of the initial purchase to which the discount applies, but which is not given at the time of sale." This safe harbor, if applicable, would protect a discount offered by a seller to a GPO, by a seller through a GPO to a buyer, and by a GPO to a buyer. Generally, to comply with the safe harbor, a GPO would have to inform the buyer, or if applicable, the individual or entity submitting a claim to a Federal health care program on behalf of the buyer, of the buyer's or other entity's obligation to report the discount, and the GPO must refrain from doing anything that would impede the buyer's or other entity's ability to meet its reporting requirements. 42 C.F.R. § 1001.952(h)(3).

As noted above, the safe harbor for GPOs is also potentially applicable to the Proposed Arrangement. It excludes from the definition of "remuneration" certain fees paid by vendors to GPOs. To qualify for protection under the GPO safe harbor, a GPO must have a written agreement with each individual or entity for which items or services are furnished. That agreement must either provide that participating vendors from which the individual or entity will purchase goods or services will pay a fee to the GPO of three percent or less of the purchase price of the goods or services provided by that vendor, or, in the event the fee paid to the GPO is not fixed at three percent or less of services, specify the amount (or if not known, the maximum amount) the GPO will be paid by each vendor (where such amount may be a fixed sum or a fixed percentage of the value of purchases made from the vendor by the members of the group under the contract between the vendor and the GPO). Where the entity that receives the goods or service from the vendor is a health care provider of services, the GPO must disclose in writing to the entity at least annually, and to the Secretary upon request, the amount received from each vendor with respect to purchases made by or on behalf of the entity. As explained in the preamble to the final regulations, the exception is not intended to protect fees to arrange for referrals or recommendations within a single entity. See Preamble to Final Rule: OIG Anti-Kickback Provisions, 56 Fed. Reg. 35,952, 35,982 (July 29, 1991). Therefore, the safe harbor provides that "GPO" means an entity authorized to act as a purchasing agent for a group of individuals or entities who are furnishing services for which payment may be made in whole or in part under Medicare, Medicaid or other Federal health care programs, and who are neither wholly owned by the GPO nor subsidiaries of a parent corporation that wholly owns the GPO (either directly or through another wholly owned entity).

Page 8—OIG Advisory Opinion No. 12-01

B. Analysis

The Requestors certified that the Proposed GPO would satisfy all the elements of the discount safe harbor set forth at 42 C.F.R. § 1001.952(h).[7] Specifically, the Proposed GPO would inform its Participants in a manner reasonably calculated to give notice to the Participants of their obligations to report any discounts—including rebates—that they receive from vendors. The Requestors assert that the terms of any distributed administrative fees would meet the definition of "rebates" under the safe harbor. The terms of the rebates would be set at the time of the first sale to which the rebate applies and would be disclosed to the Participants.

However, even if the initial discounts and administrative fees passed through the Proposed GPO to Participants as rebates would qualify for protection under the discount safe harbor, the discount safe harbor would not protect the portion of the administrative fees retained by the Proposed GPO. The administrative fees retained by the Proposed GPO also would not be protected by the GPO safe harbor, because the Proposed GPO and most of the Affiliated Participants would be wholly owned by the Parent Organization or the Subsidiary. However, absence of safe harbor protection is not fatal. Instead, such arrangements must be considered on a case-by-case basis, to determine their potential for risk to Federal health care programs.

In addressing this issue, we turn to the history of the GPO safe harbor. In 1986, Congress amended the anti-kickback statute to create an exception for amounts paid by vendors to GPOs, as long as certain conditions were met. According to the legislative history, Congress believed that GPOs could "help reduce health care costs for the government and the private sector alike by enabling a group of purchasers to obtain substantial volume discounts on the prices they are charged."[8] Subsequently, the OIG promulgated the regulatory safe harbor described above. However, in the years following, both Congress and the OIG began to question whether GPOs were achieving this key goal—i.e., whether purchases made through GPOs actually reduce health care costs for the government and the private sector.

---

[7] The Requestors also certified that discounts other than administrative fees provided by vendors through the Proposed GPO to its participants would meet the discount safe harbor requirements. This opinion is limited to the payments made by vendors to the GPO in the form of administrative fees, and the Proposed GPO's role as the offeror of the discounts. The Requestor is not in a position to certify that vendors will meet their obligations as sellers under the discount safe harbor. Therefore, we express no opinion with regard to that or other forms of remuneration potentially involved in the Proposed Arrangement.

[8] H.R. Rep. No. 99-727, at 73 (1986), reprinted in 1986 U.S.C.C.A.N. 3607, 3663.

Page 9—OIG Advisory Opinion No. 12-01

Over the past decade, the United States General Accounting Office (the "GAO") and the OIG have conducted several studies on the effect of GPOs on the marketplace. These studies have raised various concerns. For example, one GAO report noted a concern that the financial flows between hospitals, GPOs, and vendors might result in divergent interests between GPOs and hospitals. In fact, small manufacturers claimed that GPOs have an incentive not to seek the lowest price, because the GPO could earn higher administrative fees on higher-priced products.[9] An OIG report found that GPO members did not fully account for net revenue distributions from GPOs on their Medicare cost reports.[10] These are examples of ways in which GPO arrangements can hurt, rather than help, providers and payors. However, the Proposed Arrangement includes a number of protections to guard against these negative results. For the following reasons, we conclude that the Proposed Arrangement presents an acceptably low level of risk to Federal health care programs.

First, we note that the safe harbor preamble cited above explains that when a GPO is wholly owned by the same parent organization as many of the participants, there is an increased risk that administrative fees collected by the GPO could be illegal inducements to induce referrals or recommendations. As explained herein, the Proposed Arrangement includes safeguards that mitigate the risk associated with a wholly owned GPO. Although the Proposed GPO would be under the same Parent Organization as many of the entities on behalf of whom it would be contracting, each of the Nonprofit Corporations under common ownership are separate legal entities. The Proposed GPO would function as a purchasing agent for these entities, and would charge the vendors fees for these services. Moreover, the Proposed GPO would retain only that portion of the administrative fees collected that is necessary to offset its costs of centralized contracting activities and related functions and would distribute the administrative fees that exceed its costs. As discussed in greater detail below, the Participants, in turn, would be required to report their portions of the administrative fees as rebates, in accordance with the requirements of the discount safe harbor. Thus there would be no incentive for the Proposed GPO to negotiate higher administrative fees in lieu of discounts.

Second, the Requestors' certifications regarding the reporting requirements in the Participation Agreements address a particular risk area identified above—that entities purchasing through GPOs do not always fully account for net revenue distributions from the GPOs on their Medicare cost reports. Specifically, the Requestors certified that the Participation Agreements would require Affiliated Participants to: (1) report the full

---

[9] Group Purchasing Organizations: Pilot Study Suggests Large Buying Groups Do Not Always Offer Hospitals Lower Prices, GAO-02-690T, Apr. 30, 2002.

[10] Review of Revenue from Vendors at Three Group Purchasing Organizations and Their Members, A-05-03-00074, Jan. 19, 2005.

Page 10—OIG Advisory Opinion No. 12-01

amounts of their allocated administrative fees as rebates; and (2) net such amounts against the costs of purchases, whether or not the administrative fees were distributed. The Requestors also certified that the Parent Organization, the Subsidiary, the Proposed GPO, and the Affiliated Participants would comply with the Medicare cost reporting rules applicable to central purchasing activities. The Requestors further certified that the Participation Agreements would require Non-Affiliated Participants to report the full amount of actual distributions as rebates and net such amounts against the costs of purchases.[11] Although the Proposed GPO would not have control over the Non-Affiliated Participants' cost reporting activities, the Requestors have committed to provide these entities the information necessary to accurately report their costs (and would require them to engage in accurate cost reporting as part of the Participation Agreement). With respect to the Affiliated Participants, the Proposed GPO's function as a centralized purchasing organization will help ensure that the cost-reporting rules are, in fact, followed. Moreover, the Requestors further certified that the cost reports will reflect not only the cost reductions that the Affiliated Participants actually receive from their purchases, but also the amounts of any administrative fees allocated to each Affiliated Participant, even if such amount will be retained by the Proposed GPO to offset administrative costs.

Third, the Proposed GPO would inform vendors and the public generally, through disclosures on its website, that the administrative fees in excess of its costs may be passed through to Participants. In addition, the Proposed GPO would directly inform vendors that may have reporting requirements related to any administrative fees that do not qualify as bona fide service fees (such as the requirements imposed on pharmaceutical manufacturers with respect to price reporting) that administrative fees may be passed through to the Participants as rebates. As a result, those vendors would be on notice to obtain specific information regarding passed-through fees from the Participants with whom they contract, which would enable the vendors to comply with their own price reporting requirements.

Fourth, the Requestor has certified that the Proposed GPO would not be restricted to Affiliated Participants. To achieve the greater purchasing power that comes with serving a greater number of participants, the Proposed GPO has an incentive to expand its roster of participants. The goal of gaining the Non-Affiliated Participants' business should serve as additional motivation for the Proposed GPO to be competitive in the marketplace, seeking out the best prices and services for all of its Participants.

---

[11] For purposes of this advisory opinion, we rely on the Requestors' certification that they will comply, and will require the Participants to comply, with all laws, including all applicable reporting requirements as well as any contractual requirements that would allow vendors to comply with their own legal requirements. If the Requestors materially fail to comply with any such requirements, this opinion is without force and effect.

Fifth, the Requestors certified that the Parent Organization would continue to direct its purchasing volume through independent GPOs when such GPOs can obtain a better cost value from suppliers than the Proposed GPO. Similarly, the LLC would continue to contract directly on behalf of individual Nonprofit Corporations whenever necessary to meet their needs. In other words, the Requestors commit to use multiple resources to seek out the best value for the Participants, even if such purchases would not be through the Proposed GPO. Such a commitment increases the likelihood that the Participants will receive the GPO benefits intended and anticipated by Congress.

In sum, although the Proposed Arrangement cannot receive GPO safe harbor protection because of the ownership structure of the Proposed GPO, the Proposed Arrangement includes a number of features that mitigate the risks present in some GPO arrangements. Therefore, based on the totality of the facts and circumstances described herein, and for the reasons stated above, we conclude that the Proposed Arrangement presents an acceptably low risk of fraud and abuse in connection with the anti-kickback statute.

III. CONCLUSION

Based on the facts certified in your request for an advisory opinion and supplemental submissions, we conclude that, although the Proposed Arrangement could potentially generate prohibited remuneration under the anti-kickback statute if the requisite intent to induce or reward referrals of Federal health care program business were present, the OIG would not impose administrative sanctions on [Name redacted], [Name redacted], or [Name redacted] under sections 1128(b)(7) or 1128A(a)(7) of the Act (as those sections relate to the commission of acts described in section 1128B(b) of the Act) in connection with the Proposed Arrangement. This opinion is limited to the Proposed Arrangement and, therefore, we express no opinion about any ancillary agreements or arrangements disclosed or referenced in your request for an advisory opinion or supplemental submissions.

IV. LIMITATIONS

The limitations applicable to this opinion include the following:

- This advisory opinion is issued only to [Name redacted], [Name redacted], and [Name redacted], the requestors of this opinion. This advisory opinion has no application to, and cannot be relied upon by, any other individual or entity.

- This advisory opinion may not be introduced into evidence by a person or entity other than [Name redacted], [Name redacted], and [Name redacted] to provide that the person or entity did not violate the provisions of sections 1128, 1128A, or 1128B of the Act or any other law.

Page 12—OIG Advisory Opinion No. 12-01

- This advisory opinion is applicable only to the statutory provisions specifically noted above. No opinion is expressed or implied herein with respect to the application of any other Federal, state, or local statute, rule, regulation, ordinance, or other law that may be applicable to the Proposed Arrangement, including, without limitation, the physician self-referral law, section 1877 of the Act (or that provision's application to the Medicaid program at section 1903(s) of the Act.

- This advisory opinion will not bind or obligate any agency other than the U.S. Department of Health and Human Services.

- This advisory opinion is limited in scope to the specific arrangement described in this letter and has no applicability to other arrangements, even those which appear similar in nature or scope.

- No opinion is expressed herein regarding the liability of any party under the False Claims Act or other legal authorities for any improper billing, claims submission, cost reporting, or related conduct.

This opinion is also subject to any additional limitations set forth at 42 C.F.R. Part 1008.

The OIG will not proceed against [Name redacted], [Name redacted], or [Name redacted] with respect to any action that is part of the Proposed Arrangement taken in good faith reliance upon this advisory opinion, as long as all of the material facts have been fully, completely, and accurately presented, and the Proposed Arrangement in practice comports with the information provided. The OIG reserves the right to reconsider the questions and issues raised in this advisory opinion and, where the public interest requires, to rescind, modify, or terminate this opinion. In the event that this advisory opinion is modified or terminated, the OIG will not proceed against [Name redacted], [Name redacted], or [Name redacted] with respect to any action that is part of the Proposed Arrangement taken in good faith reliance upon this advisory opinion, where all of the relevant facts were fully, completely, and accurately presented and where such action was promptly discontinued upon notification of the modification or termination of this advisory opinion. An advisory opinion may be rescinded only if the relevant and material facts have not been fully, completely, and accurately disclosed to the OIG.

Sincerely,

/Lewis Morris/

Lewis Morris
Chief Counsel to the Inspector General

DEPARTMENT OF HEALTH AND HUMAN SERVICES

OFFICE OF INSPECTOR GENERAL

WASHINGTON, DC 20201

We redact certain identifying information and certain potentially privileged, confidential, or proprietary information associated with the individual or entity, unless otherwise approved by the requestor.

Issued: October 23, 2012

Posted: October 30, 2012

[Name and address redacted]

Re: OIG Advisory Opinion No. 12-15

We are writing in response to your request for an advisory opinion regarding an existing arrangement under which a hospital pays a *per diem* fee to physicians for providing on-call coverage for the hospital's emergency department (the "Arrangement"). Specifically, you have inquired whether the Arrangement constitutes grounds for the imposition of sanctions under the exclusion authority at section 1128(b)(7) of the Social Security Act (the "Act"), or the civil monetary penalty provision at section 1128A(a)(7) of the Act, as those sections relate to the commission of acts described in section 1128B(b) of the Act, the Federal anti-kickback statute.

You have certified that all of the information provided in your request, including all supplemental submissions, is true and correct and constitutes a complete description of the relevant facts and agreements among the parties.

In issuing this opinion, we have relied solely on the facts and information presented to us. We have not undertaken an independent investigation of such information. This opinion is limited to the facts presented. If material facts have not been disclosed or have been misrepresented, this opinion is without force and effect.

Based on the facts certified in your request for an advisory opinion and supplemental submissions, we conclude that, although the Arrangement could potentially generate prohibited remuneration under the anti-kickback statute if the requisite intent to induce or reward referrals of Federal health care program business were present, the Office of Inspector General ("OIG") will not impose administrative sanctions on [name redacted] under sections 1128(b)(7) or 1128A(a)(7) of the Act (as those sections relate to the commission of acts described in section 1128B(b) of the Act) in connection with the Arrangement. This opinion is limited to the Arrangement and, therefore, we express no opinion about any ancillary agreements or arrangements disclosed or referenced in your request for an advisory opinion or supplemental submissions.

This opinion may not be relied on by any persons other than [name redacted], the requestor of this opinion, and is further qualified as set out in Part IV below and in 42 C.F.R. Part 1008.

I. FACTUAL BACKGROUND

[Name redacted] ("Requestor") is a tax-exempt, charitable, not-for-profit hospital located in [city redacted], [state redacted] (the "State"). Requestor operates an emergency department ("ED") that is open 24 hours per day, 7 days per week. The Requestor certified that approximately 19% of patients seen in the ED receive uncompensated care provided by Requestor and the remaining 81% are beneficiaries of Federal health care programs, or privately insured by other third-party payors.[1]

An independent group of emergency medicine physicians provides basic staffing for the ED. At times, however, the services of specialist physicians are required, and it is necessary to have these physicians on-call. Some specialties, such as obstetrics, have restricted call arrangements, which require the physician to be physically present at Requestor's facility during call hours.[2] Most specialties are subject to unrestricted call, meaning a physician may be off-site as long as he or she can respond, in-person, to a call on Requestor's campus within 30 minutes.

Under the Arrangement, Requestor pays a *per diem* fee to specialist physicians ("Participating Physicians") to provide unrestricted call coverage for the ED. There are currently 130 Participating Physicians. Requestor offers the opportunity to participate in the Arrangement to all specialists on its staff who are subject to unrestricted call.[3]

---

[1]The Requestor certified that the percentage of ED patients who receive uncompensated care provided by physicians on Requestor's medical staff is unknown. We believe it is reasonable to assume, however, that the percentage is similar to the percentage of ED patients who receive uncompensated care from Requestor.

[2]The hospital has separate call arrangements with specialties that provide restricted call. Intensivists, hospitalists, interventional cardiologists, and general surgeons also have separate service arrangements with Requestor. We have not been asked to opine on, nor do we express an opinion about, these ancillary arrangements.

[3]The following specialties participate in the Arrangement: cardiology, otolaryngology, gastroenterology, general dentistry, hematology/oncology, nephrology, neurosurgery,

Participating Physicians enter into one-year, written agreements, containing automatic renewal provisions, with Requestor to serve on its ED call coverage panel. Participating Physicians must be available and respond by Requestor's required response times. Participating Physicians who admit ED patients must provide care to the patients during their inpatient stays and must see the patients for follow-up care in their office practices within the timeframe specified by an ED physician. These requirements apply regardless of the patient's insurance status or ability to pay. Participating Physicians must also prepare all medical records timely and participate in medical staff committee appointments.

ED physicians typically request that Participating Physicians provide one or more of the following services while on-call:

- Consultation by telephone;
- Consultation in-person by the Participating Physician at Requestor's facility and performance of any necessary inpatient care; and
- Provision of follow-up care on behalf of the patient with at least one follow-up office visit, provided that the patient arranges an appointment.

In each of these circumstances, the ED physician decides which type of assistance is needed from the Participating Physician to ensure the appropriate level of care for the patient.

Each year, Requestor allocates an aggregate annual payment amount per specialty for on-call coverage payments to Participating Physicians based on: (1) the likely number of days per month the specialty would be called; (2) the likely number of patients a Participating Physician would see per call day; and (3) the likely number of patients requiring inpatient care and post-discharge follow-up care in a Participating Physician's office. This aggregate amount per specialty is divided by 365 days per year to create the *per diem* fee for on-call coverage paid to Participating Physicians in the particular specialty. Participating Physicians receive a *per diem* fee for each day of coverage provided under the Arrangement.[4] They receive this payment regardless of whether they are contacted by the ED to treat a patient during their periods of coverage.

---

ophthalmology, oral surgery, orthopedics, pediatrics, plastic surgery, pulmonology, thoracic surgery, urology, and vascular surgery.

[4]When an ED patient has a pre-existing relationship with a staff physician in the relevant specialty, that physician is called to treat the patient, even if he or she is not the specialist on-call at the time. The Arrangement does not apply to these situations; no per diem is paid unless the physician is on-call.

Page 4—OIG Advisory Opinion No. 12-15

Requestor engaged an independent consultant to evaluate the *per diem* rates and compare them to national survey data. The consultant's analysis incorporated proprietary data concerning payment rates for each specialty. Based on this independent valuation, Requestor certified that the *per diem* rates paid under the Arrangement are, and will be, commercially reasonable and fair market value for the services provided and do not, and will not, take into account in any way the volume or value of referrals or business generated between the parties. Requestor further certified that the *per diem* payments are administered uniformly for all doctors in a given specialty without regard to the individual Participating Physician's referrals to, or other business generated for, Requestor.

Requestor uses a uniform methodology across all specialties participating in the Arrangement to ensure that call is distributed evenly among Participating Physicians. The chief of each specialty department allocates the call schedule for Participating Physicians in his or her specialty in accordance with Requestor's methodology. Requestor's Medical Executive Committee (the "Committee") oversees the equitable assignment of call among Participating Physicians. Requestor certified that every effort is made to divide the 365 days of call per year evenly among Participating Physicians within each specialty.

Requestor monitors performance by Participating Physicians under the Arrangement through medical staff department peer review processes overseen by the Committee. Requestor reviews performance of call obligations on a post hoc basis to ensure that Participating Physicians perform and adhere to the schedule. Specifically, Requestor's Performance Improvement Department tracks Participating Physicians' compliance with response times, completion of medical records, attendance at committee meetings, and participation in peer review and performance improvement activities. Requestor also monitors the Participating Physicians' obligation to provide follow-up care through patient feedback. Requestor certified that it absorbs all costs associated with the Arrangement, and that none accrue to Federal health care programs.[5]

Requestor certified that it developed the Arrangement in response to shortages it experienced in the neurosurgery and neurology specialties, and because many members of its medical staff no longer wished to take call. According to Requestor, its physicians' concerns regarding taking call included: (i) the overall amount of time devoted to call

---

[5]Under State law, costs associated with hospital payments for call coverage are not reimbursable. Additionally, Requestor certified that under Section 1814(b) of the Act, Medicare reimburses State hospitals according to the State's Federal waiver rules, which apply in lieu of Medicare reimbursement principles. Requestor certified that it excludes all payments under the Arrangement from Requestor's Health Services Cost Review Commission Annual Cost Report, which it submits to the State.

Page 5—OIG Advisory Opinion No. 12-15

availability each month; (ii) the disruption to lifestyle required by the need to remain within 30 minutes of Requestor's facility and by multiple trips to the hospital after hours or on weekends; (iii) the provision of uncompensated care for Requestor's uninsured patients; (iv) the requirement for follow-up care in a physician's office, which requires working ED patients into the physician's existing patient schedule; and (v) the adverse effect on physician malpractice premiums because of the requirement that physicians provide malpractice coverage for themselves while providing services during periods on-call. Requestor certified that it implemented the Arrangement to establish a compensated call panel to meet the needs of its ED, to meet the requirements of EMTALA,[6] and to increase physician morale.

II. LEGAL ANALYSIS

A. Law

The anti-kickback statute makes it a criminal offense to knowingly and willfully offer, pay, solicit, or receive any remuneration to induce or reward referrals of items or services reimbursable by a Federal health care program. See section 1128B(b) of the Act. Where remuneration is paid purposefully to induce or reward referrals of items or services payable by a Federal health care program, the anti-kickback statute is violated. By its terms, the statute ascribes criminal liability to parties on both sides of an impermissible "kickback" transaction. For purposes of the anti-kickback statute, "remuneration" includes the transfer of anything of value, directly or indirectly, overtly or covertly, in cash or in kind.

The statute has been interpreted to cover any arrangement where one purpose of the remuneration was to obtain money for the referral of services or to induce further referrals. See, e.g., United States v. Borrasi, 639 F.3d 774 (7th Cir. 2011); United States v. McClatchey, 217 F.3d 823 (10th Cir. 2000); United States v. Davis, 132 F.3d 1092 (5th Cir. 1998); United States v. Kats, 871 F.2d 105 (9th Cir. 1989); United States v. Greber, 760 F.2d 68 (3d Cir. 1985), cert. denied, 474 U.S. 988 (1985). Violation of the statute constitutes a felony punishable by a maximum fine of $25,000, imprisonment up to five years, or both. Conviction will also lead to automatic exclusion from Federal

---

[6]Under the Emergency Medical Treatment and Labor Act ("EMTALA") hospitals are required to provide an appropriate medical screening examination to individuals who come to an emergency department for examination or treatment for a medical condition. See, section 1867 of the Act. If an individual has an emergency medical condition, the hospital must provide either stabilizing treatment or an appropriate transfer. See id. As a condition of participation in Medicare, hospitals must provide a list of physicians who are on-call for duty after the initial examination to provide treatment necessary to stabilize an individual with an emergency medical condition. See, section 1866(a)(1)(I)(iii) of the Act.

health care programs, including Medicare and Medicaid. Where a party commits an act described in section 1128B(b) of the Act, the OIG may initiate administrative proceedings to impose civil monetary penalties on such party under section 1128A(a)(7) of the Act. The OIG may also initiate administrative proceedings to exclude such party from the Federal health care programs under section 1128(b)(7) of the Act.

The Department of Health and Human Services has promulgated safe harbor regulations that define practices that are not subject to the anti-kickback statute because such practices would be unlikely to result in fraud or abuse. See 42 C.F.R. § 1001.952. The safe harbors set forth specific conditions that, if met, assure entities involved of not being prosecuted or sanctioned for the arrangement qualifying for the safe harbor. However, safe harbor protection is afforded only to those arrangements that precisely meet all of the conditions set forth in the safe harbor.

The safe harbor for personal services and management contracts, 42 C.F.R. § 1001.952(d), potentially applies to this Arrangement. This safe harbor provides protection for personal services contracts if all of the following seven standards are met: (i) the agreement is set out in writing and signed by the parties; (ii) the agreement covers and specifies all of the services to be provided; (iii) if the services are to be performed on a periodic, sporadic, or part-time basis, the agreement exactly specifies the schedule, length, and charge for the performance intervals; (iv) the agreement is for at least one year; (v) the aggregate amount of compensation is set in advance, is consistent with fair market value in arm's-length transactions and is not determined in a manner that takes into account the volume or value of any referrals or business otherwise generated between the parties for which payment may be made by Medicare, Medicaid, or other Federal health care programs; (vi) the services performed under the agreement do not involve the counseling or promotion of a business arrangement or other activity that violates any Federal or State law; and (vii) the aggregate services contracted for do not exceed those which are reasonably necessary to accomplish the commercially reasonable business purpose of the services.

B. Analysis

1. On-Call Coverage Issues

We are aware that hospitals increasingly are compensating physicians for on-call coverage for hospital emergency rooms. We are mindful that legitimate reasons exist for such arrangements in many circumstances, including scarcity of certain physicians within a hospital's service area, and access to sufficient and proximate trauma services for local patients. Simply put, depending on market conditions, it may be difficult for hospitals to sustain necessary on-call physician services without providing compensation for on-call coverage.

As noted in our Supplemental Compliance Program Guidance for Hospitals:

> The general rule of thumb is that any remuneration flowing between hospitals and physicians should be at fair market value for actual and necessary items furnished or services rendered based upon an arm's-length transaction and should not take into account, directly or indirectly, the value or volume of any past or future referrals or other business generated between the parties.

70 Fed. Reg. 4858, 4866 (Jan. 31, 2005). Thus, with respect to compensation for on-call coverage, the key inquiry is whether the compensation is fair market value in an arm's-length transaction for actual and necessary items or services, and not determined in any manner that takes into account the volume or value of referrals or other business generated between the parties. We believe it is possible for parties to structure on-call payment arrangements that are consistent with this standard and, therefore, pose minimal risk under the anti-kickback statute. See, e.g., OIG Advisory Opinion 07-10 (Sept. 20, 2007) and 09-05 (May 14, 2009). Moreover, in some cases, it may be possible to structure on-call coverage compensation to satisfy the personal services safe harbor at 42 C.F.R. § 1001.952(d).

Notwithstanding the legitimate reasons for such arrangements, on-call coverage compensation potentially creates considerable risk that physicians may demand such compensation as a condition of doing business at a hospital, even in cases where neither the services provided, nor any external market factor (e.g., a physician shortage) support such compensation. Similarly, payments by hospitals for on-call coverage could be misused to entice physicians to join or remain on the hospital's staff or to generate additional business for the hospital.

There is a substantial risk that improperly structured payments for on-call coverage could be used to disguise unlawful remuneration. Covert kickbacks might take the form of payments that exceed fair market value for services rendered or payments for on-call coverage not actually provided. Problematic compensation structures that might disguise kickbacks could include, by way of example:

(i) "lost opportunity" or similarly designed payments that do not reflect *bona fide* lost income;

(ii) payment structures that compensate physicians when no identifiable services are provided;

(iii) aggregate on-call payments that are disproportionately high compared to the physician's regular medical practice income; or

Page 8—OIG Advisory Opinion No. 12-15

(iv) payment structures that compensate the on-call physician for professional services for which he or she receives separate reimbursement from insurers or patients, resulting in the physician essentially being paid twice for the same service.

The anti-kickback statute neither compels hospitals to pay for on-call services, nor compels physicians to provide on-call services without compensation. Rather, the statute requires that parties refrain from making unlawful kickback payments in any form. Each on-call coverage arrangement must be evaluated under the anti-kickback statute based on the totality of its facts and circumstances.

2. The Arrangement

The safe harbor for personal services and management contracts, 42 C.F.R. § 1001.952(d), potentially applies to the Arrangement. However, this safe harbor requires that the aggregate amount of compensation to the recipient to be set in advance. Although Requestor's allocation of funds to each specialty department for on-call coverage is subject to an aggregate annual cap, Requestor's monthly payments to individual Participating Physicians could vary. In addition, the safe harbor requires that, if the services are to be provided on a periodic, sporadic, or part-time basis, the agreement between the principal and the agent specifies the schedule exactly, which is not the case here. The Arrangement, therefore, does not fit squarely within the terms of the safe harbor, and we must analyze the totality of facts and circumstances to determine if the Arrangement presents minimal risk of fraud and abuse.

For a combination of the following reasons, we believe the Arrangement presents a low risk of fraud and abuse.

First, Requestor certified that, based on an independent valuation, the *per diem* payment amounts are commercially reasonable, within the range of fair market value for actual and necessary services provided without regard to referrals or other business generated between the parties. We rely on this certification in issuing this opinion.[7] We note that several features of the Arrangement appear to support the certification. The *per diem* rate paid to Participating Physicians appears tailored to reflect the burden on a Participating Physician and the likelihood that a Participating Physician in a particular specialty will actually be required to respond while on-call, as well as the likelihood that he or she will have to provide uncompensated treatment, and the likely extent of that treatment. The

[7]We are not authorized to opine on whether fair market value shall be, or was, paid or received for any goods, services, or property. See section 1128D(b)(3) of the Act. Therefore, we do not express an opinion about whether the *per diem* fee is fair market value. If the fee is not fair market value, this opinion is without force and effect.

per diem payments under the Arrangement also are tailored to cover substantial, quantifiable services, a portion of which are furnished to uninsured patients in the ED and afterwards.

Second, Requestor allocates funds for call coverage for each participating specialty and calculates the *per diem* annually, in advance, based on the methodology described herein. It uniformly administers the *per diem* payments for all Participating Physicians in a given specialty without regard to the individual Participating Physician's referrals to, or other business generated for, Requestor. These factors mitigate the risk that the payments are determined in a manner to selectively reward high-volume referrers or incentivize low-volume referrers to generate business for the Requestor.

Third, Participating Physicians provide actual and necessary services, for which they are not otherwise compensated. For instance, Participating Physicians must respond within 30 minutes to a request from the Requestor's ED and, in some cases, must provide follow-up care. A Participating Physician's obligation to provide care to any patient seen while on-call begins in the ED. In the event that the patient is admitted, the Participating Physician's obligation to provide inpatient care continues through the patient's discharge and, when applicable, an initial follow-up visit. Throughout this time, the Participating Physician remains at risk for furnishing additional services for no additional payment. In addition, the requirement that Participating Physicians document their services in patient records promotes transparency and accountability.

We recognize that in some cases a Participating Physician could collect the *per diem* payment under the Arrangement, and receive separate reimbursement from the patient or an insurer. However, the Arrangement is not intended to compensate the Participating Physicians for all care they provide to ED patients. Given the percentage of uncompensated care provided to ED patients by Requestor, it is apparent that the Arrangement requires Participating Physicians to provide a significant amount of care for which they receive no compensation, other than the *per diem* payment.

Fourth, Requestor offers the opportunity to participate in the Arrangement to all specialists on its staff who are required by its bylaws to take unrestricted call. Moreover, the method of scheduling on-call coverage is governed by Requestor's bylaws, is uniform within each specialty, and appears to be an equitable policy that is not used to selectively reward the highest referrers.

Fifth, the Arrangement is structured so that Requestor absorbs all costs and none accrue to Federal health care programs.

In short, as structured, the Arrangement appears to contain safeguards sufficient to reduce the risk that the remuneration is intended to generate referrals of Federal health care program business. In light of the totality of facts and circumstances presented, we conclude that we would not subject Requestor to administrative sanctions under sections 1128(b)(7) or 1128A(a)(7) of the Act (as those sections relate to the commission of acts described in section 1128B(b) of the Act) in connection with the Arrangement.

Finally, we note that nothing in this opinion should be construed to require a hospital or other facility to pay for on-call coverage. To the contrary, on-call coverage compensation should be scrutinized closely to ensure that it is not a vehicle to disguise payments for referrals.

III. CONCLUSION

Based on the facts certified in your request for an advisory opinion and supplemental submissions, we conclude that, although the Arrangement could potentially generate prohibited remuneration under the anti-kickback statute if the requisite intent to induce or reward referrals of Federal health care program business were present, the OIG will not impose administrative sanctions on [name redacted] under sections 1128(b)(7) or 1128A(a)(7) of the Act (as those sections relate to the commission of acts described in section 1128B(b) of the Act) in connection with the Arrangement. This opinion is limited to the Arrangement and, therefore, we express no opinion about any ancillary agreements or arrangements disclosed or referenced in your request for an advisory opinion or supplemental submissions.

IV. LIMITATIONS

The limitations applicable to this opinion include the following:

- This advisory opinion is issued only to [name redacted], the requestor of this opinion. This advisory opinion has no application to, and cannot be relied upon by, any other individual or entity.

- This advisory opinion may not be introduced into evidence by a person or entity other than [name redacted] to prove that the person or entity did not violate the provisions of sections 1128, 1128A, or 1128B of the Act or any other law.

- This advisory opinion is applicable only to the statutory provisions specifically noted above. No opinion is expressed or implied herein with respect to the application of any other Federal, state, or local statute, rule, regulation, ordinance, or other law that may be applicable to the Arrangement, including, without limitation, the physician self-referral law, section 1877 of the Act (or that provision's application to the Medicaid program at section 1903(s) of the Act).

Page 11—OIG Advisory Opinion No. 12-15

- This advisory opinion will not bind or obligate any agency other than the U.S. Department of Health and Human Services.

- This advisory opinion is limited in scope to the specific arrangement described in this letter and has no applicability to other arrangements, even those which appear similar in nature or scope.

- No opinion is expressed herein regarding the liability of any party under the False Claims Act or other legal authorities for any improper billing, claims submission, cost reporting, or related conduct.

This opinion is also subject to any additional limitations set forth at 42 C.F.R. Part 1008.

The OIG will not proceed against [name redacted] with respect to any action that is part of the Arrangement taken in good faith reliance upon this advisory opinion, as long as all of the material facts have been fully, completely, and accurately presented, and the Arrangement in practice comports with the information provided. The OIG reserves the right to reconsider the questions and issues raised in this advisory opinion and, where the public interest requires, to rescind, modify, or terminate this opinion. In the event that this advisory opinion is modified or terminated, the OIG will not proceed against [name redacted] with respect to any action that is part of the Arrangement taken in good faith reliance upon this advisory opinion, where all of the relevant facts were fully, completely, and accurately presented and where such action was promptly discontinued upon notification of the modification or termination of this advisory opinion. An advisory opinion may be rescinded only if the relevant and material facts have not been fully, completely, and accurately disclosed to the OIG.

Sincerely,

/Gregory E. Demske/

Gregory E. Demske
Chief Counsel to the Inspector General

DEPARTMENT OF HEALTH AND HUMAN SERVICES

OFFICE OF INSPECTOR GENERAL

WASHINGTON, DC 20201

[*We redact certain identifying information and certain potentially privileged, confidential, or proprietary information associated with the individual or entity, unless otherwise approved by the requestor.*]

Issued: July 16, 2013

Posted: July 23, 2013

[Name and address redacted]

Re: OIG Advisory Opinion No. 13-09

Dear [Name redacted]:

We are writing in response to your request for an advisory opinion regarding a proposal to offer members of a group purchasing organization ("GPO") an equity interest in the GPO's parent organization in exchange for the member: (1) extending its contract with the GPO for five to seven years; (2) committing not to decrease purchasing volume; and (3) relinquishing its right to a portion of the administrative fees that would otherwise have been passed through to the members (the "Proposed Arrangement"). Specifically, you have inquired whether the Proposed Arrangement would be grounds for the imposition of sanctions under the exclusion authority at section 1128(b)(7) of the Social Security Act (the "Act"), or the civil monetary penalty provision at section 1128A(a)(7) of the Act, as those sections relate to the commission of acts described in section 1128B(b) of the Act, the Federal anti-kickback statute.

You have certified that all of the information provided in your request, including all supplemental submissions, is true and correct and constitutes a complete description of the relevant facts and agreements among the parties.

In issuing this opinion, we have relied solely on the facts and information presented to us. We have not undertaken an independent investigation of such information. This opinion is limited to the facts presented. If material facts have not been disclosed or have been misrepresented, this opinion is without force and effect.

Based on the facts certified in your request for an advisory opinion and supplemental submissions, we conclude that the Proposed Arrangement could potentially generate prohibited remuneration under the anti-kickback statute and that the Office of Inspector General ("OIG") could potentially impose administrative sanctions on [name redacted] under sections 1128(b)(7) or 1128A(a)(7) of the Act (as those sections relate to the commission of acts described in section 1128B(b) of the Act) in connection with the Proposed Arrangement. Any definitive conclusion regarding the existence of an anti-kickback violation requires a determination of the parties' intent, which determination is beyond the scope of the advisory opinion process.

This opinion may not be relied on by any persons other than [name redacted], the requestor of this opinion, and is further qualified as set out in Part IV below and in 42 C.F.R. Part 1008.

I. FACTUAL BACKGROUND

[Name redacted] (the "Requestor") is a publicly traded company that provides financial and performance improvement technology-based products and services to its clients, most of which are hospitals and health systems. The Requestor's wholly owned subsidiary, [name redacted] (the "Subsidiary"), operates a GPO. The GPO serves various provider types, but its largest members are hospital systems and integrated delivery systems. Revenue earned by the GPO contributes approximately 60% of the Requestor's consolidated net revenue.

The GPO negotiates discounts and other terms in its contracts with vendors, such as manufacturers and distributors, on behalf of the GPO's members. The vendors pay administrative fees to the GPO based on the purchase price of the items and services sold to the GPO's members under the GPO contracts. The administrative fees range from 0.25% to 3% of the purchase prices.

The GPO offers various models of contracts to its members, including a fee-for-service model and a "shareback" model.[1] Under the fee-for-service model, the GPO passes through to the member 100% of the administrative fees that the GPO receives from vendors for that member's purchases. The GPO member pays the GPO a negotiated fee for the GPO's services. There are no minimum purchase requirements for members in a fee-for-service model. Under the shareback model, the GPO passes through to the member a negotiated percentage (generally 50%) of the administrative fees that the GPO collects from vendors for that member's purchases. The member does not pay any fees to the GPO in the shareback model, but does often have minimum purchase requirements.

[1] We have not been asked to opine on, and express no opinion about, the GPO's existing arrangements.

Page 3 – OIG Advisory Opinion No. 13-09

If the member does not reach its annual minimum purchase requirement, then the shareback amount is reduced pro rata (i.e., if the GPO member purchases 75% of the total amount it contracted to purchase, then the member receives 75% of the shareback amount it would have realized if it had purchased the minimum purchase amount). The Requestor certified that the GPO treats the passed-through administrative fees as discounts under both models, and that the GPO complies with the requirements of an offeror under the discount safe harbor at 42 C.F.R. § 1001.952(h).

Under the Proposed Arrangement, the Requestor would offer certain current and prospective GPO members an equity interest in the Requestor—a publicly traded company—through a private placement or, alternatively, through a secondary public offering that would require stockholder approval. In exchange for the equity interest, the GPO member would extend its current (or a new member would enter into a new) GPO agreement for a term of five to seven years. In addition to agreeing to a new five to seven year contract term, a member accepting the equity interest in the Requestor would be required to commit to not decrease the volume of its purchases through the GPO. This purchase volume would be determined based on an analysis of historical purchases made by the member. Those members electing to accept the equity interest would forego a portion of the administrative fees that otherwise would have been passed through to them. The Requestor would offer three potential options: (1) status quo (no change to the current arrangement); (2) the member would keep 66% of the current shareback and receive an amount of equity roughly equivalent to the market value of the forfeited shareback; or (3) the member would keep 33% of the current shareback and receive an amount of equity roughly equivalent to the market value of the forfeited shareback. To illustrate, assume Member A agreed to forfeit 33% of its shareback, which, based on Member A's past purchasing history, would equate to approximately $1000. If Member A agreed to extend the contract by five years, then Member A would be agreeing to forfeit $5000. Member A would receive a number of shares in the Requestor's company that equate in value to $5000. GPO members currently in fee-for-service arrangements would be permitted to enter into a shareback arrangement under these terms.

II. LEGAL ANALYSIS

A. Law

The anti-kickback statute makes it a criminal offense to knowingly and willfully offer, pay, solicit, or receive any remuneration to induce or reward referrals of items or services reimbursable by a Federal health care program. See section 1128B(b) of the Act. Where remuneration is paid purposefully to induce or reward referrals of items or services payable by a Federal health care program, the anti-kickback statute is violated. By its terms, the statute ascribes criminal liability to parties on both sides of an impermissible "kickback" transaction. For purposes of the anti-kickback statute, "remuneration"

Page 4 – OIG Advisory Opinion No. 13-09

includes the transfer of anything of value, directly or indirectly, overtly or covertly, in cash or in kind.

The statute has been interpreted to cover any arrangement where one purpose of the remuneration was to obtain money for the referral of services or to induce further referrals. See, e.g., United States v. Borrasi, 639 F.3d 774 (7th Cir. 2011); United States v. McClatchey, 217 F.3d 823 (10th Cir. 2000); United States v. Davis, 132 F.3d 1092 (5th Cir. 1998); United States v. Kats, 871 F.2d 105 (9th Cir. 1989); United States v. Greber, 760 F.2d 68 (3d Cir. 1985), cert. denied, 474 U.S. 988 (1985). Violation of the statute constitutes a felony punishable by a maximum fine of $25,000, imprisonment up to five years, or both. Conviction will also lead to automatic exclusion from Federal health care programs, including Medicare and Medicaid. Where a party commits an act described in section 1128B(b) of the Act, the OIG may initiate administrative proceedings to impose civil monetary penalties on such party under section 1128A(a)(7) of the Act. The OIG may also initiate administrative proceedings to exclude such party from the Federal health care programs under section 1128(b)(7) of the Act.

The Department of Health and Human Services has promulgated safe harbor regulations that define practices that are not subject to the anti-kickback statute because such practices would be unlikely to result in fraud or abuse. See 42 C.F.R. § 1001.952. The safe harbors set forth specific conditions that, if met, assure entities involved of not being prosecuted or sanctioned for the arrangement qualifying for the safe harbor. However, safe harbor protection is afforded only to those arrangements that precisely meet all of the conditions set forth in the safe harbor.

Two safe harbors, both of which were created by statute and interpreted by regulation, potentially apply to the Proposed Arrangement: the GPO safe harbor, 42 C.F.R. § 1001.952(j), and the discount safe harbor, 42 C.F.R. § 1001.952(h). The GPO safe harbor excludes from the definition of "remuneration" certain fees paid by vendors to GPOs. The Proposed Arrangement, however, involves not only fees paid by vendors to the GPO, but also remuneration transferred between the Requestor and the GPO members, which would not be included in the protection of the GPO safe harbor.

The discount safe harbor excludes from the definition of "remuneration" a discount on an item or service for which payment may be made in whole or in part under a Federal health care program for a buyer, seller, or offeror, as long as the relevant entity complies with certain standards. Under the safe harbor, subject to certain exceptions, the term "discount" means "a reduction in the amount a buyer (who buys either directly or through a wholesaler or a group purchasing organization) is charged for an item or service based on an arms-length transaction." A "rebate," for purposes of the safe harbor, is "any discount the terms of which are fixed and disclosed in writing to the buyer at the time of the initial purchase to which the discount applies, but which is not given at the time of sale." The Centers for Medicare & Medicaid Services ("CMS") requires that

Page 5 – OIG Advisory Opinion No. 13-09

distributions of administrative fees paid by GPOs to the GPO members be accounted for as discounts or rebates.[2]

B. Analysis

Section 1128B(b)(2) of the Act prohibits a person from knowingly and willfully offering or paying any remuneration to a person to induce such person to, inter alia, purchase or order any good, facility, service, or item for which payment may be made under a Federal health care program. When a GPO gives anything of value to its members to induce the members to order Federally reimbursable products under the GPO's contracts, the anti-kickback statute is implicated. Under the Proposed Arrangement, the Requestor seeks to transfer an equity interest in the Requestor to GPO members in exchange for the members' agreement to extend their GPO contracts under new terms. The equity interest is a form of remuneration that would not meet any safe harbor to the anti-kickback statute. It is not a discount, because it is not a reduction in price on items or services. Members would be accepting the equity interest in lieu of a portion of the administrative fees that they would have received under their previous contracts. While administrative fees passed through to GPO members could be treated as discounts on the price of goods sold by the vendors, and the GPO and GPO members could meet the reporting and other requirements of the discount safe harbor, the same is not true of an equity interest in the parent company of the GPO.

Arrangements that do not fit in safe harbors must be evaluated on a case-by-case basis based on the totality of facts and circumstances. Under the particular facts presented here, we do not believe that the Proposed Arrangement is sufficiently low risk.

Over the past decade or so, the United States Government Accountability Office ("GAO") and the OIG have conducted several studies on the effect of GPOs on the marketplace. These studies have raised various concerns. For example, one report by the GAO (then, the United States General Accounting Office) noted a concern that the financial flows between hospitals, GPOs, and vendors might result in divergent interests between GPOs and hospitals. In fact, small manufacturers claimed that GPOs have an incentive not to seek the lowest price, because the GPO could earn higher administrative

---

[2] See CMS Provider Reimbursement Manual, Part 1, Pub. No. 15-1, ch. 8, § 805: "In addition to facilitating discounts/rebates, GPOs may distribute a portion of their revenue—sometimes referred to as net revenue distributions—to providers or other organizations using the GPO. These distributions are treated like discounts or rebates on the purchases, further reducing a provider's cost of purchases facilitated through the GPO."

fees on higher-priced products.[3] When such a conflict of interest exists, then the GPO may not be serving its purpose of reducing health care costs for its members and, ultimately, for payors. However, even if the GPO did not obtain the lowest cost, members can realize cost savings if the GPO passes a portion of the administrative fees through to its members.

As explained in CMS guidance, when a GPO passes through a portion of its administrative fees to its members, those members are required to treat such distributions as discounts or rebates. See CMS Provider Reimbursement Manual, Part 1, Pub. No. 15-1, ch. 8, § 805. When the distributions are reported as rebates, they could reduce costs to Federal health care programs. Under the Proposed Arrangement, the Requestor would ask members to forego a portion of those distributions in exchange for shares of stock in the publicly traded parent of the GPO. Unlike a discount, the remuneration under the Proposed Arrangement would have no potential to benefit payors, including Federal health care programs.

Three other key elements, in combination, increase the risk of fraud and abuse posed by this particular Proposed Arrangement. First, the Requestor would require members accepting an equity interest to extend their contracts by five to seven years. Second, the equity interest offered would be tied to past purchases. Third, under this extended contract, members would not be permitted to decrease their volume of purchases under the GPO contracts. Thus, members would be locked-in to a contract for five to seven years, regardless of whether the GPO is getting them the best prices. Not only would the remuneration be tied to past purchases, but the members also would be required to maintain at least the same purchasing level going forward. Although the members' returns on investment through their equity interests would not be directly tied to their own future purchases, the GPO's revenues make up a substantial portion of the Requestor's consolidated net revenue. Under the Proposed Arrangement, the GPO would retain more administrative fees, which could boost that revenue and potentially result in higher returns for investors, including the referral source investors.

In sum, we believe that the Proposed Arrangement would allow the Requestor to give remuneration to GPO members to reward past referrals and to induce them to continue purchasing items, including those reimbursable by Federal health care programs, at equal or higher volume as in the past through the GPO, for an extended period of time. For the combination of the reasons stated herein, we cannot conclude that the Proposed Arrangement presents a minimal risk of fraud and abuse.

---

[3] Group Purchasing Organizations: Pilot Study Suggests Large Buying Groups Do Not Always Offer Hospitals Lower Prices, GAO-02-690T, Apr. 30, 2002.

Page 7 – OIG Advisory Opinion No. 13-09

III. CONCLUSION

Based on the facts certified in your request for an advisory opinion and supplemental submissions, we conclude that the Proposed Arrangement could potentially generate prohibited remuneration under the anti-kickback statute and that the OIG could potentially impose administrative sanctions on [name redacted] under sections 1128(b)(7) or 1128A(a)(7) of the Act (as those sections relate to the commission of acts described in section 1128B(b) of the Act) in connection with the Proposed Arrangement. Any definitive conclusion regarding the existence of an anti-kickback violation requires a determination of the parties' intent, which determination is beyond the scope of the advisory opinion process.

IV. LIMITATIONS

The limitations applicable to this opinion include the following:

- This advisory opinion is issued only to [name redacted], the requestor of this opinion. This advisory opinion has no application to, and cannot be relied upon by, any other individual or entity.

- This advisory opinion may not be introduced into evidence by a person or entity other than [name redacted] to prove that the person or entity did not violate the provisions of sections 1128, 1128A, or 1128B of the Act or any other law.

- This advisory opinion is applicable only to the statutory provisions specifically noted above. No opinion is expressed or implied herein with respect to the application of any other Federal, state, or local statute, rule, regulation, ordinance, or other law that may be applicable to the Proposed Arrangement, including, without limitation, the physician self-referral law, section 1877 of the Act (or that provision's application to the Medicaid program at section 1903(s) of the Act).

- This advisory opinion will not bind or obligate any agency other than the U.S. Department of Health and Human Services.

- This advisory opinion is limited in scope to the specific arrangement described in this letter and has no applicability to other arrangements, even those which appear similar in nature or scope.

Page 8 – OIG Advisory Opinion No. 13-09

- No opinion is expressed herein regarding the liability of any party under the False Claims Act or other legal authorities for any improper billing, claims submission, cost reporting, or related conduct.

This opinion is also subject to any additional limitations set forth at 42 C.F.R. Part 1008. The OIG reserves the right to reconsider the questions and issues raised in this advisory opinion and, where the public interest requires, to rescind, modify, or terminate this opinion.

Sincerely,

/Gregory E. Demske/

Gregory E. Demske
Chief Counsel to the Inspector General

DEPARTMENT OF HEALTH AND HUMAN SERVICES

OFFICE OF INSPECTOR GENERAL

WASHINGTON, DC 20201

[*We redact certain identifying information and certain potentially privileged, confidential, or proprietary information associated with the individual or entity, unless otherwise approved by the requestor.*]

Issued: May 2, 2016

Posted: May 9, 2016

[Names and addresses redacted]

Re: OIG Advisory Opinion No. 16-06

Gentlemen:

We are writing in response to your request for an advisory opinion regarding your proposal for an entity to purchase the remaining five percent ownership interest in a group purchasing organization ("GPO"), which would result in the GPO being wholly owned by an entity whose parent company also wholly owns some of the members of the GPO (the "Proposed Arrangement"). Specifically, you have inquired whether the Proposed Arrangement would constitute grounds for the imposition of sanctions under the exclusion authority at section 1128(b)(7) of the Social Security Act (the "Act"), or the civil monetary penalty provision at section 1128A(a)(7) of the Act, as those sections relate to the commission of acts described in section 1128B(b) of the Act, the Federal anti-kickback statute.

You have certified that all of the information provided in your request, including all supplemental submissions, is true and correct and constitutes a complete description of the relevant facts and agreements among the parties.

In issuing this opinion, we have relied solely on the facts and information presented to us. We have not undertaken an independent investigation of such information. This opinion is limited to the facts presented. If material facts have not been disclosed or have been misrepresented, this opinion is without force and effect.

Based on the facts certified in your request for an advisory opinion and supplemental submissions, we conclude that, although the Proposed Arrangement could potentially generate prohibited remuneration under the anti-kickback statute if the requisite intent to induce or reward referrals of Federal health care program business were present, the Office of Inspector General ("OIG") would not impose administrative sanctions on [names redacted] (collectively, the "Requestors") under sections 1128(b)(7) or 1128A(a)(7) of the Act (as those sections relate to the commission of acts described in section 1128B(b) of the Act) in connection with the Proposed Arrangement. This opinion is limited to the Proposed Arrangement and, therefore, we express no opinion about any ancillary agreements or arrangements disclosed or referenced in your request for an advisory opinion or supplemental submissions.

This opinion may not be relied on by any persons other than [names redacted], the requestors of this opinion, and is further qualified as set out in Part IV below and in 42 C.F.R. Part 1008.

I. FACTUAL BACKGROUND

[Name redacted] (the "GPO Requestor") is a GPO with over 84,000 members nationwide, including hospitals, nursing facilities, clinics, physician practices, laboratories, and home care or equipment organizations. Prior to July 1, 2015, two entities owned the GPO Requestor in equal shares: [name redacted] (the "Health System") and [name redacted] (the "Original Co-owner"). The Health System is a nonprofit corporation that owns and operates a healthcare system based in [city and state redacted]. The parent company of the Health System is [name redacted]. The Original Co-owner is a corporation that was owned by a group of approximately 120 health care providers and suppliers located principally in the [region redacted].

The Requestors certified that the Health System believed it could increase efficiencies at the GPO Requestor if it made certain changes to the GPO Requestor's operations. The Health System claimed that the most effective means to accomplish these efficiencies would be to acquire the interests of the unrelated individual entities that jointly owned half of the GPO Requestor through the Original Co-owner and replace certain management personnel at the GPO Requestor. Through a series of corporate mergers, [name redacted] (the "Subsequent Co-owner") merged with the Original Co-owner and was the surviving entity. Thus, the Subsequent Co-owner owned 50 percent of the GPO Requestor. Of the 100 shares of common stock the Subsequent Co-owner has issued, the Subsequent Co-owner sold 90 shares to the Health System and 10 shares to another corporation, [name redacted] ("Holdings"). After the mergers and stock sales, the Health System now owns a total of 95 percent of the GPO Requestor, and Holdings owns the remaining five percent. We have not been asked about, and we express no opinion regarding, the transactions related to the mergers and stock sales.

Under the Proposed Arrangement, the Health System would purchase the remaining 10 shares of the Subsequent Co-owner common stock from Holdings, which would result in the Health System being the sole owner of the GPO Requestor. The Requestors have certified that the GPO Requestor would continue to serve the same market with similar

Page 3 – OIG Advisory Opinion No. 16-06

and improved results. It would continue to operate in much the same way as in the past, including negotiating with vendors regarding products and pricing to be offered to the GPO Requestor's members, and receiving administrative fees from vendors based on a small percentage of the value of sales to members. The Requestors certified that the GPO Requestor has written agreements with each member and that those agreements specify the vendor fees in writing. Further, the GPO Requestor discloses, and would continue to disclose, in writing to each member provider or supplier, at least annually, and to the Secretary of Health and Human Services (the "Secretary") upon request, the amount received from each vendor with respect to purchases made by or on behalf of the provider or supplier. Further, the GPO Requestor maintains, and would continue to maintain, records for each member regarding reductions in price obtained by the GPO Requestor, as well as any portion of vendor administrative fees that are distributed to members ("shareback"). The Requestors certified that the GPO Requestor provides, and would continue to provide, its members with all necessary records and information to enable them to make all appropriate disclosures of discounts required to comply with the discount exception to the anti-kickback statute, and the discount safe harbor. The Requestors certified that members of the GPO Requestor that are owned or operated by the Health System (approximately 800 of the 84,000 members) are, and would continue to be, subject to GPO contract terms and conditions negotiated on the same basis as members unaffiliated with the Health System (i.e., eligible to use the same vendor discount terms and to negotiate sharebacks based on volume and commitment).

II. LEGAL ANALYSIS

A. Law

The anti-kickback statute makes it a criminal offense to knowingly and willfully offer, pay, solicit, or receive any remuneration to induce or reward referrals of items or services reimbursable by a Federal health care program. See section 1128B(b) of the Act. Where remuneration is paid purposefully to induce or reward referrals of items or services payable by a Federal health care program, the anti-kickback statute is violated. By its terms, the statute ascribes criminal liability to parties on both sides of an impermissible "kickback" transaction. For purposes of the anti-kickback statute, "remuneration" includes the transfer of anything of value, directly or indirectly, overtly or covertly, in cash or in kind.

The statute has been interpreted to cover any arrangement where one purpose of the remuneration was to obtain money for the referral of services or to induce further referrals. See, e.g., United States v. Borrasi, 639 F.3d 774 (7th Cir. 2011); United States v. McClatchey, 217 F.3d 823 (10th Cir. 2000); United States v. Davis, 132 F.3d 1092 (5th Cir. 1998); United States v. Kats, 871 F.2d 105 (9th Cir. 1989); United States v. Greber, 760 F.2d 68 (3d Cir. 1985), cert. denied, 474 U.S. 988 (1985). Violation of the statute constitutes a felony punishable by a maximum fine of $25,000, imprisonment up to five years, or both. Conviction will also lead to automatic exclusion from Federal health care programs, including Medicare and Medicaid. Where a party commits an act described in section 1128B(b) of the Act, the OIG may initiate administrative proceedings to impose civil monetary penalties on such party under section 1128A(a)(7) of the Act. The OIG may also initiate administrative proceedings to exclude such party from the Federal health care programs under section 1128(b)(7) of the Act.

The Department of Health and Human Services has promulgated safe harbor regulations that define practices that are not subject to the anti-kickback statute because such practices would be unlikely to result in fraud or abuse. See 42 C.F.R. § 1001.952. The safe harbors set forth specific conditions that, if met, assure entities involved of not being prosecuted or sanctioned for the arrangement qualifying for the safe harbor. However, safe harbor protection is afforded only to those arrangements that precisely meet all of the conditions set forth in the safe harbor.

Two safe harbors, both of which were created by statute and interpreted by regulation, potentially apply to the Proposed Arrangement. The Proposed Arrangement would involve: (1) the discounts that the GPO Requestor negotiates from vendors on behalf of its members; (2) the GPO Requestor's distribution to members of administrative fees; and (3) the administrative fees that the GPO Requestor collects from vendors. The discount safe harbor, 42 C.F.R. § 1001.952(h), could apply to the remuneration included in items (1) and (2), and the GPO safe harbor, 42 C.F.R. § 1001.952(j), could apply to the remuneration included in item (3).

The discount safe harbor excludes from the definition of "remuneration," for purposes of the anti-kickback statute, a discount on an item or service for which payment may be made in whole or in part under Medicare, Medicaid, or other Federal health care programs for a buyer, seller, or offeror of a discount who is not a seller, as long as the relevant entity complies with certain standards. Under the safe harbor, the term "discount" includes a "rebate," which is defined, for purposes of the discount safe harbor, as "any discount the terms of which are fixed and disclosed in writing to the buyer at the time of the initial purchase to which the discount applies, but which is not given at the time of sale." 42 C.F.R. § 1001.952(h)(4). This safe harbor, if applicable, would protect a discount offered by a seller to a GPO, by a seller through a GPO to a buyer, and by a GPO to a buyer. Generally, to comply with the safe harbor, a GPO would have to inform the buyer of the buyer's obligation to report the discount, and the GPO must refrain from doing anything that would impede the buyer's ability to meet its reporting requirements. Id. § 1001.952(h)(3).

As noted above, the safe harbor for GPOs is also potentially applicable to the Proposed Arrangement. It excludes from the definition of "remuneration" certain fees paid by vendors to GPOs. To qualify for protection under the GPO safe harbor, a GPO must have a written agreement with each individual or entity for which items or services are furnished. That agreement must either provide that participating vendors from which the individual or entity will purchase goods or services will pay a fee to the GPO of three percent or less of the purchase price of the goods or services provided by that vendor or, in the event the fee paid to the GPO is not fixed at three percent or less of the purchase price of the goods or services, specify the amount (or if not known, the maximum amount) the GPO will be paid by each vendor (where such amount may be a fixed sum or a fixed percentage of the value of purchases made from the vendor by the members of the group under the contract between the vendor and the GPO). Where the entity that receives the goods or services from the vendor is a health care provider of services, the GPO must disclose in writing to the entity at least annually, and to the Secretary upon request, the amount received from each vendor with respect to purchases made by or on behalf of the entity. As explained in the preamble to the final regulations, the exception is not intended to protect fees to arrange for referrals or recommendations within a single entity. See Preamble to Final Rule: OIG Anti-Kickback Provisions, 56 Fed. Reg. 35952, 35982 (July 29, 1991) (the "1991 Final Rule"). Therefore, the safe harbor provides that "GPO" means an entity authorized to act as a purchasing agent for a group of individuals or entities who are furnishing services for which payment may be made in whole or in part under Medicare, Medicaid or other Federal health care programs, and who are neither wholly owned by the GPO nor subsidiaries of a parent corporation that wholly owns the GPO (either directly or through another wholly owned entity).

B. Analysis

The Requestors certified that the GPO Requestor satisfies, and would continue to satisfy, all of the elements of the discount safe harbor set forth at 42 C.F.R. § 1001.952(h). Specifically, the GPO Requestor would continue to provide its members with all necessary records to enable them to make all appropriate disclosures of discounts negotiated by the GPO Requestor and received by the members, and would refrain from doing anything that would impede the member from meeting its obligations under this discount safe harbor.

However, even if the discounts offered and given to members, and the administrative fees passed through the GPO Requestor to members as rebates, would qualify for protection under the discount safe harbor, the discount safe harbor would not protect the administrative fees obtained by the GPO Requestor from its vendors. Those fees must be analyzed under the GPO safe harbor. According to the Requestors' certifications, the GPO Requestor and its arrangements currently meet the terms of the GPO safe harbor. Specifically, the Requestors certified that the GPO Requestor has agreements with each vendor that specify the vendor fees in writing, and the GPO Requestor discloses in writing to each provider and supplier of health care services at least annually, and to the Secretary upon request, the amount received from each vendor with respect to purchases made by or on behalf of the provider or supplier. The GPO Requestor currently is not wholly owned by the same entity that owns any of its members. The Requestors certified that, under the Proposed Arrangement, all requirements of the GPO safe harbor would continue to be met, except that the GPO Requestor would be wholly owned by the same entity that also wholly owns approximately one percent of the pool of the GPO

Requestor's members. In other words, the Proposed Arrangement would cause the GPO Requestor to fall outside the definition of a "GPO" that would be protected by the GPO safe harbor. However, absence of safe harbor protection is not fatal. Instead, such arrangements must be considered on a case-by-case basis, to determine their potential for risk to Federal health care programs.

The key question here, then, is whether the Health System's acquisition of the remaining shares of the Subsequent Co-owner's common stock, resulting in the GPO Requestor being wholly owned by the same entity that owns nearly one percent of the pool of GPO Requestor's members, increases the risk to Federal health care programs. As we explain further below, we do not believe that the Proposed Arrangement increases that risk.

To analyze this issue, we begin with the history of the GPO safe harbor. In 1986, Congress amended the anti-kickback statute to create an exception for amounts paid by vendors to GPOs, as long as certain conditions were met. According to the legislative history, Congress believed that GPOs could "help reduce health care costs for the government and the private sector alike by enabling a group of purchasers to obtain substantial volume discounts on the prices they are charged."[1] Subsequently, the OIG promulgated the regulatory safe harbor described above. The safe harbor as initially proposed in 1989 closely followed the language of the statutory exception.[2] During the notice and comment period, a commenter asked the OIG to clarify the term "GPO." As described in the 1991 Final Rule, that commenter asked whether a nursing home chain requesting percentage payments from laboratories as GPO fees would qualify for the safe harbor. As we stated in that preamble, we did not believe that "such a solicitation sanitizes the illegality when it is made indirectly by a wholly-owned subsidiary of the nursing home, instead of directly by the nursing home itself."[3] In the 1991 Final Rule, we included a definition that would prevent entities from establishing wholly owned subsidiaries as GPOs to be able to extract fees from vendors in exchange for referrals. Such an "entity" would not be the type of purchasing agent that Congress envisioned when creating the exception.

Under the Proposed Arrangement, although the GPO Requestor would be wholly owned by the same entity that also owns some of the GPO Requestor's members, the GPO Requestor's scenario is otherwise entirely different from the scenario described in the 1991 Final Rule. The members that are wholly owned by the same entity that also would wholly own the GPO Requestor constitute only approximately one percent of the GPO Requestor's total membership. The Requestors certified that all members are, and would continue to be, subject to GPO contract terms and conditions negotiated on the same

---

[1] H.R. Rep. No. 99-727, at 73 (1986), reprinted in 1986 U.S.C.C.A.N. 3607, 3663.

[2] Proposed Rule: Anti-kickback Provisions, 54 Fed. Reg. 3088 (Jan. 23, 1989).

[3] 56 Fed. Reg. 35952, 35982 (July 29, 1991).

Page 7 – OIG Advisory Opinion No. 16-06

basis as members unaffiliated with the Health System (e.g., the members of the GPO Requestor that are under common ownership would not receive more (or less) favorable discounts or shareback calculations than unaffiliated members). The Requestors' certifications indicate that, despite the GPO Requestor's proposed ownership change, the GPO Requestor would continue to operate as a purchasing agent for a group of individuals and entities, the vast majority of which are unrelated to the GPO Requestor. We therefore do not view the Health System's acquisition of the remaining five percent of the GPO Requestor as increasing the risk to Federal health care programs.

In sum, although the Proposed Arrangement cannot receive GPO safe harbor protection because of the proposed ownership structure of the GPO Requestor, based on the totality of the facts and circumstances described herein, and for the reasons stated above, we conclude that the Proposed Arrangement presents an acceptably low risk of fraud and abuse in connection with the anti-kickback statute.

III. CONCLUSION

Based on the facts certified in your request for an advisory opinion and supplemental submissions, we conclude that, although the Proposed Arrangement could potentially generate prohibited remuneration under the anti-kickback statute if the requisite intent to induce or reward referrals of Federal health care program business were present, the OIG would not impose administrative sanctions on [names redacted] under sections 1128(b)(7) or 1128A(a)(7) of the Act (as those sections relate to the commission of acts described in section 1128B(b) of the Act) in connection with the Proposed Arrangement. This opinion is limited to the Proposed Arrangement and, therefore, we express no opinion about any ancillary agreements or arrangements disclosed or referenced in your request for an advisory opinion or supplemental submissions.

IV. LIMITATIONS

The limitations applicable to this opinion include the following:

- This advisory opinion is issued only to [names redacted], the requestors of this opinion. This advisory opinion has no application to, and cannot be relied upon by, any other individual or entity.

- This advisory opinion may not be introduced into evidence by a person or entity other than [names redacted] to provide that the person or entity did not violate the provisions of sections 1128, 1128A, or 1128B of the Act or any other law.

- This advisory opinion is applicable only to the statutory provisions specifically noted above. No opinion is expressed or implied herein with respect to the application of any other Federal, state, or local statute, rule, regulation, ordinance, or other law that may be applicable to the Proposed Arrangement, including, without limitation, the physician self-referral law, section 1877 of the Act (or that provision's application to the Medicaid program at section 1903(s) of the Act).

- This advisory opinion will not bind or obligate any agency other than the U.S. Department of Health and Human Services.

- This advisory opinion is limited in scope to the specific arrangement described in this letter and has no applicability to other arrangements, even those which appear similar in nature or scope.

- No opinion is expressed herein regarding the liability of any party under the False Claims Act or other legal authorities for any improper billing, claims submission, cost reporting, or related conduct.

This opinion is also subject to any additional limitations set forth at 42 C.F.R. Part 1008.

The OIG will not proceed against [names redacted] with respect to any action that is part of the Proposed Arrangement taken in good faith reliance upon this advisory opinion, as long as all of the material facts have been fully, completely, and accurately presented, and the Proposed Arrangement in practice comports with the information provided. The OIG reserves the right to reconsider the questions and issues raised in this advisory opinion and, where the public interest requires, to rescind, modify, or terminate this opinion. In the event that this advisory opinion is modified or terminated, the OIG will not proceed against [names redacted] with respect to any action that is part of the Proposed Arrangement taken in good faith reliance upon this advisory opinion, where all of the relevant facts were fully, completely, and accurately presented and where such action was promptly discontinued upon notification of the modification or termination of this advisory opinion. An advisory opinion may be rescinded only if the relevant and material facts have not been fully, completely, and accurately disclosed to the OIG.

Sincerely,

/Gregory E. Demske/

Gregory E. Demske
Chief Counsel to the Inspector General

APPENDIX C
Selected Fraud Alerts and Special Advisory Bulletins

FINANCIAL ARRANGEMENTS BETWEEN PHYSICIANS AND HEALTH CARE BUSINESSES

REPORT TO CONGRESS

OFFICE OF INSPECTOR GENERAL
OFFICE OF ANALYSIS AND INSPECTIONS

MAY 1989

OFFICE OF INSPECTOR GENERAL

The mission of the Office of Inspector General (OIG) is to promote the efficiency, effectiveness, and integrity of programs in the United States Department of Health and Human Services (HHS). It does this by developing methods to detect and prevent fraud, waste and abuse. Created by statute in 1976, the Inspector General keeps both the Secretary and the Congress fully and currently informed about programs or management problems and recommends corrective action. The OIG performs its mission by conducting audits, investigations and inspections with approximately 1,200 staff strategically located around the country.

OFFICE OF ANALYSIS AND INSPECTIONS

This report is produced by the Office of Analysis and Inspections (OAI), one of three major offices within the OIG. The other two are the Office of Audit and the Office of Investigations. The OAI conducts inspections which are typically short-term studies designed to determine program effectiveness, efficiency, and vulnerability to fraud or abuse.

This report responds to a congressional request for information on the practice of physician ownership and self-referral contained at Section 203(c)(3) of the Medicare Catastrophic Coverage Act of 1988.

This inspection was carried out under the direction of **Barry Steeley**, Chief, Health Care Branch, Office of Analysis and Inspections. Principle participants in this study were the following people:

Office of Analysis and Inspections

Mark Krushat
Penny Thompson
Jack Molnar
Bob Katz
Natalie Coen
John Traczyk

Office of Audit

Joseph Kwiatanowski

Office of Investigations

Raisa Ottero-Cesario

Office of General Counsel

Lisa Foley

Additional contributors to the study are listed in appendix E to this report.

FINANCIAL ARRANGEMENTS BETWEEN PHYSICIANS AND HEALTH CARE BUSINESSES

REPORT TO CONGRESS

RICHARD P. KUSSEROW
INSPECTOR GENERAL

OAI-12-88-01410 MAY 1989

TABLE OF CONTENTS

EXECUTIVE SUMMARY

PURPOSE

In June 1988, Congress mandated that the Office of Inspector General (OIG), U.S. Department of Health and Human Services (HHS), conduct a study on physician ownership and compensation from health care entities to which they make referrals. Section 203(c)(3) of the Medicare Catastrophic Coverage Act (MCCA) of 1988 directed the OIG to report to Congress by May 1, 1989 on:

- physician ownership of, or compensation from, an entity providing items or services to which the physician makes referrals and for which payment may be made under the Medicare program;
- the range of such arrangements and the means by which they are marketed to physicians;
- the potential of such ownership or compensation to influence the decision of a physician regarding referrals and to lead to inappropriate utilization of such items and services; and
- the practical difficulties involved in enforcement actions against such ownership and compensation arrangements that violate current anti-kickback provisions.

BACKGROUND

Physician ownership of, and compensation from, entities to which they make referrals is a practice which has received marked attention only in the past 10 years. New trends in the way health care is delivered in the United States have created a market and impetus for investment in for-profit health care. As physicians have become investors or financial partners of health care entities for which they also generate business through referrals, public examination of the potential conflicts of such arrangements has increased.

In recent years, legislators have moved to strengthen Federal laws prohibiting payment for referrals. Certain States have acted to require disclosure of financial interests to patients; the State of Michigan has prohibited referral of patients to any entity in which the physician has a financial interest. Additional Federal and State actions are being contemplated, including a bill introduced recently in the 101st Congress, "The Ethics in Patient Referrals Act," which would generally prohibit physicians from referring Medicare patients to entities in which they hold a financial interest.

METHODOLOGY

Two surveys of health care providers were conducted to determine the prevalence of physician financial involvement with other health care entities and the nature of such arrangements. One survey was directed at physicians; the other was directed at independent clinical laboratories, independent physiological laboratories, and durable medical equipment suppliers.

Claims information from the Health Care Financing Administration's (HCFA) Part B Medicare Annual Data (BMAD) files for 1987 was used to assess utilization patterns for patients of physician-owners identified through our survey of health care businesses. Third, State officials, industry representatives, health care experts and a subsample of provider respondents to our survey were interviewed or consulted.

MAJOR FINDINGS

Many Physicians Have Financial Relationships with Health Care Businesses to Which They Refer Patients

- Twelve percent of physicians who bill Medicare have ownership or investment interests in entities to which they make patient referrals.
- Referring physicians invest in a wide range of businesses, including clinical and physiological laboratories; durable medical equipment suppliers; home health agencies; hospitals; nursing homes; ambulatory surgical centers; and health maintenance organizations.
- Eight percent of physicians billing Medicare have compensation arrangements with entities to which they refer patients. These arrangements include space rental agreements, employee arrangements, consulting agreements, and management services contracts.

Many Health Care Entities are Owned by Referring Physicians

- Nationally, at least 25 percent of independent clinical laboratories (ICLs), 27 percent of independent physiological laboratories (IPLs), and 8 percent of durable medical equipment suppliers (DMEs), are owned in whole or in part by referring physicians.
- The prevalence of ownership or investment varies by State. In some States, such as Arkansas and California, a larger than average percentage of ICLs, IPLs, and DMEs are physician owned. In other States, such as Michigan, the percentage of entities which are owned by physicians is much smaller than average.

Patients of Physician Laboratory Owners Received More Services

- Patients of referring physicians who own or invest in ICLs received 45 percent more clinical laboratory services than all Medicare patients in general, regardless of place of service. They also received 34 percent more services directly from independent clinical laboratories than all Medicare patients in general. This increased utilization of clinical laboratory services by patients of physician-owners cost the Medicare program $28 million nationally in 1987. This figure does not include any costs associated with increased utilization resulting from physician ownership interest in entities other than independent clinical laboratories.
- Patients of physicians known to be owners or investors in IPLs use 13 percent more physiological testing services than all Medicare patients in general.

Patients of Physicians Associated with DMEs Show No Difference in Receipt of Services

- Patients of physicians known to be owners or investors in DME suppliers use no more DME services than all Medicare patients in general. However, significant variation exists on a State by State basis.

PROCEDURAL RECOMMENDATIONS

Based on the results of this study, we are making recommendations that HCFA pursue the necessary legislative and regulatory changes to: (1) require entities billing Medicare to disclose the names of their physician-owners and investors to the program; and (2) require claims submitted by all entities providing services under Medicare Part B to contain the name and provider number of the referring physician.

OPTIONS FOR POLICYMAKERS

We have identified six options legislators and administrators may wish to pursue in order to address the higher use of services by patients of physician-owners and investors. These include:

1. Implement a post payment utilization review by carriers directed at physicians who own or invest in other health care entities.

2. Require physicians to disclose financial interest to patients.

3. Improve the enforcement of current anti-kickback authorities.

4. Institute a private right of action for anti-kickback cases.

5. Prohibit physicians from referring patients to certain types of entities in which they have a financial interest.

6. Prohibit physicians from referring patients to any entity in which they have a financial interest.

BACKGROUND

Physician ownership of, and compensation from, entities to which they make referrals is a practice which has received marked attention only in the past 10 years. New trends in the way health care is delivered in the United States have created a market and impetus for investment in for-profit health care. As physicians have become investors or financial partners of health care entities for which they also generate business through referrals, public examination of the potential conflicts of such arrangements has increased. The professional as well as mass media has critically examined such arrangements. Several regional studies have been conducted to determine if such arrangements lead to over use of services by physicians in a position to profit from medical decisions made for their patients.

In recent years, legislators have moved to strengthen Federal laws prohibiting payment for referrals. Certain States have acted to require disclosure of financial interests to patients; the State of Michigan has prohibited referral of patients to any entity in which the physician has a financial interest. Additional Federal and State actions are being contemplated, including a bill introduced recently in the 101st Congress, "The Ethics in Patient Referrals Act," which would generally prohibit physicians from referring Medicare patients to entities in which they hold a financial interest.

New Trends in Health Care Delivery

Many experts argue that, while self-referral has always existed, investment or ownership by physicians in other, free-standing facilities is a relatively new phenomenon that has resulted from changes in the way health care is reimbursed and delivered. These changes include: (1) the shift from inpatient to outpatient settings for the delivery of care; (2) cost containment strategies directed at physicians; and (3) the introduction of new technologies.

The Shift from Inpatient to Outpatient Settings for the Delivery of Care

Cost containment strategies implemented by the Federal Government and other third party payors have caused shifts in how, where, and at what cost health care is delivered. One of the primary agents of change has been the prospective payment system (PPS) instituted by Medicare in 1983, which established reimbursement to hospitals at predetermined fixed rates. Largely as a result of PPS, many services once performed in hospitals are now performed in outpatient settings, creating a new nexus of health care delivery in non-hospital, community settings.

Cost Containment Strategies Directed at Physicians

A number of other changes in reimbursement policy have directly affected non-hospital based physicians. The Deficit Reduction Act of 1984 (DEFRA) established the Medicare Participating Physician Program. Under this program, a participating physician agrees to accept Medicare assignment on all claims, in return for increased billing allowances and listing in a directory of physicians available to Medicare beneficiaries. The DEFRA also imposed a fee freeze for physicians from July 1984 to May 1986 for participating physicians and from July 1984 to December 1986 for non-participating physicians. In addition, a direct billing policy was implemented by Medicare for laboratory services, preventing physicians from billing for laboratory services performed in a laboratory which is independent of their offices.

While PPS has been somewhat successful in controlling expenditures under Medicare Part A (Medicare's hospital insurance program), the physician pay freeze and other measures enacted to curb Part B spending (Medicare's supplementary insurance program) have not been as successful. Medicare Part B expenditures have continued to rise despite these cost containment measures.

Because physician services account for most of the Part B expenditures (around 60 percent), Medicare administrators are continuing to pay attention to reimbursement strategies to contain costs in this area. Dr. William Roper, former Administrator of the Health Care Financing Administration (HCFA) which manages the Medicare program, stated in testimony before the Subcommittee on Health, the Committee on Ways and Means in September 1988 that "[t]otal Medicare spending on physicians' services is large and growing rapidly." He went on to say that, since the introduction of PPS, inpatient hospital costs have grown at a rate of 6 percent per year while physician costs have grown at rate of 15 percent.[1] A number of different strategies, including capitation, managed care, and a resource-based relative-value scale for reimbursement of physician services, are being considered to attack the continued growth in outlays.

The Introduction of New Technology

New technology can also affect how and where health care is delivered. Magnetic resonance imaging (MRI) is one example. Sophisticated services once found only in hospital settings can now be delivered in community settings, assuming resources are there to purchase the necessary technology. Such technology is becoming more and more important to the practice of "state of the art" medicine.

Effects on the Health Care Market

The shift from inpatient to outpatient settings for the provision of care, together with reimbursement policies which seek to contain outlays for physicians' services, have created certain market reactions which some argue have dramatically affected the rate of physician ownership in other health care entities. For example, an incentive exists for physicians or others to create additional entities that provide services once delivered in hospital settings. Physicians may establish laboratories in their offices.[2] They may pool resources to establish labs, to provide durable medical equipment, or to set up MRI facilities to meet patient needs in the community. At the same time, physicians may seek to protect or supplement their incomes by investing in such facilities providing services to their patients.

In 1980, an article in *The New England Journal of Medicine* by Dr. Arnold S. Relman, described the rise of the "medical-industrial complex," a new growth industry which supplies health care for profit. Dr. Relman wrote that the key to control of this complex lies in the hands of physicians, but noted that any financial associations between physicians and industry can undermine that role. He went on to say that "[a]s the visibility and importance of the private health care industry grows, public confidence in the medical profession will depend on the public's perception of the doctor as an honest, disinterested trustee. That confidence is bound to be shaken by a financial association between the practicing physicians and the new medical-industrial complex."[3]

Articles describing the practice of physician ownership and self-referral, most focusing on limited partnerships, have appeared in the *New York Times*, *L.A. Times*, *Business Week*, and numerous smaller publications. "The CBS Evening News" discussed the practice as it affects the laboratory industry in a segment broadcast in March 1989.

In December 1988, a series of articles on physician investment appeared in the *Christian Science Monitor*. This series of articles described the practice of ownership and self-referral as "one of the most divisive issues confronting American medicine today." It reported on one case where a private radiologist in Philadelphia had lost most of his business to a physician-owned radiological lab that opened up a block away from him. The private radiologist complained that "a few of the [doctors] just turned off the spigot" after they invested in their own facility, not allowing him to compete; the president of the physician-owned lab argued that the physicians' investment allowed them to purchase new technology that the community needed.[4]

An article in *The Wall Street Journal* entitled, "Doctor-Owned Labs Earn Lavish Profits in a Captive Market," appeared in March 1989. The article reported on a case in California in which a radiologist was threatened with the loss of referrals if he did not offer an investment opportunity to the referring physicians. The radiologist refused, and the referring physicians subsequently opened their own lab. The article also described variances in pricing between physician-owned and non-physician owned labs.[5]

Previous Studies Regarding Physician Ownership

Despite the increasing interest in the practice of physician ownership and self-referral, few studies have been conducted in this area. Among those that have been conducted are a 1981 study by the State of Michigan; a 1983 Health Care Financing Administration (HCFA) Region V study; a May 1984 Blue Cross Blue Shield of Michigan study; and a 1988 survey by the American Medical Association (AMA).

The 1981 study by the State of Michigan targeted Medicaid utilization of clinical laboratory services. It found that Medicaid recipients referred for clinical laboratory services by physician-owners had an average of 41 percent more tests than those referred by non-owners. Physician-owners also referred more of their patients for tests than did non-owners.[6]

The May 1983 HCFA Region V study did not find any appreciable difference in Medicare utilization between what they called "practice related" laboratories and "non-practice related" laboratories. However, patients of practice related laboratories had more batteries of tests done, and a greater number of "miscellaneous procedure" codes billed than patients of non-practice related laboratories.[7]

The May 1984 Blue Cross Blue Shield of Michigan study reviewed all laboratory procedures billed in a single calendar quarter. Data were analyzed for 148 laboratories as well for two subsamples of 20 laboratories each: one with known physician ownership (other than pathologist), and the other with a known absence of physician ownership. For the physician-owned group, the average number of services per patient and the average payment per patient were roughly 20 percent higher than the averages for all laboratories, and roughly 40 percent higher than the averages for the nonphysician-owned group.[8]

In response to increasing interest in financial partnerships between physicians and other health care businesses, the AMA asked questions concerning financial interests as part of its semi-annual telephone survey of physicians in Fall 1988. As a result of these interviews, the AMA estimated that 7 percent of physicians have an ownership interest in a health care entity to which they refer. The AMA also reported that an additional 3 percent of its members have ownership interests in facilities to which they *do not* refer.[9]

Other studies are now in progress. The General Accounting Office (GAO) began a review of the practice of physician ownership and self-referral in June 1988. That study is currently on-going and will report on activity in two States, Maryland and Pennsylvania.

Federal and State Activity

Federal Anti-Kickback Laws: In 1972, Congress outlawed payments for referrals of business payable under the Medicare or Medicaid programs. In 1977, Congress strengthened this prohibition when it passed the Medicare and Medicaid Anti-Fraud and Abuse Amendments. As amended in 1977, the anti-kickback law provides criminal penalties for knowingly and willfully soliciting, receiving, offering or paying anything of value in return for the referral of a health care item or service payable under the Medicare or Medicaid program. Such a transaction is deemed fraudulent and a felony punishable by a fine of up to $25,000 and imprisonment for not more than 5 years.[10]

On its face, the anti-kickback provision is very broad, covering indirect or covert bribes, kickbacks and rebates, as well as direct or overt ones. In 1985, the Third Circuit U.S. Court of Appeals dramatically demonstrated how broad the provision was intended to be. In *United States v. Greber,*[11] the court found that, "...if *one* purpose of the payment was to induce future referrals, the Medicare statute has been violated."[12] [Emphasis added.]

Greber is considered authoritative throughout the health care community. Its reasoning was recently adopted by the Ninth Circuit Court of Appeals in *United States v. Kats*. The court found that the anti-kickback statute is violated unless the payments are "wholly and not incidentally attributable to the delivery of goods and services."[13] Further, the same circuit in *United States v. Lipkis* has emphasized the importance of determining the fair market value of services rendered when analyzing ownership and compensation arrangements.[14]

It is within the framework of the *Greber, Kats* and *Lipkis* cases that physician ownership and compensation arrangements are frequently viewed, even though there are no reported court decisions which analyze the applicability of the anti-kickback statute to specific kinds of arrangements. The current view of Federal authorities is that physician ownership does not, *in and of itself*, violate the anti-kickback laws. At the same time, *Greber* and *Kats* indicate that returns on investment, whether or not related to volume of physician referrals, might constitute a violation of the statute if such returns are intended to induce referrals. The factual setting of any particular arrangement is critical to the analysis.

In 1987, Congress passed the Medicare and Medicaid Patient and Program Protection Act. This legislation expanded the anti-kickback sanctions by authorizing the Office of Inspector General (OIG) to exclude from the federal health care programs anyone who violates the anti-kickback statute.[15]

In view of the broad language of the anti-kickback statute, as well as the court's interpretation of that language under *Greber* (and later *Kats)*, the Medicare and Medicaid Patient and Program Protection Act of 1987 also required the Secretary of the U.S. Department of Health and Human Services (HHS) to develop regulations clarifying what types of arrangements or conduct would not be subject to prosecution under the anti-kickback authorities.[16] These "safe harbors" were specified in a Notice of Proposed Rulemaking (NPRM) published January 23, 1989.

The NPRM proposes a safe harbor for physicians with investment interests in large publicly held corporations, but does not do so for any other types of investment or ownership arrangements. Likewise, the proposed rule establishes a safe harbor for certain compensation arrangements (space and equipment rentals, personnel services and management contracts) that meet established criteria that limit the potential for abuse. Ownership or compensation arrangements that fall outside these safe harbors are not exempt from prosecution under the anti-kickback authorities.

The only explicit Federal prohibitions which currently exist on physician ownership and self-referral *per se* concern home intravenous (IV) drug therapy and home health agencies. The Medicare Catastrophic Coverage Act of 1988 prohibits a home IV therapy provider from providing services to a Medicare patient when such services have been ordered by a physician with a financial interest (including financial interest held through an immediate family member) in the provider. Some exceptions are made, such as for a sole rural provider or financial interest in a publicly traded company. Federal regulations also prohibit physicians from certifying the home health plan of care for a beneficiary when they own more than 5 percent of the home health agency which will provide the care.

State Laws: While many States have anti-kickback laws similar to the Federal statute, only Michigan directly forbids referral to an entity in which a physician has a financial interest. Several States are "unfriendly" to such ventures; New York, for example, has considered not certifying some physician-owned laboratories. In addition, a number of States require physicians to disclose their financial interests to patients before referral. For a more comprehensive discussion of State laws, see the OIG report "Financial Arrangements between Physicians and Health Care Businesses: State Laws and Regulations," issued in April 1989.

Laws Prohibiting Referrals to Physician-owned Facilities

One State directly forbids the referral of patients to entities in which the physician has an ownership interest. Michigan's Public Health Code forbids "directing or requiring an individual to purchase or secure a drug, device, treatment, procedure or service from another person, place, facility or business in which the licensee has a financial interest."[17]

Laws Requiring Disclosure to Patients

Arizona, California, Delaware, Florida, Massachusetts, Minnesota, Nevada, Pennsylvania, Virginia, Washington, and West Virginia specifically require disclosure of financial interests under certain circumstances to patients.

Those laws requiring disclosure of financial interest to patients vary in their stringency. For example, Florida's law only applies to equity interests of 10 percent or more.[18] Minnesota's disclosure law applies to "significant financial interest" and stipulates that the disclosure must be made "in advance and in writing to the patient and must include...a statement that the patient is free to choose a different health care provider."[19] Both the Pennsylvania and Virginia disclosure laws apply to "any financial interest in the facility or entity" to which the physician makes a referral and require that the physician "advise the patient of his freedom of choice in the selection of a facility."[20]

Additional Steps Contemplated

The Congress has expressed continued concern regarding the practice of ownership and self-referral. The Subcommittee on Oversight and Investigations, Committee on Energy and Commerce, expressed its distress regarding the emergence of such arrangements as early as 1982.[21]

In February 1989, Representative Fortney (Pete) Stark introduced H.R. 939, the "Ethics in Patient Referrals Act." This bill generally would prohibit Medicare providers from accepting referrals from physicians with an ownership interest or compensation arrangement with the provider. The bill provides for certain exceptions, including group practice arrangements, sole rural providers, and prepaid plans. The bill also authorizes the Secretary of HHS to establish other exceptions that he deems to have little risk of program or patient abuse. The Committee on Ways and Means, Subcommittee on Health, held hearings on the bill on March 2, 1989.

Several States are also reviewing the practice. The New York State Health Commissioner created an ad hoc committee to meet with the public this year and gather comments on ethical or other concerns the public may have regarding the practice. Further hearings are scheduled. The Health Care Committee of the Florida House of Representatives is currently collecting information on the practice and may conduct a study on such arrangements in Florida.

METHODOLOGY

Purpose and Objectives

In June 1988, Congress mandated that the Office of Inspector General, U.S. Department of Health and Human Services, conduct a study on physician ownership and compensation from health care entities to which they make referrals. Section 203(c)(3) of the Medicare Catastrophic Coverage Act of 1988 directed the OIG to report to Congress by May 1, 1989 on:

- physician ownership of, or compensation from, an entity providing items or services to which the physician makes referrals and for which payment may be made under the Medicare program;
- the range of such arrangements and the means by which they are marketed to physicians;
- the potential of such ownership or compensation to influence the decision of a physician regarding referrals and to lead to inappropriate utilization of such items and services; and
- the practical difficulties involved in enforcement actions against such ownership and compensation arrangements that violate current anti-kickback provisions.

Evaluability Assessment

Before beginning this study, the OIG investigated existing sources of information on ownership or investment, and referrals by physicians. The study team assessed the feasibility of using such sources of information in addressing the issues of interest to the Congress.

Currently, no complete information is held by Medicare carriers (who process Part B claims for the program), the States, or the Federal Government regarding the ownership of entities which are Medicare providers. Not all State Secretary of State offices maintain information on corporations and partnerships originating in their States. Information that is maintained generally does not include a full listing of owners, partners, or investors. Boards of Medicine do not obtain such information, although we found one (West Virginia) which maintains ownership information on all registered medical corporations which are wholly owned by medical doctors.

Another potential source of information investigated by the OIG was HCFA Form 1513, "Disclosure of Ownership and Control Interest Statement." As a condition of participation, certification, licensure or recertification under the Medicare program, a health care entity (sole proprietorship, partnership, corporation) must make disclosure of ownership and financial interest on this form. One purpose of the information is to identify entities that are owned by individuals who have been convicted of a criminal or sanctionable offense related to participation in programs established by title XVIII, XIX, or XX.

In assessing whether HCFA Form 1513 could be used as a basis of information for determining the extent of physician ownership or investment in other health care entities which are Medicare providers, the OIG discovered several limitations to its use. First, the form does not require a listing of all investors.. Instead, for the most part, only individuals having an interest of 5 percent or more must be listed. Second, physicians are not required to be expressly identified. Thus a physician owner may be identified by his name only, without a M.D. designation. Third, maintenance of the form is uneven. Forms have not always been completed in the past by providers, nor have they submitted updates when new investors are added or ownership changes hands. Lastly, the HCFA regional offices are only required to maintain this information for independent clinical laboratories, not all types of Medicare providers.

Other possible sources of ownership information that were subsequently researched during the course of this study included the Offices of the State Attorney Generals; Medicaid Fraud Control Units; local medical societies; State Public Welfare Provider Review and Sanction Offices; State revenue offices; State peer review organizations; municipal offices that maintain city or town directories; State, city, and county courthouses; State insurance commissions; State Departments of Commerce; and Medicare provider audit groups. None of these organizations maintained information on ownership of health care businesses.

At the same time, no existing information is maintained by most Medicare carriers regarding the referral activity of physicians. Claims submitted by health care entities do not generally contain the name or provider number of the referring physician.

As a result of this evaluability assessment, the OIG study team developed a study design that would collect original data on ownership and other financial arrangements between physicians and other health care entities. The OIG also developed a mechanism for assessing utilization that was patient-based, rather than physician-based, due to the lack of specific data on physician referrals and the availability of data on beneficiaries' use of services.

Study Approach

In order to gather information in all the areas outlined in Section 203(c)(3) of MCCA, the OIG study team collected data from the following sources. First, two surveys of health care providers were conducted to determine the prevalence of physician financial involvement with other health care entities and the nature of such arrangements. Second, claims information from the Health Care Financing Administration's Part B Medicare Annual Data (BMAD) files for 1987 was used to assess utilization patterns for patients of physician-owners identified through our surveys. Third, State officials, industry representatives, health care experts and a subsample of provider respondents to our survey were interviewed or consulted.

Surveys of Health Care Providers

The OIG study team conducted two surveys of Medicare-participating providers, using a two-stage random sample. During the first stage of sampling, eight Medicare carriers were randomly selected, with the probability of selection proportionate to total amounts reimbursed under Medicare in 1986. The eight carriers selected were

Travelers of Connecticut; Empire Blue Cross Blue Shield of New York; Nationwide of West Virginia; Blue Shield of Florida; Blue Shield of Michigan; Blue Shield of Kansas City; Blue Shield of Arkansas; and Occidental of California. These carriers represented approximately 30 percent of amounts reimbursed under Medicare Part B in 1986.

At the second stage of sampling, two sets of providers were selected. In the first set, 4,000 provider numbers representing physicians (500 in each carrier) were randomly selected and surveyed regarding their ownership interests in health care businesses to which they make referrals. In the second set, 1,133 provider numbers representing health care businesses (from 91 to 180 per carrier) were selected and surveyed regarding their business structure, owners, principal parties, and health care providers with whom they have compensation arrangements. The health care businesses surveyed were of three types: independent clinical laboratories (ICLs), independent physiological laboratories (IPLs), and durable medical equipment suppliers (DMEs). These three classes of providers account for approximately 50 percent of Part B claims for ancillary services.

High response rates were experienced with both surveys. The survey of physicians met with a 92 percent response rate overall, including 443 mailings (11 percent) which were undeliverable due to provider number address inaccuracies. The survey of health care businesses met with a 99.9 percent response rate including 121 (11 percent) where a response was not required because the entity had gone out of business. In total, 3,218 responses were made to the physician survey (2,690 from active Medicare providers) and 1,011 to the survey of health care entities. For further detail regarding the response rates and technical components of the surveys, see appendix A.

BMAD claims information

Based on information obtained from the entity survey described above, the OIG study team developed a list of physicians known to be owners or investors in other health care businesses. This list of physicians was matched to carrier provider number files. Physicians with designated specialty codes indicating radiology or pathology (non-referring specialties) were dropped from the IPL and ICL analysis, respectively, since such physicians are not in a position to refer patients.

Using the HCFA BMAD file, patients who had seen referring physician-owners or investors were identified. For patients associated with physicians who have investment or ownership interest in an ICL, use of laboratory services was compared to the use of such services by all beneficiaries in the file. A similar analysis was conducted for patients of physicians associated with IPLs and DMEs. For further detail regarding the BMAD file and our analysis, see appendix B.

Interviews

In order to collect detailed information concerning the nature of physician ownership and compensation arrangements, a number of providers responding to our two surveys were interviewed. Forty physician-owners identified through our physician survey were interviewed to collect detailed information on these arrangements. Twenty-four physician-owned entities and 23 non-physician owned entities identified through our survey of health care businesses were also interviewed.

In addition to these interviews, we consulted with various industry groups and associations regarding their positions on physician ownership and self-referral. These groups included the American Medical Association (AMA), the American College of Radiology (ACR), the American Society of Internal Medicine (ASIM), the College of American Pathologists (CAP), the American Clinical Laboratory Association (ACLA), and the American Imaging Association (AIA).

We also conducted interviews with 143 State officials regarding: (1) their perspectives on, and experiences with, physician ownership and self-referral; and (2) the existence and enforcement of State laws which may prohibit self-referrals, kickbacks, or require disclosure of financial interests to patients. The officials interviewed included representatives from State licensing boards, Medicaid Fraud Control Units (MFCUs), State Attorney General offices, and title XIX offices. Finally, the OIG study team consulted with knowledgeable investigators and attorneys within the OIG concerning their experiences with the enforcement of Federal anti-kickback laws as they apply to abusive ownership or compensation arrangements.

FINDINGS

Nature and Range of Arrangements

Many Physicians Have Invested In Health Care Businesses to Which They Refer Patients

- Twelve percent of physicians who bill Medicare have ownership or investment interests in entities to which they make patient referrals.
- Referring physicians invest in a wide range of businesses. They hold interests not only in independent clinical and physiological laboratories and durable medical equipment suppliers, which we specifically studied, but also in home health agencies, hospitals, nursing homes, ambulatory surgical centers, and health maintenance organizations.
- Eight percent of physicians billing Medicare have compensation arrangements with entities to which they refer. These arrangements include space rental agreements, employee arrangements, consulting agreements, and management services contracts.

Of the 2,690 active Medicare providers responding to our physician survey, 322 claimed to have an ownership interest in a health care business to which they refer patients (other than physician office laboratories). Projected and weighted nationally, then, 11.8 percent of physicians billing Medicare have an ownership or investment interest in entities to which they make referrals.

Most ownership interests are held directly by the reporting physician, although a few physicians reported that they held ownership interests indirectly through immediate family members. Eight physicians, for example, indicated that they held an ownership interest through a family member in diagnostic imaging centers, and five reported such an indirect interest in clinical or other physiological laboratories.

Interests are held in a wide array of businesses. Exhibit 1 illustrates the breakdown of interest by type of business.

Two hundred and six of the active Medicare providers surveyed reported having a compensation arrangement with an entity to which they refer. Most of these arrangements involve space rental to or from the entity, and employee or consultant fees. Exhibit 2 indicates the type of compensation arrangement reported by the physicians surveyed.

Exhibit 1

Number and Percent of Physicians Indicating Ownership by Type

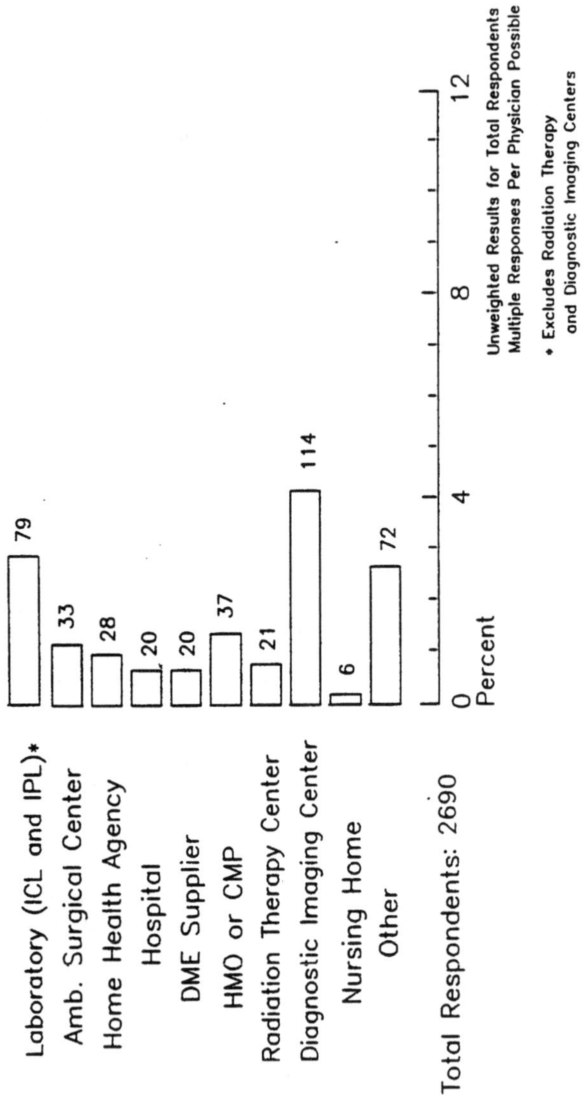

Exhibit 2

Number and Percent of Physicians Indicating Compensation Arrangements by Type

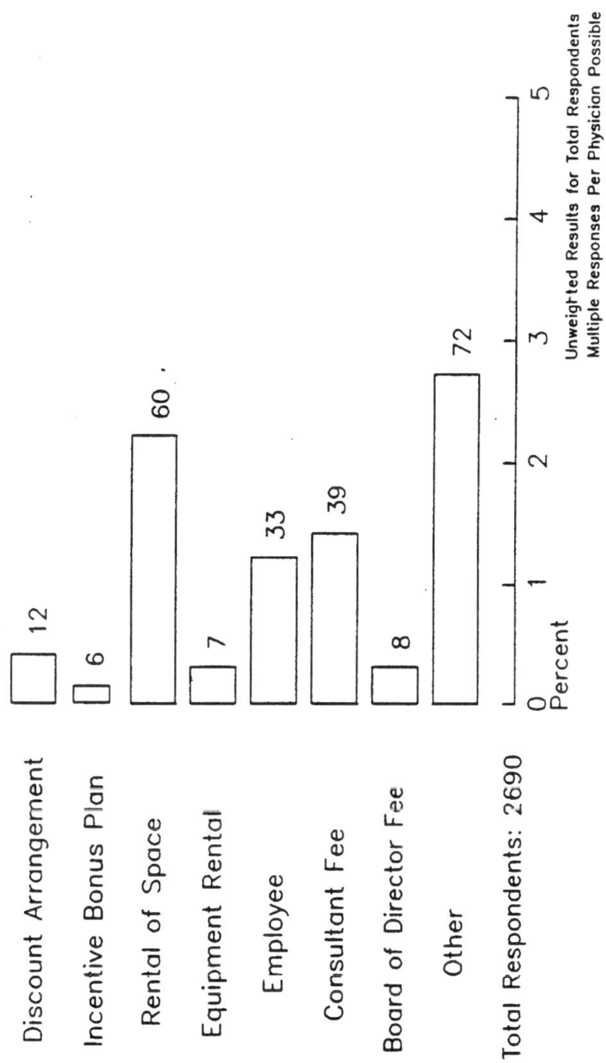

Many Health Care Entities are Owned by Referring Physicians

- Nationally, at least 25 percent of independent clinical laboratories, 27 percent of independent physiological laboratories, and 8 percent of durable medical equipment suppliers, are owned in whole or in part by referring physicians.
- The prevalence of ownership or investment varies by State. In some States, such as Arkansas and California, a larger than average percentage of ICLs, IPLs, and DMEs are physician owned. In other States, such as Michigan, the percentage of entities which are owned by physicians is much smaller than average.
- One hundred ninety-five entities in our sample (17 percent) have compensation arrangements with referring physicians. Some entities have both physician-owners and compensation arrangements with other physicians.

Of the three industries we studied, the highest rate (27 percent) of physician ownership or investment is found in the independent physiological laboratory industry. The lowest rate (8 percent) is in the durable medical equipment industry. These rates reflect conservative estimates, since they reflect only physician ownership or investment which is both direct and immediate. Physicians may also hold interests through other family members. In addition, physicians may hold interests in parent companies which in turn own other health care businesses. In such cases the owner of the entity surveyed was reported as another company; we did not attempt to collect ownership information on the parent company. (Sixteen entities in our survey reported that they are owned by another company.)

Exhibit 3 represents the rate of ownership, by industry, and indicates whether entity ownership interests are held by referring physicians (such as internists), non referring physicians (such as pathologists or radiologists), or physicians whose specialty is unknown. (Where at least one referring physician has an ownership interest, the entity is counted as referring physician owned.) As the exhibit demonstrates, a significant portion of physician ownership is accounted for by referring physicians. The actual rate of referring physician ownership is probably higher, since at least some of the physicians whose specialties are unknown can be presumed to be referring physicians.

Exhibit 4 illustrates the extent of physician ownership or investment in each industry, by State. As these figures illustrate, there is significant variability in the rate of referring physician ownership according to State. The carriers with the least amount of physician ownership are Kansas City, Michigan and New York. Differences in practice patterns in Kansas City, along with the existence of State policies unfriendly to such ventures in Michigan and New York, may help to explain these variances. Interestingly, laws in California and Florida which require disclosure of financial interests to patients do not appear to inhibit physician ownership.

One hundred ninety-five entities of the 1,133 businesses surveyed (17 percent) had one or more compensation arrangements with referring physicians. One hundred and six of the 195 entities reporting such arrangements (54 percent) were independent clinical laboratories. Types of arrangements reported by all types of entities included management/consulting agreements, space rental to and from the entity, and personnel services.

Exhibit 3

Percent of Entities Owned By Status of Physician

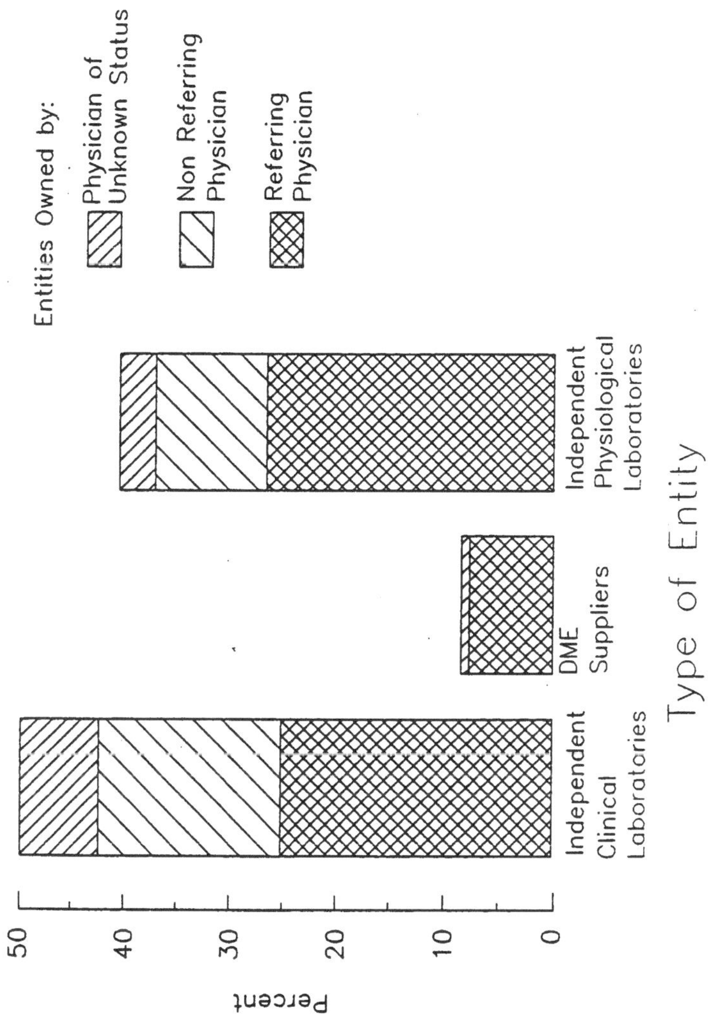

Exhibit 4

Percent Ownership by Entity Type and Carrier

Referring Physicians Only

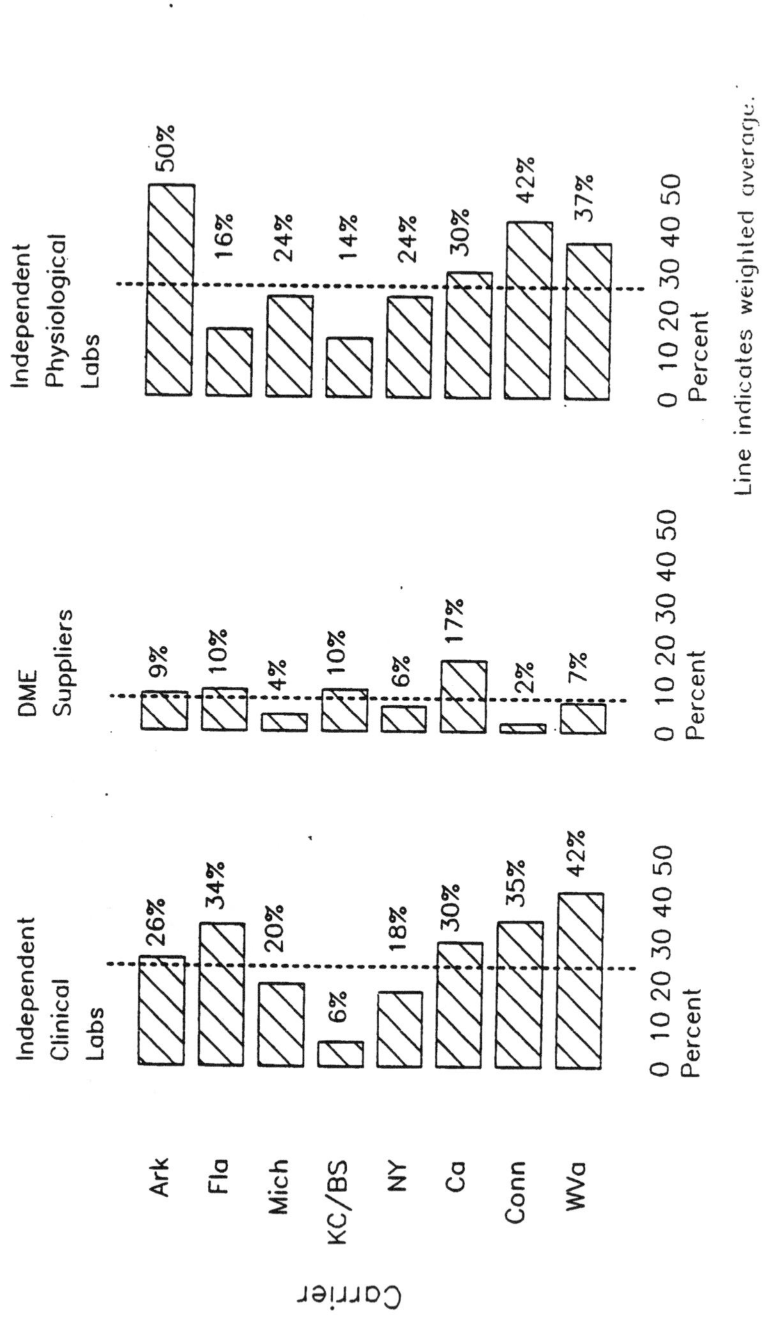

The Structure of Ownership or Investment Varies

Of the 208 entities with known physician-owners or investors in our sample of 1,133 health care businesses, 145 (70 percent) are established as corporations or similar structures, 50 (24 percent) as partnerships, and 13 (6 percent) as sole proprietorships. In contrast, 87 percent of the non physician owned entities are established as corporations, and only 4 percent as partnerships, with the remaining functioning as sole proprietorships.

Partnerships which included physicians typically have a much larger number of limited partners (average of 31) than partnerships between non physicians (average of 2). Few of the limited partners in physician partnerships were non physicians. Physician partnerships involved an average of 27 physician limited partners, with one partnership composed of 122 physician limited partners.

We requested supporting documentation (such as offerings, prospectuses, articles of incorporation and contracts) from the entities we sampled. While physician-owned companies are more likely to be structured as limited partnerships than non physician owned companies, we received few prospectuses and offerings in connection with these ventures. Of the 18 prospectuses and offerings we received for physician partnerships, none established a requirement for a specific rate of referral by investing physicians or indicated that profits are distributed in direct proportion to volume of referrals made.

Offerings and prospectuses received, however, did indicate that expectations may exist on the part of the entity with respect to physician referrals. For example, certain offerings indicated that the venture anticipated referrals from physician partners or that the viability of the business depended on such referrals. Other entities noted in their materials to us that the offering of stock or units of partnerships was made only to practicing physicians in the area. Some entities in our sample are structured in such a way as to require divestiture of financial interest by a physician upon his or her retirement from the medical profession.

Investment Opportunities are Often Identified by Physicians Themselves

Physicians reporting ownership or investment interests in health care businesses to which they refer patients most often said that they learned of such arrangements through personal contact with another associate (either a doctor, accountant, or stock broker). Only three physicians reported learning of an investment opportunity through contact from an investment firm. Although much attention has been paid to so-called "deal-makers," or third parties who act as brokers for the development of arrangements between physicians and other health care businesses, information collected through our physician survey did not suggest that this activity is prevalent. However, it is unclear to what extent the "personal associates" identified by physicians in our survey acted as agents for other third parties in soliciting interested physician-investors.

Information collected through the survey was borne out through interviews. Many of the physician-owners interviewed stated that they became aware of investment or ownership opportunities through personal contact with associates. One physician owner stated that he became aware of an opportunity to invest in a lab "at a backyard barbecue at [another] doctor's house." A large number of physician-owners stipulated that they simply saw a need in the community, and rose to meet it.

When asked whether physicians approached businesses or were sought out as investors in business, many of those interviewed indicated that both occurred. Several respondents believed that while businesses generally sought out physicians in the past, physicians have become increasingly aware of these opportunities and now seek them out or create them on their own. A consumer advocate suggested that, when such investment opportunities were new, third party brokers or "deal-makers" generally initiated them; now, he argued, the practice is common enough that financially astute physicians establish such deals on their own. One association representative stated that, in some industries, physicians are demanding investment opportunities in entities to which they refer and threatening to establish their own business if such an opportunity is not afforded them.

Impact of Arrangements on Utilization

Patients of Physician Laboratory Owners Received More Services

- Patients of referring physicians who own or invest in ICLs received 45 percent more clinical laboratory services than all Medicare patients in general, regardless of place of service. They also received 34 percent more services from independent clinical laboratories than all Medicare patients in general. This increased utilization of clinical laboratory services by patients of physician-owners cost the Medicare program $28 million in 1987. This figure does not include any costs associated with increased utilization resulting from physician ownership interests in entities other then independent clinical laboratories.

- Patients of physicians known to be owners or investors in IPLs received 13 percent more physiological testing services than all Medicare patients in general.

- The extent of increase in the use of services by patient associated with laboratory owners or investors varies by state.

Patients of referring physicians known to be owners or investors in clinical laboratories received, on the average, 45 percent more clinical laboratory services than all Medicare patients in general, regardless of place. Clinical laboratory services may be delivered in a variety of settings including independent clinical laboratories, physician's offices and hospital outpatient departments. They also received 34 percent more laboratory services from clinical laboratories than all Medicare patients in general. (See Exhibit 5.) *The actual effect is probably higher, since the control group (all patients) includes the comparison group (patients who have seen physician-owners).* If the control group consisted of patients who have *not* seen physician-owners, we would expect to see an even more dramatic effect.

Likewise, patients of physicians known to be owners or investors in physiological laboratories use 13 percent more physiological services than patients in general.[22] (See Exhibit 6.) Since physicians generally billed for physiological testing services in 1987 rather than the

Exhibit 5

Average Number* of Services Per Beneficiary By Physician Ownership Status and Place of Service

Clinical Laboratory Services

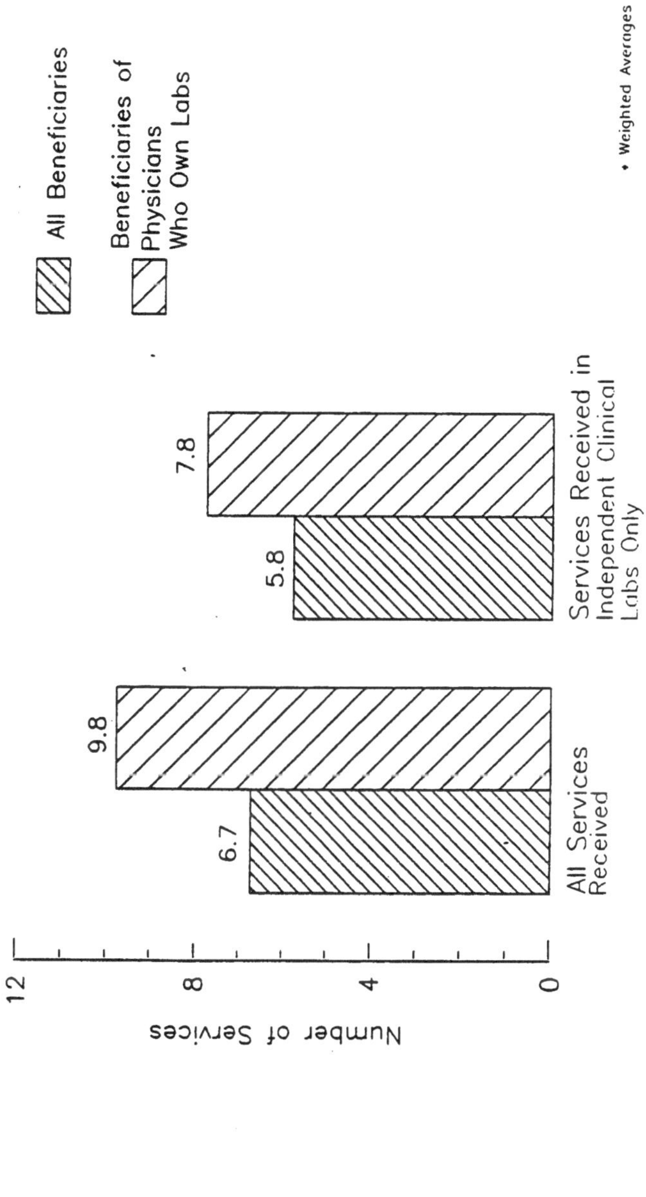

Exhibit 6

Average Number of Services Per Beneficiary By Physician Ownership Status

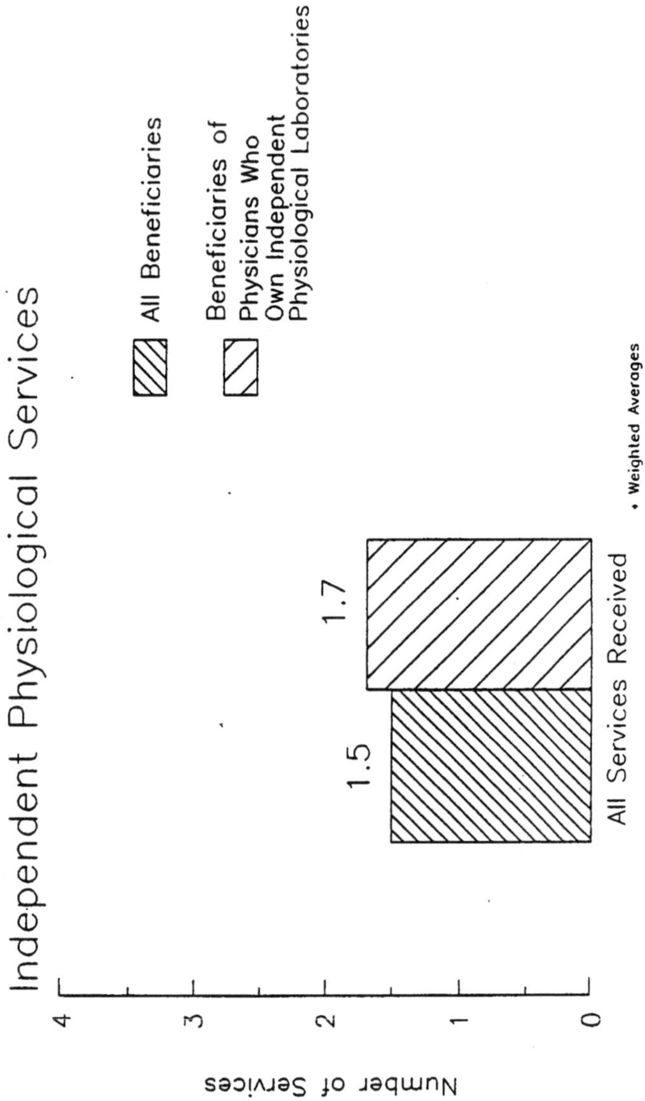

laboratories that actually performed the tests, we were unable to extend the analysis by place of service as we did with clinical laboratories, above.

The extent of difference in receipt of services varies by State. In two States, West Virginia and New York, there was no difference in experiences between patients of physician-owners of clinical laboratories and all patients in general. However, in the six remaining States there was a statistically significant increase in the use of services by patients of physician-owners. This increase ranged from a low of 30 percent in California to a high of 87 percent in Michigan. Exhibits 7 and 8 illustrate the State by State results for patients associated with physicians who are clinical and physiological laboratory owners. Again, the differences by state may be explained by local practice patterns or State law influences. It is interesting to note that the existence of disclosure laws in Florida and California, or the more stringent law in Michigan, have not prevented us from seeing increased utilization in those States.

We saw a similar effect on utilization associated with the existence of compensation arrangements between laboratories and physicians. Patients of physicians with compensation arrangements with clinical laboratories, for example, use 32 percent more laboratory services than all Medicare patients in general. See appendix B for more detail.

Based on our analysis of utilization patterns for patients of physician-owners of clinical laboratories, the difference in utilization for clinical laboratory services *alone* cost the Medicare program $28 million in 1987. This figure does not include costs associated with differences we demonstrated in utilization by patients of physician-owners in the physiological laboratory industry, or differences in utilization by patients of physicians with other types of financial arrangements (i.e., compensation arrangements).

Patients of Physicians Associated with DMEs Show No Difference in Use of Services

- Patients who saw physician-owners or investors in DMEs received no more durable medical equipment than all Medicare patients in general. However, significant variation exists on a State by State basis.

Patients of physicians who are DME owners or investors do not use any more durable medical equipment than all Medicare patients in general. In addition, we did not find any significant differences between all DME services furnished to Medicare beneficiaries or DME services furnished directly by DME suppliers. However, the data showed significant State by State variation. While in the aggregate there was no effect on the utilization of DME services, beneficiaries of physicians in Florida who own show a statistically significant increase in utilization while in West Virginia and Kansas City, this same group of beneficiaries show a significant decrease in utilization of services. Exhibits 9 and 10 illustrate the results of our analysis for DMEs.

We saw a similar effect on utilization associated with the existence of compensation arrangements between DME providers and physicians. See appendix B for more detail.

Exhibit 7

Average Number of Services Per Beneficiary
By Carrier and Ownership Status of Billing Physician

Clinical Laboratory Services

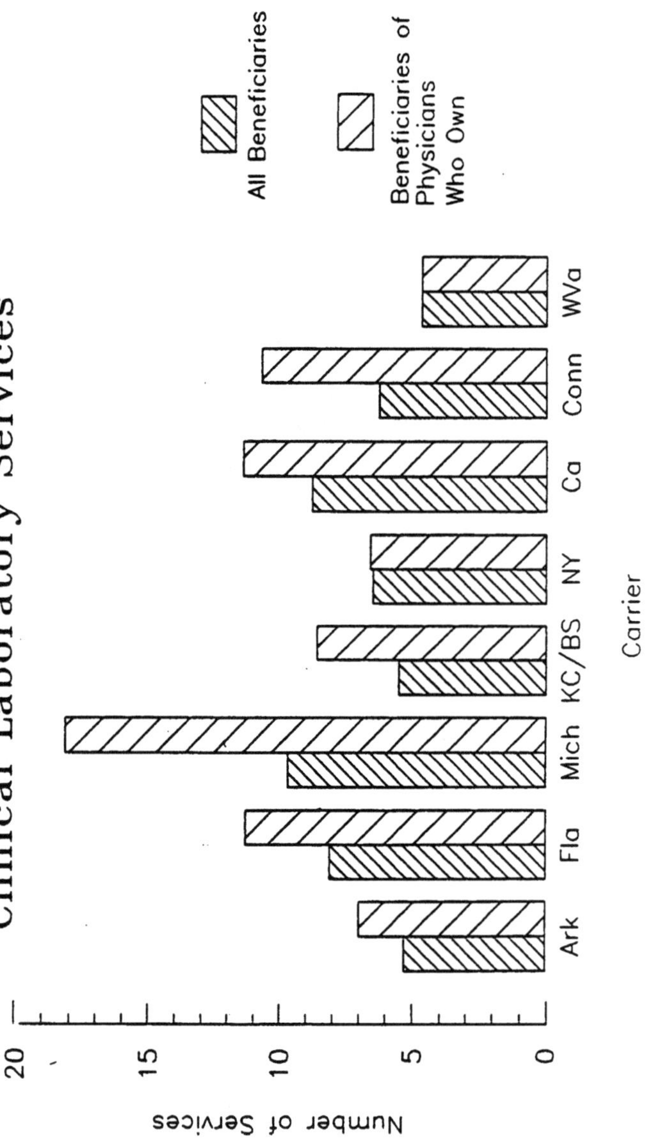

Exhibit 8

Average Number of Services Per Beneficiary
By Carrier and Ownership Status of Billing Physician

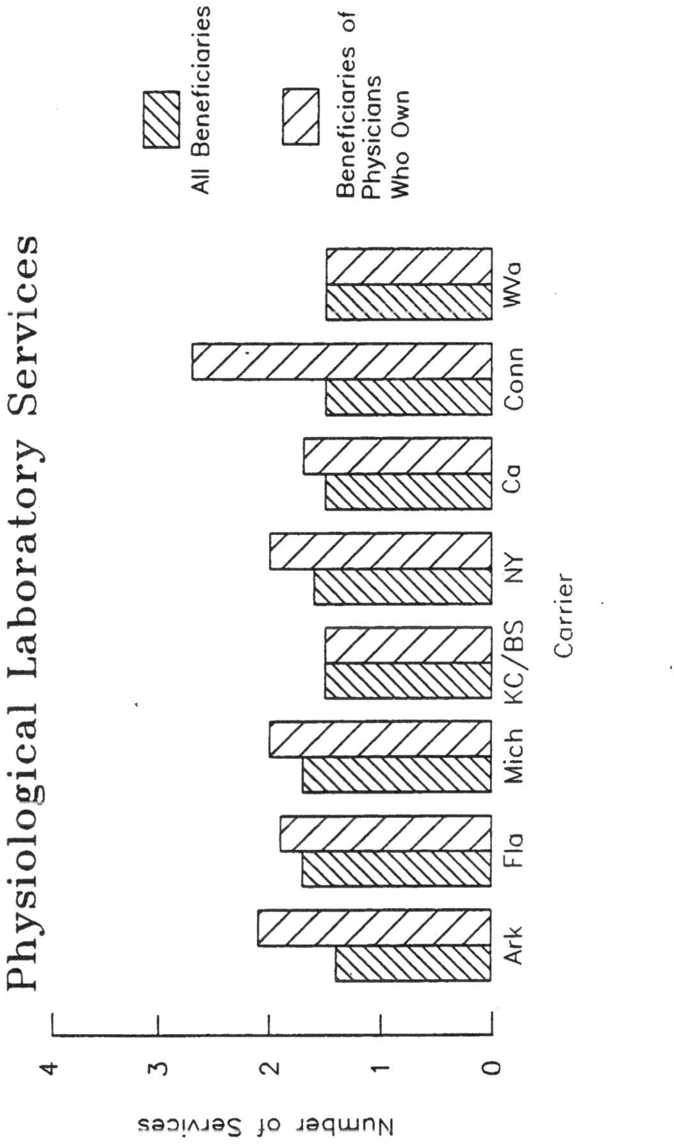

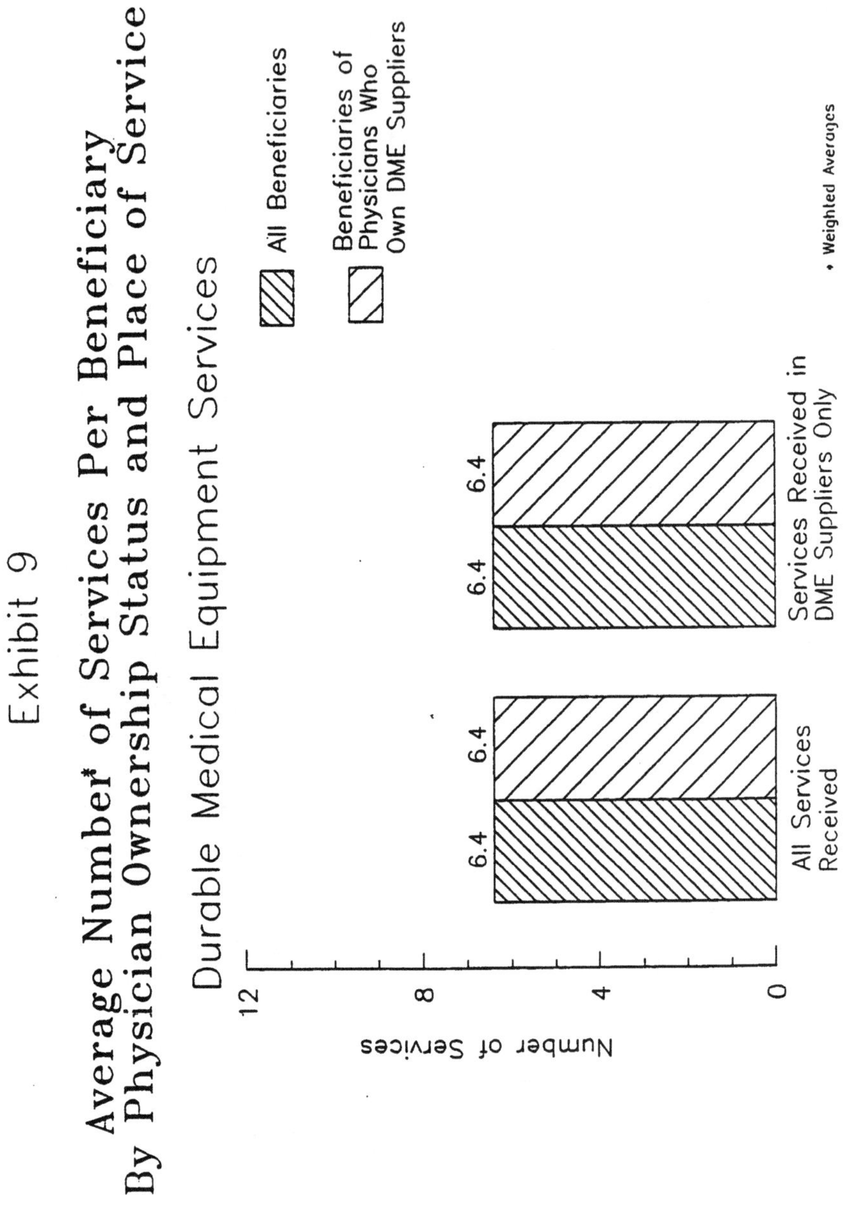
Exhibit 9
Average Number* of Services Per Beneficiary
By Physician Ownership Status and Place of Service
Durable Medical Equipment Services
All Beneficiaries
Beneficiaries of Physicians Who Own DME Suppliers
Number of Services
12
8
4
0
6.4
6.4
6.4
6.4
All Services Received
Services Received in DME Suppliers Only
* Weighted Averages

24

Exhibit 10

Average Number of Services Per Beneficiary By Carrier and Ownership Status of Billing Physician

Durable Medical Equipment Services

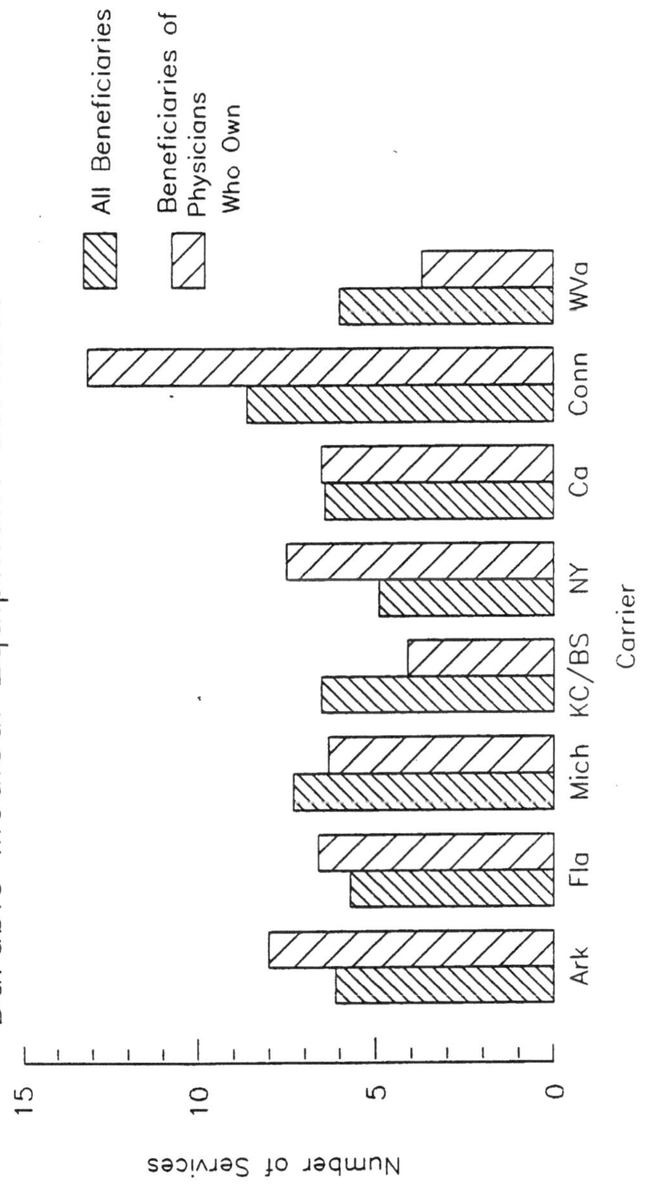

Enforcement Experiences

Enforcement of Current Federal Anti-Kickback Laws Is Challenging

- In the past two years the OIG has pursued 442 cases under the anti-kickback authorities which involve physician ownership or compensation arrangements. Most (416) were cases involving physician compensation and many (338) arose out of one large investigation in Philadelphia, Pennsylvania.

- Recent legislative and regulatory developments will aid the OIG in addressing abusive arrangements.

A number of obstacles exist which make enforcement of current anti-kickback laws, as they relate to physician ownership or compensation arrangements, challenging. Investigations of ownership arrangements are complex and labor-intensive. In order to convince a judge or jury that the anti-kickback statute has been violated, certain facts can be helpful. These include, but are not limited to:

(1) whether the amount of return is related to referral volume in any way;

(2) whether opportunities to invest are offered only to those in a position to refer business, or if those in a position to refer greater amounts of business are offered a greater investment opportunity;

(3) whether the investing physicians' referrals are monitored by the entity;

(4) whether restrictions are placed on transferability of the investment interest;

(5) whether the return on investment is excessive in light of the nature of the business risk; and

(6) whether the amounts invested reflect the capital needs of the entity, etc.

Since many of these arrangements are structured differently, such analysis requires significant legal support.

Physician compensation cases involving payments for referrals are somewhat easier to pursue, principally because they have moved from the realm of contracts and stock options to the much shadier realm of "deals"--cash payments off-the-books, paid under a veil of secrecy, exorbitant rent payments which do not reflect fair market value, or other payments which disguise their true purpose. As a result, it is easier to show that the arrangement is a sham, that medically unnecessary services were generated to receive a payoff, and that false claims were generated to obtain money. However, some of the same difficulties in enforcement exist with respect to these arrangements, including legal complexities.

Such cases are also difficult to explain to a fact-finder, unless the business arrangement clearly specifies payment for referral. Federal prosecutors are more likely to prosecute where the scheme has an element of corruption, the parties to the arrangement are involved in a number of abusive practices, or there is direct cost to the Medicare program or its beneficiaries. Even overt kickback cases are difficult to prove, where there is no "paper trail." In these instances the case must be developed with wires and interviews.

For these reasons, such cases have often been assigned a low priority at the Department of Justice. Instead, resources have been directed at criminal cases where harm to patients or the Government can be more easily demonstrated.

However, recent legislative and regulatory developments have helped pave the way for more effective and aggressive enforcement in this area. The Medicare and Medicaid Patient and Program Protection Act of 1987, which allowed the OIG to sanction providers who were previously subject only to criminal action, obviates the need for the OIG to rely on the Department of Justice to prosecute offenders. The "safe harbor" regulation, once promulgated as final rule, will help put providers on notice that they may be subject to criminal prosecution or civil sanctions if their business arrangements do not qualify for a safe harbor. The OIG Fraud Alert forewarns regional investigators, Medicare carriers, health care providers and the public as to the structural and other facts the OIG deems instructive in reviewing arrangements for potential abuse.

SUMMARY

Extent of Arrangements

Our survey data reveals that financial arrangements between physicians and health care entities to which they may make referrals are common. However, since the data presented represents a "snapshot in time" and no baseline data exists with which to judge it, it is impossible to determine if the number of financial arrangements between referring physicians and other health care entities is increasing, decreasing or remains stable. Even so, we consider the prevalence of arrangements reported in our findings as significant.

It is important to note that, while much attention is given to the percentage of physicians who are involved in such arrangements, the more relevant question for the Medicare program is the percentage of health care providers that have financial arrangements with physicians (since it is the health care providers, not the physicians, who are being reimbursed for these ancillary services). As the data demonstrates, the percentage of physician ownership or investment varies by type of provider; we have seen a greater degree of physician investment in the laboratory industries than in the DME industry. It also varies by State, with Arkansas, California, West Virginia and Connecticut markets heavily weighted with physician-owners and investors. Without baseline data, we are unable to determine if this uneven distribution represents a trend in one direction or another.

Impact on Utilization

We have also demonstrated that patients who have been seen by physician-owners or investors in the laboratory industries, or for that matter physicians with other kinds of financial arrangements with laboratories, tend to use significantly more services than Medicare patients in general. While we have demonstrated an association rather than a causality, this finding--consistent with previous small-scale studies in this area--is quite troubling.

While we have demonstrated a remarkable effect on utilization of services attributable to physician ownership in the ICL and IPL industries, no such effect occurred in the DME industry. This may be due to the elasticity and consumability of laboratory services; that is, an unlimited number of tests may be ordered for any given patient. In DME, many goods are non-consumable; hence, one patient can at the most receive one wheelchair, not an infinite number of wheelchairs. Certainly the utilization effect we have seen in the laboratory industries is cause for concern to the Medicare program, especially in light of the fact that the methodological approach supported the most conservative finding possible.

Procedural Recommendations

Regardless of action that might be taken on the options we have identified below for policymakers, certain steps should be pursued which will make further analysis and ongoing monitoring of arrangements between physicians and other health care entities possible. We are making recommendations that HCFA pursue the necessary legislative and regulatory changes to: (1) require entities billing Medicare to disclose the names of physician-owners and investors to the program; and (2) require claims submitted by all entities providing services under Medicare Part B to contain the name and provider number of the referring physician.

Options for Policymakers

A number of policy options exist which might serve to address the issue of higher utilization of services by patients of referring physician-owners. A sample of these options is delineated below. However, the choice of these options may not depend alone upon the results of this study. For example, we have not collected quantitative data regarding the impact of physician ownership and self-referral on competition, quality of care, or availability of services. These dimensions of the policy issue were outside the scope of our study. However, the choice of policy options may be driven, at least in part, on an assessment of these other factors.

1. **Implement a focused post payment utilization review by carriers.**

   Carriers now conduct post payment utilization review based on claims submitted under Medicare. One policy option is to implement such review directed at physician-owners or investors.

   This option would require several modifications to the current system of collecting information. First, in order to identify the targeted group, health care entities would have to disclose their physician-owners or investors, along with their Medicare provider numbers, to HCFA and the carriers. Second, the name and provider number of the referring physician must be entered on each claim submitted by the health care entity. Third, provider number reform must be instituted. If physicians and health care entities are allowed to use more than one provider number, the difficulty of this review is increased. Fourth, resources must be made available in the carriers to carry out such a program.

   While this approach would focus the program's attention on possible abusers only, there are several disadvantages to this approach. If the carriers found that a physician-owner ordered 20 percent more tests than his non-investing peers, it is not clear that such a finding would lead to adjudication in favor of the program. Peer review might not support a finding of "relative over-use" of tests as sufficient justification, by itself, for sanction or exclusion. In such cases, it is difficult to demonstrate that the tests ordered were in fact unnecessary; the program might experience a high reversal rate in cases before Administrative Law Judges. In addition, such focused utilization review is timely, costly and difficult to administer at the carrier level. A previous study issued by the OIG found that current post payment utilization review requirements are not being met by the carriers.[23]

2. **Require physicians to disclose financial interests to patients, as a condition of participation, when making referrals to an entity in which they have an interest.**

   As detailed earlier in the report, at least eleven States currently have laws which require physicians to make some form of disclosure to patients when they refer those patients to facilities in which they have financial interests. While we have not undertaken a causal study of the effect of disclosure requirements on physician or patient decision-making, the two States in our sample that do have disclosure laws--California and Florida--experienced the same higher utilization rate among patients of physicians owners as did other States without disclosure laws.

   While this option is perhaps the least onerous of all those described in this section, it may also be the least likely to influence actual patterns of use of services. Patients have little basis with which to judge the efficiency, quality, or even pricing of one facility versus another. Patient choice in this environment may have little meaning.

3. **Improve the enforcement of current anti-kickback authorities.**

   With recent regulatory and legislative developments which have paved the way for more aggressive enforcement of current anti-kickback laws, abusive arrangements between physicians and other health care entities may be effectively addressed. The Medicare and Medicaid Patient and Program Protection Act of 1987, the "safe harbor" regulations, and the OIG Fraud Alert have combined to create a positive environment for enforcement. Placement of additional resources at the OIG to pursue these cases would also support the goal of improved enforcement.

   While legal actions against arrangements that violate the current anti-kickback laws will deal with abusive arrangements, and perhaps deter the development of other abusive arrangements, OIG enforcement activity cannot effectively address physicians who refer patients for more services than their peers, in absence of other relevant facts. However, disclosure of financial interests by physicians to the Medicare program, together with post payment utilization review by carriers, might aid the OIG in targeting cases and reviewing arrangements under its current anti-kickback authority.

4. **Institute a private right of action for anti-kickback cases.**

   Congress may also wish to consider legislation which would allow private citizens to bring actions against other private parties engaging in conduct prohibited under current anti-kickback law. Consideration should be given to the appropriate private remedy, given the current civil enforcement scheme which only permits program exclusion. However, a private right of action would encourage self-policing among health care providers and allow the Government an additional source of cases brought against abusive arrangements. If enacted under the *qui tam* model of the

False Claims Act, the private right of action would be subject to departmental control and supervision.

5. **Prohibit physicians from referring patients to certain types of entities in which they have a financial interest.**

   This option would allow the Congress to prohibit physician referrals to certain types of entities in which they have financial involvement. This approach has precedent in the Medicare Catastrophic Coverage Act of 1988, which barred physician referrals to home IV therapy providers in which they have a financial interest. Based on our finding that patients of physician-owners in these industries use more laboratory services that patients in general, the laboratory industries are logical targets for such restrictions. However, this option may result in certain unintended consequences, such as a negative effect on availability of services; reduced competition; or a drive of services into the physician office laboratory market. In order to address some of these issues, legislation might provide exceptions for sole rural providers or others who meet a legitimate community need in providing services.

   Compliance with such legislation may be difficult to ensure. If ownership of health care entities is not disclosed to the Medicare program, then financial involvement by physicians might be unseen by the OIG or other enforcement officials. Potential for "gaming" the restriction is also evident. Financial involvement might be hidden through indirect or non-immediate interests, e.g., through family members or a holding company.

6. **Prohibit physicians from referring patients to any entity in which they have a financial interest.**

   This option, which reflects the intent of "The Ethics in Patient Referrals Act," would generally prohibit physicians from referring patients to health care entities in which they have a financial interest. As with the previous option, legislation thus constructed may result in certain unintended consequences, such as a negative effect on availability of services; reduced competition; or a drive of services into the physician-office laboratory market. In order to address some of these issues, legislation might provide exceptions for sole rural providers or others who meet a legitimate community need in providing services, as does the current bill pending before the Congress.

   Compliance with such legislation may be difficult to ensure. If ownership of health care entities is not disclosed to the Medicare program, then financial involvement by physicians might be unseen by the OIG or other enforcement officials. Potential for "gaming" the restriction is also evident. Financial involvement might be hidden through indirect or non-immediate interests, e.g., through family members or a holding company.

Additional Reports

The OIG will issue several additional reports focusing on physician ownership and other market forces in the independent clinical laboratory, independent physiological laboratory, and durable medical equipment industries in Fall 1989. Additional analysis will be conducted concerning the nature and extent of physician compensation arrangements.

ENDNOTES

1. Testimony of William L. Roper, M.D., before the Subcommittee on Health, Committee on Ways and Means, U.S. House of Representatives, September 29, 1988.

2. The OIG has recently conducted a study on physician office laboratories (POLs). *See* Office of Inspector General, Office of Analysis and Inspections, "Quality Assurance in Physician Office Laboratories," OAI-05-88-00330, March 1989.

3. Arnold S. Relman, "The New Medical Industrial Complex," *New England Journal of Medicine*, October 23, 1980.

4. Robert P. Hey and Barbara Bradley, "$450 billion industry spawns fraud, abuse," *Christian Science Monitor,* December 7, 1988; "MD's investments reap controversial profits," *Christian Science Monitor,* December 8, 1988; "Patient care vs. physicians' investments," *Christian Science Monitor,* December 12, 1988.

5. Michael Waldholz and Walt Bogdanich, "Warm Bodies: Doctor Owned Labs Earn Lavish Profits in a Captive Market," *The Wall Street Journal.* February 28, 1989, p. 1.

6. Medical Services Administration, State of Michigan Department of Social Services, "Utilization of Medicaid Laboratory Services by Physicians With/Without Ownership Interest in Clinical Laboratories: A Comparative Analysis of Six Selected Laboratories," July 9, 1981.

7. U.S. Department of Health and Human Services, Health Care Financing Administration, Division of Health Standards and Quality, Region V, "Diagnostic Clinical Laboratory Services in Region V," #2-05-2004-11, May 1983.

8. Blue Cross and Blue Shield of Michigan, Medical Affairs Division, "A Comparison of Laboratory Utilization and Payout to Ownership," May 9, 1984.

9. Mathematica Policy Research, AMA Socioeconomic Monitoring System Autumn Survey, 1988.

10. 42 U.S.C. Section 1320a-7b.

11. 760 F.2d 68 (3rd Cir. 1985). A company providing holter monitor services submitted claims to Medicare and forwarded a portion of the reimbursement to the referring physician. The operator of the holter monitoring enterprise, who was also a physician, was prosecuted. In this defense, the physician argued that the payments he made were for legitimate services, e.g., for interpreting test results.

12. 760 F.2d at 69.

13. Case No. 87-5108 (April 3, 1989). In this case, the court upheld the conviction of an owner of a clinic who received payments from a medical services company, which collected blood and urine samples and forwarded them to a laboratory. The court upheld a jury instruction that read, *inter alia,* "It is not a defense that there might have been other reasons for the solicitation of a remuneration by the defendants, if you find that one of the material purposes for the solicitation was to obtain money for the referral of services."

14. 770 F.2d 1447 (1985). In this case, the court examined a medical management company which was providing services to a physician group. This company entered into an arrangement with a laboratory which returned 20 percent of its revenue obtained from the physician group's referrals back to the management company. The defendant alleged that these payments were fair compensation for "specimen collection and handling services." 770 F.2d at 1449. The court rejected this defense, holding: "The fair market value of these services was substantially less than the [amount paid], and there is no question that [the laboratory] was paying for referrals as well as the described services." *Ibid.*

15. 42 U.S.C. Section 1320a-7(b)(7).

16. Pub.L. 100-93, Section 14.

17. Mich. Comp. Laws Ann. Section 333.16221(e)(iv).

18. Fla. Stat. Section 455.25.

19. Minn. Stat. Ann. Section 147.091(p)(3).

20. PA. Act 66, Section 2, and Va. Code Section 54-278.3.

21. Prepared statement of the Subcommittee, Subcommittee on Oversight and Investigations, Committee on Energy and Commerce, U.S. House of Representatives, March 5, 1982.

22. Unlike results associated with clinical laboratories, this number tested as statistically non-significant nationally. This is probably due to small numbers of beneficiaries in the 5 percent BMAD sample associated with physician-owners of these entities, particularly in Arkansas, Kansas City, and Connecticut.

23. Office of Inspector General, Office of Analysis and Inspections, "Medicare Carriers' Performance of Program Integrity Functions," OAI-04-88-00710, August 1988.

APPENDIX A

METHODOLOGY

This appendix presents the details of the two surveys conducted by the Office of Inspector General. Both surveys were conducted simultaneously and used the same basic design. The Office of Audit developed and administered, by mail, a survey of a sample of physicians in current practice and presumably billing the Medicare program. The Office of Analysis and Inspections surveyed, again by mail, a sample of entities providing ancillary services to the Medicare population.

Design

Both surveys used a two stage cluster design to sample the desired elements. At the initial stage, Medicare Part B carriers were selected at random, with replacement, with probability proportional to size. The size of a carrier was determined using the total Medicare dollar amounts paid by each carrier in 1986. Eight carriers were selected. The following table shows the carriers selected and the probability associated with each carrier.

Distribution of Sampled Carriers by Reimbursed Amount Source: 1986 BMAD

Carrier	Reimbursed	Probability of Selection
Arkansas BS	$ 189,533,042.00	1.0%
Florida BS	$ 1,425,407,061.00	7.4%
Michigan BS	$ 774,109,935.00	4.0%
BS of Kansas City	$ 155,282,982.00	0.8%
BS of Greater NY	$ 1,186,874,282.00	6.2%
Occidental Ca	$ 1,525,825,170.00	8.0%
Travelers CT	$ 244,404,358.00	1.3%
Nationwide WVa	$ 119,594,198.00	0.6%
Total Selected	**$ 5,621,031,028.00**	**29.4%**
All Other Carriers	$13,513,861,042.00	70.6%
National Total	$19,134,892,070.00	100.0%

The second stage differed depending upon the element of interest, either physicians or entities providing ancillary services. The second stage sampling strategy and the results of the sampling process will be discussed separately for each survey.

Office of Audit Physician Survey

For the second stage of this survey, each carrier was asked to provide a list of physician numbers used by the carrier for billing purposes. Each number on the list was considered an element for purposes of sampling. For each carrier, a simple random sample of 500 numbers was selected. The name and address of the owner of each number was identified by the carrier and a questionnaire was sent. Follow up questionnaires were sent to those physicians for whom a response had not been received within two weeks. Subsequent to the second mailing, telephone calls were made to those physicians not responding to the second mailing.
It was recognized early that the physician provider numbers we were using could represent either single physicians or groups of physicians. We were not able to distinguish between these two occurrences in all carriers prior to mailing the survey instruments. We have considered a single physician and a physician group as essentially the same. Thus, our findings represent the proportion of individual billing numbers identified to Medicare. This should be kept in mind when interpreting our results. To avoid cumbersome language, we will refer to these billing numbers as physician provider numbers.

A total of 4,024 were actually selected. Twenty-nine of these numbers were dropped prior to mailing the questionnaires. These 29 included numbers for which no address was available or the physician identified was under active investigation by our office. Overall, 81 percent of the 4,024 physicians selected responded to the questionnaire. The following table gives a breakdown of this response rate.

Office of Audit Physician Survey Responses by Category

Physician Numbers Selected		4,024	
Inappropriate numbers or Physician under Investigation		(29)	
Survey Questionnaires Mailed		3,995	
Responses Outstanding	334 (8.4%)		
Responses Returned (Undeliverable)	443 (11.1%)		
Responses Received		3,218	(80.6%)
Responses Indicating No Active Medicare Participation or Inappropriately Selected Number		528	
Active Medicare Providers		2,690	

Only active Medicare providers are used in the analysis to determine rates of ownership or compensation. The 2,690 represents 67.3 percent of the questionnaires mailed and 83.6 percent of the responses received.

Office of Analysis and Inspections Entity Survey

For this survey, a stratified design, using simple random sampling within each strata, was employed. Three types of entities were studied which constituted the three strata. Independent clinical laboratories (ICL) and durable medical equipment (DME) suppliers were identified using data supplied by the Health Care Financing Administration's (HCFA) sample of Part B services. A 5 percent sample of all beneficiaries receiving services is contained in the Part B Medicare Annual Data (BMAD) files collected by HCFA. For each of the eight carriers selected, we generated a list of ICLs and DMEs known to have billed for services in 1987. Using these lists, a simple random sample of 60 provider numbers were selected. If there were less than 60 numbers, then all of the numbers were included in the sample.

A third group of entities included in this survey are known as Independent Physiological Laboratories (IPL). These entities are independently established, non-physician providers of physiological services (Ref: HCFA Carrier Manual). Because these entities were not required to bill the Medicare program directly for services performed until April of 1988, the BMAD files could not be used to generate lists for sampling. The IPL lists were therefore generated by the carriers at our request. These lists were then used to select the 60 entities, or as many as were available, for inclusion in the survey.

In those carriers where we had less than 60 entities of one type or more, we attempted to increase the sample size of remaining group(s) of entities if possible. The sample design, as constructed, called for 1,440 entities. Because not all of the carriers had the designated minimum number of subject entities, the final sample size is 1,133. Each entity selected was mailed a survey instrument. Follow up mailings were made two weeks later and subsequent follow up by telephone was used to insure response to the survey. Due to authority vested with the Inspector General, subpoenas were issued, where necessary, to insure a complete follow up. The following three tables provide a detailed breakdown of the number of survey instruments sent and the responses received.

Results of Sampling

Independent Clinical Laboratories

Carrier	Number in BMAD	Sample Size	Responses	Lost to Followup	Percent Response
Arkansas BS	31	31	29	2	93.5%
Florida BS	141	62	60	2	96.8%
Michigan BS	88	59	58	1	98.3%
BS of Kansas City	34	34	31	3	91.2%
BS of Greater NY	102	68	65	3	95.6%
Occidental CA	273	60	51	9	85.0%
Travelers of CT	68	63	62	1	98.4%
Nationwide WVa	19	19	18	1	94.7%
TOTAL	**770**	**396**	**374**	**22**	**94.4%**
			Weighted Average	94.7%	

Durable Medical Equipment Suppliers

Carrier	Number In BMAD	Sample Size	Responses	Lost to Followup	Percent Response
Arkansas BS	60	56	54	2	96.4%
Florida BS	309	60	57	3	95.0%
Michigan BS	141	79	73	6	92.4%
BS of Kansas City	41	41	40	1	97.6%
BS of Greater NY	146	67	58	9	86.6%
Occidental CA	220	60	52	8	86.7%
Travelers of CT	50	50	48	2	96.0%
Nationwide WVa	57	57	55	2	96.5%
TOTAL	**1,024**	**470**	**437**	**33**	**93.0%**
		Weighted Average			95.7%

Independent Physiological Laboratories

Carrier	Number In Carrier	Sample Size	Responses	Lost to Followup	Percent Response
Arkansas BS	4	4	3	1	75.0%
Florida BS	275	64	41	23	64.1%
Michigan BS	42	42	32	10	76.2%
BS of Kansas City	14	14	13	1	92.9%
BS of Greater NY	45	45	35	10	77.8%
Occidental CA	90	60	44	16	73.3%
Travelers of CT	19	19	16	3	84.2%
Nationwide WVa	19	19	16	3	84.2%
TOTAL	**508**	**267**	**200**	**67**	**74.9%**
		Weighted Average			81.5%

The lost to follow up category includes: (1) those entities that were found to be out of business; and (2) those entities which we were unable to locate through efforts of our own or those of the carrier, and were presumed out of business.

Utilization Analysis

Data collected by HCFA and the Medicare carriers does not include information to determine completely ownership or compensation relationships that may exist among the various providers that bill for services to beneficiaries. Nor does information exist as to the identity of providers that have referred a beneficiary for services billed by other providers. To overcome these difficulties and use HCFA's BMAD data, the entity survey described above provided the names of any and all physicians maintaining ownership and/or compensation arrangements with the sampled entities.

The carriers were asked to divulge all provider numbers associated with each physician identified in the entity survey. Matching these provider numbers with those numbers found in the BMAD billing data allowed us to establish groups of beneficiaries known to have had services from physicians with ownership or compensation arrangements. The rates for various services in this group of beneficiaries can then be compared to the overall rates of services for all beneficiaries.

APPENDIX B

ANALYSIS

This appendix provides the detailed tables and analysis supporting the results presented in the body of this report. The data is reported in sections defined by subject matter in the title.

Proportion of Physicians Reporting Ownership and/or Compensation

Tables B1 and B2 provide detailed breakdowns by carrier of the number of physicians, or physician groups, reporting ownership (Table B1) and compensation arrangements (Table B2). For these tables, those physicians not responding to the survey were assumed to reflect the same distributions as those responding, both with respect to active participation in the Medicare program and the proportion indicating ownership and compensation arrangements. Thus, the number reported in the columns headed "Physicians Sampled" reflects those physicians who either responded or we were unable to locate and whose questionnaires were undeliverable. Physicians associated with undeliverable questionnaires were assumed to be inactive in the Medicare program for purposes of this survey.

The weighted proportion of physicians reporting ownership or compensation arrangements is based upon only those physicians also reporting that they actively bill the Medicare program. Our results estimate that there are approximately 560,000 physicians registered with Medicare carriers, of which only approximately 399,000 actually are active in Medicare. Also, Tables B1 and B2 do not give mutually exclusive counts. Approximately 26 percent of the physicians responding (unweighted percent) reported both ownership and compensation arrangements.

The data reported in this survey represents responses that are self reported by the sampled physicians or physician groups. In an attempt to verify the accuracy of the responses, two separate approaches were taken. First, two random 10 percent subsamples of all the selected physician provider numbers were drawn, by carrier. Given the physicians associated with these numbers, auditors endeavored to establish any ownership or compensation arrangements these physicians might have through independent sources. The sources used included State and local government offices as well as Federal offices located in each region.

The first subsample consisted of 402 physician provider numbers. We were able to identify five physicians, active in the Medicare program, with ownership or compensation arrangements. All five of these physicians had responded to our survey. Two of these five physicians responded to the survey that they had no ownership or compensation arrangements with other entities billing the Medicare program. We did not establish whether these two physicians referred patients to the entities so identified.

The second sample consisted of 400 physician provider numbers. With this sample, we found eight physicians meeting our criteria. Seven of these physicians had responded to our survey and again, two responded they had no ownership or compensation arrangements with entities to which they referred patients. Again, we did not establish the actual referral practices of these two physicians.

A second approach was to match the physician provider numbers obtained from this survey with those collected in the survey of entities. This match found 88 physician provider numbers. That is, 88 of the physicians selected at random from the eight carriers to receive a physician survey questionnaire were subsequently identified by the data collected in the survey of entities as physicians with either ownership or compensation arrangements from our sample of independent clinical laboratories, durable medical equipment suppliers or independent physiological laboratories. Sixty-five of these 88 physicians responded to the survey instrument. Of these 65, 14 (21 percent) indicated on the physician survey that they had no ownership or compensation arrangements with other entities to which they referred patients. As before, we could not determine actual referral patterns for these physicians.

While the conclusions that can be drawn from these two methods of verification are limited, it seems apparent that the self reported nature of the physician survey did not lead to gross misstatements of fact on the part of the physicians. At worst, we may be understating the true extent of physician financial relationships that exist. Consequently, we believe that our results are an accurate representation of the proportion of physicians who have financial relationships with other entities, to which they refer patients, and who also bill the Medicare program.

Utilization Analysis

The analysis of the effect of physician ownership and compensation arrangements on utilization of services was conducted by defining two groups of beneficiaries. The first group was defined as all beneficiaries in the carrier BMAD sample with at least one service of the type under study. For independent clinical laboratories, this was all beneficiaries with at least one service billed to Medicare using the HCFA Common Procedure Code System (HCPCS) where the first digit of the HCPCS was an '8' or a 'P'. For durable medical equipment suppliers, the first digit of the HCPCS was an 'E' and for independent physiological laboratories, the HCPCS codes listed in appendix C were used. Essentially, this group constituted the control group. The comparison group was composed of beneficiaries showing at least one service billed as in the control group and also showing a billing for services received from a physician known to have an ownership or compensation arrangement with an entity selected in the entity survey. All services for a beneficiary so identified were included in the comparison group.

This form of analysis has two important implications that should be kept in mind when interpreting the results. First, this approach represents a conservative analysis. The comparison group is not excluded from the control group and the comparison group is composed only of beneficiaries identified through the entities included in the sample. Those beneficiaries of physician owned entities not included in the sample are included in the control group but not in the comparison group. An important effect of this type of construction is to reduce any apparent difference found in utilization rates calculated for each group. Second, any differences found should be interpreted as showing an association only between groups and utilization rates. Causality cannot be established because the data lacks the information necessary to determine which physician prescribed the service billed on behalf of the beneficiary.

Tables B3 through B12 present the results of the above analysis. For clinical laboratory services and durable medical equipment services, four types of tables are given. Two tables give utilization rates by carrier where the comparison group is composed of beneficiaries seen by physicians with a known ownership interest in the entity tabled. One table uses all services, regardless of source and the second uses only those services delivered in (or by) the entity. A second set of two tables presents the same information when the beneficiary was seen by a physician with a compensation arrangement with the entity.

Only two tables are presented for services involving independent physiological laboratories, that is, all services from all sources for beneficiaries of physicians who own (Table B11) and all services from all sources for beneficiaries of physicians with compensation arrangements with IPLs (Table B12). This is due to the fact that lack of direct billing by IPLs in 1987 did not allow us to identify IPLs in the BMAD sample data.

Included in these tables is a column labeled "Ratio." This is the ratio of the utilization rate for the comparison group to that of the control group. The weighted average of this ratio, along with the upper and lower bounds of the 90 percent confidence interval, are given at the bottom of each table. This ratio gives the relative increase in the utilization rate of the comparison group when compared to the corresponding control group. If the confidence interval includes the value 1.00 then one should infer that, on the average, there is no difference in the utilization rates between the two groups. Student's t-test is provided to test the statistical significance of the differences between the utilization rates within each carrier. Large absolute values of this test statistic would indicate that the observed differences are probably not due to random chance.

Analysis of Utilization Comparison and Control Groups

Of particular concern for this utilization analysis is the occurrence of bias due to adverse selection of the comparison group of beneficiaries. This can occur either among the beneficiaries or the physicians. By using only those beneficiaries with at least one service in the calculation of the utilization rates, we have created homogenous groups, at least with respect to type and quantity of services used. This provides some protection against bias due to beneficiaries.

As to the physicians, the only information available in the BMAD data with which to test for any bias is the carrier designated specialty of the physician. Because clinical laboratory services shows the greatest increase in utilization due to physician ownership and compensation, this will be the focus of an examination of bias due to adverse physician selection. A criticism of the utilization analysis with respect to clinical laboratory services, might be that physicians, normally associated with high use of clinical laboratory services by virtue of their specialty, are the majority of those physicians establishing ownership in independent clinical laboratories. To test this, we looked at the distribution, by specialty, of the weighted proportions of physicians in both the control group and the comparison group. The weighting is across carriers. The following table gives the proportions of Medicare providers in five categories. These categories represent a recoding of the specialty codes used by Medicare carriers (see appendix D).

Weighted Distribution of Providers by Specialty and Ownership Status

Clinical Laboratory Services

Provider Type	Control Group	Comparison Group
Physicians:		
Medical, Primary Care	59.6%	50.5%
Medical, Not Primary	11.2%	10.6%
Surgeons	18.2%	16.8%
Others	4.2%	7.7%
Clinical Laboratory	3.2%	10.0%
Other Entity	3.6%	4.5%
Total	100.0%	100.0%

This table shows a decrease in the proportion of primary care physicians, an expected increase in the proportion of services delivered by clinical laboratories and an increase in the proportion of physicians in the 'Other' category. If we look at the distribution of physicians only, then the following table, again using weighted averages across carriers, is derived.

Weighted Distribution by Specialty and Ownership Status, Physicians Only

Clinical Laboratory Services

Provider Type	Control Group	Comparison Group
Physicians:		
Medical, Primary Care	64.0%	59.0%
Medical, Not Primary	12.0%	12.3%
Surgeons	19.6%	19.6%
Other	4.5%	9.0%
Total	100.0%	100.0%

This version of the table still shows the decrease in the proportion of primary care physicians and the increase among the 'Other' type of physicians. What is important in this comparison is the fact that the 'Medical, Not Primary' group of physicians contains those specialist most likely to use clinical laboratory services according to conventional wisdom. The proportion of this category in both groups is essentially equal. This would indicate that physicians normally associated with higher use of clinical laboratory services are not overrepresented in the comparison group.

Because of referrals patterns inherent in medical care delivery and the lack of referring physician identification on bills in the BMAD data, it is not possible to determine to what extent this difference in proportions might contribute to the differences seen in utilization rates for clinical laboratory services. However, the analysis represented here would indicate that the difference in utilization rates among beneficiaries is not due to any over representation of physician providers associated with greater use of these services. Thus, any bias due to adverse selection of physician providers would appear to be minimal.

Calculation of Payments

The calculation of payments associated with this report is given only for physician ownership in the case of independent clinical laboratories. To do this we must estimate a savings based on the element of selection, which for this study is the independent clinical laboratory. Thus it is not possible to make such an estimate for independent physiological laboratories as our selection was not from the BMAD data. Durable medical equipment suppliers showed no significant effect due to physician ownership.

The following table shows the number of independent clinical laboratories upon which the sampling was based, by carrier.

Carrier	Total Num. of ICLs	Number of ICLs Sampled			Prop. Owned
		Total	Unowned	Owned	
Arkansas BS	31	31	23	8	25.8%
Florida BS	141	62	41	21	33.9%
Michigan BS	88	59	47	12	20.3%
BS of Kansas City	34	34	32	2	5.9%
BS of Greater NY	102	68	56	12	17.6%
Occidental Ca	273	60	42	18	30.0%
Travelers CT	68	63	41	22	34.9%
Nationwide WVa	19	19	11	8	42.1%

Using the BMAD data, we determined the total number of beneficiaries receiving services and the total allowed amounts for all of the labs in the sample. This information is shown in the following table.

Carrier	Number of Benes.		Total Allowed	
	Unowned	Owned	Unowned	Owned
Arkansas BS	2,827	1,280	$ 110,711	$ 60,705
Florida BS	16,519	4,906	$1,075,730	$ 395,848
Michigan BS	18,629	2,180	$1,279,873	$ 176,950
BS of Kansas City	4,811	229	$ 300,417	$ 33,303
BS of Greater NY	23,390	1,633	$1,134,536	$ 80,824
Occidental Ca	8,860	1,364	$ 650,481	$ 136,146
Travelers CT	10,355	2,152	$ 543,401	$ 148,234
Nationwide WVa	830	234	$ 43,576	$ 8,864

Using these two tables, it is possible to calculate a savings per independent clinical laboratory and project this to the total estimated savings per carrier (the BMAD sample is a 5 percent sample of beneficiaries). Since each carrier, and the subsampling therein, is independent of another, a projection to the nation can be made for each carrier in the sample. The average of these individual estimates represents a valid projection to the nation for the increase in allowed amounts in 1987 that can be associated with physician ownership of independent clinical laboratories. The following table shows costs of $28.1 million due to increased utilization associated with physician ownership of independent clinical laboratories. The 90 percent confidence interval of this estimate has a lower limit of $13.7 million and an upper limit of $42.4 million.

Carrier	Sampling Fraction	Est Costs in Sample	Est Costs Per Carrier	National Estimate
Arkansas BS	1.0%	$10,577	$ 211,545	$21,154,509
Florida BS	7.4%	$76,365	$ 3,473,385	$46,937,637
Michigan BS	4.0%	$27,177	$ 810,713	$20,267,833
BS of Kansas City	0.8%	$19,004	$ 380,072	$47,509,056
BS of Greater NY	6.2%	$ 1,615	$ 48,441	$ 781,309
Occidental Ca	8.0%	$36,005	$ 3,276,421	$40,955,260
Travelers CT	1.3%	$35,303	$ 762,091	$58,622,375
Nationwide WVa	0.6%	($ 3,422)	($ 68,433)	($11,405,495)
			Average	$28,102,811
	90% Confidence Interval		Lower Limit	$13,780,546
			Upper Limit	$42,425,075

Table B1

Estimates of Rates of Physician Ownership

Carrier	Total Num. Physicians	Physicians Sampled	Active Physicians	Number Indicating Relationship	Percent of Active with Relationship
Arkansas BS	5,173	493	396	64	16.2%
Florida BS	39,905	432	313	64	20.4%
Michigan BS	21,840	420	278	25	9.0%
BS of Kansas City	3,214	449	362	19	5.2%
BS of Greater NY	38,847	474	351	18	5.1%
Occidental Ca	32,432	482	391	60	15.3%
Travelers CT	6,927	465	354	47	13.3%
Nationwide WVa	5,549	446	245	25	10.2%
			Weighted Average		11.8%

Table B2

Estimates of Rates of Physician Compensation Arrangements

Carrier	Total Num. Physicians	Physicians Sampled	Active Physicians	Number Indicating Relationship	Percent of Active with Relationship
Arkansas BS	5,173	493	396	49	12.4%
Florida BS	39,905	432	313	34	10.9%
Michigan BS	21,840	420	278	27	9.7%
BS of Kansas City	3,214	449	362	18	5.0%
BS of Greater NY	38,847	474	351	13	3.7%
Occidental Ca	32,432	482	391	26	6.6%
Travelers CT	6,927	465	354	17	4.8%
Nationwide WVa	5,549	446	245	22	9.0%
			Weighted Average		7.8%

Table B3

Comparisons based on Lab Services
All Services
Physicians with Ownership

Carrier	All Beneficiaries			Beneficiaries of Physician-Owners				
	N	Avg	Std Err	N	Avg	Std Err	Ratio	T-Test
Arkansas BS	11,135	5.3	0.06	1,196	7.0	0.25	1.32	6.612
Florida BS	73,270	8.1	0.03	7,760	11.3	0.13	1.40	23.985
Michigan BS	36,289	9.7	0.07	1,481	18.1	0.51	1.87	16.318
BS of Kansas City	8,403	5.5	0.08	274	8.6	0.59	1.56	5.207
BS of Greater NY	40,320	6.5	0.04	636	6.6	0.30	1.02	0.330
Occidental Ca	53,018	8.8	0.05	1,649	11.4	0.35	1.30	7.354
Travelers CT	14,236	6.3	0.07	1,186	10.7	0.38	1.70	11.387
Nationwide WVa	5,981	4.7	0.08	220	4.7	0.29	1.00	0.000
Weighted Averages		6.7			9.8		1.45	
	90% Confidence Interval				Lower Limit		1.28	
					Upper Limit		1.63	

Table B4

Comparisons based on Lab Services
Services from ICL Only
Physicians with Ownership

Carrier	All Beneficiaries			Beneficiaries of Physician-Owners				
	N	Avg	Std Err	N	Avg	Std Err	Ratio	T-Test
Arkansas BS	3,332	3.3	0.07	782	4.7	0.24	1.42	5.600
Florida BS	46,332	6.0	0.03	5,803	8.1	0.11	1.35	18.418
Michigan BS	22,280	8.4	0.08	1,025	12.8	0.53	1.52	8.209
BS of Kansas City	4,396	4.7	0.10	123	12.5	1.06	2.66	7.326
BS of Greater NY	25,165	5.2	0.04	455	5.0	0.26	0.96	-0.760
Occidental Ca	39,207	6.8	0.05	1,092	9.0	0.33	1.32	6.591
Travelers CT	10,121	5.5	0.08	1,013	8.5	0.34	1.55	8.589
Nationwide WVa	942	4.4	0.16	83	4.6	0.41	1.05	0.454
Weighted Averages		5.8			7.8		1.34	
	90% Confidence Interval				Lower Limit		1.04	
					Upper Limit		1.65	

Table B5

Comparisons based on LAB Services
All Services
Physicians with Compensation

Carrier	All Beneficiaries			Beneficiaries of Phy w/ Comp				
	N	Avg	Std Err	N	Avg	Std Err	Ratio	T-Test
Arkansas BS	11,135	5.3	0.06	789	6.8	0.27	1.28	5.423
Florida BS	73,270	8.1	0.03	114	8.1	0.66	1.00	0.000
Michigan BS	36,289	9.7	0.07	2,740	12.5	0.30	1.29	9.089
BS of Kansas City	8,403	5.5	0.08	178	8.5	0.93	1.55	3.214
BS of Greater NY	40,320	6.5	0.04	39	8.4	0.87	1.29	2.182
Occidental Ca	53,018	8.8	0.05	426	11.1	0.75	1.26	3.060
Travelers CT	14,236	6.3	0.07	83	10.0	1.15	1.59	3.211
Nationwide WVa	5,981	4.7	0.08	176	5.5	0.56	1.17	1.414
Weighted Averages		6.7			8.8		1.32	
	90% Confidence Interval				Lower Limit		1.21	
					Upper Limit		1.43	

Table B6

Comparisons based on LAB Services
Services from ICL Only
Physicians with Compensation

Carrier	All Beneficiaries			Beneficiaries of Phy w/ Comp				
	N	Avg	Std Err	N	Avg	Std Err	Ratio	T-Test
Arkansas BS	3,332	3.3	0.07	545	2.1	0.08	0.64	-11.289
Florida BS	46,332	6.0	0.03	83	6.2	0.58	1.03	0.344
Michigan BS	22,280	8.4	0.08	2,110	8.9	0.27	1.06	1.776
BS of Kansas City	4,396	4.7	0.10	79	6.5	1.29	1.38	1.391
BS of Greater NY	25,165	5.2	0.04	37	7.2	0.91	1.38	2.196
Occidental Ca	39,207	6.8	0.05	280	10.5	0.94	1.54	3.931
Travelers CT	10,121	5.5	0.08	72	8.2	1.08	1.49	2.493
Nationwide WVa	942	4.0	0.16	48	5.3	0.62	1.33	2.030
Weighted Averages		5.7			5.7		1.00	
	90% Confidence Interval				Lower Limit		0.82	
					Upper Limit		1.18	

Table B7

Comparisons based on DME Services
All Services
Physicians with Ownership

Carrier	All Beneficiaries			Beneficiaries of Physician-Owners				
	N	Avg	Std Err	N	Avg	Std Err	Ratio	T-Test
Arkansas BS	1,345	6.1	0.25	132	8.0	1.01	1.31	1.826
Florida BS	7,434	5.7	0.09	522	6.6	0.35	1.16	2.490
Michigan BS	3,942	7.3	0.28	24	6.3	1.57	0.86	-0.627
BS of Kansas City	776	6.5	0.36	55	4.1	0.74	0.63	-2.916
BS of Greater NY	4,703	4.9	0.15	67	7.5	1.43	1.53	1.808
Occidental Ca	5,479	6.4	0.15	247	6.5	0.60	1.02	0.162
Travelers CT	914	8.6	0.61	8	13.1	7.61	1.52	0.589
Nationwide WVa	653	6.0	0.32	29	3.7	1.03	0.62	-2.132
Weighted Averages		6.4			6.4		1.00	
	90% Confidence Interval				Lower Limit		0.79	
					Upper Limit		1.21	

Table B8

Comparisons based on DME Services
Services from DME Supplier Only
Physicians with Ownership

Carrier	All Beneficiaries			Beneficiaries of Physician-Owners				
	N	Avg	Std Err	N	Avg	Std Err	Ratio	T-Test
Arkansas BS	1,343	6.1	0.25	132	8.0	1.01	1.31	1.826
Florida BS	7,378	5.8	0.09	521	6.6	0.35	1.14	2.214
Michigan BS	3,931	7.4	0.28	24	6.3	1.57	0.85	-0.690
BS of Kansas City	773	6.5	0.36	55	4.1	0.74	0.63	-2.916
BS of Greater NY	4,671	4.9	0.15	65	7.3	1.46	1.49	1.635
Occidental Ca	5,169	6.5	0.15	230	6.1	0.60	0.94	-0.647
Travelers CT	866	8.6	0.64	7	14.1	8.71	1.64	0.630
Nationwide WVa	625	6.2	0.33	23	4.0	0.80	0.65	-2.542
Weighted Averages		6.4			6.4		1.00	
	90% Confidence Interval				Lower Limit		0.78	
					Upper Limit		1.22	

Table B9

Comparisons based on DME Services
All Services
Physicians with Compensation

Carrier	All Beneficiaries			Beneficiaries of Phy w/ Comp				
	N	Avg	Std Err	N	Avg	Std Err	Ratio	T-Test
Arkansas BS	1,345	6.1	0.25	12	7.1	2.43	1.16	0.409
Florida BS	7,434	5.7	0.09	48	6.7	1.10	1.18	0.906
Michigan BS	3,942	7.3	0.28	4	4.7	2.13	0.64	-1.210
BS of Kansas City	776	6.5	0.36	6	4.0	1.59	0.62	-1.534
BS of Greater NY	4,703	4.9	0.15	-	-	-	0.00	-
Occidental Ca	5,479	6.4	0.15	-	-	-	0.00	-
Travelers CT	914	8.6	0.61	-	-	-	0.00	-
Nationwide WVa	653	6.0	0.32	98	6.8	1.03	1.13	0.742
Weighted Averages		6.3			6.6		1.05	
	90% Confidence Interval				Lower Limit		0.74	
					Upper Limit		1.36	

Table B10

Comparisons based on DME Services
Services from DME Suppliers Only
Physicians with Compensation

Carrier	All Beneficiaries			Beneficiaries of Phy w/Comp				
	N	Avg	Std Err	N	Avg	Std Err	Ratio	T-Test
Arkansas BS	1,343	6.1	0.25	12	7.1	2.43	1.16	0.409
Florida BS	7,378	5.8	0.09	46	6.9	1.14	1.19	0.962
Michigan BS	3,931	7.4	0.28	4	4.7	2.13	0.64	-1.257
BS of Kansas City	773	6.5	0.36	6	4.0	1.59	0.62	-1.534
BS of Greater NY	4,671	4.9	0.15	-	-	-	0.00	-
Occidental Ca	5,169	6.5	0.15	-	-	-	0.00	-
Travelers CT	866	8.6	0.64	-	-	-	0.00	-
Nationwide WVa	625	6.2	0.33	93	7.0	1.07	1.13	0.714
Weighted Averages		6.4			6.8		1.07	
	90% Confidence Limit				Lower Limit		0.75	
					Upper Limit		1.38	

Table B11

Comparisons based on IPL Services
All Services
Physicians with Ownership

Carriers	All Beneficiaries			Beneficiaries of Physician-Owners				
	N	Avg	Std Err	N	Avg	Std Err	Ratio	T-Test
Arkansas BS	1,880	1.4	0.02	19	2.1	0.41	1.50	1.705
Florida BS	8,292	1.7	0.01	181	1.9	0.09	1.12	2.209
Michigan BS	10,808	1.7	0.01	183	2.0	0.10	1.18	2.985
BS of Kansas City	1,564	1.5	0.02	25	1.5	0.20	1.00	0.000
BS of Greater NY	8,417	1.6	0.01	98	2.0	0.14	1.25	2.850
Occidental Ca	9,741	1.5	0.01	712	1.7	0.04	1.13	4.851
Travelers CT	2,674	1.5	0.01	32	2.7	0.33	1.80	3.635
Nationwide WVa	1,556	1.5	0.02	94	1.5	0.10	1.00	0.000
Weighted Averages		1.5			1.7		1.13	
	90% Confidence Interval				Lower Limit		0.97	
					Upper Limit		1.29	

Table B12

Comparisons based on IPL Services
All Services
Physicians with Compensation

Carrier	All Beneficiaries			Beneficiaries of Phy w/ Comp				
	N	Avg	Std Err	N	Avg	Std Err	Ratio	T-Test
Arkansas BS	1,880	1.4	0.02	31	2.6	0.44	1.86	2.724
Florida BS	8,292	1.7	0.01	361	1.6	0.05	0.94	-1.961
Michigan BS	10,808	1.7	0.01	1,082	1.8	0.03	1.06	3.162
BS of Kansas City	1,564	1.5	0.02	134	1.9	0.12	1.27	3.288
BS of Greater NY	8,417	1.6	0.01	26	1.9	0.21	1.19	1.427
Occidental Ca	9,741	1.5	0.01	518	1.8	0.05	1.20	5.883
Travelers CT	2,674	1.5	0.01	13	1.6	0.17	1.07	0.587
Nationwide WVa	1,556	1.5	0.02	95	1.7	0.11	1.13	1.789
Weighted Averages		1.5			1.8		1.18	
	90% Confidence Interval				Lower Limit		1.01	
					Upper Limit		1.34	

APPENDIX C

HCFA COMMON PROCEDURE CODING SYSTEM (HCPCS)

Codes used to define Independent Physiological Labs.

70450	71250	71550	72125	72140
72192	72196	73200	73220	73700
73720	74150	74181	76070	76700
78000	78001	78003	78007	78010
78015	78016	78102	78103	78104
78170	78186	78202	78215	78216
78282	78290	78300	78305	78306
78310	78445	78600	78606	93258
93259	93262	93263	93266	93268
93269	93270	93720	93721	93722
93740	93850	93860	93870	93890
93910	93950	93960	M0520	M0525
M0526	M0530	M0535	M0560	M0570
M0575	M0580	M0585	M0590	M0592

Codes used to define Magnetic Resonance Imaging Services.
These Services are included in the definition of IPLs.

70540	70550	70551	70552	72141
72142	72143	72144	73221	73721
75552	76400			

APPENDIX D

RECODING OF CARRIER PROVIDER SPECIALTY

Category Created		Carrier Specialty Codes Included
Physician, Medical, Primary Care	01	General Practice
	08	Family Practice
	11	Internal Medicine
	37	Pediatrics
	38	Geriatrics
Physician, Medical, Other than Primary	03	Allergy
	06	Cardiovascular Disease
	07	Dermatology
	10	Gastroenterology
	13	Neurology
	25	Physical Medicine and Rehabilitation
	26	Psychiatry
	29	Pulmonary Disease
	30	Radiology
	36	Nuclear Medicine
	39	Nephrology
Physician, Surgeon	02	General Surgery
	04	Oncology, Laryngology, Rhinology
	14	Neurological Surgery
	16	OB - Gynecology
	18	Ophthalmology
	20	Orthopedic Surgery
	24	Plastic Surgery
	28	Proctology
	33	Thoracic Surgery
	34	Urology
	40	Hand Surgery
	48	Podiatry - Surgical Chiropody
Other Physician	05	Anesthesiology
	09	Gynecology (Osteopaths only)
	12	Manipulative Therapy (Osteopaths only)
	15	Obstetrics (Osteopaths only)
	17	Ophthalmology,Otology, Laryngology, Rhinology (Osteopaths only)
	19	Oral Surgery (Dentists only)
	21	Pathologic Anatomy; Clinical Pathology (Osteopaths only)
	22	Pathology
	23	Peripheral Vascular Diseases or Surgery (Osteopaths only)
	27	Psychiatry, Neurology (Osteopaths only)
	31	Roentgenology, Radiology (Osteopaths only)
	32	Radiation Therapy (Osteopaths only)
	35	Chiropractor, Licensed
	41	Optometrist

Category Created		Carrier Specialty Codes Included
Other Physician (cont.)	49	Miscellaneous
Clinical Laboratory	69	Independent Laboratory (Billing independently)
Other Entities	51	Medical supply company with C.O.
	52	Medical supply company with C.P.
	53	Medical supply company with C.P.O
	54	Medical supply company not included above
	55	Individual CO
	56	Individual CP
	57	Individual CPO
	58	Individuals not included in 55, 56, 57
	59	Ambulance service supplier, e.g., private
	60	Public Health or Welfare Agencies
	61	Voluntary Health or Charitable Agencies
	62	Psychologist (Billing independently)
	63	Portable X-ray Supplier (Billing independently)
	64	Audiologists (Billing independently)
	65	Physical Therapist (Billing independently)
	70	Clinic or other group practices
	87	All other, e.g., Drug and Department Store
	88	Unknown
	99	Unknown

APPENDIX E

ADDITIONAL CONTRIBUTORS TO THE REPORT

Office of Analysis and Inspections

Headquarters

Brian Ritchie
Jennifer Cryor

New York

Dawn McDonald
Tracey Kennedy
Bill Counihan

Chicago

Phillip Onofrio
Margaret Shell
Pamela May
Aquilla Box

Philadelphia

Joe Goodyear
Nancy Molyneaux

San Francisco

Neil Merino
Mollyann Brodie
Robert Gibbons
Corrinne M. Harol

Atlanta

Jim Wilson

Office of Audit

Headquarters

George Reeb
John Hapchuk
Janet Rankin
Rose Hatten

Boston

William Hornby
Herve Guerette
Hank Vanderbeek
Steve Conway
Robert Champagne

New York

Raymond J. Yak
James P. Edert
Romula Capistrano
Robert Huot
Margaret Wallace

Philadelphia

James Maiorano
Joanne Jackson
Joseph Cardamone

Atlanta

Gerald Dunhan
Bernard Rach

Chicago

Paul Swanson
Allen Peters
Tammie Anderson
Robert Templeton
Dennis Harman

Dallas

Joseph Smith
C.B. Goff

Kansas City

Dennis Dewitt
John Harrington
Gary Gunter

San Francisco

Gordon Fickel
Gerald McGee
Anna Greenhalgh
Ton Son Lam
Akop Baltayan
Paul Scott
Michael Montgomery

Office of General Counsel

Elizabeth Weiss, Thomas Crane

• B. Special Fraud Alert: Joint Venture Arrangements
(Issued August 1989)

The Office of Inspector General has become aware of a proliferation of arrangements between those in a position to refer business, such as physicians, and those providing items or services for which Medicare or Medicaid pays. Some examples of the items or services provided in these arrangements include clinical diagnostic laboratory services, durable medical equipment (DME), and other diagnostic services. Sometimes these deals are called ``joint ventures.'' A joint venture may take a variety of forms: it may be a contractual arrangement between two or more parties to cooperate in providing services, or it may involve the creation of a new legal entity by the parties, such as a limited partnership or closely held corporation, to provide such services. Of course, there may be legitimate reasons to form a joint venture, such as raising necessary investment capital. However, the Office of Inspector General believes that some of these joint ventures may violate the Medicare and Medicaid anti-kickback statute.

Under these suspect joint ventures, physicians may become investors in a newly formed joint venture entity. The investors refer their patients to this new entity, and are paid by the entity in the form of ``profit distributions.'' These subject joint ventures may be intended not so much to raise investment capital legitimately to start a business, but to lock up a stream of referrals from the physician investors and to compensate them indirectly for these referrals. Because physician investors can benefit financially from their referrals, unnecessary procedures and tests may be ordered or performed, resulting in unnecessary program expenditures.

The questionable features of these suspect joint ventures may be reflected in three areas:

(1) The manner in which investors are selected and retained;
(2) The nature of the business structure of the joint venture; and
(3) The financing and profit distributions.

Suspect Joint Ventures: What To Look For

To help you identify these suspect joint ventures, the following are examples of questionable features, which separately or taken together may result in a business arrangement that violates the anti-kickback statute. Please note that this is not intended as an exhaustive list, but rather gives examples of indicators of potentially unlawful activity.

Investor

- Investors are chosen because they are in a position to make referrals.

- Physicians who are expected to make a large number of referrals may be offered a greater investment opportunity in the joint venture than those anticipated to make fewer referrals.

- Physician investors may be actively encouraged to make referrals to the joint venture, and may be encouraged to divest their ownership interest if they fail to sustain an ``acceptable'' level of referrals.

- The joint venture tracks its sources of referrals, and distributes this information to the investors.

- Investors may be required to divest their ownership interest if they cease to practice in the service area, for example, if they move, become disabled or retire.

- Investment interests may be nontransferable.

Business Structure

- The structure of some joint ventures may be suspect. For example, one of the parties may be an ongoing entity already engaged in a particular line of business. That party may act as the reference laboratory or DME supplier for the joint venture. In some of these cases, the joint venture can be best characterized as a ``shell.''

- In the case of a shell laboratory joint venture, for example:

--It conducts very little testing on the premises, even though it is Medicare certified.
--The reference laboratory may do the vast bulk of the testing at its central processing laboratory, even though it also serves as the ``manager'' of the shell laboratory.
--Despite the location of the actual testing, the local ``shell'' laboratory bills Medicare directly for these tests.

- In the case of a shell DME joint venture, for example:
--It owns very little of the DME or other capital equipment; rather the ongoing entity owns them.
--The ongoing entity is responsible for all day-to-day operations of the joint venture, such as delivery of the DME and billing.

Financing and Profit Distribution

- The amount of capital invested by the physician may be disproportionately small and the returns on investment may be disproportionately large when compared to a typical investment in a new business enterprise.

- Physician investors may invest only a nominal amount, such as $500 to $1500.

- Physician investors may be permitted to ``borrow'' the amount of the ``investment'' from the entity, and pay it back through deductions from profit distributions, thus eliminating even the need to contribute cash to the partnership.

- Investors may be paid extraordinary returns on the investment in comparison with the risk involved, often well over 50 to 100 percent per year.

[Federal Register: December 19, 1994]

DEPARTMENT OF HEALTH AND HUMAN SERVICES

Publication of OIG Special Fraud Alerts

AGENCY: Office of Inspector General, HHS.
ACTION: Notice.

SUMMARY: This Federal Register notice sets forth the 5 previously-developed Special Fraud Alerts issued directly to the health care provider community by the HHS Office of Inspector General (OIG). In keeping with the OIG's goal and intent of publicizing its concern about possible widespread and abusive health care industry practices, and seeking wider dissemination of this information to the general public, we are republishing the main content of these Special Fraud Alerts in the Federal Register. This notice also serves to alert the general public of our intention to publish all future OIG Special Fraud Alerts in this same manner, in addition to the current method used to distribute this material to Medicare and State health care program providers.

FOR FURTHER INFORMATION CONTACT: Joel J. Schaer, Legislation, Regulations and Public Affairs Staff, (202) 619-0089.

SUPPLEMENTARY INFORMATION:

I. Background

The Use of Fraud Alerts by the OIG

Over the years, the OIG has used fraud alerts as a vehicle to identify fraudulent and abusive practices within the health care industry. The majority of these fraud alerts are disseminated internally to the OIG's Office of Investigations and other agencies within the Department. However, the OIG has also developed and issued Special Fraud Alerts intended for extensive distribution directly to the health care provider community.

Special Fraud Alerts

Since 1988, the OIG has issued 5 ``Special Fraud Alerts'' addressing specific trends of health care fraud and certain practices of an industry-wide character. Specifically, the OIG Special Fraud Alerts have served to provide general guidance to the health care industry on violations of Federal law (including various aspects of the anti-kickback statute), as well as to provide additional insight to the Medicare carrier fraud units in identifying health care fraud schemes.

In developing these Special Fraud Alerts, the OIG relies on a number of sources, such as studies or management and program evaluations conducted by the OIG's Office of Evaluation and Inspections. In addition, the OIG may consult with experts in the subject field, including those within the OIG, other agencies of the Department, other Federal and State agencies, and from those in the health care industry.

The Nature of Past Special Fraud Alerts

For the most part, the OIG Special Fraud Alerts have been reserved for national trends in health care fraud and have addressed potential violations of the Medicare and State health care programs' anti-kickback statute. The Special Fraud Alerts have addressed the following topic areas that could violate the anti-kickback statute:

- Joint venture arrangements;
- Routine waiver of Medicare Part B copayments and deductibles;
- Hospital incentives to referring physicians;
- Prescription drug marketing practices;
- Arrangements for the provision of clinical laboratory services.

II. Federal Register Publication of Special Fraud Alerts

In the past, the OIG has always printed and distributed copies of these Special Fraud Alerts directly to all Medicare program providers. While the OIG Special Fraud Alerts have been designed to be available to all affected program providers, we believe it is useful to publicize these various issues and concerns involving potential abusive health care industry practices to a more widespread audience. For this reason, we are using this Federal Register notice as a vehicle to reprint the substance of the 5 previously-issued Special Fraud Alerts cited above. It is our intention to use this same Federal Register form for publishing future Special Fraud Alerts developed by the OIG.

Because each of the previously-developed Special Fraud Alerts contained a similar brief narrative as to the nature of the OIG and a description of the Medicare and Medicaid anti-kickback statute, we will first summarize and set out this material in one section, as it is germane to all 5 subject issuances. Following that will be the main body and content of each of the Special Fraud Alerts. Lastly, we have provided the general information set forth in each of these Special Fraud Alerts addressing information on how to report information on suspected violations.

The OIG Special Fraud Alerts

A. General Background

The Office of Inspector General was established at the Department of Health and Human Services by Congress in 1976 to identify and eliminate fraud, abuse and waste in Health and Human Services programs and to promote efficiency and economy in departmental operations. The OIG carries out this mission through a nationwide program of audits, investigations and inspections. To help reduce fraud in the Medicare and Medicaid programs, the OIG is actively investigating violations of the Medicare and Medicaid anti-kickback statute, 42 U.S.C. Section 1320a-7b(b).

What Is the Medicare and Medicaid Anti-Kickback Law?

Among its provisions, the anti-kickback statute penalizes anyone who knowingly and willfully solicits, receives, offers or pays remuneration in cash or in kind to induce, or in return for:

A. Referring an individual to a person for the furnishing, or arranging for the furnishing, of any item or service payable under the Medicare or Medicaid program; or

B. Purchasing, leasing or ordering , or arranging for or recommending purchasing, leasing or ordering, any goods, facility, service or item payable under the Medicare or Medicaid program.

Violators are subject to criminal penalties, or exclusion from participation in the Medicare and Medicaid programs, or both. In 1987, section 14 of the Medicare and Medicaid Patient and Program Protection Act, PL 100-93, directed this Department to promulgate ``safe harbor'' regulations, in order to provide health care providers a mechanism to assure them that they will not be prosecuted under the anti-kickback statute for engaging in particular practices. The Department published 11 final ``safe harbor'' regulations on July 29, 1991 (42 CFR 1001.952, 56 FR 35952), and two more on November 5, 1992 (42 CFR 1001.952, 57 FR 52723). The scope of the anti-kickback statute is not expanded by the ``safe harbor'' regulations; these regulations give those in good faith compliance with a ``safe harbor'' the assurance that they will not be prosecuted under the anti-kickback statute.

B. Special Fraud Alert: Joint Venture Arrangements
(Issued August 1989)

The Office of Inspector General has become aware of a proliferation of arrangements between those in a position to refer business, such as physicians, and those providing items or services for which Medicare or Medicaid pays. Some examples of the items or services provided in these arrangements include clinical diagnostic laboratory services, durable medical equipment (DME), and other diagnostic services. Sometimes these deals are called ``joint ventures.'' A joint venture may take a variety of forms: it may be a contractual arrangement between two or more parties to cooperate in providing services, or it may involve the creation of a new legal entity by the parties, such as a limited partnership or closely held corporation, to provide such services. Of course, there may be legitimate reasons to form a joint venture, such as raising necessary investment capital. However, the Office of Inspector General believes that some of these joint ventures may violate the Medicare and Medicaid anti-kickback statute.

Under these suspect joint ventures, physicians may become investors in a newly formed joint venture entity. The investors refer their patients to this new entity, and are paid by the entity in the form of ``profit distributions.'' These subject joint ventures may be intended not so much to raise investment capital legitimately to start a business, but to lock up a stream of referrals from the physician investors and to compensate them indirectly for these referrals. Because physician investors can benefit financially from their referrals, unnecessary procedures and tests may be ordered or performed, resulting in unnecessary program expenditures.

The questionable features of these suspect joint ventures may be reflected in three areas:

(1) The manner in which investors are selected and retained;
(2) The nature of the business structure of the joint venture; and
(3) The financing and profit distributions.

Suspect Joint Ventures: What To Look For

To help you identify these suspect joint ventures, the following are examples of questionable features, which separately or taken together may result in a business arrangement that violates the anti-kickback statute. Please note that this is not intended as an exhaustive list, but rather gives examples of indicators of potentially unlawful activity.

Investor

- Investors are chosen because they are in a position to make referrals.

- Physicians who are expected to make a large number of referrals may be offered a greater investment opportunity in the joint venture than those anticipated to make fewer referrals.

- Physician investors may be actively encouraged to make referrals to the joint venture, and may be encouraged to divest their ownership interest if they fail to sustain an ``acceptable'' level of referrals.

- The joint venture tracks its sources of referrals, and distributes this information to the investors.

- Investors may be required to divest their ownership interest if they cease to practice in the service area, for example, if they move, become disabled or retire.

- Investment interests may be nontransferable.

Business Structure

- The structure of some joint ventures may be suspect. For example, one of the parties may be an ongoing entity already engaged in a particular line of business. That party may act as the reference laboratory or DME supplier for the joint venture. In some of these cases, the joint venture can be best characterized as a ``shell.''

- In the case of a shell laboratory joint venture, for example:

--It conducts very little testing on the premises, even though it is Medicare certified.
--The reference laboratory may do the vast bulk of the testing at its central processing laboratory, even though it also serves as the ``manager'' of the shell laboratory.
--Despite the location of the actual testing, the local ``shell'' laboratory bills Medicare directly for these tests.

- In the case of a shell DME joint venture, for example:
--It owns very little of the DME or other capital equipment; rather the ongoing entity owns them.
--The ongoing entity is responsible for all day-to-day operations of the joint venture, such as delivery of the DME and billing.

Financing and Profit Distribution

- The amount of capital invested by the physician may be disproportionately small and the returns on investment may be disproportionately large when compared to a typical investment in a new business enterprise.

- Physician investors may invest only a nominal amount, such as $500 to $1500.

- Physician investors may be permitted to ``borrow'' the amount of the ``investment'' from the entity, and pay it back through deductions from profit distributions, thus eliminating even the need to contribute cash to the partnership.

- Investors may be paid extraordinary returns on the investment in comparison with the risk involved, often well over 50 to 100 percent per year.

C. Special Fraud Alert: Routine Waiver of Copayments or Deductibles Under Medicare Part B
(Issued May 1991)

To help reduce fraud in the Medicare program, the Office of Inspector General is actively investigating health care providers, practitioners and suppliers of health care items and services who (1) are paid on the basis of charges\1\ and (2) routinely waive (do not bill) Medicare deductible and copayment charges to beneficiaries for items and services covered by the Medicare program.

\1\This fraud alert is not intended to address the routine waiver of copayments and deductibles by providers, practitioners or suppliers who are paid on the basis of costs or diagnostic related groups. The fact that these types of services are not discussed in this fraud alert should not be interpreted to legitimize routine waiver of deductibles and copayments with respect to these payment methods. Also, it does not apply to a waiver of any copayment by a Federally qualified health care center with respect to an individual who qualifies for subsidized services under a provision of the Public Health Service Act.

What Are Medicare Deductible and Copayment Charges?

The Medicare ``deductible'' is the amount that must be paid by a Medicare beneficiary before Medicare will pay for any items or services for that individual. Currently, the Medicare Part B deductible is $100 per year.

``Copayment'' (``coinsurance'') is the portion of the cost of an item or service which the Medicare beneficiary must pay. Currently, the Medicare Part B coinsurance is generally 20 percent of the reasonable charge for the item or service. Typically, if the Medicare reasonable charge for a Part B item or service is $100, the Medicare beneficiary (who has met his [or her] deductible) must pay $20 of the physician's bill, and Medicare will pay $80.

Why Is it Illegal for ``Charged-Based'' Providers, Practitioners and Suppliers to Routinely Waive Medicare Copayment and Deductibles?

Routine waiver of deductibles and copayments by charge-based providers, practitioners or suppliers is unlawful because it results in (1) false claims, (2) violations of the anti-kickback statute, and (3) excessive utilization of items and services paid for by Medicare.

A ``charge-based'' provider, practitioner or supplier is one who is paid by Medicare on the basis of the ``reasonable charge'' for the item or service provided. 42 U.S.C. 1395u(b)(3); 42 CFR 405.501. Medicare typically pays 80 percent of the reasonable charge. 42 U.S.C. 1395l(a)(1). The criteria for determining what charges are reasonable are contained in regulations, and include an examination of (1) the actual charge for the item or service, (2) the customary charge for the item or service, (3) the prevailing charge in the same locality for similar items or services. The Medicare reasonable charge cannot exceed the actual charge for the item or service, and may generally not exceed the customary charge or the highest prevailing charge for the item or service. In some cases, the provider, practitioner or supplier will be paid the lesser of his [or her] actual charge or an amount established by a fee schedule.

A provider, practitioner or supplier who routinely waives Medicare copayments or deductibles is misstating its actual charge. For example, if a supplier claims that its charge for a piece of equipment is $100, but routinely waives the copayment, the actual charge is $80. Medicare should be paying 80 percent of $80 (or $64), rather than 80 percent of $100 (or $80). As a result of the supplier's misrepresentation, the Medicare program is paying $16 more than it should for this item.

In certain cases, a provider, practitioner or supplier who routinely waives Medicare copayments or deductibles also could be held liable under the Medicare and Medicaid anti-kickback statute. 42 U.S.C. 1320a-7b(b). The statute makes it illegal to offer, pay, solicit or receive anything of value as an inducement to generate business payable by Medicare or Medicaid. When providers, practitioners or suppliers forgive financial obligations for reasons other than genuine financial hardship of the particular patient, they may be unlawfully inducing that patient to purchase items or services from them.

At first glance, it may appear that routine waiver of copayments and deductibles helps Medicare beneficiaries. By waiving Medicare copayments and deductibles, the provider of services may claim that the beneficiary incurs no costs. In fact, this is not true. Studies have shown that if patients are required to pay even a small portion of their care, they will be better health care consumers, and select items or services because they are medically needed, rather than simply because they are free. Ultimately, if Medicare pays more for an item or service than it should, or if it pays for unnecessary items or services, there are less Medicare funds available to pay for truly needed services.

One important exception to the prohibition against waiving copayments and deductibles is that providers, practitioners or suppliers may forgive the copayment in consideration of a particular patient's financial hardship. This hardship exception, however, must not be used routinely; it should be used occasionally to address the special financial needs of a particular patient. Except in such special cases, a good faith effort to collect deductibles and copayments must be made. Otherwise, claims submitted to Medicare mat violate the statutes discussed above and other provisions of the law.

What Penalties Can Someone Be Subject to for Routinely Waiving Medicare Copayments or Deductibles?

Whoever submits a false claim to the Medicare program (for example, a claim misrepresents an actual charge) may be subject to criminal, civil or administrative liability for making false statements and/or submitting false claims to the Government. 18 U.S.C. 287 and 1001; 31 U.S.C. 3729; 42 CFR 1320a-7a). Penalties can include imprisonment, criminal fines, civil damages and forfeitures, civil monetary penalties and exclusion from Medicare and the State health care programs.

In addition, anyone who routinely waives copayments or deductibles can be criminally prosecuted under 42 U.S.C. 1320a-7b(b), and excluded from participating in Medicare and the State health care programs under the anti-kickback statute. 42 U.S.C. 1320a-7(b)(7).

Finally, anyone who furnishes items or services to patient substantially in excess of the needs of such patients can be excluded from Medicare and the State health care programs. 42 U.S.C. 1320a-7(b)(6)(B).

Indications of Improper Waiver of Deductibles and Copayments

To help you identify charge-based providers, practitioners or suppliers who routinely waive Medicare deductibles and copayments, listed below are some suspect marketing practices. Please note that this list is not intended to be exhaustive but, rather, to highlight some indicators of potentially unlawful activity.

- Advertisements which state: ``Medicare Accepted As Payment in Full,'' ``Insurance Accepted As Payment in Full,'' or ``No Out-Of-Pocket Expense.''

- Advertisements which promise that ``discounts'' will be given to Medicare beneficiaries.

- Routine use of ``Financial hardship'' forms which state that the beneficiary is unable to pay the coinsurance/deductible (i.e., there is no good faith attempt to determine the beneficiary's actual financial condition).

- Collection of copayments and deductibles only where the beneficiary has Medicare supplemental insurance (``Medigap'') coverage (i.e., the items or services are ``free'' to the beneficiary).

- Charges to Medicare beneficiaries which are higher than those made to other persons for similar services and items (the higher charges offset the waiver of coinsurance.)

- Failure to collect copayments or deductibles for a specific group of Medicare patients for reasons unrelated to indigency (e.g., a supplier waives coinsurance or deductible for all patients from a particular hospital, in order to get referrals).

- ``Insurance programs'' which cover copayments or deductibles only for items or services provided by the entity offering the insurance. The ``insurance premium'' paid by the beneficiary is insignificant and can be as low as $1 a month or even $1 a year. These premiums are not based upon actuarial risks, but instead are a sham used to disguise the routine waiver of copayments and deductibles.

D. Special Fraud Alert: Hospital Incentives to Physicians
(Issued May 1992)

Why Do Hospitals Provide Economic Incentives to Physicians?

As many hospitals have become more aggressive in their attempts to recruit and retain physicians and increase patient referrals, physician incentives (sometimes referred to as ``practice enhancements'') are becoming increasingly common. Some physicians actively solicit such incentives. These incentives may result in reductions in the physician's professional expenses or an increase in his or her revenues. In exchange, the physician is aware that he or she is often expected to refer the majority, if not all, of his or her patients to the hospital providing the incentives.

Why Is it Illegal for Hospitals to Provide Financial Incentives to Physicians for Their Referrals?

The Office of Inspector General has become aware of a variety of hospital incentive programs used to compensate physicians (directly or indirectly) for referring patients to the hospital. These arrangements are implicated by the anti-kickback statute because they can constitute remuneration offered to induce, or in return for, the referral of business paid for by Medicare or Medicaid. In addition, they are not protected under the existing ``safe harbor'' regulations.

These incentive programs can interfere with the physician's judgment of what is the most appropriate care for a patient. They can inflate costs to the Medicare program by causing physicians to overuse inappropriately the services of a particular hospital. The incentives may result in the delivery of inappropriate care to Medicare beneficiaries and Medicaid recipients by inducing the physician to refer patients to the hospital providing financial incentives rather than to another hospital (or non-acute care facility) offering the best or most appropriate care for that patient.

Suspect Hospital Incentive Arrangements--What To Look For

To help identify suspect incentive arrangements, examples of practices which are often questionable are listed [below]. Please note that this list is not intended to be exhaustive but, rather, to suggest some indicators of potentially unlawful activity.

- Payment of any sort of incentive by the hospital each time a physician refers a patient to the hospital.

- The use of free or significantly discounted office space or equipment (in facilities usually located close to the hospital).

- Provision of free or significantly discounted billing, nursing or other staff services.

- Free training for a physician's office staff in such areas as management techniques, CPT coding and laboratory techniques.

- Guarantees which provide that, if the physician's income fails to reach a predetermined level, the hospital will supplement the remainder up to a certain amount.

- Low-interest or interest-free loans, or loans which may be ``forgiven'' if a physician refers patients (or some number of patients) to the hospital.

- Payment of the cost of a physician's travel and expenses for conferences.

- Payment for a physician's continuing education courses.

- Coverage on hospitals' group health insurance plans at an inappropriately low cost to the physician.

- Payment for services (which may include consultations at the hospital) which require few, if any, substantive duties by the physician, or payment for services in excess of the fair market value of services rendered.

Financial incentive packages which incorporate these or similar features may be subject to prosecution under the Medicare and Medicaid anti-kickback statute, if one of the purposes of the incentive is to influence the physician's medical decision as to where to refer his or her patients for treatment.

E. Special Fraud Alert: Prescription Drug Marketing Schemes (Issued August 1994)

How Does the Anti-Kickback Law Relate to Prescription Drug Marketing Schemes?

In recent years, prescription drug companies in the United States have increased their marketing activities among providers, patients and suppliers such as pharmacies. Many prescription drug marketing activities go far beyond traditional advertising and educational contacts. Physicians, suppliers and, increasingly, patients are being offered valuable, non-medical benefits in exchange for selecting specific prescription drug brands. Traditionally, physicians and pharmacists have been trusted to provide treatments and recommend products in the best interest of the patient. In an era of aggressive drug marketing, however, patients may now be using prescription drug items, unaware that their physician or pharmacist is being compensated for promoting the selection of a specific product. Prescription drugs supplied under one of these programs are often reimbursed under Medicaid. Among the specific activities, which the OIG has identified, are the following actual cases:

- A ``product conversion'' program which resulted in 96,000 brand-name conversions. In this scenario, for instance, Drug Company A offered a cash award to pharmacies for each time a drug prescription was changed from Drug Company B's product to Drug Company A's product. The pharmacies were induced to help persuade physicians, who were unaware of the pharmacies' financial interest, to change prescription.

- A ``frequent flier'' campaign in which physicians were given credit toward airline frequent flier mileage each time the physician completed a questionnaire for a new patient placed on the drug company's product.

- A ``research grant'' program in which physicians were given substantial payments for de minimis recordkeeping tasks. The physician administered the drug manufacturer's product to the patient and made brief notes, sometimes a single word, about the treatment outcome. Upon completion of a limited number of such ``studies,'' the physician received payment from the manufacturer.

If one purpose of any of these marketing schemes is to induce the provision of a prescription drug item reimbursable by Medicaid, then the criminal anti-kickback statute is implicated. There is no statutory exception or ``safe harbor'' to protect such activities. Thus a physician, pharmacy or other practitioner or supplier receiving payment under these activities may be subject to criminal prosecution and exclusion from participation in the Medicare and Medicaid programs.

A marketing program that is illegal under the anti-kickback statute may pose a danger to patients because the offering or payment of remuneration may interfere with a physician's judgment in determining the most appropriate treatment for a patient. Further, where the patient is a Medicaid beneficiary, these drug marketing practices may increase the Federal government's costs of reimbursing suppliers for the products. The OIG is investigating various drug marketing schemes, and enforcing the anti-kickback laws where these practices affect the Federal health care programs.

What To Look For

Generally, a payment or gift may be considered improper under 42 U.S.C. 1320a-7b(b) if it is:

- Made to a person in a position to generate business for the paying party;

- Related to the volume of business generated; and

- More than nominal in value and/or exceeds fair market value of any legitimate service rendered to the payer, or is unrelated to any service at all other than referral of patients.

OIG investigation may be warranted where one or more of the following features is present in prescription drug marketing activities:

- Any prize, gift or cash payment, coupon or bonus (e.g., airline discounts and related travel premiums), offered to physicians and/or suppliers (including pharmacies, mail order prescription drug companies and managed care organizations) in exchange for, or based on, prescribing or providing specific prescription products. These items are particularly suspect if based on value or volume of business generated for the drug company.

- Materials which offer cash or other benefits to pharmacists (or others in a position to recommend prescription drug products) in exchange for performing marketing tasks in the course of pharmacy practice related to Medicare or Medicaid. The marketing tasks may include sales-oriented ``educational'' or ``counseling'' contacts, or physician and/or patient outreach, etc.

- Grants to physicians and clinicians for studies of prescription products when the studies are of questionable scientific value and require little or no actual scientific pursuit. The grants may nonetheless offer substantial benefits based on, or related to, use of the product.

- Any payment, including cash or other benefit, given to a patient, provider or supplier for changing a prescription, or recommending or requesting such a change, from one product to another, unless the payment is made fully consistent with a ``safe harbor'' regulation, 42 CFR 1001.952, or other Federal provision governing the reporting of prescription drug prices.

F. Special Fraud Alert: Arrangements for the Provision of Clinical Lab Services
(Issued October 1994)

How Does the Anti-Kickback Statute Relate to Arrangements for the Provision of Clinical Lab Services?

Many physicians and other health care providers rely on the services of outside clinical laboratories to which they may refer high volumes of patient specimens every day. The quality, timeliness and cost of these services are of obvious concern to Medicare and Medicaid patients and to the programs that finance their health care services. Since the physician, not the patient, generally selects the clinical laboratory, it is essential that the physician's decision regarding where to refer specimens is based only on the best interests of the patient.

Whenever a laboratory offers or gives to a source of referrals anything of value not paid for at fair market value, the inference may be made that the thing of value is offered to induce the referral of business. The same is true whenever a referral source solicits or receives anything of value from the laboratory. By ``fair market value'' we mean value for general commercial purposes. However, ``fair market value'' must reflect an arms length transaction which has not been adjusted to include the additional value which one or both of the parties has attributed to the referral of business between them.

The office of Inspector General has become aware of a number of practices engaged in by clinical laboratories and health care providers that implicate the anti-kickback statute in this manner. Below are some examples of lab services arrangements that may violate the anti-kickback statute.

Provision of Phlebotomy Services to Physicians

When permitted by State law, a laboratory may make available to a physician's office a phlebotomist who collects specimens from patients for testing by the outside laboratory. While the mere placement of a laboratory employee in the physician's office would not necessarily serve as an inducement prohibited by the anti-kickback statute, the statute is implicated when the phlebotomist performs additional tasks that are normally the responsibility of the physician's office staff. These tasks can include taking vital signs or other nursing functions, testing for the physician's office laboratory, or performing clerical services.

Where the phlebotomist performs clerical or medical functions not directly related to the collection or processing of laboratory specimens, a strong inference arises that he or she is providing a benefit in return for the physician's referrals to the laboratory. In such a case, the physician, the phlebotomist, and the laboratory may have exposure under the anti-kickback statute. This analysis applies equally to the placement of phlebotomists in other health care settings, including nursing homes, clinics and hospitals.

Furthermore, the mere existence of a contract between the laboratory and the health care provider that prohibits the phlebotomist from performing services unrelated to specimen collection does not eliminate the OIG's concern, where the phlebotomist is not closely monitored by his [of her] employer or where the contractual prohibition is not rigorously enforced.

Lab Pricing at Renal Dialysis Centers

The Medicare program pays for laboratory tests provided to patients with end stage renal disease (ESRD) in two different ways. Some laboratory testing is considered routine and payment is included in the composite rate paid by Medicare to the ESRD facility which in turn pays the laboratory. Some laboratory testing required by the patient is not included in the composite rate, and these additional tests are billed by the laboratory directly to Medicare and paid at the usual laboratory fee schedule price.

The OIG is aware of cases where a laboratory offers to perform the tests encompassed by the composite rate at a price below fair market value of the tests performed. In order to offset the low charges on the composite rate tests, the ESRD facility agrees to refer all or most of its non-composite rate tests to the laboratory. This arrangement appears to be an offer of something of value (composite rate tests below fair market value) in return for the ordering of additional tests which are billed directly to the Medicare program.

If offered or accepted in return for referral of additional business, the lab's pricing scheme is illegal remuneration under the anti-kickback statute. The statutory exception and ``safe harbor'' for ``discounts'' does not apply to immunize parties to this type of transaction, since discounts on the composite rate tests are offered to induce referral of other tests. See 42 CFR 1001.952(h)(3)(ii).

Waiver of Charges To Managed Care Patients

Managed care plans may require a physician or other health care provider to use only the laboratory with which the plan has negotiated a fee schedule. In such situations, the plan usually will refuse to pay claims submitted by other laboratories. The provider, however, may use a different laboratory and may wish to continue to use that laboratory for non-managed care patients. In order to retain the provider as a client, the laboratory that does not have the managed care contract may agree to perform the managed care work free of charge.

The status of such agreements under the anti-kickback statute depends in part on the nature of the contractual relationship between the managed care plan and its providers. Under the terms of many managed care contracts, a provider receives a bonus or other payment if utilization of ancillary services, such as laboratory testing, is kept below a particular level. Other managed care plans impose financial penalties if the provider's utilization of services exceeds pre-established levels. When the laboratory agrees to write off charges for the physician's managed care work, the physician may realize a financial benefit from the managed care plan created by the appearance that utilization of tests has been reduced.

In cases where the provision of free services results in a benefit to the provider, the anti-kickback statute is implicated. If offered or accepted in return for the referral of Medicare or State health care plan business, both the laboratory and the physician may be violating the anti-kickback statute. There is no statutory exception or ``safe harbor'' to immunize any party to such a practice because the Federal programs do not realize the benefit of these ``free'' services. See 42 CFR 1001.952(h)(3)(iii).

Other Inducements

The following are additional examples of inducements offered by clinical laboratories which may implicate the anti-kickback statute:

- Free pick-up and disposal of bio-hazardous waste products (such as sharps) unrelated to the collection of specimens for the outside laboratory.

- Provision of computers or fax machines, unless such equipment is integral to, and exclusively used for, performance of the outside laboratory's work.

- Provision of free laboratory testing for health care providers, their families and their employees.

When one purpose of these arrangements is to induce the referral of program-reimbursed laboratory testing, both the clinical laboratory and the health care provider may be liable under the statute and may be subject to criminal prosecution and exclusion from participation in the Medicare and Medicaid programs.

G. Reporting Information

What To Do If You Have Information About Suspect Activities or Arrangements

If you have information about health care providers, practitioners, entities or other persons engaging in these types of activities or arrangements described above, contact any of the regional offices of the Office of Investigations of the Office of Inspector General, U.S. Department of Health and Human Services, at the following locations:

Regions	States served	Telephone
Boston..............	MA, VT, NH, ME, RI, CT...........	617-565-2660
New York............	NY, NJ, PR, VI...................	212-264-1691
Philadelphia........	PA, MD, DE, WV, VA...............	215-596-6796
Atlanta.............	GA, KY, NC, SC, FL, TN, AL, MS (No. District).	404-331-2131
Chicago.............	IL, MN, WI, MI, IN, OH, IA, MO....	312-353-2740
Dallas..............	TX, NM, OK, AR, LA, MS (So. District).	214-767-8406
Denver..............	CO, UT, WY, MT, ND, SD, NE, KS....	303-844-5621
Los Angeles.........	AZ, NV (Clark Co.), So. CA........	714-836-2372
San Francisco.......	No. CA, NV, AZ, HI, OR, ID, WA....	415-556-8880
Washington, DC......	DC and Metropolitan areas of VA and MD.	202-619-1900

Dated: December 2, 1994.
June Gibbs Brown,
Inspector General.
[FR Doc. 94-31157 Filed 12-16-94; 8:45 am]
BILLING CODE 4150-04-P

OFFICE OF INSPECTOR GENERAL

Special Fraud Alert

RENTAL OF SPACE IN PHYSICIAN OFFICES BY PERSONS OR ENTITIES TO WHICH PHYSICIANS REFER

February 2000

The Office of Inspector General (OIG) was established at the Department of Health and Human Services by Congress in 1976 to identify and eliminate fraud, abuse and waste in the Department's programs and to promote efficiency and economy in departmental operations. The OIG carries out this mission through a nationwide program of audits, investigations and inspections.

To reduce fraud and abuse in the Federal health care programs, including Medicare and Medicaid, the OIG actively investigates fraudulent schemes that are used to obtain money from these programs and, when appropriate, issues Special Fraud Alerts that identify practices in the health care industry that are particularly vulnerable to abuse.

This Special Fraud Alert focuses on the rental of space in physicians' offices by persons or entities that provide health care items or services (suppliers)[(1)] to patients that are referred either directly or indirectly by their physician-landlords. In this Special Fraud Alert, we describe some of the potentially illegal practices the OIG has identified in such rental relationships.

Questionable Rental Arrangements For Space in Physician Offices

A number of suppliers that provide health care items or services rent space in the offices of physicians or other practitioners. Typically, most of the items or services provided in the rented space are for patients, referred or sent, either directly or indirectly, to the supplier by the physician-landlord. In particular, we are aware of rental arrangements between physician-landlords and:

- comprehensive outpatient rehabilitation facilities (CORFs) that provide physical and occupational therapy and speech-language pathology services in physicians' and other practitioners' offices;
- mobile diagnostic equipment suppliers that perform diagnostic related tests in physicians' offices; and
- suppliers of durable medical equipment, prosthetics, orthotics and supplies (DMEPOS) that set up "consignment closets" for their supplies in physicians' offices.

The OIG is concerned that in such arrangements, the rental payments may be disguised kickbacks to the physician-landlords to induce referrals. We have received numerous credible reports that in many cases, suppliers, whose businesses depend on physicians' referrals, offer and pay "rents" -- either voluntarily or in response to physicians' requests -- that are either unnecessary or in excess of the fair market value for the space to access the physicians' potential referrals.

The Anti-Kickback Law Prohibits Any Payments to Induce Referrals

Kickbacks can distort medical decision-making, cause overutilization, increase costs and result in unfair competition by freezing out competitors who are unwilling to pay kickbacks. Kickbacks can also adversely affect the quality of patient care by encouraging physicians to order services or recommend supplies based on profit rather than the patients' best medical interests.

Section 1128B(b) of the Social Security Act (the Act) prohibits knowingly and willfully soliciting, receiving, offering or paying anything of value to induce referrals of items or services payable by a Federal health care program. Both parties to an impermissible kickback transaction are liable. Violation of the statute constitutes a felony punishable by a maximum fine of $25,000, imprisonment up to five years, or both. The OIG may also initiate administrative proceedings to exclude persons from Federal health care programs or to impose civil money penalties for fraud, kickbacks and other prohibited activities under sections 1128(b)(7) and 1128A(a)(7) of the Act.[(2)]

Suspect Rental Arrangements For Space in Physician Offices

The questionable features of suspect rental arrangements for space in physicians' offices may be reflected in three areas:

- the appropriateness of rental agreements;
- the rental amounts; and
- time and space considerations.

Below, we examine these suspect areas, which separately or together may result in an arrangement that violates the anti-kickback statute, in order to help identify questionable rental arrangements between physicians and the suppliers to which they refer patients. This list is not exhaustive, but rather gives examples of indicators of potentially unlawful activity.

Appropriateness of Rental Agreements. The threshold inquiry when examining rental payments is whether payment for rent is appropriate at all. Payments of "rent" for space that traditionally has been provided for free or for a nominal charge as an accommodation between the parties for the benefit of the physicians' patients, such as consignment closets for DMEPOS, may be disguised kickbacks. In general, payments for rent of consignment closets in physicians' offices are suspect.[(3)]

Rental Amounts. Rental amounts should be at fair market value, be fixed in advance and not take into account, directly or indirectly, the volume or value of referrals or other business generated between the parties. Fair market value rental payments should not exceed the amount paid for comparable property. Moreover, where a physician rents space, the rate paid by the supplier should not exceed the rate paid by the physicians in the primary lease for their office space, except in rare circumstances. Examples of suspect arrangements include:

- rental amounts in excess of amounts paid for comparable property rented in arms-length transactions between persons not in a position to refer business;
- rental amounts for subleases that exceed the rental amounts per square foot in the primary lease;
- rental amounts that are subject to modification more often than annually;
- rental amounts that vary with the number of patients or referrals;
- rental arrangements that set a fixed rental fee per hour, but do not fix the number of hours or the schedule of usage in advance (i.e., "as needed" arrangements);

- rental amounts that are only paid if there are a certain number of Federal health care program beneficiaries referred each month; and
- rental amounts that are conditioned upon the supplier's receipt of payments from a Federal health care program.

Time and Space Considerations. Suppliers should only rent premises of a size and for a time that is reasonable and necessary for a commercially reasonable business purpose of the supplier. Rental of space that is in excess of suppliers' needs creates a presumption that the payments may be a pretext for giving money to physicians for their referrals. Examples of suspect arrangements include:

- rental amounts for space that is unnecessary or not used. For instance, a CORF requires one examination room and rents physician office space one afternoon a week when the physician is not in the office. The CORF calculates its rental payment on the square footage for the entire office, since it is the only occupant during that time, even though the CORF only needs one examination room;
- rental amounts for time when the rented space is not in use by the supplier. For example, an ultrasound supplier has enough business to support the use of one examination room for four hours each week, but rents the space for an amount equivalent to eight hours per week;
- non-exclusive occupancy of the rented portion of space. For example, a physical therapist does not rent space in a physician's office, but rather moves from examination room to examination room treating patients after they have been seen by the physician. Since no particular space is rented, we will closely scrutinize the proration of time and space used to calculate the therapist's "rent".

In addition, rental amount calculations should prorate rent based on the amount of space and duration of time the premises are used. The basis for any proration should be documented and updated as necessary. Depending on the circumstances, the supplier's rent can consist of three components: (1) exclusive office space; (2) interior office common space; and (3) building common space.

1. Apportionment of exclusive office space - The supplier's rent should be calculated based on the ratio of the time the space is in use by the supplier to the total amount of time the physician's office is in use. In addition, the rent should be calculated based on the ratio of the amount of space that is used exclusively by the supplier to the total amount of space in the physician's office. For example, where a supplier rents an examination room for four hours one afternoon per week in a physician's office that has four examination rooms of equal size and is open eight hours a day, five days per week, the supplier's prorated annual rent would be calculated as follows:

Physician Office Rent Per Day		**% of Physician Office Space Rented by Supplier**		**% of Each Day Rented by Supplier**		**No. of Days Rented by Supplier Per Year**		
annual rent of primary lease / no. of work days per year	X	sq. ft. exclusively occupied by supplier / total office sq. ft.	X	4 hours / 8 hours	X	52 days (i.e., 1 day per week)	=	Supplier's annual rent for exclusive space

2. Apportionment of interior office common space - When permitted by applicable regulations, rental payments may also cover the interior office common space in physicians' offices that are shared by the physicians and any subtenants, such as waiting rooms. If suppliers use such common areas for their patients, it may be appropriate for the suppliers to pay a prorated portion of the charge for such space. The charge for the common space must be apportioned among all physicians and subtenants that use the interior office common space based on the amount of non-common space they occupy and the duration of such occupation. Payment for the use of office common space should not exceed the supplier's pro rata share of the charge for such space based upon the ratio of the space used exclusively by the supplier to the total amount of space (other than common space) occupied

by all persons using such common space.

3. Apportionment of building common space - Where the physician pays a separate charge for areas of a building that are shared by all tenants, such as building lobbies, it may be appropriate for the supplier to pay a prorated portion of such charge. As with interior office common space, the cost of the building common space must be apportioned among all physicians and subtenants based on the amount of non-common space they occupy and the duration of such occupation. For instance, in the example in number one above, the supplier's share of the additional levy for building common space could not be split 50/50.

The Space Rental Safe Harbor Can Protect Legitimate Arrangements

We strongly recommend that parties to rental agreements between physicians and suppliers to whom the physicians refer or for which physicians otherwise generate business make every effort to comply with the space rental safe harbor to the anti-kickback statute. (See 42 CFR 1001.952(b), as amended by 64 FR 63518 (November 19, 1999)). When an arrangement meets all of the criteria of a safe harbor, the arrangement is immune from prosecution under the anti-kickback statute. The following are the safe harbor criteria, all of which must be met:

- The agreement is set out in writing and signed by the parties.
- The agreement covers all of the premises rented by the parties for the term of the agreement and specifies the premises covered by the agreement.
- If the agreement is intended to provide the lessee with access to the premises for periodic intervals of time rather than on a full-time basis for the term of the rental agreement, the rental agreement specifies exactly the schedule of such intervals, their precise length, and the exact rent for such intervals.
- The term of the rental agreement is for not less than one year.
- The aggregate rental charge is set in advance, is consistent with fair market value in arms-length transactions, and is not determined in a manner that takes into account the volume or value of any referrals or business otherwise generated between the parties for which payment may be made in whole or in part under Medicare or a State health care program.
- The aggregate space rented does not exceed that which is reasonably necessary to accomplish the commercially reasonable business purpose of the rental.

Arrangements for office equipment or personal services of physicians' office staff can also be structured to comply with the equipment rental safe harbor and personal services and management contracts safe harbor. (See 42 CFR 1001.952(c) and (d), as amended by 64 FR 63518 (November 19, 1999)). Specific equipment used should be identified and documented and payment limited to the prorated portion of its use. Similarly, any services provided should be documented and payment should be limited to the time actually spent performing such services.

What To Do If You Have Information About Fraud and Abuse Against Medicare or Medicaid Programs

If you have information about physicians, DMEPOS suppliers, CORFs or other suppliers engaging in any of the activities described above, contact any of the regional offices of the Office of Investigations of the Office of Inspector General, U.S. Department of Health and Human Services, at the following locations:

Field Offices	States Served	Telephone
Boston	MA, VT, NH, ME, RI, CT	617-565-2664
New York	NY, NJ, PR, VI	212-264-1691

Philadelphia	PA, MD, DE, WV, VA, DC	215-861-4586
Atlanta	GA, KY, NC, SC, FL, TN, AL, MS	404-562-7603
Chicago	IL, MN, WI, MI, IN, OH, IA,	312-353-2740
Dallas	TX, NM, OK, AR, LA, CO, UT, WY, MT, ND, SD, NE, KS, MO	214-767-8406
Los Angeles	AZ, NV, So. CA	714-246-8302
San Francisco	No. CA, AK, HI, OR, ID, WA	415-437-7961

1. Persons or entities may be either suppliers or providers. For purposes of this Special Fraud Alert, we will refer to such persons as suppliers.

2. Some of the arrangements identified as suspect in this Special Fraud Alert may also implicate the Ethics in Patient Referrals Act, also known as the Stark law (section 1877 of the Act). The interpretation of the Stark law is under the jurisdiction of the Health Care Financing Administration (HCFA).

3. This Special Fraud Alert does not address the appropriateness of consignment closet arrangements under HCFA's DMEPOS supplier standards. The interpretation of the DMEPOS supplier standards is a matter under HCFA's jurisdiction.

United States Code Annotated
Title 42. The Public Health and Welfare
Chapter 7. Social Security (Refs & Annos)
Subchapter XI. General Provisions, Peer Review, and Administrative Simplification (Refs & Annos)
Part A. General Provisions (Refs & Annos)

42 U.S.C.A. § 1320a-7d

§ 1320a-7d. Guidance regarding application of health care fraud and abuse sanctions

Effective: December 21, 2000

Currentness

(a) Solicitation and publication of modifications to existing safe harbors and new safe harbors

(1) In general

(A) Solicitation of proposals for safe harbors

Not later than January 1, 1997, and not less than annually thereafter, the Secretary shall publish a notice in the Federal Register soliciting proposals, which will be accepted during a 60-day period, for--

(i) modifications to existing safe harbors issued pursuant to section 14(a) of the Medicare and Medicaid Patient and Program Protection Act of 1987 (42 U.S.C. 1320a-7b note);

(ii) additional safe harbors specifying payment practices that shall not be treated as a criminal offense under section 1320a-7b(b) of this title and shall not serve as the basis for an exclusion under section 1320a-7(b)(7) of this title;

(iii) advisory opinions to be issued pursuant to subsection (b); and

(iv) special fraud alerts to be issued pursuant to subsection (c).

(B) Publication of proposed modifications and proposed additional safe harbors

After considering the proposals described in clauses (i) and (ii) of subparagraph (A), the Secretary, in consultation with the Attorney General, shall publish in the Federal Register proposed modifications to existing safe harbors and proposed additional safe harbors, if appropriate, with a 60-day comment period. After considering any public comments received during this period, the Secretary shall issue final rules modifying the existing safe harbors and establishing new safe harbors, as appropriate.

(C) **Report**

The Inspector General of the Department of Health and Human Services (in this section referred to as the "Inspector General") shall, in an annual report to Congress or as part of the year-end semiannual report required by section 5 of the Inspector General Act of 1978 (5 U.S.C.App.), describe the proposals received under clauses (i) and (ii) of subparagraph (A) and explain which proposals were included in the publication described in subparagraph (B), which proposals were not included in that publication, and the reasons for the rejection of the proposals that were not included.

(2) Criteria for modifying and establishing safe harbors

In modifying and establishing safe harbors under paragraph (1)(B), the Secretary may consider the extent to which providing a safe harbor for the specified payment practice may result in any of the following:

(A) An increase or decrease in access to health care services.

(B) An increase or decrease in the quality of health care services.

(C) An increase or decrease in patient freedom of choice among health care providers.

(D) An increase or decrease in competition among health care providers.

(E) An increase or decrease in the ability of health care facilities to provide services in medically underserved areas or to medically underserved populations.

(F) An increase or decrease in the cost to Federal health care programs (as defined in section 1320a-7b(f) of this title).

(G) An increase or decrease in the potential overutilization of health care services.

(H) The existence or nonexistence of any potential financial benefit to a health care professional or provider which may vary based on their decisions of--

(i) whether to order a health care item or service; or

(ii) whether to arrange for a referral of health care items or services to a particular practitioner or provider.

(I) Any other factors the Secretary deems appropriate in the interest of preventing fraud and abuse in Federal health care programs (as so defined).

(b) Advisory opinions

(1) Issuance of advisory opinions

The Secretary, in consultation with the Attorney General, shall issue written advisory opinions as provided in this subsection.

(2) Matters subject to advisory opinions

The Secretary shall issue advisory opinions as to the following matters:

(A) What constitutes prohibited remuneration within the meaning of section 1320a-7b(b) of this title or section 1320a-7a(i)(6) of this title.

(B) Whether an arrangement or proposed arrangement satisfies the criteria set forth in section 1320a-7b(b)(3) of this title for activities which do not result in prohibited remuneration.

(C) Whether an arrangement or proposed arrangement satisfies the criteria which the Secretary has established, or shall establish by regulation for activities which do not result in prohibited remuneration.

(D) What constitutes an inducement to reduce or limit services to individuals entitled to benefits under subchapter XVIII or subchapter XIX within the meaning of section 1320a-7a(b) of this title.

(E) Whether any activity or proposed activity constitutes grounds for the imposition of a sanction under section 1320a-7, 1320a-7a, or 1320a-7b of this title.

(3) Matters not subject to advisory opinions

Such advisory opinions shall not address the following matters:

(A) Whether the fair market value shall be, or was paid or received for any goods, services or property.

(B) Whether an individual is a bona fide employee within the requirements of section 3121(d)(2) of the Internal Revenue Code of 1986.

(4) Effect of advisory opinions

(A) Binding as to Secretary and parties involved

Each advisory opinion issued by the Secretary shall be binding as to the Secretary and the party or parties requesting the opinion.

(B) Failure to seek opinion

The failure of a party to seek an advisory opinion may not be introduced into evidence to prove that the party intended to violate the provisions of sections[1] 1320a-7, 1320a-7a, or 1320a-7b of this title.

(5) Regulations

(A) In general

Not later than 180 days after August 21, 1996, the Secretary shall issue regulations to carry out this section. Such regulations shall provide for--

(i) the procedure to be followed by a party applying for an advisory opinion;

(ii) the procedure to be followed by the Secretary in responding to a request for an advisory opinion;

(iii) the interval in which the Secretary shall respond;

(iv) the reasonable fee to be charged to the party requesting an advisory opinion; and

(v) the manner in which advisory opinions will be made available to the public.

(B) Specific contents

Under the regulations promulgated pursuant to subparagraph (A)--

(i) the Secretary shall be required to issue to a party requesting an advisory opinion by not later than 60 days after the request is received; and

(ii) the fee charged to the party requesting an advisory opinion shall be equal to the costs incurred by the Secretary in responding to the request.

(6) Application of subsection

This subsection shall apply to requests for advisory opinions made on or after the date which is 6 months after August 21, 1996.

(c) Special fraud alerts

(1) In general

(A) Request for special fraud alerts

Any person may present, at any time, a request to the Inspector General for a notice which informs the public of practices which the Inspector General considers to be suspect or of particular concern under the Medicare program under subchapter XVIII or a State health care program, as defined in section 1320a-7(h) of this title (in this subsection referred to as a "special fraud alert").

(B) Issuance and publication of special fraud alerts

Upon receipt of a request described in subparagraph (A), the Inspector General shall investigate the subject matter of the request to determine whether a special fraud alert should be issued. If appropriate, the Inspector General shall issue a special fraud alert in response to the request. All special fraud alerts issued pursuant to this subparagraph shall be published in the Federal Register.

(2) Criteria for special fraud alerts

In determining whether to issue a special fraud alert upon a request described in paragraph (1), the Inspector General may consider--

(A) whether and to what extent the practices that would be identified in the special fraud alert may result in any of the consequences described in subsection (a)(2); and

(B) the volume and frequency of the conduct that would be identified in the special fraud alert.

CREDIT(S)

(Aug. 14, 1935, c. 531, Title XI, § 1128D, as added Pub.L. 104-191, Title II, § 205, Aug. 21, 1996, 110 Stat. 2000; amended Pub.L. 105-33, Title IV, § 4331(a)(1), Aug. 5, 1997, 111 Stat. 395; Pub.L. 105-277, Div. J, Title V, § 5201(c), Oct. 21, 1998, 112 Stat. 2681-917; Pub.L. 106-554, § 1(a)(6) [Title V, § 543], Dec. 21, 2000, 114 Stat. 2763, 2763A-551.)

Footnotes

1

So in original. Probably should be "section".

42 U.S.C.A. § 1320a-7d, 42 USCA § 1320a-7d
Current through P.L. 116-56.

End of Document

DATES: Submit written comments on the collection of information by September 30, 2002.

ADDRESSES: Submit written comments on the collection of information to the Office of Information and Regulatory Affairs, OMB, New Executive Office Bldg., 725 17th St. NW., rm. 10235, Washington, DC 20503, Attn: Stuart Shapiro, Desk Officer for FDA.

FOR FURTHER INFORMATION CONTACT: Mark L. Pincus, Office of Information Resources Management (HFA–250), Food and Drug Administration, 5600 Fishers Lane, Rockville, MD 20857, 301–827–1471.

SUPPLEMENTARY INFORMATION: In compliance with 44 U.S.C. 3507, FDA has submitted the following proposed collection of information to OMB for review and clearance.

Focus Groups as Used by the Food and Drug Administration—New Collection

FDA will collect and use information gathered through the focus group vehicle. This information will be used to develop programmatic proposals, and as such, compliments other important research findings to develop these proposals. Focus groups do provide an important role in gathering information because they allow for a more in-depth understanding of consumers' attitudes, beliefs, motivations, and feelings than do quantitative studies.

Also, information from these focus groups will be used to develop policy and redirect resources, when necessary, to our constituents. If this information is not collected, a vital link in information gathering by FDA to develop policy and programmatic proposals will be missed causing further delays in policy and program development.

In the **Federal Register** of May 24, 2002 (67 FR 36613), the agency requested comments on the proposed collection of information. FDA received four comments, but they did not pertain to the information collection though one heartily supported the use of focus groups as an instrument to help FDA better understand how well respondents comprehend health issues.

FDA estimates the burden for completing the forms for this collection of information as follows:

The total annual estimated burden imposed by this collection of information is 2,884 hours annually.

TABLE 1.—ESTIMATED ANNUAL REPORTING BURDEN[1]

Center	Subject	No. of Focus Groups per Study	No. of Focus Group Sessions Conducted Annually	Number of Participants per Group	Hours of Duration for Each Group (includes screening)	Total Hours
Center for Biologics Evaluation and Research.	May use focus groups when appropriate.	1	5	9	1.58	71
Center for Drug Evaluation and Research.	Varies (e.g., direct-to-consumer Rx drug promotion, physician labeling of Rx drugs, medication guides, over-the-counter drug labeling, risk communication).	10	100	9	1.58	1,422
Center for Devices and Radiological Health.	Varies (e.g., FDA Seal of Approval, patient labeling, tampons, on-line sales of medical products, latex gloves).	5	25	9	2.08	468
Center for Food Safety and Applied Nutrition.	Varies (e.g., food safety, nutrition, dietary supplements, and consumer education).	8	32	9	1.58	455
Center for Veterinary Medicine.	Varies (e.g., food safety, labeling, cosmetic safety and labeling).	5	25	9	2.08	468
Total		29	187		1.99	3,352

[1]There are no capital costs or operating and maintenance costs associated with this collection.

Annually, FDA projects about 29 focus group studies using 187 focus groups lasting an average of 1.99 hours each. We have allowed burden for unplanned focus groups to be completed so as not to restrict the agency's ability to gather information on public sentiment for its proposals in its regulatory as well as other programs.

Dated: August 26, 2002.

Margaret M. Dotzel,

Associate Commissioner for Policy.

[FR Doc. 02–22284 Filed 8–29–02; 8:45 am]

BILLING CODE 4160–01–S

DEPARTMENT OF HEALTH AND HUMAN SERVICES

Office of Inspector General

Publication of OIG Special Advisory Bulletin on Offering Gifts and Other Inducements to Beneficiaries

AGENCY: Office of Inspector General (OIG), HHS.

55856 **Federal Register** / Vol. 67, No. 169 / Friday, August 30, 2002 / Notices

ACTION: Notice.

SUMMARY: The OIG periodically develops and issues guidance, including Special Fraud Alerts and Special Advisory Bulletins, to alert and inform the industry about potential problems or areas of special interest. This **Federal Register** notice sets forth the recently issued OIG Special Advisory Bulletin addressing the offering of gifts and other inducements to Medicare and Medicaid beneficiaries.

FOR FURTHER INFORMATION CONTACT: Vicki Robinson or Joel Schaer, Office of Counsel to the Inspector General, (202) 619–0335.

SUPPLEMENTARY INFORMATION:

I. Background

We are issuing this Special Advisory Bulletin to help the industry better understand the prohibition on furnishing inducements to Medicare and Medicaid beneficiaries at section 1128A(a)(5) of the Social Security Act. Specifically, the Special Advisory Bulletin addresses the offering of gifts and other inducements to beneficiaries to influence their choice of a Medicare or Medicaid provider, practitioner, or supplier.

II. Special Advisory Bulletin: Offering Gifts and Other Inducements to Beneficiaries (August 2002)

Introduction

Under section 1128A(a)(5) of the Social Security Act (the Act), enacted as part of Health Insurance Portability and Accountability Act of 1996 (HIPAA), a person who offers or transfers to a Medicare or Medicaid beneficiary any remuneration that the person knows or should know is likely to influence the beneficiary's selection of a particular provider, practitioner, or supplier of Medicare or Medicaid payable items or services may be liable for civil money penalties (CMPs) of up to $10,000 for each wrongful act. For purposes of section 1128A(a)(5) of the Act, the statute defines "remuneration" to include, without limitation, waivers of copayments and deductible amounts (or any part thereof) and transfers of items or services for free or for other than fair market value. (*See* section 1128A(i)(6) of the Act.) The statute and implementing regulations contain a limited number of exceptions. (*See* section 1128A(i)(6) of the Act; 42 CFR 1003.101.)

Offering valuable gifts to beneficiaries to influence their choice of a Medicare or Medicaid provider[1] raises quality and cost concerns. Providers may have an economic incentive to offset the additional costs attributable to the giveaway by providing unnecessary services or by substituting cheaper or lower quality services. The use of giveaways to attract business also favors large providers with greater financial resources for such activities, disadvantaging smaller providers and businesses.

The Office of Inspector General (OIG) is responsible for enforcing section 1128A(a)(5) through administrative remedies. Given the broad language of the prohibition and the number of marketing practices potentially affected, this Bulletin is intended to alert the health care industry as to the scope of acceptable practices. To that end, this Bulletin provides bright-line guidance that will protect the Medicare and Medicaid programs, encourage compliance, and level the playing field among providers. In particular, the OIG will apply the prohibition according to the following principles:

- *First*, the OIG has interpreted the prohibition to permit Medicare or Medicaid providers to offer beneficiaries inexpensive gifts (other than cash or cash equivalents) or services without violating the statute. For enforcement purposes, inexpensive gifts or services are those that have a retail value of no more than $10 individually, and no more than $50 in the aggregate annually per patient.
- *Second*, providers may offer beneficiaries more expensive items or services that fit within one of the five statutory exceptions: waivers of cost-sharing amounts based on financial need; properly disclosed copayment differentials in health plans; incentives to promote the delivery of certain preventive care services; any practice permitted under the federal anti-kickback statute pursuant to 42 CFR 1001.952; or waivers of hospital outpatient copayments in excess of the minimum copayment amounts.
- *Third*, the OIG is considering several additional regulatory exceptions. The OIG may solicit public comments on additional exceptions for complimentary local transportation and for free goods in connection with participation in certain clinical studies.
- *Fourth*, the OIG will continue to entertain requests for advisory opinions related to the prohibition on inducements to beneficiaries. However, as discussed below, given the difficulty in drawing principled distinctions between categories of beneficiaries or types of inducements, favorable opinions have been, and are expected to be, limited to situations involving conduct that is very close to an existing statutory or regulatory exception.

In sum, unless a provider's practices fit within an exception (as implemented by regulations) or are the subject of a favorable advisory opinion covering a provider's own activity, any gifts or free services to beneficiaries should not exceed the $10 per item and $50 annual limits.[2]

In addition, valuable services or other remuneration can be furnished to financially needy beneficiaries by an independent entity, such as a patient advocacy group, even if the benefits are funded by providers, so long as the independent entity makes an independent determination of need and the beneficiary's receipt of the remuneration does not depend, directly or indirectly, on the beneficiary's use of any particular provider. An example of such an arrangement is the American Kidney Fund's program to assist needy patients with end stage renal disease with funds donated by dialysis providers, including paying for their supplemental medical insurance premiums. (*See, e.g.*, OIG Advisory Opinion No. 97–1 and No. 02–1.)

Elements of the Prohibition

Remuneration. Section 1128A(a)(5) of the Act prohibits the offering or transfer of "remuneration". The term "remuneration" has a well-established meaning in the context of various health care fraud and abuse statutes. Generally, it has been interpreted broadly to include "anything of value." The definition of "remuneration" for purposes of section 1128A(a)(5)—which includes waivers of coinsurance and deductible amounts, and transfers of items or services for free or for other than fair market value—affirms this broad reading. (*See* section 1128A(i)(6).) The use of the term "remuneration" implicitly recognizes that virtually any good or service has a monetary value.[3]

The definition of "remuneration" in section 1128A(i)(6) contains five specific exceptions:

- *Non-routine, unadvertised waivers of copayments or deductible amounts based on individualized determinations of financial need or exhaustion of reasonable collection efforts.* Paying the premiums for a beneficiary's Medicare Part B or supplemental insurance is *not* protected by this exception.
- *Properly disclosed differentials in a health insurance plan's copayments or*

[1] For convenience, in this Special Advisory Bulletin, the term "provider" includes practitioners and suppliers, as defined in 42 CFR 400.202.

[2] The OIG will review these limits periodically and may adjust them for inflation if appropriate.

[3] Some services, such as companionship provided by volunteers, have psychological, rather than monetary value. (*See, e.g.*, OIG Advisory Opinion No. 00–3.)

deductibles. This exception covers incentives that are part of a health plan design, such as lower plan copayments for using preferred providers, mail order pharmacies, or generic drugs. Waivers of Medicare or Medicaid copayments are *not* protected by this exception.

• *Incentives to promote the delivery of preventive care*. Preventive care is defined in 42 CFR 1003.101 to mean items and services that (i) are covered by Medicare or Medicaid and (ii) are either pre-natal or post-natal well-baby services or are services described in the *Guide to Clinical Preventive Services* published by the U.S. Preventive Services Task Force (available online at *http://odphp.osphs.dhhs.gov/pubs/guidecps*). Such incentives may not be in the form of cash or cash equivalents and may not be disproportionate to the value of the preventive care provided. (*See* 42 CFR 1003.101; 65 FR 24400 and 24409.)

• *Any practice permitted under an anti-kickback statute safe harbor* at 42 CFR 1001.952.[4]

• *Waivers of copayment amounts in excess of the minimum copayment amounts under the Medicare hospital outpatient fee schedule*. (*See* section 1128A(i)(6) of the Act; 42 CFR 1003.101.)

In addition, in the Conference Committee report accompanying the enactment of section 1128A(a)(5), Congress expressed its intent that inexpensive gifts of nominal value be permitted. (*See* Joint Explanatory Statement of the Committee of Conference, section 231 of HIPAA, Public Law 104–191.) Accordingly, the OIG interprets the prohibition to exclude offers of inexpensive items or services, and no specific exception for such items or services is required. (*See* 65 FR 24400 and 24410.) The OIG has interpreted inexpensive to mean a retail value of no more than $10 per item or $50 in the aggregate per patient on an annual basis. *Id.* at 24411.

Inducement. Section 1128A(a)(5) of the Act bars the offering of remuneration to Medicare or Medicaid beneficiaries where the person offering the remuneration knows or should know that the remuneration is likely to influence the beneficiary to order or receive items or services from a particular provider. The "should know" standard is met if a provider acts with deliberate ignorance or reckless disregard. No proof of specific intent is required. (*See* 42 CFR 1003.101.)

The "inducement" element of the offense is met by any offer of valuable (*i.e.*, not inexpensive) goods and services as part of a marketing or promotional activity, regardless of whether the marketing or promotional activity is active or passive. For example, even if a provider does not directly advertise or promote the availability of a benefit to beneficiaries, there may be indirect marketing or promotional efforts or informal channels of information dissemination, such as "word of mouth" promotion by practitioners or patient support groups. In addition, the OIG considers the provision of free goods or services to existing customers who have an ongoing relationship with a provider likely to influence those customers' future purchases.

Beneficiaries. Section 1128A(a)(5) of the Act bars inducements offered to Medicare and Medicaid beneficiaries, regardless of the beneficiary's medical condition. The OIG is aware that some specialty providers offer valuable gifts to beneficiaries with specific chronic conditions. In many cases, these complimentary goods or services have therapeutic, as well as financial, benefits for patients. While the OIG is mindful of the hardships that chronic medical conditions can cause for beneficiaries, there is no meaningful basis under the statute for exempting valuable gifts based on a beneficiary's medical condition or the condition's severity. Moreover, providers have a greater incentive to offer gifts to chronically ill beneficiaries who are likely to generate substantially more business than other beneficiaries.

Similarly, there is no meaningful statutory basis for a broad exemption based on the financial need of a category of patients. The statute specifically applies the prohibition to the Medicaid program—a program that is available only to financially needy persons. The inclusion of Medicaid within the prohibition demonstrates Congress' conclusion that categorical financial need is not a sufficient basis for permitting valuable gifts. This conclusion is supported by the statute's specific exception for non-routine waivers of copayments and deductibles based on individual financial need. If Congress intended a broad exception for financially needy persons, it is unlikely that it would have expressly included the Medicaid program within the prohibition and then created such a narrow exception.

Provider, Practitioner, or Supplier. Section 1128A(a)(5) of the Act applies to incentives to select particular providers, practitioners, or suppliers. As noted in the regulations, the OIG has interpreted this element to exclude health plans that offer incentives to Medicare and Medicaid beneficiaries to enroll in a plan. (*See* 65 FR 24400 and 24407.) However, incentives provided to influence an already enrolled beneficiary to select a particular provider, practitioner, or supplier within the plan are subject to the statutory proscription (other than copayment differentials that are part of a health plan design). *Id.* In addition, the OIG does not believe that drug manufacturers are "providers, practitioners, or suppliers" for the limited purposes of section 1128A(a)(5), unless the drug manufacturers also own or operate, directly or indirectly, pharmacies, pharmacy benefits management companies, or other entities that file claims for payment under the Medicare or Medicaid programs.

Additional Regulatory Considerations

Congress has authorized the OIG to create regulatory exceptions to section 1128A(a)(5) of the Act and to issue advisory opinions to protect acceptable arrangements. (*See* sections 1128A(i)(6)(B) and 1128D(b)(2)(A) of the Act.) While the OIG has considered numerous arrangements involving the provision of various free goods and services to beneficiaries, for the following reasons the OIG has concluded that any additional exceptions will likely be few in number and narrow in scope:

• Any exception will create the activity that the statute prohibits—namely, competing for business by giving remuneration to Medicare and Medicaid beneficiaries. Moreover, competition will not only result in providers matching a competitor's offer, but inevitably will trigger ever more valuable offers.

• Since virtually all free goods and services have a corresponding monetary value, there is no principled basis under the statute for distinguishing between the kinds of goods or services offered or the types of beneficiaries to whom the goods or services are offered. Attempting to draw such distinctions would necessarily result in arbitrary standards and would undermine the entire prohibition. Congress has provided no further statutory guidance on the bases for distinguishing and evaluating potential exceptions.

Despite these serious concerns, the OIG is considering soliciting public comment on the possibility of regulatory "safe harbor" exceptions under section

[4] For example, anti-kickback statute safe harbors exist for warranties; discounts; employee compensation; waivers of certain beneficiary coinsurance and deductible amounts; and increased coverage, reduced cost-sharing amounts, or reduced premium amounts offered by health plans. *See* 42 CFR 1001.952(g), (h), (i), and (k).

1128A(a)(5) for two kinds of arrangements:

• *Complimentary local transportation.* The OIG is considering proposing a new exception for complimentary local transportation offered to beneficiaries residing in the provider's primary catchment area. The proposal would permit some complimentary local transportation of greater than nominal value. However, the exception would not cover luxury or specialized transportation, including limousines or ambulances (but would permit vans specially outfitted to transport wheelchairs). The proposed exception may include transportation to the office or facility of a provider other than the donor; however, such arrangements may implicate the anti-kickback statute insofar as they confer a benefit on a provider that is a potential referral source for the party providing the transportation.

• *Government-sponsored clinical trials.* The OIG may propose a new exception for free goods and services (possibly including waivers of copayments) in connection with certain clinical trials that are principally sponsored by the National Institutes of Health or another component of the Department of Health and Human Services.

The OIG is reviewing its pending proposal (65 FR 25460) to permit certain dialysis providers to purchase Medicare supplemental insurance for financially needy persons in the light of the principles established in this Bulletin.

While the OIG does not expect at this time to propose any additional regulatory exceptions related to unadvertised waivers of copayments and deductibles, the OIG recognizes that such waivers occur in a wide variety of circumstances, some of which do not present a significant risk of fraud and abuse. The OIG encourages the industry to bring these situations to our attention through the advisory opinion process. Instructions for requesting an OIG advisory opinion are available on the OIG Web site at *http://oig.hhs.gov/advopn/index.htm.*

Finally, the OIG reiterates that nothing in section 1128A(a)(5) prevents an independent entity, such as a patient advocacy group, from providing free or other valuable services or remuneration to financially needy beneficiaries, even if the benefits are funded by providers, so long as the independent entity makes an independent determination of need and the beneficiary's receipt of the remuneration does not depend, directly or indirectly, on the beneficiary's use of any particular provider. The OIG has approved several such arrangements through the advisory opinion process, including the American Kidney Fund's program to assist needy patients with end stage renal disease with funds donated by dialysis providers. (*See, e.g.,* OIG Advisory Opinion No. 97–1 and No. 02–1.)

Conclusion

Congress has broadly prohibited offering remuneration to Medicare and Medicaid beneficiaries, subject to limited, well-defined exceptions. To the extent that providers have programs in place that do not meet any exception, the OIG, in exercising its enforcement discretion, will take into consideration whether the providers terminate prohibited programs expeditiously following publication of this Bulletin.

The Office of Inspector General (OIG) was established at the Department of Health and Human Services by Congress in 1976 to identify and eliminate fraud, abuse, and waste in the Department's programs and to promote efficiency and economy in departmental operations. The OIG carries out this mission through a nationwide program of audits, investigations, and inspections.

The Fraud and Abuse Control Program, established by the Health Insurance Portability and Accountability Act of 1996 (HIPAA), authorized the OIG to provide guidance to the health care industry to prevent fraud and abuse and to promote the highest level of ethical and lawful conduct. To further these goals, the OIG issues Special Advisory Bulletins about industry practices or arrangements that potentially implicate the fraud and abuse authorities subject to enforcement by the OIG.

Dated: August 8, 2002.

Janet Rehnquist,

Inspector General.

[FR Doc. 02–22124 Filed 8–29–02; 8:45 am]

BILLING CODE 4152–01–P

DEPARTMENT OF HOUSING AND URBAN DEVELOPMENT

[Docket No. FR 4736–N–12]

Notice of Proposed Information Collection for Public Comment—Lease Requirements, Recordkeeping

AGENCY: Office of the Assistant Secretary for Public and Indian Housing, HUD.

ACTION: Notice.

SUMMARY: The proposed information collection requirement described below will be submitted to the Office of Management and Budget (OMB) for review, as required by the Paperwork Reduction Act. The Department is soliciting public comments on the subject proposal.

DATES: *Comments Due Date:* October 29, 2002.

ADDRESSES: Interested persons are invited to submit comments regarding this proposal. Comments should refer to the proposal by name and/or OMB Control number and should be sent to: Mildred M. Hamman, Reports Liaison Officer, Public and Indian Housing, Department of Housing and Urban Development, 451 7th Street, SW., Room 4249, Washington, DC 20410–5000.

FOR FURTHER INFORMATION CONTACT: Mildred M. Hamman, (202) 708–3642, extension 4128. (This is not a toll-free number).

SUPPLEMENTARY INFORMATION: The Department will submit the proposed information collection to OMB for review, as required by the Paperwork Reduction Act of 1995 (44 U.S.C. Chapter 35, as amended).

This Notice is soliciting comments from members of the public and affected agencies concerning the proposed collection of information to: (1) Evaluate whether the proposed collection of information is necessary for the proper performance of the functions of the agency, including whether the information will have practical utility; (2) evaluate the accuracy of the agency's estimate of the burden of the proposed collection of information; (3) enhance the quality, utility, and clarity of the information to be collected; and (4) minimize the burden of the collection of information on those who are to respond, including through the use of appropriate automated collection techniques or other forms of information technology; e.g., permitting electronic submission of responses.

This Notice also lists the following information:

Title of Proposal: Lease Requirements—24 CFR 966.4, Recordkeeping.

OMB Control Number: 2577–0006.

Description of the need for the information and proposed use: HUD regulations 24 CFR 966.4 prescribe the provisions that shall be incorporated in leases by public housing agencies (PHAs) for dwelling units assisted under the U.S. Housing Act of 1937 in projects owned by or leased to PHAs to the tenants. This recordkeeping requirement imposed upon PHAs by HUD regulations and associated information incidental to PHAs' day-to-day operations as landlords of rental housing. If these minimal requirements were not imposed, the Federal Government would have no assurance that PHAs were adopting leases consistent with the law and regulations

OFFICE OF INSPECTOR GENERAL

SPECIAL ADVISORY BULLETIN

CONTRACTUAL JOINT VENTURES

April 2003 (C)

Introduction

This Special Advisory Bulletin addresses certain complex contractual arrangements for the provision of items and services previously identified as suspect in our 1989 Special Fraud Alert on Joint Venture Arrangements.[1] While much of the discussion in the 1989 Special Fraud Alert focused on investor referrals to newly formed entities, we observed that:

> [t]he Office of Inspector General has become aware of a proliferation of arrangements between those in a position to refer business, such as physicians, and those providing items or services for which Medicare or Medicaid pays. Some examples of the items or services provided in these arrangements include clinical diagnostic laboratory services, durable medical equipment (DME), and other diagnostic services. Sometimes these deals are called "joint ventures." *A joint venture may take a variety of forms: it may be a contractual arrangement between two or more parties to cooperate in providing services,* or it may involve the creation of a new legal entity by the parties, such as a limited partnership or closely held corporation, to provide such services. [Emphasis added.]

Notwithstanding that caution, the Office of Inspector General (OIG) is concerned that contractual joint venture arrangements are proliferating.[2]

---

[1] The 1989 Special Fraud Alert was reprinted in the Federal Register in 1994. See 59 FR 65372 (December 19, 1994). The Special Fraud Alert is also available on our web page at http://oig.hhs.gov/fraud/docs/alertsandbulletins/121994.html.

[2] The kinds of contractual arrangements addressed in this Special Advisory Bulletin are sometimes referred to as "joint ventures" or "contractual joint ventures" or may be referenced by other terminology. For purposes of the analysis set forth in this Bulletin, a "joint venture" is any

A. Questionable Contractual Arrangements

The federal anti-kickback statute, section 1128B(b) of the Social Security Act (the Act), prohibits knowingly and willfully soliciting, receiving, offering, or paying anything of value to induce referrals of items or services payable by a federal health care program. Kickbacks are harmful because they can (1) distort medical decision-making, (2) cause overutilization, (3) increase costs to the federal health care programs, and (4) result in unfair competition by freezing out competitors unwilling to pay kickbacks. Both parties to an impermissible kickback transaction may be liable. Violation of the statute constitutes a felony punishable by a maximum fine of $25,000, imprisonment up to 5 years, or both. The OIG may also initiate administrative proceedings to exclude persons from the federal health care programs or to impose civil money penalties for kickback violations under sections 1128(b)(7) and 1128A(a)(7) of the Act.

This Special Advisory Bulletin focuses on questionable contractual arrangements where a health care provider in one line of business (hereafter referred to as the "Owner") expands into a related health care business by contracting with an existing provider of a related item or service (hereafter referred to as the "Manager/Supplier") to provide the new item or service to the Owner's existing patient population, including federal health care program patients. The Manager/Supplier not only manages the new line of business, but may also supply it with inventory, employees, space, billing, and other services. In other words, the Owner contracts out substantially the entire operation of the related line of business to the Manager/Supplier – otherwise a potential competitor – receiving in return the profits of the business as remuneration for its federal program referrals.

Some examples of potentially problematic contractual arrangements include the following:

- A hospital establishes a subsidiary to provide DME. The new subsidiary enters into a contract with an existing DME company to operate the new subsidiary and to provide the new subsidiary with DME inventory. The existing DME company already provides DME services comparable to those provided by the new hospital DME subsidiary and bills insurers and patients for them.

- A DME company sells nebulizers to federal health care beneficiaries. A mail order pharmacy suggests that the DME company form its own mail order pharmacy to provide nebulizer drugs. Through a management agreement, the mail order pharmacy runs the DME company's pharmacy, providing personnel, equipment, and space. The existing mail order pharmacy also sells all nebulizer drugs to the DME company's pharmacy for its inventory.

---

common enterprise with mutual economic benefit. The application of this Bulletin is not limited to "joint ventures" that meet technical qualifications under applicable state or common law.

- A group of nephrologists establishes a wholly-owned company to provide home dialysis supplies to their dialysis patients. The new company contracts with an existing supplier of home dialysis supplies to operate the new company and provide all goods and services to the new company.

These problematic arrangements typically exhibit certain common elements. First, the Owner expands into a related line of business, which is dependent on referrals from, or other business generated by, the Owner's existing business.[3] The new business line may be organized as a part of the existing entity or as a separate subsidiary. Typically, the new business primarily serves the Owner's existing patient base.

Second, the Owner neither operates the new business itself nor commits substantial financial, capital, or human resources to the venture. Instead, it contracts out substantially all the operations of the new business. The Manager/Supplier typically agrees to provide not only management services, but also a range of other services, such as the inventory necessary to run the business, office and health care personnel, billing support, and space. While the Manager/Supplier essentially operates the business, the billing of insurers and patients is done in the name of the Owner. In many cases, the contractual arrangements result in either practical or legal exclusivity for the Manager/Supplier through inclusion of non-competition provisions or restrictions on access. While the contract terms of these arrangements may appear to place the Owner at financial risk, the Owner's actual business risk is minimal because of the Owner's ability to influence substantial referrals to the new business.

Third, the Manager/Supplier is an established provider of the same services as the Owner's new line of business. In other words, absent the contractual arrangement, the Manager/Supplier would be a competitor of the new line of business, providing items and services in its own right, billing insurers and patients in its own name, and collecting reimbursement.

Fourth, the Owner and the Manager/Supplier share in the economic benefit of the Owner's new business. The Manager/Supplier takes its share in the form of payments under the various contracts with the Owner; the Owner receives its share in the form of the residual profit from the new business.

---

[3]The Owner's referrals may be direct or indirect and may include not only ordering or purchasing goods or services, but also "arranging for" or "recommending" goods and services. See section 1128B(b) of the Act. For example, a hospital may generate business for a DME company, notwithstanding that orders for specific DME items must be signed by a physician who may or may not be a hospital employee.

Fifth, aggregate payments to the Manager/Supplier typically vary with the value or volume of business generated for the new business by the Owner. While in some arrangements certain payments are fixed (for example, the management fee), other payments, such as payments for goods and services supplied by the Manager/Supplier, will vary based on the number of goods and services provided. In other words, the aggregate payment to the Manager/Supplier from the whole arrangement will vary with referrals from the Owner. Likewise, the Owner's payments, that is, the difference between the net revenues from the new business and its expenses (including payments to the Manager/Supplier), also vary based on the Owner's referrals to the new business. Through these contractual payments, the parties are able to share the profits of the new line of business.

B. Safe Harbor Protection May Be Unavailable

Under the kickback statute, a number of statutory and regulatory "safe harbors" immunize certain arrangements that might otherwise violate the anti-kickback statute. (See 42 U.S.C. 1320a-7b(b)(3); 42 CFR 1001.952.) To qualify for safe harbor protection, an arrangement must fit squarely in one of these safe harbor provisions. Some parties attempt to carve otherwise problematic contracting arrangements into several different contracts for discrete items or services (e.g., a management contract, a vendor contract, and a staffing contract), and then qualify each separate contract for protection under a "safe harbor." Such efforts may be ineffectual and leave the parties subject to prosecution for the following reasons.

First, many of these questionable joint venture arrangements involve contracts pursuant to which the Manager/Suppliers agree to sell items and services to the Owners at a discounted price. However, where a discount is given as part of an overarching business arrangement, it cannot qualify for protection under the discount safe harbor. Simply put, the discount safe harbor does not protect – and has never protected – prices offered by a seller to a buyer in connection with a common enterprise. To be protected under the discount safe harbor, a price reduction must be based on an *arms length transaction*. (See 42 CFR 1001.952(h) under which "the term *discount* means a reduction in the amount a buyer . . . is charged for an item or service based on an arms-length transaction."). As we expressly stated in the preamble to the 1991 safe harbor regulations, the provision of items or services to a joint venture by a participant in the venture is not an "arms length" transaction:

> "Another problem exists where an entity, which is both a provider and supplier of items or services and joint venture partner with referring physicians, makes discounts to the joint venture as a way to share its profits with the physician partners. Very often this entity furnishes items or services to the joint venture, and also acts as the joint venture's general partner or provides management services to the joint venture. . . . *These*

arrangements are not arms length transactions where the joint venture shops around for the best price on a good or service. Rather it has entered into a collusive arrangement with a particular provider or supplier of items or services that seeks to share its profits with referring physician partners. [We did] . . . not intend to protect these types of transactions which are sometimes made to appear as 'discounts'. . . ." [Emphasis added] (See 56 FR 35977; July 29, 1991).

In short, a discount is not based on arms length transaction if it is provided by a seller to a purchaser in connection with a common venture, regardless of whether the venture is memorialized in separate contracts.

Second, even if the various contracts could fit in one or more safe harbors, they would only protect the remuneration flowing from the Owner to the Manager/Supplier for actual services rendered. In the contractual arrangements that are the subject of this Bulletin, however, the illegal remuneration is often the difference between the money paid by the Owner to the Manager/Supplier and the reimbursement received from the federal health care programs. By agreeing effectively to provide services it could otherwise provide in its own right for less than the available reimbursement, the Manager/Supplier is providing the Owner with the opportunity to generate a fee and a profit. The opportunity to generate a fee is itself remuneration that may implicate the anti-kickback statute.

C. Indicia of a Suspect Contractual Joint Venture

To help identify the suspect contractual joint ventures that are the focus of this Special Advisory Bulletin, we describe below some characteristics, which, taken separately or together, potentially indicate a prohibited arrangement. This list is illustrative, not exhaustive.

New Line of Business. The Owner typically seeks to expand into a health care service that can be provided to the Owner's existing patients. As illustrated in Part A, examples include, but are not limited to, hospitals expanding into DME services, DME companies expanding into the nebulizer pharmacy business, or nephrologists expanding into the home dialysis supply business.[4]

Captive Referral Base. The newly-created business predominantly or exclusively serves the Owner's existing patient base (or patients under the control or influence of the Owner). The Owner typically does not intend to expand the business to serve new

[4]These examples are illustrative only. This list is not intended to suggest that other analogous ventures are not equally suspect.

customers (i.e., customers not already served in its main business) and, therefore, makes no or few *bona fide* efforts to do so.

Little or No *Bona Fide* Business Risk. The Owner's primary contribution to the venture is referrals; it makes little or no financial or other investment in the business, delegating the entire operation to the Manager/Supplier, while retaining profits generated from its captive referral base. Residual business risks, such as nonpayment for services, are relatively ascertainable based on historical activity.

Status of the Manager/Supplier. The Manager/Supplier is a would-be competitor of the Owner's new line of business and would normally compete for the captive referrals. It has the capacity to provide virtually identical services in its own right and bill insurers and patients for them in its own name.

Scope of Services Provided by the Manager/Supplier. The Manager/Supplier provides all, or many, of the following key services:

- day-to-day management;
- billing services;
- equipment;
- personnel and related services;
- office space;
- training;
- health care items, supplies, and services.[5]

In general, the greater the scope of services provided by the Manager/Supplier, the greater the likelihood that the arrangement is a contractual joint venture.

Remuneration. The practical effect of the arrangement, viewed in its entirety, is to provide the Owner the opportunity to bill insurers and patients for business otherwise provided by the Manager/Supplier. The remuneration from the venture to the Owner (i.e., the profits of the venture) takes into account the value and volume of business the Owner generates.

Exclusivity. The parties may agree to a non-compete clause, barring the Owner from providing items or services to any patients other than those coming from Owner and/or barring the Manager/Supplier from providing services in its own right to the Owner's patients.

[5]The Manager/Supplier may also provide marketing services, although in many instances no such services are required since the Owner generates substantially all of the venture's business from its existing patient base.

As noted above, these factors are illustrative, not exhaustive. The presence or absence of any one of these factors is not determinative of whether a particular arrangement is suspect. As indicated, this Special Advisory Bulletin is not intended to describe the entire universe of suspect contractual joint ventures. This Bulletin focuses on arrangements where substantially all of the operations of a new line of business are contracted out to a would-be competitor. Arrangements involving the delegation of fewer than substantially all services, or delegation to a party not otherwise in a position to bill for the identical services, may also raise concerns under the anti-kickback statute, depending on the circumstances.

The Office of Inspector General (OIG) was established at the Department of Health and Human Services by Congress in 1976 to identify and eliminate fraud, abuse, and waste in the department's programs and to promote efficiency and economy in departmental operations. The OIG carries out this mission through a nationwide program of audits, investigations, and inspections.

The Fraud and Abuse Control Program, established by the Health Insurance Portability and Accountability Act of 1996 (HIPAA), authorized the OIG to provide guidance to the health care industry to prevent fraud and abuse and to promote the highest level of ethical and lawful conduct. To further these goals, the OIG issues Special Advisory Bulletins about industry practices or arrangements that potentially implicate the fraud and abuse authorities subject to enforcement by the OIG.

DEPARTMENT OF HEALTH AND HUMAN SERVICES

OFFICE OF INSPECTOR GENERAL

WASHINGTON, DC 20201

Fraud Alert: Physician Compensation Arrangements May Result in Significant Liability

June 9, 2015

Physicians who enter into compensation arrangements such as medical directorships must ensure that those arrangements reflect fair market value for bona fide services the physicians actually provide. Although many compensation arrangements are legitimate, a compensation arrangement may violate the anti-kickback statute if even one purpose of the arrangement is to compensate a physician for his or her past or future referrals of Federal health care program business. OIG encourages physicians to carefully consider the terms and conditions of medical directorships and other compensation arrangements before entering into them.

OIG recently reached settlements with 12 individual physicians who entered into questionable medical directorship and office staff arrangements. OIG alleged that the compensation paid to these physicians under the medical directorship arrangements constituted improper remuneration under the anti-kickback statute for a number of reasons, including that the payments took into account the physicians' volume or value of referrals and did not reflect fair market value for the services to be performed, and because the physicians did not actually provide the services called for under the agreements. OIG also alleged that some of the 12 physicians had entered into arrangements under which an affiliated health care entity paid the salaries of the physicians' front office staff. Because these arrangements relieved the physicians of a financial burden they otherwise would have incurred, OIG alleged that the salaries paid under these arrangements constituted improper remuneration to the physicians. OIG determined that the physicians were an integral part of the scheme and subject to liability under the Civil Monetary Penalties Law.

Those who commit fraud involving Federal health care programs are subject to possible criminal, civil, and administrative sanctions. For more information on physician relationships, see OIG's "Compliance Program Guidance for Individual and Small Group Physician Practices" available at http://oig.hhs.gov/authorities/docs/physician.pdf and OIG's "A Roadmap for New Physicians: Avoiding Medicare and Medicaid Fraud and Abuse" available at http://oig.hhs.gov/compliance/physician-education/roadmap_web_version.pdf.

If you have information about physicians or other providers engaging in any of the activities described above, contact the OIG Hotline at https://forms.oig.hhs.gov/hotlineoperations/ or by phone at 1-800-447-8477 (1-800-HHS-TIPS).

APPENDIX D
Selected Judicial Opinions

KeyCite Yellow Flag - Negative Treatment
Declined to Follow by U.S. ex rel. Bartlett v. Ashcroft, W.D.Pa., August 21, 2014

157 F.3d 833
United States Court of Appeals,
Eleventh Circuit.

UNITED STATES of America, Plaintiff–Appellee, Cross–Appellant,
v.
Angela F. STARKS, Defendant–Appellant,
Andrew R. Siegel, Defendant–Appellant, Cross–Appellee.

No. 96–3117.
|
Oct. 9, 1998.

Synopsis
Government employee and president of drug treatment provider were convicted in the United States District Court for the Middle District of Florida, No. 94–156–CR–T–23C, Steven D. Merryday, J., for violating anti-kickback provision of Social Security Act. Employee and president appealed, and United States cross-appealed sentence. The Court of Appeals, Birch, J., held that: (1) statute did not require knowledge that arrangement for referrals to treatment program violated the statute; (2) statute was not unconstitutionally vague; (3) president was ineligible for sentence reduction for acceptance of responsibility; and (4) district court should have used guideline for bribery of a public official, rather than guideline for fraud and deceit, in sentencing president.

Affirmed in part, reversed in part, and remanded.

Attorneys and Law Firms

***835** Miriam L. Sumpter, Tampa, FL, for Defendant–Appellant.

Arnold D. Levine, Levine, Hirsch, Segall & Northcutt, P.A., Tampa, FL, for Siegel.

Charles R. Wilson, U.S. Atty., Tamra Phipps, Terry A. Zitek and Susan H. Rothstein, Asst. U.S. Attys., Tampa, FL, Susan Humes Raab, Asst. U.S. Atty., Jacksonville, FL, for Plaintiff–Appellee, Cross–Appellant.

Appeals from the United States District Court for the Middle District of Florida.

Before ANDERSON and BIRCH, Circuit Judges, and PAINE[*], Senior District Judge.

Opinion

BIRCH, Circuit Judge:

Defendants Angela Starks and Andrew Siegel seek to overturn their convictions under the anti-kickback provision of the Social Security Act, 42 U.S.C. § 1320a–7b ("the Anti–Kickback statute"). Specifically, Starks and Siegel argue that the district court erred by refusing to instruct the jury concerning the relevant *mens rea*. In addition, Starks and Siegel contend that the Anti–Kickback statute is unconstitutionally vague. While denying the defendants' allegations of error, the government cross-appeals Siegel's sentence on the grounds that the district court should not have reduced his offense level for acceptance of responsibility, and that the district court should have applied the guideline for bribery of a public official rather than the guideline for fraud and deceit. We AFFIRM IN PART, REVERSE IN PART, and REMAND.

BACKGROUND[1]

In 1992, Andrew Siegel was both the president and the sole shareholder of Future Steps, Inc., a corporation that developed and operated treatment programs for drug addiction. On April 22, 1992, Future Steps contracted with Florida CHS, Inc. to run a chemical dependency unit for pregnant women at Florida CHS's Metropolitan General Hospital ("the Hospital"). In return, Florida CHS promised to pay Future Steps a share of the Hospital's profits from the program. As a Medicaid provider, the Hospital performed medical services for indigent and disabled persons and received payment for these activities through Consultec, the fiscal intermediary for the Florida Medicaid program. Before executing the Future Steps–Florida CHS contract, Siegel initialed each page of the agreement, which included a provision explicitly forbidding Future Steps from making any payment for patient referrals in violation of the Anti–Kickback statute.

At the time Siegel signed this contract, Angela Starks and Barbara Henry had just become community health aides in the employ of the State of Florida Department of ***836** Health and Rehabilitative Services ("HRS").[2] Although Starks and Henry were employees of HRS, they actually worked in a federally-funded research project in Tampa, Florida known as "Project Support." As part of their duties, Starks and Henry advised pregnant women about possible treatment for drug abuse. Upon beginning their work at HRS, Starks and Henry learned from their supervisor both that they could not accept any outside employment that might pose a conflict of interest with their work at HRS and that they were obligated to report any outside employment to HRS.

During the spring of 1992, Future Steps had difficulty attracting patients. One of Future Steps's salaried "liaison workers," Robin Doud–Lacher, however, identified Project Support as a potential source of referrals because of its relationship with high-risk pregnant women. When Doud–Lacher's initial efforts to establish a referral relationship between Future Steps and Project Support failed, Siegel suggested to Doud–Lacher that she spend more time at Project Support, give diapers to Project Support, take Project Support workers to lunch, and otherwise build a relationship with Project Support's employees.

During one of her subsequent visits to Project Support, Doud–Lacher learned from Starks and Henry that cuts in federal spending threatened to reduce their work hours. When Starks and Henry asked if Doud–Loucher knew of other available work, she promised to inquire for them about opportunities at Future Steps.

After discussing Starks and Henry's interest with her immediate supervisor, Doud–Lacher spoke directly with Siegel about hiring the two women. Despite Starks and Henry's extant employment with HRS, Siegel told Doud–Loucher that he would pay Starks and Henry $250 for each patient they referred: $125 when a referred woman began inpatient drug treatment with Future Steps and $125 after each such woman had stayed in Future Steps's program for two weeks.[3] After accepting Siegel's terms, Starks and Henry did not report their referral arrangement to anyone at Project Support or HRS.

At the outset of their work for Future Steps, Starks and Henry received checks written on Future Steps's account and signed by Siegel. Before issuing these checks, Siegel verified that the referred patients had actually entered the Future Steps program; he did not, though, verify that the referrals were legal. Although the checks Siegel signed were coded variously as payments for aftercare, counseling, and marketing expenses, Siegel was actually only paying Starks and Henry for their referrals. In fact, Siegel did not at any time pay Starks and Henry for any of their time, effort, or business expenses, or for any covered Medicare service.

When Doud–Lacher left Future Steps, Siegel had Michael Ix, another liaison worker, assume responsibility for the Starks and Henry referral arrangement. Generally, either Starks or Henry would call Ix and ask him to pick up a referral directly from the Project Support clinic. When Ix arrived at Future Steps with the referred patient, Siegel would give Ix a check for Starks and Henry. Later, after Henry told Ix that she did not want anyone at Project Support to see her receiving checks from Future Steps, Ix agreed to deliver the checks to Starks and Henry either in the Project Support parking lot or at a restaurant. Between June 1992 and January 1993, Future Steps wrote checks payable to Starks totaling $2750 and to Henry totaling $1975.

At the end of 1992, Future Steps began paying Starks and Henry in cash. To make these payments, Ix would withdraw cash from his personal bank account and meet Starks and Henry either at a restaurant or at a twelve-step program; Siegel and Future ***837** Steps would then reimburse Ix. On one occasion, Siegel accomplished this reimbursement by meeting Ix in a restaurant restroom and giving him $600. In total, Ix paid Starks and Henry approximately $1000 to $1200 in cash.

Beyond the impropriety of Starks and Henry's acceptance of referral payments from Siegel, the referral arrangement directly affected Starks and Henry's counseling of the pregnant women who relied on them and Project Support for help. At trial, several of Future Steps's clients testified that Starks and Henry threatened that HRS would take away their babies if they did not receive treatment for their drug addictions; in some instances, Starks and Henry threatened women with the loss of their babies if they did not go specifically to Future Steps. According to these women's testimony, Starks and Henry informed them only about Future Steps's program (eschewing discussion of alternative treatments), and most waited with Starks and Henry at the Project Support clinic until someone from Future Steps arrived to take them to the Hospital. Starks and Henry's physician supervisor also testified that she told the two HRS employees to be more evenhanded in their advice to Project Support's patients, after the number of women going to Future Steps from Project Support increased substantially.

In total, Starks and Henry referred eighteen women from Project Support to Future Steps. From these referrals, the Hospital received $323,023.04 in Medicaid payments.

On July 29, 1994, a federal grand jury indicted Siegel, Starks, Henry, and Doud–Lacher on five counts related to the referrals. Count One charged all four defendants with conspiring against the United States, in violation of 18 U.S.C. § 371, by offering to pay remuneration for referral of Medicare patients, in violation of 42 U.S.C. § 1320a–7b(b)(2)(A), and by soliciting and receiving such referral payments, in violation of 42 U.S.C. § 1320a–7b(b)(1)(A). Counts Two and Three charged Siegel and Doud–Loucher with paying remuneration to Starks and Henry to induce referrals of Medicaid patients, in violation of 42 U.S.C. § 1320a–7b(b)(2)(A). Finally, Count Four charged Starks and Count Five charged Henry with soliciting and receiving referral payments, in violation of 42 U.S.C. § 1320a–7b(b)(1)(A).

On February 22, 1996, the jury returned guilty verdicts as to all of the defendants on all five counts. Thereafter, the district court sentenced Siegel to serve three concurrent terms of twenty-four months of imprisonment and five years supervised release. In choosing this sentence, the district court reduced Siegel's offense level under U.S.S.G. § 3E1.1 for acceptance of responsibility and applied the guideline for fraud, U.S.S.G. § 2F1.1. The district court sentenced Starks to two concurrent terms of thirty months of home detention.

DISCUSSION

On appeal, defendants Starks and Siegel renew two contentions from their trial. First, they claim that the district court committed reversible error when it refused to instruct the jury that, because of the Anti–Kickback statute's *mens rea* requirement, Starks and Siegel had to have known that their referral arrangement violated the Anti–Kickback statute in order to be convicted. Second, Starks and Siegel argue that the Social Security Act's prohibition on paid referrals, when considered together with the Act's safe harbor provision, 42 U.S.C. § 1320a–7b(b)(3) ("the Safe Harbor provision"), is unconstitutionally vague. We address each of these arguments before turning to the government's cross-appeals concerning Siegel's sentence.

I. STARKS AND SIEGEL'S APPEALS

A. THE "WILLFULLY" INSTRUCTION

Starks and Siegel argue that the district court erred in its instruction concerning the *mens rea* required under the Anti–Kickback statute. According to 42 U.S.C. § 1320a–7b(b), it is illegal for a person to "knowingly and willfully solicit[ ] or receive[ ] any remuneration" for referrals for services covered by the federal government. At trial, the district court gave our circuit's pattern instruction regarding the term "willfully":

> The word willfully, as that term is used from time to time in these instructions, ***838** means the act was committed voluntarily and purposely, with the specific intent to do something the law forbids, that is with a bad purpose, either to disobey or disregard the law.

R26 at 18; *see also* 11th Cir. Pattern Jury Instr. 9.1. In reviewing the district court's charge, we determine whether the court's instructions as a whole sufficiently informed the jurors so that they understood the issues and were not misled. *See U.S. v. Hooshmand,* 931 F.2d 725, 733 (11th Cir.1991).[4]

In support of their claim, Starks and Siegel rely heavily on *United States v. Sanchez–Corcino,* 85 F.3d 549 (11th Cir.1996), and *Ratzlaf v. United States,* 510 U.S. 135, 114 S.Ct. 655, 126 L.Ed.2d 615 (1994). Since we heard oral argument on this case, however, the Supreme Court has issued an opinion in *Bryan v. United States,* 524 U.S. 184, 118 S.Ct. 1939, 141 L.Ed.2d 197 (1998), that clearly refutes Starks and Siegel's position.

In *Sanchez–Corcino,* a panel of this court held that the term "willfully" in 18 U.S.C. § 922(a)(1)(D) (requiring license for firearms), meant that the government had to prove that a defendant "acted with knowledge of the [§ 922(a)(1)(D)] licensing requirement." *Id.* at 553, 554 ("[k]nowledge of the general illegality of one's conduct is not the same as knowledge that one is violating a specific rule"). In *Bryan,* though, the Supreme Court explicitly rejected our decision in *Sanchez–Corcino. See Bryan,* 524 U.S. at ——, 118 S.Ct. at 1946. According to the *Bryan* Court, a jury may find a defendant guilty of violating a statute employing the word "willfully" if it believes "that the defendant acted with an evil-meaning mind, that is to say, that he acted with knowledge that his conduct was unlawful." *Id.* at ——, 118 S.Ct. at 1946. Further, the Supreme Court distinguished tax or financial cases, such as *Ratzlaf,* that "involved highly technical statutes that presented the danger of ensnaring individuals engaged in apparently innocent conduct." *Id.*[5] Because "the jury found that [the defendant] knew that his conduct was unlawful," the *Bryan* Court wrote, "[t]he danger of convicting individuals engaged in apparently innocent activity that motivated our decisions in the tax cases and *Ratzlaf* is not present here." *Id.* (footnote omitted). Thus, the Court held that "the willfulness requirement of § 924(a)(1)(D) does not carve out an exemption to the traditional rule that ignorance of the law is no excuse; knowledge that conduct is unlawful is all that is required." *Id.*[6]

Analogously, the Anti–Kickback statute does not constitute a special exception. Section 1320a–7b is not a highly technical tax or financial regulation that poses a danger of ensnaring persons engaged in apparently innocent conduct. Indeed, the giving or taking of kickbacks for medical referrals is hardly the sort of activity a person might expect to be legal; compared to the licensing provisions that the *Bryan* Court considered, such kickbacks are more clearly *malum in se,* rather than *malum prohibitum. Compare Bryan,* 524 U.S. at ——, 118 S.Ct. at 1946.[7] ***839** Thus, we see no error in the district court's refusal to give Starks and Siegel's requested instruction.[8] *Accord United States v. Davis,* 132 F.3d 1092, 1094 (5th Cir.1998); *United States v. Jain,* 93 F.3d 436, 440 (8th Cir.1996), *cert. denied,* 520 U.S. 1273, 117 S.Ct. 2452, 138 L.Ed.2d 210 (1997); *United States v. Bay State Ambulance and Hosp. Rental Serv., Inc.,* 874 F.2d 20, 33 (1st Cir.1989). *But cf. Hanlester Network v. Shalala,* 51 F.3d 1390, 1400 (9th Cir.1995).

B. VAGUENESS

Starks and Siegel also argue that the Anti–Kickback statute is unconstitutionally vague because people of ordinary intelligence in either of their positions could not have ascertained from a reading of its Safe Harbor provision that their conduct was illegal.[9] Under the Safe Harbor provision, the Anti–Kickback statute's prohibition on referral payments

> shall not apply to ... any amount paid by an employer to an employee (who has a bona fide employment relationship with such employer) for employment in the provision of covered items and services....
> 42 U.S.C. § 1320a–7b(b)(3); *see also* 42 C.F.R. § 1001.952. According to Starks and Siegel, this provision is vague because ordinary people in their position might reasonably have thought that Starks and Henry were "bona fide employees" who were exempt from the Anti–Kickback statute's prohibition on remuneration for referrals.

Starks and Siegel are correct that a criminal statute must define an offense with sufficient clarity to enable ordinary people to understand what conduct is prohibited. *See, e.g., Hofstatter,* 8 F.3d at 321. Both the particular facts of this case and the nature of the Anti–Kickback statute, however, undercut Starks and Siegel's vagueness argument. First, even if Starks and Siegel believed that they were bona fide employees, they were not providing "covered items or services." As the government has shown, Starks received payment from Siegel and Future Steps only for referrals and not for any legitimate service for which the Hospital received any Medicare reimbursement. At the same time, persons in either Siegel's or Starks's position could hardly have thought that either Starks or Henry was a bona fide employee; unlike all of Future Steps's other workers, Starks and Henry did not receive regular salary checks at the Hospital. Instead, they clandestinely received their checks (often bearing false category codes) or cash in parking lots and other places outside the Project Support clinic so as to avoid detection by other Project Support workers.

Furthermore, beyond these particular facts, we see no reason to view the Anti–Kickback statute as vague. In *Village of Hoffman Estates v. The Flipside,* 455 U.S. 489, 498–499, 102 S.Ct. 1186, 1193, 71 L.Ed.2d 362 (1982), the Supreme Court set out several factors for a court to consider in determining whether a statute is impermissibly vague, including whether the statute (1) involves only economic regulation, (2) provides only civil, rather than criminal, penalties, (3) contains a scienter requirement mitigating vagueness, and (4) threatens any constitutionally protected rights. As two of ***840** our sister circuits have already concluded, these factors militate against finding the Anti–Kickback statute unconstitutional. *See Hanlester,* 51 F.3d at 1398; *Bay State,* 874 F.2d at 32–33. Indeed, the statute regulates only economic conduct,[10] and it does not chill any constitutional rights. Moreover, although the statute does provide for criminal penalties, it requires "knowing and willful" conduct, a *mens rea* standard that mitigates any otherwise inherent vagueness in the Anti–Kickback statutes's provisions. *Hanlester,* 51 F.3d at 1398; *Bay State,* 874 F.2d at 33. In sum, we agree with the district court that the Anti–Kickback statute gave Starks and Siegel fair warning that their conduct was illegal and that the statute therefore is not unconstitutionally vague.

II. THE GOVERNMENT'S CROSS–APPEAL

In its cross-appeal, the government contends that the district court incorrectly granted Siegel a U.S.S.G. § 3E1.1 reduction for acceptance of responsibility. In addition, the government maintains that the district court erred by sentencing Siegel under the fraud and deceit guideline, U.S.S.G. § 2F1.1, rather than the bribery of a public official guideline, U.S.S.G. § 2C1.1.

A. ACCEPTANCE OF RESPONSIBILITY

On appeal, the government argues that Siegel should not have received a three-level reduction for acceptance of responsibility because he denied having had any guilty intent. In response, Siegel contends that he was entitled to the reduction because he admitted all the relevant facts and cooperated with the government's investigation, while preserving his legitimate legal position regarding the applicability of the statute to his conduct. We review the district court's determination that Siegel accepted responsibility for clear error. *United States v. Anderson,* 23 F.3d 368, 369 (11th Cir.1994) (per curiam).

To receive a reduction under § 3E1.1, a defendant must prove that he clearly accepted responsibility for his offense. *See id.* The reduction does not apply to "a defendant who puts the government to its burden of proof at trial by denying the essential factual elements of guilt, is convicted, and only then admits guilt and expresses remorse." U.S.S.G. § 3E1.1, comment. (n.2). Nonetheless, a defendant may, "[i]n rare situations," be entitled to this reduction if he goes to trial to assert and preserve issues unrelated to factual guilt, such as the applicability of a statute to his conduct. *Id.* Still, a defendant who contends that he did not possess fraudulent intent is making a factual, not a legal, challenge to the government's criminal allegations that precludes a sentence reduction for acceptance of responsibility. *See United States v. Smith,* 127 F.3d 987, 989 (11th Cir.1997) *(en banc) cert. denied,* 523 U.S. 1011, 118 S.Ct. 1202, 140 L.Ed.2d 330 (1998); *see also Sanchez–Corcino,* 85 F.3d at 555–56.

By its terms, 42 U.S.C. § 1320a–7b(b)(2) makes it illegal for any person knowingly to offer any payment "to induce" a referral for services covered by the federal government. Citing this provision, Siegel argues that by conceding at trial that he made payments to Starks and Henry, he admitted all the conduct prohibited by the statute. As the government correctly points out, however, Siegel has denied having had any intent *to induce referrals,* an essential element of the charges on which he was convicted. Because Siegel put the government to its burden of proof by contesting his intent to violate 42 U.S.C. § 1320a–7b(b), Siegel's arguments at trial amounted to a factual denial of guilt and were therefore inconsistent with acceptance of responsibility.[11] Given the factual positions that Siegel ***841** has taken—and continues to take—we conclude that he should not have been eligible for a reduction for acceptance of responsibility and that the district court therefore clearly erred in awarding him a three-level reduction under § 3E1.1.

B. THE FRAUD AND DECEIT GUIDELINE

Additionally, the government argues that the court erred by sentencing Siegel under the § 2F1.1 "Fraud and Deceit" guideline rather than the § 2C1.1 "Bribe" of a public official guideline. Appendix A of the Sentencing Guidelines references three guideline sections which are applicable to violations of § 1320a–7b: U.S.S.G. § 2B1.1 (larceny), U.S.S.G. § 2B4.1 (commercial bribery), and § 2F1.1 (fraud). U.S.S.G. app. A, at 384. If more than one guideline section is referenced for the particular statute, Appendix A instructs the sentencing court to use the guideline most appropriate for the nature of the conduct charged. *See* U.S.S.G. app. A, at 373 (introduction). Further, the Appendix provides that if, "in an atypical case, the guideline section indicated for the statute of conviction is inappropriate because of the particular conduct involved, [courts should] use the guideline section most applicable to the nature of the offense conduct charged in the count of which the defendant was convicted." *Id.* We review the district court's determination of the applicable guideline *de novo. United States v. Acanda,* 19 F.3d 616, 618 (11th Cir.1994).[12]

Regarding the three guidelines listed as potentially applicable in Appendix A, the government and Siegel properly agree that Siegel should not be sentenced under § 2B1.1 or § 2B4.1. Since § 2B1.1 applies to crimes involving stolen property, it clearly has no relevance. Moreover, since § 2B4.1 applies only to "bribery offenses and kickbacks that *do not involve officials* of federal, state, or local government," § 2B4.1 comment. (n.1), this guideline provision, too, cannot be appropriate for Siegel, who illegally induced referrals from a state employee working in a federal Medicare project.[13]

Siegel, however, asserts that the third listed guideline, § 2F1.1, is relevant and applicable. To support this position, which was also that of the district court, Siegel relies on *United States v. Adam*, 70 F.3d 776, 781 (4th Cir.1995). In that case, the Fourth Circuit affirmed a district court's sentence, under § 2F1.1, of a physician who had violated the Anti–Kickback statute. Although *Adam* involved application of § 2F1.1 to the Anti–Kickback statute, we find the case to be of little help to our consideration of Siegel's sentence, because the *Adam* court addressed only the district court's calculation of the government's "loss," without discussing whether § 2F1.1 or some other provision was the most appropriate guideline. *See id.* at 781–82.

Further, we see little reason to view § 2F1.1 as any more applicable to Siegel's conduct than § 2B1.1 or § 2B4.1. As a central part of any application of § 2F1.1, a district court must calculate the "loss" suffered by the defrauded or deceived victim. *See generally* § 2F1.1. Yet, in this case Siegel did not steal from anyone, including the government; Siegel did not file false Medicare claims but rather engaged in a kickback scheme that corrupted Project Support's referral process. While a district court should sentence persons committing Anti–Kickback crimes involving fraud or false statements ***842** under § 2F1.1, this provision is not appropriate for this case.

In fact, Siegel's crime presents the "atypical case" in which the listed guideline for the Anti–Kickback statute is inapposite and a court should resort to a more applicable section, in this instance § 2C1.1. First, we note that the term "induce" in 42 U.S.C. § 1320a–7b(b)(2) can be reasonably understood in this case to connote bribery. Indeed, the term "induce" is defined as "[t]o bring on or about, to affect, cause, to influence to an act or course of conduct ...," *Black's Law Dictionary* at 775; in the context of this case, "induce" and "bribe" are thus virtually synonymous, since Siegel induced Starks and Henry to refer patients to Future Steps through illicit payments. *Compare id.* at 191 ("Any money, ... preferment ... or undertaking to give any [money or preferment] ... with a corrupt intent to *induce* ... action, vote, or opinion .... ") (emphasis added). *See also United States v. Kummer*, 89 F.3d 1536, 1540 (11th Cir.1996) (discussing meaning of "bribe"). Second, the Anti–Kickback statute explicitly refers to "kickbacks, bribes, and rebates" as prohibited forms of remuneration for referrals, bringing Siegel's crime within the purview of the terms of § 2C1.1. *See* 42 U.S.C. § 1320a–7b(b)(2)(A). Thus, the indictment and jury instructions in this case referred to payment of "remuneration (including kickbacks, bribes, or rebates)." R1–2 at 3 (indictment); *see also* R26 at 24 (instruction defining remuneration). Finally, by paying Starks and Henry for referrals, Siegel sought to corrupt their execution of their duties as state employees and workers in a federal program—just the sort of corrosive activity that the Sentencing Commission designed § 2C1.1 to punish. *Cf.* § 2C1.1 comment. (background).[14] Therefore, we hold that the district court erred in applying § 2F1.1 rather than § 2C1.1 in sentencing Siegel.

CONCLUSION

In this case, Starks and Siegel ask that we reverse their convictions for violating and conspiring to violate the Anti–Kickback statute, while the government requests that we reverse the district court's application of two guideline provisions to Siegel's sentence. With regard to Starks and Siegel's appeal, we hold that the district court did not err when it refused to give their requested instruction, and that the Anti–Kickback statute is not unconstitutionally vague as applied to Starks and Siegel. Therefore, we AFFIRM these parts of the district court's judgment. With regard to the government's cross-appeal, we hold that the district court clearly erred in granting Siegel a reduction for acceptance of responsibility, and we conclude that the district court should have sentenced Siegel under § 2C1.1 rather than § 2F1.1. Therefore, we REVERSE these parts of the district court's judgment and REMAND for further proceedings consistent with this opinion.

AFFIRMED IN PART, REVERSED IN PART, and REMANDED.

All Citations

157 F.3d 833, 12 Fla. L. Weekly Fed. C 146

Footnotes

* Honorable James C. Paine, Senior U.S. District Judge for the Southern District of Florida, sitting by designation.

1 Because this case arises from a jury verdict against Starks and Siegel, we view the facts in the light most favorable to the prosecution. *See United States v. Sanchez,* 722 F.2d 1501, 1505 (11th Cir.1984).

2 Although Henry was convicted along with Starks and Siegel for violating the AntiKickback statute, she died during the course of this appeal. We have therefore vacated her sentence and instructed that she be dismissed from the case.

3 Although Starks and Henry had suggested limiting their referrals to patients living outside the area surrounding Project Support and/or restricting their recruiting for Future Steps to their non-HRS hours, Siegel imposed no bounds on the nature of their referral efforts.

4 In *Hooshmand,* we explained further that "[a] trial court's refusal to give a requested instruction is reversible error only if (1) the substance of the instruction was not covered in an instruction given, (2) the requested instruction is a correct statement of the law, (3) the requested instruction deals with an issue properly before the jury, and (4) the party seeking the requested instruction suffered prejudicial harm by the court's refusal." 931 F.2d at 734.

5 In *Ratzlaf,* the Court reviewed a gambler's conviction for illegally structuring his banking transactions so as to avoid technical reporting requirements. *See* 510 U.S. at 137–38, 114 S.Ct. at 657.

6 The *Bryan* Court thus upheld a jury instruction strikingly similar to the district court's "willfully" charge in this case:

> A person acts willfully if he acts intentionally and purposely and with the intent to do something the law forbids, that is, with the bad purpose to disobey or to disregard the law. Now, the person need not be aware of the specific law or rule that his conduct may be violating. But he must act with the intent to do something that the law forbids.

524 U.S. at ——, 118 S.Ct. at 1944. *Compare* R26 at 18 *and* 11th Cir. Pattern Jury Instr. 9.1.

7 Regardless of their knowledge of the law, Starks and Siegel should reasonably have anticipated that their kickback scheme for referrals was "immoral in its nature and injurious in its consequences," because of the obvious risk it posed of corrupting Project Support and HRS's roles as providers of medical advice to drug addicted pregnant women. *Cf. Black's Law Dictionary* 959 (6th ed.1990) (defining *malum in se*).

8 Starks and Siegel also claim that the evidence was not sufficient to prove that they acted "willfully." Given that the government only had to show that they knew that they were acting unlawfully, however, this claim is unpersuasive. The government produced ample evidence, including the furtive methods by which Siegel remunerated Starks and Henry, from which the jury could reasonably have inferred that Starks and Siegel knew that they were breaking the law—even if they may not have known that they were specifically violating the Anti–Kickback statute.

9 Starks and Siegel offer a variety of arguments to the effect that persons working in the medical field cannot anticipate what is prohibited under the Anti–Kickback statute and what is protected by that statute's Safe Harbor provision. They do not, and cannot, challenge, however, the government's contention that, since this is not a First Amendment case, we must evaluate their claim of vagueness only on an as-applied basis. *See Maynard v. Cartwright,* 486 U.S. 356, 361, 108 S.Ct. 1853, 1857–58, 100 L.Ed.2d 372 (1988). Thus, we consider Starks and Siegel's claim in light of the facts of this individual case, looking only to the constitutionality of the Anti–Kickback statute as the government has applied it to Starks and Siegel. *See United States v. Hofstatter,* 8 F.3d 316, 321 (11th Cir.1993); *United States v. Awan,* 966 F.2d 1415, 1424 (11th Cir.1992).

10 In *Hoffman Estates,* the Court explained that "economic regulation is subject to a less strict vagueness test because its subject is often more narrow, and because businesses, which face economic demands to plan behavior carefully, can be expected to consult relevant legislation in advance of action." 455 U.S. at 498, 102 S.Ct. at 1193 (footnote omitted).

11 Moreover, Siegel contested other aspects of the offense, further supporting the government's claim that he did not accept responsibility: that he signed a contract that specifically forbade him to pay for referrals or to "take any action in violation of § 1320a–7b"; that he agreed to the specifics of Starks and Henry's payment arrangements; that he reimbursed Michael Ix for cash payments made to Starks and Henry for referrals; and that he instructed his secretary to prepare referral checks for Starks and Henry.

12 At sentencing, the government did not explicitly object to the district court's application of § 2F1.1 once the court found that this provision governed Siegel's sentence. The government did, however, vigorously contend that Siegel's conduct constituted bribery. Because the government objected to this factual determination, and the decision about which guideline to apply necessarily followed from the district court's ruling, the issue has been preserved for appeal.

13 By contending that § 2B4.1 does not apply because Siegel's kickback scheme involved a public official, Siegel appears to concede that we should treat Starks and Henry as government officials in reviewing his sentence.

14 At Siegel's sentencing hearing, the district court refused to sentence him under § 2C1.1 because it "didn't charge the jury" on bribery of public employees. R29 at 30. The district court's reasoning, however, conflated two separate issues: first, whether Siegel was involved in bribery; and second, if so, whether he had been involved with bribery of a public official. If Starks and Henry were bribed but were not public officials, then § 2B4.1 (commercial bribery) would have applied. *See Jain,* 93 F.3d at 442–43 (affirming application of § 2B4.1 to a physician who violated § 1320a–7b by paying another, private physician for a referral). Since, as Siegel has conceded to this court, Starks and Henry were government officials, then, if Siegel bribed them, § 2C1.1 (bribery of a public official) should apply. It would be incongruous for this court to hold that a defendant who paid a private person for an illegal § 1320a–7b referral should be sentenced for bribery, but that another defendant who participated in the same conduct with a government official should be sentenced for fraud rather than bribery of a public official.

End of Document

106 F.Supp.2d 103
United States District Court,
D. Massachusetts.

UNITED STATES of America, Plaintiff,
v.
K. Glenn SHAW, Eileen B. Aird, and Louise Verde, Defendants.

No. Crim.A. 99–10044–RE.
|
June 19, 2000.

Synopsis
Defendant moved to dismiss indictment charging conspiracy to violate Medicare anti-kickback statute. The District Court, Keeton, J., held that: (1) government was not required to allege that defendant's conduct did not fall within the "discount exception," and (2) issues of fact as to whether defendant effectively withdrew from alleged conspiracy, and was no longer liable for acts of his coconspirators that were committed after his retirement as president of seller-supplier precluded dismissal on statute-of-limitation grounds.

Motion denied.

Attorneys and Law Firms

***104** Nancy Silverman, Martha Purcell Rogers, Ober Kaler, Washington, DC, for Eileen B. Aird.

Douglas Farquhar, Hyman, Phelps & McNamara, Washington, DC, Maria R. Durant, David M. Osburne, William H. Kettlewell, Dwyer & Collora, Boston, MA, for Glenn K. Shaw.

Sollers J. Sedwick, III, Michael E. Meece, King & Spalding, Washington, DC, for Louise Verde.

Susan G. Winkler, Diane C. Freniere, Susan C. Hanson–Philbrick, U.S. Atty's Office, Boston, MA, for U.S.

Opinion

KEETON, District Judge.

I. Pending Motions

Pending for disposition at this time are the following motions:

(1) Defendant K. Glenn Shaw's Motion to Dismiss Count 18 of Superseding Indictment for Failure to State a Crime (Docket Nos. 39, filed September 15, 1999, and 101, filed February 11, 2000) with Supporting Memoranda (Docket Nos. 41, filed September 15, 1999, and 102, filed February 11, 2000) and Appendix (Docket No. 103, filed February 11, 2000). The Government has filed a Response (Docket No. 128, filed March 15, 2000). Defendant K. Glenn Shaw filed a Reply (Docket No. 133, filed April 4, 2000). The Government filed a Surreply (Docket No. 161, filed June 5, 2000);

(2) Defendant K. Glenn Shaw's Motion to Dismiss on Statute of Limitations Grounds (Docket Nos. 43, filed September ***105** 15, 1999, and 104, filed February 11, 2000) with Memorandum in Support (Docket No. 105, filed February 11, 2000). The Government has filed an Opposition (Docket No. 112, filed February 25, 2000).

II. Procedural Background

The procedural background is relevant to the pending motions that are the subject of this Opinion.

On February 10, 1999, in a one-count indictment, a grand jury charged Dr. K. Glenn Shaw (Shaw) with a conspiracy to commit an offense against the United States in violation of 18 U.S.C. § 371. The grand jury charged, specifically, that Shaw conspired to violate the anti-kickback statute, to wit, "to induce external clinics to order and to arrange for ordering laboratory blood testing services including Non–Routine Tests for their dialysis patients from Lifechem, which services were paid for primarily by Medicare Trust Funds." Docket No. 1, ¶ 14.

Shaw entered a plea of not guilty on February 23, 1999 before Magistrate Judge Cohen.

On September 15, 1999, Shaw moved to dismiss the indictment for failure to state a crime and on statute-of-limitation grounds. *See* Docket Nos. 39 and 43.

On September 22, 1999, the grand jury returned a multi-count superseding indictment as to defendants Eileen B. Aird (Aird) and Louise Verde (Verde) and Shaw. Count One alleges that Aird and Verde conspired to defraud the government, a violation of 18 U.S.C. § 371. Count One states, specifically, that the purpose of the conspiracy was, among other things,

> to evade and frustrate efforts by Medicare to pay only for the reasonable and medically necessary blood testing of Medicare Program beneficiaries as ordered by physicians in the normal ordinary course of the treatment of their dialysis patients; and thereby to fraudulently obtain unlawful reimbursement from the Medicare Program for thousands of medically unnecessary, and therefore not lawfully reimbursable, laboratory tests performed by LIFECHEM on blood drawn from dialysis patients.

Docket No. 46, ¶ 31. Counts Two through Seventeen allege that, in conspiring to defraud the United States, as stated in paragraph one of the superseding indictment, Aird and Verde also violated 18 U.S.C. § 1341 (mail fraud) and 18 U.S.C. § 2 (aiding and abetting). *See id.* at ¶¶ 39–68.

Count Eighteen of the superseding indictment re-alleges a violation of 18 U.S.C. § 371, stating that defendant Shaw

> knowingly, willfully, and intentionally combined, conspired, confederated and agreed to commit an offense against the United States and its agency the Health Care Financing Administration, namely, to knowingly, willfully and intentionally offer and pay remuneration, directly and indirectly, overtly and covertly, in cash and in kind, to wit: by rebates and special pricing on dialysis related products, by lavish entertainment and hunting trips, by consultant fees, by grants, and by writing off debt for laboratory services for indigent and HMO patients, all such remuneration being made to induce the external dialysis facilities to order and arrange for the ordering from LIFECHEM of any service and item paid for, in whole or in part, by the Medicare Program, specifically clinical laboratory blood testing conducted for dialysis patients in the external facilities, all in violation of Title 42, United States Code, Section 1320a–7b(b)(2)(B).

Docket No. 46 at ¶ 70.

Shaw entered a plea of not-guilty before Magistrate Judge Cohen on Count Eighteen of the superseding indictment on October 15, 1999. On the same day, both Aird and Verde entered pleas of not-guilty on Counts One through Seventeen.

On February 11, 2000, Shaw moved to dismiss Count Eighteen of the superseding indictment (the only count against him) for ***106** failure to state a crime. On the same day, Shaw also moved to dismiss Count Eighteen on statute-of-limitation grounds.

On February 22, 2000, the Government dismissed Counts Two through Nine of the superseding indictment against Aird and Verde.

On February 25, 2000, the Government filed its response to Shaw's motion to dismiss Count Eighteen of the indictment on statute of limitation grounds. *See* Docket No. 112.

On March 15, 2000, the Government filed its response to Shaw's motion to dismiss Count Eighteen of the indictment for failure to state a crime. *See* Docket No. 128. On April 4, 2000, Defendant K. Glenn Shaw filed a

Reply. *See* Docket No. 133. On June 5, 2000, the Government filed a Surreply. *See* Docket No. 161.

On April 25, Magistrate Judge Cohen issued his final Status Report ordering the case returned to "the district judge to whom this case is assigned for further proceedings." Docket No. 150.

On May 25, 2000, all of the parties appeared before me for an initial pre-trial conference. At that conference, the defendants filed a list of the pending motions that remain to be resolved by the court. *See* Docket 160. Among them are Shaw's two motions to dismiss that are the subject of this Opinion.

III. Factual Background

The following recitation of relevant facts is from the superseding indictment (*see* Docket No. 46) unless otherwise stated.

A. The Players

National Medical Care (NMC), a health care company, provided through its various subsidiaries, an array of products and services to patients diagnosed with end-state renal disease ("ESRD"). From in or about 1989 through in or about December 3, 1993, Dr. K. Glenn Shaw was President of NMC Medical Products, Inc. (MPD), a wholly owned subsidiary of National Medical Care, Inc. (NMC), that manufactured, sold, and distributed products used in kidney dialysis, a primary treatment of ESRD. MPD sold these dialysis related products both to the NMC-owned clinics, called Bio–Medical Applications (BMAs) and and to dialysis facilities not owned by NMC.

NMC also had another division, called the LifeChem division (LifeChem), that provided clinical laboratory blood testing services both to the BMAs and to dialysis clinics not owned by NMC. LifeChem also specialized in performing laboratory blood tests for ESRD patients.

From August 1990 through January 1993, Eileen Aird was the General Manager of LifeChem. From January 1993 until October 1996, Aird was the president of LifeChem.

Louise Verde was the Product Manager for LifeChem from 1987 until late 1993. From late 1993 until October 1997, Verde was Senior Product Manager in Marketing at LifeChem.

On October 1, 1996, Fresneius Medical Care A.G., a German corporation, purchased NMC, and the entity formerly known as NMC continued doing business in North America under the name Fresneius Medical Care—North America.

Shaw retired from NMC's employ in 1993.

B. The Program

In 1965, Congress enacted Title XVIII of the Social Security Act ("The Medicare Program") authorizing the federal government to pay for the cost of certain medical services, including clinical laboratory blood testing services, for persons aged 65 and older. By amendment in 1972, Congress extended the coverage of the Medicare Program to include paying, under most conditions, for the cost of certain medical services for persons suffering from ESRD, regardless of the person's age.

The Department of Health and Human Services (HHS) administers the Medicare ***107** Program through the Health Care Financing Administration (HCFA). In discharging its duties, HCFA makes contracts with private insurance companies ("carriers") to receive, review, and pay lawful claims for reimbursement for the provision of clinical laboratory services to Medicare Program beneficiaries.

HCFA mandates that all ESRD patients undergo, in addition to dialysis, monthly blood testing in order to monitor the efficiency of the dialysis treatment. These tests are performed by clinical laboratories, like LifeChem, and classified by Medicare as "routine tests." The Medicare Program reimburses dialysis clinics directly for dialysis treatments and for routine tests through a monthly fixed payment per patient, per treatment. Because LifeChem was an approved provider under the Social Security Act, LifeChem was authorized to submit directly to the carriers under contract with HCFA lawful claims for reimbursement for these routine tests as well as other tests that were ordered by physicians and that were reasonable and medically necessary in the diagnosis and treatment of Medicare treatment beneficiaries.

For ESRD patients who received dialysis treatments at a dialysis unit or center, Medicare paid for the dialysis that the patient needed for the entire month through a monthly, capitated payment with money from the Medicare Program Trust Funds. That monthly payment was known as the "composite rate payment" and was usually a fixed amount that included reimbursement for the cost of dialysis as well as the cost of the routine tests. The composite rate payment for dialysis did not include payment for any non-routine test (any additional laboratory test required to diagnose or treat non-ESRD medical problems, except those that were labeled "Medicare allowable tests" by HCFA). The medicare program separately paid for non-routine tests by directly reimbursing the clinical laboratory on a fee-for-service basis. To obtain reimbursement for non-routine tests, other than Medicare allowable tests, a clinical laboratory like LifeChem would have to certify to HCFA, through the carrier, that the tests were medically necessary.

IV. The Problem

The indictment charges that Shaw, as president of MPD, conspired to pay remuneration to independent dialysis clinics for the purpose of inducing those clinics to use LifeChem's laboratory services for, among other things, non-routine tests and medically unnecessary tests that were in whole or in part reimbursable under the Medicare Program, all in violation of the health care anti-kick back statute, 42 U.S.C. § 1320a–7b(b)(2)(B).

Specifically, the Government alleges that the inducements for referring orders for LifeChem's services took the form of rebates and special pricing, grants, entertainment and hunting trips, and write-offs of bad debt for blood laboratory tests of indigent and HMO patients. With regard to the rebates and special pricing—seventy of the alleged illegal instances of remuneration—the Government alleges that beginning in 1987, Shaw, as well as other CEOs at MPD, directed employees to discontinue the practice of expressly stating that pricing or rebates on MPD's dialysis related products was contingent upon receipt by LifeChem of referrals for laboratory blood testing services, while at the same time instructing the same employees to continue to provide rebates or special pricing on MPD products in exchange for receiving referrals from the dialysis facilities to LifeChem for the laboratory blood testing. The seventy instances of alleged illegal remunerations are, defendant contends, legal "price reductions" in the form of credits applied to past due balances and future purchases of medical products purchased by the independent dialysis clinics. *See* Docket No. 102 at 5. They are listed in the superseding indictment at paragraph 73(g).

The other eight instances of alleged illegal remuneration are in the form of educational ***108** or research grants, debt write-offs, consulting fees and entertainment. As an example, the Government alleges that in the early 1990s, Shaw approved payments by MPD for lavish holiday entertainment parties, including a yacht rental worth thousands of dollars, for an external dialysis facility, in exchange for referrals of that facility's laboratory business to LifeChem. For the purpose of advancing his Motion to Dismiss for Failure to State a Crime, Shaw does not challenge these eight instances of alleged illegal remuneration (these do not include the seventy similar instances of what the defendant contends are legal "price reductions"). Shaw concedes that even if the court rules that the seventy similar instances of remuneration are not, as a matter of law, illegal under the anti-kickback statute, the trial will nevertheless go forward on the other eight instances. In that circumstance, however, the trial will be significantly abbreviated and considerably less factually complex.

V. Motion to Dismiss for Failure to State a Crime

A. Introduction

Shaw has been indicted for conspiring, under 18 U.S.C. § 371, to commit the offense of violating what has been called the Medicare Anti–Kickback Statute (hereinafter "the anti-kickback statute"). That statute reads, in relevant part,

> (b) Illegal remunerations
>
> (1) whoever knowingly and willfully offers or pays any remuneration (including any kickback, bribe, or rebate) directly or indirectly, overtly or covertly, in cash or in kind to any person to induce such person—
>
> (A) to refer an individual to a person for the furnishing or arranging for the furnishing of any item or service for which payment may be made in whole or in part under a Federal health care program, or
>
> (B) to purchase, lease, order, or arrange for or recommend purchasing, leasing, or ordering any

good, facility, service, or item for which payment may be made in whole or in part under a Federal health care program,

shall be guilty of a felony and upon conviction thereof, shall be fined not more than $25,000 or imprisoned for not more than five years, or both.

42 U.S.C. § 1320a–7b(b) (1999).

The section of the anti-kickback statute that follows the above quoted paragraphs carves out various exceptions to the activities that would otherwise be considered illegal under the statute. The exceptions are listed below.

(3) Paragraphs (1) and (2) shall not apply to—

(A) a discount or other reduction in price obtained by a provider of services or other entity under a Federal health care program if the reduction in price is properly disclosed and appropriately reflected in the costs claimed or charges made by the provider or entity under a Federal health care program;

(B) any amount paid by an employer to an employee (who has a bona fide employment relationship with such employer) for employment in the provision of covered items or services;

(C) any amount paid by a vendor of goods or services to a person authorized to act as a purchasing agent for a group of individuals or entities who are furnishing services reimbursed under a Federal health care program if—

(i) the person has a written contract, with each such individual or entity, which specifies the amount to be paid the person, which amount may be a fixed amount or a fixed percentage of the value of the purchases made by each such individual or entity under the contract, and

(ii) in the case of an entity that is a provider of services (as defined in section 1395x(u) of this title), the person ***109** discloses (in such form and manner as the Secretary requires) to the entity and, upon request, to the Secretary the amount received from each such vendor with respect to purchases made by or on behalf of the entity;

(D) a waiver of any coinsurance under part B of subchapter XVIII of this chapter by a Federally qualified health care center with respect to an individual who qualifies for subsidized services under a provision of the Public Health Service Act [42 U.S.C.A. § 201 et seq.];

(E) any payment practice specified by the Secretary in regulations promulgated pursuant to section 14(a) of the Medicare and Medicaid Patient and Program Protection Act of 1987; and

(F) any remuneration between an organization and an individual or entity providing items or services, or a combination thereof, pursuant to a written agreement between the organization and the individual or entity if the organization is an eligible organization under section 1395mm of this title or if the written agreement, through a risk-sharing arrangement, places the individual or entity at substantial financial risk for the cost or utilization of the items or services, or a combination thereof, which the individual or entity is obligated to provide.

42 U.S.C. § 1320a–7b(b)(3).

At issue for Shaw's Motion to Dismiss for Failure to State a Crime is the interpretation and application of what is commonly referred to as the "discount exception," listed in the statute and above as (3)(A).

B. The Parties' Arguments

Defendant contends that seventy remunerations described in the indictment are, as a matter of law, covered by the "discount exception" and are thus not illegal remuneration under the statute. Shaw reaches this conclusion in the following manner.

First. Shaw contends that the government does not dispute that MPD made clear in writing to its buyer-providers of health care goods and services (hereinafter "buyer-providers") how much of a price reduction was being offered and on what basis in order that they could, as is required by law, pass on those reductions to the Medicare program. In other words, Shaw contends that MPD attempted in good faith to comply with the statutory requirements by enabling the buyer-provider to report to Medicare the reductions in prices it was receiving on the goods and services purchased. *Second.* Shaw contends that MPD's communication to its buyer-providers regarding the price reductions constitutes "adequate disclosure" under the "discount exception" and that it is for the buyer-provider to "appropriately reflect" those reductions in the costs claimed to the Federal health care program. *Third.* Shaw asserts that the price reductions at issue fit within the "discount exception" in that they are a form of "discount or other reduction in price" as provided by the words of the exception and are not a "rebate" as in the prohibited "remuneration (including a kickback, bribe, or rebate)".

The government responds in the following manner. *First.* The government says that the "discount exception" is an affirmative defense that must be raised and proved at trial and is therefore not an essential element of the crime the facts of which need to be alleged in the indictment. Specifically, the government says that it is for the jury to decide, based on the court's interpretation of the statute, (1) whether transactions are rebates or discounts and therefore whether they are properly the subject of the "discount exception" and (2) if they are discounts, whether they were "properly disclosed and appropriately reflected," thereby meeting the requirements of the "discount exception." In this regard, the government argues that if the court determines that the transactions were discounts that fall within the "discount ***110** exception," the court should still construe the statute to require that for discounts to be "properly disclosed," the material terms of the discounts must appear on the face of the transaction between MPD and the providers. *Second.* The government also says that defendant misreads the statute as a matter of law. The transactions at issue are "rebates," as that word has been defined by the statute, by the promulgating regulations, and by the case law. As rebates, the government contends, they cannot fit within the "discount exception" at all.

Although the issues presented are well-briefed, each party fails to persuade me that the proposed analysis of the issues at stake in this factually and legally complex case is correct. Defendant's Motion to Dismiss for Failure to State a Crime will be denied, but on reasoning somewhat different from that in the government's submissions.

The interpretation and application of the "discount exception" to the Medicare–Medicaid Anti–Kickback Statute appears to be an issue of first impression in this circuit, and perhaps in the circuits across the country. I have found no cases, and counsel have not drawn my attention to any cases, that purport to interpret the "discount exception" to the Medicare–Medicaid Anti–Kickback Statute and, in particular, as bearing on burdens of pleading and burdens of persuasion and production at trial.

I begin with an examination of the history of the statute and the accompanying development of the "discount exception." *See* Part V.C below. The several parts of V.D explain my interpretation of the "discount exception" based on that history and in light of the few cases interpreting and applying the elements of the Medicare–Medicaid Anti–Kickback Statute. *See, e.g., United States v. Bay State Ambulance and Hospital Rental Service,* 874 F.2d 20 (1st. Cir.1989). Part V.D.5 applies that interpretation to the facts of the case against the defendant Shaw, as alleged in the indictment.

C. Legislative and Regulatory History of the Anti–Kickback Statute

In 1972, Congress amended the Social Security Act in order to improve those provisions "relating to the old-age, survivors, and disability insurance program, the hospital and medical insurance program, the medical assistance program and the child welfare program." H.R.Rep. No. 92–231, at 1 (1972), *reprinted in* 1972 U.S.C.C.A.N. 4989, 4989–90. The provisions relating to medicare, medicaid and maternal and child health programs, *see id.,* 1972 U.S.C.C.A.N. at 5052, proposed to

> provide penalties for certain practices which have long been regarded by professional organizations as unethical, as well as unlawful in some jurisdictions, and which contribute appreciably to the cost of the medicare and medicaid programs. Thus, under the committee bill, the criminal penalty provision would include such practices as the soliciting, offering, or accepting of kickbacks or bribes, including the rebating of a portion of a fee or charge for a patient referral, involving providers of health care services.

Id., 1972 U.S.C.C.A.N. at 5093.

In 1977, Congress strengthened the Social Security Act by adding to it the Medicare–Medicaid Antifraud and Abuse Amendments (a part of which is the anti-kickback statute) the purpose of which was to address the "disturbing degree [of] fraudulent and abusive practices associated with the provision of health services financed by the medicare and medicaid programs." *See* H.R.Rep. No. 95–393, pt. 2, at 44 (1977), *reprinted in* 1977 U.S.C.C.A.N. 3039, 3047. The congressional findings that supported the amendments included findings of

> a broad range of improper activities which are not restricted to one particular class of providers or treatment settings. In whatever form it is found ... ***111** fraud in these health care financing programs adversely impacts on all Americans. It cheats taxpayers who must ultimately bear the financial burden of misuse of funds in any government-sponsored program. It diverts from those most in need, the nation's elderly and poor, scarce program dollars that were intended to provide vitally needed quality health services. The wasting of program funds through fraud also further erodes the financial stability of those state and local governments whose budgets are already overextended and who must commit an ever-increasing portion of their financial resources to fulfill the obligations of their medical assistance programs.

Id., 1977 U.S.C.C.A.N. at 3047.

The primary effect of the Medicare–Medicaid Antifraud and Abuse Amendments was to turn those fraudulent acts previously classified as misdemeanors into felonies, increasing penalties to a maximum of a $25,000 fine and up to five years imprisonment. *See id.* at 39, 1977 U.S.C.C.A.N. at 3041.

As originally drafted, the anti-kickback portion of the Medicare–Medicaid Antifraud and Abuse Amendments subjected to the penalty provisions

> any person who solicits or receives any remuneration (1) in return for referring an individual to a person for the furnishing, or arranging for the furnishing of items or services; or (2) in return for purchasing, leasing, or ordering, or arranging for, or recommending the purchasing, leasing, or ordering of goods, facilities, or services. Also, any person who offers or pays any remuneration to any person to induce such person to do similar activities would be subject to the penalty provision.

Id. at 53, 1977 U.S.C.C.A.N. at 3056. The bill defined the term "remuneration"

> broadly to encompass kickbacks, bribes or rebates which may be made directly or indirectly, overtly or covertly, in cash or in kind (but would exclude any amount paid by an employer to an employee for employment in the provision of covered items or services).

Id. The bill specifically excluded from the prohibited activities, however, "the practice of discounting or other reductions in price ... but only if such discounts are properly disclosed and reflected in the cost for which reimbursement could be claimed." *Id.*

> The committee included this [discount] provision to ensure that the practice of discounting the normal course of business transactions would not be deemed illegal. In fact, the committee would encourage providers to seek discounts as a good business practice which results in savings to medicare and medicaid program costs.

Id.

From the inception of these amendments to the Social Security Act, then, a tension existed between what the anti-kickback statute defined as illegal remuneration and the common business practice of offering discounts in order to increase sales. Although the purpose and the reason for the "discount exception" was to keep costs of medical services low and to minimize the burden on the federal health subsidies, the breadth of the statute's prohibition and the ambiguity of the scope of the "discount exception" frustrated the purpose of the statute, making difficult the enforcement and prosecution of fraudulent and abusive practices as well as chilling otherwise innocuous, or even beneficial, commercial arrangements in the health care field. *See* Department of Health and Human Services, Office of Inspector General, Medicare and State Health Care Programs: Fraud and Abuse; OIG Anti-Kickback Provisions, 56 Fed.Reg. 35,952 (1991) (codified at 42 C.F.R. § 1001 et. seq.).

Congress enacted, in 1987, the Medicare and Medicaid Patient and Program Protection Act, Pub.L. No. 100–93, that added two new provisions that addressed the problems of the breadth of the anti-kickback ***112** statute. One of the provisions, section 14 of Public Law 100–93, required the promulgation of regulations specifying those payment practices that might otherwise be misconstrued as illegal remunerations under the statute but that would from then on be in a category protected from criminal liability under the new paragraph (e) of section 1320a–7b(b), the "illegal remuneration" section, of the statute. *See* 56 Fed.Reg. 35,952 (1991). These regulations have become known as "safe harbors" and have been officially codified into the anti-kickback statute at 42 U.S.C. § 1320a–7b(b)(3)(E) (excluding "any payment practice specified by the Secretary in regulations promulgated pursuant to section 14(a) of the Medicare and Medicaid Patient and Program Protection Act of 1987" from liability under paragraphs (1) and (2) of section 1320a–7b(b)).

Initially, the OIG promulgated only ten safe-harbor provisions under the authority of the 1987 Medicare and Medicaid Patient and Program Protection Act, which were all codified at 42 C.F.R. § 1001.952. Those ten safe-harbor provisions included business arrangements concerning investment interests, space rental, equipment rental, referral services, warranties, employees, group purchasing organizations, the sale of practices, and discounts. *See* 42 C.F.R. § 1001.952 (1991). By granting the Department of Health and Human Services "the authority to protect certain arrangements and payment practices under the anti-kickback statute, [however], Congress intended the regulations to be evolving rules that would be updates periodically to reflect changing business practices and technologies in the health care industry." Department of Health and Human Services, Office of Inspector General, Medicare and State Health Care Programs: Fraud and Abuse; OIG Anti-Kickback Provisions, 64 Fed.Reg. 63,518, 63,518 (1999). In years following the final rule promulgations in 1991, other "safe-harbors" have been added. *See id.*

The regulations implementing the safe-harbor provisions, 42 C.F.R. § 1001.952, set forth in detail the precise form the business arrangements must take in order to be protected under the safe-harbor provisions from the possibility of criminal prosecution under the anti-kickback statute. *See* 42 U.S.C. § 1320a–7b(b)(3)(E); 42 C.F.R. § 1001.952. The OIG was careful to state, however, that the safe harbors do "not expand the scope of activities that the statute prohibits. The statute itself describes the scope of illegal activities. The legality of a particular business arrangement must be determined by comparing the particular facts to the proscriptions of the statute." Department of Health and Human Services, Office of Inspector General, Medicare and State Health Care Programs: Fraud and Abuse; OIG Anti-Kickback Provisions, 56 Fed.Reg. 35,952, 35,954 (1991). *See also* Department of Health and Human Services, Office of Inspector General, Medicare and State Health Care Programs: Fraud and Abuse; OIG Anti-Kickback Provisions, 59 Fed.Reg. 37,202, 37,203 (1994) (clarifying the effect of the safe-harbor provisions by saying that "[w]hether a particular payment practice violates the statute is a question that can only be resolved by an analysis of the elements of the statute as applied to that set of facts. Generally speaking, however, the original final [safe-harbor provisions] did describe payment practices that would be prohibited, where the unlawful intent exists, but for the safe harbor protection that has been granted.").

Defendant Shaw does not invoke the safe-harbor provisions as a reason for why his actions, as described in count eighteen of the indictment, are not prohibited activity under the anti-kickback statute. *See* Docket No. 133 at 8 ("Dr. Shaw's motion to dismiss contends that the price reductions alleged in the Superseding Indictment were protected by the discount provision, not by a regulatory safe harbor.") Shaw invokes the statutory "discount exception" that was written into the original act by the Medicare–Medicaid Antifraud and ***113** Abuse Amendments in 1977, what is now codified at 42 U.S.C. § 1320a–7b(b)(3)(A) (emphasis added). The safe-harbor provisions, now codified at 42 U.S.C. § 1320a–7b(b)(3)(E) (emphasis added), are separate and independent bases for which certain activities may be excluded from criminal liability under the anti-kickback statute. (The fact that the safe-harbor provisions set forth an independent basis for exclusion from criminal liability under the statute does not mean, of course, that a defendant is precluded from raising both the "discount exception" and one of the safe harbors as a defense. In this case, however, Shaw raises only the "discount exception" as a reason for why the indictment fails to state a crime.)

The independent status of the safe-harbor provisions from

the "discount exception," however, does not mandate their isolation from each other when one is looking for guidance as to the proper interpretation and application of one of the statutory exceptions to criminal liability. *See, e.g., Jusino Mercado v. Commonwealth of Puerto Rico,* 214 F.3d 34, 40 (1st Cir.2000) (stating that a statute's meaning in particular instances is to be arrived at not only by a consideration of the words themselves, but by considering, as well, the context, the purposes of the law, and the circumstances under which the words were employed). On the contrary, as one of the safe-harbor provisions is a "discount safe-harbor," it is reasonable that a court charged with the task of interpreting and applying the statutory "discount exception" would look to the regulatory agency's implementation of its own "discount safe-harbor" provision as guidance for how a "discount," generally, might provide shelter from the criminal penalties under the anti-kickback statute, a statute that otherwise penalizes "any remuneration" (of which a discount is a subset) that is willfully offered, paid or solicited in order to induce business reimbursable under federal or state health care programs. This does not mean that what the OIG says in its promulgated regulations about discounts is controlling on how the word "discount" is to be interpreted and applied in the statutory "discount exception." It means only that when interpreting the "discount exception," a court is wise to consider those discounting arrangements the regulatory agency, charged with aiding the implementation of and the corporate compliance with the statute, considers non-fraudulent and non-abusive under the safe-harbor provisions promulgated under the authority granted it by congress.

By way of a caveat, however, I note that the scope of the meaning of "discount" under the discount safe harbor has changed considerably since its first official iteration in 1991, especially as "discount" relates to a "rebate." These changes are significant as supporting an inference that reliance on any one definition of "discount" or "rebate" as found in the regulations that implement the safe-harbor provisions (42 C.F.R. § 1001.952(h)) would be error if relied upon for the purposes of interpreting the "discount exception" (§ 1320a–7b(b)(3)(A)) of the anti-kickback statute. The changing nature of protected discounted (and even rebated) arrangements under the safe-harbor regulations is an expression of what the OIG has explained to be congress's intent that the regulations be "evolving rules that would be updated periodically to reflect changing business practices and technologies in the health care industry." 64 Fed.Reg. 63,518, 63,518 (1999). Thus, because the "discount exception" to the anti-kickback statute is a separate provision under which the defendant may claim an exemption from liability under the statute—one that was enacted over a decade before the safe-harbor provisions were first promulgated to provide further protection for health-care-service-and-goods providers from liability under the statute—I will interpret the "discount exception" to the anti-kickback statute in light of those discounting arrangements that the safe-harbor provisions have explicitly deemed protected from criminal liability, but I will not be limited by the ***114** definitions imposed by the safe-harbor provisions. *See, e.g.,* 42 C.F.R. § 1001.952(h)(4) (for a definition of "rebate" for the purposes of the paragraph in which the word is found); 42 C.F.R. § 1001.952(h)(5) (for a definition of "discount" for the purposes of the paragraphs in which the word is found).

D. Interpretation of the "Discount Exception"

1. *Carve–Out Structure of Statutory Drafting*

As a preliminary matter, I note that the "discount exception" is an example of the "common technique of modern legal drafting referred to in various phrases of which 'carve-out' is an example." *See Keeton, Judging in the American Legal System* (Lexis Law Publishing, 1999) § 14.5.3 (and citations therein). In paragraphs (1) and (2) of § 1320a–7b(b), the statute sets forth the activities that it makes illegal ("whoever knowingly and willfully solicits or receives any remuneration ..."), and then in its paragraph (3), the statute partially withdraws from that declaration, or "carves-out" an exception to that declaration by granting certain "discounts or other reductions in price" that define a kind of immunity from criminal liability under the statute ("Paragraphs (1) and (2) shall not apply to—(A) a discount or other reduction in price ..."). *See* 42 U.S.C. § 1320a–7b(b)(3).

This understanding of the "discount exception"—that but for the "carve-out" provision, a discount or other reduction in price would fall within the activities prohibited by paragraphs (1) or (2) of section 1320a–7b(b)—is reflected in the OIG's Final Rule promulgations. For example, in 1991, as part of its analysis of the scope of the statute, the OIG explained its understanding that a discount could be an "illegal remuneration" under the statute (as it is often made for the purpose of inducing referrals and further purchases) unless it otherwise satisfies the exception's reporting requirements. *See* 56 Fed.Reg. 35,952, 35,957 (1991) ("Congress's intent in placing the term 'remuneration' in the statute in 1977 was to cover the transferring of anything of value in any form or manner whatsoever.... Moreover, the statutory exception for discounts demonstrates that Congress prohibited transactions where there is no direct payment at all from the party receiving the referrals. The remuneration in a discount is merely a lowered price that a purchaser would otherwise obtain from a seller, which is made as an inducement to purchase larger quantities.").

Thus, the "discount exception" carves out a specific kind of remuneration from the universe of the potentially "illegal remuneration" that the statute circumscribes. This means that labeling the transaction a "discount" does not save the activity from prosecutorial scrutiny because a discount is a kind of remuneration. It means also that for a defendant to be found criminally liable for offering or soliciting illegal remunerations, all the elements of the crime as stated in paragraphs (1) and (2) of § 1320a–7b(b), including the *mens rea* element, must be found beyond reasonable doubt. *See, e.g.*, 64 Fed.Reg. 63,518, 63,519 (1999) ("The anti-kickback statute ... establishes an intent based criminal prohibition with optional statutory and regulatory 'safe harbors' that do not purport to define the full range of lawful activity. Rather, the safe harbors provide a means of assuring that payment practices are not illegal. Payment practices that do not fully comply with a safe harbor may still be lawful if no purpose of the payment practice is to induce referrals of Federal health care program business.") In other words, the fundamental analysis required of a trier of fact is "to recognize that the substance rather than simply the form of the transaction should be controlling." 56 Fed.Reg. 35,952, 35,957 (*citing* 123 Cong.Rec. 30,280 (1977), Statement of Chairman of the House Committee on Ways and Means and principal author of H.R. 3 (the Medicare–Medicaid Anti– ***115** Fraud and Abuse Amendments), Representative Rostenkowski).

For these competitively low prices (in the form of discounts or "other reductions") to be exempt from criminal liability, however, they must enure to the benefit of Medicare and Medicaid and of their beneficiaries. Thus, one essential component of this exception is that the federal or state health program share in and benefit from the reduced cost of the services or goods that are being provided at a discount or other reduced price. *See* 64 Fed.Reg. 63,518, 63,529 (1999) ("Congress intended only to protect discounts that could fairly benefit the Federal health care programs."). The only way to pass on those benefits, however, is if Medicare and Medicaid are made aware of the competitively low costs so that the federal or state system reimburses the provider the percentage of only the reduced price. This is the purpose of the phrase in the exception "properly disclose and appropriately reflected." See additional explanation below in Part V.D.3(b).

In the context of the entire statute, the discount exception makes good sense. The statute was passed to curtail fraud and abuse in Medicare and Medicaid reporting, in particular. It was passed to prevent health care service and good suppliers and providers from depriving the federal and state health care subsidy system of the benefits that a free market for health care services and goods can provide. By allowing for suppliers and providers of health care service and goods to compete with one another in limited forms, the statute strikes a balance: on the one hand, it provides for some of the benefits of a market economy by encouraging limited forms of price competition; on the other hand, it deters and penalizes other types of conduct that would lower the cost of some health care services and goods for some suppliers and providers but would not pass on that lowered cost to the federal and state health systems or to its patients.

2. *The Purpose of the "Discount Exception"*

As stated in the House Report on the Medicare–Medicaid Anti–Fraud and Abuse Amendments, the reason for excluding certain "practice[s] of discounting the normal course of business transactions" from criminal liability under the statute was to "encourage providers to seek discounts as a good business practice which results in savings to medicare and medicaid program costs." H.R.Rep. No. 95–393, pt. 2, at 54 (1977), *reprinted in* 1977 U.S.C.C.A.N. 3039, 3056. The exception, then, reflects a predictive understanding that competitive pricing schemes within the health care field will lower the cost of health care services and goods.

3. *An Analysis of the Language of the Discount Exception*

In the context of the statute's "carve-out" structure and the purpose of the "discount exception," some further points regarding the precise language and meaning of the "discount exception" deserve attention.

(a) "*discount or other reduction in price*"

Both the government and defendant fall prey to a false

dichotomy when they argue that a crucial distinction exists between "rebate" and "discount" for the purposes of understanding the scope and function of the "discount exception."

In the first instance, the label given the transaction, be it "discount" or "rebate," is not what transforms an otherwise lawful act into a crime. It is not the case, as the government argues, that any rebate is per se illegal remuneration. Nor is it the case, as defense argues, that any discount, "properly disclosed and appropriately reflected", is exempt from criminal liability. What makes the activity illegal is not the label someone attaches to the form of the transaction, even if the form may give rise to the rebuttable inference of illegality. ***116** The reason behind the transaction and the requisite state of mind underlying the criminal act are more significant than form and label. This point will be considered again in Part V.D.4 below.

Another way of explaining this point is to emphasize that the terms used in the statute are broad and are not mutually exclusive. This fact is part of the reason why the provisions defining safe harbors were promulgated in the first place. *See* 56 Fed.Reg. 35,952, 35,952 (1991). For example, a "discount or other reduction in price" as stated in the discount exception (paragraph (3) of § 1320a–7b(b)) is a kind of transferral of value, and thus a kind of remuneration (as that term is used in paragraphs (1) and (2) of § 1320a–7b(b)). *See* 56 Fed.Reg. 35,952, 35,957 (1991) (stating that "Congress's intent in placing the term 'remuneration' in the statute in 1977 was to cover the transferring of anything of value in any form or manner whatsoever" and that the "statute's language makes clear that illegal payments are prohibited beyond merely 'bribes,' 'kickbacks,' and 'rebates,' which were the three terms used in the original 1972 statute"). It cannot be the case, then, that *any* and *every* remuneration is illegal. If that were so, the various exceptions to the statute (¶¶ (A)–(E)) would be meaningless. *See, e.g., United States v. Holmquist,* 36 F.3d 154, 160 (1st Cir.1994) (stating the well-worn principle that a statute shall not be read to render words meaningless). By the same token, a rebate, the statute's example of an illegal remuneration in paragraphs (1) and (2) of § 1320a–7b(b), is also a kind of "discount or other reduction in price," as that phrase is used in the discount exception in paragraph (3) of § 1320a–7b(b). A rebate is typically given after sale and discounts are effected at the time of sale. But both discounts and rebates reduce the overall price of the item purchased and therefore, ideally, they both reduce the cost that would be reimbursed by Medicare or Medicaid. Both rebates and discounts, then, satisfy the purpose of the first exception in the statute, paragraph (A) of § 1320a–7b(b)(3).

The government argues that the difference in the time of the price reduction between a rebate and a discount is precisely the issue when, as is the case with this statute, we are concerned with curtailing opportunities for abuse and fraudulent non-disclosure with regard to reimbursement of Medicare and Medicaid costs. But, as explained above and amplified below, rebates are not *per se* illegal remunerations under the statute. A *per se* rule would make little sense in light of the expansion of the scope of activities (such as rebates) that are provided safe harbor in Part (E) of section 1320a–7b(b)(3) under certain circumstances. *See* 42 C.F.R. § 1001.952(h)(1)(iii)(A); 42 C.F.R. § 1001.952(h)(4).

Consider, as bearing on the validity of this analysis, the following evolution of the scope of "discounting" activities protected by the safe-harbor provisions.

When the final rule version of the safe-harbor regulations first came out in 1991, the OIG clarified what kinds of discounts would be within safe harbors under its rules. Those clarifications included the following.

Discounts were only transactions made on an arms length basis and not through a joint-venture or collusive contract. *See* 56 Fed.Reg. 35,952, 35,977 (1991). A discount was not a gift of free "bundled goods," those goods that were closely related to the purchased goods, such as free "surgical packs." *See id.* Discounts included rebate checks, redeemable coupons and credits subject to certain conditions, one of which is that the reductions in prices are attributable to the original good or service that was purchased or furnished. *See* 56 Fed.Reg. 35,952, 35,978 (1991) and 42 C.F.R. § 1001.952(h)(3) (1991). A discount could be an end-of-the-year payment made on the basis of charges or acquisition costs, but only for cost-report providers, and only under certain conditions. *See* ***117** 56 Fed.Reg. 56,952, 35,979 and 42 C.F.R. § 1001.952(h)(1)(i) (1991).

In 1994, the OIG issued further clarifications of its 1991 final rules. *See* 59 Fed.Reg. 37,202, 37,205. Those clarifications included a new paragraph on the scope of the discount safe harbor, saying that

> for the purposes of this regulation, a 'rebate' is any discount which is not given at the time of sale. Consequently, a rebate transaction may be covered within the safe harbor if it involves a buyer under

> § 1001.952(h)(1)(i) or (h)(1)(ii), but it is not covered if it involves a buyer under § 1011.952(h)(1)(iii) because under that provision, all discounts must be given at the time of sale.

Id. at 37,205. *See also* 42 C.F.R. §§ 1001.952(h)(1)(iii)(A) (1994) & § 1001.952(h)(4) (1994).

More recently, in 1999, the OIG issued another final-rule version of safe-harbor regulations in order to "add new safe harbor provisions under the Federal and state health care programs' anti-kickback statute, ... and to clarify various aspects of the original safe harbor provisions. Specifically, this final rule modifies the original set of final safe harbor provisions codified in 42 C.F.R. § 1001.952." 64 Fed.Reg. 63,518 (1999). In this most recent iteration of the regulations, the OIG divided the parties to the discounted transaction into three groups—buyers, sellers, and offers of discounts—in order to explain better how to comply with the regulation. *See id.* at 63,526. *See also* 42 C.F.R. § 1001.952(h) (1999).

Also, the 1999 promulgations further defined a "rebate" as not only a discount not given at the time of sale, but one that would not be within a safe-harbor if it "involves a buyer under § 1001.952(h)(1)(iii) that is neither a cost-reporter nor a HMO or CMP [competitive medical plan], because for such buyers, all discounts must be given at the time of sale." *See* 64 Fed.Reg. 63,518, 63,526 (1999). The term "rebate" was expanded, however, to include "any discount the terms of which are fixed at the time of sale of the good or service and disclosed to the buyer, but which is not received at the time of the sale of the good or service," a modification that enabled the OIG "to extend safe harbor protection to certain charge-based buyers and buyers reimbursed on the basis of fee schedules who obtain rebates." *See id.* at 63,527.

The 1999 final-rule action allowed for credits and coupons to qualify for safe-harbor protection, as long as they meet certain criteria, and also provided that in certain circumstances discounts on multiple items would qualify as a "discount" for safe harbor purposes where the reimbursement methodology for all discounted items or services is the same. *See id. See also* 42 C.F.R. § 1001.952(h)(5)(i) & (ii) (1999).

The evolution of the term "discount" over the past decade demonstrates the OIG's attempt to encourage a broad range of commercial transactions in a changing marketplace while at the same time monitoring the structure of those transactions for potential fraud and abuse. The changing scope of the meaning of the word "discount" under the safe-harbor regulation is also evidence of the fact that it is a fluid term that encompasses certain kinds of "rebates" but not others, and encompasses certain kinds of credits, but not others. Terms like "discount" and "rebate" then, contrary to how the government and defense would have it, are not mutually exclusive, even in the safe-harbor regulations that purport to be defining them in ways arguably narrower than in the statutory "discount exception."

In sum, for the purposes of interpreting the "discount exception" (paragraph (A) of § 1320a–7b(b)(3) of the anti-kickback statute, as opposed to paragraph (E), the safe-harbor regulations), a rebate is a kind of discount, as well as a kind of reduction in price. Both can be a form of remuneration that if offered or received with the ***118** requisite *mens rea,* might be considered "illegal remuneration" under the statute, and thus cannot be barred entirely from consideration under the "discount exception."

(b) *"properly disclosed and appropriately reflected "*

(i) The Parties' Arguments

Any "discount or other reduction in price" must be "properly disclosed and appropriately reflected" in order to qualify for immunity from criminal liability under the exemption. Defendant argues that this limiting language in the discount exception should be read in the disjunctive as "properly disclosed *or* appropriately reflected." Defendant so argues because, he says, a conjunctive reading would hold a seller-supplier of health care goods and services (like MPD) criminally liable for the non-reporting of the costs by the buyer-provider, as it is the buyer-provider of the goods and services who has the responsibility for filing the cost reports for proper reimbursement from Medicare and Medicare. *See, e.g.,* 42 C.F.R. § 413.20. This, defendant says, "would lead to several contradictory and even absurd results," such as nullifying the statute's scienter requirement and creating an "unprecedented executory period during which both the supplier offering a price reduction and the provider accepting the price reduction would be exposed to criminal liability for a period of time" before the cost report is filed with Medicare or Medicaid. Docket No. 102 at 13–15.

Defendant supports his argument that the phrase at issue should be read in the disjunctive with, in addition to assertions stated above, the assertion that the key distinction between a lawful price reduction and an unlawful one under the statute is full and accurate disclosure of the reduction in price. If a seller-supplier discloses the amount and method of the reduction in price to the buyer-provider whose responsibility it is to report the reduced costs to Medicare or Medicaid, then, the defendant contends, the discount exception has been satisfied and the purpose of the statute fulfilled.

The government's principal response is that disclosure is not enough. The statute calls for "proper disclosure," which the government interprets as requiring "full disclosure of the material terms of the transaction." Docket No. 128 at 23. To this the defendant says that the government's suggestion that the exception requires the disclosure of "material terms" is reading too much into the statute; "full and accurate disclosure of the price reduction" is all that is required. *See* Docket No. 133 at 12.

In response to defendant's argument about the disjunctive reading of the phrase "properly disclosed and appropriately reflected," the government does not question defendant's assertion that the "and" should be understood as an "or." Instead, the government says the absurdities that defendant suggests arise from a conjunctive reading are ameliorated by the various provisions of the regulatory safe harbor that protects a seller-supplier who offers a discount to a buyer-provider and also takes all reasonable steps to ensure that the value of the discount is passed through to Medicare or Medicaid, even when it is a buyer-provider who has the duty to report the reduction in price to the federal or state system.

It is true that the regulatory safe harbors provide detailed instructions on how a buyer-supplier may discharge its reporting duty and avoid criminal liability. *See, e.g.*, 42 C.F.R. §§ 1001.952(h)(1), 1001.952(h)(2)(ii). Those provisions, however, apply only in very specific instances, when the buyer-supplier is a certain kind of entity and the reduction in price a certain form of discount or rebate as defined by the safe-harbor provision. *See id. See also United States v. Bay State Ambulance and Hospital Rental Service*, 874 F.2d 20, 31 (1st Cir.1989). For the reasons stated previously (*see* Part V.C ***119** above), I do not consider the discount exception and the safe-harbor provisions so separate as not to be worthy of attention when determining the meaning of one or the other. They may be better understood as separate exceptions within a coordinated framework. A defendant may assert either as a defense or both as defenses. They are not irrelevant, one to the other, when the task at hand is to determine the scope and meaning of either or both. For the purposes of applying the phrase at issue in the "discount exception" to the facts of this case, however, the details of the safe-harbor provisions immunizing a specific kind of buyer from criminal liability under specific circumstances do not control a proper understanding of the "discount exception" that I am asked to interpret and apply.

(ii) A Close Reading of "*properly disclosed and appropriately reflected* "

With regard to the issue of what constitutes "proper" and "appropriate" disclosure, the memoranda of the parties speak at cross purposes. The statute requires disclosure and reflection of the costs incurred in order to satisfy the purposes of the statute—to pass on the benefits of the price reduction to Medicare or Medicaid. The government's suggested reading that the "material terms" of the transaction be disclosed is unpersuasive. It begs two questions: material to whom and in what context? The parties to the transaction might consider many more terms "material" than those needed by Medicare or Medicaid for reimbursement purposes. What the parties to the transaction may consider material, however, is not decisive as to whether the purpose of the statute is satisfied. The statute aims at reduction of the price of the goods or services through disclosure, so a lower price can be reflected in lower costs claimed from or charged to a federal health care program. In this way, the federal health program may benefit from a reduction in price offered and received. Whether disclosures are "proper" and "appropriate," as the statute requires, will depend on the details of the transaction as proved at trial and under appropriately fashioned instructions to the jury about the law they are to apply so as to understand the questions of fact they are to decide.

With regard to arguments about the conjunctive or disjunctive reading of the phrase "properly disclosed and appropriately reflected," both parties misconstrue the meaning of that phrase in the context of the "discount exception" as a whole. The phrase is properly read in the conjunctive but the effect of such a conjunctive reading does not create the conundrum that defendant suggests it does.

In order for the statute (1) to prohibit both offers and acceptances of illegal remunerations and (2) to encourage certain "discounts and other reductions in price" that would increase competition and reduce health care costs, the "discount exception" must apply to both those who offer and those who accept "discounts and other reductions in price." (The statute's criminal prohibition does, in fact, apply to both those who make offers, *i.e.*, to the seller-supplier, and those who accept offers, *i.e.*, the buyer-provider. *Compare* paragraph (1) with paragraph (2) of § 1320a–7b(b).) Defendant's argument that the "discount exception" protects only those who are asking for reimbursement directly from Medicare or Medicaid and not those who offer the "discount or other reduction in price," (for whom direct reimbursement from Medicare or Medicaid is never a part of daily business practice or an incentive) misreads the exception by misconstruing its grammatical structure.

Defendant argues that by force of the wording in the paragraph, the phrase "properly disclosed and appropriately reflected" relates only to the buyer-provider. This is not correct. To come to a proper understanding of the phrase "properly disclosed and appropriately reflected," one must read this phrase in relation to its ***120** neighboring clauses. The entire paragraph is as follows:

> Paragraphs (1) and (2) shall not apply to—
>
> (A) a discount or other reduction in price obtained by a provider of services or other entity under a Federal health care program if the reduction in price is properly disclosed and appropriately reflected in the costs claimed or charges made by the provider or entity under a Federal health care program.

42 U.S.C. § 1320a–7b(b)(3)(A). Close reading reveals that the verbs "disclose" and "reflect" describe the required activities for both "provider" and "entity". The phrase "costs claimed ... by the provider" refers to those costs claimed to Medicare or Medicaid by the buyer-provider. The phrase "charges made by the ... entity" refers to those costs charged to the buyer-provider by the seller-supplier. Both phrases are modified by the phrase "properly disclosed and appropriately reflected," which describes the required reporting activities for both the "provider" and the "entity." Thus both parties to the transaction, the seller-supplier and buyer-provider, must properly disclose and appropriately reflect the reductions in price in order to find shelter under the discount exception.

Transforming the "and" between "properly disclosed and appropriately reflected" into an "or" is both unnecessary and inappropriate under a proper reading of the paragraph. Both buyer-providers and seller-suppliers are required to "properly disclose[ ] and appropriately reflect[ ]" the reduction in price offered or received for Medicare or Medicaid reimbursable goods or services in order to avoid criminal liability.

4. *The Scienter Requirement*

The proper interpretation and application of the "discount exception," in light of the above three sections explaining its form and content, may be aided by a brief diversion into a discussion of the statute's scienter requirement. As stated above in Parts V.C and V.D.2, the "discount exception" acknowledges that profit motive does not necessarily trigger criminal liability. Offering or receiving discounts in order to compete for business does not alone mean that the entity "knowingly and willfully" induced or arranged for referrals or for other business reimbursable under the Medicaid or Medicaid programs. The "discount exception" was written into the statute from its inception in 1977 to allow for and acknowledge the benefits of competition between health care suppliers and providers, a competition that is based, in part, on a basic profit motive. *See* H.R.Rep. No. 95–393, pt. 2, at 53 (1977), *reprinted in* 1977 U.S.C.C.A.N. 3039, 3056 (stating that "discount exception" should "encourage providers to seek discounts as a good business practice which results in savings to medicare and medicaid program costs"). Thus, profit motive as evidenced by the offer or acceptance of a "discount or other reduction in price" is not sufficient to support a finding of the state of mind necessary to convict under the statute.

Consider the following discussion by the OIG regarding the importance of the intent requirement when deciding criminal liability under the statute.

> [I]t is unfortunately not possible to provide safe harbor protections for all business arrangements that are not abusive. There are certain arrangements that, although themselves legitimate, are structurally so similar to abusive arrangements that protection by way of new safe harbor provisions will inevitably also protect abusive practices as well. For example, equipment rental arrangements made between parties in a position to make and accept referrals do not receive safe harbor protection if the

> payments are based on utilization (sometimes known as the "wear and tear" clause). We recognize that equipment becomes less valuable the more it is used, and that its owner deserves compensation ***121** for such wear and tear. However, it is also a relatively easy matter to disguise such a wear and tear payment as a payment for referrals. Thus, we need to examine the intent of the parties on a case-by-case basis even though a large majority of such payments may represent only legitimate compensation to the owner of the equipment. The recent case, *United States v. Bay State Ambulance and Hospital Rental Service, Inc.*, ... emphasizes that the gravamen of the violation of the statute is "inducement" and not necessarily the structure of the arrangement. Thus, such case by case inquiries must necessarily focus on the intent of the parties.

56 Fed.Reg. 35,952, 35,955 (1991).

Several reported cases also address this issue of intent under the statute. The United States Court of Appeals for the Third Circuit, in *United States v. Greber,* 760 F.2d 68 (3d Cir.1985), held that, all other elements being satisfied, the statute is violated "if one purpose of the [remuneration] is to induce future referrals" of Medicare or Medicaid reimbursable business, "even if the payments were also intended to compensate for professional services." *Id.* at 72. In *United States v. Kats,* 871 F.2d 105 (9th Cir.1989), the court adopted the Third Circuit's reasoning and upheld a jury instruction that read:

> It is not a defense that there might have been other reasons for the solicitation of a remuneration by the defendants, if you find that one of the material purpose for the solicitation was to obtain money for the referral of services.

871 F.2d at 108 n. 1. Most recently, the United States Court of Appeals for the First Circuit upheld a district court's jury instruction charging that under the anti-kickback statute

> the defendants could only be found guilty if the payments were made primarily as inducements [for purchasing or referring medicare reimbursable business] ... If you find the payments were made for two or more purposes, then the government has to prove that the improper purpose is the primary purpose or was the primary purpose in making and receiving the payments....

Bay State Ambulance, 874 F.2d at 30. "The gravamen of Medicare Fraud is inducement," the Court of Appeals for the First Circuit declared, making it clear that the willful-and-knowing element of the crime is a touchstone for the proper evaluation of both the statute's meaning and the application of its "discount exception." *Id.* at 29.

All of these cases confirm that the issue for a jury to decide, when faced with a defendant whose contention is that the defendant is not criminally liable under the statute due to the "discount exception," is whether the reason for offering or accepting the "discount or other reduction in price" was to induce referrals of or be reimbursed for federal health care program business. It may be the case that one piece of evidence to weigh when considering whether defendant acted with the requisite intent is whether the "discount or other reduction in price" was passed on to the Medicare or Medicaid program. It also may be the case that the profit motive was so strong—the defendant was so severely in debt or the amount of profit was so enormously high—that a jury could infer that profit motive supports an inference of willful and knowing purpose to induce referrals of or be reimbursed for federal health care program business. None of this permits, however, an instruction to the jury that an inference that it makes good sense in business practice to increase profits precludes the possibility of a defendant's invoking immunity under the "discount exception."

5. *The Application of the "Discount Exception" at Trial*

For the reasons explained above in the explanation of the structure, purpose and language of the "discount exception," and of intent element of the crime, the ***122** defendant's motion to dismiss must be denied.

The indictment contains all the elements of the charged offense of conspiring to commit an offense against the United States, to wit, knowingly, willfully and intentionally to offer and pay illegal kickbacks to obtain referrals of laboratory business in violation of 42 U.SC. § 1320a–7b(b)(2)(B). *See* Docket No. 46 at ¶ 70.

Defendant's argument that he should prevail on his motion because the overt acts charged as part of the conspiracy—the allegedly illegal remunerations—are protected by the "discount exception" of the statute as a matter of law, relies on the erroneous legal premise that the statute requires that the government state in the indictment that the defendant's conduct does not fall within the "discount exception." As explained in the preceding parts of this Opinion, however, the "discount exception" does not serve as an additional element of the criminal offense. It serves, instead, as a framework around which arguments of the parties regarding the evidentiary issues, such as how the government is to prove beyond a reasonable doubt that the defendant acted with the requisite state of mind, may be presented during trial.

For example, if during trial evidence is proffered by the government or by a defendant that a discount or other reduction in price was disclosed or otherwise reflected in the costs claimed or charges made, it may be necessary for the court to make some evidentiary rulings and, depending on such proffers and rulings, it may be necessary to include in the Charge to the Jury some instruction on how disclosure of those price reductions may affect their verdict. Those matters are reserved for later determination, if they are presented at trial, and are not addressed in this Opinion.

Also, the aspects of the Charge to the Jury that concern the willfulness element of any offense charged are not decided now but will be considered immediately before and during trial.

In light of the issues that are addressed and the rulings that are made in this Opinion, Defendant Shaw's Motion to Dismiss for Failure to State a Crime will be dismissed in the order that follows this Opinion.

VI. Motion to Dismiss on Statute–of–Limitation Grounds

Defendant Shaw has also filed a motion to dismiss the indictment against him because, as he argues, it was returned after the five-year statute of limitation period expired. *See* Docket Nos. 43 and 104. Defendant argues that the limitation period began to run when Shaw effectively withdrew from the conspiracy at the time of his retirement from NMC, when he abandoned his alleged role in the conspiracy as the president of MPD, the seller-supplier. Even taking as undisputed the fact that the indictment dated February 10, 1999, was returned against Shaw five years, two months and one week after he retired from NMC on December 3, 1999, I cannot allow defendant's motion to dismiss on statute-of-limitation grounds. Reasons are identified immediately below.

First. Defendant is charged with violating 18 U.S.C. § 371, the overt act conspiracy statute. The overt acts alleged in the indictment are at paragraph 73(g), which comprises seven pages of a chart detailing the dates, amounts and form of payment from dialysis facilities external to NMC. *See* Docket No. 46 at ¶ 73(g). Many of these transactions are dated after defendants alleged retirement from NMC. *See id.* Thus, on its face, the indictment charges the commission of overt acts in furtherance of the conspiracy of which the government alleges the defendant was a part within the statute-of-limitation period. *See, e.g., United States v. Fitzpatrick*, 892 F.2d 162, 167 (1st Cir.1989); *Grunewald v. United States*, 353 U.S. 391, 396–97, 77 S.Ct. 963, 1 L.Ed.2d 931 (1957).

***123** *Second*. Defendant's contention that he effectively withdrew from the conspiracy, was no longer a member of the conspiracy, and was no longer liable for the acts of his coconspirators that were committed after his retirement in December 3, 1993, relies on issues of fact that must be submitted to a jury. *See, e.g., United States v. Sepulveda*, 15 F.3d 1161, 1190 (1st Cir.1993) (citing cases and discussing "bedrock" principles of the law of conspiracy, especially those surrounding membership that are for the jury to resolve). One factual issue to be resolved, for example, is whether his retirement effected his withdrawal from the conspiracy. Did his retirement end his involvement with NMC entirely? Although courts have recognized that a defendant can withdraw from a business conspiracy (a conspiracy carried out through the regular activities of an otherwise legitimate business enterprise) by severing his ties to the business, the effectiveness of the withdrawal depends in large part on the showing that employment at the business was essential to the defendant's involvement in the alleged conspiracy and that the defendant no longer maintained any ties with the business. *See, e.g., Morton's Market, Inc. v. Gustafson's Dairy, Inc.*, 198 F.3d 823 (11th Cir.1999); *United States v. DePeri*, 778 F.2d 963, 980 (3d Cir.1985); *United States v. Lowell*, 649 F.2d 950, 955 (3d Cir.1981). *Cf. United States v. Nerlinger*, 862 F.2d 967, 974 (2nd Cir.1988). *See also United States v. Fitzpatrick*, 892 F.2d 162, 167 (1st Cir.1989) (with regard to a statute-of-limitation defense, agreeing with the Court of Appeals for the Fifth Circuit that a conspiracy continues until anticipated economic benefits of the defendant are realized). Another factual issue to be decided, related to the first, is whether defendant's retirement from NMC was an affirmative act that disavowed or defeated the purpose of the conspiracy, in light of the case law that says that mere cessation of conspiratorial activity is not enough to effect a withdrawal. *See United States v. Juodakis*, 834 F.2d 1099, 1102 (1st Cir.1987); *United States v. Borelli*, 336 F.2d 376, 388 (2d Cir.1964), *cert. denied*, 379 U.S. 960, 85 S.Ct. 647, 13 L.Ed.2d 555 (1965).

In short, whether the prosecution of Shaw is time-barred turns on issues of fact that go to the evidence of the alleged offense itself—his membership in and alleged withdrawal from the conspiracy alleged in the indictment. For these reasons, defendant's motion to dismiss the indictment against him will be denied in the order below.

VII. Matters Remaining to be Decided

The following pretrial motions remain pending in this case:

(1) Motion of Defendants Aird and Verde to Dismiss Counts 1 and 10–17 of the Superseding Indictment for Failure to State a Crime (Docket No. 142);

(2) Motion of Defendants Aird and Verde to Strike Surplusage (Docket No. 153);

(3) Defendants' Joint Motion for Reconsideration of Magistrate's Ruling on Pretrial Motions (Docket No. 124);

(4) Defendant Shaw's Motion for Relief from Prejudicial Misjoinder Pursuant to Fed.R.Crim.P. 8(b) (Docket No. 113);

(5) Defendant Aird's Motion for Relief from Prejudicial Misjoinder Pursuant to Fed.R.Crim.P. 8(b) (Docket No. 115);

(6) Defendant Verde's Motion for Relief from Prejudicial Misjoinder Pursuant to Fed.R.Crim.P. 8(b) (Docket No. 117).

These outstanding motions will be the subject of forthcoming memoranda and orders.

All Citations

106 F.Supp.2d 103

End of Document

KeyCite Red Flag - Severe Negative Treatment
Vacated and Remanded by United States v. Luis, 11th Cir.(Fla.), June 16, 2016

966 F.Supp.2d 1321
United States District Court,
S.D. Florida.

UNITED STATES of America, Plaintiff,
v.
Sila LUIS, et al., Defendants.

Case No. 12–23588–CIV.
|
June 21, 2013.

Synopsis
Background: Government moved to convert temporary restraining order (TRO) into preliminary injunction restraining assets of defendant who was charged, in parallel criminal prosecution, with conspiracy to commit health care fraud, conspiracy to defraud United States and to commit offenses against United States, and paying health care kickbacks. Defendant moved to modify restraining order to release assets for her defense in related prosecution.

Holdings: The District Court, Paul C. Huck, J., held that:

probable cause supported issuance of preliminary injunction;

defendant was entitled to hearing at which she had opportunity to cross-examine FBI special agent;

safe-harbor provisions of Medicare's anti-kickback statute and related regulation did not apply to payments made to nurses to recruit patients for defendant's health care businesses;

court could find, in support of preliminary injunction, that defendant's conduct satisfied knowing misrepresentation element of charge of conspiracy to commit health care fraud;

government did not have to demonstrate that it had suffered a loss to obtain preliminary injunction to restrain defendant's assets;

conspiracy to pay kickbacks to receive benefits under Medicare, in violation of general conspiracy statute, could provide basis for preliminary injunction restraining defendant's assets; and

court could restrain assets that defendant sought to use to pay attorney fees in parallel criminal case, although court had discretion to release assets for payment of such fees.

Government's motion granted; defendant's motion denied.

Attorneys and Law Firms

***1325** Susan Torres, U.S. Attorney's Office, Miami, FL, for Plaintiff.

Howard Milton Srebnick, Black Srebnick Kornspan & Stumpf, Scott Alan Srebnick, Miami, FL, for Defendants.

ORDER

PAUL C. HUCK, District Judge.

THIS MATTER is before the Court upon the United States of America (the "Government['s]") Emergency *Ex Parte* Motion for Temporary Restraining Order and Preliminary Injunction under 18 U.S.C. § 1345 [D.E. # 4] and Defendant, Sila Luis ("Luis['s]") Motion to Modify the Restraining Order to Release Assets for the Defense of the Related Criminal Case [D.E. # 46]. For the reasons discussed below, the Motion for Preliminary Injunction is granted and Luis's Motion to Modify the Restraining Order is denied.

A. Background

a. *Statutory Basis for Injunctive Relief Under 18 U.S.C. § 1345*

Section 1345 allows courts to grant injunctive relief to prevent certain types of fraud and to prevent alienation of property associated with the fraud. 18 U.S.C. § 1345. Thus, a court may enter an injunction under § 1345 preventing mail fraud, wire fraud, banking laws, or the commission of a federal health care offense.[1] *Id.* Section 1345 also allows a court to enter an injunction when an individual alienates or disposes of any property obtained as a result of such violations, to prevent any person from withdrawing, transferring, removing, dissipating, or disposing of any such property or property of equivalent value.[2] *Id.* The "equivalent value" language means that when some of the assets that were obtained as a result of fraud cannot be located, a person's substitute, untainted assets may be restrained instead. *See United States v. DBB, Inc.*, 180 F.3d 1277, 1281 (11th Cir.1999).

b. *The Burden of Proof and Elements for Injunctive Relief Under § 1345*

As to the elements for injunctive relief, a reasonable reading of § 1345 indicates ***1326** that the Government bears the burden to establish that: (1) a Federal health care offense has been committed; (2) the total amount of proceeds obtained from the criminal activity; and (3) that there has been dissipation of assets received as a result of the criminal activity. *See United States v. Brown*, 988 F.2d 658, 663 (6th Cir.1993) (finding § 1345 requires the Government demonstrate that a predicate offense has been committed and the extent of the fraud); *see also* § 1345 (requiring dissipation of assets for a court to award injunctive relief).

Regarding the applicable burden of proof, there is considerable disagreement in the case law. Several courts have applied the preponderance of the evidence standard to claims for injunctive relief under § 1345. *See Brown*, 988 F.2d 658, 663 (6th Cir.1993); *United States v. Williams*, 476 F.Supp.2d 1368, 1374 (M.D.Fla.2007) (applying the preponderance of the evidence standard); *United States v. Sriram*, 147 F.Supp.2d 914, 938 (N.D.Ill.2001) (same); *United States v. Barnes*, 912 F.Supp. 1187, 1198 (N.D.Iowa 1996) (same); *United States v. Quadro Corp.*, 916 F.Supp. 613, 617 (E.D.Tex.1996) (same); *see also United States v. Legro*, 284 Fed.Appx. 143, 145 (5th Cir.2008) (recognizing disagreement about whether probable cause or preponderance of the evidence standard applies to state a claim for injunctive relief under § 1345 and declining to resolve the issue). Other courts have concluded that a showing of only probable cause is required. *See United States v. Livdahl*, 356 F.Supp.2d 1289, 1294 (S.D.Fla.2005); *United States v. Fang*, 937 F.Supp. 1186, 1197 (D.Md.1996); *United States v. Davis*, No. 88–1705–CIV–ARONOVITZ, 1988 WL 168562, at *1 (S.D.Fla.1988). This Court agrees with those courts that found probable cause is the correct burden of proof

c. *Evidence of Federal Health Care Offenses and Dissipation of Assets*

Pursuant to § 1345, the Court previously entered a temporary restraining order ("TRO") restraining all of Luis's assets. The Government seeks to convert the TRO into a preliminary injunction, and the Court held a hearing on that matter on February 6, 2013. As a basis for the requested injunctive relief, the Government points to the parallel criminal prosecution, where Luis is charged with violations of 18 U.S.C. § 1349 (conspiracy to commit health care fraud) and 18 U.S.C. § 371 (conspiracy to defraud the United States and to commit offenses against the United States). Luis is also charged with violation of 42 U.S.C. § 1320a–7b(b)(2)(B) (paying health care kickbacks) and a forfeiture count under 18 U.S.C. § 982. Luis was indicted by a grand jury on these charges. According to the indictment, the offenses resulted in $45 million of improper Medicare benefits being paid. The parties agree that Luis has much less than $45 million in personal assets.

At the hearing, the Court accepted three declarations of Federal Bureau of Investigation Special Agent Clint Warren ("Special Agent Warren") as direct testimony. Special Agent Warren investigated Luis's businesses, LTC Professional Consultants, Inc. ("LTC") and Professional Home Care Solutions, Inc. ("Professional") for Federal health care fraud. During the investigation, Special Agent Warren received information from nine cooperating witnesses ("CWs") who worked as nurses and patient recruiters for LTC, Professional, or both.

The CWs said that LTC and Professional defrauded Medicare during the period of January 2006 to June 2012. Before the fraudulent scheme was put into place, Luis signed Medicare enrollment agreements in ***1327** 2003, 2004, and 2005, whereby she agreed to abide by Medicare laws and regulations, including the Anti-kickback statute. According to the information provided to Special Agent Warren, LTC and Professional paid nurses to recruit patients. The nurses, in turn, gave the patients a portion of the kickbacks in the form of direct payments. The CWs also told Special Agent Warren that LTC and Professional fraudulently billed Medicare for services that were not medically necessary or were not actually provided. One CWs estimated that at least 90% of all Professional and LTC patients were receiving kickbacks. Eight of these CWs specifically identified patients who received kickbacks. The total paid by Medicare for claims submitted on behalf of these patients who were identified was $ 4,356,553.85. During the period of this fraud, however, LTC and Professional collected a total of approximately $45 million from Medicare billings.

Special Agent Warren's declarations also provided information about assets being dissipated. Luis and the other defendants transferred monies from LTC and Professional to themselves directly and by the use of shell corporations that were owned by Luis's family members. There was also evidence that Luis used the funds to purchase luxury items, real estate, automobiles, and to travel. According to the declarations, Luis also received approximately $4,490,000 of the funds directly. In addition, although the investigation uncovered the fact that Medicare paid LTC and Professional $45 million dollars, only a fraction of the funds were located.

B. Discussion

a. *The Indictment and Declarations of Special Agent Warren Establish Probable Cause to Satisfy the Elements of § 1345*

Initially, the indictment and declarations establish probable cause to satisfy the elements for injunctive relief under § 1345. That is, there is probable cause to believe that: (1) Federal health care offenses have been committed; (2) $45 million was obtained illegally as a result of those offenses; and (3) that there has been dissipation of those monies. An indictment is sufficient to establish probable cause that offenses have been committed and the amount of the proceeds from those offenses. *See United States v. Bissell*, 866 F.2d 1343, 1349 (11th Cir.1989). Here, the Grand Jury indicted Luis for committing Federal health care offenses and found that LTC and Professional improperly obtained $45 million from those offenses.

Furthermore, in other situations where probable cause is required, the finding of probable cause may properly rest upon the affidavit of a law enforcement officer. *See Illinois v. Gates*, 462 U.S. 213, 226, 103 S.Ct. 2317, 76 L.Ed.2d 527 (1983) (explaining that issuance of a search warrant may be based upon an affidavit of a law enforcement officer when based upon a proper information source). Section 1345 requires there be dissipation of the proceeds. As discussed above, in his investigation, Special Agent Warren discovered that Luis used the funds to purchase luxury items, real estate, automobiles, and for travel. In addition, the investigation uncovered the fact that Medicare paid LTC and Professional $45 million dollars, but only a fraction of the assets could be located. The declaration, which is based upon information discovered in the criminal investigation, establishes probable cause to believe that there has been dissipation of assets.

Thus, the initial requirement to obtain a preliminary injunction, restraining up to ***1328** $45 million of Luis's assets, has been met.[3]

b. *Luis's Right to a Hearing and Right to Challenge the Factual Basis of the Probable Cause Finding*

The parties disagree about whether Luis was entitled to a hearing and, if so, the scope of the hearing and whether she has the right to challenge the probable cause determination. The Government's position is that Luis has no right to challenge the factual basis of the probable cause finding, which is based solely upon the indictment and declarations of Special Agent Warren. Luis, on the other hand, argues that she is entitled to a full adversarial hearing where she should be allowed to cross-examine the CWs. In this case, Luis was permitted a hearing, where she was allowed to cross-examine Special Agent Warren but was not permitted to cross-examine the CWs.

As an initial matter, § 1345 does not require a hearing by its language. However, the Fifth Amendment provides "[n]o person shall ... be deprived of life, liberty, or property, without due process of law." U.S. Const. amend. V. Accordingly, the general rule is that a person cannot be deprived of property without a prior hearing. *Bissell*, 866 F.2d at 1352. However, there is an exception that exists when a criminal defendant's assets are seized or restrained. *See id.* But this exception does not mean that a criminal defendant subject to asset restraint is never permitted a hearing; a post-seizure hearing is sometimes required. *Id.*

In the criminal forfeiture context, the factors to

determine whether a hearing is required are derived from the Supreme Court's Sixth Amendment speedy trial analysis in *Barker v. Wingo*, 407 U.S. 514, 92 S.Ct. 2182, 33 L.Ed.2d 101 (1972). *Bissell,* 866 F.2d at 1352. However, because § 1345 is a civil statute, the factors from *Mathews v. Eldridge*, 424 U.S. 319, 96 S.Ct. 893, 47 L.Ed.2d 18 (1976) are determinative. These factors are: "the private interest that will be affected by the official action; ... the risk of an erroneous deprivation of such interest through the procedures used, and the probable value, if any, of additional or substitute procedural safeguards; and ... the Government's interest, including the function involved and the fiscal and administrative burdens that the additional or substitute procedural requirement would entail." *Id.* at 335, 96 S.Ct. 893.

The *Mathews* factors weigh in favor of a hearing when all of a criminal defendant's assets are restrained under § 1345, which is the case here. The Eleventh Circuit has explained that "[b]eing effectively shut out by the state from retaining the counsel of one's choice in a serious criminal case is a substantial source of prejudice." *United States v. Kaley (Kaley I)*, 579 F.3d 1246, 1258 (11th Cir.2009); *see also United States v. Kaley (Kaley II)*, 677 F.3d 1316, 1332 (11th Cir.2012) (Edmonson, J., concurring) ("Property rights, in themselves, deserve to be amply guarded by American courts. But when a citizen's liberty ... depends to a high degree on his property, the stakes are particularly high."). Moreover, there is also a risk of erroneous deprivation without a hearing: "A prosecutor has everything to gain by restraining assets that ultimately may not be forfeited. By doing so, he can stack the deck in the government's ***1329** favor by crippling the defendant's ability to afford high-quality counsel." *Kaley I*, 579 F.3d at 1266 (Tjoflat, J., concurring). Although there is no indication of prosecutorial abuse in this case, the existence of these incentives increase the likelihood the risk of an erroneous deprivation without a hearing. The third factor—the government's interest and the burdens associated with additional procedural requirements—also weighs in favor of a hearing. While the Government has an interest in not previewing its criminal case before the criminal trial, this problem can be alleviated by properly limiting the scope of the hearing.

The Government, however, contends that no hearing was required because § 1345 permits restraint of substitute assets that are not traceable to criminal activity. As discussed above, the indictment and declarations establish probable cause to believe that Luis committed Federal health care offenses, resulting in $45 million of improper Medicare benefits being paid, and that she has dissipated those assets. There is also no dispute over the fact that Luis is in possession of much less than $45 million in personal assets. As such, assuming the probable cause finding is correct, because § 1345 permits the restraint of substitute assets, there is no possibility that a preliminary injunction could reach assets that are not properly subject to restraint under § 1345. Therefore, the Government's position is that there is nothing that could be challenged at a hearing because Luis "may not challenge the validity of the indictment itself...." *Bissell*, 866 F.2d at 1349.

However, the Government's position on the due process right to a hearing was rejected by *Kaley I*. In that case, the district court found that there was probable cause to believe that certain assets were traceable to a criminal offense and, therefore, properly subject to a protective order restraining the property. *Kaley I*, 579 F.3d at 1256. Relying on *Bissell*, the district court further found that an evidentiary hearing was not required because the defendants were not permitted to challenge the validity of the indictment. *Id.* The *Kaley I* court found that the district court erred on this point. *Id.* at 1257–58. According to the opinion, "notwithstanding the ... probable cause determination, the [defendants] were entitled to challenge the restraints on their assets; in doing so, they would not be requiring the Government to establish the charged offense." *Id.* at 1258.

In accordance with her due process right to a hearing, Luis was permitted an evidentiary hearing and the opportunity to cross examine Special Agent Warren. Contrary to Luis's position, however, she had no right to cross-examine the CWs. This type of extensive hearing would be tantamount to requiring the Government to preview its entire case. However, for the reasons discussed above, the Government's position that Luis was not permitted to a hearing and is not permitted to challenge the initial probable cause finding is misplaced.

c. *Luis's Arguments Opposing a Preliminary Injunction*

Luis raises two arguments challenging the factual basis for probable cause. First, she argues that the Government has not proffered evidence of a violation of the Anti-kickback Statute, 42 U.S.C. § 1320a–7b(b)(2)(B). According to Luis, in this case, payment of kickbacks falls within the safe-harbor provision of 42 C.F.R. § 1001.952 because the payments were to employees of LTC and Professional. Luis further argues that there is no evidence of a violation of 18 U.S.C. §§ 1347, 1349 because the Medicare certifications she ***1330** signed were submitted before the alleged kickback scheme took place.

Additionally, Luis makes several other arguments challenging the entering of a preliminary injunction in this case. She argues that the application of § 1345 violates the *ex post facto* clause. Luis further argues that the Sixth Amendment requires the release of funds to pay attorney's fees and argues that the language of § 1345 does not permit the restraint of assets needed for attorney's fees. Each of these arguments is discussed below.

i. The payment of kickbacks in this case do not fall within the safe-harbor provisions of the Anti-kickback statute

Luis first contends that some of the payments made to nurse/patient recruiters do not violate the Anti-kickback statute, § 1320a–7b(b)(2)(B).[4] To support this position, she relies upon the "safe-harbor" provision contained in 42 C.F.R. § 1001.952, which provides:

> As used in section 1128B of the Act, "remuneration" does not include any amount paid by an employer to an employee, who has a bona fide employment relationship with the employer, for employment in the furnishing of any item or service for which payment may be made in whole or in part under Medicare, Medicaid or other Federal health care programs.
> 42 C.F.R. § 1001.952. A similar safe-harbor provision is contained in the statute itself. That version of the safe-harbor provides that the prohibition against paying kickbacks will not apply to "any amount paid by an employer to an employee (who has a bona fide employment relationship with such employer) for employment in the provision of covered items or services." 42 U.S.C. § 1320a–7b(b)(3)(B).

Special Agent Warren's declaration indicates that CW1, CW2, CW3, and CW6 were employees of LTC, Professional, or both. Based on this, Luis argues that these individuals fall into the ambit of the safe harbor and contends that payments to them for recruiting patients were not improper. According to Luis, the safe-harbor will apply so long as "payments to them for referring patients ... [generated revenue] for services rendered and medically necessary." As such, Luis contends that $1,826,746 of revenue generated by payment patient referrals was not generated illegally. However, Luis misinterprets the scope of the safe-harbor provisions.

For either safe-harbor provision to apply, the remuneration must have been made to the employee for furnishing or providing covered items or services or for items or services payable under Medicare. This is evident from the text of the safe-harbor provisions, as well as the Eleventh Circuit's decision in *United States v. Starks*, 157 F.3d 833 (11th Cir.1998). The text of the safe-harbor provision upon which Luis relies states that "remuneration" ***1331** does not include "any amount paid by an employer to an employee ... *in the furnishing* of any item or service for which payment may be made in whole or in part under Medicare." 42 C.F.R. § 1001.952 (emphasis added). Similarly, the safe harbor contained in § 1320a–7b states that it will apply to "any amount paid by an employer to an employee ... *for employment in the provision* of covered items or services." § 1320a–7b(b)(3)(B) (emphasis added). The emphasized language in both of these provisions makes clear that the safe-harbor provisions will only apply when payments made to an employee compensate the employee for furnishing or providing covered items or services or items or services payable by Medicare, not simply for referring patients.

This was also the Eleventh Circuit's view in *Starks*, 157 F.3d at 839, where the court considered a vagueness challenge to the employee safe-harbor provisions. In that case, two individuals (Angela Starks and Barbara Henry) were paid for referring patients to Future Steps, Inc, which was a "corporation that developed and operated treatment programs for drug addiction." *Id.* at 835. Although Starks and Henry referred patients, they did not personally provide any medical services. *Id.* at 835–36. Starks, Henry, and Andrew Siegel, the owner of Future Steps, were convicted of violations of the Anti-kickback statute. *Id.* at 837. Starks and Siegel appealed their convictions, arguing that the safe-harbor provision contained in § 1320a–7b is unconstitutionally vague. *Id.* at 839. Rejecting this argument, the court found that, even if Starks and Siegel believed they were bona fide employees, the safe-harbor was not vague, as applied, because Starks and Henry were not compensated for providing "covered items or services." *Id.; see also United States v. Borrasi*, 639 F.3d 774, 782 (7th Cir.2011) (finding as long as some portion of a payment is for referrals, the safe-harbor provisions will not apply).

Here, Special Agent Warren's declaration states that CW2, CW3, and CW6 were paid for recruiting patients.[5] Even if these patients ultimately received legitimate medical care, payments to these nurse/recruiters for referring patients to LTC and Professional violate the Anti-kickback statute. Therefore, it is irrelevant whether the nurses were bona fide employees paid for "covered items or services" because the payments to them were, at least in part, for their illegal patient referrals.

Furthermore, even if Luis's view of the scope of the safe harbor provisions were correct, her contention that the patients, who were referred by these CWs, received medically necessary services is dubious. According to the declaration, after patient recruiters were compensated for referring patients, "LTC and Professional ... would then fraudulently bill Medicare for home health services that were not medically necessary or were never provided." For this additional reason, the safe-harbor provisions do not apply here.

ii. There is probable cause to establish a knowing misrepresentation to Medicare sufficient to constitute violations of 18 U.S.C. §§ 1347, 1349

Luis further argues that there is not sufficient evidence to find that there has been a knowing misrepresentation sufficient to amount to a violation 18 U.S.C. §§ 1347, 1349[6] and, therefore, the Government cannot establish "Federal health care offenses" to restrain her assets under ***1332** § 1345. To support this argument, Luis argues that a violation of §§ 1347, 1349 requires her to submit a representation that she will comply with Medicare rules *during* the period of time she submits improper Medicare claims. This argument fails because, as discussed below, all that is required is that a certification of compliance be submitted *at some point before* a non-complying claim is knowingly submitted. That requirement is satisfied here.

Luis's erroneously relies upon *United States v. Medina*, 485 F.3d 1291 (11th Cir.2007). One issue considered in *Medina* was whether there was sufficient evidence of health care fraud to sustain convictions against four individuals who were convicted for violations of § 1347. *Id.* at 1295. The court first found that a conviction under § 1347 requires the defendant make a "knowing false or fraudulent representation to Medicare." *Id.* at 1298. The court then found that, as to one of the defendants, her conviction for violation of § 1347 that was based on claims submitted before she signed Medicare provider applications (agreeing to abide by Medicare rules) should be reversed because there was no evidence of a knowing, false representation. *Id.* at 1298. However, the convictions that were based on kickback tainted claims that were submitted after she signed Medicare provider applications were upheld. *Id.* As to those counts, there was sufficient evidence to sustain the convictions because the defendant made a knowing false or fraudulent representation to Medicare by signing the provider applications, promising to comply, and then knowingly submitted tainted claims to Medicare. *Id.*

In this case, Luis acknowledged that she signed Medicare enrollment applications in 2003, 2004, and 2005 and, by doing so, certified that she would abide by Medicare law. There is evidence that she later submitted claims that violated the law, including the Anti-kickback provision. Under *Medina*, it does not matter that the representations in certifications were made several years before the claims were submitted. All that is required is that there is a representation that one will comply with Medicare law followed by a knowingly non-compliant claim. Therefore, by allegedly submitting non-compliant claims to Medicare after signing the applications, the knowledge requirement of § 1347 and § 1349 is satisfied for purposes of § 1345.

Luis makes an additional argument that the Government must demonstrate the United States suffered a "loss" to restrain assets under § 1345. In Luis's view, despite the payment of kickbacks, the United States does not suffer a loss as long as medically necessary services are performed. This argument fails because § 1345 does not require the United States to suffer a loss. All that is necessary is that a person is "alienating or disposing of property, or intends to alienate or dispose of property" that is "obtained as a result of a ... Federal health care offense ...." § 1345.

iii. The application of § 1345 to this case does not violate the ex post facto clause

Luis further argues that the *ex post facto* clause, contained in ***1333** Article I, Section 9 of the U.S. Constitution, prohibits § 1345 from applying here. Luis points out that the statutory term "Federal health care offense" did not include payment of kickbacks until March 23, 2010. *See* 18 U.S.C. § 24 (prior to 2010 amendment). Therefore, § 1345 did not authorize the restraint of assets based upon payment of kickbacks until that date. Luis argues that because the Government's proffer of evidence relates solely to kickbacks that occurred before March 2010, restraint of assets is not permitted.

However, even assuming that the *ex post facto* clause is implicated by § 1345, Luis's argument is fundamentally flawed. The prior version of § 24, which defines the term

"Federal health care offense," included violations of the general conspiracy statute, 18 U.S.C. § 371. *Id.* A violation of § 371 was included in the definition of Federal health care offense to the extent that the crime involved "a health care benefit program." *Id.* The term "health care benefit program" was defined as "any public or private plan or contract, affecting commerce, under which any medical benefit, item, or service is provided to any individual, and includes any individual or entity who is providing a medical benefit, item, or service for which payment may be made under the plan or contract." *Id.* Accordingly, under the older version of the statute, a conspiracy to pay kickbacks to receive benefits under Medicare in violation of § 371 was a Federal health care offense and could properly result in an injunction under § 1345. *See id.*

Here, the indictment charges Luis with a count for conspiracy to pay kickbacks in violation of § 371. In addition to establishing probable cause to believe the Anti-kickback statute has been violated, the evidence before the Court is sufficient to establish probable cause to believe that § 371 has been violated and resulted in $45 million of improper Medicare benefits being paid. Thus, even under the older version of § 24, an injunction could be entered under § 1345 for violation of § 371. As such, there is no *ex post facto* issue.

iv. The Sixth Amendment does not prohibit the restraint of substitute, "untainted" assets

Luis also argues that the Sixth Amendment guarantees her a right to use assets that are not traceable to Federal health care offenses to select and retain counsel of her choice for her defense in the parallel criminal case. The Government's argument is that regardless of whether or not assets were obtained legitimately, there is no Sixth Amendment impediment to the assets being frozen as long as a statute permits restraint of substitute assets. According to the Government, because § 1345 allows substitute, untainted assets to be restrained, Luis has no Sixth Amendment right to use the assets to hire counsel of her choice.

It is undisputed that "an element of [the Sixth Amendment right to counsel] is the right of a defendant who does not require appointed counsel to choose who will represent him." *United States v. Gonzalez–Lopez,* 548 U.S. 140, 144, 126 S.Ct. 2557, 165 L.Ed.2d 409 (2006). Indeed, "[t]he Sixth Amendment comprehends a qualified right to select and be represented by counsel of choice because 'were a defendant not provided the opportunity to select his own counsel at his own expense, substantial risk would arise that the basic trust between counsel and client, which is a cornerstone of the adversary system, would be undercut.' " *Bissell,* 866 F.2d at 1351 (quoting *United States v. Koblitz,* 803 F.2d 1523, 1528 (11th Cir.1986)). However, this qualified right does not permit a criminal defendant to use assets that are the proceeds of criminal ***1334** activity to retain counsel. *Caplin & Drysdale, Chartered v. United States,* 491 U.S. 617, 626, 109 S.Ct. 2646, 105 L.Ed.2d 528 (1989); *Bissell,* 866 F.2d at 1351. This is so because "[a] defendant has no Sixth Amendment right to spend another person's money for services rendered by an attorney, even if those assets are the only way that that defendant will be able to retain the attorney of his choice." *Caplin,* 491 U.S. at 626, 109 S.Ct. 2646.

The more difficult question is the one presented here. That is, whether a criminal defendant has a Sixth Amendment right to use untainted, substitute assets to retain counsel of choice. Although the answer to this question is far from clear, the Fourth Circuit's opinion in *In re Billman,* 915 F.2d 916, 921 (4th Cir.1990) supports the Government's position. In *Billman,* a defendant was charged with racketeering and a forfeiture count, and the defendant then transferred some of the assets to another person. *Id.* at 918. The district court found that the assets that were transferred could not be directly linked to the racketeering, and the circuit court determined that it was bound to accept this finding. *Id.* As such, they were "substitute" assets. *Id.* at 920. The transferee argued that she had a Sixth Amendment right to use the funds to retain counsel of her choice. *Id.* at 921–22. The court rejected this argument because the substitute assets were subject to restraint under § 1963. *Id.* Therefore, the *Billman* court's view is that there is no Sixth Amendment impediment to the seizure of substitute assets pursuant to the statute because those assets are "contraband," even if they were not the proceeds of criminal activity. *Id.* at 922; *see also United States v. Am. Therapeutic Corp.,* 797 F.Supp.2d 1289, 1293–94 (S.D.Fla.2011) (finding no Sixth Amendment right to use untainted, substitute assets that are restrained under § 1345).

This view is common sense. An example by the Fourth Circuit that was related by the *Bissell* decision is instructive:

> Suppose a bank is robbed and $100,000 taken. A defendant is arrested in possession of $100,000

> and nothing more. The defendant protests his innocence and claims, without the slightest proof, that the $100,000 was in fact a gift from a friend. Surely no one will contend that the $100,000 must be made available to pay the defendant's lawyer, and not be kept available for return to the bank in the event the defendant is found guilty.

Bissell, 866 F.2d at 1351 (quoting *In re Forfeiture Hearing As to Caplin & Drysdale, Chartered*, 837 F.2d 637, 645 (4th Cir.1988), *aff'd sub nom., Caplin*, 491 U.S. 617, 109 S.Ct. 2646).

The reason the bank robber is not permitted to use the $100,000 to hire a lawyer is obvious. The money does not belong to him. But suppose the bank robber in the example above spent the $100,000 that he stole. It just so happens, however, that he has another $100,000 that he obtained legitimately. Should his decision to spend the $100,000 he stole mean that he is free to hire counsel with the other $100,000 when Congress has authorized restraint of those substitute assets? The reasonable answer is no. The bank has the right to have those substitute, untainted assets kept available for return as well. Therefore, in accord with the Fourth Circuit's view, the most reasonable conclusion is that there is no Sixth Amendment right to use untainted, substitute assets to hire counsel.

v. Section 1345 allows for the restraint of assets that would otherwise be used for payment of attorney's fees

Luis also argues that the purpose of § 1345 is to insure that the defendant is ***1335** not wasting or hiding assets, not to punish the defendant. As such, she argues that assets that will be used for attorney's fees should not be restrained. To the extent that Luis is arguing that the statute does not permit such assets to be restrained, this argument fails. However, the Court does have discretion to release assets for payment of attorney's fees.

In exercising its discretion for release of assets for payment of attorney's fees, the Court should consider whether the defendant is able to afford representation in the § 1345 proceedings. *See United States v. Speqtrum, Inc.*, No. CIV.A. 10–2111 JEB, 2012 WL 517526, at *2 (D.D.C. Feb. 16, 2012); *United States v. Jaime*, No. 2:10–CV–00498, 2011 WL 145196, at *1–2 (S.D.W.Va. Jan. 18, 2011). If "restrained property is a defendant's only means of securing counsel" the Court may wish to exercise its discretion to release assets to secure counsel. *See Speqtrum, Inc.*, 2012 WL 517526, at *2. In this case, Luis was represented throughout the § 1345 proceedings by competent counsel. Therefore, this consideration is no longer relevant. In the criminal prosecution, Luis will be appointed counsel if she cannot afford representation.

C. Conclusion

For the foregoing reasons, the Government's Motion for a Preliminary Injunction under 18 U.S.C. § 1345 [D.E. # 4] is GRANTED. The preliminary injunction order will be entered shortly. Luis's Motion to Modify the Restraining Order to Release Assets for the Defense of the Related Criminal Case [D.E. # 46] is DENIED.

All Citations

966 F.Supp.2d 1321

Footnotes

1 As used in this title, the term "Federal health care offense" means a violation of, or a criminal conspiracy to violate—
(1) section 669, 1035, 1347, or 1518 of this title or section 1128B of the Social Security Act (42 U.S.C. 1320a–7b);or
(2) section 287, 371, 664, 666, 1001, 1027, 1341, 1343, 1349, or 1954 of this title section 301 of the Federal Food, Drug, and Cosmetic Act (21 U.S.C. 331), or section 501 of the Employee Retirement Income Security Act of 1974 (29 U.S.C. 1131), or section 411, 518, or 511 of the Employee Retirement Income Security Act of 1974, [1] if the violation or conspiracy relates to a health care benefit program.
18 U.S.C. § 24.

2 The following is the statutory language creating the right to injunctive relief to prevent alienation of property:
(a)(2) If a person is alienating or disposing of property, or intends to alienate or dispose of property, obtained as a result of a

[Federal health care offense] or property which is traceable to such violation, the Attorney General may commence a civil action in any Federal court—

(A) to enjoin such alienation or disposition of property; or

(B) for a restraining order to—

(i) prohibit any person from withdrawing, transferring, removing, dissipating, or disposing of any such property or property of equivalent value ...

18 U.S.C. § 1345.

3 Even under the preponderance standard, the Government has carried its burden of proof to enter an injunction restraining at least $40.5 million dollars, which is 90% of $45 million. This finding is based on the indictment, as well as Special Agent Warren's affidavits detailing the crimes, receipt of Medicare funds, and dissipation of assets, including CW9's statement that 90% of LTC and Professional's patients received kickbacks.

4 Section 1320a–7b(b)(2)(B) provides:

(1) Whoever knowingly and willfully solicits or receives any remuneration (including any kickback, bribe, or rebate) directly or indirectly, overtly or covertly, in cash or in kind—

(A) in return for referring an individual to a person for the furnishing or arranging for the furnishing of any item or service for which payment may be made in whole or in part under a Federal health care program, or

(B) in return for purchasing, leasing, ordering, or arranging for or recommending purchasing, leasing, or ordering any good, facility, service, or item for which payment may be made in whole or in part under a Federal health care program,

shall be guilty of a felony and upon conviction thereof, shall be fined not more than $25,000 or imprisoned for not more than five years, or both.

42 U.S.C. § 1320a–7b(b)(2)(B).

5 Although Luis refers to CW1 when making this argument, CW1 was not a patient recruiter and, therefore, is not relevant to her argument.

6 Section 1347 provides, in pertinent part:

(a) Whoever knowingly and willfully executes, or attempts to execute, a scheme or artifice—

(1) to defraud any health care benefit program; or

(2) to obtain, by means of false or fraudulent pretenses, representations, or promises, any of the money or property owned by, or under the custody or control of, any health care benefit program.

18 U.S.C. § 1347. Section 1349 makes conspiracy to violate § 1347 a crime. *See* 18 U.S.C. § 1349.

End of Document

KeyCite Yellow Flag - Negative Treatment
Distinguished by United States v. Novartis Pharmaceuticals Corporation, S.D.N.Y., March 24, 2020

KeyCite Overruling Risk - Negative Treatment
Overruling Risk Universal Health Services, Inc. v. U.S., U.S., June 16, 2016

2016 WL 750720
United States District Court, S.D. New York.

UNITED STATES of America; the States of California, Colorado, Connecticut, Delaware, Florida, Georgia, Hawaii, Illinois, Indiana, Iowa, Louisiana, Maryland, Masschusetts, Michigan, Minnesota, Montana, Nevada, New Hampshire, New Jersey, New Mexico, New York, North Carolina, Oklahoma, Rhode Island, Tennessee, Texas, Virginia, Washington, and Wisconsin; the District of Columbia, the City of Chicago and the City of New York; ex rel., Charles Arnstein and Hossam Senousy, Plaintiffs and Relators,
v.
TEVA PHARMACEUTICALS USA, INC.; TEVA Neuroscience, Inc.; and TEVA Sales and Marketing, Inc., Defendants.

No. 13 Civ. 3702 (CM)
|
Signed February 22, 2016

Attorneys and Law Firms

Jessica Jean Hu, United States Attorney's Office, New York, NY, Brandon Joshua Lauria, Eric Leighton Young, Young Law Group, P.C., Philadelphia, PA, James Edward Miller, Karen M. Leser-Grenon, Laurie Rubinow, Shepherd, Finkelman, Miller & Shah, LLC, Chester, CT, Rosemary Farrales Luzon, Shepherd, Finkelman, Miller & Shah, LLP, San Diego, CA, for Plaintiffs.

Eric Wilson Sitarchuk, Morgan Lewis & Bockius, LLP, Philadelphia, PA, Kelly Anne Moore, Shana Ruth Cappell, Morgan, Lewis & Bockius LLP, New York, NY, for Defendants.

MEMORANDUM DECISION AND ORDER DENYING DEFENDANTS' MOTIONS TO DISMISS

McMahon, U.S.D. J.

***1** Plaintiff-relators Charles Arnstein and Hossam Senousy ("Relators") filed this *qui tam* action asserting claims arising under the False Claims Act ("FCA"), 31 U.S.C. § 3729 *et seq.*, and related state and local laws. The Defendants named in the complaint are Teva Pharmaceuticals USA, Inc. and two of its subsidiaries, Teva Neuroscience, Inc. and Teva Sales and Marketing, Inc. (collectively "Teva" or "Defendants"). Relators allege that Teva violated the FCA and the AntiKickback Statute ("AKS"), 42 U.S.C. § 1320a–7b(b), in connection with a kickback scheme.

Pending before the Court are the Defendants' motions to dismiss the Relators' Second Amended Complaint pursuant to Rules 12(b)(6) and 9(b) of the Federal Rules of Civil Procedure. For the reasons discussed below, those motions are denied. However, as was the case in a similar action before this court, *U.S. ex rel Kester v. Novartis Pharm. Corp.*, No. 11 CIV. 8196, in which I disposed of multiple motions to dismiss on the same grounds argued here, Relators need to amend their complaint either to add specificity to their assertion that certain claims are false and fraudulent or drop those claims from this lawsuit. Relators have 30 days from the date of this Order to amend their complaint.

Relators' corresponding claims under state law (Counts II through XXXIII) will be stayed pending resolution of the federal claim; the motions to dismiss those claims are denied without prejudice to renewal.

BACKGROUND

The Parties

Pursuant to the False Claims Act ("FCA"), private persons known as "relators" may file *qui tam* actions and recover damages on behalf of the United States. *See* 31 U.S.C. § 3730(b). Plaintiffs Charles Arnstein and Hossam Senousy ("Relators") originally filed this FCA action in May 2013 on behalf of the United States, 29 states, and three cities.

The defendants, collectively "Teva," are three subsidiaries of Teva Pharmaceutical Industries, Ltd., an Israeli pharmaceutical company with a global footprint that develops, manufactures, markets and sells pharmaceutical products. (SAC 4.) Defendant Teva USA is a Pennsylvania corporation with its principal place of business in North Wales, Pennsylvania; it does business nationwide. (*Id* at ¶ 5.) Defendant Teva Neuroscience is a division or operating unit of Teva USA; it is headquartered in Overland Park, Kansas. (*Id.* at ¶¶ 6, 8.) Defendant Teva Sales and Marketing is another division or operating unit of Teva USA. It is headquartered in North Wales, Pennsylvania. (*Id.* at ¶¶ 7–8.)

The Relators are pharmaceutical sales representatives who were employees of Teva Neuroscience from 2002 and 2006, respectively, until January 1, 2014, when they—along with all other Teva Neuroscience employees—were transferred to Teva Sales and Marketing. (*Id.* at ¶¶ 7–8, 12–13.)

The Relators allege that the defendants are each other's alter egos or agents, and refer to all three defendants as a single entity. (*Id.passim.*)

The Relators filed a Second Amended Complaint ("SAC" or "Complaint") on November 26, 2014. (Docket # 11.) They bring claims against Teva on behalf of the United States, 29 states, and three cities. The Relators assert a claim (Count 1) under two sections of the FCA: 31 U.S.C. § 3729(a)(1)(A) and 31 U.S.C. § 3729(a)(1)(B). They also assert claims (Counts 2–30) under 29 different state law analogues of the FCA, and three different local law analogues of the FCA (Counts 31–33).

***2** The United States has declined to intervene and assume the prosecution of this case. A number of states and municipal corporations are named plaintiffs in this action; they, too, were offered the opportunity to intervene and take over the prosecution of claims brought under corresponding state and local laws that, while similar to the FCA, are not always identical to it. They, too, elected not to intervene, and none of them has appeared by its Attorney General or other legal representative. (*See* Docket # 12).

The FCA outlaws the submission of a false or fraudulent "claim" for payment (*i.e.*, a request for reimbursement) to the government. *See* 31 U.S.C. § 3729(a)(1). Such claims may be rendered "false" in a variety of ways. In this case, the Relator's FCA claims are predicated on underlying violations of the Anti–Kickback Statute ("AKS"). Under the AKS, it is illegal to offer a person "remuneration" (*i.e.*, kickbacks) in order to "induce" that person to "recommend" the purchase of a drug covered by a federal health care program. 42 U.S.C. § 1320a–7b(b)(2). It is likewise illegal to receive remuneration "in return for ... recommending purchasing" such drugs. *Id* at § 1320a–7b(b)(1).

Generally, the Relators allege that, from 2003 through the present, the defendants violated the AKS by bribing physicians through honoraria for sham speaker programs relating to the drugs Azilect and Copaxone ("the Drugs"), which treat serious neurological diseases. At the same time, defendants allegedly caused downstream pharmacies—which were dispensing Azilect and Copaxone, possibly because of physicians' bribe-addled judgment—to submit claims to federal, state and local healthcare programs for reimbursement of the cost of those drugs.

Relators allege that, by causing downstream entities to submit claims for reimbursement for Azilect and Copaxone while at the same time paying physicians to prescribe those drugs, Teva caused the government to pay "false" claims, in violation of federal, state and local false claims acts.

Relators further allege that, by failing to take its kickback payments into account when reporting its "Best Price" and "Average Manufacturer Price" to government healthcare programs, which reports were used to calculate rebates owed to the government and to make Teva drugs eligible for purchase by certain government entities, Teva itself submitted false claims.

The Second Amended Complaint

Copaxone and Azilect

Copaxone, approved by the FDA in 1996, is used to treat relapsing-remitting Multiple Sclerosis. (SAC ¶ 88.)

Teva holds several patents relating to Copaxone. Most expired in May 2014; one will expire in September 2015. (*Id.*)

Copaxone's average annual cost for a Medicare or Medicaid patient is approximately $60,000. (*Id.*) With 40% of the market in its therapeutic class, Copaxone garnered $2.958 billion in sales for Teva in 2010, $3.570 billion in 2011, and $3,996 billion in 2012. (*Id.* ¶ 91.) It has led the market for its therapeutic class since 2008. (*Id.*)

Azilect, approved by the FDA in 2006, is used to treat symptoms of Parkinson's Disease. (SAC ¶ 89.) Teva has several patents relating to Azilect, which have expired or will expire between 2013 and 2027. (*Id.*)

Azilect's average annual cost for a Medicare or Medicaid patient is approximately $4,600. (*Id.*) The drug garnered $244 million in sales in 2010, $290 million in 2011, and $330 million in 2012. (*Id* ¶ 92.)

Together, I will refer to Copaxone and Azilect as the "Drugs."

Plaintiffs allege that the Drugs' ever-increasing sales "are hardly a coincidence —they are the direct result of a pervasive illegal kickback scheme whereby," since 2006, "Teva paid physicians to write prescriptions for the ... Drugs through an elaborate and widespread network of paid speaker programs." (*Id.* ¶¶ 94, 96.)

Speaker Programs

***3** In the United States, between 250,000 and 300,000 people suffer from Multiple Sclerosis. (*Id.* ¶ 104.) Approximately 500,000 people in the United States suffer from Parkinson's Disease. (*Id.*)

To reach those patients' doctors, Teva Neuroscience employs approximately 200 pharmaceutical sales representatives, spread over three sales areas (West, Central, and East), which are divided into 22 "regions," and then subdivided into 112 "territories." (*Id.*) Each sales representative is assigned to devote his or her attention to between 50 and 80 healthcare providers, and will make an average of five "calls" on physicians' offices daily. (*Id.*)

In addition to making "calls" on physician offices, sales representatives arrange for "speaker programs." A common feature of the pharmaceutical sales industry, "Speaker programs enlist physicians, for pay, to speak to other physicians about FDA-approved drug use." *United States v. Caronia,* 703 F.3d 149, 156 (2d Cir.2012).

In 2011, Teva representatives arranged at least 1,329 speaker programs for Azilect and Copaxone. (SAC ¶ 97.) In 2012, that number nearly quadrupled—to 5,036. (*Id.*) As of August 2013, approximately 4,600 programs had been completed or scheduled. (*Id.*)

During approximately the same time period, there were 420 "trained Copaxone speakers"—a term the Complaint does not define—and 410 "trained Azilect speakers." (*Id.* ¶ 97.) Some physicians were paid to speak at "speaker programs" several times per month. (*Id.*)

Honoraria Allegedly Dependent on the Number of Prescriptions Written by the Payee Physician

Teva paid more than $10 million annually to physicians for speaking about Azilect and Copaxone at speaker programs in 2012, 2013, and 2014. (*Id.* ¶ 97.) It pays physicians an honorarium of between $1,500 and $2,700 for each speaker program. (*Id.* ¶ 96.) The average honorarium for a single speaker program is between $2,000 and $2,500.

Prior to 2011, Teva sales representatives were permitted to decide the amount of the honorarium, and delivered the payments in green envelopes, purportedly to emphasize the lucrative nature of serving as a speaker. (*Id.*)

Relators allege that Teva added paid speakers without completing needs-assessment or similar testing. (*Id.* ¶ 98.)

Instead, Teva allegedly added paid speakers on the basis of return on investment analysis. (*Id.*) The relevant "return" variable consisted of the number of prescriptions that the physician speaker —the one being paid the honorarium— wrote for the Drugs. (*Id.* ¶¶ 98, 152.)

Teva allegedly permits a physician to continue as a paid speaker only if he or she maintains or increases the number of prescriptions he or she writes for the relevant drug. (*Id.* ¶ 96.) If a speaker-physician failed to prescribe enough Copaxone or Azilect (what was "enough" is unclear from the SAC), then "Teva refused to give them any additional speaker programs, required them to undergo 'training' in order to be added back onto the [list of physicians from whom sales representatives could choose and pay speakers], and insisted that they write more prescriptions if they were to be included on the speakers' list for the following year." (*Id.* ¶ 108.)

The SAC provides two examples of physicians who were allegedly removed from the list of approved speakers because of their failure to increase their prescribing levels for the covered drugs. (*Id.* ¶¶ 144–145.) In one instance, Teva allegedly specifically advised a physician "that he would not be given any further speaking opportunities until he increased his Copaxone prescriptions." (*Id.* ¶ 145.) The SAC does not identify who at Teva sent that particular message.

***4** The SAC provides the initials and locations of some 30 physicians situated throughout the United States who are allegedly complicit in the kickback scheme. (*Id.* ¶ 103.) Of these, one Detroit physician is a particularly prized speaker. He allegedly earns approximately $216,000 in honoraria per year, not including payments he receives from Teva for research and other consulting. (*Id.* ¶ 109.) Plaintiffs allege that Teva has gone so far as to remove that physician's name and other information from a website that tracks speakers, in order to shield him from scrutiny. (*Id.* ¶ 109.) Or perhaps his absence from the relevant database is the result of his having formed a limited liability corporation to insulate his name from scrutiny of just such payments. (*Id.*) In exchange for this largess and protection, the Detroit physician prescribes Copaxone for approximately 80% of the 5,000 patients at his clinic, meaning that he is personally responsible for $200 million of Copaxone sales annually. (*Id.*)

The SAC goes on to identify the number of claims reimbursed by Medicare Part D relating to prescriptions written by the Detroit physician as well as the 30 other physicians whose initials are used in the complaint, doing so by year. (*Id.* ¶ 110.) Those claims reach into the tens of millions of dollars. (*Id.*)

The Questionable Value of the Speaker Services Physicians Receive Honoraria to Perform

Next, Relators question the value of the speaker services that physicians provide.

Neither of the Drugs is new to the market, having been on the scene for 18 and 8 years respectively – "and there have been little, if any changes in the indications appropriate for" them. (*Id.* ¶ 100.) Teva allegedly "has not provided the sales force with any new materials to present at the programs in a number of years. Nevertheless, Teva continues to impress upon the sales force [the need] to set up more and more of these programs in order to drive the sales of the ... Drugs." (*Id.* ¶ 150.)

The speaker programs include "Journal Clubs," in which the same "journal presentations" – I assume that plaintiffs are referring to presentations that reference articles in medical journals —"occurred again and again to the same attendees." (*Id.* ¶ 99.) More recently, the majority of Teva's speaker programs have been "Peer–to–Peer Programs" and "Patient Programs" that allegedly "had few to no attendees, lacked little, if any, educational value, discussed dated and/or redundant topics, were conducted by multiple speakers from the same medical groups, and were often attended by the same physicians, patients and their families." (*Id.* ¶ 100.)

There are not a large number of canned presentations: two for Copaxone and four for Azilect. (*Id.* ¶ 100.)

It is allegedly common for physicians to alternate between giving presentations and then attending the very same canned presentation as given by another physician —allegedly because it was well nigh impossible to convince any "non-corrupt" physician to attend the same presentation more than once. (*Id.* ¶ 101.)

The SAC provides several examples of allegedly sham programs, including one in which four physicians met monthly with one another and Teva sales representatives, and rotated the duty of giving a 15 minute presentation to each other on one of a set number of rote topics. The doctors were paid $1500 each time they presented. (*Id.* ¶ 112.) In a different "program" two physicians and two Teva employees sat down to dinner; no presentation was made and no new material discussed, but each physician received $2,000 for the "program." (*Id* ¶ 113.) On another occasion, a physician sat down to dinner with a single Teva representative, presented no medical materials, and was paid $2,000. (*Id.* ¶ 114.) The Complaint provides several more examples of such generosity. (*Id.* ¶¶ 115–118.)

Teva's Efforts to Disguise the Kickback Scheme

Teva allegedly tried to "disguise the fact that the same presentations were being given against and again to the same attendees by (a) changing the titles of the programs slightly without changing the substance of the presentations, (b) changing the wording in the presentations without making any material substantive changes to the presentations, and (c) shuffling the 'slide deck' so that the presentation appeared somewhat different—even though the substance was the same." (*Id.* ¶ 100; *see also* ¶ 102 (describing the content of the presentations); ¶¶ 119–139 (offering many specific examples of speaker programs with no physician attendees, no educational content, and/or rotating speakers and attendees).)

***5** But no one was fooling the attendees. Programs for Copaxone "typically attract the same patients and their family members, who are already familiar with Copaxone and ... who will often leave once dinner is done but prior to the completion of the program." (*Id.* ¶ 143.)

Plaintiffs allege that Teva began to use speaker programs with more regularity in 2008 or 2009, when it became clear that a previous scheme to compensate physicians for prescribing Teva drugs was under scrutiny. Specifically, from approximately 2003 through 2008, Teva used "preceptorship" programs, "in which physicians were paid to allow a Teva sales representative to spend time observing their practice when, in fact, the sole purpose of the payments was to compensate physicians" for prescribing Teva drugs. (*Id.* ¶ 99.) Plaintiffs allege that Teva's paid speaker programs—as they have existed since approximately 2006—are less blatantly fraudulent, but nonetheless are simply successors to those preceptorship programs. (*Id.*)

Teva Management's Role in Orchestrating and Promoting the Kickback Scheme

This pay-to-play scheme allegedly was the result of Teva management's express direction. (*Id.* ¶ 108.)

Teva's corporate policy allegedly encouraged the kickback scheme by, *inter alia,* "evaluat[ing] and reward[ing] the sales force based on the number of speaker programs" they arranged and completed

—not on the quality of those programs. (*Id.* ¶ 149.)

Moreover, managers throughout Teva allegedly encouraged sales representatives to use honoraria to incentivize physicians to write more prescriptions, stating, *inter alia:*

- In January 2008: "We have committed as a group to try to use as many of the [speaker] programs as possible and develop our regional advocates [i.e., paid physician speakers] for outside programs." (*Id.* ¶ 147.)

- In September 2011: "AHMs [(speaker programs)], AHMS, AHMs—this is the closest thing I have to a silver bullet." (*Id.* ¶ 148.) "Invest wisely—who are your advocates? Who do you want to be your advocates?" (*Id.*)

- Intermittently, statements such as "I would like to see us [be the] # 1 region in regards to using our programs." (*Id.* ¶ 149.)

- At a regional sales meeting in October 2013, an Area director stated that 80% of all Azilect prescriptions were then being written by Azilect paid speakers. (*Id.* ¶ 96.) He "stress[ed] the need to continue paying physicians to speak (since it results in the physicians themselves writing more prescriptions) ... [and] reinforced Teva's intent to increase its use of payments to speakers as a way to drive even greater sales in 2014." (*Id.* ¶ 97.)

At the highest levels of management, Teva devised "Best Practices: Regional Approaches Seminar"—a seminar for sales associates—in which the "overarching message to Teva's leadership team [i.e., mid-level managers] was the more speaking opportunities you create to pay doctors, the more prescriptions they will write for Teva, and the more financial rewards you will receive." (*Id.* ¶ 148.)

Effect on Prescribing Habits

The SAC alleges that "the fact that doctors were paid in connection with Teva's speaker programs influenced their prescription writing with respect to the Covered Drugs." (*Id.* ¶ 153.) In Exhibit A to the SAC, the Relators provide 89 examples of physicians whose prescription-writing increased as their receipt of honoraria increased. The Relators also allege that some doctors who were kicked out of the speaker programs for failure to write an adequate number of prescriptions took the hint, and increased their prescription writing to bring themselves back into the fold. (*Id.* ¶ 145).

***6** Teva allegedly "caused many thousands of prescriptions to be written as a result of payments and/or other remuneration made in connection with speaker programs that were kickbacks to doctors. Teva paid tens of millions of dollars in kickbacks to physicians in the form of honoraria and/or other remuneration in connection with speaker programs concerning the Covered Drugs between 2006 and to date. On average each of these doctors wrote many hundreds of thousands of dollars' worth of prescriptions for the Covered Drugs that were paid for by the Government Healthcare Programs." (*Id.* ¶ 154.)

Kickback–Tainted Claims for Reimbursement

Generally, when a physician prescribes a drug, a patient is provided with a prescription, which is then filled at a pharmacy. (*Id.* ¶ 34.) The pharmacy then submits the claim for payment to the relevant Government Healthcare Program(s) for reimbursement. (*Id.*) For Copaxone in particular,

> TEVA generally first works with an MS patient to (a) establish coverage by a Government Healthcare Program or other insurance scheme, (b) ensure that the prescription is filled by a pharmacy (and delivered to the patient—usually by mail), and (c) provide training and instruction on how Copaxone should be selfadministered by injection by the patient. Once the patient is able to self-administer the drug by way of injection, Copaxone prescriptions are then filled by traditional and other pharmacies.
>
> In certain circumstances, a Government Healthcare Program may also have pharmacy facilities that directly dispense prescription drugs. In such cases, the Government Healthcare Program purchases the drug directly rather than reimbursing the pharmacy.

(*Id.* ¶¶ 34–35.)

As explained in further detail below, Relators allege that certifications and attestations signed by those seeking reimbursement from certain government healthcare programs certified compliance with the federal Anti–Kickback Statute, and that the honoraria paid to physicians prescribing the Drugs rendered those certifications and attestations false. (*Id.* ¶ 158.)

Medicare Part D

Over 50% of all patients suffering from Parkinson's Disease are on Medicare. (*Id.* ¶ 86.) Approximately 25–30% of all patients suffering from Multiple Sclerosis are on Medicare. (*Id.* ¶ 85.)

Medicare beneficiaries receive prescription drug benefits through, *inter alia,* Part D of the Medicare Program, which, through The Centers for Medicare and Medicaid Services ("CMS"), contracts with private companies known as "Part D sponsors" in order to administer prescription drug plans. (*Id.* ¶ 36.)

In turn, Part D sponsors administer the prescription drug plans through subcontracts with a variety of pharmacies. (*Id.*) "Pharmacy benefit managers" or "PBM's — who appear to work for the Part D sponsors—facilitate interactions between pharmacies and Part D sponsors. (*Id.* 37 ¶¶ 38.)

When a pharmacy dispenses drugs to a Medicare beneficiary (pursuant to a physician's prescription), the pharmacy submits an electronic claim to the beneficiary's Part D sponsor. After the pharmacy submits the electronic claim, the Part D sponsor or its PBM will reimburse the pharmacy for the "gross drug cost" of the drug dispensed—the portion of the drug cost not paid by the beneficiary, the pharmacy's dispensing fee, and any applicable sales taxes. *§ Id.* 37.)

Pursuant to CMS regulations, Part D plan sponsors must agree to comply with "Federal laws and regulations designed to prevent fraud, waste, and abuse, including, but not limited to applicable provisions of Federal criminal law, the False Claims Act (31 U.S.C. 3729 et seq.), and the *anti-kickback statute* (section 1128B(b) of the Act)." 42 C.F.R. § 423.505(h)(1) (emphasis added). Further, 42 C.F.R. § 423.505(i)(4)(iv) states: "Each and every contract must specify that the related entity, contractor, or subcontractor must comply with all applicable Federal laws, regulations, and CMS instructions."

***7** The AKS is unquestionably one of the "applicable Federal laws" governing Medicare Part D that is cited in the contractor certification. CMS regulations specifically identify the AKS as one of the "Federal laws and regulations designed to prevent fraud, waste, and abuse" that apply to Medicare Part D. 42 C.F.R. § 423.505(h)(1). Moreover, the AKS itself states that it applies to any "Federal health care program," which includes Medicare Part D. 42 U.S.C. § 1320a–7b(f).

Accordingly, downstream entities who certify compliance "with all applicable Federal laws, regulations, and CMS instructions" certify compliance with the AKS. 42 C.F.R. § 423.505(i)(4)(iv).

In Exhibit A to their Complaint, Relators provide what they describe as a "representative sample of false claims tainted by kickbacks for which reimbursement was obtained from the Medicare Part D program in 2010 and 2011 ... based upon this sample ... alone ... Medicare Part D ... paid over $63 million dollars in claims that were tainted by Teva's paid-speaker scheme." (*Id* ¶ 155.)

Exhibit A is a four-page spreadsheet listing more than 100 physicians, showing each physician's speaking engagements for Azilect or Copaxone in the years 2009, 2010, and 2011, and showing the number of Medicare Part D claims associated with each physician's prescriptions of the relevant drug during 2010 and 2011 (but not 2009). (Docket # 13–2.) It shows that at least some physicians increased the number of prescriptions written for the relevant drug as their speaker engagements (and corresponding fees) increased.

Medicaid

Medicaid is a joint federal-state program that provides health care benefits for groups including the poor and disabled. (*Id.* ¶ 57.) Each state administers a state Medicaid program that includes reimbursement for prescription drugs. (*Id.*) The federal government provides a portion of each state's Medicaid payments, known as the Federal Medical Assistance Percentage ("FMAP"). (*Id.* ¶ 58.)

The Relators' allegations regarding "false" certifications made in connection with Medicaid vary in their specificity.

The SAC identifies New York as an example of a state whose regulatory regime explicitly forbids payment to those claims resulting from "bribes and kickbacks." N.Y. Comp.Codes R. & Regs. Title 18 §§ 518.1(c), 515.2(b)(5); SAC U 60. It implies that all states have such provisions. *§ See* SAC H 60.) In Counts 2–30, the Relators allege that each of the states named as co-plaintiffs have similar regulatory regimes, and that in each, compliance with an anti-kickback statute was an express condition of payment of claims. *§ See id.* at, *e.g.*, HU 175, 187, 199.)

The SAC further alleges that "providers who participate in the Medicaid program must sign enrollment agreements with their states that certify compliance with the state and federal Medicaid requirements, including the AKS. Although there are variations among the states, the agreement typically requires the prospective Medicaid provider to agree that he or she will comply with all state and federal laws and Medicaid regulations in billing the state Medicaid program for services or supplies furnished." (SAC ¶ 61.)

Finally, the Relators allege that, "in many states, Medicaid providers, including both physicians and pharmacies, must affirmatively certify, as a condition of payment of the claims submitted for reimbursement by Medicaid, compliance with applicable federal and state laws and regulations." (SAC ¶ 62.) The Complaint cites nothing for that proposition, and only provides an exemplar certification from New York State.

TRICARE (formerly CHAMPUS)

***8** TRICARE, formerly known as CHAMPUS, is part of the United States military's health care system. (*Id.* ¶ 64.) It is administered by the Department of Defense ("DOD"). (*Id.*) TRICARE provides prescription drug benefits through military treatment facility outpatient pharmacies, TRICARE network retail pharmacies, and TRICARE's mail order service. (*Id.* ¶ 65.) TRICARE contracts with a PBM to administer its retail and mail order pharmacy programs. (*Id.*) TRICARE beneficiaries can also pay for prescriptions out of their own pockets and then submit a claim for reimbursement to TRICARE's PBM. (*Id.*) The claims process differs for each program. (*Id.*)

Pursuant to 38 U.S.C. § 8126, pharmaceutical manufacturers are required to enter into national contracts with the DOD and to make certain drugs (I presume these to include Copaxone and Azilect) available to the DOD at the Federal Ceiling Price, which is defined as no more than 76% of the manufacturer's average price for the drug. 38 U.S.C. § 8126(a)(2). (SAC ¶ 69.)

All providers that offer services to TRICARE beneficiaries, whether network providers or non-participating providers, are required to comply with TRICARE's program requirements, including its anti-abuse provisions. Kickback arrangements are included within the definition of abusive situations that constitute program fraud. 32 C.F.R. §§ 199.2(b), 199.9(a)(4), 199.9(b), 199.9(c)(12). (SAC ¶ 72.)

Additionally, while any licensed and otherwise accredited physician may provide services to TRICARE beneficiaries, some enroll in the TRICARE program as participating providers. (*Id.*) Relators allege that participating providers must expressly certify their compliance with TRICARE regulations (*id.*), but point to no program requirement of any express certification, nor do they provide any sample express certification.

Veterans Administration Health Care

The Department of Veterans Affairs ("VA") maintains a system of medical facilities from which all pharmaceutical supplies, including prescription drugs, are procured directly by the VA. (*Id.* ¶ 73.) Pursuant to 38 U.S.C. § 8126, the VA purchases the pharmaceuticals that it dispenses at the Federal Ceiling Price. (*Id.* ¶ 74.) A VA facility that requires a particular medication submits a purchase order to the VA's pharmaceutical prime vendor ("PPV"), which fills the order for the facility, then submits an invoice to the VA for payment. (*Id.*)

Relators allege that Teva entered into a contract with the VA that requires Teva to comply with all applicable federal, state and local laws. (SAC ¶ 75.)

The Claims for Reimbursement Alleged to Be False

The SAC does not identify any particular claim that is alleged to be false. Instead, it identifies (in Exhibit A), the initials of 121 physicians who wrote prescriptions for the Drugs that caused downstream entities (*i.e.*, pharmacies) to submit claims to Medicare Part D for reimbursement, which claims were submitted during a year that the physicians were receiving allegedly sham "honoraria" from Teva. Exhibit A provides the number of such claims for each physician, as well as the amount that Medicare Part D paid out for such claims during 2010 and 2011. It further provides a personal identifying number relating to each physician, and offers to provide each physician's full name if the court so instructs.

The SAC does not provide any equivalent to Exhibit A for Medicaid, TRICARE, or the VA healthcare system. Instead, it identifies the claims alleged to be false as claims listed in Exhibit A (which relates only to Medicare Part D) and "all other claims submitted to the Government Healthcare Programs for prescriptions written by these physicians for the Covered Drugs beginning from the time they began receiving honoraria payments or other remuneration and continuing to date, because the claims were the result of prescriptions induced by honoraria or other remuneration." (SAC 156.) It appears that the physicians listed in Exhibit A are not exhaustive of those who received honoraria, but are allegedly a "representative sample" of the same. (*Id.* ¶ 155.)

Pricing Violations

***9** In addition to alleging that Teva's kickback scheme caused downstream entities' certifications to be "false," the Relators allege that Teva itself made false statements to government healthcare programs that wrongly enriched Teva at the public's expense.

Pharmaceutical manufacturers who wish to participate in various government healthcare programs, described below, are periodically required to report the "Average Manufacturer Price" ("AMP") for a drug, and also the "Best Price" ("BP") for a drug to various government entities.

Alleged Avoidance of Rebate Payments Owed to State Medicaid Programs Through Failure to Exclude Kickback Payments from Calculations of Teva's "Best Price " and "Average Manufacturer Price" for the Drugs.

First, pharmaceutical manufacturers participating in Medicaid programs must rebate to the States a certain statutorily prescribed portion of the price of the drugs purchased by each Medicaid program in each state. (*Id.* ¶ 76.) The amount of the rebate is calculated, in part, using the pharmaceutical manufacturer's report of its BP and AMP. (*Id.* ¶ 77.) Thus, to participate in Medicaid, Teva entered into rebate agreements with the Department of Health and Human Services ("HHS"), in which it agreed to comply with 42 U.S.C. § 1396r–8, and therefore:

a. Agreed to report its Best Price, inclusive of cash discounts, free goods contingent upon any purchase requirements, volume discounts and rebates, etc.;

b. Agreed that it would determine its Best Price based upon its AMP, calculated as "net sales divided by numbers of units sold, excluding free goods (*i.e.,* drugs or any other items given away, but not contingent on any purchase requirements)" and that it would include in the calculation, cash discounts and all other price reductions "which would reduce the actual price paid"; and

c. Agreed that the Best Price would not take into account nominal prices, defined as prices that are less than 10% of the AMP in that quarter, so long as the sale of product at a nominal price was not contingent on any other sale.

(*Id.* ¶ 78.)

Teva made quarterly reports of its AMP and/or BP to the Medicaid Program in an electronic form, Form CMS–367. (*Id.* ¶ 79.)

The Relators allege that, when reporting its Best Price on Form CMS–367 over the last six years, Teva failed to take into account the kickbacks it paid—thereby artificially inflating its Best Price. (*Id.* ¶ 81.) That inflation of its Best Price allegedly reduced the rebate amount that Teva paid to each State Medicaid program. (*Id.*)

The SAC does not include examples of any CMS–367 form, but I take it that the Relators wish to pursue claims based on each and every allegedly undersized rebate Teva paid to State Medicaid programs based on the allegedly inaccurate CMS–367 forms submitted in the six years prior to the filing of the SAC.

The Veterans Healthcare Act

The Federal Supply Schedule ("FSS") is a price list containing more than 20,000 pharmaceutical products; the VA and other government healthcare programs depend on the FSS for most of their drug purchases. (*Id.* ¶ 83.) For a drug to be listed on the FSS, and therefore available for purchase by the patients who use the VA and other government healthcare programs, the drug's manufacturer is "required to enter a pricing agreement with HHS for the section 340B Drug Pricing Program, and with the VA and other DOD programs." (*Id.* ¶ 82.) The SAC does not define "the section 340B Drug Pricing Program."

***10** Under the Veterans Healthcare Act of 1992 ("VHCA"), drug manufacturers must comply with 38 U.S.C. § 8126, which is entitled "Limitation on prices of drugs procured by Department and certain other Federal agencies." Subsection (a)(2) of that Section requires that "the price charged during the one-year period beginning on the date on which the agreement takes effect may not exceed 76% of the non-Federal average manufacturer price (less the amount of any additional discount required under subsection (c)) ..." (*Id.* ¶ 84.)

Subsection (4) of § 8126 provides that,

> **unless the manufacturer meets the requirements of paragraphs (1), (2), and (3), the manufacturer may not receive payment** for the purchase of drugs or biologicals from
>
> (A) a State plan under title XIX of the Social Security Act, except as authorized under section 1927(a)(3) of such Act,
>
> (B) any Federal agency described in subsection (b) [i.e., the VA, the Department of Defense, the Public Health Service, including the Indian Health Service, and the Coast Guard];
>
> (C) any entity that receives funds under the Public Health Service Act.

38 U.S.C. § 8126(4) (emphasis added).

The Relators appear to argue that, by artificially inflating its Average Manufacturer Price with the cost of its kickback scheme, Teva failed to comply with the requirement that Azilect and Copaxone's pricing for the relevant government agencies "not exceed 76% of the non-Federal average manufacturer price" and therefore made it ineligible to "receive payment for the purchase of drugs" from the government entities referenced in Subsection (4). (SAC ¶ 84.)

The Relators' Causes of Action

Count 1 asserts that Teva violated two FCA subsections by: (a) "knowingly present[ing], or causing] to be presented, a false or fraudulent claim for payment or approval," 31 U.S.C. § 3729(a)(1)(A); and (b) "knowingly mak[ing], us[ing], or caus[ing] to be made or used, a false record or statement material to a false or fraudulent claim," *id.* § 3729(a)(1)(B). That Count relates to two broad theories: (1) that Teva's kickback scheme tainted downstream entities' express and/or implied certifications of compliance with the anti-kickback statute, or that Teva's kickback scheme rendered downstream claims for reimbursement false regardless of whether there was an express or implied certification; and (2) that Teva itself made false claims by failing to account for its kickback payments when reporting the Drugs' respective "Best Prices" to various government healthcare programs —where accurate reporting was required for it to receive any payments at all under 38 U.S.C. § 8126(4), and inaccurate reporting permitted it to avoid paying the full rebates it allegedly owed to State Medicaid programs.

The Relator also asserts claims (Counts 2–30) under 29 state analogues of the FCA, and claims (Counts 31–33) under three local analogues of the FCA. These state and local claims pertain to claims for repayment submitted to state and local Medicaid programs.

Procedural History

The seal on this matter was lifted on March 12, 2015, after the United States government, state governments and local governments all declined to intervene. (Docket # 22.)

Teva filed the present motions to dismiss the action under Federal Rules of Civil Procedure 9(b) and 12(b)(6) on June 5, 2015.

In addition to briefing by Teva and the Relators, this Court received a "Statement of Interest" from the United States, in which the United States disputed Teva's positions on two points of law relevant to the motion. (Docket # 43.) Teva objects to the Court's consideration of such a Statement of Interest in light of the United States' decision not to intervene. (*See* Docket # 44.)

***11** The Court has reviewed the statement of interest, but is of the mind that Relators are masters of their complaint and control what issues will and will not be pursued here. If the United States wished to pursue issues the Relators are not intending on pursuing, it should have intervened. I will not force Relators to make arguments that they did not intend on making.

DISCUSSION

I. Standard of Review

In deciding a motion to dismiss pursuant to Rule 12(b)(6), the Court must liberally construe all claims, accept all factual allegations in the complaint as true, and draw all reasonable inferences in favor of the plaintiff. *See Cargo Partner AG v. Albatrans, Inc.*, 352 F.3d 41, 44 (2d Cir.2003); *see also Roth v. Jennings*, 489 F.3d 499, 510 (2d Cir.2007).

However, to survive a motion to dismiss pursuant to Rule 12(b)(6), "a complaint must contain sufficient factual matter ... to 'state a claim to relief that is plausible on its face." ' *Ashcroft v. Iqbal*, 556 U.S. 662, 678 (2009) (quoting *Bell Atl. Corp. v. Twombly*, 550 U.S. 544, 570 (2007)). "A claim has facial plausibility when the plaintiff pleads factual content that allows the court to draw the reasonable inference that the defendant is liable for the misconduct alleged." *Id.* (citing *Twombly*, 550 U.S. at 556). "While a complaint attacked by a Rule 12(b)(6) motion to dismiss does not need detailed factual allegations, a plaintiff's obligation to provide the grounds of his entitlement to relief requires more than labels and conclusions, and a formulaic recitation of the elements of a cause of action will not do." *Twombly*, 550 U.S. at 555 (internal quotations, citations, and alterations omitted). Thus, unless a plaintiff's well-pleaded allegations have "nudged [its] claims across the line from conceivable to plausible, [the plaintiff's] complaint must be dismissed." *Id.* at 570; *see also Iqbal*, 556 U.S. at 680.

This liberal pleading standard is modified by Rule 9(b), which requires a plaintiff asserting fraud claims to meet a heightened pleading standard. While Rule 8(a) usually requires only a "short and plain statement of the claim showing that the pleader is entitled to relief," Fed.R.Civ.P. 8(a), a plaintiff asserting fraud must "state with particularity the circumstances constituting fraud or mistake." Fed.R.Civ.P. 9(b). Rule 9(b) applies to claims brought under the FCA and its state law analogues. *See Gold v. Morrison–Knudsen Co.*, 68 F.3d 1475,1476–77 (2d Cir.1995); *U.S. ex rel. Polansky v. Pfizer, Inc.*, No. 04 Civ. 704, 2009 WL 1456582, at *4 (E.D.N.Y. May 22, 2009).

II. The Relators Have Pled Their Claims with Sufficient Particularity. [1]

A. *The Complaint Sufficiently Alleges the Relationship Among the Defendants and the Role of Each in the Alleged Kickback Scheme.*

First, Defendants argue that the SAC's refusal to differentiate between them—

instead referring to all three defendants collectively as "Teva"—violates Federal Rule of Civil Procedure 9(b). (Docket # 33 at 9 (citing, *e.g., Mills v. Polar Molecular Corp.,* 12 F.3d 1170, 1175 (2d Cir.1993).)

***12** "Rule 9(b) is not satisfied where the complaint vaguely attributes the alleged fraudulent [acts] to 'defendants.' " *Mills v. Polar Molecular Corp.,* 12 F.3d 1170, 1175 (2d Cir.1993). Thus, "Where multiple defendants are asked to respond to allegations of fraud, the complaint should inform each defendant of the nature of his alleged participation in the fraud." *DiVittorio v. Equidyne Extractive Indus.,* 822 F.2d 1242, 1247 (2d Cir.1987). The Relators contend that the SAC does just that—by alleging that each defendant "participated" insofar as each is an agent and alter ego of the other, that all operated as a single joint entity and integrated enterprise, and that, therefore, the act of one is attributable to all. (SAC ¶ –8.)

Where a complaint alleges a legal relationship between fraud defendants that makes the acts of one attributable to each, "Rule 9(b) does not require Plaintiffs to allege a "specific connection between fraudulent representations ... and particular defendants ..." *Id.* (quoting *Luce v. Edelstein,* 802 F.2d 49, 55 (2d Cir.1986)) (discussing "insiders and affiliates" who all participated in alleged fraud).

"[A] bare allegation of an individual defendant's affiliation with entities allegedly committing fraudulent acts is not enough to satisfy Rule 9(b)." *Angermeir v. Cohen,* 14 F.Supp.3d 134, 147 (S.D.N.Y.2014). Thus, "Although it is a well-established principle that '[t]he fraudulent statements of an agent, when made within the scope of its agency, are attributable to the principal'," a complaint sounding in fraud against multiple defendants on an agency theory still must "plead ... facts supporting the existence of an agency relationship ..." *Woods v. Maytag Co.,* 807 F.Supp.2d 112, 121 (E.D.N.Y.2011) (quoting *Aetna Cas. & Sur. Co. v. Aniero Concrete Co.,* 404 F.3d 566, 581 (2d Cir.2005)). So too, a naked allegation that one defendant was an "affiliate" of another defendant "alone is insufficient to link [the defendant] to [the alleged fraud]" for purposes of Rule 9(b). *Ouaknine v. MacFarlane,* 897 F.2d 75, 80 (2d Cir.1990).

However, as for the Relators' allegation that the defendants are each others' alter egos, "Whether Fed.R.Civ.P. 9(b) applies to veil-piercing claims has been characterized as a 'knotty question.' " *United Feature Syndicate, Inc. v. Miller Features Syndicate, Inc.,* 216 F.Supp.2d 198, 222–23 (S.D.N.Y.2002) (quoting *Farley v. Davis,* 1992 WL 110753, at *6 (S.D.N.Y. May 8, 1992)). A "veil-piercing claim [that] rests on allegations of fraud" is required to satisfy the requirements of Rule 9(b). *Id.* (citing cases). However, "Rule 9(b) does not come into play where fraud is not" the basis of a claim for piercing the corporate veil. *Network Enters., Inc. v. APBA Offshore Prods., Inc.,* 2002 WL 31050846, at *5 (S.D.N.Y.

Sept. 12, 2002); *see also Dist. Council No. 9 v. APC Painting, Inc.,* 272 F.Supp.2d 229, 241 (S.D.N.Y.2003).

Here, the alleged fraud is the filing of false claims, not the affiliation among the named defendants. As a result, the Rule 8 pleading standard, not the heightened standard of Rule 9(b), applies.

Under Rule 8(a), I must determine if the complaint contains "sufficient factual matter," which, if accepted as true, makes allegations regarding an agency, joint enterprise, or alter ego relationship that are "plausible on [their] face." *Bell Atlantic Corp. v. Twombly,* 550 U.S. 544, 570 (2007). "Threadbare recitals of the elements of a clause" or "labels and conclusions" do not suffice. *Ashcroft v. Iqbal,* 556 U.S. 662, 678 (2009). Where "the well-pleaded facts do not permit the court to infer more than the mere possibility of misconduct," a complaint is insufficient under Fed.R.Civ.P. 8(a) because it fails to "show ... that the pleader is entitled to relief." *Id.* at 679.

***13** Defendants' opening memorandum does not challenge the sufficiency of the Relators' allegations regarding the relationships between them. In their reply brief, Defendants argue that the SAC contains nothing more than a "cursory, kitchen sink-like list of alternative possible legal relationships between Defendants." (Docket # 39 at 3 (citing SAC 8)).

Even if that objection were timely, it is inaccurate. The SAC alleges the following regarding the relationship between the three defendants, Teva USA, Teva Neuroscience, and Teva Sales and Marketing:

- All three defendants are subsidiaries of non-party Teva Pharmaceutical Industries, Ltd., an Israeli corporation with a global footprint. (SAC 4.)
- Teva USA is a Pennsylvania corporation that does business throughout the United States. (SAC ¶ 5.)
- "Defendant Teva Neuroscience is a division or operating unit of [defendant] Teva USA." (SAC ¶ 6.)
- "Teva Sales and Marketing is a new legal entity created at the direction of Teva USA and also is a division of Teva USA. Effective January 1, 2014, all Teva Neuroscience employees [including the Relators] were transferred to Teva Sales and Marketing." (SAC ¶ 7.)
- The Relators "are currently considered to be employees of Teva Sales and Marketing and take direction from Teva Sales and Marketing [yet] ... are compensated and have their expenses paid by Teva Neuroscience in its capacity as an operating unit of Teva USA." (SAC ¶ 7.)
- "At all pertinent times, Teva USA controlled, directed and supervised

the sales and marketing activities of Teva Neuroscience and Teva Sales and Marketing, as well as their employees ..." (SAC ¶ 8.)

- "At all pertinent times, the employee and labor relations, as well as the compensation and benefit activities and the sales and marketing policies and procedures of TEVA have operated from and through the centralized control of Teva USA, which has established employee and labor relations, compensation and benefits and sales and marketing policies and procedures for Teva Neuroscience and Teva Sales and Marketing." (SAC ¶ 8.)

Thus, the Relators have pleaded that the two entities that have employed them—Teva Neuroscience ("TN") and Teva Sales and Marketing ("TSM")—both function at the behest of Teva USA ("TUSA"). The Relators currently work for TSM yet are paid and reimbursed by TN (presumably including reimbursements for expenditures on speaker programs), and allege that the very sales and marketing policies that create the alleged kickback scheme, and the compensation policies that reinforce them (*i.e.*, rewarding sales representatives based, in part, on the number of speaker programs orchestrated), are created and controlled by TUSA.

These allegations are sufficient to satisfy the liberal notice pleading standard of rule 8(a).

B. *The Relators Have Sufficiently Identified the False Claims at Issue.*

Next, the defendants argue that the SAC fails to identify the "sine qua non" of a False Claims Act action: the false claims. *U.S. ex rel. Bilotta v. Novartis Pharm. Corp.,* 50 F.Supp.3d 497, 510–11 (S.D.N.Y.2014) (quoting *United States ex rel. Clausen v. Laboratory Corporation of America, Inc.,* 290 F.3d 1301, 1311 (11th Cir.2002) (emphasis in original)).

The FCA "was enacted in 1863 with the principal goal of stopping the massive frauds perpetrated by large [private] contractors during the Civil War." *Vt. Agency of Natural Res. v. United States ex rel. Stevens,* 529 U.S. 765, 781 (2000). "[T]he statute attaches liability, not to the underlying fraudulent activity or to the government's wrongful payment, but to the 'claim for payment.' " *United States v. Rivera,* 55 F.3d 703, 709 (1st Cir.1995). "Underlying schemes and other wrongful activities that result in the submission of fraudulent claims are included in the 'circumstances constituting fraud or mistake' that must be pled with particularity pursuant to Rule 9(b). However, such pleadings invariably are inadequate unless they are linked to allegations, stated with particularity, of the actual false claims submitted to the government that constitute the essential element of an FCA qui tam action." *U.S. ex rel. Karvelas v. Melrose–Wakefield Hosp.,* 360 F.3d 220, 232 (1st Cir.2004); *see also Polansky,* 2009 WL 1456582, at *5 (collecting cases). "As such, Rule 9(b)'s directive that 'the circumstances constituting fraud or mistake shall be stated with particularity' does not permit a False Claims Act plaintiff merely to describe a private scheme in detail but then to allege simply and without any stated reason for his belief that claims requesting illegal payments must have been submitted, were likely submitted or should have been submitted to the Government.... [I]f Rule 9(b) is to be adhered to, some indicia of reliability must be given in the complaint to support the allegation of an *actual false claim* for payment being made to the Government." *Bilotta,* 50 F.Supp.3d at 510 (quoting *Clausen,* 290 F.3d at 1311).

***14** "In line with the weight of authority in this Circuit," this Court already has "adopt[ed] the *Karvelas* standard —plaintiffs asserting subsection (a)(1)(A) and (a)(1)(B) claims must plead the submission of a false claim with a high enough degree of particularity that defendants can reasonably 'identify particular false claims for payment that were submitted to the government.' " *U.S. ex rel. Kester v. Novartis Pharm. Corp.,* 23 F.Supp.3d 242, 257–58 (S.D.N.Y.2014) ("*Novartis I* ") (quoting *Karvelas,* 360 F.3d at 232). Thus, "the plaintiff must provide a detailed factual basis to support his allegation that the defendant submitted a false claim in this specific instance, not just that the defendant had a custom of submitting claims." *Id.,* 23 at 255 (emphasis in original). This specificity must "provide the defendant with enough details to be able to reasonably discern which of the claims it submitted are at issue." *Id.* at 258.

This Court has cited *Karvelas* with respect to the "kind of identifying information that a plaintiff can provide in order to satisfy Rule 9(b)," which includes "dates of claims, contents of claims, identification numbers, reimbursement amounts, goods or services provided, and individuals involved in the billing." *Novartis I,* 23 F.Supp.3d at 258. In *Karvelas,* the First Circuit held that "a relator must provide details," which, although not a formulaic list, could include "the dates of the claims, the content of the forms or bills submitted, their identification numbers, the amount of money charged to the government, the particular goods or services for which the government was billed, the individuals involved in the billing, and the length of time between the alleged fraudulent practices and the submission of claims based on those practices." *Karvelas,* 360 F.3d at 233. As this Court has recognized, "In the health care fraud context, courts also note the usefulness of data such as the name of the patient who received the good or service, the name of the medical professional who provided the good or service, the date on which the good or service was delivered, the name of the employee who submitted the claim, and the government entity that reimbursed the claim." *Novartis I,* 23 F.Supp.3d at 258. For complaints alleging extensive schemes, plaintiffs may satisfy these requirements in two ways: (1) by providing sufficient identifying information about all the false claims;

or (2) by providing examples of specific false claims. *Id.* at 258.

Defendants argue that the Relators have failed to provide either examples of specific false claims or sufficient identifying information about all the false claims. In this, they argue that, "To the extent any effort is made in the SAC to specify false claims, it is in Paragraph 110 and Exhibit A," and complain that those portions of the SAC "merely set forth, in summary fashion, the number of 'Medicare Part D Claims for Drug' and cost of total 'Medicare Reimbursement' for 2010 and 2011 for each identified practitioner." (Docket # 33 at 15.) Thus, the defendants argue, "This case is fundamentally different from *Novartis I,* where the government alleged that 'every single claim' for certain drugs submitted during a particular time period involved a kickback and was therefore false." *Id.* (quoting *Novartis* 7, 23 F.Supp.3d at 265).

Actually, this case is more similar to the Novartis case than the Defendants care to admit. In *Novartis I*, the United States Government, which had intervened and taken over prosecution of the action, did not identify any particular claim that was allegedly false. 23 F.Supp.3d at 250. Rather, the Government alleged that every claim in a few "narrowly defined pools" was false. The complaint defined those pools as claims (1) for two specific drugs, (2) that were submitted by certain identified pharmacies to certain government programs, (3) during a specified time period. *Id.* at 265. The pleading was held to be sufficient under Rule 9(b).

***15** Here, Relators have alleged that all claims in a similarly defined pool are false. The pool is comprised of all claims for reimbursement (1) relating to prescriptions of Copaxone and Azilect, (2) prescribed by doctors who participated in the allegedly "sham" speaker programs, (3) that were submitted for reimbursement to certain specified government programs, (4) from 2003 [2] to the present. Relators have even identified some 30 doctors who participated in the speaker programs (SAC ¶ 103), as well as 121 speaker program participants whose prescriptions of the Drugs resulted in claims to Medicare Part D (*see* SAC Ex. A), thereby further refining the second prong of the definition. [3] Claims alleged to be false as part of that pool include claims submitted for reimbursement to four federal programs—Medicare, Medicaid, TRICARE, and the VA. There are also claims for pricing violations of the FCA, which Relators bring on the ground that Teva falsely certified information about Best Price and Average Manufacturer Price for Copaxone and Azilect.

All in all, Relators have pleaded "the submission of a false claim with a high enough degree of particularity that defendants can reasonably identify particular false claims for payment that were submitted to the government." *Novartis I,* 23 F.Supp. at 258 (internal quotation marks and citation omitted). The information in the Amended

Complaint sufficiently alleges that Teva caused false claims for reimbursement related to Copaxone and Azilect to be submitted to the government. As I held in *U.S. ex rel Kester v. Novartis Pharm. Corp.*, No. 11 CIV. 8196 CM, 2015 WL 109934, (S.D.N.Y. Jan. 6, 2015) ("*Novartis VII* "), Relators need not submit sample claims for *each government program* on behalf of which they have brought suit. *Id.* at 23. Providing sample claim information for one program with respect to the drugs at issue is a sufficient basis for the Court to infer that similar claims were submitted to the other named government programs. "Such a[n] assumption does not expose the ... defendants to baseless or speculative fraud allegations—the problem Rule 9(b) is intended to protect against." *Id.* at *24.

Thus, the allegations in the Complaint provide a basis for the allegation that false claims were actually submitted to the government programs named in the Complaint and are sufficient for Teva to identify those false claims. Teva's motion to dismiss the Complaint for failure to sufficiently identify the false claims at issue is denied.

III. The Relators Have Sufficiently Alleged a Plausible Kickback Scheme in Violation of the AKS.

A. *The Scheme Generally*

"Because the False Claims Act is an anti-fraud statute, 'claims brought under the FCA fall within the express scope of Rule 9(b).' " *United States v. New York Soc. for the Relief of the Ruptured & Crippled, Maintaining the Hosp. for Special Surgery*, No. 07 civ. 292(PKC), 2014 WL 3905742, at *7 (S.D.N.Y. Aug. 7, 2014) (quoting *Gold v. Morrison–Knudsen Co.*, 68 F.3d 1475, 1477 (2d Cir.1995)). "Rule 9(b) does not impose a 'one size fits all' list of facts that must be included in every FCA complaint." *Novartis I*, 23 F.Supp.3d at 258 (quoting *In re Cardiac Devices Qui Tam Litig.*, 221 F.R.D. 318, 337–38 (D.Conn.2004)). "Ultimately, whether a complaint satisfies Rule 9(b) 'depends upon the nature of the case, the complexity or simplicity of the transaction or occurrence, the relationship of the parties and the determination of how much circumstantial detail is necessary to give notice to the adverse party and enable him to prepare a responsive pleading.' " *Id.* (quoting *United States v. Wells Fargo Bank, N.A.*, 972 F.Supp.2d 593, 616 (S.D.N.Y.2013)). This "is a fact-specific inquiry." *Id.*

***16** Where an FCA claim is premised on violations of the anti-kickback statute, plaintiff must "plead with particularity the 'who, what, when, where and how' of the fraudulent ... scheme." *U.S. ex rel. Mooney v. Americare, Inc.*, No. 06 Civ. 1806, 2013 WL 1346022 (E.D.N.Y. Apr. 3, 2013).

"The [federal Anti–Kickback Statute] makes it illegal to 'knowingly and willfully offer[ ] or pay[ ] any remuneration (including any kickback, bribe, or rebate) ... to any person to induce such person' to 'purchase or ... recommend purchasing' a drug that is covered by a federal health care program." *Novartis I,* 23 F.Supp.3d at 262 (quoting 42 U.S.C. § 1320a–7b(b)(2)). "The [Statute] defines 'remuneration' as including 'transfers of items or services for free or for other than fair market value.' " *U.S. ex rel. Fair Lab. Practices Assocs. v. Quest Diagnostics Inc.,* No. 05 Civ. 5393(RPP), 2011 WL 1330542, at *2 (S.D.N.Y. Apr. 5, 2011), ***aff'd sub nom.,*** *United States v. Quest Diagnostics Inc.,* 734 F.3d 154 (2d Cir.2013) (quoting 42 U.S.C. § 1320a–7a(i)(6)). "[T]he AKS [also] outlaws 'knowingly and willfully solicit[ing] or receiv[ing] any remuneration (including any kickback, bribe, or rebate)' 'in return for purchasing ... or recommending purchasing' a drug covered by a federal health care program." *Novartis I,* 23 F.Supp.3d at 262 (quoting 42 U.S.C. § 1320a–7b(b)(1)). "Thus, the AKS forbids offering, paying, soliciting, or receiving kickbacks in exchange for recommending drugs covered by [federal health care programs]." *Id.*

"A 2010 amendment to the Anti–Kickback Statute, which became effective on January 1, 2011, states that a claim for services that violates the Anti–Kickback Statute also violates the FCA." *New York Soc.,* 2014 WL 3905742, at *10 (quoting 42 U.S.C. § 1320a–7b(g)).

Relators—who were themselves pharmaceutical sales representatives at Teva—have alleged that the most important sales tool available to them was the capacity to purchase doctors' loyalty by offering them "honoraria" for speaker programs that have plausibly been alleged to be shams.

Their allegations are strikingly similar to those in a complaint Judge Gardephe found sufficient under Rule 9(b) in *U.S. ex rel Bilotta v. Novartis Pharmaceuticals Corp.,* 50 F.Supp.3d 497 (S.D.N.Y. Sept. 30, 2014). In that case, Novartis allegedly

> hosted lavish events that—while ostensibly intended to "educate" attendees about Novartis cardiovascular division drugs—actually provided little to no information about the drugs. Instead, the events constituted upscale, all-expense paid social outings for the doctors, as evidenced by the fact that (1) Novartis sales representatives repeatedly invited the same participants and "speakers" to attend events concerning the same drug or topic in a short span of time; (2) Novartis spent exorbitant amounts of money on these events, both at the macro level and at the individual event level; (3) doctors

> were paid thousands of dollars to "speak" at these events, even when Novartis drugs were not discussed or the events did not take place; ...

Id. at 515.

So too here. As alleged, the speaker programs—while educational in some abstract sense—were not educational for anyone providing or attending the programs, in that they offered no new content, and were given to the same attendees repeatedly—even sometimes given to no one at all outside of Teva itself.

***17** As in *Bilotta,* physicians were continually recruited to be speakers and therefore receive generous honoraria even though allegedly Teva did no needs-assessment or similar analyses of whether it needed any more speakers to be able to staff its presentations, though it is easy to see why: it apparently had trouble finding *attendees. See id.*

Furthermore, as in *Bilotta,* the ability to make thousands of dollars in honoraria was allegedly contingent on the number of prescriptions that the physician-speaker wrote. *See id.*

B. *There is no Requirement that the Bribes Be "But-for" Causes of Prescriptions*

Defendants argue that the SAC fails to state a claim for a violation of the AKS in that it fails to "allege a factual nexus between the improper conduct and the resulting submission of a false claim to the government." (Docket # 33 at 10 (quoting *Johnson v. Univ. of Rochester Med. Ctr.,* 686 F.Supp.2d 259, 266 (W.D.N.Y.2010).) In other words, Teva asks the Court to dismiss this suit unless the plaintiffs plead facts sufficient to support the inference that the physicians would not have prescribed the drugs "but for" the fact that they were being paid pursuant to the sham speaker scheme. (*Id.*)

As this Court has already found, however, "the AKS does not require a kick-back scheme to succeed in generating new business (*i.e.,* new patient prescriptions) in order for a violation to have occurred." *Novartis I* at 263. Indeed, I have expressly rejected the argument that the AKS contains a "but for" causation requirement on a claim-by-claim basis. *See U.S. ex rel. Kester v. Novartis Pharm. Corp.,* 41 F.Supp.3d 323, 332–35 (S.D.N.Y.2014) ("*Novartis IV*"). More recently, my colleague Judge Gardephe reached the same conclusion, holding, "At the pleading stage, it is not necessary for the Government [ ] to demonstrate with precision that every prescription written by every doctor was written in exchange for a kickback." *Bilotta,* 50 F.Supp.3d at 523.

This is because the focus of the AKS is not the success of the bribe, but the bribe itself. Thus, this Court and others within this District follow the rule of the Third, Fifth, Seventh, Ninth, and Tenth Circuits:

that "the [Relator] need only prove that 'one purpose' of remuneration is to induce a person to use a service for which payment is made under a federal health care program." *U.S. v. Narco Freedom, Inc.,* No. 14–cv–8593 JGK, 2015 WL 1499265, at *10 (S.D.N.Y. Apr. 2, 2015), *U.S. v. Borrasi,* 639 F.3d 774, 781–82 (7th Cir.2011); *U.S. v. McClatchey,* 217 F.3d 823, 834–35 (10th Cir.2000); *U.S v. Davis,* 132 F.3d 1092, 1094 (5th Cir.1998); *U.S. v. Kats,* 871 F.2d 105, 108 (9th Cir.1989) (per curiam); *U.S v. Greber,* 760 F.2d 68, 71–72 (3d Cir.1985).

Defendants argue that the Relators have failed to allege that the speaker program had any single *universal* purpose of remuneration. (Docket # 39 at 7–8.) But taking all of the SAC's factual allegations as true and drawing all inferences in favor of the nonmoving party, a universal purpose of remuneration is precisely what the Relators allege for these speaker programs. The Relators have pleaded that these speaking programs were sham, provided useless information, and that the few persons in attendance were both familiar with the material already (indeed, most of them are alleged to have been presenters) and were paid to be there. By pleading facts tending to show that the speaking programs and engagements were nothing more than a means to provide money to doctors who prescribed large amounts of the Drugs, in a corporation where centralized management both oversaw the operations of a nationwide sales force and allegedly devised the scheme to defraud, Relators have done all they must at the pleading stage to advance a theory that the speaker program had a universal and improper purpose. We shall see if they can prove their case.

C. *The Allegedly Sham Honoraria – If Indeed They Are Shams – Are Not Shielded by the AKS' Personal Services Safe Harbor.*

***18** The AKS exempts certain conduct covered by statutory and regulatory safe harbors. 42 U.S.C.A. § 1320a–7b(b). Among them is a safe harbor for personal services contracts. *See* 42 C.F.R. § 1001.952(d). Defendants argue that the Relators' pleading fails to place their conduct outside of this regulatory safe harbor. (Docket # 31 at 18.)

The SAC clearly alleges facts inconsistent with the personal services safe harbor. [4]

A personal services contract must meet several conditions to qualify under the safe harbor provision. *See* 42 C.F.R. § 1001.952(d). Among them:

> The aggregate compensation paid to the [physician] over the term of the agreement is set in advance, is consistent with fair market value in arms-length transactions and is not determined in a manner that takes into

> account the volume or value of any referrals or business otherwise generated between the parties for which payment may be made in whole or in part under Medicare, Medicaid or other Federal health care programs.

42 C.F.R. § 1001.952(d)(5).

As I have explained, shot through the *entire complaint* are allegations of fact supporting the inference that the compensation paid to the physician was not "consistent with fair market value," in that the speaker programs often had no "market value" at all, and were indeed "determined in a manner that t[ook] into account the volume or value of any referrals or business otherwise generated between the parties" insofar as physicians could only *become* speakers and *remain* speakers if they generated sufficient prescriptions.

IV. The Relators Have Sufficiently Alleged the "Falsity" of Some Claims, but Are Ordered to Amend Their Pleading with Respect to Other Claims.

The Relators' federal claims arise under two subsections of the FCA, "one for *causing* false claims related to the submission of false ... certifications, in violation of Title 31, United States Code, Section 3729(a)(1)(A) ... and a second for the *use* of false statements related to the submission of ... certifications, in violation of Title 31, United States Code, Section 3729(a)(1)(B)." *United States v. Movtady,* 13 F.Supp.3d 325, 330 (S.D.N.Y.2014); (*see* SAC 163–64).

Subsection (a)(1)(A) provides for liability where the defendant "knowingly presents, or causes to be presented, a *false or fraudulent claim* for payment or approval." 31 U.S.C. § 3729(a)(1)(A) (emphasis added). To prove a claim under this subsection, a plaintiff must show that: (1) there was a false or fraudulent claim, (2) the defendant knew it was false or fraudulent, (3) the defendant presented the claim, or caused it to be presented, to the United States, and (4) it did so to seek payment from the federal treasury. *See Mikes v. Straus,* 274 F.3d 687, 695 (2d Cir.2001); *U.S. ex rel. Pervez v. Beth Israel Med. Ctr.,* 736 F.Supp.2d 804, 811 (S.D.N.Y.2010).

Subsection (a)(1)(B) provides for liability where the defendant "knowingly makes, uses, or causes to be made or used, a false record or statement material to a *false or fraudulent claim.*" 31 U.S.C. § 3729(a)(1)(B) (emphasis added). To prove a claim under this subsection, a plaintiff must show that: (1) the defendant made (or caused to be made) a false statement, (2) the defendant knew it to be false, and (3) the statement was material to a false or fraudulent claim. *See Pervez,* 736 F.Supp.2d at 811.

***19** Both subsections of the FCA at issue in this case require the existence of "false or fraudulent" claims.

A. *Definition of False or Fraudulent Claims*

In *Mikes v. Straus,* 274 F.3d 687, 696 (2d Cir.2001), the Second Circuit established the definition of a "false or fraudulent" claim in this Circuit: it is any claim "aimed at extracting money the government otherwise would not have paid." *Id.* at 696. The Second Circuit recognized two types of "falsity"—*i.e.,* two reasons that the government would not pay the claim if it knew the true facts. One is factual falsity; the other is legal falsity. *See id.* at 697.

A claim is "factually false" where the party submitting the claim supplies "an incorrect description of goods or services provided or a request for reimbursement for goods or services never provided." *Id.*; *see also Pervez,* 736 F.Supp.2d at 812. In other words, the party "bills for something it did not provide." *U.S. ex rel. Kirk v. Schindler Elevator Corp.,* 601 F.3d 94, 113 (2d Cir.2010), *rev'd on other grounds,* 131 S.Ct. 1885 (2011).

In contrast, a "legally false" claim is "false" because it has been tainted by some underlying statutory, regulatory, or contractual violation made in connection with that claim, which renders the claim ineligible for reimbursement. Under *Mikes,* a violation does not render a claim "false" unless (1) compliance with the underlying statute, regulation, or contract is a "precondition" to payment of the claim, and (2) a party falsely represents (or "certifies") compliance with the provision in connection with the claim. 274 F.3d at 697–98. The *Mikes* court distinguished between preconditions to *payment* of claims and mere conditions of *participation* in a government program; in order for a statutory violation to provide a basis for legal "falsity," the government's decision to reimburse the claim must be conditioned upon compliance with the underlying statute. *See id.* at 701–02. The preconditions to payment vary by government program.

There are also two types of false certifications: express and implied.

As the name suggests, an "express false certification" occurs when the party submitting the claim expressly and "falsely certifies compliance with a particular statute, regulation or contractual term, where compliance is a prerequisite to payment." *Id.* at 698. Generally, express certifications are made when a government program requires participants to submit forms explicitly stating that they have complied with certain statutes. *See id.* Where the party certifying compliance is, in fact, violating the statute in question, that certification is "false." The claims rendered legally "false" by such false certifications include all the claims connected to the underlying statutory violation.

Legal "falsity" can also arise on a theory of "implied false certification."

The implied false certification theory is "based on the notion that the act of submitting a claim for reimbursement itself implies compliance with governing federal rules that are a precondition to payment." *Id.* at 699. In *Mikes,* the Second Circuit stated that this theory "is appropriately applied only when the underlying statute or regulation upon which the plaintiff relies *expressly* states the provider must comply in order to be paid." *Id.* at 700 (emphasis in original). "Liability under the Act may properly be found ... when a defendant submits a claim for reimbursement while knowing ... that payment expressly is precluded because of some noncompliance by the defendant." *Id.*

***20** In 2010 Congress amended the AKS to clarify that compliance with the AKS is a precondition to payment. Pursuant to the Patient Protection and Affordable Care Act ("PPACA"), Pub.L. No. 111–148, 124 Stat. 119 (Mar. 23, 2010), the AKS now states that, "a claim that includes items or services resulting from a violation of this section constitutes a false or fraudulent claim for purposes of [the False Claims Act]." 42 U.S.C. § 1320a–7b(g). The AKS applies to all "Federal health care program[s]," including Medicare and Medicaid. *Id.* § 1320a–7b(f). The 2010 amendment therefore made clear that compliance with the AKS is a precondition to the payment of claims submitted to these programs, and not merely a condition of participation in the programs. "Accordingly, from and after March 2010 'the act of submitting a claim for reimbursement itself implie[d] compliance with' the AKS, *Mikes,* 274 F.3d at 699, even in the absence of any express certification of compliance." *U.S. ex rel. Kester v. Novartis Pharm. Corp.,* 43 F.Supp.3d 332, 364 (S.D.N.Y.2014) ("*Novartis V* "). However, because "the AKS did not 'expressly' state that it was a precondition to payment of claims submitted to federal health care programs prior to March 2010 ... it [cannot] constitute a basis for implied false certifications prior to that date." *Id.* at 365.

Relators argue that factual and legal falsity are not the only categories of false or fraudulent claims, and that, "A claim may be false or fraudulent under the FCA where it contains no certifications at all, as long as the claim is ineligible for payment, such as a claim resulting from illegal kickbacks." (Docket # 35 at 9–10). In essence, Relators argue that any claim tainted by an illegal kickback—or for that matter, any claim submitted in violation of a statute that is a precondition to payment —is *per se* a false claim. They support this argument in two ways: they point to a statement in *Mikes* to the effect that "*a false claim may take many forms,* the most common being a claims for goods and services not provided, or provided in violation of contract terms, specification, statute or regulation." 274 F.3d at 697 (emphasis added, emphasis in original omitted); and they cite *Novartis V,* in which this court held that compliance with the AKS was a precondition to payment even prior to the 2010 Amendment to the AKS. 43 F.Supp.3d at 362–364.

I decline Relators' invitation to manufacture a new type of false claims. False claims jurisprudence from and after *Mikes* and its progeny rests on analyzing whether a claim submitted to the Government for reimbursement either expressly or impliedly certified compliance with the law; that analysis would be unnecessary if there were some other type of "false claim." *Mikes,* which establishes the blueprint for analyzing false claims in this Circuit, is the law that binds this court. This court most certainly did not create any third category of false claims in *Novartis V;* rather, I concluded that the Government's pleading stated a claim under the legal falsity theory that was announced in *Mikes.*

Thus, Relators may bring a claim under the FCA for violation of the AKS if (1) submission of a claim was factually false or (2) submission of a claim was legally false because a party (a) expressly certified compliance with the AKS or (b) impliedly certified compliance with the AKS. Because the world was not on notice until March 23, 2010, that a claim tainted by an implied certification of compliance with the AKS was a "false or fraudulent" claim, Relators can prevail on a theory of implied certification only with respect to claims that were submitted after March 23, 2010. Any claims arising prior to that date would have to be accompanied by express certifications in order to be actionable under the FCA.

B. *The Pricing Violations*

The Relators allege that Teva failed to account for its kickback scheme when reporting the Drugs' "Average Manufacturer Price" and "Best Price" to various government health programs. In their briefing on this issue, the parties treat Relators allegations as express certification claims. (Docket # 35 at 18; Docket # 38 at 7). But allegations that Teva "failed to take into accounts the kickbacks it paid when it reported its Best Price" (SAC ¶ 80) or Average Manufacturing Price (*id.* ¶ 84) are allegations of *factual* falsity, not legal falsity.

***21** Specifically, Relators allege that, when reporting its Best Price on Form CMS–367 over the last six years, Teva reported a number that was too high, because it consisted, not only of the actual cost of the drug, but also some amount representing the fees paid to physician participants in the sham speaker series. (*Id.* ¶ 81.) According to Relator, the true "best price" and "average manufacturing price" for Copaxone and Azilect should have been reported by backing out the alleged kickback. The price at which (1) federal and state/local governments reimbursed Teva for providing the drug, or (2) Teva paid a rebate to the states of a certain statutorily-prescribed portion of the price of drugs purchased by each Medicaid program, *see* 42 U.S.C § 1396r–8(a)(1), was dependent on Best Price or Average Manufacturing Price (as the case may be). Thus, Relators allege that Teva caused the governments to subsidize its kickback program, by reducing the amount or the rebate that Teva had to pay to each State Medicaid program, pursuant to the rebate Agreement Teva was required to enter with HHS for its drugs to be available to Medicaid beneficiaries. (*Id.* ¶¶ 76–81.)

Relators further allege that, by artificially inflating its Average Manufacturer Price with the cost of its kickback scheme, Teva failed to comply with the requirement of its pricing agreement with HHS that Azilect and Copaxone's pricing "not exceed 76% of the non-Federal average manufacturer price" and therefore made Teva ineligible to "receive payment for the purchase of drugs" from the government entities referenced in Subsection (4), namely the VA and the DOD. (*Id* ¶ 84.)

In response, Defendants argue that they were not required to include speaker fees when calculating AMP and BP because, "Speaker fees constitute bona fide services fees ("BFSFs"), which are expressly excluded from AMP calculations. *See* 42 C.F.R. § 447.504(a) and (h); 42 C. F.R. § 447.502." (Docket # 38 at 7.)

The Court is not convinced—at least, not at the motion to dismiss stage. 42 C.F.R. § 447.502 defines bona fide service fees as "fees paid by a manufacturer to an entity; that represent fair market value for a bona fide, itemized service actually performed on behalf of the manufacturer that the manufacturer would otherwise perform (or contract for) in the absence of the service arrangement; and that are not passed on in whole or in part to a client or customer of an entity, whether or not the entity takes title to the drug." The fair import of Relators' allegations is that speaker fees paid to doctors were *not* fair market value for bona fide services. Rather, the presentations for which doctors were paid allegedly were devoid of substance (SAC ¶ 101), and the "honoraria" were, in reality, kickbacks paid in exchange for writing prescriptions of Defendants' drugs (*id.* H 96). Thus, for purposes of defeating a motion to dismiss, Relators have sufficiently alleged that honoraria fall outside of the BFSF exclusion from AMP calculations.

C. *The Reimbursement Claims (Medicare, Medicaid. VA & TRICARE)*

The Relators briefly argue that "claims tainted by kickbacks ... fit within the rubric of factually false claims, as 'the Government does not get what it bargained for when a defendant is paid by CMS for services tainted by a kickback.' " (Docket # 35 at 10 (quoting *U.S. ex. Rel. Wilkins v. United Health Grp., Inc.*, 659 F.3d 295, 314 (3d Cir.2011).) ***Wilkins,*** however was not a factual falsity case but a legal falsity case; the discussion quoted above comes from an explanation of the implied certification theory. *See* 659 F.3d at 313–14. ***Wilkins*** simply does not stand for the premise that claims tainted by kickbacks are somehow factually, as opposed to legally, false claims.

Moreover, there is no allegation of fact in the complaint supporting an inference that the reimbursement claims contained factually inaccurate information—*i.e.,* that the claims supplied "an incorrect description of goods or services provided or a request for reimbursement for goods or services never provided." *Mikes,* 274 F.3d 697. As such, the reimbursement claims allegedly in violation of the FCA must be analyzed under the theory of legal falsity.

***22** Because I have already determined that compliance with the AKS is a precondition of payment by federal healthcare programs, *supra* at 39, the only issue is whether Relators have sufficiently alleged express or (after the effective date of the PPACA) implied certifications. Relators argue that they have alleged express certification claims for each government program at issue. Thus, I will address whether Relators have sufficiently alleged express certification claims first and only reach the question of implied certification if necessary.

I. Medicare Part D

Teva argues that it cannot be held responsible for the express certifications identified in the Complaint with respect to Medicare Part D, because the express certifications at issue were not submitted by the physicians who allegedly received the kickbacks and because the certifications are too broad to be deemed "express certifications." Neither argument is persuasive. Teva also argues that submission of Prescription Drug Events ("PDEs") to the government cannot be the basis of a FCA violation because PDEs contain no certifications and Relators have failed to allege factual falsity as to any PDE data. On this point, Defendants are correct.

a. Teva Can Cause an "Upstream" [5] Entity's False Certification

Relators have described in detail the order of operations by which a doctor's kickbacktainted prescription results in a false claim: (1) a Part D sponsors enter into a subcontract with a pharmacy (SAC ¶ 36), (2) the pharmacy submits a claim to the Part D sponsor (or to its Pharmacy Benefits Manager, which submits to the Part D sponsor) when it dispenses drugs to a Medicare beneficiary (*id.* ¶ 37), (3) the pharmacy receives reimbursement from the Part D sponsor (or PBM) (*id.*), and (4) the Part D sponsor receives reimbursement from CMS (*id.* ¶¶ 40–41). Relators have even provided a chart showing the number of Medicare Part D claims and the dollar reimbursement to pharmacies associated with such claims, which were made as a result of prescriptions by allegedly compromised physicians in 2010 and 2011. (*See* SAC, Ex. A.)

Defendants contend that Relators cannot prevail on a theory by which doctors receive kickbacks from Teva but pharmacies certify compliance with the AKS, arguing that the entity making the certification must know it to be false: "For example, if upstream party Z certifies that it did not violate the AKS, and

Z in fact did not, the certification is true even if downstream entity X did. True certifications cannot support a false certification claim." (Docket # 38 at 7). This is a clever argument, but not a successful one.

First, Relators *have* alleged that the physicians did, in fact, certify compliance with the AKS – via the CMS Form 855I. That form, which Relators allege is prerequisite to participation in the Medicare program, expressly certifies the physicians will comply with the AKS in all their dealings with Medicare. (SAC ¶ 56). Defendants argue that this form applies only to the provision of physician's services (covered by Medicare Part B) and not to the provision of prescription drugs (covered by Medicare Part D). But that is incorrect. The certification states that:

> ***23** I agree to abide by the Medicare laws, regulations and program instructions that apply to me or to the organization listed in Section 4A of this application. The Medicare laws, regulations, and program instructions are available through the feefor-service contractor. I understand that *payment of a claim by Medicare is conditioned upon the claim and the underlying transaction complying with such laws, regulations, and program instructions (including, but not limited to, the Federal anti-kickback statute and the Stark law*), and on the supplier's compliance with all applicable conditions of participation in Medicare.

Medicare Enrollment Application for Physicians and Non–Physician Practitioners,

CMS.gov, https://www.cms.gov/Medicare/CMS-Forms/CMS-Forms/downloads/cms855i.pdf at 1 (last visited February 8, 2015) (emphasis added). Thus, while the form itself may be directed at a physician's services (Part B) rather than the provision of medication (Part D), the language of the certification applies to all claims made to Medicare by or at the behest of the physician. The certification under CMS Form 855I is sufficient to underpin an FCA claim for Medicare Part D reimbursement premised on a violation of the AKS.

Second, even if the physicians' CMS Form 855I did not apply to the claims at issue, Relators' argument fails because the pharmacies that filled the kickback-tainted prescriptions are alleged to have certified compliance with the AKS pursuant to 42 C.F.R. § 423.505(i)(4)(iv). Contrary to Defendants' argument, *Mikes* does not require that the party certifying compliance with a statute also be the party with knowledge that the certification is false. *See* 274 F.3d at 697. Knowledge is, of course, required for liability under the FCA, but Relators are not seeking to hold the pharmacies liable for Teva's misdeeds; they are seeking to hold Teva liable for causing the pharmacies to make false certifications. And Teva is alleged to have known exactly what it was doing.

That the pharmacies may not have known about Teva's misconduct is not fatal to the claim against Teva, because, "It is well-established that the FCA reaches claims that are rendered false by one party, but submitted to the government by another." *U.S. ex rel Feldman v. City of New York,* 808 F.Supp.2d 641, 650 (S.D.N.Y.2011) (internal quotation marks and citation omitted). Defendants concede that a downstream entity can cause an upstream entity to make a false certification. (*See* Docket # 31 at 9 n.11).

The legislative history behind the 2010 amendment to the AKS, discussed at length in *Novartis IV,* makes clear that Congress took action to clarify existing law to foreclose precisely the argument Defendants make here. In enacting the amendment, Senator Ted Kaufman, the bill's sponsor, expressly disapproved of the district court's holding in *United States ex rel. Thomas v. Bailey,* No. 06 Civ. 465, 2008 WL 4853630 (E.D.Ark. Nov. 6, 2008), a case in which a medical device company and its sales representative paid kickbacks to a surgeon for using the company's device in its surgeries. The company and the sales representative escaped liability under the FCA because the hospital—an innocent party that submitted claims to the federal government for reimbursement based on the surgeon's use of the medical device – certified its *own* knowledge of compliance with the AKS. Thus, the court determined that the hospital's certification was not, strictly speaking, false, for purposes of the FCA. Congress disapproved of this interpretation of the law and, in response, sought to clarify that "*all claims* resulting from illegal kickbacks are 'false or fraudulent' even when the claims are not submitted directly by the wrongdoers themselves." *Novartis IV,* 41 F.Supp.3d at 334 (internal citation omitted). As I stated in *Novartis* IV:

> ***24** By enacting Section 1320a–7b(g), Congress made clear that the fact that the certifications were made by an innocent party submitting a claim without knowledge of an AKS violation did not remove the taint of falsity from the certifications; any claim connected in any way to an AKS violation was ineligible

> for reimbursement, even if the party that submitted the claim had no knowledge of the AKS violation.

*Id.*at 335. Congress could hardly have intended to insulate entities whose actions violate the AKS simply because upstream entities—whose claims the violators have induced—make the actual certification. Following the 2010 amendment, Senator Kaufman left little doubt as to that intent.

Thus, this case cannot be distinguished from *Novartis IV,* in which this court denied a pharmaceutical company's motion to dismiss claims predicated on express certifications relating to the Medicare Part D program. 41 F.Supp.3d at 337. The only difference between this case and *Novartis* is that, in the latter, the FCA claims were predicated on kickbacks allegedly paid to pharmacies that certified compliance with the AKS. Here, the kickbacks were allegedly paid to doctors, who prescribed drugs that were ultimately dispensed by the pharmacies. But that is of no moment, because the kickbacks here are properly alleged to have caused doctors to prescribe the drugs, which caused pharmacies to dispense the drugs and make related claims to a Part D sponsor, which submitted claims to the federal government. The fact that there is an extra link in the causal chain does not render the claims submitted for reimbursement any less false.

b. Broad Certification Language Does Not Preclude an Express Certification Claim

Novartis IV also forecloses Defendants' argument that the certifications at issue are too "sweeping" in their language to certify compliance with the AKS. (Dockct # 31 at 7–8). Defendants argue that "generalized language, referring broadly to all applicable requirements, is insufficient to create an express certification of compliance with the AKS upon which government payment is conditioned." (*Id.*)

In *Novartis IV,* this Court held that because, "The AKS is unquestionably one of the 'applicable Federal laws' governing Medicare Part D that is cited in the subcontract certification... subcontracting pharmacies who certify compliance 'with all applicable Federal laws, regulations, and CMS instructions' certify compliance with the AKS." 42 C.F.R. § 423.505(i)(4)(iv)." 41 F.Supp.3d at 337. That certification is an express certification of compliance for purposes of the FCA. In that same case, I also held that a certification of compliance with "applicable federal and state laws and regulations" in a New York Medicaid billing certification was an express certification of compliance with the AKS. *Id.* at 338.

The case on which Defendants rely for the premise that broad certification language cannot support a claim for FCA liability, *U.S. ex rel. Conner v. Salina Reg'l Health Ctr., Inc.,* 543 F.3d 1211 (10th Cir.2008), is easily distinguishable. In that case, the relator sought to hold a hospital liable under the FCA for failure to comply with various regulations and statutes establishing conditions of participation in the Medicare program. *Id.* at 1216. The relator argued that the following certification in the hospital's annual cost reports created an express certification for purposes of the FCA: "I ... certify that I am familiar with the laws and regulations regarding the provision of health care services, and that the services identified in this cost report were provided in compliance with such laws and regulations." *Id.* at 1219. The circuit court affirmed the district court's dismissal of the express certification claim, not because the certification was too "general" to find that it attested to compliance with the Medicare regulations at issue, but because the breadth of the certification suggested that compliance with the underlying regulations *was not a precondition to payment. Id.* In contrast, here, there is no question that compliance with the AKS is a precondition to payment under all federal healthcare programs. *See Novartis V,* 43 F.Supp.3d 332, 364 (S.D.N.Y.2014). As such, a certification of compliance with "all applicable Federal laws" is express certification of compliance with a statute —the AKS—that is a precondition to payment.

c. Relators Fail to State an Express Certification Claim Premised on the Submission of Prescription Drug Events

***25** Finally, Teva argues that PDEs—data submitted by Part D Sponsors to CMS comprising 39 fields regarding the claim such as the prescriber, quantity and amount paid to the pharmacy (SAC H 38) —cannot form the basis of a FCA claim premised on violation of the AKS because PDEs contain a certification as to the factual accuracy of the data submitted, and there is no allegation in the complaint of factual inaccuracy. (Docket # 31 at 9.)

Teva is correct that there is no allegation in the Complaint that PDEs submitted to the government contained inaccurate data. Relators respond that "PDE claims for drugs tainted by kickbacks are 'false claims' for purposes of the FCA," citing *U.S. ex rel. Spay v. CVS Caremark Corp.,* 913 F.Supp.2d 125, 171 (E.D.Pa.2012). (Docket # 35 at 15). But *Spay* stands for the proposition that PDEs, if they are alleged to contain false or inaccurate data, are false claims for purposes of the FCA —not that PDEs containing accurate data allegedly tainted by kickbacks constitute false claims. Thus, the allegations in the Complaint as written do not state a claim for violation of the FCA based on the submission of PDEs.

Should Relators wish to proceed with a claim based on the submission of PDEs they must amend their Complaint to allege precisely what aspect of the

PDE forms is inaccurate. They have 30 days to do so. If, as appears to be the case, Relators cannot identify any such factually inaccurate data, then allegations of false certifications relating to the PDEs should be dropped from the Complaint.

2. TRICARE (formerly known as CHAMP US)

Compliance with the AKS is a precondition to payment under Federal Healthcare Programs, including TRICARE. *Novartis V*, 43 F.Supp.3d at 362–64 (S.D.N.Y.2014). Thus, the question is whether express or implied certifications were made in connection with claims submitted to TRICARE.

Relators allege that "physicians" and "all providers that offer services to TRICARE beneficiaries" must expressly certify compliance with various "anti-abuse" provisions. (*See, e.g.,* SAC H 72). In support of this allegation, Relators cite to 32 C.F.R. §§ 199.9(a)(4), 199.9(c)(12) and 199.2(b).

Section 199.9 is titled Administrative Remedies for Fraud, Abuse and Conflict of Interest. Section 199.9(a)(4) states in full: "Providers seeking payment from the Federal Government through programs such as [TRICARE] have a duty to familiarize themselves with, and comply with, the program requirements." 32 C.F.R. § 199.9. Section 199.9(c)(12) provides that "Examples of situations which ... are presumed to be fraud [as defined by § 199.2] include, but are not limited to: ... Arrangements by providers with employees, independent contractors, suppliers, or others which appear to be designed primarily to overcharge the [TRICARE] through various means (such as commissions, fee-splitting, and kickbacks) used to divert or conceal improper or unnecessary costs or profits." 32 C.F.R. § 199.9.

These sections do not require express certifications of compliance with the AKS. And there are no allegations that Teva entered into any TRICARE contracts or provider agreements that expressly certify compliance with the AKS. Relators have not identified any express certifications—not even exemplars. Further, this Court has held in *Novartis VII* that neither § 199.9(a)(4) nor § 199.9(c)(12) requires compliance with the AKS as a condition of payment. *See Novartis VII,* 2015 WL 109934 at *18. These provisions cannot form the basis of an implied certification claim. *Id.*

***26** In their opposition brief, Relators argue that "the SAC identifies actionable claims based upon DD Form 2642." (Docket # 35 at 18.) But reference to Form 2642 does not save Relators' claim. Form 2642 is, according to the Complaint, a form filled out by a beneficiary (that is, a patient) when filling out a prescription at a retail pharmacy outside of TRICARE's Network. The beneficiary pays the full amount for the prescription, and then submits the Form 2642 to a Pharmacy Benefit Manager, which submits a claim to TRICARE. (SAC H 67). But the form itself does not certify compliance with the AKS—or with any other statute or regulation that could conceivably relate to the conduct of a pharmaceutical company. As such, Form 2642 cannot serve as the basis for an express certification claim. *See http://www.dtic.mil/whs/directives/forms/eforms/dd2642.pdf* (last visited February 9, 2016).

Thus, Relators have not sufficiently alleged express certification claims relating to TRICARE. They also have not pointed to any basis for recognizing an implied certification claim for claims submitted to TRICARE before March 23, 2010. For claims submitted to TRICARE after March 23, 2010, the PPACA states that compliance with the AKS is a precondition for reimbursement, so to that extent, and that extent only, Relators have stated a claim for implied certification.

I note that Defendants argue that the PPACA "only addresses that subset of claims that '*resulted from* ' the kickback." (Docket # 31 at 14). Thus, according to Defendants, Relators' must allege that each prescription that caused a claim was the result of "improper financial influence," in order to state an implied certification claim. (*Id.* at 15). But, as discussed above with respect to the causation requirements of Rule 9(b), *supra* at 34–36, that argument has no merit—not least because I addressed and rejected it in *Novartis IV. See* 41 F.Supp.3d at 332–35. The PPACA clarified that the AKS is, and has always been, a precondition of payment, and it does not create a "but for" requirement as part of that precondition.

Because Relators have failed to allege any express or implied false certifications made in connection with the claims submitted to TRICARE prior to the enactment of the PPACA on March 23, 2010, Relators' FCA claim may not go forward insofar as it relates to those claims for repayment. Relators have 30 days to replead their TRICARE claims, invoking the specific certification forms, statutes, or regulations that provide a basis upon which this Court can find that false certifications (either express or implied) rendered those claims "false."

3. *Veterans Administration Healthcare*

Relators allege that Defendants entered into a contract with the VA that "requires TEVA to comply with all applicable federal, state and local laws, executive orders, rules and regulations applicable to performance of TEVA's duties" under the contract. (SAC ¶ 75). Relators allege that the contract also specifically identifies seven statutes with which TEVA is required to comply. Though Relators appear to concede that the statutes specifically identified by contract have no bearing on this suit, they argue that a certification of compliance with "all applicable federal ... laws" is an express certification of compliance with the AKS. (Docket # 35 at 18.) Defendants argue that this language is too broad to be deemed an express certification.

As discussed above, because the AKS is a precondition to suit and, by its own terms, applies to federal healthcare programs, certification of compliance with all applicable laws in a contract for services under the Veterans Administration Healthcare program is express certification of compliance with the AKS. Relators have sufficiently alleged express certification claims with respect to the VA healthcare program.

4. Medicaid

***27** Relators allege a variety of express certifications with respect to Medicaid. The SAC alleges that "providers who participate in the Medicaid program must sign enrollment agreements with their states that certify compliance with the state and federal Medicaid requirements, including the AKS." (SAC ¶ 61.) The SAC does not contain sample language from any enrollment agreement. Further, Relators allege that, "in many states, Medicaid providers, including both physicians and pharmacies, must affirmatively certify, as a condition of payment of the claims submitted for reimbursement by Medicaid, compliance with applicable federal and state laws and regulations." (SAC ¶ 62.) The Complaint provides an exemplar certification from New York State. The Complaint also alleges that Teva "caus[ed] the States to submit false claims to the United States Government on Form CMS–64 (Quarterly Medicaid Statement of Expenditures for the Medical Assistance Program), which falsely certified that all drugs for which federal reimbursement was sought ... were paid for in compliance with federal law, including the AK[S] ... " (*Id.* ¶ 165), and that Teva knowingly caused pharmacies and other healthcare providers to submit false CMS–1500 claims for payment. (*Id.* ¶ 164).

Defendants argue that (1) Relators have failed to allege express certifications for all state Medicaid programs except for New York's, (2) allegations that the states submitted false claims to the United States Government on Form CMS–64 fail because the form's certification is "forward-looking" and too broad to constitute an express certification, and (3) Form CMS–1500 contains no express certification.

In *Novartis IV,* I held that "conclusory allegations that 'many states' require express AKS compliance certifications" were insufficient to state a claim premised on express certification. 41 F.Supp.3d at 338–39. To state a claim, Relators must *identify* the express certification. Here, Relators here have not actually identified any express certification with respect to enrollment agreements. Nor have they identified certifications with respect to billing, with the exception of billing certifications for New York's Medicaid program. (See SAC ¶ 63).

As for the alleged express certification in form CMS–1500, neither party has provided the Court with a sample form (the link provided by Defendants in their reply brief does not lead to the form itself), but the Court endeavored to find the CMS

1500 claim form 08/05 (the form in effect during the relevant time period) itself. It appears to contain no certification as to compliance with the AKS.[6]

However, Relators have sufficiently alleged express certifications with respect to state Medicaid programs on Form CMS–64. Because Form CMS–64 contains an express certification of compliance with federal laws (Compl.¶ 164), and Relators allege that states submitted this form in conjunction with Medicaid claims submitted to the federal government for reimbursement, Relators' FCA claim premised on express certifications with respect to Medicare withstands Defendants motion to dismiss. As discussed above, Defendants' argument that such a certification is too broad, per *Conner,* fails. Further, Defendants' contention that Form CMS–64 cannot form the basis of an express certification claim because it is "forward-looking" has no merit. Neither party has provided the exact language of the CMS–64 form, but the parties seem to agree that this form contains language similar to the CMS–855I form, which says, "I agree to abide by the Medicare laws, regulations and program instructions." (*See* Docket # 31 at 13 n.16; Docket # 35 at 16.) In *Novartis VII,* I held that the phrase "I *agree* to abide by" applicable laws and regulations "does not predict future behaviors; it obligates the provider to behave in a certain manner." 2015 WL 109934, at *19. Form CMS–64 (assuming it contains the same language, as the parties suggest) is therefore an express certification of compliance with the AKS.

***28** Should Relators wish to proceed with their Medicaid-based allegations on a certification other than that contained in Form CMS–64, they must amend their Complaint to state the express certifications from the enrollment agreement or billing certifications upon which they rely. They may do so by providing exemplar certifications for each relevant state, as they have done for New York. They have 30 days to do so.

V. The Relators Have Sufficiently Alleged That the Defendants "Willfully" and "Knowingly" Caused the Submission of False Claims.

"[T]he text of the FCA expressly states that it does not require 'proof of specific intent to defraud.' " *New York Soc.,* 2014 WL 3905742, at *8 (quoting 31 U.S.C. § 3729(b)(1)(B)). Rather, a defendant violates the FCA if it "knowingly ... causes to be presented[ ] a false or fraudulent claim for payment or approval," or "knowingly ... causes to be made or used, a false record or statement material to a false or fraudulent claim." 31 U.S.C. § 3729(a)(l)(A)-(B).

Defendants argue that, to meet this standard, a complaint must allege facts sufficient to draw the inference that a defendant had specific knowledge that he was violating the Anti-Kickback Statute and then had specific knowledge of the submission of false claims. (*See* Docket

#31 at 20-22.) That is simply not the standard.

A defendant acts knowingly within the meaning of the FCA if it "(i) has actual knowledge of the information; (ii) acts in deliberate ignorance of the truth or falsity of the information; or (iii) acts in reckless disregard of the truth or falsity of the information." 31 U.S.C. § 3729(b)(l)(A) (emphasis added). " '[T]his does not conflict with Rule 9(b),' since '[m]alice, intent, knowledge, and other condition of mind of a person may be averred generally.' " *New York Soc.*, 2014 WL 3905742, at *8 (quoting *Gold*, 68 F.3d at 1477).

As Judge Gardephe found in *Bilotta*, so this Court finds that, considered together,

> the allegations raise a strong inference that [Teva] caused the submission of false claims to federal ... healthcare programs and that it acted with actual knowledge in doing so or, at the very least, in deliberate ignorance or reckless disregard of that fact. This strong inference arises from the abundant evidence—as pled in the complaints—that the purpose of the speaker program was not to disseminate medical or scientific information to doctors, but rather to reward those who prescribed large quantities of [Teva] drugs, and to encourage other doctors to prescribe larger quantities of [Teva] drugs. This inference also arises from evidence demonstrating that [Teva] intentionally encouraged these sham speaker events ...

Id. at 528-29 (citing 31 U.S.C. § 3729(b)(l)). Defendants' arguments to the contrary uniformly ask the Court to draw all inferences in their favor, rather than in the favor of non-movant Relators.

VI. The Relators' State and Municipal FCA Claims Are Stayed and the Motions to Dismiss Counts II Through XXXIII are Denied Without Prejudice

In addition to alleging that Defendants caused false Medicaid claims to be submitted to the federal government in violation of the FCA, Relators claim that Teva caused the submission of false Medicaid claims to state and local governments in violation of the false claims acts of 32 different states and municipalities, each of which has its own laws and regulations, not all of which are identical to the AKS.

In the interest of judicial economy and docket management, these claims (Counts II through XXXIII) are stayed until the federal FCA claims have been resolved. If the federal claims are ultimately dismissed, this Court will decline to exercise jurisdiction over the several state and local claims and they can be adjudicated in fora where local laws are well known and frequently applied. If Relators prevail on the federal claims, we will address the resolution of these pendent claims as part of an overall resolution. However, there is no reason for this Court to spend a lot of time delving into the arcana of myriad (as in, more than 30) state and local false claims laws before the factual record in this case is developed and the federal claims are resolved one way or another.

Accordingly, Teva's motions to dismiss the state and local claims are denied without prejudice to renewal after the federal claims have been resolved; Counts II through XXXIII are severed and placed on the Court's suspense calendar.

CONCLUSION

For the foregoing reasons, Defendants' motions to dismiss are denied. As I have held that certain of the certifications alleged in the complaint are an insufficient basis for FCA liability, Relators must amend their pleading with respect to those claims as directed *supra* in sections IV.C.1.c, IV.C.2, and IV.C.4. They have 30 days to do so. The Clerk of the Court is directed to remove Docket Nos. 30 and 32 from the Court's list of pending motions.

All Citations

Not Reported in Fed. Supp., 2016 WL 750720, Med & Med GD (CCH) P 305,554

Footnotes

1 In addition to the two arguments discussed below, Defendants' opening 9(b) memorandum briefly complains that the Relators have failed to identify certifications by physicians themselves. (Docket # 33 at 17.) This contention has no merit. Defendants flesh out this argument further in their 12(b)(6) memoranda, (*see* Docket # 31 at 8–9, Docket # 38 at 3–4), and I therefore address (and reject) it in greater detail below. *See infra* at 45–48.

2 Relators allege that Teva has knowingly and willfully violated the FCA "from 2003 to the present" (SAC ¶ 163), though they note that sham speaker programs became more prevalent in 2008 and 2009 (SAC ¶ 99).

3 These lists do not purport to be exhaustive; there may come a time when they will be deemed exhaustive, however.

4 Because the SAC, if believed, precludes application of the personal services safe harbor, I need not decide the question whether it is a plaintiff's burden to allege facts that remove a defendant's conduct from all possible safe harbors, or instead a defendant's burden to prove entitlement to a safe harbor as an affirmative defense after the pleadings stage.

5 Throughout this opinion, the Court has referred to all entities, such as pharmacies, that are below the Part D sponsor and "first tier entity" *(i.e.,* the party that contracts with the Part D sponsor) in the chain of claim submission as "downstream" entities, consistent with the definitions provided in 42 C.F.R. § 423.4. Pharmacies, however, are "upstream" from the physicians who allegedly received kickbacks from Teva, in that they are further up the causal chain of claim submission. I will therefore refer to such pharmacies as "upstream" to demonstrate their position in the causal chain relative to physicians and Teva, for purposes of this section only.

6 See https://www. google.com/url?sa=t & rct=j & q= & esrc=s & source =web & cd= 1 & ved= Oah UKEwiTg faGnfDKAhUW4GMKHYKkBXwQFgg2MAA & url=https #®%2 F www. cms. gov®Medic are®CMS-Forms®CMS-Forms®downloads%2 Fcms1500805.pdf & usg=AFQjCNEdWVkcMSjOhJOjVjmq 7ufMnZ8vO & sig2=miL3gxD0RI4IxMaIBKkD 7A & cad=rja

End of Document

2017 WL 1344365
United States District Court, E.D. Pennsylvania.

The UNITED STATES of America, et al., EX REL. Catherine A. BROWN and Bernard G. Vezeau
v.
PFIZER, INC.

CIVIL ACTION NO. 05-6795
|
Filed 04/12/2017

Attorneys and Law Firms

Eric L. Young, McEldrew Young, Margaret L. Hutchinson, Susan Dein Bricklin, U.S. Attorney's Office, Philadelphia, PA, Frederick M. Morgan, Morgan Verkamp LLC, Cincinnati, OH, John R. Mininno, Cahill, Wilinski & Cahill, Haddonfield, NJ, Rita L. Hanscom, Deputy Attorney General, San Diego, CA, Ronald J. Styka, Assistant Attorney General, Lansing, MI, John Ellingson, Assistant Attorney General, Helena, MT, for the United States of America, et al., ex rel. Catherine A. Brown and Bernard G. Vezeau.

Loren H. Brown, DLA Piper LLP, New York, NY, Adam D. Brown, Jayne Risk, DLA Piper Rudnick Gray Cary US, LLP, Richard L. Scheff, Montgomery McCracken Walker & Rhoads LLP, Philadelphia, PA, Andrew J. Hoffman, II, DLA Piper LLP, Los Angeles, CA, Carlton E. Wessel, DLA Piper LLP, Douglas H. Hallward-Driemeier, Kelly O'Connell, Ropes & Gray LLP, Washington, DC, Joshua S. Levy, Ropes & Gray LLP, Boston, MA, for Pfizer, Inc.

MEMORANDUM

R. BARCLAY SURRICK, District Judge

***1** Presently before the Court is Defendant Pfizer Inc.'s Second Motion to Dismiss. (ECF No. 103.) For the following reasons, Defendant's Motion will be denied.

I. BACKGROUND

A. Procedural History

On March 1, 2016, we ruled on Defendant's First Motion to Dismiss Plaintiffs' First Amended Complaint. *United States v. Pfizer, Inc.*, No. 05-6795, 2016 WL 807363 (E.D. Pa. Mar. 1, 2016); (ECF Nos. 93, 94.) The factual background surrounding this matter is set forth in that Memorandum.

On March 15, 2016, Relators filed a Second Amended Complaint. (SAC, ECF No. 98.) On May 6, 2016, Defendant filed the instant Motion to Dismiss. (Def.'s Mot., ECF No. 103.) Relators filed a Memorandum in Opposition to Defendant's Motion to Dismiss on June 24, 2016. (Rels.' Mem. Opp., ECF No. 107.) On July 13, 2016, Defendant filed a Reply Memorandum in Support of its Motion. (Def.'s Reply, ECF No. 109.) On July 27, 2016, Relators filed a Reply Memorandum in Opposition to Defendant's Memorandum. (Rels.' Reply, ECF No. 111.) Since that time, Defendant has submitted three separate "notices of supplemental authority," and Relators have submitted one "notice of supplemental authority." On October 31, 2016, Defendant filed the first Notice of Supplemental Authority (ECF No. 115), and on December 22, 2015, Relators filed a response (ECF No. 116). On January 30, 2017, Defendant filed a second Notice of Authority (ECF No. 117), and on March 6, 2017, Relators filed a response (ECF No. 118). On March 15, 2017, Defendant filed a third Notice of Authority (ECF No. 119), and on March 25, 2017, Relators filed a response (ECF No. 120). On April 7, 2017, Relators filed a Notice of Supplemental Authority. (ECF No. 121.) The Second Motion to Dismiss is now ready for disposition.

B. Parties' Contentions

Defendant advances four arguments in support of its Second Motion to Dismiss. First, Defendant contends that the Court lacks subject matter jurisdiction over portions of Relators' SAC. In the prior Memorandum, we concluded that Relators' claims were barred by the first-to-file rule. However, we permitted Relators to file an amended complaint. *Pfizer*, 2016 WL 807363, at *8. Defendant now argues that Relators lack subject matter jurisdiction because Relators are required to file a separate action in order to cure the jurisdictional defect. Defendant further argues that even if Relators were to file a new action, it would be time-barred under the False Claim Act's ("FCA") six-year statute of limitations. Second, Defendant maintains that its off-label use of Vfend on neutropenic patients and for empiric therapy is covered by Medicare and other healthcare programs. Third, Defendant alleges that Relators have failed to state a claim that Defendant paid kickbacks to physicians and pharmacists. Defendant argues that its actions do not qualify as illegal kickbacks because they are protected by a safe harbor regulation. Fourth, Defendant argues that Relators have not stated a claim under the FCA because Relators did not allege that Defendant submitted reimbursement claims to the FDA that contained expressly false statements. Defendant argues that Relators must rely on the implied false certification theory, and that Relators have failed to properly state a claim under that theory. Defendant further argues that Relators have failed to satisfy the materiality requirement of the FCA because the government continued to pay for Vfend after Relators' allegations in 2005.

***2** Relators reject each of Defendant's arguments, citing our previous Memorandum, which Relators claim addressed many of the same arguments that Defendant raises in the instant Motion. With regard to Defendant's jurisdictional argument, Relators argue that this Court specifically permitted Relators to file the SAC to reassert their claims. Relators argue that because they added no additional factual allegations in their SAC, and filed the SAC pursuant to the Court's Order, Defendant's argument is invalid. Further, Relators argue that they have pled facts sufficient to state a claim of fraudulent inducement under the FCA. Relators argue that they have satisfied the FCA's materiality requirement because they alleged that Defendant presented false and misleading statements to the FDA, which in turn caused the FDA to approve Vfend to treat Candida infections. With regard to Defendant's other allegations, Relators maintain that these allegations merely restate the arguments that Defendant made in its First Motion to Dismiss, and should accordingly be dismissed.

II. LEGAL STANDARD

Under Federal Rule of Civil Procedure 8(a)(2), "a pleading that states a claim for relief must contain a short and plain statement of the claim showing that the pleader is entitled to relief." Failure to state a claim upon which relief can be granted is basis for dismissal of the complaint. Fed. R. Civ. P. 12(b)(6). "To survive a motion to dismiss, a complaint must contain sufficient factual matter, accepted as true, 'to state a claim to relief that is plausible on its face.' " *Ashcroft v. Iqbal*, 129 S. Ct. 1937, 1949 (2009) (quoting *Bell Atl. Corp. v. Twombly*, 550 U.S. 544, 570 (2007)). "A claim has facial plausibility when the plaintiff pleads factual content that allows the court to draw the reasonable inference that the defendant is liable for the misconduct alleged." *Iqbal*, 129 S. Ct. at 1949 (citing *Twombly*, 550 U.S. at 556). While a court "must accept all factual allegations as true, construe the complaint in the light most favorable to the plaintiff, and determine whether, under any reasonable reading, the plaintiff may be entitled to relief," *Phillips v. Cnty of Allegheny*, 515 F.3d 224, 233 (3d Cir. 2008), "a court need not accept as true 'legal conclusions' or '[t]hreadbare recitals of the elements of a cause of action, supported by mere conclusory statements...." *Wilson v. City of Philadelphia*, 415 Fed.Appx. 434, 436 (3d Cir. 2011) (quoting *Iqbal*, 129 S. Ct. at 1949). "A complaint may not be dismissed because it appears unlikely that the plaintiff can prove those facts or will ultimately prevail on the merits." *McTernan v. City of York, Pa.*, 564 F.3d 636, 646 (3d Cir. 2009). However, a plaintiff's claims "must contain more than an unadorned, the-defendant-unlawfully-harmed-me accusation." *Fowler v. UPMC Shadyside*, 578 F.3d 203, 210 (3d Cir. 2009) (quoting *Iqbal*, 129 S. Ct. at 1949).

An FCA complaint must meet the heightened pleading standard set forth by Federal Rule of Civil Procedure 9(b), which demands that a plaintiff "state with particularity the circumstances constituting the fraud or mistake." Fed. R. Civ. P. 9(b). Therefore, a plaintiff must allege "the who, what, when, where and how of the events at issue." *In re Rockefeller Ctr. Props., Inc. Secs. Litig.*, 311 F.3d 198, 217 (3d Cir. 2002) (citation and internal quotation marks omitted). There is a split among the Circuit Courts with regard to the "particularity" requirement of Rule 9(b). The Third Circuit has adopted the approach of the First, Fifth, and Ninth Circuits, which "have taken a more nuanced reading of the heightened pleading requirements of 9(b)." *Foglia v. Renal Ventures Mgmt., LLC*, 754 F.3d 153, 156 (3d Cir. 2014). Under *Foglia*, "it is sufficient for a plaintiff to allege 'particular details of a scheme to submit false claims paired with reliable indicia that lead to a strong inference that claims were actually submitted.' " *Id.* (citations and quotation marks omitted).

III. DISCUSSION

A. Subject Matter Jurisdiction

1. Amended Complaint

In its First Motion to Dismiss, Defendant argued that Relators' claims were barred by the FCA's first-to-file rule. We noted that a relator is only entitled to relief under the FCA if the relator is the first person to file the complaint. *Pfizer*, 2016 WL 807363, at * 6; *see* 31 U.S.C. § 3730(b)(5) ("When a person brings an action under this subsection, no person other than the Government may intervene or bring a related action based on the facts underlying the pending action."). We cited the Supreme Court's decision in *Kellogg Brown & Root Servs. v. United States ex rel. Carter*, 135 S. Ct. 1970, 1979 (2015), which held that a *qui tam* suit under the FCA is no longer deemed "pending" once it is dismissed. *Pfizer*, 2016 WL 807363, at *8. Since the first action, the *Worsfold* action had been dismissed, we granted Relators leave to file an amended complaint to assert claims that had previously been barred by the first-to-file rule. *Id.* Defendant argues, however, that an amended complaint does not cure the first-to-file jurisdictional bar. Defendant argues that if a case was barred by the FCA's first-to-file rule, a relator must file a new action.

***3** The First Circuit Court of Appeals is the only circuit court to have addressed this issue. *See U.S. ex rel. Gadbois v. PharMerica Corp.*, 809 F.3d 1 (1st Cir. 2015). In *Gadbois*, the relators filed a complaint in the District of Rhode Island; however, the district court dismissed the relator's claim for lack of subject matter jurisdiction. 809 F.3d at 3. The district court dismissed the claim pursuant to the FCA's first-to-file rule because there was already a similar case pending in the Eastern District of Wisconsin. *Id.* However, while the case was pending on appeal in the First Circuit, the case in the Eastern District of Wisconsin was dismissed. *Id.* at 4. Citing *Kellogg*, the First Circuit permitted the relators to supplement their complaint pursuant to Rule 15(d) in order to cure the jurisdictional defect. (*Id.* at 4-5.) The court justified its decision by stating that Rule 15 helps "courts and litigants to avoid pointless formality." *Id.* at

4. The First Circuit also noted that courts are encouraged to allow parties to supplement their pleadings "when doing so will promote the economic and speedy disposition of the entire controversy between the parties, will not cause undue delay or trial inconvenience, and will not prejudice the rights of any of the other parties to the action." *Id.* (internal quotation marks and citation omitted).[1] We agree with the reasoning of the First Circuit.

Like the facts in *Gadbios*, the pending *Worsfold* case was dismissed, and therefore was no longer "pending" for purposes of the first-to-file rule under the FCA. We are satisfied that Relators were permitted to file the SAC as a cure for the jurisdictional defect present with the FAC. Accordingly, the SAC is not jurisdictionally barred under the FCA's first-to-file rule.

2. Statute of Limitations

Defendant argues that even if this Court determines that the SAC cures jurisdictional defects in light of the *Worsfold* dismissal, the Relators' claims are nonetheless time-barred. Defendant argues that the FCA has a six-year statute of limitations, and therefore Relators' pediatric and prophylactic claims are time-barred. Defendant states that Relators seek recovery for pediatric and prophylactic reimbursement claims submitted between 2002 and 2009. Relators filed the SAC on March 15, 2016. The original complaint was filed on December 29, 2005. Defendant contends that the operative complaint that courts should use when determining if a claim is time-barred under the FCA is the complaint filed following dismissal of the first-filed action. Here, that would be the SAC, which would result in Relators' pediatric and prophylactic claims being time-barred. Relators respond that for statute of limitations purposes, the SAC should relate back to the date of the original complaint. Defendant argues that the SAC cannot relate back to the original complaint because (1) the original complaint does not allege claims of off-label pediatric or prophylactic use of Vfend and (2) this Court lacked subject-matter jurisdiction over the original complaint.

***4** Rule 15(c) provides that "[a]n amendment to a pleading relates back to the date of the original pleading when ... the amendment asserts a claim or defense that arose out of the conduct, transaction, or occurrence set out—or attempted to be set out—in the original pleading." *See also ASARCO, LLC v. Union Pac. R. Co.*, 765 F.3d 999, 1004 (9th Cir. 2014) ("An otherwise time-barred claim in an amended pleading is deemed timely if it relates back to the date of a timely original pleading."). The Supreme Court has held that "relation back depends on the existence of a common core of operative facts uniting the original and newly asserted claims." *Mayle v. Felix*, 545 U.S. 644, 646 (2005). The Third Circuit has held that an amended complaint relates back "only where the opposing party is given fair notice of the general fact situation and the legal theory upon which the amending party proceeds...." *Glover v. F.D.I.C.*, 698 F.3d 139, 146 (3d Cir. 2012) (internal quotation marks and citation omitted). "If the amendment relates back to the date of the filing of the original complaint, the amended complaint is treated, for statute of limitations purposes, as if it had been filed at that time." *Garvin v. City of Phila.*, 354 F.3d 215, 220 (3d Cir. 2003) (citation omitted). The relation back provision "aims to ameliorate the harsh result of the strict application of the statute of limitations." *Id.*

Relators argue that the pediatric and prophylactic off-label claims alleged in the SAC arise out of the conduct alleged in the original complaint. Relators cite to their allegations in the original complaint, which state that Defendant engaged in illegal off-label promotion of Vfend. Relators argue that this behavior arises out of a common set of operative facts—namely off-label promotion of Vfend (original complaint) and, more specifically, off-label promotion of Vfend for pediatric and prophylactic use (SAC). Defendant argues that Relators' SAC does not relate back to their original complaint because the original complaint does not specifically mention off-label promotion of Vfend for pediatric or prophylactic use.

As noted above, Relators filed the original complaint on December 29, 2005. (Compl., ECF No. 1.) Relators' original complaint alleged Defendant's violations under the FCA, pointing to Defendant's off-label promotion of Vfend. (*Id.* ¶¶ 12, 14-15.) Relators stated that Vfend was not approved to treat patients with Candida infections, and that physicians were only permitted to prescribe Vfend to non-neutropenic patients. (*Id.* ¶ 24.) Relators pled that Defendant promoted Vfend illegally, specifically that Defendant alleged that "Vfend is equally efficacious against all species of Candida, despite having irrefutable evidence that it is not." (*Id.* ¶ 152.) These pleadings support allegations that Defendant engaged in illegal off-label promotion of Vfend, in violation of the FCA. While Relators did not allege that Defendant promoted Vfend off-label for pediatric and prophylactic purposes specifically, they did plead that Defendant "marketed Vfend off-label for empiric therapy...." (*Id.* ¶ 171.) Relators' original complaint also contained allegations that Defendant provided misleading information to the FDA. Relators' allegations in the SAC state more specifically that Defendant promoted Vfend off-label for pediatric and prophylactic use. We find that Relators' allegations in the SAC arise out of the conduct that Relators alleged in their original complaint, namely that Pfizer promoted Vfend for impermissible off-label uses. We also find that Relators' original complaint gave Defendant fair notice of the general fact situation that Relators allege in the SAC.

Defendants also argue that this Court did not have subject-matter jurisdiction over the original complaint because of the first-to-file rule. We reject this argument because "a district court does not lack subject matter jurisdiction over an action that may be barred on the merits by the first-to-file rule." *United States ex rel. Hayes v. Allstate Ins. Co.*, No. 16-705, 2017 WL 1228551, at *3 (2d Cir. Apr. 4, 2017). Interpreting the FCA, the Second Circuit in *Hayes* noted that "[b]ecause the FCA 'clearly state[s]' that *other* limitations on *qui tam* actions are jurisdictional, but does not 'clearly state[ ]' that the first-to-file rule is jurisdictional, we must treat the first-to-file rule 'as nonjurisdictional in character.' " *Id.* (quoting *Sebelius v. Auburn Reg'l Med. Ctr.*, 133 S. Ct. 817, 824 (2013)). The D.C. Circuit also held that the first-to-file bar "does not speak in jurisdictional terms or refer in any way to the jurisdiction of the district courts." *U.S. ex rel. Heath v. AT & T, Inc.*, 791 F.3d 112, 120 (D.C. Cir. 2015), *cert. denied sub nom.AT&T, Inc. v. U.S. ex rel. Heath*, 136 S. Ct. 2505 (2016) (quoting *Arbaugh v. Y & H Corp.*, 546 U.S. 500, 515 (2006)); *see also* *Allergan*, 2017 WL 1233991, at *11 ("[T]he first-to-file rule bears only on whether a *qui tam* plaintiff has properly stated a claim, rather than on the scope of courts' jurisdiction." (citation and internal quotation marks omitted)). *But see*, *U.S. ex rel. Branch Consultants v. Allstate Ins. Co.*, 560 F.3d 371, 376-77 (5th Cir. 2009); *Walburn v. Lockheed Martin Corp.*, 431 F.3d 966, 970 (6th Cir. 2005). Since we did not lack subject-matter jurisdiction over Relators' original complaint, we reject Defendant's argument that the SAC cannot relate back to the original complaint for lack of jurisdiction.

***5** Accordingly, we conclude that the SAC relates back to the date of the original complaint—December 29, 2005—and therefore Relators' clams are not time-barred by the FCA's six-year statute of limitations.

B. Off-Label Promotion

1. Medicare

In our previous Memorandum, we determined that "any of Relators' claims that are based on prescriptions reimbursed *by Medicaid* for 'Empiric Therapy in Febrile Neutropenic Patients' cannot form the basis of an FCA claim, and will be dismissed." *Pfizer*, 2016 WL 807363, at *12 (emphasis in original). However, we did not similarly dismiss Relators' Medicare claims. *Id.* Rather, we found that in order for Vfend's off-label use for empiric therapy to be reimbursable by Medicare, it must (1) be supported by a recognized compendium, and (2) must not be identified as "not indicated for 'Empiric Therapy in Febrile Neutropenic Patients' " in one or more statutorily-recognized compendia. *Id.* (citing 42 U.S.C. § 1395x(t)(2)(B)). We therefore granted Relators the opportunity to explore through discovery whether such statutorily-recognized compendium existed. *Id.*

Defendant argues that we should have dismissed Relators' Medicare claims. Defendant argues that "[c]ontrary to the Court's suggestion" the statutory provision that we cited—42 U.S.C. § 1395x(t)(2)(B)—does not apply to Vfend. (Def.'s Mot. 14.) Defendant contends that the statute we cited to relates "solely to" anticancer drugs. (*Id.*) Defendant argues that, like Medicaid, Medicare covers Vfend when used for empiric therapy. We rejected that argument in our previous Memorandum, and we reject it here.

The statutory provision does not state that it applies "solely to" drugs or biologicals used in an anticancer regimen, as Defendant suggests. Rather, the text states the following: "the term 'drugs' *also includes* any drugs or biologicals used in an anticancer chemotherapeutic regimen for a medically accepted indication." 42 U.S.C. § 1395x(t)(2)(A) (emphasis added). Defendant's contention that this statutory provision is limited to anticancer drugs is misguided. "Courts must presume that a legislature says in a statute what it means and means in a statute what it says there. When the words of a statute are unambiguous, then this first canon is also the last: judicial inquiry is complete." *In re Phila. Newspapers, LLC*, 599 F.3d 298, 304 (3d Cir. 2010) (quoting *Conn. Nat'l Bank v. Germain*, 503 U.S. 249, 253-54 (1992)). The statute does not state that it only applies to anticancer drugs. The statute makes clear that it *also* applies to anticancer drugs, and we therefore interpret the statute to encompass drugs such as Vfend.

Accordingly, we continue to hold that Relators should be given the opportunity to engage in discovery to identify any statutorily-recognized compendium which states that Vfend is "not medically appropriate" for empiric therapy in Neutropenic Patients.

2. Other Federal Programs

Defendant also alleges that four other federal healthcare programs cover Defendant's use of Vfend for empiric therapy. These federal programs are: TRICARE, the Federal Employees Health Benefits Program ("FEHBP"), the Civilian Health and Medical Program of the Department of Veterans Affairs ("CHAMPVA"), and the Railroad Retirement Medicare Program ("RRM"). We addressed Defendant's arguments in our previous Memorandum and stated that "Defendant ha[d] not alleged that the statutory and regulatory authority governing payments of claims by [the four] federal health care providers refer to drug compendia like the AHFS-DI for determining whether the use of a drug is medically necessary." *Pfizer*, 2016 WL 807363, at *12 n.17. Accordingly, we held that Relators' claims should not be dismissed. *Id.* Similarly, we maintain that if Defendant does not cite to any relevant statutory authority that is instructive in this case, we will not dismiss Relators' claims.

***6** TRICARE—Defendant argues that TRICARE will reimburse off-label drugs when it is "medically necessary." Defendant cites to the TRICARE Policy Manual, stating that TRICARE considers "nationally accepted standards of practice in the medical community." (Def.'s Mot. 17.) However, Defendant fails to cite to any statutory authority which states that support from AHFS-DI and DRUGDEX —the compendia Defendant cites to in support of its off-label use—deems Vfend medically necessary for empiric use. Consistent with our previous ruling, we will not dismiss Relators' claim.

FEHBP—Defendant argues that FEHBP covers use of Vfend for empiric therapy because multiple compendia support such use. However, Defendant acknowledges that "[t]here is no law or regulation mandating when a prescription drug is insurable and reimbursable under FEHBP." (*Id.* at 18 (citation omitted).) Defendant attempts to argue that because AHFS-DI and DRUGDEX support empiric use of Vfend, this Court should deem it medically necessary. Consistent with our previous ruling, we will not dismiss Relators' claim.

CHAMPVA—Defendant argues that CHAMPVA covers empiric use of Vfend for the same reasons that TRICARE does so. Since Defendant has failed to identify any statutory authority dictating coverage for CHAMPVA in this circumstance, we reject Defendant's argument and will not dismiss Relators' claim.

RRM—Defendant argues that the RRM applies the same coverage standards as Medicare. Since we will permit Relators to engage in discovery to identify other compendium for their Medicare claim, we similarly permit Relators to engage in discovery for their RRM claim.

C. Kickbacks

1. Rule 9(b) Requirements

Defendant argues that Relators have failed to state a claim under the Anti-Kickback Statute. Defendant argues that Relators' allegations simply contain conclusory statements and do not provide factual allegations that raise Relators' claims above a speculative level. In our prior Memorandum, we ruled that Relators' FAC contained "thorough allegations of a complex scheme to defraud the federal Government with false claims." *Pfizer*, 2016 WL 807363, at *13. As support that Relators satisfied Rule 9(b)'s pleading requirements, we cited Relators' allegations, which included the following:

> Defendant misrepresented and concealed the true import of the 608 Study which was used to obtain approval in 2004 for use of Vfend in treating invasive Candida fungal

> infections, paid physicians to submit an article to the New England Journal of Medicine advocating for off-label use of Vfend in 2002, distributed misleading marketing materials to sales representatives and doctors starting in May of 2002, and provided illegal kickbacks to physicians and pharmacists for the purpose of influencing their behavior. Relators allege that as a result of these unlawful acts, Defendant contributed to the filing of over $250 million in false claims.

Id. (internal citations and quotation marks omitted).

Relators have pled similar facts in the SAC. Relators' SAC states the following: Defendant "misrepresented and concealed the true import of the 608 Study which was used to obtain approval in 2004 for use of Vfend in treating invasive Candida fungal infections" (SAC ¶ 69); Defendant paid physicians to write and submit an article to the New England Journal of Medicine advocating for the off-label use of Vfend for empiric therapy when they "well knew that the 603 Study results showed that Vfend was not suitable for [such a] use" (*id.* ¶ 125); Defendant distributed "misleading materials ... urging physicians to prescribe Vfend" and similarly "encouraged its sales representatives to promote Vfend for 'early and aggressive therapy' " (*id.* ¶¶ 126, 128); and Defendant "participated in, encouraged, and authorized the unlawful payment of illegal kickbacks to physicians and pharmacists in order to increase sales of Vfend, a substantial percentage of which were for 'off-label' uses" (*id.* ¶ 166). Relators claim that the federal Government paid "in excess of $250 million in false claims for the purchase of Vfend" since 2002. (*Id.* ¶ 8.)

*7 Defendant argues that these allegations fail to state a claim because Relators have not alleged that any of Pfizer's speakers or sales representatives paid physicians to specifically market Vfend. Defendant cites *United States v. Celgene Corp.*, No. 10-3165, 2016 WL 7626222 (C.D. Cal. Dec. 28, 2016), in which the alleged Anti-Kickback Statute violations were dismissed because penalizing the defendant's generalized promotion of a drug "would effectively criminalize all promotion of medical goods and services." *Id.* at *18. Further, the *Celgene* court noted that "there [was] no evidence that speakers did anything other than convey truthful scientific information about the drugs." *Id.* Relators note that *Celgene* was decided at the summary judgment stage, and that it in essence rejects Defendant's argument that Relator's allegations would effectively criminalize the promotion of prescription drugs.

We are satisfied that Relators' allegations are sufficient to state a claim. Moreover, we find that Relators' allegations do not give rise to a concern that the Anti-Kickback Statute would be penalizing a "general promotion" of Vfend. Relators have alleged that Pfizer told its sales representatives to use *misleading* materials in order to encourage physicians to prescribe Vfend. (SAC ¶ 126.) Relators allege that Defendant "illegally promoted" Vfend, telling physicians to "choose Vfend first." (*Id.* ¶ 127.) Clearly, Realtors' allegations that Defendants' marketing tactics utilized deceit and misrepresentations distinguish this case from *Celgene*. In addition, contrary to Defendant's assertions, Relators alleged that Defendant paid physicians in order to encourage them to prescribe a particular drug. Furthermore, Relators allege that "[i]n addition to paying the aforementioned speaking fees to doctors for convincing other doctors to prescribe Vfend off label," Pfizer established a program "created to reward doctors who are willing to do whatever it takes to write Vfend." (*Id.* ¶¶ 187-88.) For the same reasons that we found Relators' claims sufficient to meet Rule 9(b)'s pleading requirements in our previous Memorandum, we find that Relators have sufficiently met the pleading requirements here.

2. Safe Harbor Regulation

Defendant argues that its financial arrangements with physicians, consultants, and promotional speakers fall within the Department of Health and Human Services' safe harbor regulation found at 42 C.F.R. § 1001.952. Defendant argues that under the safe harbor regulation, Defendant's payments for physicians' services do not constitute "illegal remuneration." Defendant bears the burden of proving that its conduct was protected by the safe harbor regulations. *U.S. ex rel. Kosenske v. Carlisle HMA, Inc.*, 554 F.3d 88, 95 (3d Cir. 2009). Relators argue that it is impossible for Defendant to prove that it is entitled to the safe harbor protection at the pleadings stage.

In order for Defendant to be protected by the safe harbor regulation for "personal services and management contracts," it must prove all seven of the elements listed. The elements are as follows:

> (1) The agency agreement is set out in writing and signed by the parties.
>
> (2) The agency agreement covers all of the services the agent provides to the principal for the term of the agreement and specifies the services to be provided by the agent.
>
> (3) If the agency agreement is intended to provide for the services of the agent on a periodic, sporadic or part-

time basis, rather than on a full-time basis for the term of the agreement, the agreement specifies exactly the schedule of such intervals, their precise length, and the exact charge for such intervals.

(4) The term of the agreement is for not less than one year.

(5) The aggregate compensation paid to the agent over the term of the agreement is set in advance, is consistent with fair market value in arms-length transactions and is not determined in a manner that takes into account the volume or value of any referrals or business otherwise generated between the parties for which payment may be made in whole or in part under Medicare, Medicaid or other Federal health care programs.

***8** (6) The services performed under the agreement do not involve the counselling or promotion of a business arrangement or other activity that violates any State or Federal law.

(7) The aggregate services contracted for do not exceed those which are reasonably necessary to accomplish the commercially reasonable business purpose of the services.

42 C.F.R. § 1001.952.

In its brief, Defendant mentions only elements 1, 2, 5, and 7. *See* Def.'s Mot. 22 (noting the elements as "set out in writing, specifies the services to be provided, aggregate compensation is consistent with fair market value, and aggregate services do not exceed those which are reasonably necessary to accomplish the commercially reasonable business purpose of the services"). In addition, Defendant does not affirmatively state how it satisfies each of the seven elements. Rather, Defendant merely asserts that Relators did not "identify any contractual arrangement that failed to comply with the personal services safe harbor...." (Def.'s Mot. 23.) Relators argue that this is insufficient. Specifically, Relators argue that the fifth element is not met because the payments Defendant made to physicians were specifically made to increase the volume of prescriptions for Vfend.

With regard to the fifth element, at the very least, Relators' allegations call into question whether the compensation Defendant paid to physicians and pharmacists was "consistent with fair market value in arms-length transactions." 42 C.F.R. § 1001.952 (5). Relators allege the following in the SAC: Defendant "gave its sales representatives large budgets to compensate physicians to promote Vfend's efficacy for various off label uses" (SAC ¶ 167); Defendant gave "pharmacists gifts in exchange for insights into what medications physicians were using" (*id.*); Defendant paid physicians bills for "travel, first-rate lodging, extravagant meals and entertainment" (*id.* ¶ 173); Defendant paid "in kind" kickbacks to physicians (*id.* ¶ 174); Defendant created "sham" speaker programs where Defendant paid doctors to convince other doctors to prescribe Vfend (*id.* ¶ 175); Defendant established an annual entertainment budget to impress physicians' business (*id.* ¶ 176); Defendant paid physicians $1,500 for each training session (*id.* ¶ 179); and Defendant paid one physician $44,800.35 in one year alone to promote Vfend to other physicians (*id.* ¶ 180). Absent any argument to the contrary by Defendant, we are compelled to conclude that Relators' allegations call into question whether the types of compensation that Defendant paid to its medical agents was actually consistent with a fair market value. Accordingly, at this point Defendant's actions do not meet the safe harbor requirements.

D. FCA Liability

Defendant contends that in light of the recent Supreme Court decision in *Universal Health Services, Inc. v. United States*, 136 S. Ct. 1989 (2016), Relators' allegations that Defendant concealed clinical trial data pertaining to Vfend are insufficient to state a claim under the FCA. Defendant argues that Relators must rely on an implied certification theory in asserting their FCA claim because Relators' SAC does not allege that their reimbursement claims contained false statements. Relators argue that they need not rely on an implied certification theory to state a claim under the FCA. Realtors maintain that they alleged FCA liability under the fraudulent inducement theory.

***9** "Under a fraudulent inducement theory, although [a defendant's] subsequent claims for payment made under the contract [are] not literally false, because they derived from the original fraudulent misrepresentation, they, too, [become] actionable false claims." *U.S. ex rel. Longhi v. United States*, 575 F.3d 458, 468 (5th Cir. 2009) (internal quotation marks omitted). Under the "implied certification theory," a defendant would be liable under the FCA if "a claimant seeks and makes a claim for payment from the Government without disclosing that it violated regulations that affected its eligibility for payment." *U.S. ex rel. Wilkins v. United Health Grp., Inc.*, 659 F.3d 295, 305 (3d Cir. 2011) (citation omitted). The Eighth Circuit distinguishes the two theories as follows:

> [*Escobar*] was about implied false certifications, claims for payment that do not say anything untrue but are misleading because of what they leave out, whereas [the relator's] claims are based on the rule that when a government contract is secured through fraud, claims for payment later submitted under the contract can count as false claims even if they are not fraudulent

> themselves. Because the fraud that matters for [the relator's] theory is whatever [the defendant] initially induced the government to enter into the ongoing relationship, not any misrepresentations—implicit or explicit—in the claims for payment themselves, the Court's analysis of when such claims can be actionably misleading is irrelevant here.

Olson v. Fairview Health Servs. of Minn., 831 F.3d 1063, 1079 n.20 (8th Cir. 2016) (citation and internal quotation marks omitted).

Defendant argues that Relators must rely on an implied certification theory in an attempt to establish falsity because Relators did not allege that their claims contained expressly false statements. Relators argue that they did allege that Defendant made false representations in its New Drug Application to obtain FDA approval of Vfend to treat Candida infections, which was needed to allow Pfizer to obtain government reimbursement. For the following reasons, we find that Relators have sufficiently stated a claim under the fraudulent inducement theory. [2]

1. Falsity

"Under fraudulent inducement, FCA liability attaches to each claim submitted to the government under a contract so long as the original contract was obtained through false statements or fraudulent conduct." *Weston*, 840 F.3d at 499 (citation and internal quotation marks omitted). We find, as we did in our previous Memorandum, that Relators have alleged that Defendant "embarked on a marketing campaign that cynically exploited the switched endpoints of the 608 Study by repeatedly, and falsely, claiming that Vfend was a superior antifungal treatment." *Pfizer*, 2016 WL 807363, at *10 (internal quotation marks omitted). Furthermore, Relators' SAC alleges the following: that Pfizer submitted "a false and misleading New Drug Application ("NDA") to the Food and Drug Administration ("FDA") for approval of Vfend" (SAC ¶ 3); that "[a]fter the FDA's rejection of the Empiric Therapy indication for Vfend and its limited approvals in 2002 and 2004, Pfizer could only maximize its Vfend sales by marketing Vfend for a broad range of off-label uses and by misrepresenting and concealing key aspects of the 608 Candida Study" (*id.* ¶ 67); that "[t]he net effect of Pfizer's misrepresentations about the efficacy of Vfend in treating C. glabrata is that the medical community was misled into believing that Vfend was the antifungal drug of choice ... In fact, those patients were more likely to die with Vfend." (*id.* ¶ 153); and that "Pfizer made these false and misleading survival rate claims about Vfend...." (*id.* ¶ 149). In addition, Relators specifically allege that "Pfizer misrepresented and concealed the true import of the 608 Study which was used to obtain approval in 2004 for use of Vfend in treating invasive Candida fungal infections" by "[f]alsely cit[ing] the 608 Study as evidence that Vfend was more effective ... despite the fact that, as Pfizer well knew, the 'primary endpoint' of the 608 study upon which its claims were based was totally invalid for that purpose," and "[m]isrepresenting the 608 Study results to add credibility to Pfizer's illegal marketing of Vfend ... to falsely suggest that Vfend was suitable for 'Empiric Therapy.' " (*Id.* ¶ 69.)

***10** We find that Relators have sufficiently established the element of "falsity" pursuant to the FCA. We agree that Relators alleged that Defendant withheld or concealed adverse test results from the FDA, however Relators have *also* alleged that Pfizer made expressly false statements to the FDA for approval of Vfend in order to induce Medicare and Medicaid payments. Therefore, the falsity element is satisfied.

2. *Materiality*

The Supreme Court refined the FCA's definition of materiality in *Escobar*. 136 S. Ct. 2002 ("We now clarify how that materiality requirement should be enforced."). The Court noted that "[u]nder any understanding of the concept, materiality looks to the effect on the likely or actual behavior of the recipient of the alleged misrepresentation." *Id.* at 2003 (citation and internal quotation marks omitted). The Court held that "[t]he materiality standard is demanding" and "cannot be found where noncompliance is minor or insubstantial." *Id.* Relators argue that the results of the 608 Study that Pfizer presented to the FDA for approval of Vfend for Candida infections were material to the FDA's subsequent approval. Defendant cites the First Circuit's decision in *D'Agostino v. ev3, Inc.*, 845 F.3d 1 (1st Cir. 2016) in arguing against materiality. Similar to this case, the court in *D'Agostino* was analyzing a relator's fraudulent inducement theory under the FCA. *Id.* at 7-10. The court held that the relator's alleged false representations did not have a tendency to influence the FDA into approving the drug. *Id.* The court held that the relator's allegations that the defendant's false representations "could have" influenced the FDA were insufficient to make the false representations material. *Id.*

Here, Relators alleged that the misrepresentations that Defendant made in its application to the FDA in 2004 did in fact cause the FDA to approve Vfend to be used to treat Candida infections. Unlike the relator in *D'Agostino*, Relators here provide factual allegations that demonstrate how Defendant's misrepresentations caused the FDA to approve Vfend for Candida infections. Relators allege in their SAC that in 2002, the FDA rejected Pfizer's application to approve Vfend to treat serious Candida infections. (SAC ¶ 56.) Relators allege that the FDA refused to approve Vfend to treat Candida infections because the 608 Study showed that Vfend was not as effective as another antifungal drug, to which Vfend was being compared. (*Id.*) In 2004, Pfizer again attempted to obtain FDA approval for Vfend in treating Candida infections. (*Id.* ¶ 68.) Relators allege that this second time, however, Pfizer misrepresented the 608 Study by doing the following: falsely citing the 608 study as evidence that Vfend was more effective than other antifungal medications in treating Candida infections, claiming that the 608 Study revealed that Vfend was effective in treating a Candida infection despite the fact that the 608 Study showed the opposite results, misrepresenting the 608 Study results to add credibility to Pfizer's illegal marketing tactics, and supporting the publication of "ghost written" articles in medical journals, which cited the 608 Study as evidence that Vfend should be used to treat Candida infections. (*Id.* ¶ 69.) We find that Relators have pled sufficient facts to demonstrate that Defendant's misleading and false statements were material to the FDA's approval of Vfend for treating Candida infections.

***11** Defendant also argues that since both the federal and state governments have continued to pay for Vfend despite Relators' allegations against Defendant, Relators cannot satisfy the materiality requirement. Defendant cites *Escobar*, which noted that "if the Government regularly pays a particular type of claim in full despite actual knowledge that certain requirements were violated, and has signaled no change in position, that is strong evidence that the requirements are not material." 136 S. Ct. at 2003-04. Relators argue that there is no evidence that the government had actual knowledge of Pfizer's misrepresentations when making their decisions to pay for Vfend and that courts must take a holistic approach to determining materiality, since no one factor is dispositive.

On remand from the Supreme Court, the First Circuit in *Escobar* further defined what "actual knowledge" meant within the context of determining materiality. *Escobar*, 842 F.3d 103, 112 (1st Cir. 2016). The First Circuit noted that "mere awareness of allegations concerning noncompliance with regulations is different from knowledge of actual noncompliance." *Id.* Further, the court held that even if the government had actual knowledge that certain requirements were violated, "such knowledge is not dispositive." *Id.* at 110. Highlighting the Supreme Court's emphasis on "applying the holistic approach to determining materiality," the First Circuit ultimately held that the relators had satisfied the FCA's materiality requirement. *Id.* Defendant cites *D'Agostino* to support its argument that Relators' allegation against Pfizer in 2005 is sufficient to constitute "actual knowledge" of an FCA violation. The First Circuit in *D'Agostino* held that "[t]he fact that CMS has not denied reimbursement for [the drug] in the wake of [the relator's] allegations casts serious doubt on the materiality of the fraudulent representations that [the relator] alleges." *Id.* at 7. Both First Circuit cases were published after the Supreme Court's instructions on materiality in *Escobar*. As noted above, we distinguish the facts in *D'Agostino* from the current case before us. We find, as the First Circuit found in *Escobar*, that Relators have satisfied the materiality requirement. Here, the SAC alleges that:

> Plaintiff United States, unaware of the false or fraudulent nature of the records and/or statements caused to be made and used by Pfizer, and in reliance on the accuracy thereof, has paid and approved, and continue to pay and approve, claims for Vfend that were ineligible for reimbursement and would not have been paid or approved if any part of the truth were known.

(SAC ¶ 211.)

The mere fact that the government has continued to pay and approve claims for Vfend even after Relators' allegations in 2005 is insufficient to establish that Relators' claims lack materiality. As the First Circuit held, mere knowledge of allegations regarding noncompliance is insufficient to prove actual knowledge of noncompliance. Moreover, Relators allege that the United States was "unaware of the false or fraudulent nature" of Pfizer's statements and actions, and therefore due to this ignorance, continued to pay for reimbursement claims for Vfend. Absent evidence that the government had actual knowledge of Defendant's fraud, we find the government's continued payments of Vfend claims insufficient to establish that Relators' claims fail for lack of materiality.

Accordingly, we find that Relators have sufficiently pled materiality.

3. *Scienter*

The Supreme Court in *Escobar* highlighted the FCA's scienter requirement, stating that "[w]hat matters is not the label that the Government attaches to a requirement, but whether the defendant knowingly violated a requirement that the defendant knows is material to the Government's payment decision." 136 S. Ct. at 1996. Defendant argues that even assuming that Relators have satisfied the falsity and materiality requirements, they have failed to adequately allege scienter. Defendant argues that Relators' allegations are insufficient to prove that Defendant knowingly violated the FCA. As support, Defendant argues that Relators admit that the swapped endpoints in the 608 Study were the result of Pfizer's mistake, and that Pfizer alerted the FDA as soon as it discovered its mistake.

***12** We rejected this argument in our previous memorandum, and we reject that argument here. In our Memorandum denying Defendant's First Motion to Dismiss we stated the following;

> Defendant's argument that Relators' claims should be dismissed because the switched endpoints in the 608 Study was merely a mistake that was ultimately disclosed to the FDA is rejected. While it may be true that Defendant disclosed the switched endpoints to the FDA, the Complaint alleges a fraud much larger in scope than Defendant invites us to believe. Relators allege that Defendant's submission of the 608 Study with the mistaken endpoints caused the FDA to grant Defendant approval to treat Candida infections and that such approval would not have been given if the proper endpoint had been submitted to the FDA. (Am. Compl. ¶¶ 75, 83-100, 105.) More importantly, however, Relators allege that "Pfizer knew that the 608 Study was seriously flawed and its results grossly misleading," (*id.* at ¶ 71), and despite this, "hid from view the lower efficacy and higher mortality rates among the patients in the 608 Study who had C. glabrata infections" (*id.* at ¶ 87), and concealed the adverse test results from the FDA and the medical community. According to Relators, despite knowledge of the dangers of Vfend revealed by the 608 study, Defendant embarked on a marketing campaign that "cynically exploited the switched endpoints of the 608 Study by repeatedly, and falsely, claiming that Vfend was a superior antifungal treatment." (*Id.*) These allegations are sufficient.

Pfizer, 2016 WL 807363, at *10.

We again determine that Relators' allegations are sufficient to allege that Defendant acted with the requisite scienter pursuant to the FCA. Accordingly, we find that Relators have stated a claim against Defendant under the FCA.

IV. CONCLUSION

For the foregoing reasons, Defendant's Second Motion to Dismiss will be denied.

An appropriate Order follows.

All Citations

Not Reported in Fed. Supp., 2017 WL 1344365, Med & Med GD (CCH) P 305,917

Footnotes

1 Defendant cites the district court case of *United States v. Medco Health Sols., Inc.*, No. 11-684, 2017 WL 63006, at *12 (D. Del. Jan. 5, 2017) as authority for the proposition that filing an amended complaint does not correct a first-to-file jurisdictional defect. The case notes that there is a split in authority among various district courts, and held that the reasoning in *Gadbois* and in our previous denial of Defendant's First Motion to Dismiss "does not hold up under scrutiny." *Id.* at 12.

We note that several district courts have held that relators are not required to re-file a case to cure a jurisdictional defect, and are instead permitted to file an amended complaint with the court. *See, e.g.*, *United States ex rel. Wood v. Allergan, Inc.*, No. 10-5645, 2017 WL 1233991, at *15 (S.D.N.Y. Mar. 31, 2017) (concluding "that a violation of the rule is curable through the filing of an amended or supplemental complaint after the earlier-filed action was dismissed"); *United States v. Cephalon, Inc.*, 159 F. Supp. 3d 550, 558 (E.D. Pa. 2016) (finding that "it would be unjust to require relators to refile their claims even though their only procedural roadblock was dismissed over two years ago and they have amended their complaint since then"); *U.S. ex rel. Kurnik v. PharMerica Corp.*, No. 11-01464, 2015 WL 1524402, at *6 (D.S.C. Apr. 2, 2015) (holding that the relator was permitted to file an amended complaint after the first-filed case was dismissed, and that doing so "does not run afoul of the policy behind the FCA because it does not threaten [the defendants] with double recovery").

2 After *Escobar*, appellate courts have analyzed relators' FCA claims under the fraudulent inducement theory. *See, e.g.*, *Weston Educ., Inc.*, 840 F.3d 494, 499 (8th Cir. 2016); *Olson*, 831 F.3d at 1074 (8th Cir. 2016).

End of Document

INDEX

Note: Page numbers followed by "*f*" indicate figures.

I

R

V

W